EXAM✓PREP

PHR
Third Edition

Cathy Winterfield

PHR Exam Prep, Third Edition

ISBN-13: 978-0-7897-5612-1

ISBN-10: 0-7897-5612-9

Library of Congress Cataloging-in-Publication Number: 2015939395

Printed in the United States on America

First Printing: August 2015

Trademarks

All terms mentioned in this book that are known to be trademarks or service marks have been appropriately capitalized. Pearson cannot attest to the accuracy of this information. Use of a term in this book should not be regarded as affecting the validity of any trademark or service mark.

Warning and Disclaimer

Every effort has been made to make this book as complete and as accurate as possible, but no warranty or fitness is implied. The information provided is on an "as is" basis. The author and the publisher shall have neither liability nor responsibility to any person or entity with respect to any loss or damages arising from the information contained in this book or from the use of the CD or programs accompanying it.

Special Sales

For information about buying this title in bulk quantities, or for special sales opportunities (which may include electronic versions; custom cover designs; and content particular to your business, training goals, marketing focus, or branding interests), please contact our corporate sales department at corpsales@pearsoned.com or (800) 382-3419.

For government sales inquiries, please contact governmentsales@pearsoned.com.

For questions about sales outside the U.S., please contact international@pearsoned.com.

Associate Publisher
Dave Dusthimer

Acquisitions Editor
Betsy Brown

Development Editor
Box Twelve Communications

Managing Editor
Sandra Schroeder

Project Editor
Seth Kerney

Copy Editor
Gill Editorial Services

Indexer
Lisa Stumpf

Proofreader
Megan Wade-Taxter

Technical Editor
Susan F. Alevas

Editorial Assistant
Vanessa Evans

Multimedia Developer
Lisa Matthews

Book Designer
Mark Shirar

Composition
Trina Wurst

Contents at a Glance

Table of Contents

About the Author

Cathy Lee Pantano Winterfield, MBA, MSHE, SPHR, ACC, is president of NovaCore Performance Solutions, a coaching firm dedicated to enhancing the performance of individuals and teams in the workplace. This enterprise represents the culmination of more than 25 years of experience in human resources, training, consulting, management, and coaching in businesses, not-for-profit organizations, and governmental entities.

Previously, Cathy served as a member of the extension faculty of Cornell University—School of Industrial and Labor Relations, where she was the director of human resource management programs.

Cathy has written numerous books:

- *Performance Appraisals*, for Silver Lining Publications, a division of Barnes & Noble
- *Mission-Driven Interviewing: Moving Beyond Behavior Based Questions*, by PTI Publishing
- *PHR Exam Prep* (First, Second, and Third Editions)
- *SPHR Exam Prep* (Third Edition), by Pearson IT Certification
- *PHR/SPHR Quick Reference*, by Pearson IT Certification

Cathy has presented at national and local conferences on a variety of topics related to human resources and management development. In addition, she has coauthored more than a dozen online courses in leadership, human resources, management development, and organ donation.

Cathy holds a bachelor of arts degree from Ithaca College; an MBA from Pace University; and a master's degree in higher education from Kaplan University, with a specialty in Online College Teaching. She has earned the Associate Certified Coach (ACC) credential from the International Coach Federation. She is also a certified administrator of the Myers-Briggs Type Indicator (MBTI) Assessments. Cathy has likewise earned the Senior Professional in Human Resources (SPHR) designation from the Human Resource Certification Institute; and the CCP (Certified Compensation Professional) designation from WorldatWork. She is a member of the Society for Human Resources Management, the American Society for Training & Development, and the International Coach Federation.

You can reach Cathy at Cathy@CathyWinterfield.com.

Dedication

"Aunt Barbara" (Barbara Flynn)

Having been in my life for nearly 50 years, Aunt Barbara has known me longer than—and better than—anyone on this earth. While I do not remember the moment I first met her (as I was only 3 years old), I remember clearly so many moments that we have shared since then.

Together, we have journeyed into birth…into death…and through nearly a half century of life. She has given me love, laughter, and the gift of family. Her daughter is my sister…her grandchildren are my nephews…her house is my home.

Aunt Barbara, you are a gift and an inspiration—to me and to countless others. You have earned the respect and admiration of friends and even of strangers who hear your remarkable story of living with multiple sclerosis. You have chosen to live fully despite the challenges and losses you have faced. You have chosen to embrace each moment and to see the gift that each offers.

In short, you have chosen "yes," and you have inspired me beyond all measure.

For the gift of "you," I am forever grateful.

Acknowledgments

I've learned many things from writing this book—one of which is that I'll never again skip past the "Acknowledgments" section of a book that I'm reading. I've come to realize that an author (at least this author) is a person fortunate enough to be surrounded by a team of talented and committed individuals without whom there would be no book—and therefore without whom there would be no authorship.

So, in recognition of those who wove together the tapestry that you now hold in your hand, I would like to express my appreciation to the following individuals:

Betsy Brown, acquisitions editor: For her leadership, expertise, sound advice, open-mindedness, and kindness throughout the editorial transition and the actual publication of this book. Betsy is one of the most supportive, competent, inspiring professionals with whom I've ever worked.

Susan Alevas, technical editor: For her guidance, perspective, discernment, support, and insight—along with her willingness to be a sounding board—all of which yielded far better ideas and results than I could have generated on my own. Drawing on her decades of experience as a practitioner, academic professional, writer, attorney, and author, Susan kept me on the technical straight and narrow.

David Dusthimer, associate publisher: For his belief, confidence, and support of this project, from concept to product(s).

Jeff Riley, development editor, and Seth Kerney, project editor: For their eagle-eyed scrutiny and for their simultaneous—yet single-minded—attention to the "forest" as well as to the "tree."

Sandra Schroeder, managing editor, and Karen Davis, copy editor: For their individual and collective contributions.

Please note that the many enhancements that have been made to this edition are due to the creativity, diligence, and vision of this editorial team. Any errors or omissions that remain are my sole responsibility.

Many family members, friends, and colleagues: For, in myriad ways, making a difference in my personal and professional life, helping make this book possible, and "cheering me on" during its actual creation.

Nugget: For forsaking many walks and adventures to keep me company throughout the writing of nearly every page of this book.

^Clarence^ and Barbara: For building Crow's Nest with their own loving hands, never knowing it would one day be someone else's beloved writer's retreat.

My husband Craig: For making Crow's Nest ours and supporting me lovingly and patiently throughout all the many highs, lows, challenges, and milestones of writing this book.

P&L: "I'll still be loving you." - Restless Heart

About the Reviewer

Susan F. Alevas is a seasoned management/training consultant and is licensed to practice law in the states of New York and Florida. Spanning more than 25 years, her previous management career included 15 years of executive leadership in human resources and labor relations in both the private and public sectors, in addition to serving as in-house attorney for several organizations. Ms. Alevas's leadership was consistently marked by ethical, creative, and cost-effective business solutions. Her experience in human resources management includes employee/labor relations, budgeting, contract negotiations, conflict resolution, recruitment and staffing, HRIS operations, performance management, staff development, succession planning, and benefits administration. She also is an adjunct instructor at Cornell University's School of Industrial and Labor Relations extension program, New York University, and the State University of New York at Stony Brook, and teaches business ethics, human resources management, employment/labor law and conflict management/dispute resolution. In 2004, she founded her management/training consulting company.

We Want to Hear from You!

As the reader of this book, *you* are our most important critic and commentator. We value your opinion and want to know what we're doing right, what we could do better, what areas you'd like to see us publish in, and any other words of wisdom you're willing to pass our way.

We welcome your comments. You can email or write to let us know what you did or didn't like about this book—as well as what we can do to make our books better.

Please note that we cannot help you with technical problems related to the topic of this book.

When you write, please be sure to include this book's title and author as well as your name, email address, and phone number. I will carefully review your comments and share them with the author and editors who worked on the book.

Email: feedback@pearsonitcertification.com

Mail: Pearson IT Certification
            ATTN: Reader Feedback
            800 East 96th Street
            Indianapolis, IN 46240 USA

Reader Services

Visit our website and register this book at www.pearsonitcertification.com/title/9780789756121 for convenient access to any updates, downloads, or errata that might be available for this book.

Introduction

Welcome to *PHR Exam Prep*, Third Edition. Whether this is the first Exam Prep book you've ever picked up or you've used Pearson's prep resources before, this book will provide valuable information, unique perspectives, and perceptive insights—as well as helpful suggestions—as you prepare to take the Professional in Human Resources (PHR) examination. We'll even include a bit of moral support!

This introduction will explain the PHR exam in a general sense and explore ways in which this Exam Prep product can help you as you prepare to take the exam. It will begin to give you an idea of the various topics you'll be exploring in greater detail in this book as well as important information about how the book is structured. Then it will get into some specific study tips. (These are not as complete as the ones you'll find in Pearson's coaching video titled *HRCI Certification Exams: A Coach's Approach to Preparing and Passing the Exams*, but they will give you a good start.)

About the PHR Credential

Performing HR-related transactions well is important, but by itself it's not enough. Those of us who truly want to succeed in the ever-evolving HR profession must thoroughly understand the HR body of knowledge and be well equipped and well prepared to apply that knowledge in effective, meaningful, impactful, and appropriate ways. Passing the PHR exam is one way that HR professionals can demonstrate to themselves, to their employers, and to their potential employers that they do, in fact, possess fluency and knowledge in the HR profession. Passing the PHR also serves to establish a foundation of credibility with other HR colleagues—in a sense, even before one is personally acquainted with them. Separate and apart from how others might perceive this accomplishment, earning the PHR certification also represents a level of professionalism and will inspire a measure of self-confidence that is uniquely attainable through this achievement.

The PHR exam is administered by the Human Resource Certification Institute (HRCI). Since 1976, more than 135,000 HR professionals in over 100 countries have earned certification. By maintaining this rigorous and integrity-driven standard that is relevant as well as appropriately challenging, HRCI has contributed immeasurably to the advancement of the profession.

The HRCI certification exams constitute an important part of what makes our profession *a true profession*. HRCI offers the opportunity for qualified HR professionals to earn well-recognized, well-respected credentials that have "stood the test of time." As such, these exams are also a near-universal indicator of achievement. So, by purchasing this book, you have taken an important first step toward earning the distinction that accompanies the PHR designation.

Composition of PHR Exam

The PHR exam assesses certificants' knowledge and application of the HR body of knowledge. Questions are drawn from each of the six functional areas in accordance with the following percentages:

- ▶ Business Management and Strategy—11%
- ▶ Workforce Planning and Employment—24%
- ▶ Human Resource Development—18%
- ▶ Compensation and Benefits—19%
- ▶ Employee and Labor Relations—20%
- ▶ Risk Management—8%

About This Book

Most of the exam preparation materials on the market today don't distinguish exam prep for the PHR exam from exam prep for the Senior Professional in Human Resources (SPHR) exam. We do. Why? Because the exams are different. And it's our belief that because the PHR and SPHR exams are different, your preparation should be a bit different as well. Thus, by tailoring your preparation to more closely reflect what will be covered on the PHR exam, you are positioning yourself to focus on those areas that matter most to you and that are most likely to ensure that you will pass the exam.

Like so many other things in life (and in HR), this isn't necessarily as clear cut as it sounds. Certain questions that you'll encounter on the PHR exam will seem quite senior or strategic in nature—almost more like what you would expect to see on the SPHR exam instead of on the PHR exam. As such, we're not going to limit our questions in this book to those that represent what the PHR exam is "supposed to" contain because this exam—like our profession—can be anything but typical at times.

For this reason, we've taken the following approach in this book: although it's true that the PHR exam contains more fact-based questions than scenario-based questions, the reality is that it's impossible to know exactly which topics will be covered in terms of "just the facts" and which will be placed in the context of a workplace scenario. We're committed to helping you prepare for whatever you might encounter on the PHR exam, which is why we've included more scenario-based questions than you might encounter on the actual exam.

We believe that if you can answer a scenario-based question correctly, it's almost certain that you understand the raw knowledge behind it (assuming you haven't guessed at the answer, that is). Answering a strictly fact-based question successfully, however, doesn't necessarily mean that you could answer a scenario-based question that has been built around those same facts. And on the PHR exam, you might be called upon to do exactly that.

In short, we hope to test your limits (if you will pardon the expression). We are committed to helping you prepare as thoroughly as possible, even if that means that some people might find the exam prep to be a bit more challenging than the actual PHR exam. In a way, in fact, we would consider that to be very good news.

Chapters

We've devoted one full chapter to each of the six functional areas covered on the PHR exam. Please note that we've taken a different (and we believe more straightforward) approach in structuring the third edition of the book:

Chapter 1: Business Management and Strategy (BM & S) (formerly Chapter 3)

Chapter 2: Workforce Planning and Employment (formerly Chapter 4)

Chapter 3: Human Resource Development (formerly Chapter 5)

Chapter 4: Compensation and Benefits (formerly Chapter 6)

Chapter 5: Employee and Labor Relations (formerly Chapter 7)

Chapter 6: Risk Management (formerly Chapter 8)

Please note an important change to the third edition of the book: There is no longer a separate chapter addressing the HRCI-identified areas of Core Knowledge. Instead, these areas of Core Knowledge have been woven into the book.

Why did we make this change? For the same reason that we restructured this book: to better reflect the actual PHR exam.

Consider this: If you look at the HRCI website, you'll see "PHR EXAM WEIGHTING BY FUNCTIONAL AREA." This includes the breakdown of the way the test is built, with the percentage of test questions drawn from each functional area. No questions are drawn specifically from the Core Knowledge section—even though questions do cover those topics. As such, we have incorporated each area of Core Knowledge into the functional area with which it is most commonly associated, and through which it is most likely to be applied.

Please note, however, that—as with all areas of this test (and, of "real life HR")—there can be crossover. As such, think of each area of Core Knowledge creatively, and with an openness to where it might "show up" on the exam.

And just to confirm that we're all on the same page, we're talking about the following:

- *76:* Needs assessment and analysis

- *77:* Third-party or vendor selection, contract negotiation, and management, including development of requests for proposals (RFPs)

- *78:* Communication skills and strategies (for example: presentation, collaboration, sensitivity)

- *79:* Organizational documentation requirements to meet federal and state guidelines

- *80:* Adult learning processes

- *81:* Motivation concepts and applications

- *82:* Training techniques (for example: virtual, classroom, on-the-job)

- *83:* Leadership concepts and applications

- *84:* Project management concepts and applications

- *85:* Diversity concepts and applications (for example: generational, cultural competency, learning styles)

- *86:* Human relations concepts and applications (for example: emotional intelligence, organizational behavior)

- *87:* Ethical and professional standards

- *88:* Technology to support HR activities (for example: HR Information Systems, employee self-service, e-learning, applicant tracking systems)

- *89:* Qualitative and quantitative methods and tools for analysis, interpretation, and decision-making purposes (for example: metrics and measurements, cost/benefit analysis, financial statement analysis)

- *90:* Change management theory, methods, and application

- *91:* Job analysis and job description methods

- *92:* Employee records management (for example: electronic/paper, retention, disposal)

- *93:* Techniques for forecasting, planning, and predicting the impact of HR activities and programs across functional areas

- *94:* Types of organizational structures (for example: matrix, hierarchy)

- *95:* Environmental scanning concepts and applications (for example: Strengths, Weaknesses, Opportunities, and Threats [SWOT], and Political, Economic, Social, and Technological [PEST])

- *96:* Methods for assessing employee attitudes, opinions, and satisfaction (for example: surveys, focus groups/panels)
  - *97:* Budgeting, accounting, and financial concepts
  - *98:* Risk-management techniques

At the end of the book, there is a practice PHR exam, as well as an answer key and explanations about why each choice was—or wasn't—the best answer. Use these tests as a way to test your knowledge and understanding and to map out areas in which you want to invest additional study time.

But let us be clear about one very important point: *This book is neither designed nor intended to cover everything you need to know to pass the PHR exam.* Instead, we've brought together as much information as possible to help you prepare for the PHR exam—as well as lists of resources where you can get more information about particular topics. We'll also give you more practice—lots of it.

You can also use this book to brush up on particular areas in which you want a bit more review or practice. To do this, use the index or the table of contents to go straight to the specific topics, sections, and questions you want to reexamine. We've structured the book according to headings and subheadings to facilitate the process of providing straightforward, outlined, easy-to-reference information about each specific topic. In fact, after you've taken the PHR exam, you can use this book as a tightly focused reference tool that will serve you well as a day-to-day resource for HR-related information.

Chapter Formats

The third edition of this book has been completely restructured and redesigned to more closely reflect the HR body of knowledge. As such, as you move through each chapter, you'll be able to review content within the overarching context of the most relevant competencies and areas of knowledge around which the test is built.

Within this overarching framework, each content-driven Exam Prep chapter follows a regular structure. Please note that we'll cluster related competencies and areas of knowledge together to make it easier to make sense of related concepts, facts, laws, and cases.

Notes

We've also included several Notes in each chapter that serve as "reflective inserts" to challenge you to look more deeply into the topic that is being discussed—perhaps from a different perspective that encourages you to consider and weigh the "voice of experience."

Chapter Summaries

At the end of each chapter, you'll find a comprehensive summary of the material covered in that chapter.

Key Terms

A list of key terms appears at the end of each chapter. As part of your review, make sure you understand and can recognize, define, or explain each of those terms and that you are prepared to apply each of them within the context of a specific scenario if you're called on to do so.

Exercises

Located at the end of each chapter in the "Apply Your Knowledge" section, the exercises include additional tutorial material and more chances to apply the knowledge and practice the skills that were presented earlier in the chapter.

Study Tips

Each chapter will offer study tips that are particularly relevant to that functional area. Feel free to be creative, however, and apply tips from each chapter to other chapters.

Review Questions

These open-ended, short answer/essay-type questions will elicit your explanation of important chapter concepts.

Exam Questions

This section presents a short list of exam questions based on a sampling of the content that was covered in the chapter.

Review and Exam Question Answers and Explanations

The next two sections will include the Review Questions and Exam Questions answers and explanations.

Suggested Readings and Resources

Each chapter concludes with a listing of suggested books, websites, or other resources through which you can explore the topics covered in that particular chapter in greater detail.

Information About the PHR Exam

You can find the best, most complete, and most up-to-date source of information about the HRCI suite of exams at HRCI.org. Check out this website for firsthand information about the different HRCI tests available, test eligibility, testing dates, prices—*everything* you need ever wanted to know (and then some) about HR certification.

Accreditation

Not all certification tests are created equal, and not all hold the same value (and, potentially, worth). It's important to ensure that the test in which you invest your time, money, and efforts is accredited.

According to HRCI:

> "The HR Certification Institute was accredited by the National Commission for Certifying Agencies (NCCA) in 2008. NCCA is an independent, third-party organization that accredits more than 300 programs from 120 organizations in a variety of industries. Certification programs must demonstrate compliance with rigorous standards that represent the best practices in the professional certification industry to earn and maintain accreditation status. For more information on NCCA accreditation, visit www.credentialingexcellence.org."

> —2014 Certification Policies and Procedures Handbook, p. 5

PHR Exam Structure

According to HRCI:

"All exam questions are multiple choice, which means they contain a stem (or premise) and four (4) answer choices including only one (1) correct answer.

"The premise states the problem or the question to be answered. You can expect two (2) main types of premise statement, including a statement posing a question (example: "Which type of psychological test measures a person's overall ability to learn?") and an incomplete statement (example: "A person's overall ability to learn is best measured by a[n]...").

"The correct answer is one (1) of the four (4) options representing the correct response **or** the best correct response. In this case, **best means** that a panel of experts would agree to this judgment. Some answer choices are written to look correct, but they are not the **best** answer. This is done to assess your ability to make the right decision and apply knowledge in an actual work experience.

"Some of the multiple-choice questions are formatted as scenarios. Scenario questions present typical HR situations, followed by questions based upon them. These scenarios require you to integrate facts from different areas of the HR body of knowledge. They are particularly well suited for SPHR candidates because the scenarios often present typical situations encountered by senior-level HR practitioners.

"All questions are classified according to the following levels:

- ▶ knowledge/comprehension: recalling factual material, translation or interpretation of a concept

- ▶ application/problem solving: applying familiar principles or generalizations to solve real-life problems

- ▶ synthesis/evaluation: combining distantly related elements by making critical judgments that require accuracy or consistent logic

"After the exam, the performance data of the exam overall and each question is carefully evaluated. A number of statistical measures are routinely calculated and reviewed for each question. Questions that do not perform to established standards are discarded or revised. This continuous review of questions ensures that exams are valid and reliable."

PHR Exam Format

In addition to studying the actual content within each of the six functional areas, you need to be familiar with the format of the PHR exam.

The PHR exam is a computerized test consisting of 175 multiple-choice questions. You'll have three hours to complete the exam, which is administered by a computer at a testing center.

Of the 175 test questions, only 150 will count toward your overall score. The other 25 questions, called "pre-test questions," are being piloted for possible use in future exams, and your answers to these questions will not count toward your overall score. The catch, however, is that you won't know which questions will count toward your overall score and which won't—so you would be wise to assume that every question is a scored question and to approach every question with focus and attention.

As described earlier, each question has four possible answers. Often, more than one answer will make some degree of sense or may initially seem correct. You must, however, choose the best answer.

NOTE

It has been said that "close only counts in horseshoes and hand grenades." Close doesn't count on the PHR exam either. Take your time and evaluate all four options before selecting the best answer.

NOTE

Be particularly careful not to automatically default to the response that most closely approximates how your employer would handle a particular situation or how you've handled a similar situation in the past. Every organization has its own way of handling HR-related situations; however, your employer's way of handling a situation isn't necessarily the best way or the way that HRCI has deemed the best.

Examples of multiple-choice questions appear at the end of each chapter in this book.

Study and Exam Prep Tips

Now that you've got a sense of how this book is designed, how the PHR is designed, and how this book will support you in your efforts to pass the PHR, close your eyes and imagine yourself in this situation. (Well, first read this paragraph, and then close your eyes.)

It's the day before you're scheduled to take the PHR exam. Your legs, arms, and fingertips tingle as you experience a rush of adrenaline. Beads of sweat dot your forehead. If you've scheduled the exam on a workday or on a day that follows a workday, you may find yourself dreading the tasks you normally enjoy because, in the back of your mind, you're wishing you could read just a few more pages, review your notes one more time, or complete a couple more practice questions. You cram in a few more pages of reading—perhaps along with a few more French fries from the to-go dinner you picked up on the run.

Now let's imagine a different scenario. Please read this, and then close your eyes and visualize this image instead:

It's the day before you're scheduled to take the PHR exam. You're going about your daily routine—either at work or at home—calmly and confidently looking forward to (yes, we said *looking forward to*) taking the PHR exam the next day. You're confident in your knowledge that you did everything you set out to do when you made your PHR study plan months earlier. You've eaten a favorite meal for dinner—something healthy and delicious. You're going to have a relaxing evening and get a good night's rest. As you drift off to sleep, a slight smile plays about your lips as you relax in the knowledge that you are well prepared to take—and pass—the PHR exam.

If you like the second scenario more than the first, you're not alone. And it doesn't have to be just a dream. In fact, you have already taken one of the first steps toward creating that reality, and you're holding it in your hands right now.

With this book, along with your other prep materials, you can develop an evenly paced study plan that will help you avoid most of these pretest jitters. Although no one book or product (*including this one*) should ever serve as your only preparation tool, know that your commitment to buying this book—and, especially, to using it to prepare for the PHR exam—brings you one step closer to attaining your objective of passing the PHR exam.

This section of the book provides you with some general guidelines for preparing for any certification exam and for the PHR exam in particular. It's organized into three sections. The first section addresses learning styles and how they affect you as you prepare for an exam. The second section covers exam-preparation activities as well as general study and test-taking tips. This is followed by a closer look at the PHR certification exam, including PHR-specific study and test-taking tips.

Learning Styles

To better understand the nature of test preparation, it is important to understand the learning process. You're probably already aware of how you best learn new material; if you're not, right now would be a great time to figure it out.

There are three primary learning styles: visual, kinesthetic, and auditory. If you're more of a visual learner, you might need to see things for them to sink in. If so, you might find that creating outlines works well for you. If you're a kinesthetic learner, a hands-on approach will likely serve you well, so you might prefer to work with homemade flash cards. Auditory learners may want to create their own audio recordings of key facts and information they can listen to on a cassette or digital voice recorder.

Whatever your preferred learning style, test preparation is always more effective when it takes place over a period of time. It goes without saying (well, perhaps it does need to be said) that it's not a good idea to study for a certification exam by pulling an all-nighter the night before the exam. It's also not advisable to postpone your study until the week before the exam. Solid preparation means more than that. It requires consistent preparation—at a steady pace over a period of months, not days or even weeks. As you begin your preparation, it's important to keep in mind that learning is a developmental, evolving process. Taking a planned, deliberate approach to studying and learning material that will be on the exam will help you recognize what you already know well, what you need to know better, and what you still need to learn—in other words, what you don't know very well at all—at least not yet.

Learning takes place when you incorporate new information into your existing knowledge base. And remember—even if this book is the first PHR study tool you've looked at so far, you already do have an existing knowledge base. How can you (and, for that matter, how can we) be so certain of that? Because you're required to have at least one year (and, in many cases, two or more) of professional-level experience to sit for the PHR exam. That represents at least one year of knowledge, skills, and experience—which means you're already on your way to passing the PHR.

> **NOTE**
>
> Again, don't rely on any single resource—even this book—to prepare for the PHR exam. No matter how good a resource might be, it provides only one perspective, and it can provide only a limited amount of material. *PHR Exam Prep*, Third Edition should serve as a supplement to your other study resources, not as a replacement for them. There is more knowledge and information required to pass the PHR exam than could ever be included in this book or any other single resource. So, in short, don't put all your eggs in one basket—even this one.

As you prepare for the PHR exam, this book, along with many of the other study materials you'll use, will serve three purposes:

▶ It will add incrementally to your existing knowledge base.

▶ It will facilitate the process of drawing meaningful connections between the test content and your own professional experience.

▶ It will enable you to restructure and translate your existing knowledge and experience into a format that's consistent with the PHR exam.

Perhaps without even realizing it, you'll be adding new information to your existing knowledge base—all of which will then be organized within the framework of the six functional areas of HR around which the PHR exam is designed. This process will lead you to a more comprehensive understanding of important concepts, relevant techniques, and the human resources profession in general. Again, all this will happen only as a result of a repetitive and self-reinforcing process of study and learning, not as the product of a single study session.

Keep this model of learning in the forefront of your mind as you prepare for the PHR exam. It will help you make better decisions about what to study and about how much more studying you need to do.

General Study Tips

There's no one "best" way to study for any exam. There are, however, some general test-preparation strategies and guidelines that have worked well for many test takers and that might work well for you, too.

Before we get into that, however, one important principle to keep in mind is that learning can be broken into various depths:

▶ Recognition (of terms, for example) represents a somewhat superficial or surface level of learning in which you rely on a prompt of some sort to elicit recall.

▶ Comprehension or understanding (of the concepts behind the terms, for example) represents a deeper level of learning than recognition does.

▶ Analysis of a concept, along with the ability to apply your newly expanded understanding of that concept, represents an even deeper level of learning.

This is not to say that recognition isn't important. It is—particularly for multiple-choice exams, and particularly for the PHR exam.

NOTE

This is in significant part a function of the level of knowledge that PHR candidates are expected to have mastered, which is not as advanced or complex as what is expected of SPHR candidates. As such, recognition (by itself) is a somewhat less relevant level of learning on the SPHR exam because the SPHR exam focuses on more complex and strategic applications of the same body of knowledge.

In addition to ensuring that you are able to recognize terms, you should build a study strategy through which you will develop the ability to process, digest, and absorb the material at a level or two deeper than that. In this way, you'll know the material so thoroughly that you'll be able to perform well on a variety of types of questions—for instance, on questions that require you to apply your knowledge to specific problems, as well as on questions that only require you to be able to recognize and identify the correct (meaning, the best) answer from among a series of possible answers. The PHR contains questions of both types, along with a variety of other types of questions.

Macro and Micro Study Strategies

One strategy that can enhance and support learning at multiple levels is outlining (especially for visual learners, as we mentioned earlier). Creating your own study outline that incorporates concepts covered on the PHR will support your efforts to absorb and understand the content more fully, to make connections between related topics, and to map together information that you have gleaned from a variety of study sources. For instance, it will help you make connections between the six functional areas, the core areas of knowledge, and the HR-related responsibilities associated with each of those six functional areas. Your outline will also help you dig a bit deeper into the material if you choose to include a level or two of detail beyond what you might find on most generic, summary-style study tools. You can add more value to your outline, for instance, by expanding it to include information such as definitions, details, analyses, examples, related laws, related cases, key historical events, key thinkers, and the like.

An outline such as this can support your study efforts in a variety of ways. For instance, as you build the points and subpoints of your outline, you'll be able to better appreciate how they relate to one another. You'll also gain a better understanding of how each of the main objective areas outlined in this book is similar to—and different from—the other main objective areas. If you do the same thing with the subobjectives, you'll also gain a fuller understanding of how each subobjective relates to its objective and how those subobjectives relate to one another. It's also important to understand how each of the HR-related responsibilities is similar to—or different from—other HR-related responsibilities, which an outline can help you clarify. The same holds true for the areas of knowledge that span the six functional areas and for the HR-related knowledge required for each of the functional areas—each of which is identified within each chapter.

Next, work through your completed outline. Focus on learning the details. Take time to refamiliarize yourself with—and, in some cases, memorize—and understand terms, definitions, facts, laws, cases, and so forth. In this pass-through of the outline, you should attempt to focus on learning detail rather than on just an overview of the big picture (on which you already focused your attention as you built your outline).

It's not a good idea to try to accomplish both of these strategies at once. Research has shown that attempting to assimilate both types of information (macro and micro) at the same time interferes with the overall learning process. If you consciously separate your studying into these two approaches, you are likely to perform better on the exam.

Active Study Strategies

The process of writing down and defining objectives, subobjectives, terms, facts, and definitions promotes a more active learning strategy than you'd experience by just reading study materials. In human information-processing terms, writing forces you to engage in more active encoding of the information. Conversely, simply reading the information results in more passive processing. Using this study strategy, focus on writing down (or typing out) the items that are highlighted throughout this book.

You might want to consider doing the same for your other study sources. Try to merge your notes whenever possible to take an integrated approach to your test prep. (But always keep track of your sources. Color coding or shading might help with staying organized.)

Another active study strategy involves applying the information you have learned by creating your own examples and scenarios. Think about how or where you could apply the concepts you're learning. You could even try your hand at writing your own questions, which you could share with a study partner or group. Again, write everything down to help you process the facts and concepts in an active fashion.

The multiple review and exam questions at the end of each chapter provide additional opportunities to actively reinforce the concepts you are learning, so don't skip them.

Common Sense Strategies

As you study your test prep materials, use good common sense. (Most of us have learned the hard way that common sense can be all too uncommon.) For instance, study when you are alert. Reduce or eliminate distractions. (Put that smartphone away, and log out of your social media accounts.) Eat when you are hungry, reward yourself when you reach a milestone, and take breaks when you get tired. Pushing through when your body really needs a break can sometimes result in frustration, anxiety, and physical exhaustion—none of which will enhance your performance on the exam.

Design Your Own Personal Study Plan

And do it now. There is no single best way to prepare for any exam. Different people learn in different ways, so it's important to develop a personal study plan that's right for you. As you do so, establish long-term and short-term goals for yourself. Know exactly what you will accomplish and by what date. You'll experience a sense of accomplishment each time you reach a milestone, so allow yourself the opportunity to celebrate. You will have earned the right to revel a bit—plus, taking a little celebratory break will help you feel more refreshed as you move into the next stage of your prep.

And, as you develop this plan, you might want to build in some cushion of time. As we've all experienced from time to time, "things happen." Life happens. And, sometimes, those "things" can throw our calendars, our emotions, even our physical bodies off track. Plan for those unexpected events so that they don't derail you.

Questions to Ask Yourself

As you develop your personal study plan, ask yourself the following questions:

- How much time do I have to invest in preparing for the exam?

- How much money do I have to invest in preparing for the exam?

- Do I learn better on my own or when I have the chance to interact with others? Or, does some combination of both work best for me?

- Am I comfortable with an online study environment, or do I prefer a traditional classroom setting?

- Does my schedule afford me the opportunity to attend regularly scheduled classroom-based exam prep workshops?

- What is my preferred learning style?

- If I've taken this test before and didn't pass, what have I learned? What was effective about my original study plan? What was ineffective? What could I have done differently?

> **NOTE**
>
> And for those readers who didn't pass the PHR exam the first time around, let the experience go. Take the lessons that you learned and put them to good use now. It's your time to shine.

Assessment Testing

One of the most important aspects of learning is what has been called meta-learning. Meta-learning has to do with realizing when you know something well or realizing when you need to study some more. In other words, you assess and recognize the degree to which you have learned the material you've been studying.

For most people, this can be a difficult assessment to make independently in the absence of study tools. Pretesting is one tool that can help you in this way by establishing a baseline of what you already know before you start your study regime and as you proceed through different phases of your study plan. Pretesting tools can include review questions, practice questions, practice tests, and the like.

You can then use the insights you obtain from these pretesting assessment tools to guide and direct your studying because developmental learning takes place as you cycle (and recycle) through your study plan. So begin by assessing how well you already know or have learned a particular topic. Use that assessment to decide what you need to continue studying. Then conduct another assessment, followed by more review. Repeat this process until you feel confident in your knowledge and understanding of the topic.

You might have already noticed that there are two practice exams included with this book: one in the book and one online. We strongly suggest that you consider incorporating these into your study plan.

General Test-Taking Tips

Taking exams can be stressful. This is especially true if it's been a while since you've been in school or taken tests. There are, however, steps you can take to reduce the level of stress you are experiencing as you prepare for—and take—the exam. As you prepare and answer lots of practice questions, your comfort level with test taking will likely increase. Be patient with yourself; your rustiness *will* fade away. In addition, consider other stress-reducing techniques, such as visualization. Just as Olympic athletes visualize themselves performing in their events as part of their preparation, visualize yourself progressing comfortably and confidently through the questions on the PHR exam.

The structure, format, and style of the exam may be unfamiliar to you. Test taking is a skill all its own—separate and apart from the material that the test covers—and every test is different. This is why so many individuals and organizations offer test-preparation services. You've probably seen the advertisements for test-prep services for the SAT, LSAT, GRE, GMAT—the alphabet soup of test taking goes on and on. The specific attributes of each exam, however, are unique, as are the quality and value of various test prep services and resources. Collect as much information as possible, and choose wisely before availing yourself of test-prep services.

PHR-Specific Information, Study, and Test-Taking Tips

We've all heard of "the fear of the unknown." Well, knowledge dispels fear (or at least it helps to do so). Knowing as much as you can about how the PHR exam is designed, formatted, administered, and delivered will help you as you prepare to take the exam.

PHR Preparation Options

You can choose from many options as you prepare for the PHR exam. Please visit the HRCI website for current information on exam preparation providers.

Here are some considerations to keep in mind when choosing from among the many available providers and delivery modalities:

Online Programs

Check out online college/university programs carefully before signing up to ensure that you choose a format that's right for you. Be particularly alert to real-time ("synchronous") participation requirements if you have limited time availability or if you are available to study only during nontraditional classroom hours (in which case you might find "asynchronous" participation to be a better option).

Self-Study

If being part of a cohort group isn't the best choice for you, you might want to consider a self-study option. SHRM offers a self-study learning system, which has preparation materials and tools on each functional area and on the entire HR body of knowledge.

The self-study format allows you maximum flexibility to prepare for the PHR at a time and a place that's most convenient for you. It also contains an online component that offers lots of additional questions in a computerized format, thereby more closely replicating what you will experience during the actual PHR exam.

Study Partners and Teams

Whether you're preparing for the PHR using a classroom, online, or self-study format, you may find it helpful to find another test taker with whom you can partner as you prepare for the test. Ideally, you'll want to find someone whose schedule is similar to—and whose learning style is compatible with—your own. Even more important, look for a buddy who has strengths in those functional areas in which you need the most development and who would benefit from the assistance of someone who is well versed in those functional areas in which you are strongest. You may want to look for a buddy with whom you'll study in person or someone with whom you can confer online. Study partners and teams can be found through colleagues at work, through a prep course, or through other reputable sources.

Online Study Groups

Be open to the idea of forming an online study group. Multiple online study groups, for instance, are registered with www.groups.yahoo.com. (As always, of course, be prudent and cautious when creating online relationships.)

PHR-Specific Test Preparation Tips

Make no mistake: the PHR exam challenges your knowledge, your HR skills, and your test-taking abilities. Here are some tips to help you as you prepare for the PHR exam:

- Be prepared to combine your skill sets with your experience and to identify solutions using that combined insight because the PHR exam tests your knowledge as well as your skill. You will be called on to resolve problems that may draw on different dimensions of the material covered. For example, you could be presented with a realistic workplace scenario about a layoff that requires you to understand when—and how—the Age Discrimination in Employment Act (ADEA) needs to be taken into consideration. Why is this type of question likely to appear? In this particular example, it's one thing to know the provisions of the ADEA, but it's something else entirely to understand its application and relevance to a layoff situation. More broadly, these types of scenario-based questions are reflective of real life. And, to be an effective HR professional, you'll need to be able to successfully make these kinds of connections and applications.

- Get used to delving into minute details. Each exam question can incorporate a multitude of details. Try thinking of each detail as a potential clue. Some of these details will prove to be ancillary. Some of them will help you rule out possible answers but not necessarily enable you to identify the best answer. Other details will provide you with a more complete picture of the situation being described. The reality is that you may be called on to combine this information with what you know and what you have experienced to identify the best answer. If you don't pay attention to how the information that you're given helps you eliminate certain responses, the best answer might elude you.

- Hold yourself to time limits when taking practice tests. You must complete the PHR exam within three hours. To get used to this time constraint, use a timer when you take practice tests. Learn to pace yourself.

- Peruse the HRCI (www.hrci.org) website—early and often.

- Talk with others who have already taken the PHR exam—whether or not they passed. Although PHR test takers are prohibited from divulging specific types of information about the exam, they can tell you about their overall test-taking experience. You may find that their insights, ideas, and suggestions hold great value for you as you prepare to take the test. Be careful, however, not to let yourself feel anxious on the basis of anything that you might hear. Just use it as a way to make better choices relative to developing your own exam-prep plan and relative to taking the actual exam.

Strategies and Tips for PHR Exam Day

Your studying is done, you've familiarized yourself with the test center (online virtual tours are available), you're wearing comfortable clothing, and you've arrived at least 30 minutes early with ID in hand. Now what? First, breathe. Remember that you have thoroughly prepared yourself for the PHR exam.

You are ready for this.

Now prepare yourself mentally. Focus on your feelings of confidence. There's no one "right" way to do this. Some people, however, find it helpful to consider one (or perhaps both) of the following two mindsets:

1. **"If you can see it, you can be it."** As discussed earlier, continue to visualize yourself confidently answering test questions—just as you did during your test preparation. Start by writing your name with the letters "PHR" after it on the mini whiteboard you've been given to use as a scratch pad. You're self-assured, relaxed, and ready to demonstrate what you know. Then see yourself leaving the test center, a smile on your face, having just learned that you have passed the exam.

2. **"What's the worst that can happen?"** Remind yourself that the worst thing that could possibly happen is that you do not pass the PHR exam. If that does happen, many choices are available to you, the most obvious of which is retaking the test. So, even if the worst possible thing happens, you'll get through it, and you will have learned valuable lessons along the way—lessons you can use to help you pass the test the next time.

Here are some additional suggestions to consider as you sit down to take the PHR exam:

- ▸ **Take your time:** Determine how much time you can spend on each question while still allowing yourself time to check your responses afterward. Most importantly, read every question—and every answer—deliberately and completely. Don't skip over even one word. Remember that you will need to identify the best answer, not just a good answer.

- ▸ **Collect yourself:** When you actually sit down at the computer terminal, take a few moments to collect yourself before you jump right into the test. Again, breathe. Set aside any internal distractions and focus on the exam. You're ready for this, so take a moment or two to remind yourself of that.

- ▸ **Take a break if you need one:** You have three hours to complete the exam, so give yourself some time to get some air, stretch your legs, and reenergize yourself.

- ▸ **Remember that you might be audiotaped or videotaped:** Don't allow this to distract you; instead, remember that taping test takers is "business as usual" for Prometric testing facilities. Don't take it personally; just let it go. You have more important things to focus on than a camera or microphone.

- ▸ **Don't rush, but don't linger too long on difficult questions, either:** The questions will vary in their degree of difficulty and complexity. Don't let yourself be flustered by one particularly difficult, wordy, or (seemingly) tricky question.

- ▸ **Read every word of every question:** Just like in real life, one word or one minute detail can make all the difference in selecting the best answer.

- ▸ **Don't look for patterns in answer selections:** There aren't any.

- ▸ **Don't assume the longest answer is the best answer:** Don't assume the shortest answer is the best answer either.

- **Answer every question:** Unanswered questions are 100% likely to be wrong. If you make a wild guess, you have a 25% chance of getting it right. If, however, you can narrow down your choices to two or three possible responses, you can double or triple your chances of answering the question correctly.

- **Take advantage of the fact that you can "mark," return to, and review skipped or previously answered questions:** When you reach the end of the exam, return to the more difficult questions. You may even want to deliberately skip some of the more difficult questions along the way, knowing that you can return to them after you have successfully answered many, many other exam questions.

- **Try to build in time to review your answers after you have answered all the questions:** Pay particular attention to questions that contain a lot of detail or those that seemed particularly straightforward the first time around. (It's possible you might have initially overlooked something important.)

- **When rechecking your responses, you may be tempted to question every answer you've made, but be careful not to fall into the trap of second-guessing yourself too much:** If you read the question carefully and completely the first time through, and you felt like you knew the right answer, you probably did. If, however, as you check your answers, a response clearly stands out as incorrect, change it. You also might want to consider changing a response if you missed, misread, or misinterpreted details in the questions the first time around or if you jumped to a clearly incorrect conclusion. If you are left feeling completely unsure whether you should change your original response, however, it's usually a good idea to go with your first impression.

And, last—but perhaps most important—believe in yourself: now, when you study, and when you sit down to take the test. It's your turn. So roll up your sleeves. You're about to begin the process of earning your PHR designation.

Contacting the Author

On a somewhat more personal note, please know that the highly talented team of Exam Prep editors and I have worked diligently to create a real-world tool that you can integrate into your overall personalized PHR study strategy. We take this responsibility seriously and would greatly appreciate hearing back from you about your experiences with this book, along with any feedback you have—positive as well as constructive. For instance, let us know the degree to which you found this book to be helpful in your preparation efforts. And, for those of you who have purchased an earlier edition of this booked, we'd be curious to hear your thoughts on the new design.

We also recognize that—despite our best efforts—there's always room for improvement. In that spirit, each of us is keenly interested in hearing your suggestions for changes or additions that could enhance the value of this book for future PHR candidates. We'll consider everything you say carefully and respond to all reasonable suggestions and comments.

And, of course, we love good news. So, even if you just want to tell us that you passed your PHR exam and share the story of your success, let us know. We'll celebrate with you!

Whatever the nature of your comment, I invite you to reach out to me at Cathy@CathyWinterfield. com. Thank you in advance for doing so.

NOTE

Please note that I wrote the first and second editions of this book under the name Cathy Lee Gibson. (My name has changed, but the author remains the same.)

Last, let me offer a word of thanks for including us in your exam prep strategy. Enjoy the book and your experiences with it. We would wish you luck on the exam, but we don't think you really need it. Using this book as part of a larger test-prep plan, we know you'll do well on the strength of your knowledge, skills, and ability to apply those skills to real-life workplace situations. With all that going for you, there's no need for luck.

Frequently Asked Questions

As you prepare for the test, you might have some general questions. To support you, we've pulled together some of the questions that we've been asked before by HR professionals who are studying for the PHR and that you might have as well:

Question: What I'm reading about here, in this book, is called something different where I work. Which words are right?

Answer: Keep in mind that you are studying to pass a test that is predicated on HRCI's definition of the HR body of knowledge. So, regardless of how a particular program might be labeled (or handled) at your current/prior organization(s), it's important to think about it within the context of HRCI's HR body of knowledge. Don't worry too much if your organization uses different terminology. Instead, focus on understanding the ideas and how they play out in your own experience.

Question: I'm supposed to apply my own experience, right? But my own experience doesn't line up with what is in these books.

Answer: This can happen. In fact, it happens to a lot of people who are studying for the PHR/SPHR exam. And it can be frustrating when it does.

Try keeping two things in mind. First, if there is a gap between what you've experienced and the HRCI body of knowledge, go with what is in the HRCI body of knowledge. You can reconcile the differences later on. For now, understand what HRCI considers the recommended approach and follow that.

Second, keep in mind that you will be asked to choose the best possible response when you take the test—not the response that is most familiar to you. As such, going with your initial answer might not be the best approach for this particular test because your initial response might be more of a measure of what you are familiar with rather than what HRCI would consider the best answer to be.

Lastly, please keep in mind—this doesn't mean that your employer is necessarily wrong. For a variety of reasons, the best approach for one organization might be different from the best approach overall. However, you are studying not only to learn; you are studying to pass a test. Know what HRCI is looking for and choose accordingly.

Question: Why are some things in more than one place in this book?

Answer: Many of the concepts and ideas in this book relate to more than one functional area. That's not only okay, it's actually good because it reflects the interrelatedness of the HR profession. It's not a profession in which we can put things into neat boxes. The "messiness" of our work help keeps it vibrant, interesting, and ever-evolving.

Having said that, some concepts and laws pertain to functional areas in very different ways. Some of those areas of overlap are not clear. And, in some cases, leaving out a particular law or concept might constitute a misleading or incomplete omission. As such, they warrant dual inclusion.

Question: Why are some concepts in just one place if they can apply to more than one functional area?

Answer: That's a good question. Ultimately, part of what you are called upon as a certificant—and as an HR professional—is to do some of this mapping yourself, as you prepare for this test and in the workplace. We've started this process for you, and encourage you to keep moving forward with it as you do your test prep, either on your own or with your study partners.

Question: Do I have to know the functional area that a particular topic or law aligns with?

Answer: Often, as you come to understand the focus of each functional area, these connections will become easier to make. It might not seem that way at first, but keep the faith. This 1,000-piece puzzle will fall into place, more and more, as you move through your study plan.

Having said that, don't box yourself in. There are many possible applications and ways to map this. We'll get into this more in the full-length books, as mentioned earlier.

Question: I used a different test prep resource, and it put ideas in different functional areas. Who is right, and who is wrong?

Answer: There are different ways to look at the HRBOK. And, although we can't comment on the relative value or worth of different test prep tools, we do suggest that you apply your own logic and analysis to this. What makes sense? And, more importantly, why?

No test prep resource has all the answers. And any valuable test prep resource should encourage you to think more, rather than less. Use your own reasoning ability to think through what makes sense to you.

Question: Where does this HRBOK come from? Does SHRM endorse it?

Answer: HRCI publishes the HR body of knowledge. Although HRCI and SHRM once had a close and collaborative relationship, SHRM is now wholly separate from HRCI. Said differently, HRCI is a certifying organization that offers an accredited credential that has met the National Commission for Certifying Agencies' (NCAA's) rigorous standards. SHRM is a professional membership association that began offering newly created HR certifications in 2015.

Question: There's a lot of legal content in this book. Does that mean I don't need to hire a lawyer? (Whew—that would be a relief.)

Answer: No! This author is not a lawyer and does not play one on TV, in the classroom, or when she writes. Nothing in this book should be considered legal advice. Qualified legal counsel should always be contacted with any questions of legal relevance. (Yes, this is the fine print. And it's really important. Pay close and careful attention to it.)

Question: There are so many laws, so many cases. I can't keep them all straight in my mind. Can't I just learn everything but the laws?

Answer: Part of being an HR professional—especially in the United States—involves knowing the laws, the cases, and the implications of both. Excluding these will likely result in your failing the exam (I've seen this before. Trust me—this strategy just doesn't work.) More importantly, doing so may result in your being a far less effective HR professional than you otherwise could have been.

CHAPTER ONE

Business Management and Strategy (BM & S)

There is a familiar saying that goes something like this: "Some people make things happen, some people watch things happen, and some people wonder what happened." In our profession, we are fortunate to have the opportunity to choose which of those paths we will follow. Although this choice holds true for every functional area within HR (and for every chapter of this book), it is particularly true of strategic management.

The Evolving Role of HR

HR has been on a long and sometimes challenging journey through which it has redefined itself as a profession and redefined itself with respect to its role in the organization. Before we focus more explicitly on HR's current role and impact, let's briefly review the earlier legs of this evolutionary journey.

A Brief Historical Scan of HR

Much has changed about our profession in the past 50+ years, during which an ongoing discussion around professionalism and certification has continued to evolve. Perhaps the most outwardly recognizable sign of the journey in which we have been engaging is how we refer to our profession.

Originally, our profession was known as "Industrial Relations" (the "I" and the "R" in Cornell's "ILR" come from "industrial relations"; the "L" comes from "labor"). Sometime back in the 1950s, it started to be called "Personnel." Today, for the most part, we know it as "Human Resources" or "Human Capital." Tomorrow, who knows what it will be called; in some organizations, a "chief people officer" or a "VP of people" already leads our function.

One thing is certain: our name hasn't changed just to keep up with the times. Rather, these changes reflect the transformation of our role from a job or a support function to a bona fide profession—from administrative support roles to strategic organizational partners.

Of course, just as the name of our department has not changed in all organizations, neither has our role evolved at an even pace in all organizations. Let's take a closer look at what this means and at what its true impact is on how we carry out our roles.

HR As It Was, and HR As It Is (or Can Be)

As mentioned previously, the way in which HR professionals carry out their functions has changed and evolved over the years. Table 1.1 highlights some indicators of this shift.

TABLE 1.1   HR: Then and Now

Then	Now
Reactive	Proactive
Gatekeeper (or gate closer)	Facilitator
Policy enforcer	Policy strategy consultant
Authoritarian	Consultative
Focused on HR and its goals	Focused on the organization and its mission
Employee advocate (from managers' perspective) and/or management advocate) (from the employee's perspective)	"Truth advocate" (© D'Amato)

The distinctions between then and now, however, aren't always quite as absolute and clear as this chart may indicate:

▶ Many organizations fall somewhere along the spectrum between then and now in terms of how their HR departments function in an overall sense.

▶ Other organizations might more closely resemble Then with respect to some areas of responsibility and more closely resemble Now with respect to others.

▶ So, too, each of us might function in some ways closer to the Then end of the spectrum and function in other ways closer to the Now.

This can be true on an organizational, functional, or even individual level.

Larger, overarching questions can and should emerge through contemplation of where we fall (individually and collectively) along the Then and Now spectrum. These questions include the following:

▶ How does the organization perceive HR?

▶ How does HR perceive itself?

We can begin to explore and address these questions by developing a broader, more holistic understanding of the myriad required roles of HR within the organization. The HR Impact Model provides one road map within which to begin to develop this understanding.

The HR Impact Model

The HR Impact Model in Figure 1.1, developed by this author and Dr. Robert K. Prescott, SPHR, of Rollins College Crummer Graduate School of Business, uses four categories to explore the functional responsibilities of HR professionals:

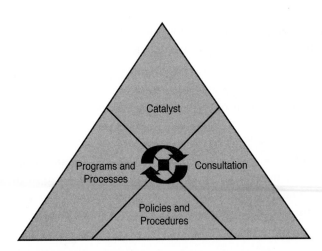

FIGURE 1.1

HR Impact Model. © 2005, Prescott and Winterfield.

Traditionally, many HR professionals operate only within the Policies and Procedures and Programs and Processes categories. For many of us, these categories represent our anchors—the zones within which we are most comfortable, and the ones within which many of our organizations traditionally (and sometimes currently) expected us to function.

We must now, however, migrate away from the familiar comfort offered by those two sectors we have inhabited for so long. This impact model illustrates and explains the other roles required of today's—and tomorrow's—HR professionals.

Policies and Procedures

Policies and procedures represent the dimension of the HR Impact Model with which many of us, as HR professionals, are most familiar. It is, in essence, our comfort zone. And although we must be prepared to expand beyond it, we also must ensure that we master our performance within it.

> ▶ **Organizational role:** Create and implement HR policies and procedures. There is no doubt that this is an important role for the HR function. However, even though they're perceived as policy experts, HR professionals who focus only on policies and procedures tend not to be integrally involved in their organization's strategic planning or change efforts.

> ▶ **Organizational impact:** Influence the creation, appropriate interpretation, and implementation of organizational policy; ensure fair treatment of employees; and provide a decision-making framework.

In the next section, we'll discuss the importance—and potential impact—of programs and processes.

Programs and Processes

Traditionally, HR professionals have been regarded as "people experts" who can help build and maintain effective work relationships, motivate performance, and develop employees. Those focused on programs and processes tend to work in functional-oriented teams (for example, employee relations, compensation, or training) to support the effective execution of those processes.

> ▶ **Organizational role:** Oversee programs and processes to attract, motivate, develop, and retain employees.

▶ **Organizational impact:** Promote employee satisfaction and enhance performance. Provide effective process guidelines for the organization to follow in implementing people-management practices.

Next, let's take a look at the consultative dimensions of the HR Impact Model.

Consultation

In this client-oriented role, HR professionals help define the overall organizational strategy, structure, and culture as well as enhance the effectiveness of individuals within the organization. HR professionals who assume these roles within the organization improve their working relationships with their constituents and increase their credibility throughout the organization.

▶ **Organizational role:** Respond to or identify the needs of management and work in partnership to enhance the management team's effectiveness, both individually and collectively.

▶ **Organizational impact:** Support, coach, develop, and challenge clients to take appropriate action on identified problems, issues, challenges, initiatives, or programs.

Last, let's take a closer look at the tremendous impact that HR can wield as true catalysts for change.

Catalyst

In this role, the HR professional stays abreast of market demographics, business needs, and employee attitudes and values as well as of state-of-the-art approaches to HR management. The HR professional points out emerging HR issues and trends both within the company and in the external market and identifies their impact on the organization and how management might best respond to them.

In this context, it is also important to note that HR professionals do not work within any one dimension in isolation. It is the unique, customized mix of services for a given organization that yields the greatest impact. HR professionals have to assess their proper mix of requirements for their respective organization.

▶ **Organizational role:** Focus on the long-term, strategic needs of the organization to identify relevant trends and ensure that management is prepared to act appropriately in guiding the organization for the long term.

▶ **Organizational impact:** Help position the organization for the future, especially by designing a working environment and organizational culture that meets the changing needs, preferences, and demographics of current and future employees and by helping the organization address changes in its business and operating environments.

Next up: we'll look at the administrative, strategic, and operational/tactical dimensions of HR.

The Dimensions of HR: The Three Legs of a Stool

With the HR Impact Model as one backdrop, another way to consider our evolving roles as HR professionals is to think of our function as a three-legged stool, where administrative, strategic, and operational/tactical elements are the legs.

- ▶ **Leg #1:** Administrative
- ▶ **Leg #2:** Strategic
- ▶ **Leg #3:** Operational/Tactical

Leg #1: Administrative

These are the transactions—the "things" that need to be done. Over the years, some of the transactions we used to perform have gone away. Or they have been and will likely continue to be outsourced. More often, however, those functions manifest themselves dramatically differently today than they did yesterday or are being handled in different—and often more in streamlined or more technologically sophisticated—ways (such as self-serve kiosks, intranets, HRIS applications, outsourcing, and so on).

Leg #2: Strategic

The difference between the administrative functions in HR and the strategic functions in HR is like the difference between being a person who designs automobiles and the person who's a passenger in an automobile. Both are important and, ultimately, each needs the other. Were there no automobile designers, the current generation of cars would become the future generation of cars, leaving certain safety and efficiency needs unmet (not to mention ever-changing stylistic trends). Were there no passengers, there would be no need for cars in the first place, and certainly no need for anyone to invest time and energy into looking toward the future of the automotive industry.

Strategic HR management speaks to HR's overall commitment, in both word and deed, to meeting the ever-evolving short-term, long-term, and strategic objectives of the organization. Strategic HR takes a long-term, future-focused approach to the ways in which it will partner with the organization to attain its organizational mission. Strategic HR looks at business and organizational issues rather than just HR issues because all HR issues are, ultimately, business issues. Said differently, rather than endeavoring to maintain the status quo, strategic HR cultivates, nurtures, and embraces change. It is dynamic, effective, consultative, and ever-evolving—just like the HR profession.

Leg #3: Operational/Tactical

Somewhere in between the administrative functions that must be performed and the inventive and creative life force that is part of strategic HR management lies the operational—or tactical—dimension of the HR function.

One definition of the word "tactical" offers a militaristic reference, which might help to explain its particular relevance to the HR profession. The American Heritage Dictionary of the English Language defines "tactical" as follows:

(a) Of, relating to, used in, or involving military or naval operations that are smaller, closer to base, and of less long-term significance than strategic operations.

(b) Carried out in support of military or naval operations: tactical bombing.

This definition aligns well with the application of this term in the HR profession. The operational, tactical, or day-to-day performance and execution of the HR role can be accomplished in many ways—some of which place us more closely toward the administrative end of the spectrum, whereas others demonstrate more vividly how, and whether, the overarching strategic objectives of HR (and, therefore, of the organization) are being brought to life. In the automotive metaphor used previously, the tactical area might be depicted by the role of the driver. Passengers wouldn't get anywhere without drivers—even if a car had the most evolved designs and finest appointments imaginable. Also, the performance and safety features that were woven into the design would come to life only in the hands and feet of the driver—the person who plays a more active, involved, and immediately impactful role than any passenger.

RESPONSIBILITY

BM & S Responsibility 01

Interpret and apply information related to the organization's operations from internal sources, including finance, accounting, business development, marketing, sales, operations, and information technology, to contribute to the development of the organization's strategic plan.

KNOWLEDGE

Knowledge 08

Elements of a cost-benefit analysis during the life-cycle of the business (such as scenarios for growth, including expected, economic stressed, and worst-case conditions) and the impact to net worth/earnings for short-, mid-, and long-term horizons.

SWOT Analysis (Strengths, Weaknesses, Opportunities, and Threats)

A SWOT analysis is conducted to ascertain the strengths and weaknesses that are inherent to an organization, as well as the opportunities and threats that it faces from external forces. Although it sounds relatively simple and straightforward, the process of conducting a SWOT analysis can become challenging, in part because it is often difficult for organizations—as it is for people—to see themselves objectively.

When examining strengths and weaknesses, it is necessary for analysis to be directed inward. This clear and objective assessment would ascertain the resources of the organization, including the following:

- ▶ Human
- ▶ Financial
- ▶ Technological
- ▶ Capital
- ▶ Brand image

Opportunities and threats, conversely, look outward at factors such as competition, economic trends, customer needs and wants, and legislative or regulatory activity. This process, known as environmental scanning, is explored earlier in this chapter.

Minding Our Own Business

As HR professionals, there is much specific business-related information we need to know about the various structural elements of organizations. In addition to everything else addressed in this chapter (and, in a sense, in this book), here are some of the business concepts with which HR professionals need to be familiar.

Accounting/Finance Functions and Concepts

Developing a solid understanding of financial and accounting concepts is an essential component to being a valuable HR professional. Knowing how they manifest within one's organization is even more essential. Remember—we're not just "people people"—we're businesspeople. For that reason, this section will set forth important financial descriptors that are key concepts for savvy HR professionals to understand.

- **Acid test:** A mathematical calculation/metric that divides current liabilities into the sum of the following: cash, accounts receivable, and short-term investments. This calculation is intended to measure an organization's ability to cover liabilities without selling off inventory or liquidating other long-term investments.

- **Accounts payable:** Money that the organization owes to others. This could include—but is not necessarily limited to—outstanding bills from vendors, suppliers, lenders, and the like. Accounts payable constitutes a liability to the organization and is reflected as such on an organization's balance sheet.

- **Accounts receivable:** Money that is owed to the organization. Accounts payable refers to invoices that have been sent/given to customers but that have not yet been paid. Accounts receivable constitutes an asset and is generally recorded as such on an organization's balance sheet.

- **Asset:** Anything owned by an organization that has, or has the ability to generate, economic value to that organization.

- **Balance sheet:** A financial statement that itemizes assets, liabilities, and shareholder/ owners' equity as of a particular point (date) in time. On a balance sheet, the total of the assets must equal the sum of the liabilities + shareholder/owners' equity. A balance sheet is sometimes referred to as a *statement of financial position*.

- **Budgeting:** The process by which a financial plan is developed for an organization, or one or more portions of an organization, for a specified period of time. A budget includes expected costs and expenses and revenues within the specific context of resource requirements (human and nonhuman). Budgets are created as a way of further supporting organizational objectives and stated milestones.

- **Activity-based budgeting:** An approach to budgeting in which the costs of individual activities are individually assessed, compared to other activities performed within the organization, and looked at within the context of the overarching organizational objectives and the degree to which those activities contribute to the attainment of those objectives.

- **Formula budgeting:** An approach to budgeting in which the proposed budget is developed by applying a consistent formula to the current budget figures (for instance, 3% increase).

- **Incremental budgeting:** A process by which a new budget is developed using the budget for the current period as a starting point. This form of budgeting constitutes a "tweaking" of the current budget rather than an approach that starts from the beginning.

- **Zero-based budgeting:** A process by which the proposed budget is not based on current or prior expenses, revenues, or performance. Rather, the budgeting process begins, each time, "from scratch."

- **Business activity ratios:** Mathematical calculations/metrics that provide information on the pace at which different balance sheet items have been converted into either cash or sales (depending upon which balance sheet item is being measured).

- **Cash flow statement (statement of cash flows):** A financial tool that captures the inflows and outflows of cash during a stated period of time. A cash flow statement is one tool that can be used to ascertain and predict the financial soundness and strength of an organization.

- **Current ratio:** A mathematical calculation/metric that divides current assets by current liabilities. This calculation is considered to reflect the organization's ability to pay its creditors and meets its current and short-term financial obligations.

- **Debt ratios:** A mathematical calculation/metric that divides total debt by total assets. Debt ratios are often one tool (of several) used to assess the level of risk associated with moving forward with a financial transaction/venture with an organization.

- **Equity:** The value (in financial terms) of the owners' interest in an organization.

- **Financial ratios:** Mathematical calculations/metrics in which different items from the financial statement are divided, one into another, to provide information on organizational performance. This information can subsequently be analyzed to reach conclusions and inform organizational decision-making.

- **Gross profit margin:** A mathematical calculation/metric that divides gross profit by revenues. The resulting quotient is a measure of the organization's profitability.

- **Income statement:** A financial instrument that enumerates and documents revenues and expenses over a particular period of time.

- **Liability:** Any financial obligation that an organization must pay, either presently or in the future.

- **Liquidity:** A calculation of available cash or assets that could be quickly converted to cash with no loss in value.

- **Profitability ratios:** A mathematical calculation/metric that measures how well an organization has been able to generate profit (revenues less expenses) during a particular period of time.

- **Return on investment (ROI):** A metric that calculates the absolute or relative worth, value, and effectiveness. This is calculated as follows:

$$\frac{\text{Financial gain from investment} - \text{Cost of investment}}{\text{Cost of investment}}$$

Technical Activities/Operations

HR professionals also need to develop an understanding of the operational dimensions of the organization. Failing to do so could potentially undermine an HR professional's credibility in the eyes of their clients, as well as their effectiveness.

- **Capacity:** A manufacturing term that speaks to the maximum volume of goods or services that can be produced/delivered within a specified timeframe based on current human and nonhuman organizational resources.

- **Inventory:** The supply of goods and materials that is poised for production, sales, or to support customer service.

- **Span of control:** The number of individuals ("direct reports") who report to a specific supervisor/manager/leader within an organization.

Cost/Benefit Analysis

$$\frac{\text{Financial gain that will be—or has been—generated from investment}}{\text{Cost of investment}}$$

> **NOTE**
>
> This financial gain can be projected or actual, depending upon the nature of the calculation one is making.

Commercial Activities/Sales and Marketing

The 4 Ps: The 4 Ps refer to the categories into which components of marketing plans can be divided.

- ▸ **Product:** The item (tangible) or service (intangible) that is being marketed.
- ▸ **Place:** Any location—real or virtual—at which a product or service can be purchased/procured.
- ▸ **Price:** The amount that a customer pays/will pay for a product or service.
- ▸ **Promotion:** All the ways in which an organization seeks to communicate with customers and potential customers about its products and services, and the benefits thereof.

BM & S Responsibility 02

Interpret and apply information related to the organization's operations from internal sources, including finance, accounting, business development, marketing, sales, operations, and information technology, in order to contribute to the development of the organization's strategic plan.

RESPONSIBILITY

Business Processes 10

(For example: operations, sales and marketing, data management)

RESPONSIBILITY

Strategic planning helps the organization look toward the future and begin to shape how it will position itself for that future.

One element of strategic planning is external scanning. Let's take a closer look at that particular component.

Environmental Scanning: An External Perspective

Environmental scanning is the process through which organizations maintain awareness of the opportunities and threats presented by the surroundings—both macro and micro—within which they operate.

For information that is obtained through an environmental scan to be truly valuable, leaders within the organization must use the data that is collected to modify, as appropriate, organizational objectives or strategies. The ability to demonstrate organizational agility in response to environmental information is essential; the willingness to act on that information is perhaps even more important.

Some organizations conduct environmental scans on an ad hoc basis, often in response to crises or other unexpected events. Other organizations plan to conduct environmental scans on a more regular basis. Still other organizations choose to conduct scanning on a continuous basis—always collecting, processing, and analyzing data. Although there is no one right approach, in today's highly turbulent (and sometimes even volatile) business and organizational environments, it may be prudent to consider conducting environmental scanning more frequently rather than less frequently.

External Trends: Things to Keep an Eye On

Organizations need to monitor trends of a wide and varying nature, including the following:

- ▶ Economic
- ▶ Competitive
- ▶ Political
- ▶ Global
- ▶ Business
- ▶ Industry
- ▶ Employment
- ▶ Technological
- ▶ Demographic
- ▶ Legislative/Regulatory

RESPONSIBILITY

BM & S Responsibility 04

Establish strategic relationships with key individuals in the organization to influence organizational decision-making.

To perform this responsibility effectively, HR professionals must develop effective internal consulting skills. Just as importantly, they must know how to leverage those skills within the structure of their organization, as well as the "place" where the organization finds itself within the organizational life cycle. This section will explore each of these areas in greater depth.

The HR Professional as Internal Consultant

Throughout the sectors of the HR Impact Model and all three legs of the stool, HR professionals must make choices relative to how they will portray and conduct themselves within the organization. Within any of those sectors and any of those legs, one of the most critical choices that must be made is the degree to which an HR professional will function in a truly consultative manner.

So what is consulting? According to Peter Block, in the first edition of his must-have book *Flawless Consulting*:

"You are consulting any time you are trying to change or improve a situation but have no direct control over the implementation. If you have direct control you are managing, not consulting. The consultant's lack of direct control and authority is what makes our task difficult and, at times, drives us crazy."

The HR profession is difficult and may even feel a little bit crazy at times. It is also challenging, meaningful, and highly impactful. Through the role of internal consultants, each HR professional can magnify and leverage his contributions at the transformational, tactical, and even transactional level. One way to do this is by applying a consistent, well-thought-out consulting process. The seven stages of internal consulting represent one such model.

The Seven Stages of Internal Consulting

The Seven Stages of the Internal Consulting model (Prescott, 2005) include Exploring the Situation; Gaining Agreement to the Project Plan; Gathering Data, Analyzing, and Identifying Findings; Developing Recommendations; Presenting the Findings and Recommendations; Implementing; and Reviewing, Transitioning, and Evaluating the Project.

Stage 1—Exploring the Situation: Seek to gain a better understanding of the situation. Meet with the client to discuss the situation and to determine whether the project should go forward.

Stage 2—Gaining Agreement to the Project Plan: Step 1: Develop a draft project plan that defines the project and its goals. The plan should also include roles and responsibilities, information and resources needed, tasks required, data collection methods, measurements, and a project timeline. Step 2: Meet with the client to gain agreement to move forward with the project based on the project plan. This plan is a dynamic document, and it should be adjusted, as needed and appropriate, throughout the project.

Stage 3—Gathering Data, Analyzing, and Identifying Findings: Collect, aggregate, and analyze information related to the project goals.

Stage 4—Developing Recommendations: Formulate realistic and measurable recommendations based on the findings and goals of the project.

Stage 5—Presenting the Findings and Recommendations: Present the findings and recommendations to the client. Gain the client's agreement to implement the recommendations, and explore ways to approach the implementation process.

Stage 6—Implementing: Work collaboratively with the client to plan and implement the recommendations. Project management, communication, and monitoring are key components of this stage.

Stage 7—Reviewing, Transitioning, and Evaluating the Project: Review the project and transition it to the client. Assess (and self-assess) what was accomplished, what worked well, and what may be done differently in the future.

Organizational Structure and HR

As we've stated numerous times, to be effective in our profession, we have to be savvy businesspeople. It's not enough to be skilled in our craft as HR professionals. Although our profession is our craft, we also need to be prepared to knowledgeably practice that craft within our organizations and our industries. To do so, one of the many things we need to understand is how organizations are structured. Organizational structure speaks to the various ways in which organizations can be designed to attain maximum levels of effectiveness and efficiency. Understanding organizational structure will also enable HR professionals to establish more effective strategic relationships with key individuals within the organization.

The "Roots" of Organizational Structure

As we begin to take a look at how organizations are structured, it's important to understand the work of Henri Fayol, whose work we will study in greater depth later in this chapter. Fayol identified six functional groups within organizations and suggested that all organizational activities can fit into one of those six functional areas:

▶ Technical activities

▶ Commercial activities: sales and marketing

▶ Financial activities

▶ Security activities

▶ Accounting activities

▶ Managerial activities

Despite the ongoing relevance of Fayol's theories, a few things have changed since Fayol's time. One is the role of human resources in the organization, which at first glance is not well reflected in these six areas. Another is information technology, nonexistent in the early twentieth century when Fayol set forth his ideas. Something that can be said to hold true for both of these areas is that while each constitutes its own independent function, each also supports and reinforces the efforts of and impacts the success of every other area within the organization. This is important in and of itself because it reinforces the idea that these areas—although illustrative—are not necessarily as clearly dichotomized as they were when Fayol originally set forth his ideas.

The Functional Organizational Structure

As the name implies, functional organizations are composed of departments, each of which is dedicated to a different function. This approach, the most common organizational structure, often consists of highly centralized departments, such as HR, operations, sales/marketing, accounting, and so on.

The functional organizational structure is generally hierarchical in nature—with each employee reporting to one, and only one, individual, as shown in Figure 1.2.

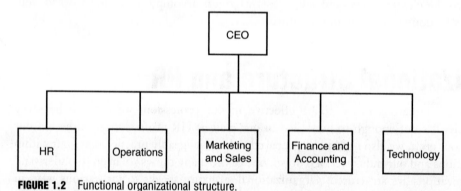

FIGURE 1.2 Functional organizational structure.

The Divisional Organizational Structure

A more decentralized approach to organizational structure, divisional structures are segmented on the basis of some shared characteristic—for instance, geographic region, customer base, product line, and so on. Each division would encompass all the people and functions needed to attain its objectives (objectives pertaining to its designated geographic region, customer base, product line, and so on).

Although still primarily hierarchical in nature, it is also possible for dotted-line reporting relationships to exist within a divisional organizational structure. By dotted line, we mean that while a straight-line reporting relationship exists to the division head, another, dotted-line relationship can also exist to traditional functional leaders. (In the case of HR, for instance, this might mean a dotted-line reporting relationship to the VP of HR.) An example of divisional organization structure is shown in Figure 1.3.

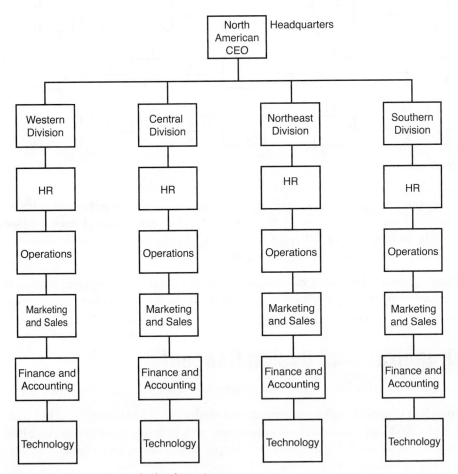

FIGURE 1.3 Divisional organizational structure.

The Matrix Organizational Structure

A matrix organizational structure is, in one sense, a combination of functional and divisional structures, as shown in Figure 1.4. It attempts to draw on the strengths of each, while minimizing the potential downside of "silos" that can emerge in a traditional hierarchical organization.

Example of Matrix Organizational Structure

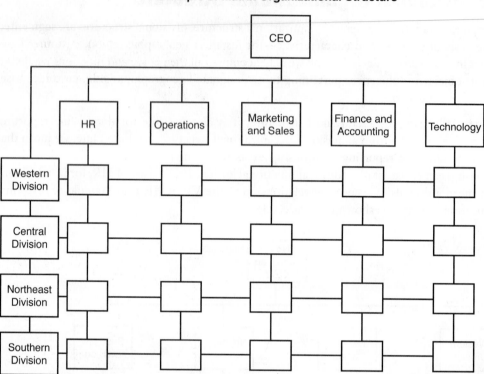

FIGURE 1.4 Matrix organizational structure.

Unlike in a functional or divisional organizational structure, employees who work within a matrix structure may report to two managers rather than to just one. Although each manager may be primarily accountable for different dimensions of the employee's work, neither is superior to the other; there are two chains of command.

Although affording their own unique challenges, matrix organizational structures tend to be particularly effective in project-driven environments (for instance, consulting, construction, and so on).

Other Organizational Design Concepts

HR professionals also need to know these other concepts related to organizational design:

▶ **Boundaryless organization:** An organizational model that relies modestly on the traditional, hierarchical approach and instead functions with little attention to reporting lines or relationships, functional distinctions or silos, or barriers (real, or imagined) between or even outside the organization.

▶ **Bureaucracy:** An organizational model in which clearly defined lines of authority and areas of responsibility are created within a hierarchical structure. Bureaucracies are often characterized by many rules, approval guidelines, and—often—a degree of rigidity.

▶ **Departmentalization ("departmentation"):** The process of dividing related tasks and responsibilities between different units within the organization. Such units are often referred to as "departments." Although each department might address a variety of tasks, all of those tasks are related in some meaningful way.

▶ **Formalization, or formal authority:** The rights, privileges, and power that are inherent to a particular position, and which thus are granted to an individual upon selection for or appointment to a particular position. This type of authority is often codified in some way. It is often historically present in the same position, but such authority can be imbued to—or even taken away from—positions as intentional organizational changes are implemented.

▶ **Virtual organization:** An organizational model in which the organization does not reside in any one particular "brick and mortar" location but rather exists and conducts business on the Internet.

The Organizational Life Cycle

It's particularly important for HR professionals to be familiar with organizational life cycles, in part because each phase will warrant different interventions, different approaches, and perhaps even different relationships.

An organizational life cycle consists of the four evolutionary stages of birth, growth, maturity, and decline experienced by organizations over the course of time. These phases or stages are roughly approximate to the phases of life experienced by humans, thereby further bolstering the perspective of the organization as a living, breathing entity. Each phase of the organizational life cycle will warrant different HR systems or interventions.

The four stages of the life cycle—though referred to slightly differently by different experts—are as follows:

▶ **Stage 1: Introduction (or "birth"):** Excitement and energy are high and cash flow may be low. Struggling start-ups often find themselves searching for solid footing, financially as well as operationally. The core group of highly talented employees may focus fixedly on the founder as a source of direction, wisdom, and inspiration.

In the introduction phase, employees may find themselves paid above market rates as a reflection of the founder's desire to lure them onboard. Alternatively—and somewhat conversely—if money is in short supply, employees in the introduction phase may earn less cash compensation and have those diminished earnings offset by other noncash rewards (equity, intrinsic rewards, and so on).

Depending on the organization, HR may or may not have a presence in this phase of the organizational life cycle.

▶ **Stage 2: Development (or growth):** The organization grows in so many ways during the development phase. Market share, facilities, equipment, revenues, and the number of employees are all likely to expand, to varying degrees. Along with that growth, the organization is likely to experience some growing pains.

Although it may be a challenging process for some organizations—and one that might be met with resistance—it is important that policies and procedures are formalized as a way of fostering equity, compliance, and consistency.

▶ **Stage 3: Maturity:** The growing pains have passed, and the culture is well established. In fact, it's important to ensure that certain elements of the culture do not become a bit too well established. If this were to happen, an entitlement mentality could begin to emerge relative to pay, benefits, performance standards/expectations, and the like. The organizational structure could evolve in a somewhat rigid manner, and resistance to change initiatives could be high.

As is the case with us humans, organizations must resist the onset of inertia during these years of maturity lest they begin to atrophy. In close partnership with senior leadership, HR must play a key role in ensuring that this doesn't happen.

▶ **Stage 4: Decline:** If that inertia does set in, and if the organization or its employees begin to atrophy, decline is likely not far behind. There are many examples of the demise of long-standing organizations—retailers, in particular, and anchors in local and national communities—that just weren't able to keep up with the changing times. This can happen for any number of reasons, such as salaries that are beyond what the organization can truly afford to pay, inflexible management, disengaged workers—the list goes on and on. In the wake of such decline, downsizing is likely to occur, either in pockets or across the organization as a whole.

RESPONSIBILITY

BM & S Responsibility 05

Establish relationships/alliances with key individuals and outside organizations to assist in achieving the organization's strategic goals and objectives (for example: corporate social responsibility and community partnership).

Organizations—for profit, not-for-profit, as well as municipal—are growing progressively more cognizant of themselves as members of the communities in which they operate. Many employers—particularly of newly established entities—seek to establish active community partnerships. These partnerships could be described as relationships that are forged between employers and community organizations (usually not-for-profit or municipal) in support of the mission of the community-based organization. These relationships often benefit the community organization, the employer, and its employees. It also helps build positive public relations and goodwill for the organization within the community by contributing in a meaningful way that reaches beyond seeking profits (and which, perhaps ironically, might therefore contribute to generating incremental profit).

A related concept is that of corporate responsibility, an organization's choice to share responsibility for the environment—physical as well as social—in which it operates. That environment can be defined in a micro sense (such as the town or city in which the employer operates) or in a more macro sense (such as the global environment and green initiatives). Corporate responsibility constitutes a form of corporate citizenship, commitment to, and engagement that is optional and that, presumably, will result in a better quality of life in the community.

There are many relevant dimensions to creating alliances and establishing relationships that need to be considered—one of which is to understand the principles behind motivation.

Motivation cuts across all six functional areas. Motivation, for instance, is often associated with why—and how—employees learn. It's also highly relevant, however, to how employees perceive and value salaries, wages, and benefits and to establishing and sustaining positive relationships in the workplace. And, within the context of this functional area, it is particularly relevant to influencing, creating alliances, and building strategic relationships.

Motivation theory directly affects employee performance in the workplace. As such, HR professionals need a keen understanding of the various motivation theories to incorporate them—in a practical sense—into their initiatives and into their consulting relationships with managers. Some of the key theories in which HR professionals must be well versed are the following:

▶ Maslow's Hierarchy of Needs

▶ B.F. Skinner—Operant Conditioning

▶ Frederick Herzberg—Motivation-Hygiene Theory

▶ Douglas McGregor—Theory X and Theory Y

▶ David McClelland—Acquired Needs Theory

▶ J. Stacy Adams—Equity Theory

▶ Victor Vroom—Expectancy Theory

The following subsections will describe each of these critical theories to help you build your knowledge.

Maslow's Hierarchy of Needs, 1954

Maslow's theory presents five levels of need experienced by humans. People move into higher levels of need as lower levels of need are sufficiently satisfied. Those levels, from most fundamental to most evolved, are

▶ **Basic physical needs:** Basic physical needs include food, water, shelter, acceptable working conditions, and other fundamental, foundational needs.

▶ **Safety and security:** Safety and security needs speak to the need to live and work in an environment that feels—and is—safe.

▶ **Belonging and love:** In the workplace, this need can manifest itself through membership in a department, a profession, a division, clubs, affinity groups, or simply through friendships and relationships.

▶ **Esteem:** Esteem manifests in two dimensions: self and others. Self-esteem refers to valuing one's own self, personally and professionally. Esteem from others relates to receiving recognition and approval from others.

▶ **Self-actualization:** Through self-actualization, individuals want to, and strive to, reach their full potential. Self-actualization is, very often, its own reward.

Maslow at Work

HR professionals need to look for creative ways to address the motivational needs identified by Maslow—even though employees may not be fully aware of them.

Addressing needs doesn't mean trying to move everyone to the next level. It is important not to impose expectations on employees that they do not want to embrace. It is equally important to afford workplace-appropriate opportunities for those who do.

On that note, be sure to keep all applications of Maslow's theory firmly grounded in the workplace. Link it clearly and unambiguously to performance—of the organization, the department, and the individual. Always maintain your focus on the organization's goals, and always be prepared to articulate job-related reasons for motivation-based initiatives.

Last, as you focus on creating opportunities that enable employees to move to higher-level needs, don't lose track of whether and how well employee's lower-level needs are being met. A compensation system, for instance, that allows employees to meet their basic physical needs at one point in time may eventually become problematic and fall well below what labor market competitors are paying. How can this happen? Well, if you stop monitoring how competitors are paying their employees—even for a short period of time—and you might find that your data (and pay rates and practices) quickly become outdated.

B.F. Skinner, Operant Conditioning, 1957

B. F. Skinner's theory of operant conditioning assumes that the ways people choose to behave in the future are a function of the consequences that have resulted from their past behavior. Skinner identifies four types of consequences:

▶ **Positive reinforcement (praise):** Demonstrating desired behavior results in a desirable outcome or consequence. This may encourage the individual to choose to engage in desired behaviors again.

Workplace example: A customer service supervisor observes a customer service representative skillfully resolve a complaint from an irate customer and praises that person for successfully defusing a potentially volatile situation.

▶ **Negative reinforcement:** When an individual believes that specific behaviors will result in a specific undesirable outcome or consequence, she may choose to demonstrate more desirable behaviors instead. In this way, the individual will behave in a way that prevents that undesirable consequence from happening.

Workplace example: An employee chooses to use his own email address and computer—rather than the company's email system—for jokes or other correspondence that could potentially be viewed as inappropriate for the workplace.

▶ **Punishment:** Demonstrating undesirable behavior results in an undesirable outcome or consequence. This may encourage the individual to choose not to engage in that undesired behavior again.

Workplace example: An employee who continues to answer incoming personal cell phone calls during a training session, even after being asked to stop, is asked to leave the training session and is not permitted to register for a make-up program for at least three months.

▶ **Extinction:** An individual's behavior—whether desired or undesired—elicits no outcomes or consequences at all. The individual may choose not to demonstrate that behavior again.

Workplace example: An employee persists in trying to engage coworkers in counterproductive conversations about other coworkers (that is, gossip). If the coworkers do not join in, the employee might choose not to initiate these sorts of (undesired) conversations in the future.

Frederick Herzberg, Motivation-Hygiene Theory, 1959

Herzberg identified two separate and distinct types of needs:

▶ **Motivation factors:** Motivation factors relate specifically to the job itself—for instance, the nature of the work, the challenge inherent to the work, and the perceived or real value of the work.

▶ **Hygiene factors:** Hygiene factors relate to everything else an employee might experience in the workplace—everything associated with the work, but not the work itself. This includes—but is not limited to—pay, benefits, nature of supervision, relationships with coworkers, and so forth.

Dubbed "The Father of Job Enrichment," Herzberg distinguished between factors that can generate positive feelings about work (motivation factors) and factors that can result in negative feelings about work (hygiene factors). So, although unacceptable motivation factors won't cause an employee to be unhappy at work, unacceptable hygiene factors could. Conversely, acceptable or positive motivation factors will cause an employee to be happy at work, but acceptable or positive hygiene factors won't. However, motivation factors will have a positive impact on an employee's motivation level if, and only if, hygiene factors are acceptable.

Herzberg's theory challenged employers—and personnel departments—to look at employees' satisfaction at work in a completely new and different way. No longer was job satisfaction viewed as existing along a single continuum. Herzberg transformationally defined it as a function of two related, but wholly different, factors—both of which warranted attention.

Douglas McGregor, Theory X and Theory Y, 1960

Building on Maslow's work, Theory X and Theory Y refer to two approaches to management:

- ▶ Theory X managers manage in accordance with the general belief that employees are uncommitted, uninterested, hesitant to assume any additional responsibility, and essentially lazy.

- ▶ Theory Y managers manage in accordance with the general belief that employees will take on—and even look for—additional work if the employee perceives that the work is satisfying and rewarding.

David McClelland, Acquired Needs Theory, 1961

McClelland's theory identified and focused on one particular need: achievement. According to McClelland, achievement is not a universal motivator for everyone, and the degree of need varies from individual to individual.

Individuals who experience—or, perhaps more appropriately, possess—the need for achievement are neither risk averse nor risk embracing. More frequently, they take a middle-of-the-road approach when it comes to risk—calculated and conscious. Those motivated by the need for achievement, therefore, will assume an acceptable and tolerable level of risk that allows the opportunity for upside potential, confident all the while that their skills, abilities, and contributions will have the greatest impact in determining the outcome of a situation. Interestingly, individuals with a high achievement need are less concerned with the rewards of achievement than they are with the actual attainment of that achievement.

With respect to performance management, individuals who have a high need for achievement may gravitate toward stretch goals, which are explored further in Chapter 5, "Employee and Labor Relations." They would also be more likely to focus on the goals portion of a performance management system or form than the competencies portion.

J. Stacy Adams, Equity Theory, 1963

Equity theory, as the name implies, is predicated on the assumption that people want to be treated fairly, particularly when compared to how others around them are treated. It also purports that such comparisons will be made frequently.

In the context of employment, equity theory asserts that employees will compare their inputs (everything they bring to the job and invest in the job) and outputs (how they are rewarded—both intrinsically and extrinsically—for what they invest in the job) to others' inputs and outputs. If employees come away from this process feeling as though they are being treated fairly in comparison to others, they will continue to put forth effort. Conversely, employees who come away from this process with the belief that they are being treated unfairly will seek to make a change. That change might include trying to change their own inputs, trying to change their own outputs, or trying to change the inputs or outputs of others. Any of these options could manifest themselves in either productive or unproductive ways. And, of course, that same employee could quit—the most dramatic way that an employee can change inputs.

Victor Vroom—Expectancy Theory, 1964

Vroom's expectancy theory is all about weighing options and making choices. It asserts, in essence, that people will put forth effort when they believe that such effort will result in an outcome and that that outcome is worthwhile. This theory is composed of three key elements and resulting questions that individuals (in this case, employees) ask themselves:

- **Expectancy:** "How likely is it that I'll be able to attain a particular goal (in this case, a certain level of performance) if I put forth the required effort?"

- **Instrumentality:** "Assuming that I do attain this level of performance, how likely it is that I'll be recognized or rewarded in some way?"

- **Valence:** "Assuming that I am recognized or rewarded, what is that recognition or reward really worth to me?"

RESPONSIBILITY

BM & S Responsibility 07

Develop, influence, and execute strategies for managing organizational change that balance the expectations and needs of the organization, its employees, and other stakeholders.

HR's Role in Change Management

It has been said that the only constant is change. That is particularly—and at times poignantly—evident in the workplace.

Organizationally, change is all around us and can manifest itself in many ways: downsizings, redeployments, introductions of new processes, reassignment among staff, mergers and acquisitions—the list goes on and on. Without a doubt, HR plays a major role with respect to managing that change positively and productively. (In those organizations where HR has truly earned a "seat at the table," HR will ideally have an important role with respect to initiating, driving, and shaping change, as well.)

HR's role, in this regard, is inextricably linked to the attainment of organizational objectives and the furtherance of the organization's mission. During times of change, HR is called on to lead people-management processes. HR professionals—individually and collectively within the organization—must align their people-management efforts with the strategic goals of the organization. HR must also be prepared to measure the degree of success that has been attained.

To meet the ever-accelerating pace of change, HR professionals must understand change, as well as the environments that cause change. This understanding will be particularly important when HR is called upon to adapt the organization's people-management practices to evolving workplace-based realities while maintaining and improving on current levels of organizational performance. As such, successfully designing, aligning, and implementing adaptive people-management practices is an essential component of being a strategic HR partner.

Change Management

The organization is a complex human system that must be continually examined and reexamined. Leaders in organizations must, as such, be able to take the vision of the organization and translate it into goals, which in turn should become the foundation for managing the organization, for assessing performance, and for distributing rewards.

Change management activities involve: "(1) defining and instilling new values, attitudes, norms, and behaviors within an organization that support new ways of doing work and overcome resistance to change; (2) building consensus among customers and stakeholders on specific changes designed to better meet their needs; and (3) planning, testing, and implementing all aspects of the transition from one organizational structure or business process to another" (www.gao.gov).

Changes on the Horizon: How Might They Impact HR and Our Organizations

In many ways, HR trends are best identified by looking first at business/organizational, industry, and societal trends. As a microcosm of the outside world, organizations are directly impacted by what happens in the external environment. It logically follows that because HR exists to support the attainment of organizational objectives, it is impossible—or at least extremely ill-advised—for us to isolate ourselves—from the organization or from the world.

For this reason, HR professionals must keep their fingers on the pulse of the world around them and on the world at large. Workplaces can change almost instantaneously, and trends can develop almost as quickly.

NOTE

One devastatingly illustrative example of this can be found in the aftermath of Hurricane Katrina. In 2004, many of us gathered for the national SHRM (Society for Human Resource Management) conference at the New Orleans conference center to learn, to network, to groove to the music of the Doobie Brothers, and to be moved and inspired by the now stilled—but never silenced—voice of Christopher Reeve. Slightly more than one year later, that same building in which we congregated was overflowing with individuals displaced from their jobs, their homes, their loved ones, and nearly every other recognizable dimension of their lives. Years later, many are still experiencing this displacement and disconnection. Hurricane Katrina and its aftermath thrust many concerns to the forefront—issues that may not have been on everyone's radar screen just a few weeks earlier. As HR professionals, we cannot forget the lessons of Katrina; rather, we must leverage them as a reminder to vigilantly prepare for the unexpected, the unimagined, and the hard-hitting impact of events that take place in our ever-shrinking world.

Here are just a few of the trends that all HR professionals should monitor and revisit on a regular basis:

- Globalization
- Technology
- Safety and security
- Terrorism
- Aging workforce

- Polygenerational workplaces
- Work/life balance
- Changing technology
- Contingent workforces
- Climate changes
- Political shifts (global, national, and local)
- Remote teams/workplaces (telecommuting)

There are two types of change management theory with which HR professionals need to be familiar: change process theory and implementation theory.

Change Process Theory

Change process theory looks at the dynamics behind how change happens within organizations. Kurt Lewin took a close look at the change process and is an important contributor in the area of change process theory. He identified two primary motivational sources of change:

- Change that is driven within an individual, arising out of her own needs
- Change that is imposed upon an individual from the environment

In this discussion of change management, we will focus on the second motivational source of change—environmental (meaning, external).

Lewin first described the change process as one that involves three stages: unfreezing, moving, and refreezing:

- **Unfreezing:** "The bus is leaving, so get on board." During the unfreezing stage, everyone who is involved with and affected by the change must be brought to the point where he can understand and accept that a particular change will happen. (Understanding and accepting the change, however, does not necessarily mean agreeing with the change—nor does it have to.) An important part of that acceptance involves letting go of behaviors that reflect resistance to change or that can actually impede the change process.

- **Moving:** "You're on the bus; now let's get moving." Moving, in this context, represents the process through which people are brought to accept the change and the process through which they are brought to the point where they actually experience the new state that the change was designed to bring about.

- **Refreezing:** "You know, I almost can't remember a time when we didn't take this bus." In this phase, what once represented a change has now become, in simplest terms, the new normal.

Implementation Theory

The other change-related theory with which HR professionals need to be familiar is implementation theory. Implementation theory focuses on carrying out specific strategies—in this case, OD (organization development) interventions—that are designed to bring about the unfreezing, moving, and refreezing described previously.

Let's take a look at four categories of OD interventions that might be executed as part of that implementation process:

▶ **Human processual interventions:** Seek to effect change and impact relationships within (and between) groups and individuals.

▶ **Technostructural interventions:** Focus on improving what work gets done, as well as the ways and processes through which the work gets done. It looks at job design, job redesign, job restructuring, work content, workflow, work processes, and the like.

▶ **Sociotechnical interventions:** Focus on groups in the workplace and the ways in which those groups can become more (or, at least, semi-) autonomous with respect to the performance and execution of work. Examples of this might include job enrichment, work rescheduling, and participative management.

Mission

BM & S Responsibility 09

Facilitate the development and communication of the organization's core values, vision, mission, and ethical behaviors.

RESPONSIBILITY

Knowledge 01

The organization's mission, vision, values, business goals, objectives, plans, and processes.

KNOWLEDGE

To effectively develop and communicate the organization's values, vision, mission, and ethical behaviors, we must first understand what those are.

An organization's mission statement articulates, in essence, the reason the organization is in existence. It may speak to the nature of the organization's business or purpose, its customers, and sometimes even its employees and its role in the community. A mission statement should be broad (but not overly generalized), brief, clear, unambiguous, and designed to last for "the long haul."

Values

Values constitute the beliefs on which the organization has been built. They are the tenets that shape and guide strategic and day-to-day decision-making, as well as the behaviors that are exhibited in the organization. Organizations identify values, in part, as a way to clearly guide those decisions and behaviors. Values are often represented in terms and principles such as integrity, honesty, and respect.

Vision

An organization's vision is a brief yet comprehensive descriptive and inspirational statement that articulates where the organization wants to be and what it wants to become in the future.

With these in mind, let's focus on communication.

Communication

In the course of performing our jobs, HR professionals need to possess and demonstrate a variety of skills and abilities—analytical, problem solving, decision-making, interpersonal, intrapersonal, conflict resolution—just to name a few. Underscoring all these is the ability to communicate effectively and strategically. Again, this concept spans all six areas of HR. Doing our jobs well just isn't enough—we have to ensure that the work that we do is appropriately communicated to and understood by the people with whom we partner. For instance, we might design a compensation program that is designed to lead the market. (See Chapter 4, "Compensation and Benefits," for more information on what this means.) We might accomplish that posture by establishing competitive base-pay rates, along with an incentive program that is—potentially—lucrative for employees who meet or exceed certain goals. If we don't communicate with managers and employees about how we designed the program, however, and about how the incentive program really puts us ahead of our labor market competitors in terms of compensation, the impact and power of our design might be unappreciated or, even worse, misunderstood or misapplied.

Communication can be described as the exchange or conveyance of information, ideas, feelings, thoughts, or questions between two or more individuals or groups. Communication can take many forms and can be accomplished with or without technical or mechanical devices. Communication can also vary in its level of effectiveness and creates a shared responsibility between the person who conveys the communication and the person who receives the communication.

One way to look at this is to consider this within the context of the five Ws and one H that news reporters have traditionally sought to answer:

▶ *Why* **communicate:** First, think about why you are communicating this message. If you don't clearly convey a reason for the message, others within the organization will undoubtedly ascribe a reason. Not surprisingly, that reason will not always be accurate or positive.

▶ *What* **to communicate:** Balancing employees' "need to know" (and some would say "right to know") against the organization's legal or ethical obligations relative to the dissemination of information presents a delicate and precarious situation. If you find yourself in a situation like this (and it is likely that sooner or later you will), be truthful. Lies or half-truths will always surface. And, once lost, credibility can rarely be regained. Even then, it must be earned—a slow and costly process. Sometimes, telling the truth means that you can't reveal every detail of every situation—and that you might need to acknowledge this.

CAUTION

It's critical (and sometimes painfully difficult) for HR professionals to remember that confidential information is just that—confidential! This may be especially true if you have friends within the organization who may come to you looking for "the inside scoop." Reminding employees (regardless of the nature of your personal relationship with them) of your commitment to maintaining confidentiality is part of truth telling, as well.

▶ *When* **to communicate:** Timing may not be everything when it comes to communication, but it is critically important. First, consider the content of the message you will be communicating. How much urgency is there for communicating the message? Is there a benefit to waiting? Think about other considerations as well. In a micro sense, be aware of the day of the week and the time of the day when you choose to communicate a message. In a macro sense, consider what's going on in the organization, in the industry, in society, and even in the world before you share critical information.

▶ *Where* **to communicate:** Think about where you want people to be when they receive the message. Attending a face-to-face meeting, which is largely presentation driven? Or participating from a satellite location in a teleconference that permits questions and answers? Or alone, behind their computers, reading an email? There is no one right approach or solution for all situations, so it's important to consider the totality of the exact situation in which you find yourself.

▶ *Who* **will communicate, and to whom:** Sometimes HR professionals prepare messages that they will communicate directly. At other times, HR professionals will collaborate with managers to put together a particular message that the managers will deliver personally. Or, HR professionals will deliver messages that—in some form or fashion—others have created for us. And, of course, there are times when we ghost write information that someone else will actually communicate.

TIP

There's no one right answer for any situation, so think through the cast of characters—those who will construct the message, deliver the message, and receive the message—thoroughly and carefully.

▶ *How* **to communicate:** It's not enough to rely on one method of communication. Identify multiple ways to communicate important messages. Different media are available to you, including in person, print, email, teleconference, and live streaming video, to name just a few.

"How to communicate" addresses another important consideration: the directional flow of communication. Are methods in place within the organization to ensure that information can flow up as well as down? Can individuals across different units or divisions of the organization communicate with each other? And are meaningful feedback mechanisms in place to enable you to accurately gauge the impact and effectiveness of your communication efforts?

"I'm a People Person"

The answers to why, where, when, who, and how can convey just as powerfully as "what" the message is. HR professionals must be keenly aware not only of what they communicate, but that how one communicates, by itself, constitutes another level of communication. You must be keenly aware of the nuances of these underlying messages and approach them strategically.

This approach constitutes a significant departure from the stereotypical image of the HR professional as a "people person." That image evokes, in part, the idea of a "touchy-feely" person, armed and ready with a shoulder to cry on.

In reality, there is nothing soft or natural about communicating in your role as an HR professional, and there is much justification for HRCI to identify it as a core area of knowledge. With respect to the ways in which you communicate as an HR professional, you must be an ear to listen, not a shoulder to cry on.

BM & S Responsibility 10   **RESPONSIBILITY**

Reinforce the organization's core values and behavioral expectations through modeling, communication, and coaching.

Coaching and mentoring are highly specialized skills. They can only be developed with diligent study, extensive practice, and—some would assert—specialized training. Coaching, in fact, is a profession in much the same way that HR is a profession.

Having said all of this, coaching and mentoring are also standalone skills that constitute an important subset of those required to be an effective HR professional.

Coaching

Coaching is a professional relationship in which one individual listens, mirrors, "walks with," and "makes space" for another individual to learn, to grow, to explore, and to make empowered choices.

Executive Coaching

Executive coaching is a professional relationship in which a senior level of the organization works with an individual who helps her to identify and eradicate blind spots, to explore potentially challenging experiences or relationships, and to temper confidence and boldness with other required executive-level professional competencies.

Mentoring

Mentoring is a professional relationship in which one person shares his insights and personal experiences with individuals who are usually less experienced and who may work at a lower hierarchical level within the organization. Mentors often offer advice, guidance, and direction.

> **NOTE**
>
> In this context, *mentoring* refers to relationships within the organization. Mentoring can also take a different shape as a form of community partnership and service when mentoring is performed with younger or at-risk individuals within the community. In addition, mentoring, in terms of the professional relationship already discussed, need not be limited to those working within the employee's organization. Rather, mentors often work at other organizations, for labor market competitors, or even in different industries.

Modeling

The concept of modeling is also closely related to coaching. In this context, *modeling* refers to individuals at all levels of the organization—especially the upper levels, in organizations that are not flat—demonstrating behaviors that are reflective of the organization's values and the behaviors that are considered to be appropriate, consistent with, and supportive of the organization's overarching vision and missions.

RESPONSIBILITY

BM & S Responsibility 11

Provide data such as human capital projections and costs that support the organization's overall budget.

Formulating sound human capital projections requires specialized skills in research, analysis, and projections.

We will discuss some of these methods and techniques here and strongly suggest that you also peruse the resources listed at the end of this chapter.

Predicting "human capital projections and costs is more involved than it might appear. Accurate forecasting requires selecting from among numerous nonmathematical (qualitative) as well as mathematical (quantitative) analyses.

Nonmathematical Forecasting Techniques

In most organizations, qualitative judgments are made all the time. These judgments can relate to a whole host of issues—marketing, product development, philanthropy, staffing, or any other business-related issues. These judgments can be structured or unstructured, informal or formal.

Management Forecasts

Sometimes individuals who perform qualitative analysis draw on the knowledge and experience of the organization's managers—and the institutional knowledge that those managers have acquired in their roles. Savvy managers—especially those who couple their awareness of the organization with knowledge of the industry and of the economy in general—can provide HR with a wealth of information. As a caution, however, it's important to remember that the information derived from this somewhat unstructured approach may not always be accurate. Relying too heavily on managerial predictions can result in significant errors in judgment, so they should ideally be coupled with other, more structured mathematical and nonmathematical approaches.

The Delphi Technique

The Delphi technique is an example of a structured nonmathematical technique in which expert opinions from a variety of individuals are sought, distilled, and distilled again. An objective, neutral, uninvolved leader recaps what the experts submit, summarizes that information, and condenses it into a more concise format. (The leader is not one of the "experts" and does not inject her opinions or interpretations into the process.) This happens several times until a final position is identified—one that incorporates the evolving and iterative input of many individuals but that does not unduly reflect any one position or viewpoint.

A distinguishing—and critical—element of the Delphi technique is that the "experts" from whom opinions are sought and ideas are culled down never meet in person and never discuss their submissions—all of which are made in writing. Rather, their submissions are collected and processed by an objective third party. In this way, the Delphi technique ensures that factors such as group dynamics, overpowering personalities, or just plain politics do not taint the assessment process. The anonymity of the process further encourages individuals to take a risk and submit their ideas without fear of reprisal, retribution, or judgment. The sanitized nature of this process puts expert contributors on a more even footing, further ensuring the integrity of this process.

Nominal Group Technique

Like the Delphi technique, the nominal group technique takes a nonmathematical approach to forecasting. The nominal group technique is similar to the Delphi technique in that it calls upon the expertise and predictive ability of experts. Most of the similarities between these two techniques, however, end there. With the nominal group technique, experts meet in person and process their ideas as a group. Led by a facilitator, the meeting begins with each expert writing down and presenting his ideas to the group. Neither discussion nor assessment of ideas, however, is permitted at this point—only presentation is acceptable. The group then comes together to discuss each others' ideas, after which each group member is called on to independently rank the ideas. The meeting facilitator will then combine all the individual rankings to determine which are the most important and valued to the group. Through this process, the forecast is made.

Mathematical Forecasting Techniques

Mathematical—or quantitative—forecasting techniques are predicated on the belief that the best predictor of future performance is past performance. (Think "behavior-based interviewing," which we'll explore later in Chapter 2.

Trend Analysis

Trend analysis looks at and measures how one particular factor changes over a period of time. Trend analysis, for instance, can provide information—albeit unrefined—that can be helpful in developing a better understanding of business cycles, which in turn will affect staffing needs.

Ratio Analysis

Ratio analysis is similar to trend analysis in that it examines changes, movements, and trends over a period of time. Instead of looking at just one variable alone, it looks at two variables (one of which, for instance, could relate to staffing levels) and how the relationship between those two variables has evolved over time. This becomes the basis for a number of applications, which could include forecasting staffing needs.

For example, a rental car company might look at how the number of cars rented per day or per shift compares to the number of employees assigned to work per day or per shift. This might help the car rental company predict future staffing requirements.

> **NOTE**
>
> Ratio analysis assumes that the relationship between the two factors being looked at will hold constant. In this example it also assumes that there will not be any turnover (which, of course, is not usually a reasonable assumption). Other assumptions may be operating as well—consciously or unconsciously. Because the degree to which those assumptions are identified—and are sound—will significantly affect the overall quality of the ratio analysis, these underlying assumptions must be surfaced and factored into the analysis. Also, ratio analysis—like any other analysis—usually should not be the only type of analysis that you use. A combination of analyses will generally yield a more reliable result.

Turnover Analysis

Human capital projections are impacted by turnover and the ability to accurately calculate and predict turnover. As discussed elsewhere in this book, turnover measures the percentage of the workforce that has left the organization during a specified period of time. Most often expressed on an annual basis, turnover is calculated as follows:

$$\frac{\text{Number of terminations during a specified period of time}}{\text{Average \# of employees in the workforce during that same period of time}}$$

This information can be used in a number of ways—one of which is to help predict future turnover rates, which can affect staffing needs. Turnover can be voluntary (for instance, an employee accepts employment at another organization) or involuntary (for instance, an employee is laid off). Turnover can be broken down in any number of ways:

- ▶ Total for the entire organization

- ▶ Total for one—or more—particular departments

- ▶ FLSA (Fair Labor Standards Act) (exempt or nonexempt) status

- ▶ Length of service

- ▶ Unionized/nonunionized status

Good Turnover and Bad Turnover

Despite popular opinion, turnover is not inherently bad. Just like cholesterol, there is "good turnover" and "bad turnover." An example of good turnover might be an individual who accepts a more challenging or appropriate position in a different unit or division within the organization. An example of "bad turnover" might be a relatively new employee who quits after two weeks because she did not accurately understand the requirements of the position for which she was hired.

Whether turnover is deemed "good" or "bad," of course, involves making value judgments, which will vary from organization to organization. In one organization, for instance, an employee resigning to pursue higher education on a full-time basis or to serve the nation (through military service or the Peace Corps, for instance) might be counted as "good" turnover. In other organizations, these same reasons might be counted as "bad" turnover. Some organizations use the terms "acceptable" and "unacceptable" rather than "good" or "bad" to downplay the value judgments inherent to these labels. It's also possible to look at turnover in terms of controllability. Controllable turnover might include voluntary terminations, and noncontrollable turnover might include death or retirement.

Simple Linear Regression

Simple linear regression provides a different way of looking at statistical relationships. It examines the past relationship between two factors (in this case, one of which is staffing), determines the statistical strength of that relationship, and—on the basis of that analysis—projects future conditions. In the previous example of the rental car company, the relationship between car rentals and staffing levels would be measured, and—on the basis of the strength of that relationship—would be extrapolated into the future.

Multiple Linear Regression

Multiple linear regression is similar to simple linear regression, except that several factors are taken into consideration. In the rental car example, for instance, other factors that could be looked at in addition to staffing levels might be the number of vehicles that were actually available to be rented, the number of customers who "no-showed," or the number of potential customers who were turned away.

Simulations

Simulations create scenarios through which different realities can be tested mathematically to see what could happen under a variety of changing conditions.

Legislative Framework, Considerations, and Opportunities

BM & S Responsibility 15

RESPONSIBILITY

Monitor the legislative and regulatory environment for proposed changes and their potential impact to the organization, taking appropriate proactive steps to support, modify, or oppose the proposed changes.

Knowledge 02

KNOWLEDGE

Legislative and regulatory processes.

At the introduction of this chapter, we referenced a familiar saying: "Some people make things happen, some people watch things happen, and some people wonder what happened." This is perhaps no more apparent than in our legislative process, created hundreds of years ago, yet perhaps more vibrant and vital now than ever before.

As HR professionals, understanding the legislative process helps us to more effectively affect that process. It is both our right and our responsibility to do this. Why? Because the employment-related laws that are passed in our nation directly impact our profession, the organizations for which we work, and the way we perform our jobs. (Hint: think HIPAA, FMLA, and so forth.)

How a Bill Becomes a Law

Some readers may recall the *Schoolhouse Rock* series from the 1970s and 1980s that explained—quite entertainingly (at the time, it seemed)—how a bill becomes a law. Although "I'm Just a Bill" may not grace our televisions anymore, the following 13-step process still accurately describes how laws are passed. It's a process that is worth revisiting now, as we reaffirm our commitment to being strategic and effective business and organizational partners.

Although anyone can draft a bill, only a member of Congress can actually introduce legislation. In so doing, that member of Congress becomes the sponsor of the bill.

There are four basic types of legislation: bills, joint resolutions, concurrent resolutions, and simple resolutions.

- ▶ **Bills:** Statutes, in their draft format, while they are on their way to becoming law.

- ▶ **Joint resolutions:** A resolution passed by the Senate as well as the House of Representatives that has the force of law after it has been either signed by the president or passed over the veto of the president.

- ▶ **Concurrent resolutions:** A legislative measure that addresses a concern that pertains to the Senate as well as the House of Representatives. Concurrent resolutions, however, are not submitted to the president and thus do not have the force of law.

- ▶ **Simple resolutions:** A legislative measure that pertains to either the Senate or the House of Representatives. Simple resolutions offer a nonbinding opinion, are not submitted to the president, and do not have the force of law.

The legislative process officially begins when a bill or resolution is given a number. (The number is preceded by "H.R." if it is a House bill, and "S." if it is a Senate bill.) After a number is assigned, the following steps will ensue. What follows speaks to federal law. A similar—although not identical—process is followed in each of the states.

1. **Referral to committee:** Bills are usually referred to standing committees in the House or Senate according to carefully delineated rules of procedure.

2. **Committee action:** One of three things can happen to a bill after it reaches a committee: it can be sent to a subcommittee; it can be considered by the committee as a whole; or it can be ignored (at which point the bill dies, or is killed, depending upon one's point of view).

3. **Subcommittee review:** Bills are often referred to subcommittee for study and hearings. Hearings provide the opportunity to put views of the executive branch, experts, other public officials, supporters, and opponents officially on the record. Testimony can be in person or submitted in writing.

4. **Mark up:** When the hearings are completed, the subcommittee may meet to mark up the bill—that is, make changes and amendments prior to recommending the bill to the full committee. If a subcommittee votes not to report legislation to the full committee, the bill dies.

5. **Committee action to report a bill:** After receiving a subcommittee's report on a bill, the full committee has two choices: it can conduct further study and hearings, or it can vote on the subcommittee's recommendations and any proposed amendments. The full committee then votes on its recommendation to the House or Senate. This procedure is called "ordering a bill reported."

6. **Publication of a written report:** After a committee votes to have a bill reported, the chairman instructs staff to prepare a report on the bill. This report describes the intent and scope of the legislation, impact on existing laws and programs, position of the executive branch, and views of dissenting members.

7. **Scheduling floor action:** After a bill is reported back to the chamber where it originated, it is placed in chronological order on the calendar. The House has several legislative calendars, and the speaker and majority leader largely determine if, when, and in what order bills come up. In the Senate, only one legislative calendar exists.

8. **Debate:** When a bill reaches the floor of the House or Senate, there are rules or procedures governing the debate. These rules determine the conditions and amount of time that will be allocated for debate.

9. **Voting:** After the debate and the approval of any amendments, the bill is passed or defeated by the members voting.

10. **Referral to other chamber:** When the House or the Senate passes a bill, it is referred to the other chamber, where it usually follows the same process through committee and floor action. This chamber can choose from four courses of action: approve the bill as is, reject the bill, ignore the bill, or change the bill.

11. **Conference committee action:** If only minor changes are made to a bill by the other chamber, it is common for the legislation to go back to the first chamber for concurrence. However, when the actions of the other chamber significantly alter the bill, a conference committee is formed to reconcile the differences. If the conferees cannot reach agreement, the legislation dies. If agreement is reached, a conference report describing the committee members' recommendations for changes is prepared. Both the House and the Senate must approve the conference report.

12. **Final actions:** After the House and Senate have approved a bill in identical form, it is sent to the president. At this point, there are two ways in which the legislation can become law:

    ▶ If the president approves of the legislation, he or she signs it and it becomes the law of the land.

    ▶ If the president takes no action for 10 days while Congress is in session, the legislation automatically becomes law.

▶ Alternatively, if the president opposes the bill, he can veto it; or, if he takes no action after the Congress has adjourned its second session, it is considered a pocket veto and the legislation dies.

13. **Overriding a veto:** If the president vetoes a bill, Congress may attempt to override the veto. This requires a two-thirds roll-call vote of the members who are present in sufficient numbers for a quorum.

Be Heard—Reach Out to Your Elected Officials

There are a variety of ways to reach out to the members of Congress and other elected officials who represent you.

Write (Early, But Not Too Often)

Morris K. Udall (1922–1998), a congressman from Arizona, composed *The Right to Write— Some Suggestions on Writing to Your Representative in Congress*. Although Udall retired from Congress in 1991 before the advent of the Internet as a popular method of day-to-day communication, his suggestions are as valid today as they were years ago:

▶ Address your correspondence properly (for instance, when writing to a member of Congress, address it to "The Honorable ____ _____").

▶ Use the correct physical address.

▶ Identify the bill or issue you're writing about, ideally using the bill number as well as the name by which it is popularly known.

▶ Send letters in a timely manner while there is still time for your member of Congress to consider your input.

▶ Communicate with those members of Congress who represent you.

▶ Be brief, and be legible. Our elected officials are busy and receive a great deal of communication to sort through.

▶ Personal letters may have greater impact than form letters or petitions.

▶ Be specific about why you hold your opinion and how the legislation would affect you.

▶ When possible, offer suggestions.

▶ If you have expertise in a particular area, say so—and then share it.

▶ Provide your elected officials with positive, as well as constructive, feedback.

(One might be well advised to reach out to state representatives as well.)

Udall offers some basic "don'ts" as well:

▶ Don't threaten.

▶ Don't promise.

▶ Don't engage in name-calling.

▶ Don't speak for others you claim to represent (unless you actually do).

- ▸ Don't become a "pen pal."

- ▸ Don't demand commitment—especially before all the facts are in.

Lobbying

Lobbying is the process of reaching out to your elected officials to express your beliefs and opinions with the hope of influencing a governmental body.

> **NOTE**
>
> Before beginning any lobbying activities, it is essential to do your homework. Know the subject matter and draft your message clearly and concisely. Be firm, be knowledgeable, and be confident. Know the issue, explain your concerns relative to the consequences of the issue, and suggest a specific course of action. In addition, consider coordinating your efforts with others who share a similar viewpoint.)

Personal Visits

Consider meeting with your elected official or perhaps with one of her staff members.

Stay Informed

Perhaps most important, stay up-to-date on the issues that can potentially affect the HR profession, the organization in which you work, or the ways in which you will carry out the role of HR. Affiliate with organizations—such as SHRM—that are committed to shaping the laws that influence our profession and our workplaces. Sign up to receive "e-lerts"—legislative updates from organizations. Seek such e-lerts from organizations toward whose beliefs you feel inclined, as well as from organizations whose beliefs may not align as closely with your own predispositions. Forge relationships with legal resources at your organization (in house or outside counsel). And don't stop paying attention after a law is passed—court interpretations can also have a big impact on how you execute your role.

Strategic Planning

Knowledge 03

Strategic planning process, design, implementation, and evaluation

KNOWLEDGE

Knowledge 04

Management functions, including planning, organizing, directing, and controlling.

KNOWLEDGE

Strategic planning is a step-by-step process through which an organization defines and describes its long-term mission and vision and engages in expansive, far-reaching, and systematic planning to achieve that mission and vision. Specifically, the organization identifies where it wants to be and what it wants to accomplish long term (often 3–5 years, or even longer). The organization will subsequently begin to map out how its vision and mission for those years will be attained.

In an oversimplified sense, strategic planning is the process of looking into the future, painting a picture of where we want to be and what we want to achieve in that future, and ascertaining how we will get there. It is a type of extreme proactivity rather than reactivity, of planning for the future rather than simply responding to it as it unfolds.

There are a number of compelling reasons for organizations to engage in a strategic planning process, just a few of which follow:

▶ By methodically looking toward the future, the organization creates an opportunity to proactively shape and influence its own future.

▶ The organization will develop a clearer awareness of how it is positioned externally and how it measures up internally.

▶ It creates (or reaffirms) the overall vision, mission, and values of the organization and refocuses attention on how to bring these potentially ambiguous tenets to life in a meaningful, tangible way.

▶ It engages individuals throughout the organization in a meaningful and impactful initiative.

Strategic Planning: A Four-Phase Process

Many theorists describe and define the strategic planning process in different ways and as containing different steps and components. The following is one way of looking at the strategic planning process.

Phase 1: Establish a foundation for the strategy

Phase 2: Develop the strategic plan

Phase 3: Implement the strategic plan

Phase 4: Evaluate the plan, process, and performance

Phase 1: Establish a Foundation for the Strategy

To be effective, the strategic planning process must be grounded in the organization's mission, vision, and values.

▶ **Mission:** An organization's mission statement articulates, in essence, its reason for being. It may speak to the nature of the organization's business or purpose, its customers, and sometimes even its employees and its role in the community. A mission statement should be broad (but not overly generalized), brief, clear, unambiguous, and designed to last for the long haul. The goals of an organization should cascade from its mission, so the mission is far bigger than any goal—and thus must be able to withstand the test of time.

▶ **Vision:** An organization's vision is a brief yet comprehensive descriptive and inspirational statement that articulates where the organization wants to be and what it wants to become in the future. The vision should resonate in the hearts, minds, and day-to-day endeavors of the organization's employees. It should give those employees an awareness that they have a meaningful opportunity to be part of something bigger than themselves. It must motivate them to aspire to the legacy that the vision can create and that it ultimately can leave behind.

▶ **Values:** Values are the beliefs on which the organization has been built. They are the tenets that shape and guide strategic, tactical, and day-to-day decision-making (the three legs of that stool again). These same tenets affect the behaviors that employees within the organization demonstrate as they carry out their responsibilities. Organizations identify values, in part, as a way to clearly guide those decisions and behaviors. Values are often represented in terms and principles such as integrity, honesty, and respect.

Phase 2: Develop the Strategic Plan

Formulating a strategy on the basis of deliberately crafted statements that articulate the mission, vision, and values of the organization is critical, but it's only the first step. The next step is to actually develop the strategic plan.

There are several key components to the development phase of the strategic plan.

SWOT Analysis (Strengths, Weaknesses, Opportunities, and Threats)

A SWOT analysis is conducted to ascertain the strengths and weaknesses that are inherent to an organization, as well as the opportunities and threats that it faces from external forces. Although it sounds relatively simple and straightforward, the process of conducting a SWOT analysis can become challenging, in part because it is often difficult for organizations—as it is for people—to see themselves objectively.

When examining strengths and weaknesses, it is necessary for analysis to be directed inward. This clear and objective assessment would ascertain the resources of the organization, including the following:

- ▶ Human
- ▶ Financial
- ▶ Technological
- ▶ Capital
- ▶ Brand image

Opportunities and threats, conversely, look outward at factors such as competition, economic trends, customer needs and wants, and legislative or regulatory activity. This process, known as environmental scanning, is explored earlier in this chapter.

Strategic Objectives

After the SWOT analysis is completed, the outputs of that analysis can and should be scrutinized and, to the degree possible, addressed. After that process is finished—or at least begun—it's time to begin generating ideas that will eventually grow, develop, and be cultivated into overarching organizational initiatives.

These overarching organizational initiatives must then cascade into specific strategies that enable each department, division, or other organizational units to contribute directly to the attainment of the organization's overall objectives and mission. For this to happen, a top-down/bottom-up approach similar to that described in the performance management process must be implemented throughout the organization (see Chapter 5). To oversimplify the process, like any pyramidal structure—and even like Maslow's hierarchy of needs (see Chapter 2, "Workforce Planning and Employment")—goals at the lower, more functional levels of the organization must ultimately support the more overarching objectives of the organization.

Keep this process building, and you'll be well on your way to bringing the vision, mission, and values of the organization to life in a highly tangible and visible manner.

Phase 3: Implement the Strategic Plan

Similar to Fayol's directing stage, the implementation phase is, again, the defining moment… and the moment at which the true value and impact of interventions are made manifest. Strategies become tactics and tactics become operationalized. Management functions—from planning through controlling—are used to make the strategies part of the day-to-day fabric and functioning of the organization. Because, at this level, we have also reached the point at which individuals will have a very real, albeit somewhat indirect, impact on whether the organization's objectives are attained, performance management principles become critical as well.

Three factors that are essential to successfully implementing any strategic plan are commitment, credibility, and communication.

Commitment

It is critical to secure the support and commitment of leaders at all levels of the organization—particularly the upper levels—before even entertaining the idea of creating (let alone implementing) a strategic plan. This commitment can and should encompass everything from seeing the strategic process through to its conclusion to striving to achieve the goals and implementing the changes that are generated through this process.

In short, strategic plans that sit on a shelf are useless. Talking the talk is not enough. Walking the walk is mandatory. Without commitment, a strategic plan is not only useless—it might even do more harm than good. It may serve to heighten awareness of needs, as well as of potential, that will subsequently remain unaddressed.

Credibility

Credibility is created and sustained through the following:

▸ Representative participation from all levels of the organization

▸ A commitment to follow through on every step of the process (rather than short cutting the process)

▸ Clear, complete, and appropriate documentation of the process

Communication

Communication is the lifeblood of any relationship—personal or professional. It can enhance strong relationships, and it can weaken relationships that appear to be otherwise strong.

Responsibility for communication cannot be relegated to the person who receives the message, nor can it be solely assigned to the person who delivers the message. Rather, communication represents a shared responsibility—one that must take the vehicle of communication into consideration, as well.

Phase 4: Evaluate the Plan, Process, and Performance

Evaluating how well a strategic plan was envisioned, designed, and implemented is an involved process, as is any evaluative process. In Chapter 5, we provide a more in-depth discussion of evaluative processes (in a more general sense) as explored through ADDIE (Needs Analysis and Assessment, Design, Development, Implementation and Evaluation). Revisit the "E" in ADDIE and seek other sources and ideas for evaluating a plan, the process for developing that plan, and the overall performance against that plan.

Perhaps most important, be prepared to incorporate changes, insights, and revisions. Holding on to a flawed design or an ineffective implementation process is like "spending good money after bad." In an organization, the currency in question may be your own reputation and credibility, so be prepared to flex.

Perhaps an unlikely guru, Henri Fayol was hired at the age of 19 to work as an engineer for a French mining company. He worked there for many years, ultimately serving as its managing director from 1888 to 1918. Based on the experience he gained at the mining company, Fayol, known as the Father of Modern Management, identified five functions of a manager, which he referred to as the following:

- Prevoyance
- To organize
- To command
- To coordinate
- To control

In more contemporary parlance, these five functions are often referred to as planning, organizing, directing, coordinating, and controlling. Let's take a closer look at each of these so we can better understand organizational structure and the context within which our clients carry out their roles.

Planning

Planning lays the groundwork for how managers will work toward accomplishing the organization's goals. Through planning, managers decide what needs to get done, when it needs to get done, who will do it, how it will get done, and where it will be done. In the absence of planning, the organization—and the people in it—will lack direction and perhaps even just coast along. In other words, to quote the immortal words of the great philosopher (and baseball Hall of Famer) Yogi Berra, "If you don't know where you are going, you will end up somewhere else."

Organizing

Organizing speaks to the ways in which the manager obtains and arranges the resources that he needs to implement the plans (the output of the planning function). Those resources could include people, facilities, and materials. During the organizing function, the manager must also designate reporting relationships within the organization. In short, the linkages between people, places, and things must be established.

Directing

During the directing phase, the actual work is performed—goods are produced or services are provided. In addition to ensuring that things go smoothly from a technical perspective, in the directing phase, the manager must also focus attention on leading and motivating the human resources who are actually performing the work.

Coordinating

Through the coordinating function, the manager brings together all the resources that he or she has organized to accomplish the stated plan. The manager must also ensure that the pieces continue to fit.

Controlling

Controlling assumes more of an oversight role, and in some senses an evaluative role (in an ongoing, iterative sense). In this phase, the manager ascertains the degree to which the planning he engaged in actually produced the desired results. If the manager determines that there is a gap between the targeted goals and the actual results, he must then focus on ways to bridge that gap.

Fayol subsequently further broke down these five functions into 14 principles of management:

1. Division of work
2. Authority and responsibility
3. Discipline
4. Unity of command
5. Unity of direction
6. Subordination of individual interests to general interests
7. Remuneration of personnel
8. Centralization
9. Scalar chain
10. Order
11. Equity
12. Stability of tenure of personnel
13. Initiative
14. Esprit de corps (union is strength)

Leadership Concepts

Developing leaders within the organization is a key objective for HR professionals, especially for those who are involved in organizational development.

Leadership is difficult to define because many different individuals have set forth just as many different definitions. Leadership is also very different from management, although those terms are often used (or misused) interchangeably. In simplest terms, *leadership* can be defined as the ability to encourage "followership" to attain specific objectives. *Followership*, in this sense, does not refer to unthinkingly submissive imitators; rather, it speaks to highly dedicated devotees who are passionately and wholeheartedly committed to the vision of someone else. That someone else, in this case, is the leader. For without followers, there can be no leaders. Without effective leaders, there will be no followers, and there will be no organized, implemented strategy for attaining organizational objectives.

Over time, the following four theories have emerged on the subject of leadership, each evolving from the prior:

▶ Trait theories

▶ Behavioral theories

▶ Situational leadership theories

▶ Contingency theories

Trait Theories

Trait theories support the idea that leaders are born, not made. Being a great leader, then, was more a function of nature than nurture. It had to do with being a great person—and being born that way. Research in support of this theory, however, was neither consistent nor complete. For instance, no one set of leadership traits could be identified. Additionally, different leaders using very different approaches in different situations could effect a successful outcome. Enter behavioral theories.

Behavioral Theories

Beginning in the 1940s, a new school of thought on leadership began to emerge: leadership can be taught. All it would take to develop nonleaders into leaders would be a willing student who would receive proper instruction relative to essential and appropriate leadership behaviors.

Ohio State University and the University of Michigan both conducted considerable research on behavioral management theories. Their research yielded similar results by identifying two critical dimensions of leadership behavior:

▶ **"Consideration" (Ohio State) or "Employee-Centered" (University of Michigan)**— Refers to the interpersonal, trust, respect, and social dimensions of leadership.

▶ **"Initiating Structure" (Ohio State) or "Job-Related" (University of Michigan)**— Refers to factors related to the work itself—specifically, what employees need to do and how they need to do it to attain objectives.

As with trait theories, questions about leadership still remained unanswered by the behavioral theory approach. Situation leadership theories represented the next evolution of thought.

Situational Leadership Theories

Situational leadership theories demonstrate a greater appreciation for the complexity of the leadership role. They suggest that no single leadership approach is right for every situation. Situational leadership theories also suggest that part of what is required to be a good and effective leader is having the ability to select and utilize the most effective leadership approach for each specific situation.

The following sections will present three key situational leadership theories.

Paul Hersey and Ken Blanchard's Situational Leadership Theory

How does a leader encourage followership? According to Paul Hersey and Ken Blanchard, "it depends." Hersey and Blanchard's theory of situational leadership suggests that leaders must use different approaches, at different times, with different employees. These approaches will depend on each employee's maturity and proficiency at performing specific functions. Maturity or proficiency relate to the technical skills required to perform a particular task, as well as the nontechnical skills (or behavioral competencies) required to bring a task to its successful conclusion.

Hersey and Blanchard identify four approaches:

- **Telling:** Leaders must provide the employee with precise instruction and fairly close supervision while the employee is learning to perform the new task. Feedback must be specific and frequent.

- **Selling:** As the employee begins to develop proficiency at the new task, an effective leader will begin to provide additional background information or explanation relative to the nuances of the task. At this stage, the employee has moved beyond the basics and can function with a bit less supervision.

- **Participating:** By now, the employee has developed a certain level of skill at performing the task and can comprehend many of the underlying principles of the task. The employee still, however, requires support, encouragement, and reinforcement. In this phase, leaders need to make the employee more aware of what she can do and encourage the employee to perform the tasks in an increasingly confident, independent, and self-sufficient manner.

- **Delegating:** By now, in addition to being able to perform the technical aspects of the task, the employee possesses the behavioral characteristics and competencies required to bring the task to a successful conclusion. The leader needs to communicate the goal (ideally, after collaboratively developing it with the employee) and must allow the employee to accomplish it independently. In short, at this point, an effective leader lets go.

See Figure 1.5, which describes directive and supportive behaviors.

BLANCHARD SITUATIONAL LEADERSHIP MODEL LEADER BEHAVIOR CATEGORIES	
DIRECTIVE BEHAVIOR	**SUPPORTIVE BEHAVIOR**
• One-way communication • Followers' roles spelled out • Close supervision of performance	• Two-way communication • Listening, providing support & encouragement • Facilitating interaction • Involving follower in decision-making

FIGURE 1.5 Examples of directive and supportive behaviors.

In addition to Figure 1.5, Figure 1.6 illustrates the Hersey-Blanchard Situational Leadership Model.

The Hersey-Blanchard Situational Leadership Model also represents a different relationship between task and relationship. As described previously, each of these considerations will be "low" or "high" depending on the maturity and proficiency of the employee. In other words, the emphasis that a leader should place on task and relationship considerations will be different for each quadrant.

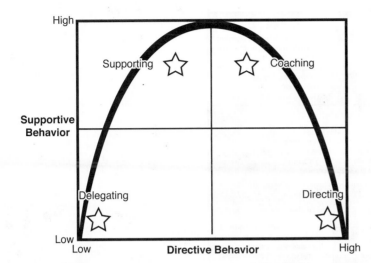

FIGURE 1.6 The Hersey-Blanchard Situational Leadership Model.

NOTE

It is important to note that—at any one point in time—the same employee can function in different quadrants relative to different tasks/responsibilities. An employee should not be assigned to or identified as performing in any one particular quadrant. (In other words, don't pigeon-hole your employees.) Instead, recognize that each task performed by the employee may fall into a different quadrant and would therefore warrant a different leadership approach.

Robert R. Blake and Jane S. Mouton's Situational Leadership Theory

Blake-Mouton's situational leadership theory depicts leadership behavior along a two-axis grid:

▸ Concern for people (vertical axis)

▸ Concern for task/production (horizontal axis)

Each axis uses a one-to-nine scale on which to chart the degree of concern that leaders demonstrate for each dimension (see Figure 1.7).

Unlike Hersey and Blanchard's model, there is room for gradations within each of the four quadrants in this model. Looking at the extremes, however, does afford insight into the leadership style that each of the four quadrants (to one degree or another) represents:

▸ **Authority-Obedience** (Task Managers) (nine on production, one on people) are demanding and authoritarian. They rarely, if ever, admit to being wrong. They shift blame away from themselves. They focus entirely on what needs to be attained, with little concern for the human dimensions that speak to how the task will be attained.

▸ **Team Managers** (nine on production, nine on people) focus on attaining tasks as well as maintaining and enhancing relationships with those who will be performing those tasks.

▸ **Country Club Managers** (one on production, nine on people) are more like cheerleaders than coaches. They focus almost exclusively on cultivating positive relationships with employees—within a positive work environment—and pay little if any attention to the tasks at hand. Relationships become the exclusive goal; organizational objectives become almost—if not completely—irrelevant.

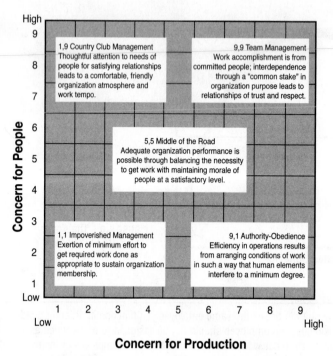

FIGURE 1.7 The Blake-Mouton Situational Leadership Model.

From Blake, R.R., and J.S. Mouton, The Managerial Grid. Gulf Publishing, Houston, 1964. RMW 2/10/02

▶ **Impoverished Managers** (one on production, one on people) take the laissez-faire management style to an unproductive extreme. They delegate work (the task) and are often not seen again until there is more work to be delegated. They are absentee leaders in every sense—with respect to what needs to get done, who will do it, and how it will get done.

In the center of the grid is "organization man management" (five on production, five on people). This is a more middle-of-the-road (or middle-of-the-grid, to be precise) approach that balances concern with production for concern for people and for morale.

Contingency Theories

Evolving out of situational leadership theory, the fourth stage in this evolutionary process involves contingency theories, the best known of which was developed by Fred Fiedler. Like some of the earlier theories, Fiedler devised a method of ascertaining the degree to which leaders were concerned with tasks and the degree to which leaders were concerned with people. Fiedler then used that measure to determine situations in which different leaders would be most effective or, in other words, the situations that would be most favorable for specific leadership styles.

The factors that determine that level of favorableness follow:

▶ **Leader-members relations:** How strong and how significant are the relationships between the leader and the team members? To what degree will those relationships make the leader more or less effective and influential?

▶ **Task structure:** How structured is the work that the team members are performing?

▶ **Position power:** How much power or influence does the leader's position hold, or how much can it exert? To what degree can the leader ensure accountability for performance and authority to delegate?

A leader's effectiveness will be impacted by the relative strength or weakness of these three factors. In general, the higher the factors, the more effective the leader will be.

Although leadership styles vary widely, they can be grouped into two primary categories—transactional leadership and transformational leadership:

▶ **Transactional leadership:** The transactional leadership style is characterized by the possibility of rewards and the threat of punishment. This is a "no news is good news" approach to leadership—leaders get involved only when goals are not met or when employees are not adhering to stated rules.

▶ **Transformational leadership:** Transformational leaders are coaches, not enforcers. They model the behavior they expect the group to emulate, and they focus on relationships as well as tasks. These two concerns are not mutually exclusive; rather, they coexist and are complementary. Both are essential, and neither is expendable.

Management and Leadership: Bridging the Gap

Managers are seen as those individuals who manage the process or the activities of a department or organization. Leaders are those who provide the vision and direction that lead to a motivating force of accomplishment. To be an effective manager, you need to bridge both.

As described in a leadership-management model developed by Anthony Panos (Principal, OPG.), "Success is an anesthetic that dulls the drive for change." We see evidence of this phrase in many organizations and more specifically in many managers and potential leaders. As with employees, some managers feel that if things are going well, there is no need for change. Leaders who allow themselves to fall into the same trap, however, are destined to a fate of mediocrity or failure.

According to Panos's model, there are five components to building the bridge between management and leadership:

1. Commit to achieve.

2. "It's not about you."

3. Establish credibility.

4. Align people.

5. Impact people significantly.

1. Commit to Achieve

The first component to building the bridge between management and leadership is developing and embracing a commitment to achieve. You can accomplish this by understanding the organization's goals and striving with your staff to attain them, while being aware of and incorporating the personal goals and aspirations of your staff members. Furthermore, and possibly more importantly, be honest with yourself about what kind of organization you want to create. There needs to be honesty of purpose and intent. Ensuring consistency between intent and reality will eliminate the confusion that occurs often between what employees thought they signed up for and what is really going on.

2. "It's Not About You"

Next, it's important to remember that "it's not about you." Your focus must remain on the success of the employees who report to you, not on your success. That will come later. For now, spotlighting your employees is key. Leave the headlining for someone else, and give recognition to those who are excelling. When you allow your employees to do their jobs and do them well, they become responsible and empowered. And you, in turn, attain success.

3. Establish Credibility

To continue in this process you must establish credibility. This does not occur by the application of your authority; rather, it comes from consistency, competence, dedication, and commitment. For you to lead, you must have the permission of the people whom you lead. You get that permission by the establishment of your credibility.

4. Align People

The next step is the alignment of people. Often, after the strategic planning is done, we put (hopefully) the right people in the right jobs to accomplish the plan. To properly align people, you first must align them with the vision, mission, and values of the organization. Build a team of staff members that share common values. Align their professional needs with the organization's needs. Cascade the organization's strategic plan so that it manifests itself in some way into every employee's individual objectives.

5. Impact People Significantly

Last, impact people significantly. How can you do that? Everyone is different, but through communication and understanding, you know what triggers people have. Without being manipulative, push those buttons. Be sensitive and responsive to their needs and tie them to the needs of the organization. Make connections between how their interests, skills, talents, and developmental needs tie to the organization and vice versa.

According to Panos, managers must provide direct reports with feedback, development, a sounding board. In short, managers help clear the path to their direct reports' success. Those who can bridge the gap between leader and manager do all of the above and look out over the horizon to see where the next bump or opportunity is coming from. Leadership development, and the specific interventions that will accomplish it, should be aimed at attaining these end results.

Let's take a look at one other related topic: project management.

Project Management

No discussion of leadership and management would be complete without the topic of project management.

More and more, work is project based. For many of us and for many of our clients, project management is a critical skill needed to perform our own work and to support the work that our clients are performing.

In the vernacular of project management, a project is a special and temporary undertaking designed to accomplish a specific goal and yield a specific output. The management portion of this term speaks to the overall process required for ensuring the successful accomplishment of this goal, rather than the goal itself.

Projects are usually deadline driven. Although the project timeline may be demanding, it is common for projects not to have additional resources devoted to their accomplishment.

A common difficulty of project-based work is the inherent challenge of balancing the day-to-day workload with efforts to complete high-priority special projects. Projects are frequently delegated with nothing more than a deadline—and with no additional resources for the individuals to whom those projects are delegated. Understandably, the person to whom the project has been delegated will seek additional resources—perhaps human and perhaps capital. However, such resources are often already being utilized to carry out the day-to-day responsibilities of the operation. As such, in addition to slowing down productivity with respect to the day-to-day ongoing workload, it is also possible that the project may not be accomplished within its stated time frame because of the impact of limited or insufficient resources.

As HR professionals, it is likely that we will undertake projects in addition to our regular responsibilities rather than being afforded a temporary hiatus from those responsibilities. Balancing day-to-day workload, therefore, while working to complete a special project can be challenging and requires a unique skill set—one that is often separate and distinct from the skills needed to execute the project itself.

Like HR, project management is a profession. Although HR managers may not be members of the project management profession, we still must develop many of the unique skills associated with project management to successfully accomplish our objectives—which, again, will span all six functional areas of HR. Some of those skills will include the following:

- ▶ Clarifying goals

- ▶ Analyzing a project and developing a workable plan to complete it on time .

- ▶ Managing the project according to the plan

- ▶ Ensuring that other work expectations are still met

Project Management: Definition and Processes

The Project Management Institute (PMI) defines project management as "the application of knowledge, skills, tools, and techniques to a broad range of activities to meet the requirements of a particular project." Project managers seek to accomplish their objectives by gaining control over five factors: time, cost, quality, scope, and risk. To do this, those who undertake a project must clarify the needs and scope of the project, work out a plan for meeting those needs, and manage the project according to that plan. These steps, however, are sometimes easier to talk about than they are to execute.

PMI goes on to identify five distinct (yet overlapping) processes within project management:

- ▶ **Initiation processes:** Initiation processes are those that secure approval or authorization to undertake the project.

- ▶ **Planning processes:** Through planning processes, objectives are established, as are the best alternatives that will support the attainment of those objectives.

- ▶ **Executing processes:** Everything comes together through the executing processes; the scope, the objectives, and the deliverables all fall into place. To attain this level of successful execution, the right resources need to be in the right place at the right time.

▶ **Controlling processes:** Controlling processes include managing the scope of the project and making sure the project stays in line with the original objectives. A significant degree of follow-up is required to carry out controlling processes.

▶ **Closing processes:** Closing processes involve "sign-off" processes and mark the end of the project. As part of closing processes, stakeholders must determine whether, and to what degree, the project met its obligations.

These processes, although separate, are interrelated. The output from one set of processes contributes significantly to the inputs of subsequent processes. Although the processes are not wholly finite and discrete, they are more or less sequential, following the order presented here. Perhaps the best way to describe these processes is that they are interdependent, yet separate and somewhat sequential, though not linear.

KNOWLEDGE

Knowledge 05

Corporate governance procedures and compliance (for example, Sarbanes-Oxley Act).

The Sarbanes-Oxley Act (SOX) was created in 2002 in the wake of huge corporate accounting scandals, including Enron and Tyco, to name just two. Designed to protect investors, SOX enacted reforms designed to enhance corporate responsibility and financial disclosures and to combat corporate and accounting fraud. For more information on the Sarbanes-Oxley Act, see Chapter 6, "Risk Management."

There are a number of SOX provisions that HR professionals needs to be particularly concerned with, four of which include the following:

▶ Prohibition against insider trading during certain pension plan blackout periods—section 306(a).

▶ Requirement that plan administrators must provide 30-day written notice in advance of blackout periods to individual account plan participants and beneficiaries—section 306(b).

▶ Requirement to disclose whether the company has adopted a code of ethics that applies to the company's key officers (at a minimum, this code must apply to the company's principal executive officer, principal financial officer, principal accounting officer or controller, or persons performing similar functions)—section 406.

▶ Establishment of whistleblower protection in a wide variety of situations for employees who report fraud against shareholders—section 806(a).

KNOWLEDGE

Knowledge 09

Business concepts (for example: competitive advantage, organizational branding, business case development, corporate responsibility).

Competitive Advantage

Competitive advantage speaks to the way in which an organization can operate, sell, manage, produce, or somehow function in a way that is measurably and meaningfully superior to that of its competitors.

Business Case Development

Business case development speaks to the process of developing a proposal in support of the modification of an existing business approach or the introduction of a new program/initiative. The business case must be made on the basis of careful and supported analysis, sound projections, financial metrics, realistic assessments, and always—always—with an eye toward how the initiative will advance the overarching business objectives and attainment of the organization's mission in a manner that is consistent with the values of the organization.

Organizational Branding

Organizational branding speaks to the process by which an organization creates, establishes, and maintains a distinct and differentiating image of itself in the minds and memories of consumers in an effort to create positive associations and, in turn, to increase brand loyalty.

RESPONSIBILITY

BM & S Responsibility 17

Participate in enterprise risk management by ensuring that policies contribute to protecting the organization from potential risks.

Proactively identifying and making choices relative to the potential consequences of various levels of risk is a practice known as risk management. Although it's a key focus—and the title—of Chapter 6, let's begin to explore this topic here. Specifically, let's establish a foundation from which we can develop an appreciation of the unique role that HR professionals can play with respect to risk management.

Organizations face potential exposure in many employment-related areas; allegations can be made relative to sexual harassment, wrongful discharge, unlawful discrimination, or negligent hiring and retention, to name just a few.

Legal actions stemming from employment-related issues cost organizations untold dollars in attorneys' fees, court fees, settlements, and judgments. These monetary costs do not even begin to recognize other costs that are far more difficult to calculate—costs resulting from diminished employee morale, decreased productivity, allocation (or misallocation) of internal resources, and perhaps even the organizations' reputation as a labor market competitor, vendor, or community member.

HR professionals are uniquely positioned to anticipate, identify, and intervene before problems become "cases." Look for areas of potential exposure. In our roles, we see more, hear more, and know more about situations that have the potential to escalate. De-escalation of potentially litigious situations constitutes one of the most valuable contributions that HR professionals can make to their organizations.

NOTE

The following BM & S responsibilities/areas of knowledge are established as part of the SPHR responsibilities/areas of knowledge, so they are not covered in this book. They are addressed and explored in Pearson's *SPHR Exam Prep.*

- **BM & S Responsibility 03:** Participating as a contributing partner in the organization's strategic planning process (for example, provide and lead workforce planning discussion with management, develop and present long-term forecast of human capital needs at the organizational level).

- **BM & S Responsibility 06:** Develop and utilize business metrics to measure the achievement of the organization's strategic goals and objectives (for example, key performance indicators, balanced scorecard).

- **BM & S Responsibility 08:** Develop and align the human resource strategic plan with the organization's strategic plan.

- **BM & S Responsibility 12:** Develop and execute business plans (that is, annual goals and objectives) that correlate with the organization's strategic plan's performance expectations to include growth targets, new programs/services, and net income expectations.

- **BM & S Responsibility 13:** Perform cost/benefit analysis on proposed projects.

- **BM & S Responsibility 14:** Develop and manage an HR budget that supports the organization's strategic goals, objectives, and values.

- **BM & S Responsibility 16:** Develop policies and procedures to support corporate governance initiatives (for example, whistleblower protection, code of ethics).

- **BM & S Responsibility 18:** Identify and evaluate alternatives and recommend strategies for vendor selection and outsourcing.

- **BM & S Responsibility 19:** Oversee or lead the transition and implementation of new systems, service centers, and outsourcing.

- **BM & S Responsibility 20:** Participate in strategic decision-making and due diligence activities related to organizational structure and design (for example, corporate restructuring, mergers and acquisitions [M&A], divestitures).

- **BM & S Responsibility 21:** Determine strategic applications of integrated technical tools and systems (for example: new enterprise software, performance management tools, self-service technologies).

- **Knowledge 06:** Due diligence processes (for example, M & A, divestitures).

- **Knowledge 07:** Transition techniques for corporate restructuring, M & A, offshoring, and divestitures.

Chapter Summary

Functioning effectively requires a number of areas of knowledge and expertise, all of which could be grouped into three critical categories: knowing our business (organization), knowing our profession (craft), and knowing our customers. Although simply stated, much goes into mastering these three areas if they are to be performed at a highly efficient and effective level. In fact, that mastery should never end, as our organizations—and our roles—will never stop evolving.

This chapter addresses some of the specific areas of knowledge with which HR professionals need to become fluent and specific responsibilities that HR professionals must perform with competence as well as credibility. It is intended as a starting point, not an ending point. Strategic management is also an area within which many HR professionals will gain greater understanding, fluency, and competence as they gain experience and expertise within their careers. So if you aren't quite where you want to be yet, be patient with yourself. Keep studying, learning, and growing. Even the most seasoned and expert HR professional is committed to doing this.

Key Terms

- Business Management and Strategy (BM & S)
- Policies and procedures
- Consultation
- Catalyst
- Administrative
- Strategic
- Operational/tactical
- SWOT analysis
- Acid test
- Accounts payable
- Accounts receivable
- Asset
- Balance sheet
- Budgeting
- Activity-based budgeting
- Formula budgeting
- Incremental budgeting
- Zero-based budgeting
- Business activity ratios
- Cash-flow statement
- Current ratio
- Debt ratios
- Equity
- Financial ratios
- Gross profit margin
- Income statement
- Liability
- Profitability ratios
- Return on investment (ROI)
- Capacity
- Inventory
- Span of control
- Cost/benefit analysis
- Product
- Place
- Price
- Promotion
- Environment scanning
- Internal consulting
- Henri Fayol
- Functional organizational structure
- Divisional organizational structure
- Matrix organizational structure
- Boundaryless organization
- Bureaucracy
- Departmentalization ("departmentation")

- Formalization, or formal authority
- Virtual organization
- Organizational Life Cycle
  - Stage 1: Introduction (or "birth")
  - Stage 2: Development (or "growth")
  - Stage 3: Maturity
  - Stage 4: Decline
- Corporate social responsibility
- Community partnership
- Motivation
- Maslow's hierarchy of needs
  - Basic physical needs
  - Safety and security
  - Belonging and love
  - Esteem
  - Self-actualization
- B.F. Skinner—operant conditioning
  - Positive reinforcement (praise)
  - Negative reinforcement
  - Punishment
  - Extinction
- Frederick Herzberg—Motivation—Hygiene Theory
  - Motivation factors
  - Hygiene factors
- Douglas McGregor—Theory X and Theory Y
- David McClelland—Acquired Needs theory
- J. Stacy Adams—Equity Theory
- Victor Vroom—Expectancy Theory
  - Expectancy
  - Instrumentality
  - Valence
- Change management

- Change Process Theory
  - Unfreezing
  - Moving
  - Refreezing
- Implementation Theory
  - Human processual interventions
  - Technostructural interventions
  - Sociotechnical interventions
- Mission
- Values
- Vision
- Communication
- Coaching
- Executive coaching
- Mentoring
- Modeling
- Nonmathematical forecasting techniques
  - Management forecasts
  - The Delphi technique
  - Nominal group technique
- Mathematical forecasting techniques
  - Trend analysis
  - Ratio analysis
  - Turnover analysis
  - Simple linear regression
  - Multiple linear regression
- Simulations
- Legislative framework, considerations and opportunities
- Bills
- Joint resolutions
- Concurrent resolutions
- Simple resolutions
- Lobbying
- Strategic planning

- ▶ Phase 1: Establish a Foundation for the Strategy
- ▶ Phase 2: Develop the Strategic Plan
- ▶ Phase 3: Implement the Strategic Plan
- ▶ Phase 4: Evaluate the Plan, Process, and Performance
- ▶ Planning
- ▶ Organizing
- ▶ Coordinating
- ▶ Directing
- ▶ Controlling
- ▶ Leadership concepts
  - ▶ Trait Theories
  - ▶ Behavioral Theories
- ▶ Situational Leadership Theories (Paul Hersey and Ken Blanchard, Robert R. Blake and Jane S. Mouton)
- ▶ Contingency Theories
- ▶ Transactional leadership
- ▶ Transformational leadership
- ▶ Anthony Panos
- ▶ Project management
  - ▶ Initiation processes
  - ▶ Planning processes
  - ▶ Executing processes
  - ▶ Controlling processes
  - ▶ Closing processes
- ▶ Sarbanes-Oxley (SOX), 2002

Apply Your Knowledge

This chapter focuses on issues relating to strategic management. Complete the following review questions and exam questions as a way of reviewing and reinforcing the knowledge and skills you'll need to perform your responsibilities as an HR professional and to increase the likelihood that you will pass the PHR examination.

Review Questions

1. Describe the managerial function "planning."

2. Describe what the mission of an organization means.

3. Would transactional leaders be best described as coaches, directors, enforcers, or captains? Why?

4. Describe the introduction phase of the organizational life cycle.

5. Describe the controlling processes of project management.

Exam Questions

1. Which of the following is not a category of processes within project management?

   ○ **A.** Planning

   ○ **B.** Executing

   ○ **C.** Coordinating

   ○ **D.** Controlling

2. Which of the following statements about change is most true?

   ○ **A.** HR professionals must proactively seek to understand change and what causes it.

   ○ **B.** HR must serve as an employee advocate during times of change.

   ○ **C.** HR must ensure that the pace of change does not exceed the organization's ability to adapt to it.

   ○ **D.** HR must serve as a management advocate during times of change.

3. Which of the following statements about values is not true?

   ○ **A.** Values are often expressed through terms such as "communication" and "decision-making."

   ○ **B.** Values affect behaviors that are exhibited on a day-to-day basis in the workplace.

   ○ **C.** Values are the beliefs on which an organization is built.

   ○ **D.** Values shape and guide strategic as well as day-to-day decision-making.

4. What is the first step in the scientific method?

   ○ **A.** Develop a hypothesis.

   ○ **B.** Question and observe.

   ○ **C.** Scan existing secondary research.

   ○ **D.** Conduct a needs analysis.

5. What is one overarching purpose of an HR audit?

   ○ **A.** To ascertain how well the HR department—through all its various functional areas—has aligned itself with the organization's strategic objectives

   ○ **B.** To ascertain the degree to which the HR department has complied with all legal requirements and the potential financial exposure associated with existing levels of noncompliance

   ○ **C.** To ascertain the performance of the HR department with respect to the nature and quality of the consultative services it provides to its internal clients

   ○ **D.** To ascertain the degree to which the HR department is poised to meet the current, future, and emerging human capital and talent needs of the organization

6. The transformational leadership style

   ○ **A.** Places greater emphasis on relationships than on tasks

   ○ **B.** Places greater emphasis on tasks than on relationships

   ○ **C.** Is characterized by the possibility of rewards and by the threat of punishment

   ○ **D.** Encourages a coaching style of leadership

7. Effectiveness can be defined as

   ○ **A.** A ratio of inputs to outputs

   ○ **B.** The degree to which goals are met

   ○ **C.** The degree to which goals reflect desired outputs

   ○ **D.** A ratio of outputs to inputs

8. Which of the following is not specifically recognized as being critically important to successfully implementing a strategic plan?

   ○ **A.** Commitment

   ○ **B.** Credibility

   ○ **C.** Collaboration

   ○ **D.** Communication

9. Project managers seek to accomplish their objectives by gaining control over five factors, one of which is the following.

   ○ **A.** Regulatory compliance

   ○ **B.** Risk

   ○ **C.** Reward structures

   ○ **D.** Staffing

10. All of the following are compelling reasons for organizations to engage in a strategic planning process except this one.

   ○ **A.** Developing a clearer awareness of how the organization measures up, internally and externally

   ○ **B.** Engaging individuals throughout the organization in a meaningful organizational effort

   ○ **C.** Enabling employees to prepare themselves to react positively and constructively to future events

   ○ **D.** Creating—or reaffirming—the vision, mission, and values of the organization

Answers to Review Questions

1. Planning, the first of five managerial functions, lays the groundwork for how managers will work toward accomplishing the organization's goals. Through planning, managers decide what needs to get done, when it needs to get done, who will do it, how it will get done, and where it will be done. In the absence of planning, the organization—and the people in it—will lack direction and perhaps even just coast along.

2. An organization's mission statement articulates, in essence, its reason for being. It may speak to the nature of the organization's business or purpose, its customers, and sometimes even its employees and its role in the community. A mission statement should be broad (but not overly generalized), brief, clear, unambiguous, and designed to last for "the long haul." Because the goals of an organization must be based on the mission, the mission is far bigger than any goal—and thus must be able to withstand the test of time.

3. Of these four choices, the term "enforcer" would best characterize transactional leaders. Transactional leaders use a system built on "the carrot and the stick" approach—and mainly the stick. Coaching doesn't reflect this approach and instead is more characteristic of the transformational leadership style. The image of a captain might more closely reflect the role a leader plays in the selling quadrant of Hersey and Blanchard's Situational Leadership Model. A director could imply a wider variety of leadership approaches under transactional as well as transformational styles.

4. Introduction (or "birth") is the first step in the organizational life cycle. During this phase, excitement and energy run high and cash flow may be quite tight. Struggling start-ups often find themselves searching for solid footing—financially as well as operationally. The core group of highly talented employees who are part of a start-up operation may focus fixedly on the founder as a source of direction, wisdom, and inspiration.

   In the introduction phase, employees may find themselves paid above market rates as a reflection of the founder's desire to entice them to come on board. Alternatively, if money is in short supply, during the introduction phase of the life cycle employees may earn less cash compensation and have those diminished earnings offset by other noncash rewards (equity, intrinsic rewards, and so on).

   Depending on the organization, HR may or may not have a formal presence in this phase of the organizational life cycle.

5. Controlling processes include managing the scope of the project and making sure the project stays in line with the original objectives. A significant degree of follow-up is required to carry out controlling processes.

Answers to Exam Questions

1. Answer C is the best answer. Coordinating is a management function, not a project management process. Answers A, B, and D are not the best answers because they each identify a project management process. (Those processes include initiation, planning, executing, controlling, and closing.)

2. Answer A is the best answer. HR professionals must seek to understand change and what causes it—ideally before change descends upon the organization. Change, itself, brings considerable challenges of its own—and often does not afford HR professionals the luxury of time to study change theory or process. (Those are lessons that HR professionals need to undertake in advance.) Answer C is not the best answer because HR's role is not to regulate the pace of change. At times, the pace of change may not be controllable. At other times, the pace of change may, in fact, be controllable, but the organization's leaders may decide that it is not appropriate or advisable to slow the pace of change. Answers B and D are not the best answers; HR must serve as a "truth advocate" during times of change (in fact, at all times), not as dedicated advocates of management or employees.

3. Answer A is the best answer. Terms like "communication" and "decision-making" are often used to describe competencies (also called success factors), not values. Answers B, C, and D are not the best answers because each makes a true statement about values.

4. Answer B is the best answer. Question and observe is, in fact, the first step in the scientific method. Answer A is not the best answer because developing a hypothesis is the second step in the scientific method. Answer C is not the best answer because the scientific method is a form of primary research and is therefore separate and distinct from secondary research. Answer D is not the best answer because conducting a needs analysis and assessment is the first step in the ADDIE process, not the scientific method.

5. Answer A is the best answer. The primary and overarching purpose of an HR audit is to ascertain how well the HR department has aligned itself with the organization's strategic objectives. Answers B, C, and D are not the best answers; although each identifies a possible component of an HR audit, none of these is broad enough to encompass the overarching purpose of an HR audit.

6. Answer D is the best answer. The transformational leadership style places greater emphasis on relationships than on tasks. Answer A is not the best answer; transformational leaders concern themselves with relationships as well as task dimensions—neither is emphasized to the exclusion of the other. Answer B is not the best answer; the transactional leadership style is characterized by the possibility of rewards and the threat of punishment, whereas the transformational leadership style focuses on coaching rather than enforcement (or threats of enforcement).

7. Answer B is the best answer. Effectiveness is a measure of the degree to which goals—carefully established goals—are met.

8. Answer C is the best answer. Although collaboration is an important element of the strategic planning process, it is not recognized as one of the three Cs—the most important keys to successful strategic planning. Those three Cs are commitment (answer A), credibility (answer B), and communication (answer D).

9. Answer B is the best answer. The five factors over which project managers seek to establish control are time, cost, quality, scope, and risk. (Answer B is "risk.") Project managers do not specifically seek to establish control over regulatory compliance (answer A), reward structures (answer C), or staffing (answer D), although all of those elements will be considerations as they work to attain their objectives.

10. Answer D is the best answer. The focus of strategic planning is on proactivity, not reactivity. Therefore, through strategic planning, the organization creates an opportunity for individuals at all levels of the organization to proactively shape and influence the future rather than just react to it. Answers A, B, and C are not the best answers because each one articulates a compelling reason to engage in strategic planning.

Suggested Readings and Resources

Alevas, S. (2005). *The Ethical Enabler: Empowering Employees to Become Chief Ethics Officers.* Retrieved from http://alevasconsulting.com/ethical_enabler.htm.

Becker, Brian E., Mark A. Huselid, and Dave Ulrich. *The HR Scorecard: Linking People, Strategy, and Performance* (hardcover). Cambridge, MA: Harvard Business School Press, 2001.

Block, P. (2011). *Flawless Consulting: A Guide to Getting Your Expertise Used* (3rd ed.). San Francisco, Calif.: Pfeiffer.

Business Literacy for HR Professionals: Essentials of Strategy. (2006). Boston, Mass: Harvard Business School Press.

Harvard Business Literacy for HR Professionals: The Essentials of Managing Change and Transition. (2005). Boston, Mass.: Harvard Business School Press in partnership with Society for Human Resource Management.

Johnson, C. (2012). *Organizational Ethics: A Practical Approach* (2nd ed.). Thousand Oaks, Calif.: SAGE Publications.

Martin, V. (2006). *Managing Projects in Human Resources, Training and Development.* London: Kogan Page.

Pynes, J. (2013). *Human Resources Management for Public and Nonprofit Organizations: A Strategic Approach* (4th ed.). San Francisco, Calif.: Jossey-Bass.

Ulrich, D. (2013). *Global HR Competencies: Mastering Competitive Value from the Outside In.* New York: McGraw-Hill.

Ulrich, D. (2012). *HR from the Outside In: The Next Era of Human Resources Transformation.* New York: McGraw-Hill.

Ulrich, D. (2009). *HR Transformation: Building Human Resources from the Outside In.* Chicago: McGraw-Hill.

Ulrich, D., and Smallwood, W. (2008). *The Leadership Code: Five Rules to Lead By.* Boston, Mass.: Harvard Business Press.

Ulrich, D., and Ulrich, W. (2010). *The Why of Work: How Great Leaders Build Abundant Organizations to Deliver Value for Customers, Investors, and Communities.* Chicago: McGraw-Hill.

CHAPTER TWO

Workforce Planning and Employment

Workforce planning and employment (WPE) speaks to HR's responsibility to ensure integrated, seamless, and effective recruitment, hiring, orientation, and exit processes that support the short-term, long-term, emerging, and strategic objectives of the organization.

An organization's overall success will be determined to a significant degree by its ability to have the right people, with the right skills, in the right places, at the right times. Although this statement sounds somewhat straightforward, let's take a closer look at what it actually means.

"To have" in this context can refer to hiring employees to work a traditional work arrangement, hiring employees to work some sort of nontraditional work arrangement, or retaining nonemployees to perform services on an as-needed basis (consultants). Although most organizations secure their "people resources" through traditional employment relationships, many organizations are also augmenting this approach with nontraditional arrangements, such as consulting services.

"The right people, with the right skills" refers to employing or contracting with individuals who possess and demonstrate the knowledge, skills, abilities, and behavioral characteristics needed to support the organization's mission and to attain the organization's objectives. Employing individuals who don't have the necessary knowledge, skills, abilities, and behavioral characteristics can be problematic (or, at the very least, challenging). Employing—and retaining—individuals who possess skills that they want to put to use but that aren't needed can be equally—and sometimes even more—problematic.

"In the right places, at the right times" speaks to the importance of analyzing short-term and long-term organizational needs to ensure that the organization is neither overstaffed nor understaffed at any given moment. In this context, the terms "overstaffing" and "understaffing" can refer to the number of people employed, as well as the skills that those individuals bring to the organization.

Achieving this delicate balance requires a considerable amount of planning. It also requires that HR professionals continually maintain awareness of the organization's mission, as well as its short-term, long-term, and emerging goals. In this way, HR professionals—in close collaboration with the leaders and managers of the organization—can determine how to strategically support the organization's goals.

Effective workforce planning ensures that the organization has the "people resources" in place that will enable it—through those very same people—to fulfill its mission and achieve its objectives. Workforce planning encompasses myriad activities relating to how employees enter into—and exit from—the organization. It looks at these functions primarily from the perspective of meeting the organization's needs and ideally takes a long-term (more tactical, or perhaps transformational, in nature)—and a short-term (more transactional in nature)—approach.

By effectively performing responsibilities relating to workforce planning and development, HR professionals can seize another opportunity to forge a business partnership with their internal clients. For this to happen, HR professionals must take a deliberate and consistent approach to workforce planning that starts with the organization's strategic plan and with how HR can align its efforts and work product with that plan.

Determining "what" and "who" the organization needs to achieve its goals is more involved than it might appear. Accurate forecasting requires selecting from among numerous nonmathematical (qualitative) and mathematical (quantitative) analyses.

RESPONSIBILITY

WPE Responsibility 01

Ensure that workforce planning and employment activities are compliant with applicable federal laws and regulations.

KNOWLEDGE

Knowledge 11

Applicable federal laws and regulations related to workforce planning and employment activities (for example: Title VII, ADA, EEOC Uniform Guidelines on Employee Selection Procedures, Immigration Reform and Control Act).

To formulate and execute these plans, HR professionals must be well versed in those laws that impact our profession and that affect the ways in which we source, hire, promote, and separate/terminate employees. Equal employment opportunity is the foundation on which these laws have been built and constitutes one critical element of every HR professional's knowledge base.

Laws, however, are not static. Rather, they are continually interpreted and reinterpreted—by the courts and even by administrative agencies. As such, HR professionals have a professional and ethical mandate to familiarize themselves with important cases from the past and to monitor new cases, proposals, and regulations. In this way, we will be better equipped to understand and appreciate new interpretations of these laws and thus maintain currency with respect to how they will affect the workplace and the ways in which we choose to carry out our strategic, tactical, and transactional roles.

NOTE

The "best answer" to all questions on the PHR exam that relate to laws and cases will be determined by laws and regulations that are in effect at the start of each exam period. Be sure that you keep updated on new laws, new cases, and changed regulations. Also note that proposals are not "official" until they are officially adopted.

Congress has passed numerous pieces of federal legislation specifically designed to eradicate discrimination on the basis of a variety of factors. This legislation—while diverse in terms of the areas that are spanned—shares one thing in common: none of the characteristics or traits addressed by these laws has any affect on a person's ability to do the job. Each piece of legislation has brought the workplace one step closer to ensuring that hiring, promotional, and all other employment-related decisions are based solely on job-related factors.

EXAM ALERT

When it comes to employment law, HR professionals must tread carefully. To function effectively, we need a solid understanding of the laws that affect our profession, our clients, and our organizations. We must maintain currency with respect to the way the courts interpret—and reinterpret—existing laws, and we must understand the impact of new laws and cases. There is, however, a line over which we cannot cross under penalty of law. Ultimately, a person who is not an attorney cannot practice law or dispense legal advice. We must be cautious that our efforts do not unintentionally overstep this line.

Relevant Laws and Executive Orders

As you move into this section, keep in mind that it includes relevant laws, case law, and executive orders (EOs). Unlike laws, which are passed by Congress, EOs are enacted by the president. They do carry, however, the same weight as law. EOs provide guidance and assistance to federal agencies relative to the execution of their duties and to employers relative to what they must do to be in compliance with the executive order. HR professionals need to be fluent with respect to EOs pertaining to employment issues.

Title VII of the Civil Rights Act, 1964

Although it wasn't the first antidiscrimination law, Title VII of the Civil Rights Act of 1964 was a landmark piece of legislation prohibiting employment discrimination on the basis of race, color, religion, sex, or national origin. It was the most inclusive piece of antidiscrimination legislation up to that time (and, some might argue, perhaps even up to *this* time). In short, Title VII radically changed the workplace.

Title VII applies to private employers with 15 or more employees. Title VII, as amended, also specifically applies to federal, state, and local governments, as well as to employment agencies and labor organizations, education institutions that employ 15 or more individuals, private and public employment agencies, labor organizations, and joint labor management committees controlling apprenticeship and training.

According to the EEOC:

> "This law makes it illegal to discriminate against someone on the basis of race, color, religion, national origin, or sex. The law also makes it illegal to retaliate against a person because the person complained about discrimination, filed a charge of discrimination, or participated in an employment discrimination investigation or lawsuit. The law also requires that employers reasonably accommodate applicants' and employees' sincerely held religious practices, unless doing so would impose an undue hardship on the operation of the employer's business" (www.eeoc.gov).

The Civil Rights Act of 1964 established the first "protected classes" and created the Equal Employment Opportunity Commission (EEOC). As published on its website, the EEOC's mission is "to promote equal opportunity in employment through administrative and judicial enforcement of the federal civil rights laws and through education and technical assistance" (www.eeoc.gov).

Title VII of the Civil Rights Act of 1964 prohibits discrimination in all aspects of the employment relationship, including

- ▶ Hiring and firing
- ▶ Compensation, assignment, or classification of employees
- ▶ Transfer, promotion, layoff, or recall
- ▶ Job advertisements
- ▶ Recruitment
- ▶ Testing
- ▶ Use of company facilities
- ▶ Training and apprenticeship programs
- ▶ Fringe benefits
- ▶ Pay, retirement plans, and disability leave
- ▶ Other terms and conditions of employment

Title VII also prohibits retaliation against an employee who files a charge of discrimination, who participates in an investigation, or who opposes discriminatory practices.

Under rare circumstances, exceptions can be made to Title VII requirements. Table 2.1 includes some of these exceptions.

TABLE 2.1   Exceptions to Title VII

Type of Exception	Definition	Example
Bona fide occupational qualification (BFOQ)	Certain job requirements that are mandated by business necessity may have an unintended discriminatory (disparate) impact upon applicants or employees on the basis of gender, religion, or national origin.	Hiring females to be bathroom attendants in a women's restroom. Hiring a person of a particular religious denomination to be a minister to members of that faith.
Professionally developed test of abilities	Job-related tests that ascertain skill or ability may have an unintended discriminatory (disparate) impact upon people on the basis of gender, religion, or national origin.	Strength or physical skills or agility tests if those tests assess skills that have been shown to be necessary for successful performance of a particular position—as determined by the actual performance of current or former employees.
Seniority systems	Bona fide seniority or merit-based systems that are not intended or designed to discriminate unlawfully.	Bona fide collective bargaining agreements.
Piece-rate systems	Compensation programs under which individuals are paid according to their production volume.	Certain assembly line or factory assignments.

Executive Order 11246, 1965

EO 11246, the first employment-related EO, is administered by the Office of Federal Contract Compliance Programs (OFCCP). It established two key requirements for federal contractors and subcontractors that have contracts in excess of $10,000 during any one-year period:

▶ These employers are prohibited from discriminating in employment decisions on the basis of race, color, religion, sex, or national origin. This requirement reconfirmed the nondiscrimination requirements established by Title VII of the Civil Rights Act of 1964. "Contractors and subcontractors who hold a single federal contract or subcontract in excess of $10,000 or who hold contracts or subcontracts with the federal government in any 12-month period that have a total value of more than $10,000 are required to post the EEO notice, Equal Employment Opportunity is the Law (PDF). Federal contractors and subcontractors who (1) hold government bills of lading; (2) serve as a depository of federal funds in any amount; or (3) act as issuing and paying agents for U.S. savings bonds and notes must also post the EEO notice" (www.dol.gov).

▶ These employers must take affirmative steps—or actions—in advertising open positions, recruiting, employment, training, promotion, compensation, and termination of employees to ensure the elimination of employment barriers for women and minorities (individuals who we might refer to today as "people of color").

NOTE

Additional information about Affirmative Action Plans (AAPs) is included later in this chapter.

Uniform Guidelines on Employee Selection Procedures, 1978

The Uniform Guidelines on Employee Selection Procedures was intended to address the need to establish a uniform set of principles relative to all elements of the selection process—including interviewing, preemployment testing, and performance appraisal. One key purpose of the Uniform Guidelines was to deal with the concept of "adverse impact" (also known as "disparate impact") as it pertains to the employment process. Another was to ensure that interview and selection processes are reliable (consistent) and valid:

"These guidelines incorporate a single set of principles which are designed to assist employers, labor organizations, employment agencies, and licensing and certification boards to comply with requirements of Federal law prohibiting employment practices which discriminate on grounds of race, color, religion, sex, and national origin. They are designed to provide a framework for determining the proper use of tests and other selection procedures.

These guidelines do not require a user to conduct validity studies of selection procedures where no adverse impact results. However, all users are encouraged to use selection procedures which are valid, especially users operating under merit principles" (www.dol.gov).

As mentioned earlier, the key purpose of the Uniform Guidelines was to deal with the concept of "adverse impact" (also known as "disparate impact") as this concept pertains to the employment process and to ensure that interview and selection processes are reliable (consistent) and valid. For more information on this concept, see the section titled "Disparate (or "Adverse") Impact."

Reliability

The degree to which a selection process or instrument is consistent is reflective of the degree to which that instrument is reliable.

All interviews for a position should generate consistent information for decision-making—even if several interviewers are involved, and even when all interviewers don't meet every candidate.

In this context, one important function of a well-defined and well-documented interviewing process is to ensure the most reliable results possible, even given the inevitable differences among interviewers. This is one reason why it is critical that interviewers prepare and consistently use a list of job-related questions that will be asked of all candidates for a particular position.

Validity

Employment interviews measure applicants' skills. Valid interviews ensure that those skills relate meaningfully and clearly to the skills that are required to perform a particular job.

Validity establishes and demonstrates a clear relationship between performance on the selection procedure and performance on the job. Although it is difficult to establish good measures of validity, it is possible to make a case for validity if the interview has the following characteristics:

- ▶ It is based on job analysis.
- ▶ It contains questions that provide evidence about important job-related skills.
- ▶ Interview information is systematically related to a specific job.

HR professionals need to be familiar with at least the following four types of validity.

Content Validity

A selection procedure has content validity if it assesses a candidate's ability to perform representatively sampled significant parts of the job.

Example: A typing test for an administrative assistant's position would demonstrate content validity.

Criterion-Related Validity

A selection procedure has criterion-related validity if scores achieved by incumbents correlate highly with their respective job performance.

Example: A requirement that candidates have fluency in a particular foreign language would have criterion-related validity if it were shown that people who demonstrate fluency in that language actually perform better on the job than those who do not demonstrate fluency.

Construct Validity

A selection procedure has construct validity if it measures the degree to which the test taker possesses a particular psychological trait (if, of course, it can be shown that the trait is required for successful performance of the position). More specifically, according to the EEOC Uniform Employee Selection Guidelines:

> "Evidence of the validity of a test or other selection procedure through a construct validity study should consist of data showing that the procedure measures the degree to which candidates have identifiable characteristics which have been determined to be important in successful performance in the job for which the candidates are to be evaluated" (www.eeoc.gov).

Example: An instrument that assesses the degree to which candidates for a car salesperson's position are persistent would demonstrate construct validity.

Predictive Validity

A selection procedure has predictive validity if the predictions that it makes actually manifest themselves in the test takers' subsequent performance.

Example: An instrument that is designed to assess the degree to which candidates for a position possess and demonstrate empathy would have predictive validity if individuals who scored well on this test demonstrated, after being hired, that they actually did possess and demonstrate this characteristic.

A Closer Look at Testing

The Uniform Guidelines set forth—quite literally—uniform guidelines to ensure that the selection process remains focused on job-related criteria. The Uniform Guidelines may also, however, serve as an opportunity to look more closely at our selection processes—even if we have not found that adverse impact exists—so as to ensure that our processes are truly focused on the job and not on other extraneous factors. This does not, by itself, necessarily include or exclude the use of instruments that we commonly refer to as "tests." It does, however, challenge HR professionals and hiring managers to ensure that the use of any such tests remains fixedly (and statistically) focused on job-related qualifications and requirements.

It might also challenge us to revisit tests that we have already incorporated into the selection process, perhaps applying a closer degree of scrutiny or a greater degree of rigor to our design or selection of each particular test. Testing is often seen as a panacea, of sorts, in the selection process—a black-or-white, make-or-break decision point (unless or until, of course, we aren't comfortable with a particular set of test results).

In addition to challenging us to look closer at the validity and reliability of the tests we use, consider allowing the Uniform Guidelines to serve as a challenge to rethink testing in general because, in the most literal sense, every step in the selection process constitutes a test of one sort or another and could be interpreted/analyzed/scrutinized as such by the EEOC.

NOTE

This applies even to the interview itself—even though this step in the selection process is often perceived as a semistructured (or even unstructured) opportunity to just "get a feel" for the candidate. Try to keep this perspective in mind as you take a closer look at the "Interviews and the Interview Process" section later in this chapter.

The EEOC has published the fact sheet shown in the following sidebar on "Employment Tests and Selection Procedures."

Employment Tests and Selection Procedures

Employers often use tests and other selection procedures to screen applicants for hire and employees for promotion. There are many different types of tests and selection procedures, including cognitive tests, personality tests, medical examinations, credit checks, and criminal background checks.

The use of tests and other selection procedures can be an effective means of determining which applicants or employees are most qualified for a particular job. However, use of these tools can violate the federal antidiscrimination laws if an employer intentionally uses them to discriminate based on race, color, sex, national origin, religion, disability, or age (40 or older). Use of tests and other selection procedures can also violate the federal antidiscrimination laws if they disproportionately exclude people in a particular group by race, sex, or another covered basis unless the employer can justify the test or procedure under the law.

On May 16, 2007, the EEOC held a public meeting on employment testing and screening. Witnesses addressed legal issues related to the use of employment tests and other selection procedures. (To see the testimony of these witnesses, please see the EEOC's website at http://eeoc.gov/eeoc/meetings/archive/5-16-07/index.html.)

This fact sheet provides technical assistance on some common issues relating to the federal anti-discrimination laws and the use of tests and other selection procedures in the employment process.

Background

▶ Title VII of the Civil Rights Act of 1964 (Title VII), the Americans with Disabilities Act of 1990 (ADA), and the Age Discrimination in Employment Act of 1967 (ADEA) prohibit the use of discriminatory employment tests and selection procedures.

▶ There has been an increase in employment testing due in part to post 9-11 security concerns as well as concerns about workplace violence, safety, and liability. In addition, the large-scale adoption of online job applications has motivated employers to seek efficient ways to screen large numbers of online applicants in a nonsubjective way.

▶ The number of discrimination charges raising issues of employment testing, and exclusions based on criminal background checks, credit reports, and other selection procedures, reached a high point in FY 2007 at 304 charges.

Types of Employment Tests and Selection Procedures

Examples of employment tests and other selection procedures, many of which can be administered online, include the following:

▶ Cognitive tests assess reasoning, memory, perceptual speed and accuracy, and skills in arithmetic and reading comprehension, as well as knowledge of a particular function or job.

▶ Physical ability tests measure the physical ability to perform a particular task or the strength of specific muscle groups, as well as strength and stamina in general.

▶ Sample job tasks (for example, performance tests, simulations, work samples, and realistic job previews) assess performance and aptitude on particular tasks.

▶ Medical inquiries and physical examinations, including psychological tests, assess physical or mental health. (Per ADA requirements, employers with 15 or more employees can only make such inquiries/exams after a conditional offer of employment has been extended.)

▶ Personality tests and integrity tests assess the degree to which a person has certain traits or dispositions (dependability, cooperativeness, safety) or aim to predict the likelihood that a person will engage in certain conduct (theft, absenteeism).

▶ Criminal background checks provide information on arrest and conviction history.

▶ Credit checks provide information on credit and financial history.

▶ Performance appraisals reflect a supervisor's assessment of an individual's performance.

▶ English proficiency tests determine English fluency.

Governing EEO Laws

This section will focus on laws that relate to Equal Employment Opportunity in the workplace. These laws span more than 50 years—and growing.

Please note: the laws discussed in this book are effective at the federal level. Although state or local laws cannot be less generous, they can—and in many cases are—more generous. The HRCI certification exam will not address state and local laws, but HR professionals must be well versed with the laws that affect the geographic areas for which they are responsible.

Title VII of the Civil Rights Act of 1964

Title VII prohibits employment discrimination based on race, color, religion, sex, or national origin.

With respect to tests in particular, Title VII permits employment tests as long as they are not "designed, intended or used to discriminate because of race, color, religion, sex or national origin." 42 U.S.C. § 2000e-2(h). Title VII also imposes restrictions on how to score tests. Employers are not permitted to (1) adjust the scores of, (2) use different cutoff scores for, or (3) otherwise alter the results of employment-related tests on the basis of race, color, religion, sex, or national origin. Id. at §2000e-2(l).

Title VII prohibits both "disparate treatment" and "disparate impact" discrimination.

Title VII prohibits intentional discrimination based on race, color, religion, sex, or national origin. For example, Title VII forbids a covered employer from testing the reading ability of African American applicants or employees but not testing the reading ability of their white counterparts. This is called "disparate treatment" discrimination. Disparate treatment cases typically involve the following issues:

▶ Were people of a different race, color, religion, sex, or national origin treated differently?

▶ Is there any evidence of bias, such as discriminatory statements?

▶ What is the employer's reason for the difference in treatment?

▶ Does the evidence show that the employer's reason for the difference in treatment is untrue and that the real reason for the different treatment is race, color, religion, sex, or national origin?

Title VII also prohibits employers from using neutral tests or selection procedures that have the effect of disproportionately excluding persons based on race, color, religion, sex, or national origin, where the tests or selection procedures are not "job-related and consistent with business necessity." This is called "disparate impact" discrimination.

Disparate impact cases typically involve the following issues:

▶ Does the employer use a particular employment practice that has a disparate impact on the basis of race, color, religion, sex, or national origin? For example, if an employer requires that all applicants pass a physical agility test, does the test disproportionately screen out women? Determining whether a test or other selection procedure has a disparate impact on a particular group ordinarily requires a statistical analysis.

▶ If the selection procedure has a disparate impact based on race, color, religion, sex, or national origin, can the employer show that the selection procedure is job related and consistent with business necessity? An employer can meet this standard by showing that it is necessary to the safe and efficient performance of the job. The challenged policy or practice should therefore be associated with the skills needed to perform the job successfully. In contrast to a general measurement of applicants' or employees' skills, the challenged policy or practice must evaluate an individual's skills as related to the particular job in question.

▶ If the employer shows that the selection procedure is job related and consistent with business necessity, can the person challenging the selection procedure demonstrate that there is a less discriminatory alternative available? For example, is another test available that would be equally effective in predicting job performance but would not disproportionately exclude the protected group?

See 42 U.S.C. § 2000e-2 (k). This method of analysis is consistent with the seminal Supreme Court decision about disparate impact discrimination, Griggs v. Duke Power Co., *401 U.S. 424 (1971)*.

▶ In 1978, the EEOC adopted the Uniform Guidelines on Employee Selection Procedures or "UGESP" under Title VII. See 29 C.F.R. Part 1607. UGESP provided uniform guidance for employers about how to determine if their tests and selection procedures were lawful for purposes of Title VII disparate impact theory.

▶ UGESP outlines three different ways employers can show that their employment tests and other selection criteria are job related and consistent with business necessity. These methods of demonstrating job relatedness are called "test validation." UGESP provides detailed guidance about each method of test validation.

Title I of the Americans with Disabilities Act

Title I of the Americans with Disabilities Act (ADA) prohibits private employers and state and local governments from discriminating against qualified individuals with disabilities on the basis of their disabilities.

The ADA specifies when an employer may require an applicant or employee to undergo a medical examination (a procedure or test that seeks information about an individual's physical or mental impairments or health). The ADA also specifies when an employer may make "disability-related inquiries" (inquiries that are likely to elicit information about a disability).

When hiring, an employer may not ask questions about disability or require medical examinations until after it makes a conditional job offer to the applicant. 42 U.S.C. §12112 (d)(2).

After making a job offer (but before the person starts working), an employer may ask disability-related questions and conduct medical examinations as long as it does so for all individuals entering the same job category. Id. at § 12112(d)(3).

With respect to employees, an employer may ask questions about disability or require medical examinations only if doing so is job related and consistent with business necessity. Thus, for example, an employer could request medical information when it has a reasonable belief, based on objective evidence, that a particular employee will be unable to perform essential job functions or will pose a direct threat because of a medical condition, or when an employer receives a request for a reasonable accommodation and the person's disability or need for accommodation is not obvious. Id. at § 12112(d)(4).

The ADA also makes it unlawful to do the following:

▶ Use employment tests that screen out or tend to screen out an individual with a disability or a class of individuals with disabilities unless the test, as used by the employer, is shown to be job related and consistent with business necessity. 42 U.S.C. § 12112(b)(6).

▶ Fail to select and administer employment tests in the most effective manner to ensure that test results accurately reflect the skills, aptitude or whatever other factor that such test purports to measure, rather than reflecting an applicant's or employee's impairment. Id. at § 12112(b)(7) .

► Fail to make reasonable accommodations, including in the administration of tests, to the known physical or mental limitations of an otherwise qualified individual with a disability who is an applicant or employee, unless such accommodation would impose an undue hardship. Id. at § 12112(b)(5).

The Age Discrimination in Employment Act

The Age Discrimination in Employment Act (ADEA) prohibits discrimination based on age (40 and over) with respect to any term, condition, or privilege of employment. Under the ADEA, covered employers may not select individuals for hiring, promotion, or reductions in force in a way that unlawfully discriminates on the basis of age.

The ADEA prohibits disparate treatment discrimination, i.e., intentional discrimination based on age. For example, the ADEA forbids an employer from giving a physical agility test only to applicants over age 50, based on a belief that they are less physically able to perform a particular job, but not testing younger applicants.

The ADEA also prohibits employers from using neutral tests or selection procedures that have a discriminatory impact on persons based on age (40 or older), unless the challenged employment action is based on a reasonable factor other than age. *Smith v. City of Jackson, 544 U.S. 228 (2005).* Thus, if a test or other selection procedure has a disparate impact based on age, the employer must show that the test or device chosen was a reasonable one (www.eeoc.gov).

Age Discrimination in Employment Act, 1967

The Age Discrimination in Employment Act (ADEA) prohibits discrimination on the basis of age for employees and job applicants who are age 40 and above. There is no upper cap on age limit (although there initially was). Under the ADEA, it is unlawful to discriminate against a person because of her age with respect to any term, condition, or privilege of employment, including hiring, firing, promotion, layoff, compensation, benefits, job assignments, and training.

The ADEA also makes it unlawful to retaliate against an individual for opposing employment practices that discriminate based on age or for filing an age discrimination charge, testifying, or participating in any way in an investigation, proceeding, or litigation under the ADEA.

The ADEA does permit employers to favor older workers based on age even when doing so adversely affects a younger worker who is 40 or older.

ADEA covers private employers with 20 or more employees, state and local governments (including school districts), employment agencies, and labor organizations.

The EEOC has published the following Facts About Age Discrimination Fact Sheet:

The Age Discrimination in Employment Act of 1967 (ADEA) protects individuals who are 40 years of age or older from employment discrimination based on age. The ADEA's protections apply to both employees and job applicants. Under the ADEA, it is unlawful to discriminate against a person because of his age with respect to any term, condition, or privilege of employment, including hiring, firing, promotion, layoff, compensation, benefits, job assignments, and training. The ADEA permits employers to favor older workers based on age even when doing so adversely affects a younger worker who is 40 or older.

It is also unlawful to retaliate against an individual for opposing employment practices that discriminate based on age or for filing an age discrimination charge, testifying, or participating in any way in an investigation, proceeding, or litigation under the ADEA.

The ADEA applies to employers with 20 or more employees, including state and local governments. It also applies to employment agencies and labor organizations, as well as to the federal government.

ADEA protections (www.eeoc.gov) include the following:

▶ Apprenticeship programs

▶ Job notices and advertisements

▶ Preemployment inquiries

▶ Benefits

▶ Waivers of ADEA rights

Apprenticeship Programs

It is generally unlawful for apprenticeship programs, including joint labor-management apprenticeship programs, to discriminate on the basis of an individual's age. Age limitations in apprenticeship programs are valid only if they fall within certain specific exceptions under the ADEA or if the EEOC grants a specific exemption.

Job Notices and Advertisements

The ADEA generally makes it unlawful to include age preferences, limitations, or specifications in job notices or advertisements. A job notice or advertisement may specify an age limit only in the rare circumstances in which age is shown to be a BFOQ that's reasonably necessary to the normal operation of the business.

Preemployment Inquiries

The ADEA does not specifically prohibit an employer from asking an applicant's age or date of birth. However, because such inquiries may deter older workers from applying for employment or may otherwise indicate possible intent to discriminate based on age, requests for age information will be closely scrutinized to make sure that the inquiry was made for a lawful purpose rather than for a purpose prohibited by the ADEA.

Benefits

The Older Workers Benefit Protection Act of 1990 (OWBPA) amended the ADEA to specifically prohibit employers from denying benefits to older employees. Congress recognized that the cost of providing certain benefits to older workers is greater than the cost of providing those same benefits to younger workers and that those greater costs would create a disincentive to hire older workers. Therefore, in limited circumstances, an employer may be permitted to reduce benefits based on age as long as the cost of providing the reduced benefits to older workers is the same as the cost of providing benefits to younger workers.

Employers are permitted to coordinate retiree health benefit plans with eligibility for Medicare or a comparable state-sponsored health benefit.

Waivers of ADEA Rights

An employer may ask an employee to waive her rights or claims under the ADEA either in the settlement of an ADEA administrative or court claim or in connection with an exit incentive program or other employment termination program. However, the ADEA, as amended by OWBPA, sets out specific minimum standards that must be met for a waiver to be considered knowing and voluntary and, therefore, valid. Among other requirements, a valid ADEA waiver must

- ▶ Be in writing and be understandable
- ▶ Specifically refer to ADEA rights or claims
- ▶ Not waive rights or claims that may arise in the future
- ▶ Be in exchange for valuable consideration
- ▶ Advise the individual in writing to consult an attorney before signing the waiver
- ▶ Provide the individual at least 21 days to consider the agreement and at least 7 days to revoke the agreement after signing it

If an employer requests an ADEA waiver in connection with an exit incentive program or other employment termination program, the minimum requirements for a valid waiver are more extensive.

Fair Credit Reporting Act, 1970

The Fair Credit Reporting Act (FCRA) was the first law passed with the intention of ensuring fair and accurate consumer reporting. This law is particularly relevant to workforce planning and employment because some employers base hiring and promotion decisions, in part, on credit reports.

The FCRA is administered by the Federal Trade Commission, which has published the following information for employers:

> https://www.ftc.gov/tips-advice/business-center/guidance/using-consumer-reports-what-employers-need-know

Equal Employment Opportunity Act, 1972

The Equal Employment Opportunity Act of 1972 expanded the reach of Title VII of the Civil Rights Act of 1964 to include educational institutions; state, local and federal governments; and private employers who employ 15 or more employees. This Act also allows charging parties a longer period of time within which to file claims, and "amends its sex discrimination guidelines to prohibit employers from imposing mandatory leaves of absence on pregnant women or terminating women because they become pregnant. EEOC also states it is sex discrimination for an employer to give women disabled by pregnancy less favorable health insurance or disability benefits than that provided to employees disabled by other temporary medical conditions" (www.eeoc.gov).

Rehabilitation Act, 1973

The Rehabilitation Act of 1973 prohibits discrimination on the basis of physical and mental disabilities.

▶ **Section 503:** Requires affirmative action and prohibits employment discrimination by federal government contractors and subcontractors with contracts of more than $10,000. According to the EEOC, "Section 503 of the Rehabilitation Act of 1973, as amended, protects qualified individuals from discrimination on the basis of disability in hiring, promotion, discharge, pay, fringe benefits, job training, classification, referral, and other aspects of employment. Disability discrimination includes not making reasonable accommodation to the known physical or mental limitations of an otherwise qualified individual with a disability who is an applicant or employee, barring undue hardship. Section 503 also requires that Federal contractors take affirmative action to employ and advance in employment qualified individuals with disabilities at all levels of employment, including the executive level" (www.eeoc.gov).

▶ **Section 504:** States that "no otherwise qualified individual with a disability in the United States shall be excluded from, denied the benefits of, or be subjected to discrimination under" any program or activity that either receives federal financial assistance or is conducted by any executive agency or the United States Postal Service.

▶ **Section 508:** Requires that federal agencies' electronic and information technology is accessible to people with disabilities, including employees and members of the public.

Pregnancy Discrimination Act, 1978

The Pregnancy Discrimination Act of 1978 (PDA) amended Title VII of the Civil Rights Act of 1964 to specifically prohibit discrimination on the basis of pregnancy, childbirth, or related medical conditions.

In short, it requires that employers treat applicants or employees who are pregnant or otherwise affected by related conditions in the same manner as other applicants or employees with other short-term conditions. This Act covers employers with 15 or more employees, including state and local governments. It applies to employment agencies, labor organizations, and the federal government.

Pregnancy-related protections include the following.

Hiring

An employer cannot refuse to hire a pregnant woman because of her pregnancy, because of a pregnancy-related condition, or because of the prejudices of coworkers, clients, or customers.

Pregnancy and Maternity Leave

An employer may not single out pregnancy-related conditions for special procedures to determine an employee's ability to work. However, if an employer requires its employees to submit a doctor's statement concerning their inability to work before granting leave or paying sick benefits, the employer may require employees affected by pregnancy-related conditions to submit such statements.

▶ If an employee is temporarily unable to perform her job due to pregnancy, the employer must treat her the same as any other temporarily disabled employee. For example, if the employer allows temporarily disabled employees to modify tasks, perform alternative assignments, or take disability leave or leave without pay, the employer also must allow an employee who is temporarily disabled due to pregnancy to do the same.

▶ Pregnant employees must be permitted to work as long as they are able to perform their jobs. If an employee has been absent from work as a result of a pregnancy-related condition and recovers, her employer may not require her to remain on leave until the baby's birth. An employer also may not have a rule that prohibits an employee from returning to work for a predetermined length of time after childbirth.

▶ Employers must hold open a job for a pregnancy-related absence the same length of time jobs are held open for employees on sick or disability leave.

Health Insurance

Any health insurance provided by an employer must cover expenses for pregnancy-related conditions on the same basis as costs for other medical conditions. Health insurance for expenses arising from abortion is not required, except where the life of the mother is endangered.

▶ Pregnancy-related expenses should be reimbursed exactly as those incurred for other medical conditions, whether payment is on a fixed basis or a percentage of reasonable-and-customary-charge basis.

▶ The amounts payable by the insurance provider can be limited only to the same extent as amounts payable for other conditions. No additional, increased, or larger deductible can be imposed.

▶ Employers must provide the same level of health benefits for spouses of male employees as they do for spouses of female employees.

Fringe Benefits

Pregnancy-related benefits cannot be limited to married employees. In an all-female workforce or job classification, benefits must be provided for pregnancy-related conditions if benefits are provided for other medical conditions.

▶ If an employer provides any benefits to workers on leave, the employer must provide the same benefits for those on leave for pregnancy-related conditions.

▶ Employees with pregnancy-related disabilities must be treated the same as other temporarily disabled employees for accrual and crediting of seniority, vacation calculation, pay increases, and temporary disability benefits.

▶ It is unlawful to retaliate against an individual for opposing employment practices that discriminate based on pregnancy or for filing a discrimination charge, testifying, or participating in any way in an investigation, proceeding, or litigation under Title VII.

Immigration Reform and Control Act, 1986

The Immigration Reform and Control Act (IRCA) prohibits employers from discriminating against job applicants on the basis of national origin and from giving preference to U.S. citizens. IRCA also established penalties for those who knowingly hire illegal aliens (people who are referred to, by some individuals and organizations, as "undocumented workers," rather than "illegal aliens").

IRCA accomplishes these objectives through several means. The most visible process requires employers to review and record information/documentation submitted by employees that establish that employee's identity and eligibility to work in the United States. The form used to record this information is known as the I-9 form. The I-9 form must be completed within three business days of the employee's date of hire (but not before the employer starts). Certain portions of the I-9 must be completed by the employee, and certain portions must be completed by the employer.

NOTE

The I-9 lists acceptable documents for establishing identity and eligibility to work in the United States. Employees must provide either one document from Column A or one document each from Column B and Column C. Under no circumstances can an employer express preference for any particular document.

The government revised the I-9 form in 2013 (see Figure 2.1).

Drug-Free Workplace Act, 1988

The Drug-Free Workplace Act requires federal contractors (with contracts of $100,000 or more) and individuals and organizations that are awarded federal grants (of any size) to agree to maintain a workplace free of illegal drugs.

> The Department of Labor (DOL) provides the following guidelines relative to the Drug-Free Workplace Act: "The Act does not apply to those who do not have, nor intend to apply for, contracts/grants from the Federal government. The Act also does not apply to subcontractors or subgrantees."

Because the Act applies to each contract or grant on a case-by-case basis, you will need to determine coverage for each federal contract or grant you have or for which you are applying. If your company has a grant that is covered under the Act and a contract that is not, the Act does not cover the entire company but rather only employees working on the covered grant. Even though you may not be required to provide a drug-free workplace for all your employees, you may find it cost effective to do so — and a good way to protect your workers and your business profits.

Although all individuals with federal contracts or grants are covered, requirements vary depending on whether the contractor or grantee is an individual or is an organization (www.dol.gov).

These requirements can vary substantially. According to the DOL, "Although all covered contractors and grantees must maintain a drug-free workplace, the specific components necessary to meet the requirements of the Act vary based on whether the contractor or grantee is an individual or an organization. The requirements for organizations are more extensive, because organizations have to take comprehensive, programmatic steps to achieve a workplace free of drugs."

HR professionals should partner with organizational leadership/counsel to ascertain the requirements that pertain to them (if any) under this Act.

Employment Eligibility Verification

Department of Homeland Security

U.S. Citizenship and Immigration Services

USCIS
Form I-9
OMB No. 1615-0047
Expires 03/31/2016

▶START HERE. Read instructions carefully before completing this form. The instructions must be available during completion of this form.

ANTI-DISCRIMINATION NOTICE: It is illegal to discriminate against work-authorized individuals. Employers **CANNOT** specify which document(s) they will accept from an employee. The refusal to hire an individual because the documentation presented has a future expiration date may also constitute illegal discrimination.

Section 1. Employee Information and Attestation *(Employees must complete and sign Section 1 of Form I-9 no later than the **first day of employment**, but not before accepting a job offer.)*

Last Name *(Family Name)*	First Name *(Given Name)*	Middle Initial	Other Names Used *(if any)*		
Address *(Street Number and Name)*	Apt. Number	City or Town		State	Zip Code
Date of Birth *(mm/dd/yyyy)*	U.S. Social Security Number	E-mail Address		Telephone Number	

I am aware that federal law provides for imprisonment and/or fines for false statements or use of false documents in connection with the completion of this form.

I attest, under penalty of perjury, that I am (check one of the following):

☐ A citizen of the United States

☐ A noncitizen national of the United States *(See instructions)*

☐ A lawful permanent resident (Alien Registration Number/USCIS Number): _____

☐ An alien authorized to work until (expiration date, if applicable, mm/dd/yyyy) _____ . Some aliens may write "N/A" in this field. *(See instructions)*

For aliens authorized to work, provide your Alien Registration Number/USCIS Number **OR** Form I-94 Admission Number:

    1. Alien Registration Number/USCIS Number:_____

               OR

    2. Form I-94 Admission Number: _____

    If you obtained your admission number from CBP in connection with your arrival in the United States, include the following:

      Foreign Passport Number: _____

      Country of Issuance: _____

    Some aliens may write "N/A" on the Foreign Passport Number and Country of Issuance fields. *(See instructions)*

3-D Barcode
Do Not Write in This Space

Signature of Employee:	Date *(mm/dd/yyyy)*:

Preparer and/or Translator Certification *(To be completed and signed if Section 1 is prepared by a person other than the employee.)*

I attest, under penalty of perjury, that I have assisted in the completion of this form and that to the best of my knowledge the information is true and correct.

Signature of Preparer or Translator:	Date *(mm/dd/yyyy)*:	
Last Name *(Family Name)*	First Name *(Given Name)*	
Address *(Street Number and Name)*	City or Town	State	Zip Code

🛑 *Employer Completes Next Page* 🛑

FIGURE 2.1 The I-9 form.

Employee Polygraph Protection Act, 1988

Administered by the Department of Labor, the

"EPPA prohibits most private employers from using lie detector tests, either for pre-employment screening or during the course of employment. Employers generally may not require or request any employee or job applicant to take a lie detector test, or discharge, discipline, or discriminate against an employee or job applicant for refusing to take a test or for exercising other rights under the Act. Employers may not use or inquire about the results of a lie detector test or discharge or discriminate against an employee or job applicant on the basis of the results of a test, or for filing a complaint, or for participating in a proceeding under the Act. Subject to restrictions, the Act permits polygraph (a type of lie detector) tests to be administered to certain job applicants of security service firms (armored car, alarm, and guard) and of pharmaceutical manufacturers, distributors and dispensers.

"Subject to restrictions, the Act also permits polygraph testing of certain employees of private firms who are reasonably suspected of involvement in a workplace incident (theft, embezzlement, etc.) that resulted in specific economic loss or injury to the employer. Where polygraph examinations are allowed, they are subject to strict standards for the conduct of the test, including the pretest, testing and post-testing phases. An examiner must be licensed and bonded or have professional liability coverage. The Act strictly limits the disclosure of information obtained during a polygraph test."

Worker Adjustment and Retraining Notification Act, 1988

The Worker Adjustment and Retraining Notification Act (WARNA) mandates employer notification requirements under specific circumstances involving mass layoffs and plant closings, thus giving displaced workers time to make arrangements for other employment. ("Arrangements," in this context, span a spectrum of possibilities ranging from transferring to another worksite to participating in retraining programs, or anything in between or beyond.)

WARNA covers employers with 100 or more full-time employees (or the equivalent—100 or more full-time and part-time employees who work a combined total of 4,000 or more hours per week).

NOTE

Exceptions and clarifications abound when it comes to determining whether an employer is covered by WARNA. Review www.dol.gov for more information about how to make this determination.

WARNA requires these employers to give employees at least 60 days' written notice before either a mass layoff or plant closing. According to the DOL, a mass layoff occurs under the following sets of circumstances:

▶ A covered employer must give notice if there is to be a mass layoff that does not result from a plant closing but that will result in an employment loss at the employment site during any 30-day period for 500 or more employees, or for 50–499 employees if they make up at least 33% of the employer's active workforce. Again, this does not count employees who have worked less than 6 months in the last 12 months or employees who work an average of less than 20 hours a week for that employer. These latter groups, however, are entitled to notice.

▶ An employer also must give notice if the number of employment losses that occur during a 30-day period fails to meet the threshold requirements of a plant closing or mass layoff, but the number of employment losses for 2 or more groups of workers, each of which is less than the minimum number needed to trigger notice, reaches the threshold level, during any 90-day period, of either a plant closing or mass layoff. Job losses within any

90-day period will count together toward WARN threshold levels unless the employer demonstrates that the employment losses during the 90-day period are the result of separate and distinct actions and causes.

WARNA is also triggered in the event of a plant closing, which occurs when a covered employer determines that an employment site (or one or more facilities or operating units within an employment site) will be shut down, if the shutdown will result in an employment loss (as defined later) for 50 or more employees during any 30-day period. This does not count employees who have worked less than 6 months in the past 12 months or employees who work an average of less than 20 hours a week for that employer. These latter groups, however, are entitled to notice.

Within the context of WARNA, the DOL defines an employment loss as

▶ An employment termination, other than a discharge for cause, voluntary departure, or retirement

▶ A layoff exceeding 6 months

▶ A reduction in an employee's hours of work of more than 50% in each month of any 6-month period

The DOL also cites certain exceptions to WARNA:

"An employee who refuses a transfer to a different employment site within reasonable commuting distance does not experience an employment loss. An employee who accepts a transfer outside this distance within 30 days after it is offered or within 30 days after the plant closing or mass layoff, whichever is later, does not experience an employment loss. In both cases, the transfer offer must be made before the closing or layoff, there must be no more than a 6 month break in employment, and the new job must not be deemed a constructive discharge. These transfer exceptions from the "employment loss" definition apply only if the closing or layoff results from the relocation or consolidation of part or all of the employer's business" (www.dol.gov).

Under WARNA, notice must be given to

"…the chief elected officer of the exclusive representative(s) or bargaining agency(s) of affected employees and to unrepresented individual workers who may reasonably be expected to experience an employment loss. This includes employees who may lose their employment due to 'bumping,' or displacement by other workers, to the extent that the employer can identify those employees when notice is given. If an employer cannot identify employees who may lose their jobs through bumping procedures, the employer must provide notice to the incumbents in the jobs which are being eliminated. Employees who have worked less than 6 months in the last 12 months and employees who work an average of less than 20 hours a week are due notice, even though they are not counted when determining the trigger levels.

"The employer must also provide notice to the State dislocated worker unit and to the chief elected official of the unit of local government in which the employment site is located" (www.doleta.gov).

The DOL provides the following guidance with respect to required notification periods under WARN Act:

"With three exceptions, notice must be timed to reach the required parties at least 60 days before a closing or layoff. When the individual employment separations for a closing or layoff occur on more than one day, the notices are due to the representative(s), State dislocated worker unit and local government at least 60 days before each separation. If the workers are not represented, each worker's notice is due at least 60 days before that worker's separation.

"The exceptions to 60-day notice are:

"(1) Faltering company. This exception, to be narrowly construed, covers situations where a company has sought new capital or business in order to stay open and where giving notice would ruin the opportunity to get the new capital or business, and applies only to plant closings;

"(2) Unforeseeable business circumstances. This exception applies to closings and layoffs that are caused by business circumstances that were not reasonably foreseeable at the time notice would otherwise have been required; and

"(3) Natural disaster. This applies where a closing or layoff is the direct result of a natural disaster, such as a flood, earthquake, drought or storm.

"If an employer provides less than 60 days advance notice of a closing or layoff and relies on one of these three exceptions, the employer bears the burden of proof that the conditions for the exception have been met. The employer also must give as much notice as is practicable. When the notices are given, they must include a brief statement of the reason for reducing the notice period in addition to the items required in notices" (www.doleta.gov).

NOTE

Some states, such as California, have "baby WARN" laws in effect, which may have different notification thresholds or requirements. So, as always, be sure to check for—and ensure you are in adherence with—any relevant state laws.

Americans with Disabilities Act, 1990

The Americans with Disabilities Act (ADA) guarantees equal opportunity for qualified individuals with disabilities in public accommodations, employment, transportation, state and local government services, and telecommunications.

The EEOC has proudly described the ADA as "the world's first comprehensive civil rights law for people with disabilities" and likens it to the Emancipation Proclamation for people with disabilities.

The ADA covers employers with 15 or more employees, including state and local governments. It also applies to employment agencies and to labor organizations. In addition, the ADA's nondiscrimination standards apply to federal sector employees under section 501 of the Rehabilitation Act, as amended, and its implementing rules. According to the EEOC, Title I of the ADA prohibits private employers, state and local governments, employment agencies, and labor unions from discriminating against qualified individuals with disabilities in job application procedures, hiring, firing, advancement, compensation, job training, and other terms, conditions, and privileges of employment.

Title I also covers medical examinations and inquiries, as well as drug and alcohol abuse:

- ▶ **Medical examinations and inquiries:** Employers may not ask job applicants about the existence, nature, or severity of a disability. Applicants may be asked about their ability to perform specific job functions. A job offer may be conditioned on the results of a medical examination, but only if the examination is required for all entering employees in similar jobs. Medical examinations of employees must be job related and consistent with the employer's business needs.

- ▶ **Drug and alcohol abuse:** Employees and applicants currently engaging in the illegal use of drugs are not covered by the ADA when an employer acts on the basis of such use. Tests for illegal drugs are not subject to the ADA's restrictions on medical examinations. Employers may hold illegal drug users and alcoholics to the same performance standards as other employees (www.eeoc.gov).

Title V of the ADA provides additional instructions with respect to its enforcement of the ADA by the EEOC, the federal agency charged with enforcing the employment provisions of the ADA.

The ADA also renders it unlawful to retaliate against an individual for opposing employment practices that discriminate based on disability or for filing a discrimination charge, testifying, or participating in any way in an investigation, proceeding, or litigation under the ADA.

At a minimum, HR professionals need to develop a solid understanding of the basic terminology used throughout the ADA to be able to effectively implement its provisions—and to move beyond simple compliance ("transactional") toward a more strategic application of the ADA ("tactical," or perhaps even "transformational").

Individual with a Disability

According to the EEOC, an "individual with a disability" is a person who

- ▶ Has a physical or mental impairment that substantially limits one or more major life activities

- ▶ Has a record of such an impairment

- ▶ Is regarded as having such an impairment

Qualified Person

To be a considered a "qualified person," a candidate must meet minimum job requirements (education, experience, licenses, and so forth) and must be able to perform the essential functions of the position with or without reasonable accommodation.

Reasonable Accommodation

A reasonable accommodation represents a change in the way that one or more responsibilities relating to the execution of a position is performed, so as to enable a person with a disability to perform the essential functions of the position. Accommodations, however, do not have to be adopted if they cause undue hardship to the organization.

Undue Hardship

An undue hardship would be caused by an accommodation that would create significant difficulty (enough to disrupt business operations), result in a significant financial outlay, or change something about the essential nature of the business. If this language seems unclear, it is. Even the language drawn directly from the EEOC website relative to undue hardship is somewhat ambiguous: "Undue hardship is defined as an action requiring significant difficulty or expense when considered in light of factors such as an employer's size, financial resources, and the nature and structure of its operation." Perhaps this could be rephrased to say "it depends"—because it does.

> **NOTE**
>
> In this context, the word "organization" is often interpreted to encompass more than just the location at which the employee who needs the accommodation works. Thus, the definitions of "reasonable accommodation" and "undue hardship" might vary substantially from what one might initially assume. This, like all decisions of a legal nature, should be made only after consulting with qualified counsel. Said differently, things are not always what they initially appear to be, so don't make unilateral determinations about what constitutes undue hardship. Confer with legal counsel, client managers, or senior HR colleagues, as appropriate.

Major Life Activities

According to the EEOC, "major life activities" include—but are not necessarily limited to— walking, seeing, hearing, breathing, caring for oneself, performing manual tasks, sitting, standing, lifting, learning, and thinking. Major bodily functions are also considered to be a major life activity. Furthermore, according to the EEOC, "the determination of whether an individual's (condition) substantially limits a major life activity is based on the limitations imposed by the condition when its symptoms are present (disregarding any mitigating measures that might limit or eliminate the symptoms)" (www.eeoc.gov).

Civil Rights Act of 1991

The Civil Rights Act of 1991 significantly expanded employees' rights and remedies under Title VII of the Civil Rights Act of 1964. In addition to establishing the right for plaintiffs in Title VII cases to enjoy jury trials, it allowed for plaintiffs to be awarded compensatory and punitive damages (which is limited according to the size of the employer's workforce and which caps at $300,000 per individual for compensatory and punitive damages, combined).

Compensatory damages are designed to "make the employee whole" with respect to lost wages, benefits, and other expenses and losses. Punitive damages, as the name implies, are intended to punish employers who violate the Act.

"In addition, the 1991 Act added a new subsection to Title VII, codifying the disparate impact theory of discrimination, essentially putting the law back as it had been prior to Wards Cove. And in response to Price-Waterhouse, the Act provided that where the plaintiff shows that discrimination was a motivating factor for an employment decision, the employer is liable for injunctive relief, attorney's fees, and costs (but not individual monetary or affirmative relief) even though it proves it would have made the same decision in the absence of a discriminatory motive. The Act also provided employment discrimination protection to employees of Congress and some high-level political appointees. Lastly, Title VII and ADA coverage was extended to include American and American-controlled employers operating abroad" (www.eeoc.gov).

Family and Medical Leave Act, 1993

The Family and Medical Leave Act (FMLA) entitles eligible employees (who work for covered employers) up to 12 weeks of unpaid, job-protected leave during any 12-month period for one or more of the following reasons:

▶ The birth and care of the newborn child of the employee

▶ Placement with the employee of a son or daughter for adoption or foster care

▶ Care for an immediate family member (spouse, child, or parent) with a serious health condition

▶ Medical leave when the employee is unable to work because of a serious health condition

The DOL has published a fact sheet on the FMLA at www.dol.gov/whd/regs/compliance/whdfs28.pdf.

Uniformed Services Employment and Reemployment Rights Act, 1994

The Uniformed Services Employment and Reemployment Rights Act (USERRA) provides reinforcement rights for individuals who miss work because of "service in the uniformed services," which is defined as voluntary or involuntary uniformed service.

According to the Department of Justice: "USERRA is a federal statute that protects servicemembers' and veterans' civilian employment rights. Among other things, under certain conditions, USERRA requires employers to put individuals back to work in their civilian jobs after military service. USERRA also protects servicemembers from discrimination in the workplace based on their military service or affiliation" (www.doj.gov).

HR professionals must be fluent with the contents of the USERRA Fact Sheet 3, published by the DOL: www.dol.gov/vets/programs/userra/userra_fs.htm.

Congressional Accountability Act, 1995

Touted on the informational poster as "advancing safety, health, and workplace rights in the legislative branch," the Congressional Accountability Act (CAA) protects Congress and Legislative Branch agency employees with coverage under 11 laws (which has subsequently been expanded to include 13 laws), including these:

▶ Fair Labor Standards Act (FLSA), 1938

▶ Title VII of the Civil Rights Act (Title VII), 1964

▶ Age Discrimination in Employment Act (ADEA), 1967

▶ Occupational Safety and Health Act (OSHA), 1970

▶ Rehabilitation Act, 1973

▶ Federal Service Labor-Management Relations Statute (FSLMRA), 1978

▶ Employee Polygraph Protection Act (EPPA), 1988

▶ Worker Adjustment and Retraining Notification Act (WARNA), 1988

▶ Americans with Disabilities Act (ADA), 1990

▶ Family and Medical Leave Act (FMLA), 1993

▶ Uniformed Services Employment and Reemployment Act (USERRA), 1994

▶ Veterans' Employment Opportunities Act (VEOA), 1998

▶ Genetic Information Nondiscrimination Act (GINA), 2008

Americans with Disabilities Act Amendments Act, 2008

The Americans with Disabilities Act Amendments Act (ADAAA) amended the ADA of 1990 by codifying a broader interpretation of the ADA, particularly with respect to the definition of a disability. Specifically, this Act established two new entitlements for military families: "qualifying exigency leave" and "military caregiver leave":

"Qualifying exigency leave "may be taken for any qualifying exigency arising out of the fact that a covered military member is on active duty or call to active duty status" (www.dol.gov).

Military caregiver leave

"may be taken by an eligible employee to care for a covered servicemember with a serious injury or illness" (www.dol.gov).

"The Act emphasizes that the definition of disability should be construed in favor of broad coverage of individuals to the maximum extent permitted by the terms of the ADA and generally shall not require extensive analysis." (www.eeoc.gov)

Also:

"The Act makes important changes to the definition of the term "disability" by rejecting the holdings in several Supreme Court decisions and portions of EEOC's ADA regulations. The effect of these changes is to make it easier for an individual seeking protection under the ADA to establish that he or she has a disability within the meaning of the ADA" (www.eeoc.gov).

Genetic Information Nondiscrimination Act, 2008

Under Title II of the Genetic Information Nondiscrimination Act (GINA), it is "illegal to discriminate against employees or applicants because of genetic information. Title II of GINA prohibits the use of genetic information in making employment decisions, restricts employers and other entities covered by Title II (employment agencies, labor organizations and joint labor-management training and apprenticeship programs — referred to as 'covered entities') from requesting, requiring or purchasing genetic information, and strictly limits the disclosure of genetic information" (www.eeoc.gov).

"The law forbids discrimination on the basis of genetic information when it comes to any aspect of employment, including hiring, firing, pay, job assignments, promotions, layoffs, training, fringe benefits, or any other term or condition of employment. An employer may never use genetic information to make an employment decision because genetic information is not relevant to an individual's current ability to work" (www.eeoc.gov).

HR professionals must be fluent in the following information about GINA, provided by the EEOC: www.eeoc.gov/eeoc/newsroom/wysk/gina_nondiscrimination_act.cfm.

Lilly Ledbetter Fair Pay Act, 2009

The Lilly Ledbetter Fair Pay Act amended the Civil Rights Act of 1964 and was the first bill signed into law by President Barack Obama.

> "Under the Act, an individual subjected to compensation discrimination under Title VII of the Civil Rights Act of 1964, the Age Discrimination in Employment Act of 1967, or the Americans with Disabilities Act of 1990 may file a charge within 180 (or 300) days of any of the following:
>
> when a discriminatory compensation decision or other discriminatory practice affecting compensation is adopted;
>
> when the individual becomes subject to a discriminatory compensation decision or other discriminatory practice affecting compensation; or
>
> when the individual's compensation is affected by the application of a discriminatory compensation decision or other discriminatory practice, including each time the individual receives compensation that is based in whole or part on such compensation decision or other practice" (www.eeoc.gov).

In this sense, this Act expanded the procedural standing of employees (and former employees) who were negatively impacted by discriminatory wage decisions made in the past but which still impact current pay rates/earnings, to retain "standing" necessary to bring a lawsuit. How did it do so? By establishing that each paycheck event starts the statute of limitations anew.

Said differently, this "codifies the EEOC's longstanding position that each paycheck that contains discriminatory compensation is a separate violation regardless of when the discrimination began. The Ledbetter Act recognizes the 'reality of wage discrimination' and restores 'bedrock principles of American law. Particularly important for the victims of discrimination, the Act contains an explicit retroactivity provision" (www.eeoc.gov).

Relevant Case Law

HR professionals must be well versed in key precedent-setting cases relating to EEO, as a subset of workforce planning and employment. The following summaries (presented in chronological order) describe the significance of some of those landmark cases.

Griggs v. Duke Power, 1971

Key issue: Adverse impact.

Significance: Discrimination need not be deliberate or observable to be real. Rather, it can exist if a particular policy or practice has a statistically significant adverse impact on members of a protected class. This is true even when the same requirement applies to all employees or applicants, as was the situation in this case. When a particular requirement does have an impact on members of a protected class, the burden of proof rests with the employer to demonstrate that the requirement is, in fact, job related and consistent with business necessity.

McDonnell Douglas Corp v. Green, 1973

Key issue: Disparate treatment/prima facie.

Significance: The initial burden of proof for establishing a prima facie (Latin for "at first view") case of discrimination against an employer (or potential employer) under Title VII of the Civil Rights Act of 1964 rests with the employee (or applicant), who must be able to establish four key elements:

- ▶ The person is a member of a protected class.

- ▶ The person applied for a job for which the employer was seeking applicants.

- ▶ The person was rejected, despite being qualified for the position.

- ▶ After this rejection, the employer continued to seek other applicants with similar qualifications.

After the employee establishes a prima facie case for disparate treatment, the burden of proof then shifts to the employer, who must provide a nondiscriminatory reason for its decision.

This case falls under the category of "reverse discrimination" because it alleged race discrimination and was brought by individuals who were not minorities/people of color.

Albemarle Paper v. Moody, 1975

Key issue: Employment tests — job relatedness and validity of employment tests.

Significance: Any tests that are used as part of the hiring or promotional decision-making process must be job related. This applies to any instrument that is used as a "test," even if that was not its original purpose. This case also established that employment tests must demonstrate predictive validity, consistent with the Uniform Guidelines for Employee Selection Procedures.

Washington v. Davis, 1976

Key issue: Employment tests and disparate impact.

Significance: A test that has an adverse impact on a protected class is still lawful as long as the test can be shown to be valid and job related.

Regents of California v. Bakke, 1978

Key issue: Affirmative action.

Significance: The Supreme Court ruled that although race could be a factor in college admission decisions, quotas could not be established.

Although this case was based on a college admissions program, its significance extended to workplace affirmative action programs.

This case falls under the category of "reverse discrimination" because it alleged race discrimination and was brought by someone who was not a minority/person of color.

United Steelworkers v. Weber, 1979

Key issue: Affirmative action.

Significance: Affirmative action plans that establish voluntary quotas that have been jointly agreed to by an organization as well as its collective bargaining unit do not constitute race discrimination under Title VII of the Civil Rights Act of 1964 if they are designed to remedy past discrimination that has resulted in current underutilization.

This case falls under the category of "reverse discrimination" because it alleged race discrimination and was brought by someone who was not a minority/person of color.

Meritor Savings Bank v. Vinson, 1986

Key issue: Sexual harassment.

Significance: This was the first ruling to establish that sexual harassment (whether quid pro quo or hostile environment) constitutes a violation of Title VII of the Civil Rights Act of 1964. In addition, the court ruled that it isn't enough for an organization to have a policy prohibiting discrimination. Instead, the ruling stated, "Reasonable care requires effective communication of policies and training. The employer has the burden of proof."

Johnson v. Santa Clara County Transportation Agency, 1987

Key issue: Affirmative action.

Significance: Gender can be used as a factor in the selection process if there is underrepresentation in a particular job classification, as long as the AAP does not set forth a quota.

This case falls under the category of "reverse discrimination" because it alleged sex discrimination and was brought by a man.

Martin v. Wilks, 1988

Key issue: Affirmative action.

Significance: Current employees who are negatively affected by consent decrees that were established in an earlier time and that sought to resolve discrimination that was present in an earlier time may challenge the validity of such decrees.

This case falls under the category of "reverse discrimination" because it alleged race discrimination and was brought by individuals who were not minorities/people of color.

Automobile Workers v. Johnson Controls, 1990

Key issue: Title VII of the Civil Rights Act of 1964, as amended by the Pregnancy Discrimination Act.

Significance: The Supreme Court ruled that Johnson Controls' fetal protection policy constituted a violation of Title VII of the Civil Rights Act of 1964, as amended by the Pregnancy Discrimination Act. As such, even rules that are well intentioned are unlawful if such rules result in discrimination on the basis of sex.

Harris v. Forklift Systems, 1993

Key issue: Sexual harassment.

Significance: The court clarified the standard relative to what constitutes a sexually hostile work environment: "This standard, which we reaffirm today, takes a middle path between making actionable any conduct that is merely offensive and requiring the conduct to cause a tangible psychological injury. Conduct that is not severe or pervasive enough to create an objectively hostile or abusive work environment—an environment that a reasonable person would find hostile or abusive—is beyond Title VII's purview. Likewise, if the victim does not subjectively perceive the environment to be abusive, the conduct has not actually altered the conditions of the victim's employment, and there is no Title VII violation."

Taxman v. Board of Education of Piscataway, 1993

Key issue: Affirmative action.

Significance: The U.S. Court of Appeals for the Third Circuit ruled that—in the absence of underrepresentation as demonstrated and documented through an affirmative action plan—organizations cannot take race into account when making decisions relative to who will be laid off and who will be retained. Doing so would constitute a violation of Title VII of the Civil Rights Act of 1964.

This case falls under the category of "reverse discrimination" because it alleged race discrimination and was brought by a person who was not a minority/person of color.

St. Mary's Honor Center v. Hicks, 1993

Key issue: Burden of proof.

Significance: To ultimately prevail in an allegation of discrimination under Title VII of the Civil Rights Act of 1964, the charging party (meaning, the employee who filed the charge) must go beyond a prima facie case and actually prove that the employer's actual reasons for an employment action are, in fact, discriminatory.

McKennon v. Nashville Banner Publishing Co., 1995

Key issue: After-acquired evidence.

Significance: An employer will be held accountable for discriminatory employment actions even if it discovers evidence after taking the discriminatory employment action that would have led the employer to that same employment action for legitimate, nondiscriminatory reasons.

This case falls under the category of "reverse discrimination" since it alleged race discrimination and was brought by someone who was not a minority/person of color.

Faragher v. City of Boca Raton, 1998, and Ellerth v. Burlington Northern Industries, 1998

Key issue: Sexual harassment.

Significance: If an employee is subjected to a tangible adverse employment action because of a supervisor's sexually harassing behavior, the employer is liable. The employer is also vicariously liable when its supervisors create a sexually hostile work environment, even if the employee is not subjected to an adverse employment action. This is true whether or not the employer itself was negligent or otherwise at fault. However, if the employee is not subjected to tangible adverse employment action, the employer may be able to raise as a defense that he acted reasonably to prevent or promptly correct any sexually harassing behavior and that the plaintiff unreasonably failed to take advantage of the employer's preventive or corrective opportunities.

Oncale v. Sundowner Offshore Services, 1999

Key issue: Sex discrimination, by members of one sex against a person of the same sex.

Significance: Title VII's prohibition of sex discrimination does include harassment of individuals by others who happen to be the same sex.

Kolstad v. American Dental Association, 1999

Key issue: Punitive damages under the Civil Rights Act of 1991.

Significance: Punitive damages can be awarded only when the employer has acted with malice and reckless indifference to the employee's federally protected rights.

This subjective standard was considered to be easier to establish than the more objective standard that would be required if employees had to prove that the nature of the actual behavior to which they had been subjected reached a level in which it would be considered "egregious."

Circuit City Stores, Inc. v. Adams, 2001

Key issue: Mandatory arbitration agreements as a condition of employment.

Significance: The Supreme Court confirmed the legality of requiring employees to sign mandatory arbitration agreements as a condition of employment and that such agreements are enforceable under the Federal Arbitration Act (FAA), with the exception of seamen and railway workers.

Grutter v. Bollinger and Gratz v. Bollinger, 2003

Context: Barbara Grutter was applying for admission to the University of Michigan Law School, and Jennifer Gratz was applying for admission to the University of Michigan as an undergraduate student. Lee Bollinger was the president of the University of Michigan.

Key issue: Affirmative action.

Significance: Race can be taken into account as an admissions factor because it furthers the establishment of diversity—a "compelling state interest"—as long as the admissions process is "narrowly tailored" to achieve the objective of achieving a diverse student body.

Interestingly, Supreme Court Justice Sandra Day O'Connor indicated that cases of this sort will likely be ruled differently at some point in the future: "Race-conscious admissions policies must be limited in time. The Court takes the Law School at its word that it would like nothing better than to find a race-neutral admissions formula and will terminate its use of racial preferences as soon as practicable. The Court expects that 25 years from now, the use of racial preferences will no longer be necessary to further the interest approved today."

These cases fall under the category of "reverse discrimination" because they alleged race discrimination and were brought by people who were not minorities/people of color.

General Dynamics Land Systems v. Cline, 2004

Key issue: Age discrimination (relative).

Significance: Younger employees (even if they are over the age of 40) cannot allege age discrimination because of the establishment of programs or decisions that favor older employees. As Justice David Souter wrote in the opening of his opinion, "The Age Discrimination in Employment Act of 1967 (ADEA or Act), 81 Stat. 602, 29 U.S.C. § 621 et seq., forbids discriminatory preference for the young over the old. The question in this case is whether it also prohibits favoring the old over the young. We hold it does not."

This case falls under the category of "reverse discrimination" because it alleged age discrimination and was brought by a person who was relatively younger.

Ricci v. DeStefano, 2009

Key issue: Disparate impact.

Significance: The Supreme Court confirmed that, "fear of litigation alone cannot justify an employer's reliance on race to the detriment of individuals who passed the examinations and qualified for promotions."

Equal Employment Opportunity Commission v. Abercrombie & Fitch Stores, Inc., 2015

Key issue: The need for religious accommodation, when such need has not been explicitly communicated to the employer.

Significance: According to the Supreme Court, "motive and knowledge are separate concepts. An employer who has actual knowledge of the need for an accommodation does not violate Title VII by refusing to hire an applicant if avoiding that accommodation is not his motive. Conversely, an employer who acts with the motive of avoiding accommodation may violate Title VII even if he has no more than an unsubstantiated suspicion that accommodation would be needed."

This case involved an applicant named Samantha Eluef. Eleuf, a practicing Muslim, wore a hijab to her interview but did not specifically request a religious accommodation to wear it on a daily basis at work.

Legal Concepts/Definitions Relevant to Workplace Planning and Employment

In addition to knowing the laws listed earlier, it's also essential to know, understand, and be able to identify the relevance of a variety of legal concepts and definitions. In this section, we'll explore and discuss those that pertain primarily to Workforce Planning and Employment.

Equal Employment Opportunity: The Basics

EEO represents a commitment to ensure that equal opportunity throughout all dimensions of the employment relationship serves as the backdrop to employment-related legislation. To be effective in their roles (and to ensure compliance with the law), HR professionals need to understand certain fundamental Equal Employment Opportunity (EEO)-related concepts. This section will address and discuss some basic EEO-related concepts.

Protected Class

A *protected class* is a group of people who share a common characteristic and who are protected by law from discrimination and harassment on the basis of that shared characteristic.

Discrimination

Discrimination, in the truest sense of the word, is not necessarily illegal. To discriminate is to make a distinction, or to discern. When distinctions or discernments are made on the basis of factors, traits, or characteristics that are protected by law, however, discrimination becomes unlawful.

Types of Unlawful Discrimination

HR professionals must be knowledgeable about the following types of discrimination:

▶ Disparate (or "adverse") treatment

▶ Disparate (or "adverse") impact

▶ Perpetuating past discrimination

Disparate (or "Adverse") Treatment

Disparate (or "adverse") treatment is a type of unlawful discrimination that occurs when an employer intentionally treats applicants or employees differently on the basis of their race, color, sex, religion, national origin, age, disability, military or veteran status, or any other characteristic protected by law. The following would constitute examples of disparate treatment:

▶ Candidates who indicate on their employment application that they speak Spanish are interviewed (in part or in whole) in Spanish, but all other candidates are interviewed in English.

▶ Female members of a team or department are asked to take meeting minutes or provide refreshments, whereas male members are not.

▶ The quality or quantity of work that is performed by employees who request a modified work schedule so they can attend religious services is more closely scrutinized than the quality or quantity of work performed by employees who do not make such a request.

Disparate (or "Adverse") Impact

Disparate (or adverse) impact occurs when a seemingly neutral policy or practice has a disproportionately negative effect upon one or more members of a protected class. In this context, policies or practices that do not reflect legitimate job requirements but do have a statistically significant impact on members of a protected class may constitute unlawful discrimination. For instance:

▶ An organization requires that all newly hired employees have a college degree, even though a degree is not required to perform some of the jobs that exist within the organization. If members of protected classes are "screened out" at a statistically higher rate, an allegation of disparate impact might be upheld.

▶ An organization requires that all newly promoted managers spend the first six months on the job working at six different—and geographically dispersed—locations throughout the country. If members of a protected class are eliminated from consideration for employment at a statistically higher rate because of this policy, and if this policy is found to be unrelated to successful performance of the position, an allegation of disparate impact might be upheld.

Determining Whether Adverse Impact Exists Within a Selection Process

It's important to know how to mathematically determine whether adverse impact exists within a selection process. The Uniform Guidelines on Employee Selection Procedures (1978), which is explored in the "Uniform Guidelines on Employee Selection Procedures (1978)" section in this chapter, discusses and defines adverse impact in two separate—but interrelated—ways. First, let's take a look at the "bottom-line" concept":

"If the information called for by sections 4A and B of this section shows that the total selection process for a job has an adverse impact, the individual components of the selection process should be evaluated for adverse impact. If this information shows that the total selection process does not have an adverse impact, the Federal enforcement agencies, in the exercise of their administrative and prosecutorial discretion, in usual circumstances, will not expect a user to evaluate the individual components for adverse impact, or to validate such individual components, and will not take enforcement action based upon adverse impact of any component of that process, including the separate parts of a multipart selection procedure or any separate procedure that is used as an alternative method of selection. However, in the following circumstances the Federal enforcement agencies will expect a user to evaluate the individual components for adverse impact and may, where appropriate, take enforcement action with respect to the individual components: (1) where the selection procedure is a significant factor in the continuation of patterns of assignments of incumbent employees caused by prior discriminatory employment practices, (2) where the weight of court decisions or administrative interpretations hold that a specific procedure (such as height or weight requirements or no-arrest records) is not job related in the same or similar circumstances. In unusual circumstances, other than those listed in paragraphs (1) and (2) of this section, the Federal enforcement agencies may request a user to evaluate the individual components for adverse impact and may, where appropriate, take enforcement action with respect to the individual component" (www.dol.gov).

Next, let's take a look at the "four-fifths" rule:

"A selection rate for any race, sex, or ethnic group which is less than four-fifths (4/5) (or eighty percent) of the rate for the group with the highest rate will generally be regarded by the Federal enforcement agencies as evidence of adverse impact, while a greater than four-fifths rate will generally not be regarded by Federal enforcement agencies as evidence of adverse impact. Smaller differences in selection rate may nevertheless constitute adverse impact, where they are significant in both statistical and practical terms or where a user's actions have discouraged applicants disproportionately on grounds of race, sex, or ethnic group. Greater differences in selection rate may not constitute adverse impact where the differences are based on small numbers and are not statistically significant, or where special recruiting or other programs cause the pool of minority or female candidates to be atypical of the normal pool of applicants from that group. Where the user's evidence concerning the impact of a selection procedure indicates adverse impact but is based upon numbers which are too small to be reliable, evidence concerning the impact of the procedure over a longer period of time and/or evidence concerning the impact which the selection procedure had when used in the same manner in similar circumstances elsewhere may be considered in determining adverse impact. Where the user has not maintained data on adverse impact as required by the documentation section of applicable guidelines, the Federal enforcement agencies may draw an inference of adverse impact of the selection process from the failure of the user to maintain such data, if the user has an underutilization of a group in the job category, as compared to the group's representation in the relevant labor market or, in the case of jobs filled from within, the applicable work force" (www.dol.gov).

Thus, whereas disparate treatment is an intentional form of discrimination, disparate impact may be either intentional or unintentional. Ultimately, however, the question of intent has limited importance in that lack of intent neither alters nor excuses the fact that unlawful discrimination has occurred.

Perpetuating Past Discrimination

Unlawful discrimination also occurs when an employer's past discriminatory practices are perpetuated through current policies or practices—even those that appear to be nondiscriminatory. When linked in some way with past discrimination, seemingly nondiscriminatory practices can have a discriminatory effect.

One of the most commonly recognized examples of how past discrimination can be perpetuated through current policy or practice can be found in the use of employee referral programs. Here's how this can happen: if discriminatory hiring decisions have been made in the past, an employer's workforce may now be primarily composed of people who are not members of protected classes—perhaps people who are white or male. If that same employer uses referrals from current employees as the primary means of recruiting new employees, it is likely that the individuals who will subsequently be brought into the workforce may also be primarily white or male —thus perpetuating the potentially discriminatory (albeit unintentional) staffing decisions that were made in the past.

Harassment: (Yet) Another Type of Unlawful Discrimination

Unlawful workplace discrimination can also manifest itself as harassment of a person on the basis of her membership in a protected class. Although most of the landmark court cases and media coverage on this topic focus on sexual harassment, HR professionals must be cognizant of the fact that harassment on the basis of any protected class—not just sex—may constitute unlawful discrimination.

The EEOC has issued the following information/guidelines around harassment:

"Harassment becomes unlawful where 1) enduring the offensive conduct becomes a condition of continued employment, or 2) the conduct is severe or pervasive enough to create a work environment that a reasonable person would consider intimidating, hostile, or abusive. Anti-discrimination laws also prohibit harassment against individuals in retaliation for filing a discrimination charge, testifying, or participating in any way in an investigation, proceeding, or lawsuit under these laws; or opposing employment practices that they reasonably believe discriminate against individuals, in violation of these laws.

"Petty slights, annoyances, and isolated incidents (unless extremely serious) will not rise to the level of illegality. To be unlawful, the conduct must create a work environment that would be intimidating, hostile, or offensive to reasonable people.

"Offensive conduct may include, but is not limited to, offensive jokes, slurs, epithets or name calling, physical assaults or threats, intimidation, ridicule or mockery, insults or put-downs, offensive objects or pictures, and interference with work performance. Harassment can occur in a variety of circumstances, including, but not limited to, the following:

"The harasser can be the victim's supervisor, a supervisor in another area, an agent of the employer, a co-worker, or a non-employee.

"The victim does not have to be the person harassed, but can be anyone affected by the offensive conduct.

"Unlawful harassment may occur without economic injury to, or discharge of, the victim."

Prevention is the best tool to eliminate harassment in the workplace. Employers are encouraged to take appropriate steps to prevent and correct unlawful harassment. They should clearly communicate to employees that unwelcome harassing conduct will not be tolerated. They can do this by establishing an effective complaint or grievance process, providing antiharassment training to their managers and employees, and taking immediate and appropriate action when an employee complains. Employers should strive to create an environment in which employees feel free to raise concerns and are confident that those concerns will be addressed.

Employees are encouraged to inform the harasser directly that the conduct is unwelcome and must stop. Employees should also report harassment to management at an early stage to prevent its escalation.

Employer Liability for Harassment

The employer is automatically liable for harassment by a supervisor that results in a negative employment action such as termination, failure to promote or hire, and loss of wages. If the supervisor's harassment results in a hostile work environment, the employer can avoid liability only if it can prove that: 1) it reasonably tried to prevent and promptly correct the harassing behavior; and 2) the employee unreasonably failed to take advantage of any preventive or corrective opportunities provided by the employer.

"The employer will be liable for harassment by non-supervisory employees or non-employees over whom it has control (e.g., independent contractors or customers on the premises), if it knew, or should have known about the harassment and failed to take prompt and appropriate corrective action.

"When investigating allegations of harassment, the EEOC looks at the entire record: including the nature of the conduct, and the context in which the alleged incidents occurred. A determination of whether harassment is severe or pervasive enough to be illegal is made on a case-by-case basis" (www.eeoc.gov).

Sexual Harassment

Sexual harassment is a form of sex discrimination, which was rendered illegal by Title VII of the Civil Rights Act of 1964. The EEOC defines sexual harassment as follows:

"Unwelcome sexual advances, requests for sexual favors, and other verbal or physical conduct of a sexual nature constitute sexual harassment when:

1. Submission to such conduct is made either explicitly or implicitly a term or condition of an individual's employment.

2. Submission to or rejection of such conduct by an individual is used as the basis for employment decisions affecting such individual.

3. Such conduct has the purpose or effect of unreasonably interfering with an individual's work performance or creating an intimidating, hostile, or offensive working environment."

There are two categories of sexual harassment:

▶ **Quid pro quo:** As previously articulated in point 2, quid pro quo harassment occurs when an individual's submission to or rejection of sexual advances or conduct of a sexual nature is used as the basis for employment-related decisions. Quid pro quo harassment, therefore, originates from a supervisor or from others who have the authority to influence or make decisions about the employee's terms and conditions of employment.

▶ **Hostile work environment:** Hostile work environment harassment occurs when unwelcome sexual conduct unreasonably interferes with an individual's job performance or creates a hostile, intimidating, or offensive work environment. Hostile work environment harassment can be found to exist whether or not the employee experiences (or runs the risk of experiencing) tangible or economic work-related consequences. By definition, a hostile work environment can be created by virtually anyone with whom an employee might come in contact in the workplace (or "workspace," in the event of remote harassment through electronic means such as emails, faxes, instant messages (IMs), and so on).

Key EEO-Related Terms

In going through this section, and as you prepare for the PHR exam, there are some terms that you'll need to be familiar with:

- **Charge:** A formal complaint, submitted to an agency, that alleges unlawful discrimination.

- **Charging party:** A person who alleges that he has experienced unlawful discrimination (also called the complainant).

- **Complainant:** A person who alleges that she has experienced unlawful discrimination (also called the charging party).

- **EEOC:** The government agency responsible for enforcing Title VII of the Civil Rights Act of 1964 (Title VII), the Equal Pay Act (EPA), the Age Discrimination in Employment Act (ADEA), and the Americans with Disabilities Act (ADA).

- **Plaintiff:** A party who files a lawsuit alleging unlawful discrimination.

- **Respondent:** The employer, person, or party against whom a charge of unlawful discrimination has been filed.

- **Fair Employment Practices Agencies (FEPAs):** State or local agencies responsible for enforcing EEO laws that are specific to their respective jurisdiction. At the state level, 47 states (all except Alabama, Arkansas, and Mississippi) have agencies that respond to charges of EEO violations.

Federal, State, and Local Jurisdictions

On the federal level, the agency charged with enforcing many of the laws that are aimed at eliminating discrimination is the EEOC.

Sometimes charges can be filed under two or even three jurisdictions. For instance,

- If a charge is filed with a FEPA but is also covered by federal law, the FEPA "dual files" the charge with EEOC to protect federal rights. In this scenario, the FEPA will usually maintain responsibility for handling the charge.

- If a charge is filed with EEOC but is also covered by state or local law, EEOC "dual files" the charge with the state or local FEPA. In this scenario, the EEOC will usually maintain responsibility for handling the charge.

At other times, when a state or local EEO law is more protective than the corresponding federal law (or when a corresponding federal law does not exist), a charge may be filed only with the FEPA, whose laws offer greater protection to employees.

Filing Charges: Time Limits and Related Information

The EEOC offers the following guidelines relative to filing charges of discrimination (www.eeoc.gov):

Filing a Charge of Employment Discrimination

Federal employees or applicants for federal employment should see Federal Sector Equal Employment Opportunity Complaint Processing.

Who Can File a Charge of Discrimination?

Any individual who believes that her employment rights have been violated may file a charge of discrimination with EEOC.

In addition, an individual, organization, or agency may file a charge on behalf of another person to protect the aggrieved person's identity.

How Is a Charge of Discrimination Filed?

A charge may be filed by mail or in person at the nearest EEOC office.

Individuals who need an accommodation to file a charge (such as a sign language interpreter or print materials in an accessible format) should inform the EEOC field office so appropriate arrangements can be made.

Federal employees or applicants for employment should see Federal Sector Equal Employment Opportunity Complaint Processing.

What Information Must Be Provided to File a Charge?

The following information must be provided to file a charge:

▶ The complaining party's name, address, and telephone number.

▶ The name, address, and telephone number of the respondent employer, employment agency, or union that is alleged to have discriminated, and the number of employees (or union members), if known.

▶ A short description of the alleged violation (the event that caused the complaining party to believe that his or her rights were violated).

▶ The date(s) of the alleged violation(s).

Federal employees or applicants for employment should see Federal Sector Equal Employment Opportunity Complaint Processing.

What Are the Time Limits for Filing a Charge of Discrimination?

All laws enforced by EEOC, except the Equal Pay Act, require filing a charge with EEOC before a private lawsuit may be filed in court. There are strict time limits within which charges must be filed:

▶ A charge must be filed with EEOC within 180 days from the date of the alleged violation to protect the charging party's rights.

▶ This 180-day filing deadline is extended to 300 days if the charge also is covered by a state or local antidiscrimination law. For ADEA charges, only state laws extend the filing limit to 300 days.

▶ These time limits do not apply to claims under the Equal Pay Act because under that Act persons do not have to first file a charge with EEOC to have the right to go to court. However, because many EPA claims also raise Title VII sex discrimination issues, it may be advisable to file charges under both laws within the time limits indicated.

▶ To protect legal rights, it is always best to contact EEOC promptly when discrimination is suspected.

▶ Federal employees or applicants for employment should see Federal Sector Equal Employment Opportunity Complaint Processing.

What Agency Handles a Charge That Is Also Covered by State or Local Law?

Many states and localities have antidiscrimination laws and agencies responsible for enforcing those laws. EEOC refers to these agencies as FEPAs. Through the use of "work sharing agreements," EEOC and the FEPAs avoid duplication of effort while ensuring that a charging party's rights are protected under both federal and state law.

▶ If a charge is filed with a FEPA but also covered by federal law, the FEPA "dual files" the charge with EEOC to protect federal rights. The charge usually will be retained by the FEPA for handling.

▶ If a charge is filed with EEOC but also covered by state or local law, EEOC "dual files" the charge with the state or local FEPA but ordinarily retains the charge for handling.

How Is a Charge Filed for Discrimination Outside the United States?

U.S.-based companies that employ U.S. citizens outside the United States or its territories are covered under EEO laws, with certain exceptions. An individual alleging an EEO violation outside the U.S. should file a charge with the district office closest to her employer's headquarters. However, if you are unsure where to file, you may file a charge with any EEOC office.

EEOC—Handling Charges

After a charge of discrimination has been filed, the EEOC sends a letter to the employer notifying it that a complaint has been filed. At this point, some employers will decide to "settle." There are any number of reasons why an organization might decide to settle, just a few of which include the following:

▶ To elude the requirement of providing information to the EEOC.

▶ To avoid allocating resources (financial, human, emotional, and otherwise) to the process of responding to a charge of discrimination, especially if it appears that the costs of fighting may outweigh the benefits of prevailing ("winning")—even if the organization believes that no unlawful discrimination has taken place.

▶ To prevent the possibility of bad press that can, at times, be generated even by the mere filing of a charge of discrimination.

▶ To seek a resolution to a situation in which the employer believes that there may be exposure (in other words, where the charge of discrimination may be valid).

Alternatively, many employers choose not to seek a settlement agreement when a charge of discrimination is first filed. In such situations, there are four primary ways that the EEOC can handle the charge:

- ▶ **Investigate it:** Investigations can be designated as "high priority" or "non-high priority," depending upon the strength of the facts that have been presented in the charge. An EEOC investigation can take myriad forms, including written requests for information, in-person interviews, document reviews, and even a visit to the location where the discrimination allegedly occurred.

- ▶ **Settle it:** A charge can be settled at any stage of the investigation if the charging party and the employer are both interested in doing so. If no settlement is reached, the investigation resumes.

- ▶ **Mediate it:** The EEOC offers a confidential mediation program as an alternative to a lengthy investigative process. For a charge to be mediated, the charging party and the employer must both be willing to participate. If the mediation process is not successful, the charge will be investigated.

- ▶ **Dismiss it:** A charge can be dismissed at any point in the process if the agency determines that further investigation will not be able to establish that the alleged unlawful discrimination actually occurred. When a charge is dismissed, a notice is issued in accordance with the law that gives the charging party 90 days within which to file a lawsuit on his own behalf.

EEOC Determinations

The EEOC determines whether there is "reasonable cause" to believe that unlawful discrimination has occurred.

When the EEOC determinates that discrimination has likely occurred, it issues a finding of "reasonable cause." This determination is based on the evidence gathered during the investigation. If the EEOC determines that there is reasonable cause, the EEOC will attempt conciliation with the employer in an effort to develop a remedy for the discrimination. If the EEOC cannot conciliate the case, the EEOC will decide whether to take the case to court. (The EEOC chooses to litigate a very small percentage of cases.) If the EEOC does not take the case to court, it will close the case and issue the charging party a "right to sue" letter.

If the EEOC determines that there is no reasonable cause, the case is closed, the parties are notified, and the charging party is given a "right to sue" letter. The charging party then has 90 days to file a private lawsuit.

The charging party can also request a right to sue letter from the EEOC 180 days after the charge was filed (60 days for ADEA). A charging party may not bring a case to court if the charge has been successfully conciliated, mediated, or settled.

EEO—Going to Court

If a case does proceed to court, HR's role will vary significantly, depending on a host of factors. For instance, in some organizations, HR may be called on to assist in-house or outside counsel with responding to a complaint, to collect data as part of the discovery process, or to be available to assist and facilitate the process. Depending on HR's role in the actual case,

HR professionals may be deposed, testify, or represent the organization during the trial—in a sense, being the "face" of the organization to the judge and jury.

> **NOTE**
>
> It is important to keep in mind the critical and unique role of juries. A "jury of one's peers" might be more likely to identify with a plaintiff than with an organization. In short, from the perspective of the organization, the turf is a bit less friendly and the stakes are higher than they were before 1991.

Relief or Remedies

When a plaintiff prevails in an EEO lawsuit, she may be awarded various forms of "relief" or remedies (whether the discrimination was intentional or unintentional):

- ▶ Back pay

- ▶ Hiring, or front pay (instead of hiring the individual)

- ▶ Promotion

- ▶ Reinstatement, or front pay (instead of rehiring the individual)

- ▶ Reasonable accommodation

- ▶ Other actions that will make an individual "whole" (in the condition that she would have been but for the discrimination)

- ▶ Attorneys' fees

- ▶ Expert witness fees

- ▶ Court costs

Compensatory and punitive damages may also be available when the discrimination is found to be intentional (and in rare cases, even when the discrimination is found to be unintentional).

Understanding Front Pay

The concept of front pay is one with which HR professionals should be familiar. According to the EEOC (www.eeoc.gov):

> "The remedy of front pay compensates a victim in situations where reinstatement or nondiscriminatory placement would be an available remedy, but is denied for reasons peculiar to the individual claim. The compensation of front pay makes the victim of discrimination whole generally until such nondiscriminatory placement can be accomplished. See *Romero v. Department of the Air Force.*"

Numerous decisions of the Commission have recognized the Commission's authority to award front pay as a remedy and have discussed the propriety of such an award under the particular facts of those cases. The Commission decisions discussed in this article were selected to illustrate the Commission's treatment of the front pay remedy.

Reinstatement or nondiscriminatory placement is preferred over the remedy of front pay. See Romero. However, front pay may be determined to be more appropriate in certain situations. The Court in *EEOC v. Prudential Federal Savings and Loan Association* stated that front pay should be awarded "when the employer has exhibited such extreme hostility that, as a practical matter, a productive and amicable working relationship would be impossible."

The Commission in *Finlay v. United States Postal Service*, and in earlier cases cited in Finlay, set out three circumstances in which front pay may be awarded in lieu of reinstatement: (1) Where no position is available; (2) Where a subsequent working relationship between the parties would be antagonistic; or (3) Where the employer has a record of long-term resistance to discrimination efforts.

NOTE

This highlights the reality that any situation could potentially devolve into a lawsuit. Sometimes there is nothing you can do to prevent that from happening. It's also not helpful to worry excessively about the possibility of litigation. The best that any of us can do is to ensure that we handle situations well (and consistently), that we seek to deescalate situations whenever possible, that we invite employees to raise concerns internally, and that we—along with the clients with whom we consult—conduct ourselves in a manner that will, if subjected to scrutiny, hold up.

HR professionals play various roles in the organization; one of the most important is the role of proactive observer. In short, if you believe that a situation has the possibility to produce a charge of discrimination or any other legal challenges, notify your senior HR colleagues and, as appropriate, counsel. Depending on the culture of your organization, you may want to consider seeking input from counsel along the way. Also remember the fine line that HR cannot cross—HR professionals cannot practice law. We must, however, recognize when we need to call in someone who can (such as in-house or outside counsel). This can, at times, be a fine line to walk.

Equal Opportunity…for Whom?

Ensuring EEO is an ever-evolving concept. As such, it might be more accurate to say that, as of today, these laws ensure equal opportunities for "most," rather than for "all."

There are still individuals who—at a federal level—can be excluded from consideration for employment on the basis of shared characteristics or traits—even though those characteristics or traits are not job related. For instance, as of the time when this book was published, no federal law exists prohibiting employment discrimination on the basis of sexual orientation or on the basis of marital status, even though certain states do offer those additional protections.

This chapter is based upon the assumption that all workforce planning and employment decisions should be based on job-related factors. Doing so will help ensure that we do not run afoul of the law. Additionally—and perhaps just as important—this will also ensure that we do not eliminate qualified individuals on the basis of factors that have nothing to do with whether they can perform the jobs for which they are applying.

RESPONSIBILITY

WPE Responsibility 02

Identify workforce requirements to achieve the organization's short- and long-term goals and objectives (for example: corporate restructuring, workforce expansion, or reduction).

RESPONSIBILITY

WPE Responsibility 03

Conduct job analyses to create and/or update job descriptions and identify job competencies.

RESPONSIBILITY

WPE Responsibility 04

Identify, review, document, and update essential job functions for positions.

WPE Responsibility 05

Influence and establish criteria for hiring, retaining, and promoting based on job descriptions and required competencies.

RESPONSIBILITY

WPE Responsibility 15

Develop, implement, and evaluate employee retention strategies and practices.

RESPONSIBILITY

Knowledge 23

Internal workforce assessment techniques (for example: skills testing, skills inventory, workforce demographic analysis).

KNOWLEDGE

HR professionals must partner with management and leadership to determine functionally—and on a job-by-job basis—what these employees will need to do to move the organization to where it needs to go. These are the all-important workforce analysis and planning functions. It is in this context that we will look at jobs.

It's important to note that not all organizations conduct this process in the same order. And that's okay. It's more important to ensure that all these steps are taken in a logical way that will yield solid results than it is to mandate a particular process.

Job Analysis

Job analysis is the process by which information about a specific position is collected. Job analysis produces three important outputs that are critical to the workforce planning process:

▶ Job description

▶ Job specifications

▶ Job competencies

Job Description

Job descriptions are a key tool for many of the functions that HR professionals perform. Although they can take many different formats, most job descriptions have several elements in common:

▶ **Identifying information:** This includes job title, department or division name, reporting relationship, FLSA status, the date on which the description was written, the name of the person who wrote it, and so on.

▶ **Scope information:** This is the area of responsibility for, over, or within which this position has authority or responsibility.

▶ **Responsibility for supervision, if applicable:** This includes any positions whom the position incumbent supervises.

▶ **Physical work conditions or physical demands:** Although easy to overlook, it's critical to include this information in the job description.

- ▶ **Minimum requirements:** Often, this refers to experience, education, or other mandatory credentials required to perform the position successfully. These are often the factors that will be initially used to screen candidates in or out during the résumé review process and to determine who will be interviewed.

- ▶ **Knowledge, skills, and abilities required:** These are acceptable levels of knowledge, skills, and abilities (also known as KSAs). These may include items that organizations or interviewers sometimes mistakenly take for granted and do not explore enough with candidates during the selection process.

  - ▶ **Knowledge:** Simply stated, knowledge is what the incumbent needs to know about a specific body of information to be able to perform the position successfully. For instance, an instructor who conducts training onsite at a particular organization may need to have knowledge of organizational dynamics. An automotive mechanic may need to have knowledge of mechanical, electronic, and computer technology.

  - ▶ **Skills:** Skills refer to the ability to perform a particular task. For instance, the instructor may need to possess the ability to engage participants in facilitated discussions about the workshop topics. The automotive mechanic may needs to possess the ability to drive a standard (or "stick") shift.

  - ▶ **Abilities:** Abilities refer to specific traits or behavioral characteristics required to perform successfully in a position. For instance, an instructor may need to demonstrate a willingness and comfort to engage quickly with people with whom she is not previously acquainted (which could perhaps be referred to as "outgoing"). The automotive mechanic might need to be mechanically inclined.

- ▶ **Overall purpose of the position:** This is a short (usually less than a paragraph, and maybe even as short as a sentence) statement summarizing why the position exists and what it is intended to accomplish.

- ▶ **Overall purpose/mission of the organization:** Some organizations choose to include the mission of the organization on each job description as a way of ensuring that the mission of the position is—and remains—meaningfully linked to and aligned with the mission of the organization.

- ▶ **Duties and responsibilities:** These are tasks and functions that the incumbent is expected to perform. Sometimes job descriptions also indicate the percentage of time that is spent on each major responsibility or group of responsibilities (which may or may not correlate to the importance of the responsibility).

Although there is no one definitive, or master, list of what should be included in a job description, selecting and including appropriate elements (such as those listed here) ensures that the job description is accurate, thorough, and on target to serve (ultimately) as a valuable resource for other projects and initiatives.

Essential and Nonessential Job Functions

For ADA and other purposes, duties and responsibilities should be divided into two categories: essential and nonessential job functions.

The ADA states that "consideration shall be given to the employer's judgment as to what functions of a job are essential, and if an employer has prepared a written description before advertising or interviewing applicants for the job, this description shall be considered evidence of the essential functions of the job" (www.eeoc.gov). Failure to have a job description in place, therefore, could diminish the strength of the employer's position in defending an allegation that an employee or applicant has been discriminated against on the basis of disability. In short, employers can't "make up" (or look like they are making up) requirements after the fact.

Essential functions are those that are inherently fundamental and necessary to a position. Together—and perhaps even on their own—they constitute part (or even most, or all) of the reason that the job exists. Often, an essential function cannot be performed by many —or perhaps even by any —other employees in the organization.

Conversely, nonessential functions are more peripheral to the position. They generally constitute a smaller and relatively unimportant part of the position and could fairly easily be performed by other employees.

> **NOTE**
>
> Confer with managers, senior HR staff, and counsel—as appropriate—relative to delineating essential from nonessential functions. This decision should never be made in a vacuum.

Job Specifications (or "Specs")

Job specifications refer to the qualifications that a successful candidate must possess or demonstrate to perform effectively in a position. These could refer to the skills, knowledge, abilities, behavioral characteristics, and other credentials and experience necessary to perform a position successfully. They do *not*, however, refer to the qualifications that the best-qualified candidate might possess or bring to a role; instead, they refer to what it will take to get the job done in a manner that fully meets expectations of the position.

Job specs can be expressed as

- ▶ **KSAs:** The minimally acceptable levels of knowledge, skills, and abilities required to successfully perform a position

- ▶ **Credentials:** Years of experience, educational requirements, and so on

- ▶ **Requirements:** Physical or mental

> **NOTE**
>
> Credentials, although important to establish and consider, can be misleading. Said differently, a person who possesses or has earned a particular credential doesn't necessarily have the knowledge or skills that one might assume go along with that credential. Earning a four-year degree in accounting, for instance, doesn't necessarily mean that a candidate can perform certain accounting functions. Similarly, the greatest accomplishment of a candidate who has five years of related professional-level experience may, in fact, be that she was not terminated during those five years. Or, she might have one year's worth of professional-level experience that she has repeated five times. The bottom line—don't make assumptions. Credentials should be a starting point, not an ending point, for making selection decisions.

Job Competencies

Job competencies speak to broad categories of skills, abilities, or behavioral characteristics that are required to perform successfully in a particular position, department, or organization. These are often embraced by organizations with terms such as "key success factors," "competencies for success," or "performance factors." They could include things such as "communication skills," "teamwork," or "initiative." The same competencies may manifest themselves differently in different positions or departments throughout the organization.

BFOQs are legitimate job requirements mandated by business necessity that can have an unintended discriminatory (disparate) impact on applicants or employees.

Job Analysis

Job analysis is the process through which information about a position is inventoried. The elements that compose each job in the organization are identified through this process. These elements often include

- ▶ Responsibilities, duties, and tasks performed by the position incumbent.

- ▶ How those responsibilities, duties, and tasks relate to each other and to other jobs within the organization. This includes how frequently each of those activities is performed as well as how activities relate to each other in terms of importance.

Job analysis also identifies the KSAs required for successful performance of the position.

> **NOTE**
>
> Although HR professionals usually lead job analysis initiatives, "leadership" must not become confused with "ownership." HR professionals perform job analysis on behalf of clients. The clients are the ones, however, who own the initiatives and must live with the results. HR must function in a consultative manner to ensure support and buy-in from internal clients.

Job analysis is not about completing a form. It is also not just about the job description that will be produced as a byproduct of the job analysis. Rather, it is a building block as you continue to form relationships with your internal clients. It will either enhance or diminish how others within your organization perceive you.

> **NOTE**
>
> There may be a temptation to define a job according to the skills, abilities, or behavioral characteristics that the current—or former—incumbent brings to it. However, job analysis must focus on the job, not on the individual who holds, or held, that particular position. It must also not be unduly influenced by the current labor market—real or perceived.

How to Conduct a Job Analysis

There are many ways to collect information that will be used in conducting a job analysis. Depending on what is appropriate in your organization, consider the following:

- ▶ Interviewing the incumbent, or the prior incumbent, if that person is available

- ▶ Interviewing the person who supervises the position

- ▶ Interviewing the supervisor's supervisor

- ▶ Interviewing coworkers

- ▶ Interviewing direct reports, if applicable

- ▶ Interviewing clients or customers with whom the position interacts

▶ Interviewing vendors with whom the position interacts

▶ Observing the incumbent performing the position, if possible and appropriate

▶ Reviewing work product

▶ Reviewing any documentation, reports, or performance-related statistics or records generated by—or about—the position

> **NOTE**
>
> Another option is to consider taking a 360-degree/multi-rater approach to conducting a job analysis for the position. This would involve collecting input from multiple individuals (up to, and possibly including everyone) with whom the position interacts.

Conducting Job Analysis Interviews

Interviews can be conducted in person, through written or emailed surveys, or by a combination of both. Either way, be sensitive to the amount of time you ask people to invest in this process. Work to ensure that this process remains as streamlined and efficient as possible, while still ensuring that you collect the information you need.

Interviews/questionnaires may vary in length and content, depending on the nature and amount of involvement and contact that the interviewee has with the position. Also be certain that you explain the purpose of the interview/questionnaires and the way in which participating in this process will ultimately benefit the interviewee.

Job Descriptions

One of the primary results generated by a job analysis is a job description. A job description is an inventory of important information gathered about the position during the job analysis process.

Different organizations structure their job descriptions differently. In large part, this is a function of the job evaluation system that will be used. Job descriptions, however, incorporate stylistic as well as substantive considerations. They reflect, to a degree, the culture of the organization.

How to Create a Job Description

However the job description is designed, certain elements should be included:

▶ Job title

▶ Date on which the description was completed

▶ Name of person preparing the description

▶ Department, unit, or division

▶ Supervisory reporting relationship(s)

▶ Direct reporting relationships, if applicable

▶ Essential functions

▶ Nonessential functions

- ► Working conditions and environment
- ► Physical requirements of the position
- ► Degree of financial accountability
- ► Qualifications required to perform the position

Although there is no one definitive, or master, list of what should be included in a job description, selecting and including appropriate elements (such as those listed above) in the job description ensures that the job description is accurate, thorough, and on target to serve (ultimately) as a valuable resource for other projects and initiatives.

RESPONSIBILITY

WPE Responsibility 06

Analyze labor market for trends that impact the ability to meet workforce requirements (for example: federal/state data reports).

RESPONSIBILITY

WPE Responsibility 07

Assess skill sets of internal workforce and external labor market to determine the availability of qualified candidates, utilizing third-party vendors or agencies as appropriate.

RESPONSIBILITY

WPE Responsibility 08

Identify internal and external recruitment sources (for example, employee referrals, diversity groups, social media) and implement selected recruitment methods.

RESPONSIBILITY

WPE Responsibility 10

Brand and market the organization to potential qualified applicants.

KNOWLEDGE

Knowledge 13

Recruitment sources (for example, employee referral, social networking/social media) for targeting passive, semi-active and active candidates.

KNOWLEDGE

Knowledge 14

Recruitment strategies.

KNOWLEDGE

Knowledge 15

Staffing alternatives (for example, outsourcing, job sharing, phased retirement).

Knowledge 16

Planning techniques (for example, succession planning, forecasting).

Knowledge 25

Employer marketing and branding techniques.

Recruiting Candidates

"Recruiting and selection" are often thought of as a single process. In fact, however, they are two separate components of the staffing process and need to be approached and carried out separately. Recruiting is the process of attracting and creating a pool of qualified candidates. Selection is the process of identifying the candidate(s) to whom the position will be offered.

Employer Branding

Before an employer goes out in search of new employees, it needs to consider how potential candidates in the labor market will perceive the organization. Organizations create a "brand" as an employer in much the same way they create a brand for the product or service that they market to their customers. So, just as an organization markets its products or services deliberately and intentionally, it must deliberately and intentionally decide on a marketing strategy that will be used to promote the employer's brand within the labor market.

Relevant Labor Market

In looking at drawing from an external pool of candidates, it is important to first define the relevant labor market. This refers to the size and scope of the geographic area within which an organization would seek to attract qualified candidates for a particular position(s).

Even within the same organization, the relevant labor market for different positions can vary widely depending upon the skills, knowledge, abilities, and behavioral characteristics required to perform each position successfully. Other factors that impact how an organization defines the relevant labor market might be the degree of competition that exists among employers for particular skills or knowledge and the degree to which certain skills or knowledge requirements are industry specific.

Selection Criteria

The first step that must be taken to begin the process of creating a pool of qualified candidates is to identify and develop selection criteria for the position. Selection criteria can be likened to a "shopping list" of what you're looking for in the individuals who will populate your candidate pool (and, ultimately, the candidate(s) who will join the organization). This could—and often will—include KSAs, job specifications, and specific requirements stemming from the job competencies.

Never Go Shopping—or Recruiting—Without a List

If you go grocery shopping without a list, you can lose your focus, forget items you need, purchase things you don't really need, or be attracted to items that are marketed well but that might lack substance. If this happens when you're going grocery shopping, it's no big deal—you can just go back to the store again to get what you missed the first time around. However, if you begin the recruitment and selection process without a clear idea of the qualifications that your successful candidate must ultimately possess, the stakes can be a bit higher.

Sometimes our ideas about the requirements for a particular position are unintentionally tainted by other factors—for instance, the qualifications that the prior incumbent possessed, or the qualifications of the individuals in the broader labor pool or who are actually applying for an open position. The best, most objective, and most legally defensible way to establish selection criteria is to do so objectively, within the context of the job-related information that has been generated through the job description, job specs, and the like. It's critical to do this up front before you look at a single résumé.

Internal and External Recruiting

After you've determined (in collaboration with your internal client—most likely the hiring manager, in this case) the selection criteria for a particular position, the next step is to decide whether to seek to create a candidate pool internally, externally, or through a combination of both approaches.

Recruiting Internal Candidates

Many—in fact, most—organizations embrace the idea of promoting current employees from within the organization. This begins by creating a pool of qualified candidates from among current employees. Three primary mechanisms for seeking internal candidates for positions within the organization are job posting, job bidding, and succession planning.

Job Posting

Job posting systems announce position openings to current employees within the organization. Candidates who believe that they meet the minimum requirements of the position (as posted) are invited to apply for positions—sometimes even before external candidates are sought.

Job Bidding

Although the job posting process isn't triggered until a job opens, job bidding systems invite employees to express interest in positions at any time, even if a position is not currently available. Candidates who are determined to meet the qualifications for a position in which they have expressed interest will automatically be put into consideration when that position becomes available.

Succession Planning

In addition to job posting and job bidding, many organizations take further proactive steps toward succession planning: the detailed, ongoing process through which an organization identifies individuals who might be able to fill higher-level positions that could become available in the future.

Succession plans are "living, breathing" tools that impact individual and group professional development planning and that —through predictive efforts and proactive planning —strive to ensure that the overarching mission and goals of the organization will not be derailed by the inevitable departure of individuals from the organization.

You can find more information about succession planning in Chapter 3, " Human Resource Development."

Internal Candidates: Advantages and Disadvantages

Recruiting internal candidates can benefit employees as well as employers. Through internal recruitment, employees can grow and develop without leaving the organization. Employers can select from a pool of internal candidates about whom they have more job-related knowledge than they would normally have about an external candidate. Both employees and employers can build on the investments they have already made in each other and may even experience an enhanced sense of loyalty and dedication to each other.

Recruiting internal candidates, however, also presents certain risks, such as these:

► Relying too heavily on performance appraisals that, for a variety of reasons, may not be reflective of actual past performance (see Chapter 3).

► Relying too heavily on performance appraisals that, even when accurate, may reflect KSAs that are not wholly relevant to the position for which the candidate is applying.

Particular risk exists when a position is posted for which a strong internal candidate has already been identified. If it is fully expected (in other words, predetermined) that a particular individual will be selected for an open position, the integrity of the job posting or bidding system could be seriously—and perhaps irreparably—compromised.

Policy Considerations

The organizational policies surrounding internal recruiting systems must be thought through carefully and administered consistently. For instance

► Is an employee who posts or bids for a position required to notify her current supervisor? Is the supervisor required to grant "permission" for the employee to post for another position?

► If an employee is selected for a position, how long must that employee wait before being "allowed" to start his new job? Must a replacement for the employee's former position be found before the employee can move on to his new position?

► Must an employee be performing satisfactorily in her current position to be considered for another position within the organization? Would certain areas of unsatisfactory performance be acceptable, such as those that are unrelated to the new position?

► Must an employee work for a specified period of time in one position before posting for a different position within the organization?

► Are employees who currently hold exempt-level positions subject to different requirements than employees who hold non-exempt–level positions?

Any of these considerations, depending on how they are handled, can either strengthen or diminish the ultimate effectiveness of the job posting or bidding system.

Recruiting External Candidates

There are various options available for recruiting external candidates. A few of these options include

- Internet job listing websites
- Newspaper advertisements
- Radio advertisements
- ".jobs" websites
- College and university career development/placement offices
- Job fairs
- Open houses
- Alumni networks (alumni of colleges/universities, as well as alumni of companies)
- Former employees
- Walks-ins
- Professional organizations
- Referrals from current employees or industry network colleagues
- State unemployment offices
- Organizational websites
- Prior applicants
- Social media

Perhaps the newest and least traditional of these methods is the use of social media. Let's explore this in more detail.

Using Social Media to Find Candidates

There are many social media platforms, the most popular of which (as of this printing) are considered LinkedIn, Facebook, and Twitter. Of these three platforms, LinkedIn is the most professionally oriented, and Facebook is the most personally oriented —although that is shifting quickly, as Facebook is quickly becoming a way for candidates and employers to "find" each other.

"Finding" each other is one of the great potential benefits of social media. Although active candidates —those who are actively seeking a new position —will look for new opportunities, passive job seekers —by definition —will not. Social media (particularly LinkedIn, at the moment) provide a way for employers to find individuals who might not currently be seeking a new job but who might be well suited for a job opening and who might be willing to consider new opportunities.

In this overlap between these two types of candidates are semi-active candidates: those who occasionally look for a new position (perhaps when feelings of dissatisfaction or lack of appreciation relative to their current positions mount) but who do not make a full-time, concerted effort to do so. These individuals can also be reached through social media and might be more receptive to considering new employment than passive candidates would be.

Using Social Media to Learn About Candidates

Of potential greater concern —and greater debate —is the use of social media (especially Facebook) as a way to gather information about current candidates. There are legal, as well as ethical, questions surrounding this practice —and the "jury is still out" (literally, as well as figuratively).

Here are some things to keep in mind as you consider using Facebook to gather information about candidates:

- ▶ To what degree is the information you are gathering reflective of the individual?

- ▶ To what degree is the information you are gathering related to the qualifications of the position?

- ▶ To what degree can you be confident that the candidate created/posted the content on his page?

- ▶ To what degree is the information you are gathering likely to expose you to information that is covered by EEO laws?

- ▶ To what degree might gathering such information unlevel the playing field for candidates?

- ▶ What would your measure of comfort be if you were required to discuss this practice with counsel? Or what if you were on the witness stand and were called to testify?

HR professionals —and all who are involved in the hiring process —are advised to speak with counsel before incorporating social media into the candidate evaluation process.

They *Are* External Candidates, But...

Considering prior candidates for openings for which they did not specifically apply can have repercussions relative to who is considered to be an applicant, particularly with respect to EO 11246 and EEO-1 reporting. Repercussions can also result from allowing walk-in candidates who are filling out applications for any position, rather than for one particular job opening. These considerations can even affect the way in which employers phrase rejection letters. For this reason, HR professionals need to familiarize themselves with guidelines and possible ramifications before committing to candidates in their "rejection letters" that they will be "considered for any future job openings for which they may be qualified," or before digging through files to find a great candidate that previously interviewed for a different position.

Employment Agencies

There are several different types of employment agencies of which HR professions must have knowledge.

Employment Agencies—State

Each state has a service through which unemployed individuals who are currently looking for work are often required to register, thus providing a potentially rich pool of candidates to employers. These public agencies will also provide preliminary screening and candidate referral services to employers.

Employment Agencies—Temporary

Many organizations utilize temporary employment agencies to secure services that are needed on a short-term basis. This allows organizations the flexibility to meet temporary, short-term, or unexpected needs. Some organizations also use a "temp to hire" model to try out the employee before extending an offer of regular employment. This also gives the employee the opportunity to try out the organization before deciding whether to make a commitment to a particular organization or position.

This process used to be referred to as "temp to perm." It is no longer advisable to use this language, however, because there is no such thing as permanent employment. Employers — and HR professionals, in particular — should be careful not to say anything or use any verbiage that could potentially imply otherwise or that could unintentionally create an implied contract.

Private Employment Agencies (Also Known as Private Search Firms)

Employers may also enlist the services of private employment agencies to assist them in finding regular employees. There are two primary options:

- ▶ **Contingency employment agencies/search firms:** The employer pays a fee to the firm only when a candidate is hired through its efforts. This type of agency would be selected more often for entry-level professional or supervisory recruiting efforts.

- ▶ **Retained employment agencies/search firms:** The employer pays a fee to the firm whether or not a candidate is hired. This type of agency would be selected more often for executive-level recruiting efforts.

NOTE

Different terms, conditions, and "guarantees" apply to different types of agencies. Terms can differ from employer to employer or even from position to position. It's important to negotiate knowledgeably, to finalize terms before beginning a search, and to review any agreements carefully before signing.

It is also advantageous for HR professionals to maintain awareness of less traditional and nontraditional sources for recruiting external candidates—such as prisons, houses of worship, displaced homemaker services, and so on.

Employee Referral: A Hybrid Approach

Many organizations embrace employee referral systems—a recruiting technique whereby current employees are used as a source for recruiting external candidates into the applicant pool.

This approach offers distinct advantages—and potential disadvantages, as well. Some potential advantages include

- ▶ Candidates who are referred by current employees may have a better understanding of the culture and values of the organization and thus have more realistic expectations about the job and about the organization.

- ▶ Current employees are more likely to refer individuals who they believe (rightly or wrongly) have a high likelihood of succeeding. This happens because current employees often believe that the performance of the person whom they refer will have an impact on how they are perceived by the organization.

- ▶ Employee referral programs—even those that offer rich rewards—are significantly more cost-effective than most other forms of recruiting.

Employee referral programs also have the potential for significant disadvantages:

- ▶ If the current organization is not particularly diverse (with respect to gender, age, race, education background, or a host of other factors), employee referral programs might perpetuate that lack of diversity.

- If an affirmative action plan is in place, and if there are areas of underutilization, an employee referral program is not likely to demonstrate "good faith efforts" to recruit candidates who are women or minorities.

- In organizations where there are prior patterns of hiring discrimination, employee referral programs are likely to reinforce those patterns.

In many cases, organizations will not rely exclusively on employee referral programs for creating pools of candidates. Instead, employee referral programs are one of several techniques used to create a pool of qualified and, ideally, diverse candidates.

Nontraditional Staffing Alternatives

HR professionals also need to be familiar with other, more flexible, less traditional staffing arrangements. These arrangements do not necessarily fall within "internal" or "external" sources because these options could be offered to existing employees within the organization, could be used as a way to attract external candidates, or could even result in the outsourcing of functions that were formerly performed within the organization.

Examples of nontraditional staffing alternatives could include the use of temporary help, temp-to-hire arrangements, outsourcing to third-party vendors (any entity or person outside the organization to whom work can be outsourced), off-shoring (a specific type of outsourcing that uses vendors located overseas), or contracting with consultants. Current or newly hired employees can also participate in flexible staffing programs through part-time employment, telecommuting, job sharing arrangements, or seasonal employment.

Outsourcing

More and more organizations are deciding to have certain services performed by individuals or entities that are external to the organization rather than by employees. Welcome to the ever-expanding world of third-party contracts.

Third-party relationships are no longer a phenomenon; rather, they are progressively becoming a standard—and even expected—way of conducting business. Some services that are outsourced represent new initiatives or projects. At other times, work that is currently being performed by employees is outsourced to individuals or entities outside the organization.

Different organizations may choose to outsource different functions. Many functions (and some people would argue that almost any function) within an organization can be outsourced.

Many HR departments outsource significant functions as well. Some of the HR functions that are often partially—or fully—outsourced include the following:

- 401(k) or 403(b) programs
- Pensions/benefits
- Stock option administration
- Learning and development
- Payroll
- Safety and security

Request for Proposal

The Request for Proposal (RFP) is a written document that invites third-party contractors to propose written solutions that address the organization's needs—ideally, within a price that the customer is willing to pay. Developing a solid and carefully constructed RFP is critical; a poorly designed or overly vague RFP may yield proposed solutions that do not address the organization's actual problems. Worse yet, those solutions may appear to be workable and appropriate—until they have been implemented.

KNOWLEDGE

Knowledge 17

Reliability and validity of selection tests/tools/methods.

KNOWLEDGE

Knowledge 18

Use and interpretation of selection tests (for example, psychological/personality, cognitive, motor/physical assessments, performance, assessment center).

Preemployment Testing

Preemployment testing is another way of ascertaining the degree to which a candidate possesses and can demonstrate the knowledge, skills, and abilities/behavioral characteristics required to successfully perform the position. Any tests that are used must be job related and valid. (See the section "Uniform Guidelines on Employee Selection Procedures" earlier in this chapter.)

Some of the most commonly used types of preemployment exams are discussed in this section.

Agility Tests

Agility tests are preemployment tests that are used to ascertain whether the candidate can perform the physical requirements of the position for which she is applying.

Aptitude Tests

Aptitude tests are preemployment tests that are used to ascertain whether the candidate possesses the skills or knowledge required to perform the position for which he is applying.

Assessment Center

Assessment centers are facilities that assess evaluate candidate's absolute and relative qualifications for open positions within an organization, or with respect to overall potential/talent.

Cognitive Ability Tests

Cognitive ability tests are preemployment tests that are used to assess the candidate's intelligence or current skill level with respect to a job-related function. Cognitive tests could be administered to assess skills such as problem-solving, mathematical skill, or numerical ability.

Integrity, or Honesty, Tests

These tests are preemployment tests that are used to ascertain the degree to which a candidate would be likely to engage in behavior that is dishonest or that reflects a potential lack of integrity.

Medical Tests

These tests are preemployment medical tests, or exams, that can be conducted only if the exam is job related and consistent with business necessity, and even then only after an offer (or a conditional offer) of employment has been extended to the candidate. It is important to note that an offer of employment cannot be rescinded simply because a medical test reveals that a candidate has a disability. Instead, in this situation, the employer would then determine the feasibility of extending a reasonable accommodation that does not cause undue hardship.

Personality Tests

Personality tests are preemployment tests that are used to gather information about a candidate's personality traits, motivation, discipline, and other characteristics.

Preemployment Drug Testing

Preemployment drug testing is urine (or, less often, blood or hair sample) that is subjected to testing to identify the presence of illegal drugs. When used in a preemployment context, drug tests are not considered to be medical tests. Most employers, however, do not conduct drug testing until a conditional offer of employment has been extended to, and accepted by, the candidate.

Prepromotion Drug Testing

Prepromotion drug testing is conducted to decrease the likelihood of promoting someone who is currently using/abusing illegal drugs.

> **NOTE**
>
> This may not apply to public-sector employers unless permitted by the collective-bargaining agreement or for safety-sensitive positions.

WPE Responsibility 09

RESPONSIBILITY

Establish metrics for workforce planning (for example, recruitment and turnover statistics, costs).

Knowledge 12

KNOWLEDGE

Methods to assess past and future staffing effectiveness (for example, costs per hire, selection ratios, adverse impact).

Measuring Recruiting Costs and Effectiveness

There are numerous ways to calculate the costs associated with recruiting as well as the overall effectiveness of the recruiting process. Some of those measures focus on the actual recruiting process (for instance, cost per hire or time to file), while others take a more forward-looking approach (for instance, voluntary or involuntary turnover percentage for new hires within the first 3, 6, or 12 months).

The most critical points to keep in mind about measuring recruiting costs and interviewing effectiveness are these:

1. Do it.

2. Do it consistently.

Historically, HR professionals can —and often have — become their own worst enemies by settling for subjective and qualitative answers to the question, "How am I doing?" The good news, however, is that this offers us yet another opportunity to learn to be more strategic. So, in conjunction with your clients and with HR leadership, determine which measures will be most relevant and valuable. Ask questions such as these:

▶ Which recruiting sources yield the most applicants?

▶ Which recruiting sources yield the best qualified applicants?

▶ On that note, how do you define a "good applicant"? Is it one who meets the minimum qualifications of the position? One to whom an offer of employment is extended? One who accepts an offer of employment? Or one who is still with the organization 3, 6, or 12 months after being hired?

▶ Which recruiting sources are the least expensive on a cost-per-hire basis?

▶ How much time, effort, and attention does each recruiting source require from HR, or from the manager, during the recruiting process?

To calculate many of these measures, you'll need to calculate yield ratios. A yield ratio calculates the percentage of applicants from a particular recruiting source who advance to a particular stage in the recruiting process. For instance, one pertinent yield ratio might refer to the number of résumés from minimally (at least) qualified candidates as a percentage of the number of total résumés received (from particular recruiting sources). It might also be helpful to compare this yield ratio for different recruiting sources.

Cost per Hire

HR professionals must be well versed in calculating accurate cost per hire metrics. The formula for calculating cost per hire follows:

$$\frac{\text{Total of all costs associated with recruiting, selecting, and hiring employees}}{\text{Number of individuals hired}}$$

Generally, this calculation will be made over a one-year period.

One of the most crucial considerations for calculating cost per hire accurately is ensuring that all costs —internal as well as external, and direct as well as indirect —are included in the numerator of this calculation. Otherwise, the cost per hire will be inaccurate (and understated). Review, and perhaps even use, cost-per-hire calculators that are available online through reputable sources.

Turnover Analysis

HR professionals must also be well-versed in calculating turnover. Turnover measures the percentage of the workforce that has left the organization during a specified period of time.

Most often expressed on an annual basis, turnover is calculated as follows:

Number of terminations during a specified period of time divided by the average

Number of employees in the workforce during that same period of time

This information can be used in a number of ways—one of which is to help predict future turnover rates, which can affect staffing needs. Turnover can be voluntary (for instance, an employee accepts employment at another organization) or involuntary (for instance, an employee is laid off). Turnover can be broken down in any number of ways:

▶ Total for the entire organization

▶ Total for one—or more—particular departments

▶ FLSA (exempt or nonexempt) status

▶ Length of service

NOTE

Despite popular opinion, turnover is not inherently bad. Just like cholesterol, there is "good turnover" and "bad turnover." An example of good turnover might be an individual who accepts a more challenging or appropriate position in a different unit or division within the organization. An example of "bad turnover" might be a relatively new employee who quits after two weeks because he did not accurately understand the requirements of the position for which he was hired.

Whether turnover is deemed "good" or "bad," of course, involves making value judgments, which will vary from organization to organization. In one organization, for instance, an employee resigning to pursue higher education on a full-time basis or to serve the nation (through military service or the Peace Corps, for instance) might be counted as "good" turnover. In other organizations, these same reasons might be counted as "bad" turnover. Some organizations use the terms "acceptable" and "unacceptable" rather than "good" or "bad," so as to downplay the value judgments inherent to these labels.

It's also possible to look at turnover in terms of controllability. Controllable turnover might include voluntary terminations, and noncontrollable turnover might include death or retirement.

Adverse Impact

Please also ensure that you review information about adverse impact, discussed earlier in this chapter.

WPE Responsibility 11

Develop and implement selection procedures (for example, applicant tracking, interviewing, reference and background checking).

RESPONSIBILITY

Knowledge 19

Interviewing techniques (for example, behavioral, situational, panel).

KNOWLEDGE

The Selection Process

After you've put together a pool of candidates who—at the very least—meet the minimum qualifications for the position, the recruiting process is essentially complete. At this point, the selection process can begin.

The Employment Application

In most cases, candidates submit résumés during the recruiting process. (This may not be true for all positions, such as for certain entry-level positions.) From the candidate's perspective, résumés are essentially advertisements that are designed to get the candidate's foot in the door. This statement is actually quite literal because the candidate's goal at this point is to be invited for an interview.

Résumés: Fact or Fiction?

A résumé is often written by someone other than the candidate who is submitting it —someone who may have great skill at presenting the candidate in the best possible light and can perhaps make the candidate look stronger than she actually is. Résumés can also be created as the product of highly structured and preformatted software programs. These programs provide a host of possible qualifications, accomplishments, and responsibilities for hundreds of different positions that a candidate can choose to include in her résumé. Although software such as this can be helpful in constructing a résumé, it can also enable candidates to craft résumés that are not wholly reflective of reality. In other words, candidates can end up appearing much better on paper than they actually are in person.

HR professionals and hiring managers must recognize that although résumés are intended to provide a record of candidates' employment, education, skills, and job-related experiences, they are sometimes more "story" than "history." In addition, there is nothing on the résumé itself that requires the candidate to formally attest to the truthfulness of its contents—so relying on it to make employment-related assessments (beyond selecting whom to interview) may be ill advised.

In addition to requesting a résumé, most organizations require candidates to complete an application form, usually before being interviewed. Like all other recruiting and selection tools, the application must seek information that is job related and that is valid with respect to its ability to predict the applicant's ability to successfully perform the position.

Treating Applicants Differently —Proceed with Caution (Better Yet...Don't Proceed At All)

Some organizations may require some, but not all, candidates to complete an evaluation form before being interviewed. When this happens, individuals applying for "lower-level" positions are often more likely to be required to complete the application before the first face-to-face interview, whereas applicants for "higher-level" positions are sometimes more likely to be permitted to postpone that requirement until it is determined that they will move forward in the selection process. Although commonplace, this practice is potentially problematic on a number of levels. First, it is unfair and inconsistent. Second, if more women and people of color apply for lower-level positions (and are therefore required to complete an application form), this policy could have an adverse impact against women or people of color.

The EEOC considers the employment application to be a test—so be sure to scrutinize and assess it the same way you would scrutinize or assess any other test.

Types of Employment Applications

Employment applications provide a means for ensuring that all candidates present information about their work history, education, and experience—in a consistent format. Be careful on this point, however, especially if the same organization operates in different states in which different laws might be in effect. In addition, different types of applications are sometimes used for different types of positions within the same organization. This practice is generally considered to be permissible as long as similarly situated applicants are required to complete the same type of application form at the same point in the selection process.

Short-Form Employment Applications

Short-form employment applications are shorter versions of an organization's standard employment application. In this sense, the word "short" is used in a relative sense; even the short-form application could still be several pages in length.

Short-form employment applications may be used as a prescreening tool or for certain "lower-level" positions within the organization that require fewer, less complex, or less technical skills. Short-form employment applications could also be used at an early phase in the selection process. In this case, candidates who progress to a later stage of the selection process might be required to complete a longer application at that time.

Long-Form Employment Applications

Long-form employment applications require candidates to provide more detailed and comprehensive information.

Job-Specific Employment Applications

Job-specific employment applications are sometimes used when an organization does high-volume recruiting for a particular position or for particular types of positions. In such cases, the application would be tailored to seek highly specific and relevant information pertaining to the specific position or job category for which the candidate is seeking employment.

Weighted Employment Applications

Weighted employment applications are intended to facilitate the process of evaluating candidates' qualifications in a consistent and objective manner by assigning relative weights to different portions of the application. These different weights will vary depending on the relative importance of each section, as determined by the requirements of the position.

> **NOTE**
>
> Weighted employment applications are difficult and time consuming to create and maintain because positions are almost constantly evolving and changing in some way. They can also run afoul of EEO guidelines (for example, if extra credit is granted for factors that are not truly related to the job or that are not as important/unimportant as the weighting might imply).

Critical Parts of the Employment Application

Whatever type of employment application an organization chooses, many applications share a variety of elements. As such, the application will often require the candidate to provide information relative to the following areas:

- Personal data (name, address, contact information)
- Education
- Training
- Credentials/certificates/job-related skills
- Employment history (including organizations, dates of employment, titles, supervisors' names, and reasons for leaving prior positions)

- Names of professional references

- The candidate's ability to provide proof during the first three days of employment of her identity and eligibility to work in the United States (in the event that she is hired)

The application also serves as a vehicle to formally secure permission from or communicate information to the candidate—and to require the candidate to acknowledge the granting of that permission or the receipt of that information by signing the application. Examples of this might include

- Permission to verify information provided on the application.

- Permission to check references (former employers, supervisors, or professional references).

- Employment-at-will statement. This statement articulates and reaffirms that in almost every state the organization can terminate the individual's employment at any time, with or without cause. Most employment applications also confirm and articulate that the employee also has the right to leave the organization at any time, with or without notice.

- EEO statement (and, if applicable, affirmative action statement).

- Acknowledgement that the organization reserves the right not to hire the candidate if it is determined that he has provided any information that is not truthful.

- Acknowledgement that the organization may, or will, terminate candidacy or employment if it is determined (before or after the candidate has been hired) that she provided any information on the application that was not truthful at the time the application was completed.

NOTE

Whoever accepts applications from the candidate (whether electronically or face to face) must ensure that the application is fully completed before it is accepted. What this means, in practice, is that the candidate may not write the words "see résumé" on any portion of the application. It also means that all questions have been answered completely. Sometimes candidates will leave a question blank that they do not want to answer. This way they can still attest to the truthfulness of the information they have provided on the application but attempt to avoid the sanctions that can stem from lying on an application.

Interviews and the Interview Process

From the perspective of the candidate, the purpose of a résumé is to get a job interview. From the perspective of the organization, the purpose of a résumé is to decide whom to interview. Taking this a step further, the purpose of an interview is to collect information that will enable the interviewer and the organization to determine the degree to which each candidate possesses and demonstrates the knowledge, skills, abilities, and other job specifications required to successfully perform the position.

Interviewing is one of those skills that many people learn by observation or through independent practice. Unfortunately, however, this skill is too critical to be learned through osmosis—in other words, the "sink or swim" approach doesn't always work. Sometimes what happens instead is that interviewers will learn to swim but will swim poorly (and perhaps even risk drowning —themselves, and maybe even others). In addition, sometimes the people whom new interviewers observe (and emulate) may not be skilled in the process.

Increased knowledge about and skill in interviewing can have a significant impact on the quality of the selection process.

Styles of Selection Interviews

Interviews fall into two primary types of styles—directive and nondirective.

- **Directive interviews:** Directive interviews take a more structured approach by asking consistent questions of all candidates. The interviewer maintains control of the interview—despite the fact that candidates sometimes make significant attempts to seize that control away from them.

- **Nondirective interviews:** Nondirective interviews are relatively unstructured. The candidate, not the interviewer, ends up guiding the interview and therefore ends up controlling the flow and content of information.

To Direct, or Not to Direct

Which style is better to use in selection interviews: directive or nondirective? Generally speaking, a directive style is more effective and appropriate than a nondirective style for a number of reasons:

- If a résumé is equivalent to a candidate's advertisement, giving a candidate control of the interview is like letting her broadcast an infomercial. Candidates will unfailingly present and highlight information that is most flattering to them—but that information won't necessarily coincide with the information that the interviewer needs to collect and assess relative to each candidate's ability to perform the job. It also isn't likely to be consistent with information provided by other candidates, which can lead to unfair and even flawed comparisons between candidates—comparisons that would be difficult to defend in the event of a legal challenge.

- To conduct a fair, reliable, and legally defensible interview, interviewers must ask candidates consistent questions. This is exceedingly difficult, if not impossible, to accomplish during a nondirective interview.

- Perhaps the most effective approach is a combination of both of these approaches—a combination that, in a sense, reflects the reality that selection interviewing is an art as well as a science. Developing a style that reflects a structured conversation ensures that all candidates are asked consistent questions, yet allows for related follow-up questions that keep the interaction lively, dynamic, revealing, and informative (all within a consistent and job-related context).

Types of Selection Interviews

There are a variety of selection interviews. In this section, we'll look at some of the better-known types of preemployment interviews:

- Phone interviews
- Prescreen interviews
- Behavior-based interviews
- Stress interviews
- One-on-one versus panel/team interviews

Phone Interviews

Sometimes organizations choose to conduct a short phone interview before deciding whether to bring a candidate onsite for a face-to-face interview. This can be particularly helpful in surfacing legitimate job-related "knock-out" factors that could either cause the employer to decide to eliminate a candidate from consideration or that could cause a candidate to self-select out of the selection process. Factors that might be discussed could involve job requirements (such as overtime or work conditions), salary requirements, or basic technical knowledge or skill, just to name a few possibilities.

> **NOTE**
>
> Phone interviews can be an efficient and effective way of showing respect for your candidates, your internal clients, and yourself. Just be certain to be consistent in the questions you ask each candidate—even at this point in the process.

Prescreen Interviews

In many organizations, HR conducts initial prescreening interviews with candidates. The purpose of prescreen interviews is to determine which candidates meet specific job requirements—the same ones that were identified in advance. This can include the process of verifying that the candidate actually meets the minimum requirements for the position and establishing whether the candidate meets other specific fundamental requirements. (We have used the word "actually" in light of the recognition, once again, that a résumé might be more "story" than "history.")

> **NOTE**
>
> Here, too, the HR professional has an opportunity to partner with line managers. Don't make assumptions about what qualifications you should try to assess during a prescreen interview; instead, work collaboratively with your clients to develop an effective, streamlined, cohesive strategy.

Behavior-Based Interviews

Behavior-based interviews require the candidate to describe past experiences that demonstrate the degree to which he possesses the knowledge, skills, and behavioral characteristics that are required to successfully perform the position for which the candidate is applying.

Behavior-based questions ask the candidate to describe a specific situation in which he demonstrated a particular job requirement. In his responses, the candidate should describe the situation, the specific way in which he behaved in the situation, and the outcome that resulted from his actions.

> **NOTE**
>
> Behavior-based questions are effective only if the candidate provides a thorough and complete answer. Candidates, however, often are not conditioned to respond in this way, so it's incumbent upon the interviewer to ask probing follow-up questions. Probing follow-up questions must focus on the original question and not allow the candidate to stray into a different area about which the candidate might prefer to speak. Probing questions must also be asked with the intention of getting the information the interviewer needs (the information that the original question sought to obtain), even if the interviewer doesn't get the information she wants.

Stress Interviews

During stress interviews, the interviewer (or interviewers) deliberately creates a high-stress environment in an effort to ascertain how the candidate would respond in a high-stress work situation.

Concerns Regarding Stress Interviews

There are (at least) two primary concerns with respect to stress interviews. First, interviewers run the risk of jeopardizing the degree to which they can ascertain all the other KSAs required for the position. In some jobs, where the ability to handle extreme levels of stress is essential and foundational (such as homeland security), this may be wholly appropriate. In other situations where extreme stress is a factor—but is not a constant, immutable, or defining element of a position—stress interviews may not be the most effective choice.

A second area of potential concern with respect to stress interviews is consistency. The interviewer must be certain that a consistent level of stress is created in each employment interview, that the stress that is created in different interviews is of a consistent nature, and that it is created in a consistent manner. Otherwise, the "stress test" element of the interview could be found to be inconsistent and, therefore, unreliable. This could, in turn, increase the possibility of a legal challenge or allegations of unlawful discrimination.

One-on-One Versus Panel/Team Interviews

Sometimes, for a variety of reasons, organizations choose to conduct panel or team interviews—interviews in which more than one interviewer interviews a candidate at the same time. Panel interviews can save time and money. They can also backfire. To help ensure that panel interviews are successful and productive, keep the following ideas in mind:

▶ Let the candidate know ahead of time that she will be participating in a panel interview. Eliminating the element of surprise will help prevent additional unnecessary anxiety.

▶ Plan—even choreograph—the interview in advance. Make sure all participants know their respective responsibilities. Plan who will ask which questions and how probing follow-up questions will be handled. Arrange for "hand-offs" from one interviewer to another, much the same way as is done during a team-based television newscast.

▶ Consider the seating arrangements. If possible, interview in a room that has a round table. If you must interview in a room with an oval or rectangular table, position the chairs in a way that creates the feeling of a round table. At all costs, avoid placing all the interviewers on one side of the table and the candidate on the other side of the table. It is also best to avoid placing the candidate at the head of the table when there are multiple interviewers, as this can lead to a "tennis match" need to continually look from one side of the table to the other.

Key Components of Selection Interviews

An interview is part science, part art, and part architecture. The interview process must be carefully structured to support its overall purpose: to provide the interviewer and the candidate with information that can be used to make accurate assessments and, ultimately, sound decisions. The interviewer needs to assess the degree to which the candidate possesses the qualifications for the position. The candidate needs information to make an informed decision about whether to join the organization in the event that an offer of employment is extended.

And, throughout all of this, interviewers have to be careful not to give away the answers before they even ask the questions. (This becomes particularly important when an organization uses a sequential interview process.)

Although there is no single best way to structure an interview, the following presents one effective approach.

1. Establish Rapport

It's important to help the candidate feel welcome at the beginning of the interview. Establishing rapport through a warm greeting, an offer of a glass of water, or brief "chit chat" about the weather can help the candidate to relax—and, in turn, hopefully summon more candid, honest responses.

CAUTION

Rapport-building is a way of breaking the ice—just be careful that you don't fall though. Don't let your chit chat stray into areas about which you should not be conversing with candidates. Avoid, for instance, discussions about children, hobbies, mode of transportation, world events, or political happenings. Don't allow the conversation to stray into small talk that would reveal information that is unrelated to the position.

In addition, recognize and remember that you will (hopefully) be interviewing a diverse pool of candidates and may encounter individuals who dress, speak, behave, or interact in ways that are different from your own. A candidate, for instance, may choose not to shake your hand or may choose not to make eye contact with you. Don't inappropriately read into these or any other potentially unexpected behaviors. Be open and inclusive of these differences, and make sure you base your assessments solely on job-related factors.

2. Ask Primary and Probing Questions

Primary questions are asked of all candidates for a particular position during a particular interview process. They are designed to elicit relevant information about how well the candidate possesses and can demonstrate the skills, knowledge, and behavioral characteristics required to perform the position successfully.

Probing questions are the follow-up questions to those primary questions. Because they are asked in response to each candidate's initial response to a primary question, probing questions will vary from interview to interview. Interviewers can still ensure consistency, however, by only asking probing questions that relate to the original primary question. Don't get derailed by an evasive candidate, an interesting tangent, or a candidate's inability to answer the original primary question.

NOTE

Probing is a double-edged sword. We need to probe until we get what we need, not until we get what we want. Make sure that your probing stays focused on the original primary question, and don't get distracted or derailed. Furthermore, after you get the answer to your primary question, stop probing. Be particularly careful not to let your curiosity get you to probe too deeply.

3. Invite the Candidate to Ask Questions

After you have finished asking your primary and probing questions, invite the candidate to ask you any questions she might have. It is important to provide this opportunity only after you have asked your questions to ensure that the candidate does not obtain information from you that will enable her to better answer your questions. In other words, as already mentioned, interviewers need to be careful not to give away the answers before they even ask the questions.

NOTE

A candidate's questions can also provide insight into his motivations, professional interests, or the seriousness with which he is approaching the job search. Pay careful attention to what you hear. Be equally careful not to be overly impressed by well-developed questions; many candidates understand that one of the rules of interviewing is to have good questions prepared in advance. Remember that there can be a vast difference between a candidate's ability to interview well for a job and a candidate's ability to perform the job for which he is interviewing.

4. Realistically Describe the Position and the Organization

Provide each candidate with complete, honest, realistic, and consistent information about the position and the organization. Ensure that you share information in a consistent manner with all candidates—those in whom you preliminarily think you might be more interested, as well as those in whom you think you might be less interested. "Pitching" the position more positively or enthusiastically to one candidate over another could raise questions later about why you did not share information in a consistent manner and why you chose to encourage or discourage particular candidates.

TIP

The interview is a time to collect information—assessment comes later. Maintain an open mind about all candidates at this point, and focus on what is taking place in the actual interview. Evaluate the information you collect during the interview after it's over. During the interview, make a conscious effort not to be distracted by anything that might cause you to make a snap judgment about the candidate or about her qualifications for the position. Recognize any such items/distractions and set them aside to think about later—after the interview is over. Remaining nonjudgmental and remaining "in the moment" are two of the most important keys to being an effective interviewer.

5. Close the Interview

In that same spirit, end all your interviews in a consistent and nonjudgmental manner. Let the candidate know what will happen next in the process, and provide the candidate with a reasonable time frame during which he can expect to hear back from you. Make no promises, offer no assessments, and provide no "feedback" relative to how the candidate performed during the interview. An interviewer's role is one of information gatherer, not career counselor (at least with respect to external candidates). And any career counseling for internal candidates should take place after the interview/selection process is completed—not during the actual process.

Essential Intrapersonal/Interpersonal Skills Required to Conduct an Effective Interview

Within this structure, interviewers must bring the interview to life. They must use their skills—interpersonal and otherwise—to attain a variety of goals, including ensuring the following:

▶ All needed information is obtained.

▶ All interviews are conducted in a consistent manner and yield consistent information.

▶ The interview is positive, upbeat, and affirming and does not assume a robotic tone.

▶ The rapport that was established at the beginning of the interview is maintained—or, as necessary, rebuilt—throughout the interview.

- ▶ They do not allow personal feelings or biases that are unrelated to the position to enter into the interview process.

- ▶ They remain within both the letter and the spirit of the law.

The following section highlights some of the skills essential for conducting an effective interview.

Intrapersonal/Interpersonal Skills

Listen carefully, attentively, and effectively. Paraphrase what you hear the candidate saying. When you do, preface your statements with phrases like these:

- ▶ "What I think I hear you saying, and please feel free to correct me if I am mistaken, is…"

- ▶ "So what I'm getting from you on this point, and please let me know if I'm on track with this, is…"

- ▶ "Let me know if I've heard this correctly… …"

In this way, you actually give the candidate permission to correct your understanding (something that most candidates are probably reluctant to do). You invite them, essentially, to tell you if you're wrong. This approach—and any clarifying information that you elicit from candidates—will help you attain your objective of ensuring that you leave the interview with an accurate understanding of each candidate's qualifications for the position.

Nonverbal Communication Cues ("Nonverbals")

Observe each candidate's nonverbal behavior. When you notice a significant change in that behavior, pay attention and consider probing for more information around whatever question the candidate was answering when that change occurred. Be careful not to assign specific meaning to any specific gesture. For instance, folding one's arms across one's chest may not necessarily mean that a candidate is distant, aloof, or "hiding something." In reality, it may simply indicate that the candidate is cold (literally, not figuratively). And be careful that any probing questions you ask remain strictly job related. Curiosity has the potential to land an employment interview in hot water.

It's also important to be aware of the messages that you may be transmitting to candidates through your own nonverbal behavior. Try to convey openness through your posture and movements. Deliberately use your nonverbal communication cues to encourage the candidate's engagement. Make sure you do not unintentionally communicate any sort of judgment—either positive (for example, through nodding) or negative (for example, through a frown or furrowed brow).

Take Notes

During the interview, jot down keywords or phrases that the candidate offers in response to your primary and probing questions. If you leave whitespace in between your list of questions, you'll have a convenient place where you can jot down keywords that pertain to the specific questions you are asking. Be careful not to take too many notes—this could detract from your connection with the candidate. You can—and should—go back after the interview is complete to fill in any gaps and details that will provide a more complete picture around the key words that you already wrote down.

> **NOTE**
>
> It's important to let the candidate know at the beginning of the interview that you will be taking notes. Otherwise, the minute you jot something down, the candidate may assume that she said something "wrong" and may spend time and energy trying to determine what that was and how she can back her way out of whatever she shouldn't have said. When you let the candidate know you will be taking notes, you can use it as a rapport-building opportunity. Let the candidate know, in your own words, that what she'll be telling you during the interview is important, and you want to be sure that you accurately capture, and remember, what she says.

> **NOTE**
>
> All notes must be strictly job related. Do not use any sort of code that will help you recognize individual candidates. In addition, do not take any notes on the résumé; instead, use the whitespace that you have left between each of the primary questions you prepared (including two or three questions on each 8-1/2 by 11 sheet of paper serves as a good starting point).

Manage Your Biases: Individual, Organizational, and Societal

Although we each have the right to think or feel however we choose, we don't always have the right to act on those feelings. This is particularly true in an employment context and with respect to interviewing. Interviewers are human beings, and, like all human beings, we have biases. However, we should not make—and are often barred by law from making—assessments or decisions that are based on those biases rather than on predetermined job-related factors.

As interviewers, it is incumbent upon us to vigilantly recognize how our individual biases could taint our assessments and decisions. Biases at the organizational level—and even at the societal level—could also affect our assessments and must be recognized, managed, and set aside.

Interviewers must develop the ability to recognize and eliminate from consideration factors that are not job related when making employment-related recommendations and decisions. These factors can relate to legally protected classes, such as a person's race or religion, or could relate to things that are (for the most part) generally unrelated to the law, such as a candidate's appearance, personal mannerisms, name, or even cologne.

Manage Your Biases: Interviewer Errors

Another category of interviewer bias warrants attention. These biases essentially constitute "errors"—meaning "errors in judgment"—that are sometimes made by interviewers. Interestingly, these errors are similar to those that are sometimes made by HR professionals or managers during the performance management and appraisal process. Learning to address and prevent these errors up front, therefore, can yield benefits throughout the entire employment life cycle. Table 2.2 describes some types of interviewing bias.

TABLE 2.2   Interviewing Bias or Errors

Types of Interviewing Bias or Errors	How It Manifests Itself in the Interviewing Process
Contrast	The interviewer compares candidates to each other instead of comparing them to the requirements of the position.
	Although it is essential to eventually compare candidates to each other, this comparison—by itself—can be misleading. Even the "best-qualified candidate" won't necessarily meet the requirements of the position. Becoming professionally enamored with a candidate because he is "the best of the bunch" could result in a substandard hire, and, ultimately, an unsatisfactory hiring decision. Before comparing candidates to each other, therefore, interviewers should compare each candidate's qualifications to the requirements of the position.
First impression	The interviewer places an inordinate level of emphasis on the impression that the candidate makes on her during the first few minutes or even seconds of the interview.
	It has been said that "first impressions last." Although the impression may last, that impression may be incorrect. At best, it is incomplete. Interviewers need to remind themselves that good candidates, at times, get off to a slow start during the interview. So, too, poor candidates may initially appear quite polished and impressive.
Halo	The interviewer evaluates the candidate disproportionately positively on the basis of one outstanding and impressive qualification or characteristic.
	This evaluation, however, is often incomplete and inaccurate. One positive quality or qualification—no matter how impressive it may be—is not reflective of all of the KSAs required to perform a position successfully.
Horns	The interviewer evaluates the candidate disproportionately negatively on the basis of one poor qualification or characteristic.
	This evaluation, however, is often incomplete and inaccurate. One negative quality or qualification—no matter how unimpressive it may be—is not necessarily reflective of all of the KSAs required to perform a position successfully.
Leniency	The interviewer applies an inappropriately lenient standard to one or more candidates resulting in a higher overall assessment of the candidate.
	Being "nice" to one or more candidates doesn't help the organization and is unfair to the candidate.
	Instead, an organization needs to hire qualified candidates to fulfill its mission and attain its overarching objectives. Extending offers to unqualified or less qualified candidates as a way of being "nice" undermines those efforts.
	In addition, it's important to keep in mind that a candidate who is invited to accept a position for which she is not truly qualified is, in one sense, being set up to fail.
Strictness	The interviewer applies an inappropriately harsh and demanding standard to one or more candidates, resulting in a lower overall assessment of the candidate.
	Being "strict" with one or more candidates doesn't help the organization and is unfair to the candidate.
	An organization needs to hire qualified candidates to fulfill its mission and attain its overarching objectives. Eliminating qualified candidates from consideration because of unrealistically high standards undermines those efforts.
	A candidate who is denied the opportunity to join the organization and perform a position for which he or she is truly qualified can end up with a negative impression of the organization. If enough candidates have an experience such as this and share it with enough individuals, the organization's reputation in the labor market could ultimately end up being damaged.

Recency	The interviewer recalls the most recently interviewed candidates more vividly than candidates who were interviewed earlier in the process.
	Again, this error allows unfairness to enter into the process. The random scheduling of candidate interviews should not result in any candidate being unduly favored or discounted.
Similar-to-me	The interviewer evaluates a candidate on the basis of how much that candidate is similar to, or different from, the interviewer.
	If interviewers recognize characteristics or attributes in candidates that they dislike about themselves, this recognition—whether conscious or unconscious—can have a negative impact on how the interviewer evaluates the candidate. Conversely, if interviewers recognize characteristics or attributes in candidates that they like about themselves, this recognition—whether conscious or unconscious—can have a positive impact upon how the interviewer evaluates the candidate. Either way, the impression is personal in nature, unrelated to the candidate's qualifications, and is therefore inappropriate.

Showing Respect Throughout the Recruiting and Selection Processes

Sometimes, in the heat of the recruiting and selection process, HR professionals overlook the reality that candidates are not the only ones being assessed or interviewed. At every stage of the recruitment and selection processes, candidates are paying careful attention to how they are treated by the employees with whom they come into contact. As such, professionalism is essential—as is discretion and respect. It might be helpful to remember the "golden rule" when it comes to how you treat a candidate.

Throughout the recruiting and selection processes, try to empathize with the candidate. For instance, ask yourself—if you were a candidate, what kind of voice-mail message would you like a potential employer to leave for you? Would you want a telephone interviewer to just jump into her questions, or would you prefer her to set up a time that is mutually convenient? And always remember that when you participate in the recruiting and selection process, you are representing more than just yourself individually. To candidates, you represent and define—to a significant degree—the entire organization.)

Legal Considerations for Interviewing and Selection

Interviewers need to be cautious not to wander intentionally or unintentionally into areas that present potential legal pitfalls.

The following tables (Tables 2.3 through 2.6) provide examples of questions you might consider asking during an interview and why they're permissible or not. It also suggests some questions you might want to ask instead.

For all the tables, the Color column corresponds to the following definitions:

▶ **Red:** STOP! Do not ask this question/make this statement. It is just generally not advisable, and which is likely to invite significant legal risk/exposure.

▶ **Yellow:** Proceed with caution. You may be asking a question/making a statement that could expose you to legal risk/exposure. Ask yourself, what do you really need to know, or what do you really want to say? If what you want to know or to say poses acceptable legal risk to you and to your organization, proceed. If not, ask the question in a different way.

▶ **Green:** Look both ways first, then ask the question or make the statement, as it is unlikely to raise significant legal risk/exposure.

TABLE 2.3   Rapport-Building

Question	Color	Potential Considerations/Concerns	Possible Alternative Phrasing
Your last name, Doe-Soprano-Rodriguez, is interesting. I've never seen a double-hyphenated last name before.	Red	**Legal** May elicit information about national origin. Depending upon state/ local laws, may elicit information about marital status. **Nonlegal** Likely to elicit information that is not job related. May allow the interview to get "off track." Less-than-optimal use of time.	There is no lawful way to rephrase this question. Instead, ask a different rapport-building question.
What a unique and interesting tie/pin. Is there a story or some special meaning behind it?	Yellow	**Legal** May elicit information that could reveal membership in a protected class, including (but not limited to) national origin, race, disability, marital status. **Nonlegal** Likely to elicit information that is not job related. May allow the interview to get "off track." Less-than-optimal use of time.	There is no lawful way to rephrase this question so that it is more appropriate. Instead, consider asking a different rapport-building question.
How was your trip here today? Were the directions okay?	Green	This is a permissible question.	(None)
The weather has been so warm lately, hasn't it? Maybe there really is something to this "global warming."	Yellow	**Legal** Speaking about weather is fine. Speaking about the climate, climate patterns, or global warming, however, introduces an issue that is more charged —politically, as well as emotionally. **Nonlegal** Likely to encourage conversation that is not job related and that may touch on strongly held beliefs that are irrelevant to the job.	"Is it still as humid outside as it was this morning?"
So, tell me a little bit about yourself.	Yellow	**Legal** Open-ended and nondirected, the question may unintentionally invite self-disclosures that could reveal membership in a protected class. **Nonlegal** Likely to elicit information that is not job related. May allow the interview to get "off track." Less-than-optimal use of time. Potential for "halo effect."	Think about what types of job-related "broad-based" questions might be more effective.

TABLE 2.4   Job Qualifications

Question	Color	Potential Considerations/Concerns	Possible Alternative Phrasing
What type of military discharge did you receive?	Red	**Legal** Unlawful to ask about the type or condition of military discharge.	There is no lawful way to rephrase this question. Candidates, however, can incorporate relevant skills and knowledge that they have gleaned from their military experience as they answer primary questions (that are being asked of all candidates for the position).
We strongly encourage associates to maintain work/life balance. To that end, what was the title of the last book you read that was unrelated to your work?	Yellow	**Legal** The titles —and contents —of books that a candidate reads could reveal information relative to membership in almost any protected class. **Nonlegal** Likely to elicit information that is not job related. May allow the interview to get "off track." Less-than-optimal use of time. Potential for "halo effect."	If the interviewer is concerned about ascertaining whether candidates for employment have maintained professional currency, ask a primary question like this, "Based on your review of current literature, what do you see as the top three challenges facing our industry/profession?"
I see that your name is Garcia-Menendez. Do you speak Spanish? Some of our clients are Spanish speaking.	Red	**Legal** Likely to elicit information related to national origin. **Nonlegal** If fluency in Spanish is required for the position, all candidates should be asked the same primary question about their proficiency in this area.	"This job requires the ability to read, speak, and write Spanish fluently. Can you meet this requirement of the position?" (Ask of all candidates at the same point in the interview process.)
I noticed that you are on the Board of the American Cancer Society. What skills have you developed from that role that could enhance your qualifications for this job?	Yellow	**Legal** The interviewer "opens the door" for the candidate to share information that could reveal membership in a protected class. **Nonlegal** Does not maintain a level playing field, as a question such as this does not give all candidates the opportunity to showcase relevant skills and qualifications (regardless of the volunteer activities that a candidate chooses to put on a résumé). Likely to elicit information that isn't job related. May allow the interview to get "off track." Less-than-optimal use of time. Potential for "halo effect."	Candidates can incorporate relevant skills and knowledge that they have gleaned from volunteer or community experience as they answer the primary questions that are being asked of all candidates for the position. It is more advisable to avoid asking specifically about any particular job or organization listed on a résumé —instead, consider allowing candidates to make their own meaningful, relevant connections.

Question	Color	Potential Considerations/Concerns	Possible Alternative Phrasing
Are you prevented from becoming legally employed because of visa or immigration status?	Red	**Legal** May reveal information relative to national origin (on a preemployment basis). **Nonlegal** Framed in a negative way.	"If hired, would you be able to prove your identity and eligibility to work in the United States?"

TABLE 2.5   Job Requirements

Question	Color	Potential Considerations/Concerns	Possible Alternative Phrasing
This job can require up to 30 hours of mandatory overtime each week, after regular business hours. Can you meet this requirement of the position?	Green	This is a permissible question.	(None)
This job requires some unplanned, but mandatory, overtime. To be quite candid, we've found that some associates with child or elder care responsibilities find this difficult. So, can you meet this requirement of the job?	Red	**Legal** Specifically links the job requirement to child/elder care responsibilities, which could elicit information revealing membership in a protected class (and that is unrelated to the job). That, in turn, could subsequently lead to an allegation of discrimination on the basis of gender or some other protected class.	"This job requires some unplanned, mandatory overtime. Can you meet this requirement of the position?"
This position requires periodic unplanned overtime. What would you do if you were called at home on the weekend and told to be at work within one hour to work the overnight shift?	Yellow	**Legal** The interviewer "opens the door" for the candidate to share information that could reveal membership in a protected class. **Nonlegal** Likely to elicit information that isn't job related. Hypothetical questions are less effective than behavior-based questions at predicting how a candidate will behave in this actual work situation. Behavioral characteristics play a key role in this job requirement.	First, be clear about what information you are trying to gather from the candidate. If you simply want to know if the candidate is available for periodic, unplanned overtime, ask: "This position requires periodic unplanned OT. Can you meet this requirement of the job?" However, if you are trying to get at a different behavioral characteristic (such as commitment or loyalty), be more direct with the question you choose to ask: "Tell me about a time when you went above and beyond your routine job requirements in response to a workplace situation."

Question	Color	Potential Considerations/Concerns	Possible Alternative Phrasing
This job requires lifting 10-pound boxes of paper about four hours each day. Do you have any conditions that would restrict you from meeting this requirement of the job?	Red	**Legal** May reveal a disability or a condition that could be regarded as a disability. **Nonlegal** "Conditions" that a candidate may have aren't important. What is important is whether the candidate can perform the essential functions of the position for which she is applying (with or without reasonable accommodation).	"This job requires lifting 10-pound boxes of paper about four hours each day. Can you meet this requirement of the position, with or without reasonable accommodation?" *Please note that an assessment should be made relative to whether the candidate could meet this requirement of the position "with or without reasonable accommodation." Seek additional assistance/input when making such determinations.
We operate 24/7 with frequent shift assignment changes. Do you have any obligations that would prevent you from working this type of variable schedule?	Yellow	**Legal** Likely to elicit information relative to membership in protected classes (such as disability or marital status). **Nonlegal** Likely to elicit information that is not job related and which could taint the interviewer's assessment of the candidate's overall ability to perform the job. May elicit information that, although not directly covered by law, could be related or linked to membership in a protected class.	"We operate 24/7 with frequent shift assignment changes, with little or no notice. Can you meet this requirement of the position?"

TABLE 2.6   Marketing the Position

Question	Color	Potential Considerations/Concerns	Possible Alternative Phrasing
Our company is committed to providing associates with the resources they need to grow and cultivates an environment where each associate can reach his full potential.	Green	The language used in this question is factual, appropriate, descriptive, and neither makes nor implies any promises relative to the length or nature of the employment relationship.	(None)
Our company makes a significant commitment to providing associates with ongoing learning and development opportunities, enabling them to add breadth and depth to their contributions.	Green	The language used in this question is factual, appropriate, descriptive, and neither makes nor implies any promises relative to the length or nature of the employment relationship.	(None)
Our company believes in maintaining a healthy work–life balance, and we offer a wide variety of programs to support that commitment.	Green	The language used in this question is factual, appropriate, descriptive, and neither makes nor implies any promises relative to the length or nature of the employment relationship, nor does it invite self-disclosures that could be unrelated to the job.	(None)

> **NOTE**
>
> Any preemployment conversations that candidates have must adhere to all legal guidelines—regardless of whether the conversations were held with HR professionals, managers, or potential colleagues. This includes any casual conversations that take place over meals, walking through hallways, or as part of rapport-building.

Realistic Job Previews

At some (consistent) point in the interview process, it is critical that candidates be given—and, perhaps more important, process and understand—a realistic picture of the position and the organization. This, in turn, will help the candidate make a realistic and accurate assessment of whether he will be willing and able to function effectively within the day-to-day realities of the position, the department or unit, and the organization. (In other words, it will help the candidate determine whether he is likely to "fit.")

> **NOTE**
>
> Different methods of communicating a realistic job preview (RJP) can be used at different phases of the interview process. Whatever techniques are used, however, must be used at a consistent point in the interview process, and in a consistent manner.

RJPs can be conveyed and communicated in a number of ways, including through

- ▶ Verbal descriptions of the work, the work environment, and the work conditions

- ▶ Facility tours

- ▶ The opportunity to read the employee handbook

- ▶ Opportunities to speak with current employees, particularly those who would be the incumbent's peers or colleagues

> **NOTE**
>
> Any and all employees who are involved in the interview process must be fully trained in how to conduct/ participate in preemployment interviews (and conversations) in a legally sound manner.

Background Checks

After the interview process is complete and any appropriate and relevant tests have been successfully completed, the final candidate(s) should be subjected to a rigorous background-checking process.

In a sense, conducting a background check is almost like starting the interviewing process all over again. This is sometimes easier said than done, especially because managers (and HR professionals) have invested a great deal of time, energy, and interest in the final candidate by this point in the process. It can be most challenging to open-mindedly embark upon a journey that might disprove what one believes one has already learned about the specifics of a candidate's employment history.

The person conducting a reference check must maintain—or regain, if necessary—a wholly objective perspective on the candidate. This person must be completely open to the fact that a reference check can yield a variety of possible outcomes. It could confirm, for instance, that the information that was collected through the interview (and testing processes, if relevant) was accurate. This is, of course, a good thing. Alternatively, the background check may reveal previously unidentified problems or concerns with the candidate's past performance or credentials. Because past performance is, in many ways, the best predictor of future performance, obtaining such information at any point before an offer of employment is extended is also a good thing.

Background checks can explore any or all of the following areas:

- **Work history:** Employers, dates of employment, titles, salaries, and performance records.

- **Academic records:** Degrees, diplomas, certificates, certifications, and the dates when they were earned.

- **Criminal background checks:** Many employers seek information relative to whether the final candidate(s) has been convicted of, pled guilty to, or pled no contest to a crime. In addition to identifying potentially serious performance issues, the organization may discover convictions related to prior instances of workplace violence.

> **TIP**
> In the event that you learn of a conviction at any point in the selection process, consult with senior HR leadership and counsel, as appropriate, before making any assessments, judgments, or decisions.

> **CAUTION**
> Remember, though, that an arrest is not a conviction and cannot be treated as such. In our justice system, individuals are innocent until proven guilty. Discriminating on the basis of arrest record could lead to adverse impact on the basis of race. From a nonlegal perspective, it could also lead to losing a really good candidate.

- **Driving history:** Employers may—and should—choose to review the motor vehicle reports for candidates who are applying for positions for which driving is an essential job function.

- **Credit history:** Employees who will have access to financial resources or who are entrusted with certain types of financial responsibility may be required to permit the potential employer to review their credit report.

> **CAUTION**
> Some organizations assert that there is a connection between a candidate's integrity and the candidate's credit rating. Other organizations assert that a candidate's individual financial habits provide insight into how that person would handle the organization's financial resources. Before implementing credit-checking procedures, consult with senior HR leadership and counsel, as appropriate, to ensure that these assumptions—along with all other reasons for requiring candidates to submit to a review of their credit report—are accurate and defensible in the event of a challenge. It is also critical to ensure that all activities relating to credit checks are conducted in a manner consistent with the Fair Credit Reporting Act.

RESPONSIBILITY

WPE Responsibility 12

Develop and extend employment offers and conduct negotiations as necessary.

RESPONSIBILITY

WPE Responsibility 13

Administer post-offer employment activities (for example, execute employment agreements, complete I-9/e-Verify process, coordinate relocations, and immigration).

RESPONSIBILITY

WPE Responsibility 14

Develop, implement, and evaluate orientation and onboarding processes for new hires, rehires, and transfers.

KNOWLEDGE

Knowledge 24

Employment policies, practices, and procedures (for example, orientation, on-boarding, and retention).

KNOWLEDGE

Knowledge 26

Negotiation skills and techniques.

Employment: Extending the Offer

The story doesn't end when you decide whom you want to hire—you still need to extend the offer. And then, of course, the candidate needs to decide whether to accept it. The way you extend the offer will say a lot to the candidate about the organization—not just about you. (One of the exciting and challenging things about interviewing allows us to be a part of something that is bigger than any of us individually. "You" represent more than just "you.") The way you extend an offer will also have a big impact on whether the candidate accepts the offer.

Tips for Extending an Employment Offer

Many organizations extend a verbal offer of employment over the phone and then follow that up with a formal written offer of employment. Other organizations meet with candidates personally and hand them an offer letter immediately upon extending an offer of employment.

Whichever method your organization uses, the manner in which an offer of employment is extended is important and must be approached with the same degree of care that has been infused into the rest of the preemployment process. The following are some particular considerations to keep in mind:

► Avoid expressing earnings in annual terms. Some organizations choose to indicate what the candidate would earn each pay period, whereas others choose to express earnings in monthly, daily, weekly, or even hourly rates.

- Be sure to take any potential FLSA-status ramifications into consideration when calculating "breakdowns" that are shorter than one week in duration.

- Avoid language that alludes to guarantees or assurances of earnings or ongoing employment or dates through which the employee will be paid.

- Avoid language that hints of any sort of a long-term employment relationship or that speaks of the employer as a "family." (Although not impossible, it's a lot harder to fire a family member than it should be to fire a noncontracted, "at will" employee. Don't make things more challenging by mixing metaphors. Work is work. Family is family. And, to that point, be careful not to hire anyone whom you cannot fire —especially if that person is a family member.)

- Use the offer letter as an opportunity to reaffirm that the employment relationship is "at-will," and—if counsel agrees—define what that means.

- State that the only agreements or promises that are valid are those that are included in the offer letter.

- State the date by which the candidate must either accept or decline the offer of employment. Ensure that you permit a reasonable period of time—not too much time and not too little.

In short, an overly exuberant offer of employment can cause more harm than good. Such letters must be carefully crafted, and counsel should review and approve the template for such letters before implementation.

Employment Contracts

Some organizations use employment contracts for individuals in certain (often "higher-level") positions. The contract addresses and outlines different aspects of the employment relationship and is binding on the organization as well as the employee.

Here are some of the boilerplate items that are likely to appear in an employment contract :

- Identifying information and contact information for the employer and the employee

- Position title, as well as the duties and responsibilities of the position

- Duration of the contract, or a specific statement that the contract is indefinite

- Type of compensation (salary, commission, and so on), frequency of compensation, and formulas for calculating compensation (if appropriate)

- Benefits, including vacation allotment

- Clauses covering terms of noncompete agreements, confidentiality, nonsolicitation of clients or customers, and so on

- Termination clause, which could include conditions under which the employee could be terminated, as well as any mandatory notice requirements that would apply

NOTE

Familiarize yourself with oral, written, implied, and express contracts as they pertain to the employment relationship.

Onboarding

Onboarding, formerly referred to as "employee orientation," refers to the process by which an employee is supported as she transitions into the organization. This support can—and should—be provided by HR as well as by the hiring manager, and it can encompass a number of different components including the following:

▶ Introduction (or, assuming the interview process was conducted effectively, "reintroduction") to the mission and overarching objectives of the organization, as well as how this position contributes to the fulfillment of that mission and the attainment of those objectives.

▶ Introduction (or, ideally, reintroduction) of the values of the organization.

▶ Discussion of the performance management system, in a macro as well as a micro sense. Macro would refer, for instance, to the structure and design of the performance management system, as well as expectations relative to how the employee will actively engage in the system. Micro might refer to each employee's specific goals or the competencies against which he will be evaluated.

▶ Personal introductions to coworkers and peers.

▶ A tour of the facilities. Be sure not to forget the rest room, copy machine, printers, and fax machine (if your organization still uses one) —the little things can make a big difference, especially at the beginning of the employment relationship.

▶ Review of safety guidelines.

▶ Review of "rules and regulations."

▶ Completion of required paperwork.

Unfortunately, many organizations still focus primarily or even exclusively on the completion of required paperwork rather than on critical nonadministrative elements, such as those inventoried here. This is not to imply that paperwork is not important. It is. But it's not enough. Work with managers to build an onboarding program that will capture and channel the nervous excitement that new employees often experience during their first days and weeks in a new job. Get the employee started in the right way. Make sure the employee's first days, weeks, and months on the job are positive, memorable, and meaningful.

The Importance of New Hire Paperwork

New-hire paperwork is very important—strategically, administratively, and even (potentially) legally.

Although the paperwork that newly hired employers are required to complete will vary from organization to organization, all employers are required to complete the I-9 form as part of IRCA requirements. A full and proper I-9 verifies identify, as well as eligibility to work in the United States.

Closely related to the I-9 form is E-verify, "an Internet-based system that compares information from an employee's Form I-9, Employment Eligibility Verification, to data from U.S. Department of Homeland Security and Social Security Administration records to confirm employment eligibility" (www.uscis.gov). E-Verify is a voluntary program for some employers and a mandatory one for others, such as federal contractors.

Wise employers —and HR professionals —will ensure that employees somehow acknowledge that their employment relationship is "at will." Employment-at-will is a common-law tort doctrine under which the employer and the employee are both granted broad rights, most of which focus on the right of either party to terminate the employment relationship at any time for any lawful reason. A number of important exceptions to the employment-at-will doctrine exist, including lawful reasons, public policy exceptions, wrongful terminations, and implied contracts.

Although everyone involved in the hiring /employment/termination process shares in this responsibility, HR must be particularly diligent about ensuring that a lawful, legitimate, nondiscriminatory reason exists and can be articulated when a decision to terminate an employee is being contemplated.

Noncompete Agreements

Many employers require newly hired employees to sign noncompete agreements, which prohibit current and (within stated limitations) former employees from competing against the employer. "Competing" can manifest itself in a number of ways and must be defined within the agreement, with language similar to this:

> The term "not compete" as used herein shall mean that the employee shall not own, manage, operate, consult, or be employed in a business substantially similar to or competitive with the present business of the company or such other business activity in which the company may substantially engage during the term of employment.

In return for signing the noncompete agreement, the employee is given the opportunity to work for the organization.

The strength, enforceability, and even legality of noncompete agreements depends on state and local laws, precedents that have been set by court cases, and a variety of other factors, such as these:

▶ Whether there is a time frame established in the agreement, and, if so, how long it is in effect

▶ The existence (and reasonableness) of any geographic limitation within which the employee cannot compete

▶ Whether there is anything in the agreement that would preclude the employee from earning a living in her chosen field

▶ Whether the employee is fairly compensated for signing the noncompete agreement, particularly if the employee was already employed at the time that he was asked to sign the agreement

Confidentiality Agreements

Newly hired employees are often required to sign confidentiality agreements . Confidentiality agreements prohibit employees from revealing any confidential information to which they might be exposed during the course of their employment. This could include trade secrets, patent information, and the like. It also prohibits employees from using confidential information in any way other than the purposes for which it was intended and is necessary within the context of the employee's job.

Relocation

As part of the employment/promotion process, some employers will move a current or existing (or, less frequently, newly hired) employee's primary residence from one location to another. Relocation happens more frequently in some organizations than in others. Organizations, and the HR professionals who work within them, must be familiar with relevant laws, policies, and past practices to ensure sound decision-making and consistent, nondiscriminatory treatment of employees.

Organizations may decide to outsource the administrative dimensions of relocation. This is often a strategic decision, and one that would be addressed more frequently at the SPHR level.

RESPONSIBILITY

WPE Responsibility 17

Develop and implement the organization exit/off-boarding process for both voluntary and involuntary terminations, including planning for reductions in force (RIFs).

KNOWLEDGE

Knowledge 22

Voluntary and involuntary terminations, downsizing, restructuring, and outplacement strategies and practices.

Termination: The End of the Employment Life Cycle...or Is It?

Terminations reside at the other end of the spectrum of the employment life cycle. They are often not given the degree of attention they deserve and require. Knowing how to effectively facilitate the process of employee terminations—whether voluntary or involuntary — is just as critical as knowing how to effectively facilitate the process of bringing employees into the organization. Whatever the reason or cause, an employee's exit from the organization should be just as positive and respectful as the onboarding process for that employee's replacement will be.

Involuntary Terminations

Involuntary terminations—regardless of the specific reasons for the terminations—are challenging. There are several types of involuntary terminations.

Layoffs

Most HR professionals—at one time or another in their careers—will participate in the process of laying off employees. No matter what you call them—downsizing, rightsizing, RIFs, or any of the other monikers in use these days—layoffs are never easy. The decision to lay off one or more employees should not be made lightly, and the manner in which the layoff is conducted is absolutely critical.

Determining Who Will Be Laid Off

Layoffs are handled differently in different organizations and under different conditions. When the employment relationship is governed by a collective bargaining agreement, the terms and conditions governing who will be selected for layoff will likely be clearly spelled out and are

137

Termination: The End of the Employment Life Cycle...or Is It?

usually heavily weighted toward seniority ("last in, first out," or LIFO). In the absence of a collective bargaining agreement, decisions relative to who will stay and who will go may be based less on seniority and more on skills, past performance, job function, or perceived potential.

> **NOTE**
>
> Before choosing to rely on performance appraisal information or ratings when making employment decisions, it is critical to ensure the integrity and accuracy of the performance system. Any number of rater or process errors could significantly skew performance ratings and could therefore diminish the legitimacy and defensibility of layoff decisions made under these assumptions. Don't assume that performance ratings are meaningfully and accurately calibrated across the organization—or even within a particular department. Instead, take a closer—and open-minded—look.

The Role of HR in the Layoff Process

HR's role in the layoff process can vary greatly from organization to organization. Often, HR professionals help prepare for the layoff in an administrative (transactional or "paperwork") capacity. This may include calculating severance pay or vacation entitlements or preparing COBRA paperwork. In addition, HR is often a primary source within the organization for information about outplacement services, in the event those services are being provided to assist employees as they transition out of the organization and as they begin the process of seeking new employment. (Outplacement support consists of resources and assistance provided to employees who are being involuntarily terminated for reasons unrelated to cause. The purpose of this assistance is to empower departing employees to find new employment. This could include résumé preparation, mock interviewing, networking assistance, coaching, and more.)

HR's role often extends beyond administrative responsibilities such as these. Sometimes HR professionals participate in meetings that are held with employees who will be terminated as part of the layoff. These meetings must be conducted with respect, consideration, empathy, integrity, and alacrity. This is a difficult situation for the employees who are leaving the organization as well as for the employees who are staying. It is also a difficult process for the managers and HR professionals who are involved in the process.

> **NOTE**
>
> As difficult as it may be, HR professionals cannot allow themselves to become lost in the emotional dimensions of the layoff process. Ultimately, all layoffs should occur because of business necessity, and only after all other viable options have been considered. As strategic business partners, however, HR professionals are called upon to participate in even the most difficult parts of carrying out that business strategy. We can, however, commit ourselves to performing this role in a compassionate and professional manner.

Those Who Remain

It's critical not to overlook those employees who are still employed after the layoff. Although these individuals have not been laid off, they did witness the layoff and are significantly affected by it. The impact on these individuals can be tangible as well as intangible. In a tangible sense, employees who are left behind may now face heavier workloads. They may also be concerned about their former colleagues and about what the future—both short term and long term—holds in store for them. Their fear of the unknown can be distracting and can significantly diminish morale. Also, employees who remain after a layoff may feel some degree of uncertainty and may even begin looking for employment elsewhere. If decisions relative to whom to lay off and whom to retain were made in part or in whole on the basis of performance, the organization risks losing its most valuable talent.

There is no single roadmap for handling this situation. Two tenets, however, should always be observed:

▶ Communicate clearly, frequently, and in a truthful manner. Credible communication about the layoff and its impact on the organization is essential to rebuilding some sense of comfort and security.

▶ No matter how much you might want to, and no matter how much you believe it, do not offer assurances or make promises to the effect that the layoffs are over or that no one else will be laid off. The reality of an employment-at-will relationship—particularly one that is not governed by a contract or other agreement—is that anyone can be let go at any time for any lawful reason. Make no promises that you cannot keep—and make no statements that could unintentionally create an implied contract.

You also might want to consider eliminating the term "survivor" when referring to "employees who remain." The term "survivor" implies that some did not "survive." Such language can serve to unintentionally escalate an already negative situation by overlaying unnecessarily dramatic language.

CAUTION

There aren't many "nevers" or "no brainers" when it comes to HR, but here's one: Never, under any circumstances, reveal the names of individuals who are on a layoff list unless and until you are explicitly directed to do so within the context of the overall communication strategy that has been developed. First and foremost, HR professionals cannot, under any circumstances, break the commitment to confidentiality with which they have been entrusted. Second, on a more practical note, such lists often change multiple times before the actual layoffs occur.

Other Involuntary Terminations

Many, if not most, employers have the legal right to terminate an employee at any time, for any lawful reason—or for no reason at all. In reality, however, using employment-at-will principles in a "willy-nilly" manner can seriously damage morale, diminish loyalty, increase turnover, and damage the employer's reputation in the labor market. It could also increase the likelihood of litigation.

Most of the time, the decision to terminate an employee is well thought out, carefully scrutinized, and based on legitimate performance-related issues. It should also be made only after whatever progressive discipline process is in place within the organization has been followed—and followed with the expectation, hope, and intention of empowering employees to bring about a positive outcome, rather than with the sole intention of creating a paper trail that will let you terminate an employee with a greater degree of comfort. (Although that is one possible outcome, it shouldn't be the initial objective.)

Managers—HR's clients—make termination decisions. Sometimes (and ideally) they make these decisions in conjunction with HR. At other times, they make these decisions independently and bring HR into the process only when it comes time to execute the decision. In either scenario, HR can add value to this process. Sometimes, when it appropriate to do so, HR can suggest alternative approaches. HR can also ensure that the termination has been made in accordance with the organization's policies and practices and that it is nondiscriminatory. At times, HR can also point out information that has been unintentionally overlooked, such as consistently positive performance appraisals in the file of a person who is being terminated for poor performance. In short, HR can provide a "second set of eyes" and can help managers think through this all-important business decision. Perhaps most importantly, HR can remind clients that counsel must be consulted before any layoff is implemented.

Voluntary Terminations

There are a number of reasons why an employee might decide to voluntarily terminate her employment with the organization. Among these could be the following:

- Acceptance of employment elsewhere ("other" or "different" employment, not necessarily "better" employment)
- Return to school
- Retirement, whether at an expected point in time, or earlier
- Avoidance of an anticipated involuntary termination
- Dissatisfaction with the current employer, manager, or job
- Health- or disability-related reasons
- Enrollment in the military
- Personal reasons (birth or adoption of a child, illness of a family member)

CAUTION

Early retirement can present a positive alternative to involuntary layoffs. Early retirement, however, presents multiple risks—in particular, the possibility of allegations of age discrimination. Consult with counsel before implementing any retirement program to ensure that the program is lawful and defensible in the event of a challenge.

Constructive Discharge

Constructive discharge does not fit neatly into either "voluntary" or "involuntary" terminations. It may, however, constitute wrongful discharge. (Wrongful termination happens when an employer discharges or dismisses an employee in violation of federal, state, or local laws or statutes. Wrongful termination/discharge is a tort doctrine that speaks to the employer having ended the employment relationship for wrongful reasons. One possible basis for wrongful termination could exist if an employee was terminated in violation of an individual employment contract. Others could apply as well and would vary from state to state. Wrongful termination can be related to discrimination, contract considerations, or other common law/tort violations.)

An employee who alleges constructive discharge asserts that she was subjected to such intolerable working conditions that remaining employed with the organization had become an impossibility. Essentially, the employee is saying that she was forced to quit. Claiming constructive discharge, however, does not make it so—instead, this must be proven.

Exit Interviews

HR's responsibility extends beyond replacing an employee who has been terminated, whether voluntarily or involuntary.

> **NOTE**
>
> Replacing an employee should not be a knee-jerk reaction in the wake of a termination. HR professionals are not order takers or order fillers and should not behave as such. Partner with your clients to explore creative options. Determine whether a position truly needs to be replaced. If it does, explore whether it should be replaced in its current form. Use terminations as an opportunity to revisit old assumptions and to support your clients by exploring new and creative approaches.

HR professionals are often called on to participate in the exit interview process. Exit interviews provide employers with an invaluable opportunity. If departing employees are assured—and if they believe—that their comments will not be attributed personally to them in any way, they will be more likely to provide candid and valuable feedback relative to their employment experiences with your organization.

Exit interviews should focus on job-related factors rather than feelings. An exit interviewer may want to ask for feedback relative to myriad topics, just a few of which could include the following:

- The interview and selection process and whether it provided a realistic and accurate depiction of the job

- The degree to which the employee felt as though he was making a valuable contribution that ultimately furthered, in some way, the mission of the organization

- The nature of the supervision received and the employee's relationship with her supervisor

- Training opportunities, and the degree to which the employee was truly encouraged (and permitted) to take advantage of those opportunities

> **CAUTION**
>
> Although some organizations conduct exit interviews using forms that the employee is asked to complete, many organizations find that in-person exit interviews yield more valuable results. The quality and the information provided will also be enhanced if the exit interviewer maintains a neutral and nonjudgmental demeanor during the interview—regardless of what the departing employee might say. In fact, many of the same intra personal and interpersonal skills that enhance the preemployment interview process can enhance the exit interview process.

Severance Packages

HR might also be called upon to create, and inform employees about, their severance packages. A severance package consists of monies (and, in some cases, other benefits) granted to an involuntarily terminated employee for reasons unrelated to individual performance in recognition of the end of the employment relationship and of the years that the employee worked for her employer.

RESPONSIBILITY

WPE Responsibility 18

Develop, implement, and evaluate an AAP as required.

Affirmative Action Plans

AAPs refer to programs created to overcome the effects of past societal discrimination by identifying areas of underutilization. AAPs may be required for Executive Order 11246, the Rehabilitation Act of 1973 (covered earlier in the chapter), and the Vietnam Era Veterans' Readjustment Assistance Act (VEVRAA) of 1974.

AAPs set forth (and require documentation of) good faith efforts to address and resolve that underutilization.

Any and all nonconstruction federal contractors and subcontractors are required to design and maintain formal AAPs for each of their establishments if they have 50 or more employees and any of the following is true:

 (i)   They have a subcontract of $50,000 or more.

 (ii) They have government bills of lading which, in any 12-month period, total or can reasonably be expected to total $50,000 or more.

 (iii) They serve as a depository of government funds in any amount.

 (iv) They are a financial institution that is an issuing and paying agent for U.S. savings bonds and savings notes in any amount (www.dol.gov).

> **NOTE**
>
> In 1967, EO 11375 was enacted, adding sex to the list of protected classes. In 1969, EO 11478 was enacted, adding age and people with a "handicap" to the list of protected classes. In 1998, EO 13087 was enacted, adding sexual orientation to the list of protected classes. Parental status was added as a protected class in 2000 through EO 13152.

Executive Order 11246

A good place to start your review is with the fact sheet that the DOL has developed: www.dol.gov/ofccp/regs/compliance/aa.htm.

It's important to familiarize yourself with all the elements of an AAP and, specifically, with how to prepare each of them. Some of the elements that are required to be in an AAP are detailed in the following sections.

Designation of Responsibility

This person—identified by name—is often an HR professional. He must have the necessary authority and resources to implement the AAP successfully. This must include the support of, and access to, top management. This is particularly important because the DOL is quite direct in its position that commitment to affirmative action should be an integral part of the organization's functioning rather than an administrative add-on.

Organizational Display or Workforce Analysis

Nonconstruction contractors must prepare an organizational profile, which can be presented as either the new "organizational display" or the older workforce analysis. The proposed organizational profile is a shorter, simpler format, which in most cases would be based on the contractor's existing organizational chart(s) to provide a depiction of the contractor's workforce. This profile is essentially an organizational chart that includes summary information about incumbents' race, gender, and wages. As per the DOL:

> "The Organizational Display is a detailed chart of the contractor's organizational structure. For each organizational unit, the display must indicate the following:
>
> ▶ The name of the unit and the job title, race and gender of the unit supervisor
>
> ▶ The total number of male and female incumbents and the total number of male and female incumbents in each of the following groups: Blacks, American Indians, Asians, Hispanics, and whites other than Hispanics"

Job Group Analysis

Nonconstruction contractors must also prepare a "job group analysis" intended to begin the process of comparing the employer's representation of women and minorities to the estimated availability of qualified women and minorities who are available to be employed.

Availability Analysis

The new regulations still require contractors to determine the availability of minorities and women for jobs in their establishments, compare incumbency to availability, declare underutilization, and establish goals to eliminate the underutilization.

Utilization Analysis

Availability is then compared to incumbency, and if the percentage of minorities or women is lower than the availability—"less than would reasonably be expected given their availability percentage in that particular job group"—the contractor must establish a "placement goal" (41 C.F.R. §60-2.15); that is, the contractor must set goals to correct the underutilization.

Placement Goals

Placement goals are established for areas in which underutilization exists. Placement goals must be pursued through good faith efforts—not through the establishment of quotas. The "bottom line" is that, when underutilization exists, the placement goal must be set at an annual percentage rate equal to the availability figure for women or minorities. (It may be necessary, at times, to set goals for particular minority groups where significant underutilization exists.)

Action-Oriented Programs

The employer must develop and execute action-oriented programs that are specifically designed to correct any problem areas and to attain established placement goals. These action-oriented programs cannot just be "more of the same" less than fully effective procedures that resulted in these problem areas in the first place. Instead, the employer must demonstrate good faith efforts to remove identified barriers, expand employment opportunities, and produce measurable results.

Identification of Problem Areas

The contractor must perform in-depth analyses of its total employment process to determine whether and where impediments to equal employment opportunity exist.

Internal Audit and Reporting System

The contractor must develop and implement an auditing system that periodically measures the effectiveness of its total affirmative action program. The following actions are identified by the DOL as key to a successful affirmative action program:

1. Monitor records of all personnel activity—including referrals, placements, transfers, promotions, terminations, and compensation—at all levels to ensure the nondiscriminatory policy is carried out.

2. Require internal reporting on a scheduled basis as to the degree to which equal employment opportunity and organizational objectives are attained.

3. Review report results with all levels of management.

4. Advise top management of program effectiveness and submit recommendations to improve unsatisfactory performance.

Vietnam Era Veterans' Readjustment Assistance Act, 1974

Vietnam Era Veterans' Readjustment Assistance Act (VEVRAA) requires employers with federal contracts or subcontracts of $25,000 or more to provide equal opportunity and affirmative action for Vietnam-era veterans, special disabled veterans, and veterans who served on active duty during a war or in a campaign or expedition for which a campaign badge has been authorized.

> **NOTE**
>
> Don't let the name mislead you—VEVRAA affords protection to veterans from other than the Vietnam era. Be familiar with the definitions of "special disabled veteran," Vietnam era veterans, and all other veterans covered by VEVRAA.

For purposes of VEVRAA, a Vietnam era veteran is a person who (1) served on active duty for a period of more than 180 days, any part of which occurred between August 5, 1964 and May 7, 1975, and was discharged or released with other than a dishonorable discharge; (2) was discharged or released from active duty for a service connected disability if any part of such active duty was performed between August 5, 1964 and May 7, 1975; or (3) served on active duty for more than 180 days and served in the Republic of Vietnam between February 28, 1961 and May 7, 1975.

VEVRAA requires employees with federal contracts or subcontracts of $100,000 or more must file a VETS-100A report by September 30 each year. The DOL has published the following information on the VETS-100 and VETS-100A forms.

Background

The U.S. DOL Veterans' Employment and Training Service (VETS) is responsible for administering the requirement under the Vietnam Era Veterans' Readjustment Assistance Act of 1974 (VEVRAA), 38 U.S.C. 4212(d), that federal contractors and subcontractors track and report annually to the Secretary of Labor the number of employees in their workforces who belong to the categories of veterans covered under the affirmative action provisions of the Act.

VETS has published implementing regulations at 41 CFR Part 61-250 that require federal contractors with a federal contract or subcontract of $25,000 or more that was entered into prior to December 1, 2003 to file a completed Federal Contractor Veterans' Employment VETS-100 Report form ("VETS-100 Report") annually.

The VETS-100 Report calls for federal contractors and subcontractors to report the number of employees and the number of new hires during the reporting period who are

(1) Special disabled veterans

(2) Veterans of the Vietnam era

(3) Veterans who served on active duty in the U.S. military during a war or a campaign or expedition for which a campaign badge has been authorized

(4) Recently separated veterans (veterans within one year from discharge or release from active duty)

The Jobs for Veterans Act (JVA), enacted in 2000, amended the reporting requirements under VEVRAA by increasing the dollar amount of the Federal contract and subcontract that triggers coverage and changing the categories of veterans that contractors and subcontractors are to track and report. The regulations at 41 CFR Part 61-300 implement the JVA amendments to the reporting requirements under VEVRAA and require federal contractors and subcontractors with a contract or subcontract of $100,000 or more awarded or modified on or after December 1, 2003, to file a VETS-100A Report.

Federal contractors and subcontractors completing the VETS-100A Report are to provide information on the number of employees and new hires during the reporting period who are

(1) Disabled veterans

(2) Veterans who served on active duty in the U.S. military during a war or campaign or expedition for which a campaign badge is awarded

(3) Veterans who, while serving on active duty in the Armed Forces, participated in a United States military operation for which an Armed Forces service medal was awarded pursuant to Executive Order 12985

(4) Recently separated veterans (veterans within 36 months from discharge or release from active duty)

Mandatory Job Listings

The OFCCP administers and enforces the affirmative action provisions of VEVRAA, which require federal contractors and subcontractors to employ and advance in employment qualified covered veterans. To implement the affirmative action requirement, VEVRAA and the implementing regulations at 41 CFR Part 60-250 and Part 60-300 issued by OFCCP require federal contractors and subcontractors to list most employment openings with the appropriate employment service delivery system, and each such employment service delivery system is required to give covered veterans priority in referrals to such openings. Executive and senior management positions, positions to be filled from within the contractor's organization, and positions lasting three days or fewer are exempt from the mandatory job listing requirement. Listing jobs with the state workforce agency job bank or with the local employment service delivery system where the opening occurs will satisfy the requirement to list job openings with the appropriate employment service delivery system. Additional information on the mandatory job listing requirement is available on the OFCCP website.

Affirmative Action

OFCCP regulations implementing VEVRAA also require certain federal contractors and subcontractors to develop and maintain a written AAP. The AAP sets forth the policies and practices the contractor has in place to ensure that its personnel policies and practices do not limit employment opportunities for covered veterans. The AAP also spells out the steps the contractor will take to recruit, train, and promote covered veterans. Additional information about the written AAP is also available on the OFCCP website.

Knowledge 20

Impact of compensation and benefits on recruitment and retention

KNOWLEDGE

Compensation and Benefits

HR professionals need to be familiar with how compensation and benefits relate to recruitment and retention. As with many areas we have explored, there are legal and nonlegal dimensions to this discussion.

Sherman Antitrust Act, 1890

The Sherman Antitrust Act of 1890 was a law that was passed in an effort to curb the growth of monopolies. Under the Act, any business combination that sought to restrain trade or commerce would from that time forward be illegal. Specifically, the Act states that

▶ **Section 1:** "Every contract, combination in the form of trust or otherwise, or conspiracy, in restraint of trade or commerce among the several States, or with foreign nations, is declared to be illegal."

▶ **Section 2:** "Every person who shall monopolize, or attempt to monopolize, or combine or conspire with any other person or persons, to monopolize any part of the trade or commerce among the several States, or with foreign nations, shall be deemed guilty of a felony."

The Sherman Antitrust Act is relevant to compensation's impact on recruitment and retention because an improperly conducted salary survey (or even information attempts to gather data on competitor's wage rates) can constitute a violation of this Act.

Equal Pay Act, 1963

The Equal Pay Act of 1963 prohibits discrimination on the basis of sex in the payment of wages or benefits to men and women who perform substantially equal (but not identical) work, for the same employer, in the same establishment, and under similar working conditions. (An establishment generally refers to one specific physical location.) Similar to the way in which the Fair Labor Standards Act (FLSA) status is determined, substantial equality is determined by job content, not job titles.

Compensation Strategies

An often-embraced "default" position is that an organization "should" pay more than any other labor market competitor. This is not, however, the only option, nor is it necessarily the best option. Rather, there are three potentially valid strategies to consider, as discussed in this section.

Lag the Market

This is a compensation strategy in which an organization chooses, by design, or simply because of budgetary constraints, to offer total compensation packages that are less competitive than the total compensation packages that are being offered by their labor market competitors. Organizations that lag the market might offset this potential disadvantage by reinforcing and maximizing the intrinsic rewards that it offers—long-term potential growth opportunities, the ability to contribute to a particularly significant organizational mission, and so on.

Lead the Market

This is a compensation strategy in which an organization offers total compensation packages that are better than packages being offered by their labor market competitors. Organizations that lead the market may believe that higher compensation packages will attract higher-performing employees who will, in turn, pay for themselves, and then some. In short, these organizations want the best of the best and are willing to pay for it.

Match the Market

This is a compensation strategy in which an organization chooses to offer total compensation packages that are comparable to the total compensation packages being offered by their labor market competitors. Organizations that match the market make a conscious choice to be "externally competitive" with respect to total compensation.

RESPONSIBILITY

WPE Responsibility 19

Develop and implement a record retention process for handling documents and employee files (for example: pre-employment files, medical files, and benefits files).

Documentation Strategies for HR Professionals

This particular responsibility, perhaps more than any other responsibility addressed in this chapter, takes a high -level overview of this portion of our function. By this, we mean that the records that must be maintained will vary —by law, by industry, by state, by jurisdiction —and by a dozen other factors.

Within an organization, maintaining documentation is dreaded by many, postponed by most, enjoyed by few, and viewed suspiciously by others. HR's role in establishing and maintaining legal and effective documentation practices is particularly pivotal.

With respect to WPE-related record keeping, HR is responsible for maintaining much of the information and documentation required to ensure compliance with federal, state, and local laws. A few examples of some of these record-keeping requirements stemming from this functional area include, but are in no way limited to, applicant flow data, veteran status, AAP-related data, and I-9 reporting.

A primary takeaway for this responsibility is that HR professionals must take great care in ensuring that they learn, know, and follow the unique retention requirements to which they are subject. This is not a responsibility that can be performed intuitively, nor is it one that can be adequately addressed within a book of this scope.

Also, keep in mind that maintaining documentation means more than just "being organized." In a sense, this responsibility can be a "Catch-22" for HR professionals. By definition, the actions associated with maintaining documentation are transactional. They are not strategic in nature. They are also driven, in large part, by compliance requirements. But if we don't perform this portion of our job well, it is unlikely that we will be given the opportunity to perform functions that are more strategic in nature. Why? One reason is fairly self-evident: if we cannot demonstrate the ability to successfully execute tasks of a more mundane and administrative nature, it is unlikely that we will be entrusted with initiatives that are more strategic or visible. The second reason can become painfully obvious: documentation, when mishandled, can lead to very real and tangible costs (human, as well as monetary) to the organization. These costs can, and often do, have a strategic impact.

Some documentation basics that HR professionals need to think about include these:

- **Know what needs to be documented:** This includes federal, state, and local requirements—as well as documentation mandated by collective bargaining agreements, employment contracts, and performance management programs.

- **Know how to document:** Many forms must be completed in accordance with specific, detailed, and mandatory guidelines. Those specific requirements can also impact the ways in which documents are maintained, stored, retrieved, and distributed.

- **Know what not to document:** Documentation takes two main forms—documentation that pertains to collecting and maintaining legally mandated record keeping, and documentation that pertains to performance management (in the broadest sense of that term). For purposes of this discussion, our focus will remain on the first type of documentation.

Here are some hands-on ideas to consider:

- Set up streamlined processes and procedures for handling routine and repetitive documentation requirements.

- Utilize technological tools, as appropriate and helpful.

- Maintain ongoing awareness of evolving laws and regulations to ensure they maintain continual compliance with potentially changing regulations.

- Incorporate fail-safe mechanisms into those processes. Even in the best-designed systems, it's inevitable that things will go wrong. Make sure there is a way to identify and resolve insufficient or noncompliant documentation.

- Look for ways to use existing documentation more strategically. Ascertain how you can turn data into information and how you can use that information as you work to earn, or maintain, a seat at the table.

Employment Litigation Is No Laughing Matter

There's an old joke that goes something like this:

Question: "What's the difference between true love and employment litigation?"

Answer: "Employment litigation lasts forever."

In truth, there is nothing funny about employment litigation. However, there's a valuable reminder that can be taken away from this quip: any written or electronic communication you create, in any form, is—for all intents and purposes—forever subject (potentially) to subpoena. This is particularly true for electronic communications—emails and even instant messages. Our most contemporary communications are, in some ways, even more permanent than the stone tablets of ages gone by—so be extremely prudent and careful about the documentation you maintain. You may one day have the opportunity to review it again—in a courtroom, in front of a jury, or on the front page of a newspaper.)

NOTE

The following WPE Responsibilities/Areas of Knowledge—WPE Responsibility 16 and Knowledge 21—are not covered in this book because they are covered in Pearson's SPHR Exam Prep.

RESPONSIBILITY

WPE Responsibility 16

Develop, implement, and evaluate the succession planning process.

KNOWLEDGE

Knowledge 21

International HR and implications of global workforce for workforce planning and employment.

Chapter Summary

Responsibilities relating to workforce planning and employment provide HR professionals with the opportunity to have a lasting impact on the organization. Whether this impact is positive, however, depends in large part on the way in which HR professionals execute these responsibilities.

To function successfully with respect to the functional area of workforce planning and employment, HR professionals must develop an understanding of and an appreciation for equal employment opportunity (EEO).

It's also critical for HR professionals to understand the many laws and cases that shape this functional area and to commit to maintaining currency with respect to emerging cases that offer additional interpretation, and reinterpretation, of these laws. In addition, HR professionals must be prepared to contribute meaningfully to ensuring that the organization will be able to meet its future goals by making sure the right people, with the right skills, are in the right places at the right times.

The ability to execute this functional area effectively is also predicated on knowing and understanding the organization's strategic plan. HR professionals who have already earned a "seat at the table" in their organization are likely to have a good grasp of where the organization is going. HR professionals must proactively seek opportunities for learning about the organization's long-term objectives. Unless we do, our efforts may be less productive, less relevant, less valued, and less impactful.

Ultimately, the choice of how we will perform in this area rests with us. The choices that we make will go a long way toward defining how we are perceived by the organization, our overall effectiveness in the organization, and the degree to which we will participate in a transformational manner within the organization.

Key Terms

- Workforce planning and employment (WPE)
- Executive orders
- Title VII of the Civil Rights Act, 1964
- Bona fide occupational qualification (BFOQ)
- Seniority systems
- Piece-rate systems
- Protected classes
- Equal Employment Opportunity Commission (EEOC)
- Executive Order 11246, 1965
- Office of Federal Contract Compliance Programs (OFCCP)
- Uniform Guidelines on Employee Selection Procedures (UGESP), 1978
- Adverse impact (also known as " disparate impact")
- Reliability
- Validity
  - Content validity
  - Criterion- related validity
  - Construct validity
  - Predictive validity
- Age Discrimination in Employment Act (ADEA), 1967
- Fair Credit Reporting Act (FCRA), 1970
- Equal Employment Opportunity Act, 1972
- Rehabilitation Act, 1973
  - Section 503

- ▶ Section 504
- ▶ Section 508
- ▶ Pregnancy Discrimination Act, 1978
- ▶ Immigration Reform and Control Act (IRCA), 1986
  - ▶ I-9 form
- ▶ Drug-Free Workplace Act, 1988
- ▶ Department of Labor (DOL)
- ▶ Worker Adjustment and Retraining Notification Act (WARNA), 1988
  - ▶ Mass layoff
  - ▶ Plant closing
- ▶ Americans with Disabilities Act (ADA), 1990
  - ▶ Individual with a disability
  - ▶ Qualified person
  - ▶ Reasonable accommodation
  - ▶ Undue hardship
  - ▶ Major life activities
- ▶ Civil Rights Act of 1991
  - ▶ Compensatory damages
  - ▶ Punitive damages
- ▶ Family and Medical Leave Act (FMLA), 1993
  - ▶ Covered employers
  - ▶ Eligible employees
  - ▶ Leave entitlement
  - ▶ Serious health condition
- ▶ Uniformed Services Employment and Reemployment Rights Act (USERRA), 1994
- ▶ Department of Justice
- ▶ Congressional Accountability Act (CAA), 1995
- ▶ Americans with Disabilities Act Amendments Act (ADAAA), 2008
  - ▶ Qualified exigency leave
  - ▶ Military caregiver leave
- ▶ Genetic Information Nondiscrimination Act (GINA), 2008
- ▶ Lilly Ledbetter Fair Pay Act, 2009

- ▶ *Griggs v. Duke Power, 1971*
- ▶ *McDonnell Douglas Corp v. Green, 1973*
- ▶ *Albemarle Paper v. Moody, 1975*
- ▶ *Washington v. Davis, 1976*
- ▶ *Regents of California v. Bakke, 1978*
- ▶ *United Steelworkers v. Weber, 1979*
- ▶ *Meritor Savings Bank v. Vinson, 1986*
- ▶ *Johnson v. Santa Clara County Transportation Agency, 1987*
- ▶ *Martin v. Wilks, 1988*
- ▶ *Automobile Workers v. Johnson Controls, 1990*
- ▶ *Harris v. Forklift Systems, 1993*
- ▶ *Taxman v. Board of Education of Piscataway, 1993*
- ▶ *St. Mary's Honor Center v. Hicks, 1993*
- ▶ *McKennon v. Nashville Banner Publishing Co., 1995*
- ▶ *Faragher v. City of Boca Raton, 1998*, and *Ellerth v. Burlington Northern Industries, 1998*
- ▶ *Kolstad v. American Dental Association, 1999*
- ▶ *Grutter v. Bollinger* and *Gratz v. Bollinger, 2003*
- ▶ *Circuit City Stores, Inc. v. Adams, 2001*
- ▶ *General Dynamics Land Systems v. Cline, 2004*
- ▶ *Ricci v. DeStefano, 2009*
- ▶ Protected class
- ▶ Discrimination
  - ▶ Disparate (or "adverse") treatment
  - ▶ Disparate (or "adverse") impact
  - ▶ Bottom-line approach
  - ▶ "Four-fifths" rule:
  - ▶ Perpetuating past discrimination
- ▶ Harassment:
  - ▶ Sexual harassment
  - ▶ Quid pro quo sexual harassment
  - ▶ Hostile work environment sexual harassment
- ▶ Equal Employment Opportunity (EEO)

- Charge
- Charging party
- Complainant
- Plaintiff
- Respondent
- Fair Employment Practices Agencies (FEPAs)
- Reasonable cause
- Right to sue letter
- Relief
- Remedies
- Back pay
- Front pay
- Job analysis
- Job description
- Job specifications
- Job competencies
- Knowledge
- Skills
- Abilities
- KSAs
- Essential and nonessential job functions
- Job specifications (or "specs")
- Credentials
- Recruiting
- Selection
- Employer branding
- Relevant labor market
- Selection criteria
- Internal and external recruiting
- Job posting
- Job bidding
- Succession planning
- Social media
- Employment agencies
  - Employment agencies — state
  - Employment agencies —temporary
  - Private employment agencies (also known as private search firms

- Contingency employment agencies/ search firms
- Retained employment agencies/ search firms
- Employee referral
- Nontraditional staffing alternatives
- Outsourcing
- Request for Proposal (RFP)
- Preemployment testing
  - Agility tests
  - Aptitude tests
  - Assessment center
  - Cognitive ability tests
  - Integrity, or honesty, tests
  - Medical tests
  - Personality tests
  - Preemployment drug testing
  - Prepromotion drug testing
- Yield ratio
- Cost per hire
- Turnover analysis
- Employment application
- Résumés
- Short- form employment applications
- Long- form employment applications
- Job- specific employment applications
- Weighted employment applications
- Interview
  - Directive interviews
  - Nondirective interviews
  - Phone interviews
  - Prescreen interviews
  - Behavior-based interviews
  - Stress interviews
  - One-on-one versus panel/team interviews
- Nonverbal communication cues ("nonverbals")
- Interviewer errors
  - Contrast error

- First impression error
- Halo error
- Horns error
- Leniency error
- Strictness error
- Recency error
- Similar-to-me error
- Realistic job previews (RJP)
- Background checks
- Employment contracts
- Onboarding (also referred to as "employee orientation")
- Relocation
- Involuntary terminations
- Layoffs
- Voluntary terminations
- Constructive discharge
- Wrongful termination/ discharge
- Exit interviews
- Severance packages
- EAP

- Outplacement support
- Severance package
- Affirmative Action Plan (AAP)
  - Designation of responsibility
  - Organizational display or workforce analysis
  - Job group analysis
  - Availability analysis
  - Utilization analysis
  - Placement goals
  - Action- oriented programs
  - Identification of problem areas
  - Internal audit and reporting system
- Vietnam Era Veterans' Readjustment Assistance Act (VEVRAA), 1974
- VETS-100/VETS 100A
- Sherman Antitrust Act, 1890
- Equal Pay Act, 1963
- Lag the market
- Lead the market
- Match the market

Apply Your Knowledge

This chapter focuses on issues relating to workforce planning and employment. Complete the following review questions and exam questions as a way of reviewing and reinforcing the knowledge and skills you'll need to perform your responsibilities as an HR professional and to increase the likelihood that you will pass the PHR examination.

Review Questions

1. Describe directive and nondirective interviews. In general, which is the preferred approach?

2. What are some of the factors that need to be considered when using performance as a criterion for determining who will be let go in a layoff situation?

3. What are some best practices with respect to taking notes during an interview?

4. Describe sexual harassment that takes the form of a hostile work environment.

5. Define and describe the differences between a mass layoff and a plant closing (according to WARNA).

Exam Questions

1. Which of the following forms of discrimination is not covered by Title VII of the Civil Rights Act of 1964?

   ○ **A.** Age

   ○ **B.** Color

   ○ **C.** Race

   ○ **D.** National origin

2. Which of the following statements is true about quid pro quo sexual harassment?

   ○ **A.** It can be exacted by any employee on any other employee.

   ○ **B.** It creates a hostile work environment that can ultimately lead to constructive discharge.

   ○ **C.** It creates a situation in which an employee's terms and conditions of employment are affected by acceptance or rejection of sexual advances.

   ○ **D.** It cannot occur during the preemployment selection process because it refers to tangible or economic work-related consequences that, by definition, can be experienced only by current employees.

3. Which of the following employers would be required to prepare formal affirmative action plans?

   ○ **A.** Federal contractors who receive federal grants of any amount

   ○ **B.** Federal contractors with $50,000 or more in federal contracts

   ○ **C.** Federal contractors with at least 50 employees who have federal contracts of at least $50,000 per year

   ○ **D.** All federal contractors, regardless of the size or scope of the contract

4. In the event of a mass layoff or plant closing, WARNA requires employers to notify all the following individuals or entities except

   ○ **A.** Affected employees or their representatives (such as a collective bargaining unit)

   ○ **B.** The State Dislocated Worker Unit

   ○ **C.** The appropriate local government unit

   ○ **D.** The EEOC, which will conduct an adverse impact analysis before layoffs are implemented

5. A defining Supreme Court case for interpreting the Civil Rights Act of 1991 was

   ○ **A.** *Kolstad v. American Dental Association, 1991*

   ○ **B.** *Grutter v. Bollinger and Gratz v. Bollinger, 2003*

   ○ **C.** *St. Mary's Honor Center v. Hicks, 1993*

   ○ **D.** *United Steelworkers v. Weber, 1979*

6. A manager with whom you have not previously worked comes to you for help with implementing two different solutions she has come up with to fix a turnover problem in her department. This manager is highly regarded—and highly visible—in the organization. You are eager to perform well on this project because you are confident it will help you strengthen your relationship with her. You are also certain that the manager will tell her peers about her experience with you, which makes it particularly critical that you handle yourself well. Your first response should be to

- ○ **A.** Communicate your commitment to implementing the manager's solutions.
- ○ **B.** Offer alternative solutions based on experience you have had with similar situations.
- ○ **C.** Ask questions to obtain more information about the problems the manager is experiencing.
- ○ **D.** Ask questions to obtain information that will help you implement the manager's solution more effectively.

7. A properly conducted job analysis will produce all of the following except:

- ○ **A.** Job competencies
- ○ **B.** Job postings
- ○ **C.** Job specifications
- ○ **D.** Job description

8. Which of the following is not one of the main elements in a job description?

- ○ **A.** Scope information
- ○ **B.** Physical work conditions and physical demands
- ○ **C.** Compensation rates
- ○ **D.** Minimum requirements

9. Which of the following would be least likely to be considered a job competency?

- ○ **A.** Communication skills
- ○ **B.** Reading skills
- ○ **C.** Teamwork skills
- ○ **D.** Interpersonal skills

10. All of the following represent benefits of employee referral programs except

- ○ **A.** Highly cost-effective recruiting
- ○ **B.** Employees who are more likely to succeed
- ○ **C.** Demonstration of good faith efforts to remedy underutilization
- ○ **D.** Increased candidate familiarity with the organization

Answers to Review Questions

1. Directive interviews take a more structured approach. The interviewer(s) asks the same questions of all candidates and maintains control of the interview. Conversely, nondirective interviews are more conversational and relatively unstructured. In a nondirective interview, the candidate—not the interviewer—ends up controlling the interview and primarily determines what will be discussed.

   Generally speaking, a directive style is more effective and appropriate than a nondirective style because it yields more consistent results, facilitates the process of comparing candidates to the job requirements and to each other, and generally provides greater defensibility in the event of a legal challenge. Although the directive approach is the better one, the interview must still remain dynamic and interactive.

2. Before choosing to rely solely on employees' prior performance ratings to determine who should be laid off and who should be retained, the organization needs to carefully examine its performance appraisal system and assess its validity and overall worth. The system itself could be flawed, or—even if it is sound—there could be problems with the way in which individual raters have applied it over time. Either factor could result in misguided assessments, which could consequently diminish the legitimacy (and defensibility) of layoff decisions made on the basis of employees' past performance.

3. At the beginning of the interview—perhaps at the end of the formal "rapport- building" process—let the candidate know that you will be taking notes. The candidate may otherwise assume that she has said something wrong the minute your pen hits the paper. Letting the candidate know you will be taking notes can actually constitute another element of rapport- building: you are interested in and care about what she is going to tell you and want to be certain that you remember it correctly.

   Note taking should not interfere in any way with the interview process. It also should not diminish the personal connectedness that the interviewer establishes with the candidate during the initial rapport- building portion of the interview. Jotting down key words and phrases that the candidate offers in response to the interviewer's questions will help the interviewer remember the candidate's responses after the interview is over. Interviewers can then go back after the interview is done and "flesh out" more details around each of the candidate's answers.

4. Sexual harassment that manifests itself as a hostile work environment exists when unwelcome sexual conduct unreasonably interferes with an employee's job performance or creates a hostile, intimidating, or offensive work environment. A hostile work environment can be found to exist whether or not the employee experiences (or runs the risk of experiencing) tangible or economic work-related consequences.

   Hostile work environment harassment is unrelated to any decisions that are made relative to the employee's employment. As such, hostile work environments can be created by virtually anyone with whom an employee might come in contact in the workplace or "workspace."

5. According to WARNA, a "mass layoff" occurs under the following sets of circumstances:

   ▸ Mass layoff: A covered employer must give notice if there is to be a mass layoff that does not result from a plant closing but that will result in an employment loss at the employment site during any 30-day period for 500 or more employees, or for 50–499 employees if they make up at least 33% of the employer's active workforce. Again, this does not count employees who have worked less than 6 months in the past 12 months or employees who work an average of less than 20 hours a week for that employer. These latter groups, however, are entitled to notice.

   An employer also must give notice if the number of employment losses that occur during a 30-day period fails to meet the threshold requirements of a plant closing or mass layoff, but the number of employment losses for 2 or more groups of workers, each of which is less than the minimum number needed to trigger notice, reaches the threshold level, during any 90-day period, of either a plant closing or mass layoff. Job losses within any 90-day period will count toward WARNA threshold levels unless the employer demonstrates that the employment losses during the 90-day period are the result of separate and distinct actions and causes.

WARNA defines a "plant closing" as follows:

▶ Plant closing: A covered employer must give notice if an employment site (or one or more facilities or operating units within an employment site) will be shut down, and the shutdown will result in an employment loss (as defined later) for 50 or more employees during any 30-day period. This does not count employees who have worked less than 6 months in the past 12 months or employees who work an average of less than 20 hours a week for that employer. These latter groups, however, are entitled to notice.

Answers to Exam Questions

1. Answer A is the best answer. Title VII of the Civil Rights Act of 1964 established five protected classes: color (answer B), race (answer C), national origin (answer D), religion, and sex. Age did not become a protected class until 1967, with the passage of the Age Discrimination in Employment Act (ADEA).

2. Answer C is the best answer. Quid pro quo harassment occurs when an individual's submission to or rejection of sexual advances or conduct of a sexual nature is used as the basis for employment-related decisions. Because this sort of impact can usually only be brought about by a supervisor or someone else in a position of authority in the organization, answer A is not the best answer. Answer B is not the best answer; quid pro quo harassment is a separate concept from hostile work environment harassment (although both types of harassment could potentially lead to constructive discharge). Answer D is not the best answer; either quid pro quo or hostile work environment harassment could occur during the recruiting or selection processes.

3. Answer B is the best answer. Federal contractors with $50,000 or more in federal contracts would be required to prepare formal affirmative action plans. Answer A is not the best answer; Executive Order 11246 does not specifically use the awarding of federal grants as a factor that determines whether an organization needs to prepare a formal affirmative action plan. Answer C is not the best answer; this threshold refers to an organization's obligation to file annual EEO reports, not to the organization's obligation to prepare a formal affirmative action plan. Answer D is not the best answer; not all contractors are required to prepare formal affirmative action plans.

4. Answer D is the best answer. There is no WARNA requirement to notify the EEOC of impending mass layoffs or plant closings. The organization should, however, conduct an adverse impact analysis before making any layoff decisions. Answers A, B, and C are not the best answers; each one indicates individuals or entities who are required to be notified in the event that WARNA is triggered.

5. Answer A is the best answer. In *Kolstad v. American Dental Association, 1991*, the court ruled that punitive damages can be awarded only when the employer has acted with malice and reckless indifference to "the employee's federally protected rights." Answers B, C, and D each address different legal principles.

6. Answer C is the best answer. HR adds value to this process by asking questions that help to ascertain the underlying problems—and that help distinguish problems from symptoms. Answer A is not the best answer; although a manager may be convinced of the true nature of a problem and what the solution should be, the manager's assessment is not necessarily correct, so you shouldn't unthinkingly commit to implementing it. Answer B is not the best answer for a related reason; you don't really know what the problem is, so it is not possible to suggest a solution. Additionally, if you use this approach, you are dismissing the manager's opinions and experience—and you risk damaging your relationship with the manager. Answer D is not the best answer; it assumes that the manager's assessment of the problem is correct and that the proposed solution is the best possible intervention.

7. Answer B is the best answer. A properly conducted job analysis will produce job competencies (answer A), job specifications (answer C), and a job description (answer D). Although information generated through the job analysis should be used to write a job posting, this is not one of the specific outputs of the job analysis process.

8. Answer C is the best answer. Compensation rates are generally not included in a job description. Scope information (answer A), physical work conditions and physical demands (answer B), and minimum requirements (answer C) do constitute important parts of the job description for each position.

9. Answer B is the best answer. Job competencies speak to broad categories of skills that are required to perform successfully in a particular position, department, or organization. Of the four answers, "reading skills" is least likely to be defined in this way because it is more of a discrete, observable, and measurable skill. Communication skills (answer A), teamwork skills (answer B), and interpersonal skills (answer D) are all more likely to be considered "key success factors" or "performance factors."

10. Answer C is the best answer. If underutilization exists within an organization, employee referral programs are not likely to remedy that problem. Answers A and D are not the best possible answers; "highly cost-effective recruiting" and "increased candidate familiarity with the organization" both represent benefits of employee referral programs. Answer B is not the best answer; although the employee who makes the referral may believe that the candidate whom they refer will succeed, that assessment is not necessarily accurate.

Suggested Readings and Resources

Alexander, D., & Hartman, L. (2012). *Employment law for business* (7th ed.). New York: McGraw-Hill.

Arthur, D. (2012). *Recruiting, Interviewing, Selecting & Orienting New Employees* (5th ed.). New York: AMACOM, American Management Association.

Department of Justice. www.usdoj.gov.

Department of Labor. www.dol.gov.

Equal Employment Opportunity Commission (EEOC). www.eeoc.gov.

Flynn, N. (2012). *The Social Media Handbook: Policies and Best Practices to Effectively Manage Your Organization's Social Media Presence, Posts, and Potential Risks.* San Francisco: Pfeiffer.

Gibson, C. (2006). *Mission- Driven Interviewing: Moving Beyond Behavior- Based Questions: Strategies for Managers & HR Professionals.* Huntington, Conn.: PTI Publishing.

Gottlieb, B., and Kelloway, E. (1998). *Flexible Work Arrangements: Managing the Work- Family Boundary* (1st ed.). Chichester, England: Wiley.

Moran, J. (2014). *Employment Law: New Challenges in the Business Environment* (6th ed.). Upper Saddle River, New Jersey: Pearson Education.

Robertson, K. (1999). *Work Transformation: Planning and Implementing the New Workplace.* New York: HNB Pub.

Schweyer, A. (2004). *Talent Management Systems: Best Practices in Technology Solutions for Recruitment, Retention, and Workforce Planning.* Toronto, Ont.: Wiley.

Steingold, F. (2011). *The Employer's Legal Handbook* (10th ed.). Berkeley, Calif.: Nolo.

Walsh, D. (2013). *Employment Law for Human Resource Practice* (4th ed.). Mason, Ohio: South-Western Cengage Learning.

CHAPTER THREE

Human Resource Development

Human resource development (HRD) can be defined, in its simplest terms—well...it actually isn't all that easy to define. A review of the research describes HRD in myriad and sometimes ambiguous ways. If you have studied and reviewed HRD-related books, articles, and documents as part of your preparation for the PHR exam and still aren't 100% clear in your understanding of where and how it fits within the broader field of HR, you are not alone. And when you add organization development (OD) into the mix, things can seem even more unclear.

In an effort to lend as much clarity as possible to this critically important HR functional area, let's approach HR development with this working definition:

> HRD consists of training, development, change management, career development and performance management strategies, functions, and initiatives to ensure that the skills, knowledge, abilities, and performance of the workforce (and the individuals who comprise it) will meet the short-term, long-term, emerging, and strategic objectives of the organization.

Said differently, HRD is composed of processes and initiatives that improve current—and prepare for future—organizational effectiveness by ensuring that those who work within the organization will be prepared to demonstrate levels of performance consistent with current and emerging organizational needs. To bridge the gap between where employees are at any point in time with where they need to be at a targeted, subsequent point in time, myriad interventions could be used, including training, career development, change management, performance management, and organization development initiatives. These interventions are "the stuff" of which HRD is made.

Now let's take a look at OD:

> OD refers to the process through which the overall performance, growth, and effectiveness of an organization is enhanced through strategic, deliberate, and integrated initiatives. The interesting and complex area of OD incorporates four academic disciplines: psychology, sociology, anthropology, and management.

Effective OD does not "happen" haphazardly. Instead, it represents a systematic, planned, and (usually) multifaceted approach to organizational enhancement. OD interventions are intended to identify and leverage an organization's competitive advantages and to ensure the organization's success.

OD helps maintain the organization's focus on this one truth: it is the people within organizations—literally, its human resources—who accomplish the work. This, in turn, significantly affects the overall success of the organization. In that sense, a big part of OD is human development, or in this case, employee development. As such, OD is inextricably related to the HR function and to human resource development.

Two other areas that contribute to the overall effectiveness of HRD are leadership development and performance management. Although both areas are inextricably woven into the tapestry of HRD, each maintains its own presence and uniqueness—even in those organizations that do not openly espouse HRD initiatives.

To understand, appreciate, and begin to perform HRD more effectively, HR professionals need to be familiar with key foundational concepts as well as relevant legal dimensions of human resource development. HR professionals also need to be able to knowledgeably navigate the five primary areas of HRD:

- ▶ **Organization development (OD):** The development of effective and productive organizations that simultaneously develop, empower, and support their employees.

- ▶ **Training (also known as "learning and development"):** The learning and (when successful) transfer of skills and knowledge that will enable an employee to perform her current job more effectively, thus contributing to the overall effectiveness of the organization.

- ▶ **Career development:** The deliberate preparation for and unfolding of the professional pathway along which each individual travels during his adult working life.

- ▶ **Leadership development:** The strategic investment in the managers and leaders who work within the organization.

- ▶ **Performance management:** The embedded structures, complemented by the periodic and day-to-day activities in which managers engage with their employees, which are established to support the organization and its employees as each works to achieve organizational objectives.

Although each of these areas is inextricably woven into the tapestry of HRD, each also maintains its own presence and uniqueness, and each has the potential to stand alone in the absence of the others (although perhaps not as effectively or impactfully).

RESPONSIBILITY

HRD Responsibility 01

Ensure that human resources development activities are compliant with all applicable federal laws and regulations.

KNOWLEDGE

Knowledge 27

Applicable federal laws and regulations related to human resources development activities (for example: Title VII, ADA, Title 17 [Copyright law]).

Understanding HR-Related Laws

In addition to the HR-related laws that are explored in the other HR functional areas, there are several other laws—ones that are not exclusively (or even primarily) HRD related—that must be considered carefully because of the impact they can have on the way we perform our jobs (such as the Civil Rights Act of 1964, the Age Discrimination in Employment Act, and the Americans with Disabilities Act Amendments Act). As you go through your test prep, consider each law and ask yourself how it could apply to HRD. And be sure to make connections to laws explored in the other chapters in this book.

This section also includes relevant legal principles/concepts.

U.S. Patent Act, 1790

In addition to being familiar with copyrights, HR professionals need to have a working understanding of patents.

Patents confer certain rights upon the individual to whom the patent is granted. Specifically, a patent holder has "the right to exclude others from making, using, offering for sale, or selling" the invention in the United States or "importing" the invention into the United States. Interestingly, a patent does not grant the patent holder the right to take any specific action relative to the patent that she has been granted or relative to the invention for which the individual was granted the patent. Instead, it prohibits others from taking the preceding actions. The responsibility for enforcing those rights, however, falls squarely upon the individual to whom the patent has been granted (with no assistance from the U.S. Patent Office).

There are six types of U.S. patents. (The first three listed next are the "primary" ones.)

Utility Patent

Issued for the invention of a new and useful process, machine, manufacture, or composition of matter, or a new and useful improvement thereof, a utility patent generally permits its owner to exclude others from making, using, or selling the invention for a period of up to 20 years from the date of patent application filingsubject to the payment of maintenance fees. Approximately 90% of the patent documents issued by the USPTO in recent years have been utility patents, also referred to as "patents for invention."

Design Patent

Issued for a new, original, and ornamental design embodied in or applied to an article of manufacture, a design patent permits its owner to exclude others from making, using, or selling the design for a period of 14 years from the date of patent grant. Design patents are not subject to the payment of maintenance fees. Please note that the 14-year term of a design patent is subject to change in the near future.

Plant Patent

Issued for a new and distinct, invented, or discovered asexually reproduced plant including cultivated spores, mutants, hybrids, and newly found seedlings, other than a tuber-propagated plant or a plant found in an uncultivated state, a plant patent permits its owner to exclude others from making, using, or selling the plant for a period of up to 20 years from the date of patent application filing. Plant patents are not subject to the payment of maintenance fees.

Reissue Patent

Issued to correct an error in an already issued utility, design, or plant patent, a reissue patent does not affect the period of protection offered by the original patent. However, the scope of patent protection can change as a result of the reissue patent.

Defensive Publication

Issued instead of a regular utility, design, or plant patent, a defensive publication (DEF) offers limited protection, defensive in nature, to prevent others from patenting an invention, design, or plant. The Defensive Publication was replaced by the Statutory Invention Registration in 1985–1986.

Statutory Invention Registration

The statutory invention registration (SIR) document replaced the DEF in 1985–1986 and offered similar protection. Please note that the America Invents Act (AIA), which was signed into law on September 16, 2011, repeals provisions pertaining to statutory invention registrations; the issue of these documents will be discontinued (www.uspto.gov).

> **NOTE**
>
> HR professionals and the organizations for which they work need to understand and consider patent issues, particularly if employees might [or do] create inventions in the course of their work. To avoid costly and time-consuming litigation—which could even affect the marketability of the invention—organizations should consult with counsel, in advance, relative to drafting and implementing written agreements governing patent-related issues.

> **NOTE**
>
> Be mindful that these same protections do not necessarily exist in other countries. Be cautious about any agreements that you make—explicit and implicit—when creating or delivering HRD initiatives in/for nations other than the United States.

Copyright Act of 1976

The Copyright Act of 1976 protects the work of authors, artists, and others who create original materials. This law also addresses fair use and public domain, which will be explored soon.

First, though, a bit of relevant history. The idea of protecting the work of authors, artists, and others who create original materials dates back all the way to the Constitution. Article I, Section 8 of the United States Constitution states: "The Congress shall have Power…to promote the Progress of Science and useful Arts, by securing for limited Times to Authors and Inventors the exclusive Right to their respective Writings and Discoveries."

Now fast forward 189 years to the Copyright Act of 1976.

What's Covered and What Rights Are Granted

A copyright grants certain rights to authors and others who create original works. According to Section 102 of the Act, this protection extends to "original works of authorship fixed in any tangible medium of expression, now known or later developed, from which they can be perceived, reproduced, or otherwise communicated, either directly or with the aid of a machine or device." Works of authorship that are protected include the following:

- ▶ Literary works

- ▶ Musical works, including any accompanying words

- ▶ Dramatic works, including any accompanying music

- ▶ Pantomimes and choreographic works

- ▶ Pictorial, graphic, and sculptural works

- ▶ Motion pictures and other audiovisual works

- ▶ Sound recordings

- ▶ Architectural works (this category was added in 1990)

The Act grants copyright holders exclusive rights to the following six specific categories of activities:

▶ The right to duplicate/reproduce/copy the work

▶ The right to create derivative works that are based on the original work

▶ The right to sell, lease, rent, or otherwise distribute copies of the work to the public

▶ The right to perform the work publicly

▶ The right to display the work publicly

▶ The right to digital performance in sound recordings

In so doing, the Act also prohibits those who do not hold the copyright from engaging in those activities without permission of the copyright holder.

Copyright Holders

Most of the time, the author, artist, or individual who created the work owns the copyright to the work. The Copyright Act, however, does establish two important "work-for-hire" exceptions to this rule. These exceptions pertain specifically to work product created by the following:

▶ **Employees:** The work product that an employee generates in the normal course of his employment is automatically owned by the employer.

▶ **Consultants/independent contractors:** The work product generated by a consultant or independent contractor is usually automatically owned by the organization with whom the consultant contracts. From the perspective of the organization that has contracted with the consultant, it is important to have a signed written agreement that states that a work-for-hire arrangement has been established and that the organization owns all work product that is produced.

Copyright law covers only the particular form or manner in which ideas or information were first fixed. Copyrights do not, however, cover the actual ideas, concepts, or facts that are included in the fixed work.

Copyrights last for the lifetime of the author, plus 70 years. After that, the work passes into the public domain. Anonymous works and works that were created under work-for-hire agreements enter the public domain either 95 years after the first year of publication or 120 years after the year in which they were created, whichever comes first.

Public Domain

As previously indicated, copyrights—and the protections afforded by copyrights—eventually expire. After a copyright for a particular work expires, that work enters the public domain. This means that the copyright holder no longer enjoys the six areas of protection cited previously and that the works are available, and free, for all to use.

TIP

Most work created by the federal government is, by definition, considered to be in the public domain. This provision of the Act can be helpful to HR professionals, especially with respect to work product that is generated relative to legal and compliance-related issues.

> **NOTE**
>
> Just because a work is publicly accessible does not mean that it is in the public domain. With access to countless numbers of websites, combined with the ability to copy, paste, and save text and images on almost any topic, the temptation may exist to incorporate existing materials into HRD/training presentations, handouts, or other work-related documents. For legal, professional, and ethical reasons, resist the temptation. Don't do it.

Fair Use

In addition to works that are in the public domain, HR professionals (and anyone else, of course) can use copyrighted works under certain circumstances. This is known as fair use. According to the Copyright Act, portions of copyrighted works can be used without the permission of the author for purposes of "criticism, comment, news reporting, teaching (including multiple copies for classroom use), scholarship, or research." Even then, however, what constitutes fair use is contingent upon a number of factors:

- ▶ Whether the work will be used for commercial purposes or for not-for-profit or educational purposes

- ▶ The nature of the way in which the work will be used

- ▶ How much of the work is used, both in terms of the overall size of the portion of the work that is being used, as well as the percentage of the total work that is being used

- ▶ Whether the use could affect the potential market or the market value of the work

Common Law

Common law is a system of law in which traditions, customs, and precedents have the same force of law as existing laws or statutes that have been enacted as a result of the full legislative process. With a common law system, laws and statutes are, quite literally, interpreted and reinterpreted on a case-by-case basis. In practice, each interpretation (and each case) sets a new precedent but can also be reinterpreted, thus setting (yet another) new precedent.

As it evolves, this process results in rights being granted to employees on an individual basis.

Let's take a look at some of the concepts most closely related to HRD.

Negligent Training

This tort doctrine refers to an employer's failure to provide proper training to an employee when that failure results in some sort of unfit performance by the employee. Negligent training can emerge as an issue either when an employee who was hired for one position assumes another position for which she may not be fully and appropriately trained or when an employee's job duties and responsibilities change over time, thus requiring additional training if the employee is to continue performing the job in a fit manner.

> **NOTE**
>
> When calculating costs of training, the cost of *not* conducting training must also be considered. Negligent training is one possible, if seemingly nebulous, cost of not conducting training.

HRD Responsibility 02

Conduct a needs assessment to identify and establish priorities regarding human resource development activities.

Knowledge 32

Task/process analysis.

ADDIE: An Overview

ADDIE is a five-phase model (often used within a context of instructional design) that includes analysis/assessment (of needs), design, development, implementation, and evaluation. The acronym ADDIE represents the following five steps:

A: Analysis/assessment (of needs)

D: Design

D: Development

I: Implementation

E: Evaluation

Although the ADDIE model can be applied in any of the functional areas within HR (in fact, it is one of HRCI's 23 areas of core knowledge), it is perhaps most frequently referenced with respect to HRD (specifically, training and instructional design). Therefore, much of the information in this chapter (and, perhaps, on the PHR exam) relating to ADDIE uses training-specific examples. As you move through the chapter, however, and continue to prepare for the PHR exam, keep in mind the broader applications of ADDIE.

ADDIE: "A" Is for Analysis/Assessment

Needs assessment and analysis is a way of defining problems. Taking this a step further, a problem could be defined as the difference between a situation or condition as it currently is compared to what that situation or condition needs to be. If needs assessment is faulty, the solution will be faulty as well because it will address the wrong problem (and might even contribute to creating a new one).

With respect to HR initiatives, ADDIE can serve as an excellent tool to ascertain where the organization "is," where it needs to be, and how the HR initiative can specifically serve to bridge that gap.

As we begin to explore needs analysis/assessment—the first step in the ADDIE model—it's helpful to keep in mind that HR professionals have the greatest impact and add the greatest value when they seek to carry out their responsibilities (whatever those responsibilities might involve) in a consultative manner. As such, it's helpful to proactively think about the kinds of questions you might encounter as you prepare for and work your way through this phase. In this way, you'll be better able to recognize and respond to these questions when you hear them, and—even more important—you can look for opportunities to ask them yourself. Some representative questions that might come up in the needs analysis/assessment phase might include the following:

- ▶ Why is an HRD/training initiative being considered?

- ▶ Why is one particular type of HRD/training initiative being favored (if applicable)?

- ▶ If the HRD/training initiative under consideration is being motivated by a perceived performance problem, what is the nature of the substandard performance? (We need to recognize that reason before we can begin to determine whether an HRD/training initiative might constitute an appropriate intervention.)

- ▶ What level of subject matter knowledge and skill do employees possess?

- ▶ What level of subject matter knowledge and skill do employees need?

- ▶ What is the gap between current performance levels and desired or expected performance levels?

- ▶ What are the learning objectives that the HRD/training initiative would need to attain to bridge that gap?

- ▶ What level of organizational/leadership support exists to bridge that gap? (This may be a function of how closely the "missing" skills or knowledge relates to the mission and goals of the organization.)

- ▶ By what date must the organization begin to address the gap?

- ▶ By what date must the organization fully bridge the gap?

- ▶ What are the costs of various HRD/training options, and what would be the benefits?

- ▶ What resources are available to address this gap? (Resources can include people, money, and time.)

- ▶ What costs would accrue/consequences result if this gap remains unaddressed?

Analysis/Assessment: Theoretical/Scholarly Foundation

Before getting into the nuts and bolts of needs analysis/assessment, it's helpful and important to understand what's behind it.

In 1961, McGehee and Thayer identified three levels of HRD/training needs analysis and assessment: organizational analysis, task or work (operations) analysis, and individual or person (man) analysis:

- ▶ **Organizational-level analysis:** Level 1 of McGehee and Thayer's three levels of HRD/training needs analysis and assessment. Organizational-level analysis determines where HRD/training can and should be used within the overall organization.

- ▶ **Task or work (operations) level analysis:** Level 2 of McGehee and Thayer's three levels of HRD/training needs analysis and assessment. Task- or work (operations)-level analysis collects and addresses data about a particular job or group of jobs.

- ▶ **Person (man)-level analysis:** Level 3 of McGehee and Thayer's three levels of HRD/training needs analysis and assessment. Person (man)-level analysis assesses performance of a particular individual.

EXAM ALERT

More than five decades later, McGehee and Thayer's theory still constitutes an important tool for HRD/training needs analysis/assessment (although some of the terminology has evolved a bit over time, as indicated in Table 3.1).

TABLE 3.1   Needs Analysis/Assessment

Level of Needs Analysis (1961 Verbiage)	Level of Needs Analysis (Contemporary Verbiage)	Definition/Description of the Level of Analysis	Examples of What the Analysis Looks at
Organizational analysis	N/A	Determine where HRD/training can and should be used within the overall organization	What is the organization's mission? What are its objectives? In the future, what knowledge, skills, and abilities (KSAs) will the organization's employees need to possess and demonstrate?
			What is the pool of skills currently available within the organization?
			What is the gap between those two?
			What is the organization's culture like?
Operations analysis	Task or work analysis	Collect data about a particular job or group of jobs	What are the performance standards for a particular job?
Man analysis	Individual or person analysis	Assess performance of a particular individual	How well is a particular employee performing?
			Where does the employee's performance fall below the expected standards of the position?
			Is that lag attributable to skills or knowledge the employee needs to attain or develop? How might training or other HRD initiatives address any performance issues (areas in which actual performance does not match the level of performance required to attain established job standards)?

NOTE

Be familiar with how internal and external factors affect a needs analysis/assessment and how they can affect the recommendations that are generated through that needs analysis/assessment. Know what those environmental considerations could be as well as how to conduct an effective scan using strengths, weaknesses, opportunities, and threats (SWOT) analysis.

Needs Analysis/Assessment: Why Do It?

There are several compelling reasons to conduct a needs analysis/assessment before embarking on an HRD/training initiative. Following are some of those reasons:

▶ To identify—objectively and factually—performance-related problems within the organization. (Engaging in this process with internal clients constitutes another concrete example of how HR can truly function as strategic and consultative business partners, even on seemingly transactional or tactical related matters.)

▶ To collect facts with which to establish a baseline level of performance. This baseline will then provide a valid comparison for pretraining/post-training (or, more broadly, pre-HRD initiative/post-HRD initiative) assessments.

▶ To generate increased involvement with and, therefore, buy-in for the HRD/training solution that is ultimately implemented. Securing buy-in at all levels of the organization (especially at the senior leadership level) is critical.

▶ To ensure that your decisions and recommendations are based on facts rather than on assumptions. This is another way to help dispel the "fuzzy-wuzzy, touchy-feely, party-planning, people-people" stereotype, which many HR professionals are still wrestling to redefine. This process provides HR professionals with an opportunity to enhance their reputation in the organization as legitimate business partners—not as people who rely solely on their ability to intuitively read a situation.

▶ To increase the likelihood of identifying a solution that will truly bridge the performance gap.

▶ To ensure that a legitimate cost-benefit analysis is conducted before a commitment is made to any particular HRD/training solution. The costs associated with implementing the HRD/training initiative must also be compared to the costs that would accrue if the current situation were allowed to persist without implementing the HRD/training intervention.

An unintended, but potentially significant, benefit of conducting a needs analysis/assessment is that you may also identify other organizational issues that had previously gone unnoticed. Even if these concerns are not best addressed by an HRD/training-based initiative—and even if they do not fall within the purview of HR—you still will have made a meaningful contribution to the overall effectiveness of your organization.

Needs Analysis/Assessment: What Are the Risks of Not Doing It?

Having looked at the benefits of conducting a needs analysis/assessment, it's also important to look at the situation from a different perspective—specifically, the risks associated with not conducting a needs analysis/assessment. A few of these risks might include the following:

▶ Misidentifying problems

▶ Overlooking problems

▶ Eliminating the only means of establishing a basis from which to make meaningful assessments of the impact of an HRD/training initiative

▶ Possibly increasing skepticism relative to the value of—and necessity for—the HRD/training initiative

▶ Damaging HR's reputation, either collectively or relative to specific individuals, by contributing to the impression that HR folks just try to "get a feel for things" instead of making rigorous, fact-based business decisions

Here's one more note to keep in mind before we move into "how" to do this. Managers—and even other HR professionals—may come to you with definite ideas of how to resolve a particular problem. When this happens, pause, ask questions, and—above all—listen. It's critical at this point in the process to collaboratively identify the actual—rather than the perceived—problem and to ascertain the underlying causes of that problem. Therein lies an important difference between assessment (identifying the problem) and analysis (identifying the causes of that problem). Skipping either of those steps is likely to influence the effectiveness of the remaining steps in the ADDIE process.

Needs Analysis/Assessment: How Do You Do It?

Although experts may differ on the specifics, and different models might include different steps, a well-constructed needs analysis should include the following four steps:

1. Gather data that will enable you to identify specific needs.

2. Determine which of those needs can be addressed through HRD/training interventions.

3. Propose/select a solution (depending on HR's role in the organization and in this process) for those needs that are best addressed through HRD/training interventions.

4. Compare the costs of implementing an HRD/training initiative to the benefits that will accrue from delivering the HRD/training initiative.

Let's look at each of these steps more closely.

Step 1 of Needs Analysis/Assessment: Gather Data

Data gathering can be performed by someone within the organization or with some level of support and assistance from external experts (for instance, consultants). Regardless of who gathers the data, however, establishing trust is essential. Otherwise, the overall objective of enhancing organizational performance and attaining overarching organizational objectives could be undermined by mistrust or morale problems engendered by flawed data-gathering processes (see Table 3.2).

> **NOTE**
>
> It's essential to make a commitment to following through on the information you collect through the data-gathering phase, even if the organization ultimately decides not to launch an HRD/training initiative. In short, the first time that employees tell you about their concerns cannot be the last time that you communicate with them about those concerns. The process of gathering data, especially through survey or focus group techniques, raises awareness and thus raises expectations. Don't let those expectations be ignored—even if the answer ends up being that they will not be addressed through an HRD initiative at this time.

TABLE 3.2 Data Collection

Data Collection Techniques	Sample Strengths	Sample Weaknesses
General surveys (closed-ended questions)	Easier to tabulate (especially if done electronically). Confidentiality can be ensured, which may lead to greater candor of response.	Information may be overly general in nature, in part because of the nature of closed-ended questions.

Data Collection Techniques	Sample Strengths	Sample Weaknesses
"Felt-needs" employee surveys (asking people to identify the areas in which they feel they need training)	Can reach a large number of employees in a short time frame.	Employees may identify wants instead of needs. The training that the employees are requesting, therefore, may not directly translate into enhanced work performance that supports attainment of organizational objectives.
"Organizational challenges" employee surveys (asking employees to identify individual, group, or organizational performance issues)	Can reach a large number of employees in a short time frame. Ensures a focus on performance issues, which can then be translated by those who administer the survey into HRD/training solutions.	Because these questions are more open ended in nature, results may take longer to tabulate.
Review of published business documents	Provides factual, objective data with which many decision makers should already be familiar (and in which they likely already have confidence).	Reflects past situations, which may not be reflective of more recent trends.
Interviews	Obtain in-depth information from individuals at all levels of the organization (thus providing a variety of valuable perspectives).	Time consuming and labor intensive. Requires a skilled interviewer (who also can establish trust).
Focus groups	Provides a qualitative approach. A skilled facilitator may be able to extract particularly valuable information. The synergy present in a well-functioning group may generate more valuable and insightful data than would have been generated by the same members individually.	Labor intensive and time consuming. More difficult to reach large numbers of people within a relative short time frame. Direction of discussion may be swayed by group dynamics or by the presence or contributions of one or more influential individuals. It may be challenging to replicate identical conditions across various focus groups, which could theoretically taint/affect the consistency of the data that is collected. May be prohibitive because of limited resources (time, cost, or facilitator availability).
Observation	Provides a realistic viewpoint rather than one that might be "sanitized," obsequious, or self-serving.	Labor intensive and time consuming. Requires a trained observer (trained in making observations, as well as in the work that is being observed).
Performance appraisals	If done well, the performance management and appraisal process can establish criteria.	Performance appraisals—for myriad reasons—do not always provide an accurate reflection of actual performance (or of that performance as it compares to standards). (See "Performance Appraisal and Management—Pitfalls to Avoid.")
Skills assessment	Results are easily quantified.	Does not measure whether the skills that are being assessed are actually being used on the job.

As indicated, each data-gathering method has advantages and disadvantages. For this reason, a combination of two or more methods might be more effective.

Step 2 of Needs Analysis: Identify Needs That Can Be Addressed Through Specific HRD/Training Initiatives

Organizations implement different HRD/training initiatives for a variety of reasons. Ultimately, however, these reasons fall into two primary categories: to gain knowledge and to develop skills. Both of these, ultimately, are intended to change behavior, to enhance performance, and to achieve the organization's stated goals:

▶ **Knowledge:** HRD/training initiatives that are implemented for the purpose of expanding upon employees' knowledge base will expose participants to a body of information they must know or with which they must be familiar to perform their jobs effectively. Sometimes knowledge training is even mandated by law (for instance, sexual harassment training in California). Knowledge-based training generally focuses more on what a person knows than on how he applies that knowledge. Knowledge-based training can also be implemented to educate employees about organization-specific topics that are unrelated to specific skills or to general areas of knowledge. Either way, this acquisition of knowledge is directly intended to manifest as specific desired behaviors (that employees now know more about), which in turn will produce desired results (that employees now know how to deliver).

▶ **Skills:** As the word "skills" implies, skills training is designed to teach participants how to do something related to their job. That "something," however, can span a wide spectrum of possibilities.

Skills training can address certain specific, discrete functions that are important to the individual's ability to perform her job and that contribute to the organization's ability to attain its overall objectives. Skills training can also, however, address and cultivate behaviors that are reflective of the values of the organization or that support demonstration of organizational competencies.

Attitude Versus Behavior

Attitude is important to consider—particularly with respect to training and performance management. It's also exceedingly difficult, however, to get one's hands around the concept of "attitude" in any sort of concrete, consistent, objective manner. In short, attitude is subjective and personal. By defining attitude behaviorally, however, an organization can accomplish two objectives: it can create a basis for designing HRD/training interventions that will cultivate behaviors that manifest desired attitudes, and it can provide a framework within which to evaluate employees in a more objective and more defensible manner (for performance management purposes, or should any other need arise).

For instance, consider the attitudinal characteristic "flexibility." This word can, of course, mean different things to different people—particularly to managers and their direct reports. By identifying flexibility behaviorally, however, within the context of the results that the employee is expected to produce, it's easier to discuss, address, and resolve attitude problems relating to flexibility. In this case, some behavioral definitions of flexibility might be these:

▶ Displays agility, openness, and responsiveness in the face of rapidly changing conditions

▶ Performs a wide range of assignments accurately, efficiently, and willingly

▶ Handles multiple projects simultaneously without experiencing a decline in quality or quantity of performance

By framing and defining the words that we use—and the expectations that we have—in terms of behaviors, attitudes become easier to address, discuss, and resolve.

Step 3 of Needs Analysis: Propose/Select a Solution (Depending upon HR's Role in the Organization and in This Process)

In proposing/selecting a solution, it is essential to use a logical, fact-based approach. One dimension of that approach will include comparing the resources that are available to the resources that are required to deliver each specific HRD/training initiative. Resources, in this context, could mean financial, human, temporal, and technological, to name a few.

If the resources required to implement a particular solution would be truly impossible to secure, however, it would be counterproductive to continue considering a particular solution. That's the kind of information that you're better off knowing up front before making a commitment to any particular course of action.

It is also critical to prepare a cost-benefit analysis as part of the process of proposing/selecting a solution. As with other dimensions of needs analysis, there is no one right way to conduct a cost-benefit analysis. Calculating return on investment (ROI), however, is essential. ROI can be calculated by considering the following:

1. Calculate the costs associated with the current situation, as is, if no HRD/training intervention were implemented (in other words, the cost of *not* implementing the HRD/training initiative).

2. Calculate the costs associated with implementing the HRD/training intervention. Be sure to consider all direct and indirect costs, including (but not limited to):

   ▶ The trainer's/facilitator's salary (prep time, delivery, and follow-up) and fees

   ▶ Wages and salaries paid to participants during the HRD/training session

   ▶ Lost revenue from nonproduction of goods or nondelivery of services during the HRD/training session

   ▶ Any overtime expenses that might result because of work that was not completed during the HRD/training session

   ▶ Food and beverages

   ▶ Materials

   ▶ Facility fees

   ▶ Travel

3. Calculate the financial gains that will accrue from implementing the HRD/training initiative. Financial gains could accrue from a variety of sources, such as these:

   ▶ The value of the skills that employees develop and the knowledge that employees gain through the HRD/training intervention (after those skills and that knowledge is applied in the workplace).

   ▶ Costs (or potential costs) that will not be incurred (or that will no longer be incurred) after the HRD/training initiative is delivered.

   ▶ Benefits that are less tangible (but no less real). Please note that some of these benefits might be more difficult to attribute directly to the HRD/training initiative (for instance, increased morale, retention, and customer satisfaction, to name a few).

Step 4 of Needs Analysis: Compare the Costs of Implementing the HRD/Training Initiative to the Benefits That Will Accrue from Conducting the HRD/Training Initiative

In doing this, it's important to keep in mind that the objective is not to sell anyone on a particular initiative—including ourselves. The objective is to make a well-informed decision that focuses on meeting the needs of the organization.

In addition to conducting this analysis, many organizations use a measure referred to as "cost per trainee" or "cost per participant," which is calculated as follows:

$$\frac{\text{Total of all costs associated with the HRD/training initiative}}{\text{Number of individuals who participate in the HRD/training initiative}}$$

This formula can provide valuable information that can be used to make a variety of HRD/training-related decisions. For instance, just a few of the decisions that this analysis could help you make might be the following:

▶ Whether to sponsor an in-house HRD/training initiative or send participants to publicly offered training programs

▶ Whether to develop an HRD/training initiative internally or purchase/license it externally

▶ Whether the initiative will be online, on ground, or hybrid

▶ Whether the HRD/training initiative will be secured through a source that is external to the organization:

  ▶ Whether to purchase or license the product

  ▶ Whether to have the vendor supply trainers or implement a "train the trainer" program

  ▶ Whether to use the external product "as is" or pay for customization

  ▶ The length of the HRD/training initiative

  ▶ Who will attend the HRD/training initiative

  ▶ The frequency with which HRD/training initiatives—on any single topic and across the board—will be delivered

  ▶ Whether to hold the HRD/training initiative onsite at the organization's facility or secure conference space at an offsite location, such as a hotel or conference center

By changing one or more than one variable, HR professionals will generate a variety of scenarios for comparison. This will enable you to do a more effective job of making rigorous, fact-based recommendations that will truly help bolster your role as a business partner.

HRD Responsibility 03

RESPONSIBILITY

Develop/select and implement employee training programs (for example: leadership skills, harassment prevention, computer skills) to increase individual and organizational effectiveness.

KNOWLEDGE

Knowledge 30

Training program development techniques to create general and specialized training programs.

KNOWLEDGE

Knowledge 31

Facilitation techniques, instructional methods, and program delivery mechanisms.

ADDIE: "D" Is for Design

In the design phase (the first "D" in ADDIE), you will plan—and prepare to build—the HRD/training initiative that will address the specific needs that were identified through the needs analysis/assessment phase. More specifically, the design phase of the ADDIE process will generate a design plan.

Looking at this phase of the process within the framework of the 5 Ws and an H, some of the questions that are likely to be addressed during the design phase include these:

- ▶ Who:

    - ▶ Who is the target population?

    - ▶ Who will develop the HRD/training initiative?

    - ▶ Who will deliver the HRD/training initiative?

    - ▶ Who will evaluate the HRD/training initiative?

- ▶ What:

    - ▶ What will the HRD/training initiative accomplish? In other words, what are the HRD/training objectives?

    - ▶ What content will be included to meet those HRD/training objectives?

    - ▶ What methodologies will be incorporated into the HRD/training initiative?

    - ▶ In what order will the various components of the HRD/training initiative be delivered?

    - ▶ What delivery method(s) will be used?

    - ▶ By what means and measures will the attainment (or nonattainment) of objectives be evaluated?

- ▶ When:

    - ▶ When will the HRD/training initiative be delivered?

    - ▶ When must the delivery of the HRD/training be completed (by what date and before what organizational milestone)?

    - ▶ When will the HRD/training initiative be announced?

- ▶ Where:

    - ▶ Where will the HRD/training program be delivered?

    - ▶ What logistical considerations/requirements are associated with each specific location?

- How:

    - Within each method, how will content specifically be addressed?

    - How will the learning objectives be attained through the HRD/training initiative?

Design—The Theoretical/Scholarly Foundation

What is design? Like so much of the information that can be found about ADDIE, the definition of the design component differs from expert to expert. In 1992, Gagne described instructional design (ISD) as a systematic process with a strong planning component. He also identified three commonalities that exist. He found that most instructional design models do the following:

- Identify what the outcomes of the HRD/training will be

- Develop the actual instructional methods and materials

- Create a component that will serve to evaluate the effectiveness of a program/initiative

In 1998, Hannafin and Peck put forth the idea that the instructional design process consists of a series of interrelated steps based on principles derived from educational research and theory. The three phases that they identify in their model (needs assessment, design, and development/implementation) involve a process of continual evaluation, reevaluation, and revision as the program is being developed.

Design: The Steps

Combining the wisdom of these and other experts, let's look at the design process as consisting of four distinct steps:

1. Identify outcome objectives.

2. Identify learning methodologies.

3. Establish a time frame.

4. Gain agreement and sign-off.

Let's take a closer look at each of these four steps.

Design Step 1: Identify Outcome Objectives

Similar to performance management applications, learning objectives should follow the acronym SMART. Although numerous definitions of this acronym exist, one particularly effective one is

- **S: Specific:** The HRD/training objectives must be clearly articulated, unambiguous, and understood in the same way by everyone involved in the HRD/training process (the instructional designer, the manager, the facilitator, the participant, and so forth).

- **M: Measurable:** If an HRD/training intervention is to be considered a valid solution that will truly support the overall performance objectives of the organization—and of the individuals in the organization—then the outcomes of that HRD/training initiative must be measurable and must be able to withstand the rigor to which those measures will ultimately be subjected through the assessment phase.

▶ **A: Action-oriented:** Objectives should be written so that the behaviors/actions that the learner is expected to demonstrate at the conclusion of the HRD/training initiative are described using strong, robust action verbs (generate, produce, resolve, demonstrate, complete, apply, and so on). Don't write objectives with verbs that are not as effective at articulating observable or measurable behaviors (understand, appreciate, value, and so forth).

▶ **R: Realistic:** Writing realistic training objectives means avoiding both ends of the "difficulty spectrum." At one end of the spectrum, HRD/training objectives that are too easy to attain aren't challenging enough and may not hold the attention and interest of participants. In addition, overly easy objectives might not generate desired results. (It may be helpful to keep in mind that if the results could be attained that easily, there would have likely been a less-formal solution than a full-blown HRD/training initiative.) At the other end of the spectrum, HRD/training objectives that are virtually impossible to attain will serve only to discourage participants. Despite the belief that some individuals have that setting unrealistically high expectations results in an overall higher level of attainment than would have been achieved if goals were set lower, the reality is often quite different. Setting objectives that are consistently unrealistically high will create an inevitable cycle of failure. Over time, this could result in employees feeling frustrated, resentful, or even manipulated or exploited. No matter what results have been attained through overly aggressive goal setting, they won't be worth the long-term negative repercussions of this approach—including morale issues, disengagement, and even higher turnover (possible of your better employees, which is often the "bad kind" of turnover).

▶ **T: Time-bound:** Time is a valuable resource—often, more valuable than money. Ensure that the HRD/training objectives identify goals that can be attained and applied to the actual performance of the position within a period of time that is acknowledged and agreed to in advance. This time frame should be determined collaboratively, taking the input of all stakeholders into consideration.

Design Step 2: Identify and Select Learning Methodologies

Identifying and selecting appropriate learning methodologies means deliberately choosing specific techniques and activities that will be most effective at giving participants the opportunity to learn and practice their enhanced skills and apply their expanded knowledge. There are many methodologies from which you might choose, some of which are the following:

▶ Lecture/lecturette

▶ Demonstration

▶ Reading

▶ Small group discussions/instructor-facilitated large group discussions

▶ Individual, small-group, or large-group activities/applications

▶ Case study

▶ Role play

Let's take a closer look at each of these methodologies.

Lecture/Lecturette

Lectures or lecturettes (min-lectures) are primarily one-way delivery mechanisms through which instructors/speakers present information to participants. Often, this information is detailed or technical in nature. It often consists of material that is substantially new, so the participants probably need some time to absorb it.

Lectures/lecturettes afford the opportunity for participants to take detailed notes, which can be particularly helpful for those learners for whom note taking is an effective means of reinforcing and retaining content. These notes can be taken freely, without the expectation that learners will contribute conversationally to a topic about which they may not be very knowledgeable (yet). Lectures/lecturettes might also be particularly valuable for auditory learners. In addition, note taking may reinforce learning for kinesthetic learners.

When lectures/lecturettes are overused, participants may lose interest. Boredom (or even fatigue) can set in, in significant part because of the minimal degree of interaction permitted by the didactic format inherent to most lectures/lecturettes.

So, how long is too long for a classroom-based (brick-and-mortar or online) training lecture? As is so often the case, that depends. Some experts say—especially for online applications—that any lecture longer than 5 minutes is too long. Others assert that, in a classroom setting, lectures can last as long as 20 minutes without becoming excessive. Before deciding on a particular length of time for a lecture/lecturette, however, it's important to weigh a variety of factors, a few of which follow:

▶ The nature and complexity of the topic

▶ The time of day

▶ How much time has passed since the last break

▶ What learning methodology preceded the lecture

▶ The overall effectiveness of the lecturer

▶ How the participants normally spend their day when they are actually performing their jobs (rather than participating in a training session)

▶ The overall percentage of lecture in the training program

Demonstration

Lectures are to demonstrations as "tell me" is to "show me." During a demonstration, the instructor/facilitator shows the participants how to perform a particular function, duty, or role.

For many learners, demonstrations are more engaging than lectures because something is actually happening. The skill is not just being referenced—it is being exhibited. Visual learners, in particular, might benefit greatly from demonstrations.

TIP

Demonstrations might be of even greater value if participants are also invited to try out—through an exercise or case study—what they are being shown. This multiple-step approach moves the activity from passive to active and thus appeals to visual as well as tactile/kinesthetic learners.

Reading

In recent years, reading hasn't been used much during training programs. In fact, it has often been given a "bad rap." Perhaps this is because some working adults still recall unpleasant experiences from grade school during which they were directed by a teacher to spend long periods of class time reading. Or, perhaps some participants think of in-class reading as a waste of time because they feel that they could read on their own time.

However, dedicating short periods of time during a training session to reading can reap numerous benefits. First, it appeals to visual learners who effectively process and retain printed information. Reading can also provide a welcome change of pace during a training session. For instance, if participants have completed some sort of self-analytical instrument, they may appreciate having a few minutes to review information that will help them begin to process and interpret what their results mean (particularly when compared to the option of sharing those results aloud and having them interpreted in front of the rest of the group). Reading printed material can also be extremely helpful when the content contains details that participants must refer to repeatedly, such as instructions for a case study or role play.

Small Group Discussions/Instructor-Facilitated Large-Group Discussions

When considering discussions as a learning methodology, it may be helpful to reflect upon Malcolm Knowles's tenets about adult learning: the role of a learner's experience. (We'll explore this in detail later in this chapter.) This is the principle that says that adult learners believe they have a significant amount of valuable experience on which they can draw to enhance their own learning—and from which others can benefit as well. Skillfully facilitated discussions will allow participants to do exactly that and to feel more engaged in the learning experience. What's even better is that these feelings are legitimate. Participants can learn a great deal from each other during small- and large-group discussions.

Individual, Small-Group, or Large-Group Activities/Applications

Hearing information is one thing; seeing it demonstrated is another—and following up one or both of those techniques with an activity that requires hands-on involvement can be an extremely effective way of reinforcing learning. Giving participants the chance to immediately apply the knowledge or skills about which they have just learned can also lead to significantly higher retention rates than lecture or demonstration alone.

Case Studies

Case studies draw on two of Knowles's other theories:

- **Learner's self-concept:** "I'm an adult, and I can direct myself. That includes in a classroom setting, so please treat me accordingly."

- **Orientation to learning:** "What I learn today needs to be able to help me solve problems in the workplace tomorrow—not at some unspecified time in the future."

Case studies present participants with real-life situations that allow them to apply the knowledge they have learned and practice the skills they have developed during the training session. In the safe environment of the classroom, learners can try out their newly acquired knowledge and newly expanded skills before they must return to the workplace (where it might not be quite as safe to make mistakes). Participants will benefit from receiving feedback from the instructor/facilitator relative to those aspects of the case study that were handled well. Participants will also benefit (perhaps even more) from receiving feedback from the instructor/facilitator relative to those aspects of the case study that could have been handled differently, or better. In both cases, the participant will be able to incorporate this feedback before bringing the knowledge and skills learned during the training back to the workplace. This can, potentially, increase the value of the training experience even more.

Role Plays

Role plays are similar to case studies and can even be used as a natural culmination of a case study. Role plays, in one sense, take case studies one step further, in that participants actually act out the ways in which they would apply their knowledge and practice their skills in particular situations.

One of the advantages of role playing is that—when well executed—they can provide one of the most realistic re-creations of workplace conditions that is possible in a training situation. It also presents participants with the opportunity to practice skills and apply knowledge—opportunities that they otherwise might not be afforded for quite some time. This is particularly important because, as reviewed earlier, retention levels are higher if training is followed closely by opportunities to put that training into practice.

> **CAUTION**
>
> Role plays can backfire if they're not handled delicately by the trainer. For instance, although feedback must be candid and honest, it also must be delivered in a way that does not diminish the self-esteem of the role-play participants or negatively affect the way in which others will perceive participants after the training ends. Role playing is risky—for the participant, for the instructor, and ultimately for the HR or training professional who designed and pitched the training. Role plays should be led by skilled instructors/facilitators who are adept at providing positive, constructive, and productive feedback in classroom settings and who have the ability to defuse a variety of (potentially sensitive) situations.

> **NOTE**
>
> Please note that many of the more active approaches to learning may be unfamiliar to—and even initially uncomfortable for—individuals of certain cultures.

> **NOTE**
>
> Cultural considerations will also strongly affect how adult learners approach learning and how they interact/behave during the delivery of OD initiatives.

Design Step 3: Establish a Time Frame

As explored previously, it's critical to make sure that HRD/training objectives are time bound. At this point in the process, timing continues to be just as important. Establishing and agreeing on a time frame for the development, implementation, and evaluation of the learning processes is critical. Establishing a time frame for implementing the entire project—as well as for reaching important milestones along the way—helps to ensure accountability, increase management support, and treat HRD/training with the same level of rigor as any other organizational (meaning, business) initiative.

Design Step 4: Gain Agreement and Sign-off

Often, this step of the design process may be minimized or even overlooked. Without a signed agreement that specifies all the elements and terms of the HRD/training initiative, however, you are more likely to experience misunderstandings (and all the problems that go along with them). There may be perceptions that you didn't deliver what you promised, when you promised it, and how you promised it. One incident like this can significantly damage your credibility (or the credibility of HRD/training initiatives, or even the credibility of HR in general). Don't allow room for misunderstandings; even if it may at first feel a bit formal, secure formal written agreement of the design plan before you begin the development phase of ADDIE.

Training

After an overall strategy has been established for developing the organization and the individuals within the organization, training is one possible intervention that can be considered. Training is one way, but not the only way, to cultivate learning within an organization.

Learning organizations are ones in which individuals at all levels strive to acquire knowledge and develop skills that will enable them, individually and collectively, to attain higher levels of performance. The concept of a "learning organization" is fundamental to HRD and is often supported through training initiatives. In his pivotal work *The Fifth Discipline*, Peter Senge identifies five disciplines, or overarching principles, that synergistically foster learning within learning organizations:

- **Systems thinking:** The ability to identify patterns and to recognize how those patterns can be impacted or changed.

- **Personal mastery:** Subject matter expertise that an individual possesses and demonstrates in a particular area, along with a commitment to maintain that expertise through lifelong learning.

- **Mental models:** Deeply rooted, firmly held beliefs and assumptions that affect how we perceive the world around us, as well as the actions we choose to take.

- **Shared vision:** A forward-looking perspective that inspires and secures a commitment to working toward a common vision.

- **Team learning:** The ability of a team to work wholeheartedly toward creating and attaining its stated objectives and desired results.

The Adult Learner

Even when training is an appropriate intervention, it can be effective only when it is learner centered and when the learners/participants are treated as adults.

An adult learner is an individual who has (usually) exceeded the primary/secondary levels of education (United States) and who is engaged in learning activities in an academic or organizational setting. Andragogy, the study and science of adult learning, is significantly different from pedagogy, the study and science of how children learn. One of the key contributors to andragogy was Malcolm Knowles (whose principles are referenced earlier). In 1978, Knowles stated:

"Andragogy assumes that the point at which an individual achieves a self-concept of essential self-direction is the point at which he psychologically becomes adult. A very critical thing happens when this occurs: The individual develops a deep psychological need to be perceived by others as being self-directing. Thus, when he finds himself in a situation in which he is not allowed to be self-directing, he experiences a tension between that situation and his self-concept. His reaction is bound to be tainted with resentment and resistance."

Based upon this observation, Knowles identified and developed five key assumptions about how adults learn:

- **Learner's need to know**: "I understand why I need to learn this. It makes sense to me."

- **Learner's self-concept**: "I'm an adult, and I can direct myself. That includes in a classroom setting, so please treat me that way."

- **Role of learner's experience**: "I've got lots of valuable experience that I want to draw upon to help me as I learn. Maybe I can help others learn through that experience as well."

- **Readiness to learn**: "I'm ready to learn this because what I learn will help me function better in some way."

- **Orientation to learning**: "What I learn today will help me solve problems at my workplace tomorrow—not at some unspecified time in the future."

As we move into this topic, we would like to mention two "realities": first, organizations continually change and evolve, thereby demanding more and different things from the people they employ. Second, those employees must be willing and able to learn new skills to perform their expanding roles in a fully proficient manner. With respect to an employee's performance within the organization, maintaining a current level of performance often equates to stagnation or even atrophy (which can result in progressive discipline or even termination).

This is true for employees who want to grow into higher-level positions within the organization as well as for employees who want to continue successfully performing in their current positions. Even the "Steady Eddies" and "Steady Bettys" within organizations will find that they must learn and grow within their jobs to keep them. Few individuals can say that they are performing their current job in the same way they performed it 10 or even 5 years ago. During those years, much has been learned, and most likely more will be learned as they remain employed with the organization. This requires the organization to understand adult learners and the realities of teaching adults new skills.

Adults learn very differently from children, however. HR professionals must understand these differences and incorporate them into their instructional design of training programs. Training, like documentation and so many other areas of HR, is more than just a function. The way you carry out your role with respect to training will have a tremendous impact on how you are perceived and how you are defined within the organization—both individually and as a member of HR. Treat a roomful of employees or managers like children, and you'll have a captive audience—but not in a good sense. They'll be looking for ways to duck out early for breaks, surreptitiously answer emails on a handheld wireless device under the table, or—worse yet—just leave and not return.

NOTE

Every training session provides you with an opportunity to partner. But be cautious—don't unintentionally patronize your participants. Training can help define you as an inspiring and motivating facilitator, or it can reinforce the negative adage that "those who can't do, teach."

Learning Styles: How We Learn

When designing training, it's also important for HR professionals to have an understanding of learning styles. Learning styles refer to different ways in which people learn and process ideas and information. There are three different learning styles. (We've also included examples of how those styles might manifest in terms of the PHR exam.)

▶ **Visual learners:** Visual learners learn most effectively through what they see. They might best benefit from videos or DVDs, the use of presentation software, easel pad notes, printed binders that include significant amounts of printed information, extensive note taking, and the like.

  PHR Exam Prep application: Reading this book, highlighting this book (perhaps with color-coded highlighters), preparing study cards, and using self-sticking color-coded flags.

▶ **Auditory learners:** Auditory learners learn most effectively through what they hear. They might best benefit from lectures, facilitated discussions, "ask the expert" -style lecturettes on e-learning platforms, and the like.

  PHR Exam Prep application: Audio recordings (self-made or otherwise) of materials from study guides.

▶ **Tactile/kinesthetic learners:** Tactile/kinesthetic learners learn best when they can be hands on, in the most literal sense of the word. They like to touch, to feel, to explore, and to experience the world around them. Kinesthetic learners are most likely to enjoy—and learn best from—role plays that reinforce and synthesize key learning points. They like to move around during training sessions and to be physically involved in the learning process.

  PHR Exam Prep application: In studying for the PHR exam, tactile learners might be most likely to use note cards as a study tool (especially if they created the cards).

> **NOTE**
>
> Trainers will likely have all types of learners in every training session—whether brick-and-mortar, online, or hybrid. Design and develop training programs accordingly rather than based on the trainer's preferred style or even leadership's preferred style.

Learning Curves

Learning curves refer to the patterns through which individuals learn new material. There are four types of learning curves with which HR professionals need to be familiar.

Negatively Accelerating Learning Curve

Initially, learners process and absorb information quickly. Subsequently, the pace of learning tapers off as the learner becomes more skilled and comfortable. Negatively accelerating learning curves, as shown in Figure 3.1, are commonly associated with training for repetitive or routine tasks.

Negatively accelerating learning curve

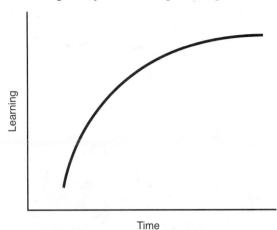

Time

FIGURE 3.1 Negatively accelerating learning curve.

Positively Accelerating Learning Curve

Initially, learners process and absorb information relatively slowly. Ultimately, the pace of learning picks up as the learner masters the complexities of whatever it is about which she is learning. Positively accelerating learning curves, as shown in Figure 3.2, are more commonly associated with training for material or content that is more complex.

Positively accelerating learning curve

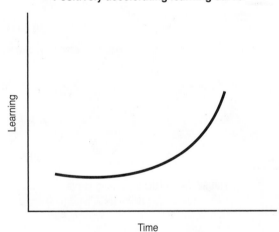

Time

FIGURE 3.2 Positively accelerating learning curve.

S-Shaped Learning Curve

S-shaped learning curves, as shown in Figure 3.3, combine elements of negatively and positively accelerating learning curves. With s-shaped learning curves, the pace of learning ebbs and flows as learners attain greater levels of competence through training as well as through hands-on experience.

S-shaped learning curve

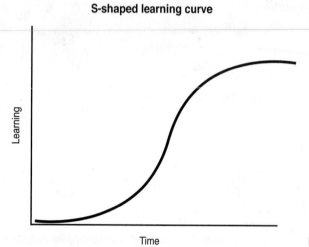

FIGURE 3.3 S-shaped learning curve.

Plateau Learning Curve

Plateau learning curves, as shown in Figure 3.4, are similar to positively accelerating learning curves in that learners process and absorb information quickly at first, but then the pace of learning slows significantly, or even stops—at least temporarily.

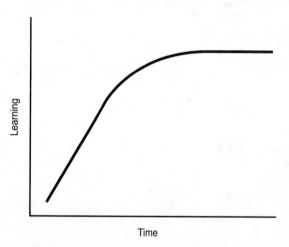

FIGURE 3.4 Plateau learning curve.

Training Modalities/Techniques

We HR professionals, in collaboration with the clients we serve, can choose from a variety of training approaches. Having familiarity with as many of these modalities as possible will enable the HR professional to develop a training solution that is most appropriate for each unique problem while taking into account individual, departmental, and organizational considerations.

Brick-and-Mortar Learning

Brick and mortar training is one of the most traditional types of training that organizations conduct. It constitutes a training/learning program that is delivered face to face and in person, either at the workplace or at an offsite location.

Multiple learners participate in brick-and-mortar learning at the same time and can—ideally—learn from each other as well as from the instructor/facilitator.

On-the-Job Training

On-the-job training takes place in the actual workplace and is predicated on learning what one needs to know, when one needs to know it, by learning precisely what needs to be done in the moment, at the actual location where the "real" work is done

On-the-job training is usually less expensive than other forms of learning because it does not require incremental resources beyond the time of the learner and the trainer. It is important, however, to remember that a less expensive intervention is not always more cost effective, so additional analysis between cost must be undertaken to identify the best intervention.

E-learning

E-learning is a form of training/learning that is delivered completely online. E-learning can be synchronous (everyone learns the same content at the same time) or asynchronous (each learner moves through the program at his own pace). E-learning programs can also be facilitated (by a leader who engages actively in the course content) or nonfacilitated (experienced by learners without the involvement of an instructor to facilitate the learning process).

Hybrid Learning

Hybrid learning is delivered partially online and partially in a traditional classroom.

> **NOTE**
>
> If e-learning/hybrid learning classes include individuals from multiple nations—or even multiple cultures within the same nation—be cognizant of how that might affect the dynamics that emerge during the course. Even more importantly, if e-learning courses will be delivered globally, be careful that the design does not overly or inappropriately reflect the biases, laws, or cultural norms of the nation where the learning was developed or the cultural beliefs that the course designer holds to be true.

Retaining What Is Learned

Effective trainers will incorporate into their programs experiences and methodologies appealing to a variety of learning styles to increase participant involvement and improve the degree to which participants will retain what they learn. Although this may vary from person to person, the following statement generally holds true: the greater the level of learner participation, the greater the level of retention. Consider the percentages outlined in Table 3.3 when designing your learning program.

TABLE 3.3 Learning Experience/Retention Levels

Learning Experience	Level of Retention
Lecture	5%
Reading	10%
A/V	20%
Demonstration	30%
Discussion	50%
Practical/application	70%
Teaching others	90%

Environmental Factors/Elements to Consider—"Brick and Mortar" Classroom Learning

There are some nuts-and-bolts considerations relative to training programs that, even though they may initially appear to be somewhat mundane in nature, can have a big impact on the ultimate success of a training program and which, therefore, should be carefully considered when designing a training program.

Seating Configurations

One of the factors that must be considered is how the training space will be physically arranged. There are many seating arrangements from which to choose. Figure 3.5 illustrates the symbols used in the models that follow.

O = Instructor

X = Participant

— = Table

FIGURE 3.5   Instructor/participant legend.

Classroom/Theater

Classroom/theater style works well if there are a large number of participants in the training session (see Figure 3.6). By design, however, this style reduces the opportunity for participation by, and instructor interaction with, attendees. In some cases, especially when the size of the training group is particularly large or when the training is conducted in a room that has particularly bad acoustics, the instructor (who will likely become more of a lecturer in a setting like this) may require a microphone, or lavaliere microphone ("mic").

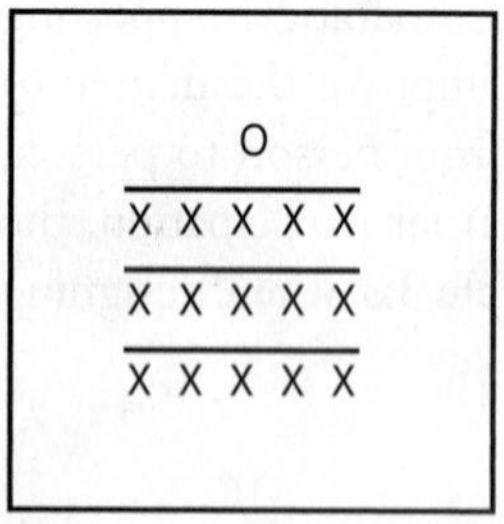

O

X X X X

X X X X

X X X X

FIGURE 3.6   The classroom/theater seating style.

Chevron

Chevron style works well for narrower rooms (see Figure 3.7). It allows for more participation and interaction and facilitates the process of participants working in small groups.

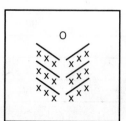

FIGURE 3.7   The Chevron seating style.

Modified Restaurant

A modified restaurant style works well when participants will be engaging in a number of small group activities during the training session (see Figure 3.8). This arrangement will provide the instructor with easy access to groups as well as individual participants during individual and small group activities.

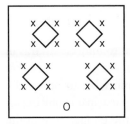

FIGURE 3.8 Modified restaurant seating style.

U-Shaped

The U-shaped style encourages interaction and participation through increased visual contact among participants and with the instructor (see Figure 3.9). Participants sit in chairs that are placed by tables (usually rectangular and narrow) set up in the shape of a letter "U."

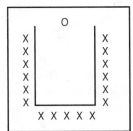

FIGURE 3.9 The U-shaped seating style.

By moving forward and backward through the U, an instructor may be able to move closer to individuals from whom he would be farther away in a classroom or chevron style. This movement and proximity may encourage engagement and interaction. Although this style works particularly well with small groups, it may also provide a viable alternative (sometimes the only viable alternative) for long, relatively narrow training spaces where there is no large center table.

Boardroom

The boardroom setup is similar to the U-shaped setup except that there is a large table in the center of the room around which participants sit (see Figure 3.10). Sometimes the boardroom setup is the only option if training is to be held in a room that has one large table.

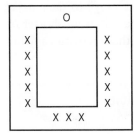

FIGURE 3.10 The boardroom seating style.

> **TIP**
>
> Most trainers have a preferred room setup, which may vary from program to program depending on the nature, content, and level of interaction needed. When possible, know what your preferred style is for a particular program and request it. Recognize, however, that you may not have a choice relative to room configuration. Be prepared to train in a variety of settings. Also, be flexible—the training setup you expect may not be the training setup in which you must deliver the program.

Room Temperature

Room temperature may or may not be within your control. It's important to understand this in advance. Also, as the instructor, you may be so involved in leading the training experience that you may not be aware of changes in room temperature that are uncomfortable to others. Be sensitive to cues that a temperature adjustment might be needed (such as participants putting on or removing layers of clothing). If you have any degree of control over the temperature in the room, invite participants to tell you when the temperature needs to be adjusted. Just remember that "you can't please everyone" when it comes to room temperature; the best that you can do is to try to maintain the room temperature within a reasonable range that is acceptable to most people in the room. If you have no control over the temperature in the room, be up-front with participants about this as soon as possible (ideally, before the start of the session so they can wear appropriate clothing—which usually means dressing in layers). In this way, participants won't mistakenly think that you are being insensitive or unresponsive to their needs.

Air Flow/Movement/Freshness

Know whether there are windows in the training room and whether those windows can safely be opened. If there are no windows, determine whether the room has sufficient airflow. If not, determine whether you can bring a fan (a quiet one) into the room to increase air movement.

Noise

Distracting noises can emanate from inside or outside the building in which you are conducting training. Unwanted noise can come from factors that are controllable, uncontrollable, or semicontrollable, depending upon the situation. Do what you can to anticipate possible noise-based distractions, and try to eliminate them in advance.

Breaks

Short breaks should be scheduled, ideally, once every 90 minutes. However, it's also important to create an environment in which participants are free to leave the room if they need to. (Adults don't like to have to ask permission to use the bathroom or to get a drink of water—and shouldn't have to do so.) Allow enough time during breaks to use the restroom, chat with a colleague, and perhaps check voicemail or email. Generally, 10 to 15 minutes is sufficient and appropriate. Allowing longer breaks might tempt participants to "steal away" to their desks or laptops—in which case, it may be difficult to get them back on time. Allowing shorter or fewer breaks might unintentionally encourage participants to engage in these activities anyway (perhaps even while you are trying to deliver the program).

Smartphones, Personal Technology, and Training Expectations

As communication technology has evolved, etiquette hasn't always evolved along with it. More and more, instructors are encountering situations in which beepers, cell phones, handheld email devices, text messaging, pagers, laptop computers, and the like are being used during instructional portions of training sessions.

Communicate your expectations about electronic communication devices up front, at the beginning of the training program. Encourage participants to give themselves as well as those around them the gift of an uninterrupted training experience. Gently remind them that their organization wants them to be there and that is where they should focus their attention. Also, however, let participants know that you recognize that life goes on outside the training room, that emergencies do occur, and that you understand participants might need to be reachable during a session. Encourage participants to find the least disruptive way in which to do this—ideally, they will choose to turn off their electronic devices and ensure that someone knows where to find them in the event of an emergency. If participants decide that they must keep their devices turned on, encourage them to set them to vibrate or silent and to leave the room if they must take a call or respond to a text.

Food

Another decision that must be made is whether to provide meals, snacks, or beverages to participants. Different organizations have different philosophies on this topic. Some organizations feel that they should not have to "bribe" individuals to attend a program that will benefit them and the organization. Other organizations take a more hospitable approach, seeing training as an opportunity for them to demonstrate their appreciation while adding a bit of celebration and festivity (or, as some organizations say, "If you feed them, they will come").

To varying degrees, food-related decisions will be a function of organizational culture as well as of budgetary considerations. Whatever choice you make, try to make it one that the organization feels comfortable committing to for the foreseeable future. (Otherwise, you'll never stop hearing, "We used to have such great meals at training sessions, but now they expect us to buy our own food in the cafeteria.") Additionally, be aware that some people have dietary preferences and restrictions that relate to religion, health conditions, or other factors.

Training: Not a Panacea

Training is a solution that can be easily overused or underused by organizations.

Training may be overused when it is seen as a cure-all for problems that may be unrelated to skills or areas of knowledge that are required to perform a particular task or function or achieve a particular level of performance. It is not the act of sponsoring, providing, or attending a training program that improves individual or organizational performance; rather, it is the experience of participating in a program that will develop specific skills or affect specific areas of knowledge that are needed, at that moment, to support organizational success. Implementing a training solution when it is not appropriate to do so could diminish the likelihood that a more appropriate training initiative might be accepted at a later time, when it might be more successful.

Training may be underused if an organization chooses not to avail itself of training options that could remedy performance issues relating to gaps between current and needed levels of skill or knowledge. There are also circumstances that reach beyond the question of whether individuals have specific skills or knowledge. In those cases, training may not be effective or helpful. Here are a few of those:

▶ When there are systemic issues that would exist even if all employees were fully proficient with the proposed content

▶ When there are underlying cultural issues or problems that the training would not address

▶ When there are leadership issues, such as lack of trust

▶ When organizational missions, visions, or values are either not clearly defined or are incongruous with each other or with reality

▶ When training has been used before as a "flavor of the month" approach to problem solving

> ▶ When training is viewed as or has been used as a symbolic gesture rather than a means of creating real organizational change
>
> In short, training is not a cure-all. It is, however, an effective way of addressing issues involving skills development and requiring transfer of knowledge.

ADDIE: "D" Is for Development

In this phase of Addie, you will develop (or oversee/participate in the development of) the design plan that was created in the previous phase. This will include the development of the actual materials. Alternatively, you may decide that the best way to execute the design plan is to purchase or license materials from a source outside the organization. Either way, during this phase, every exercise, resource, handout, activity, and training element is created, built, or otherwise secured. The outputs from this phase, therefore, will include program materials (for participants and instructors/facilitators) as well as instructional guides (for instructors/facilitators).

ADDIE: "I" Is for Implementation

By now, the HRD/training program has been designed and developed. You've made sure that it is practical rather than overly theoretical in a balance that is consistent with the culture and expectations of your organization. It has been designed and built to deliver knowledge and skills that participants will be able to use in the workplace, not just in the classroom. Now it's time to prepare for the actual launch—in the classroom, online, or through some blended (hybrid) combination of both.

Pilot Programs

By the time an HRD/training program is ready to be implemented (or delivered), a great deal of time, talent, and financial resources have probably been invested in its successful launch. As such, it may be difficult (or even painful, at moments) to entertain the possibility that some dimension of the program, as conceived or designed, may need to be refined, overhauled, or even scrapped. Yet it is precisely this possibility to which we must be open—and that we must even consciously invite.

It is for this reason that—assuming a program will be delivered more than one time—it is critical to run a pilot program before launching a full-fledged HRD/training initiative.

Options for Running Pilot Programs

A pilot program is generally delivered to a subsection of the population of individuals who would ultimately be expected to participate in the HRD/training initiative. It's also delivered to decision makers, senior managers (from whom you want to re-secure buy-in), and other key stakeholders.

Pilot sessions can be run in a number of different ways, two of which follow:

- ▶ **Identical Program Format:** In this scenario, the pilot program is identical to the actual training program you have designed and developed. In this way, the attendees of the pilot program will be able to experience and assess the same program that subsequent attendees will attend.

- ▶ **Abbreviated Program Format:** In this format, the pilot program enables participants to experience some, but not all, of the program elements. Some portions might be described or discussed, and others might be introduced but not executed. Certain portions of the program might be skipped entirely.

Ideally, an HRD/training pilot should be identical to the actual training program that subsequent participants will experience (the first option). Realistically, however, this will not always be possible, nor will your clients always be open to this option. So, as an alternative, be prepared to deliver an abbreviated format.

Collecting and Using Feedback from Pilot Programs

With either pilot program format, a critical component of the pilot involves receiving feedback from those who attend the pilot program. This feedback should be far more extensive than the single-page workshop evaluation forms (sometimes called "smile sheets") that participants are often asked to complete at the end of training sessions. Ideally, pilot evaluation will afford the opportunity for a candid exchange of ideas with all stakeholders. Encourage your pilot participants to share their feedback during a post-training feedback session, at which time they could present questions, comments, and thoughts about which they have made notes during and after the session. Be prepared, however, that your client may not be open to scheduling a formal follow-up session after the pilot. Instead, you may be asked to move in and out of role (instructor versus training designer/developer), as appropriate, during the actual pilot program.

After pilot program participants have provided you with their feedback and insights, the next step is to review, assess, and incorporate (as appropriate) that feedback into the next iteration of the training program. This feedback—and even your own observations—may help you address issues relating to any number of potential concerns, including content, exercises, use of specific methodologies, pace, complexity, clarity, the order in which the content is delivered, and so forth.

NOTE

Yes, you've invested a lot of time and effort into the HRD/training initiative by this point. It can even be said that you have invested a lot of yourself. And yes, this process of scrutiny and review may feel a bit frustrating. But know that you are not wasting your time. Instead, think of it this way—you are being provided with insights and reactions that will make the time you have already invested pay off even more because it will enable you to produce an even better training program.

CAUTION

On a related note, stay positive. Demonstrating defensiveness at this point in the process can harm you in two ways—it can keep you from delivering the best training product possible, and it can diminish your credibility as an HR professional and consultative business partner, something that goes well beyond the scope of even the broadest HRD/training initiative. So, as you are being provided with feedback, be sure to practice your active listening skills—even if it hurts. The end result, for all involved (including you), will be of a higher quality because of your efforts, your willingness to listen, your flexibility, and your commitment to the outcome and to your clients.

Facilitator/Instructor

Now that we've taken a close look at content, let's take a close look at delivery. Another important dimension of effective implementation focuses on the facilitator/instructor. Effective facilitation is an artful science and a scientific art. There are myriad factors that can be considered when selecting a trainer. Different factors might be more relevant or important in different situations. The following list represents a partial inventory of skills that are crucial to effective facilitation/instruction in the traditional "brick-and-mortar" setting (and provides a basis from which to evaluate actual performance).

Clarity of Presentation

The clarity of an instructor/facilitator's presentation refers to the effective use of practices that foster better understanding of the subject matter and prevent confusion. An instructor or facilitator who has strong clarity of communication would likely do the following:

▶ Provide a written outline of the key points that will be addressed during the workshop.

▶ Regularly define new terms, concepts, and principles when they are introduced (rather than assuming a certain level of audience knowledge or putting participants on the spot relative to who does or does not understand a particular concept). Be particularly careful of using acronyms before explaining what they mean. It can be challenging to remain mindful of this, especially when an instructor knows a topic "inside and out." It is, however, critically important.

▶ Explain why particular processes, techniques, or formulas are incorporated into the program (rather than just "throwing" information at participants).

▶ Use real-world examples to bring workshop concepts to life.

▶ Relate new ideas and concepts covered in the program to more familiar ones and to participants' own experiences.

▶ Provide occasional summaries and restatements of important ideas and ensure smooth transitions to new, yet related, topics.

▶ Adjust the pace of delivery when introducing complex and difficult material.

▶ Avoid excessive digressions from the outline or key topics.

▶ Use materials and visual aids to support and clarify concepts.

▶ Use well-organized and well-written handouts, workbooks, computerized presentations, and the like.

▶ Keep a "parking lot"—a list of topics to address either later in the program or "offline." This will help you remain on task, on time, and organized.

Presentation Effectiveness

Some of the behaviors that might indicate presentation effectiveness could include the following:

▶ Clearly stating the objectives of the workshop.

▶ Presenting subjects in a logical order.

▶ Allowing ample time for participants to grasp, explore, and practice concepts.

▶ Periodically confirming with participants that they are "with you." (Of course, paraphrasing and asking discussion questions represent far more effective ways of accomplishing this than literally asking participants if they are with you.)

▶ Designing and using exercises that are practical and helpful to participants and that support concepts and objectives.

▶ Referring to and utilizing training materials (including the participant manual) throughout the program.

▶ Using videos, music, or other special audio/visual aids to enhance the learning experience and to appeal to auditory or visual learners.

- Ensuring that writing on boards/easel pads is organized, legible, and captures important points of the subject matter.

- Summarizing major points throughout, and at the conclusion of, the workshop (in an interactive manner, whenever possible).

Participant Dynamics

Effective learning experiences maintain participants' interest and strive for a high level of involvement. Instructors who are skilled with respect to engaging participants might do the following:

- Periodically modify the pace of the program to maintain—or recapture—participants' interest and engagement.

- Use instructional techniques that promote interactivity.

- Address participants by name. (Using table tents can help facilitate this.)

- Encourage participant feedback.

- Provide constructive feedback in a nonthreatening and affirming manner.

- Utilize activities and exercises that are challenging and that encourage participants to reach above their previous level of skill or knowledge.

- Utilize techniques, methods, and logic that can be applied back at the workplace.

Question/Answer Technique

Effective presentations incorporate questions that challenge participants to analyze information and to apply their newly acquired (or enhanced) skills and knowledge. Effective question/answer facilitation techniques might include the following:

- Ask factual questions to provide participants with the opportunity to demonstrate their knowledge—existing, as well as expanding.

- Ask open-ended, thought-provoking questions that engage participants.

- Ask questions that afford participants the opportunity to apply information or principles addressed during the workshop.

- Ask questions that challenge participants to exercise analysis or judgment relative to the instructional materials.

- Ask follow-up questions to clarify and interpret instructional materials, as well as participants' responses and comments.

- Allow ample opportunity (silence) for participants to think through their responses before answering a question.

- Rephrase and repeat difficult questions as appropriate.

▶ Respond to unclear (or wrong) participant responses in an honest, yet affirming, manner.

▶ Repeat participants' questions and answers when they have not been heard by all participants. (It's usually important to acknowledge the reason for this, acoustic or otherwise, at an appropriate time.)

▶ Redirect participant questions to other program participants, as appropriate.

▶ Defer difficult, irrelevant, or time-consuming questions or comments from participants for discussion outside the workshop. (In other words, know when to take a discussion offline.)

Verbal and Nonverbal Communication

Communicating effectively verbally and nonverbally (and combining those two expressions of communication in an effective manner) would require behaviors such as the following:

▶ Speaking audibly and clearly

▶ Modulating voice level to ensure variety of emphasis

▶ Not using an excessive amount of "minimal encouragers" as speech fillers (okay, ah, uh-huh, um)

▶ Speaking at a pace that is neither too fast nor too slow

▶ Projecting excitement and enthusiasm about the program and the materials

▶ Establishing and maintaining eye contact with workshop participants as appropriate

▶ Moving throughout the room/area in an engaging (rather than distracting) way

▶ Using facial expressions and hand gestures to reinforce and emphasize verbal messages

▶ Listening carefully to participants' comments and questions

---

KNOWLEDGE

Knowledge 36

Techniques to assess training program effectiveness, including use of applicable metrics (for example: participant surveys, pre- and post-testing).

ADDIE: "E" Is for Evaluation

The evaluation phase allows for—and in fact mandates—a comparison of the results or outputs of the HRD/training to the learning objectives that were established during the needs analysis/assessment phase. In this way, the degree to which the specific HRD/training objectives were met can be ascertained through measurement, not guesswork. There will be no question, either way, whether the gap between actual performance (pretraining) and desired performance (post-training) has been bridged.

The Theoretical/Scholarly Foundation

The works of two experts—Donald L. Kirkpatrick and Robert Brinkerhoff—are particularly relevant to evaluation of training (and—through transferability—of other HRD) initiatives.

Kirkpatrick: Four Levels of Evaluation

Kirkpatrick's theory takes a "summative" approach to evaluation in that it is predicated on the interpretation of data that is collected after the initiative has been implemented. Kirkpatrick's approach allows for a complete analysis of the entire initiative on four different levels: reaction, learning, behavior, and results.

Kirkpatrick's Level 1: Reaction

Reaction-level evaluation measures participants' responses and reactions to the program immediately after the program has been delivered. This level of evaluation often takes the form of a short survey that participants are asked to complete at the end of a training session.

Reaction-level evaluation is fast, relatively easy, and frequently utilized. Its value lies in its ability to provide insights into participants' immediate reactions to instructor delivery, training environment, refreshments, and other immediately apparent factors of the HRD/training experience.

> **CAUTION**
>
> Although post-evaluation training forms may ask participants to speculate relative to the degree to which they will be able to transfer content learned during the training program back to the job, this process of speculation is not factual, nor is it necessarily accurate. As such, don't be tempted to assess the ultimate success of a training program on the results of those initial "smile sheets." Instead, remember that true success can only be determined by the long-term attainment of the learning objectives, the transfer of learning to the workplace, return on investment (ROI), and the like.

> **NOTE**
>
> The transfer of skills and knowledge will enable an employee to perform her current job more effectively, thus contributing to the overall effectiveness of the organization, but training does not ensure transfer of learning. Explore evaluation techniques to ensure that training initiatives have had an impact—ideally a measurable or observable one—upon the workplace.

Kirkpatrick's Level 2: Learning

Learning-level evaluation measures whether—and to what degree—participants have mastered skills or acquired knowledge points that were identified in the learning objectives. Pretests and post-tests—frequently seen in e-learning applications—are one means of assessing the development of skills and the acquisition of knowledge.

▶ A pretest is an assessment instrument that is administered to participants prior to engaging in the training, learning, or OD session.

▶ A post-test is an assessment instrument that is administered to participants after engaging in the training, learning, or OD initiative. This instrument must be identical to the pretest that was administered to the group before the training/OD session. To provide valuable feedback, this instrument should be completed as soon after the completion of the training/OD program as possible to generate a more valid measure of the learning that was achieved during the session (rather than as a result of independent research in which participants might engage afterward).

Kirkpatrick's Level 3: Behavior

Behavior-level evaluation measures whether participants' on-the-job behaviors have changed in a manner consistent with training objectives. In short, it measures transfer of training—the degree to which participants apply the skills and knowledge covered in the training session back to the workplace.

In conducting behavior-level assessment, it is important to recognize that individuals can choose to change their workplace behavior for a variety of reasons—some of which are completely unrelated to the training in which they participated. A few of these reasons might relate to the following:

▶ Receiving positive reinforcement for demonstrating desired behaviors in the workplace

▶ Experiencing progressive disciplinary actions as a result of demonstrating substandard behavior in the workplace

▶ Receiving explicit feedback as part of a performance management or appraisal process—feedback that described the performance problem in explicit terms: terms that, to the employee, might ultimately motivate change

Kirkpatrick's Level 4: Results

Results-level evaluation looks specifically at whether the business or organizational results that were expected to occur as a result of the HRD/training initiative did, in fact, occur. This level of results-based evaluation is measurable, concrete, and usually of keen interest to the leaders of the organization because results speak volumes.

As with Kirkpatrick's level 3 analysis, however, it is important to recognize the degree to which other factors (for instance, a direct competitor going out of business) could have affected the results. It's important that ROI calculations made as part of results-level analysis truly reflect the implementation of HRD/training initiatives and not other unrelated factors.

Brinkerhoff: Formative Evaluation Model

As discussed previously, Kirkpatrick's model takes a summative evaluation approach that is implemented only after training has been delivered. Robert O. Brinkerhoff's approach is different. Published in *Achieving Results Through Training*, Brinkerhoff's model incorporates formative evaluation. Within a formative evaluation model, evaluative feedback and input is sought throughout the development and implementation phases in an effort to strengthen the ultimate training initiative through real-time incorporation of evaluative feedback. Brinkerhoff's formative evaluation model mandates an iterative process in which feedback, analysis, and assessment conducted at one phase of the process will be used to make enhancements throughout the current and subsequent phases.

Brinkerhoff's model identifies six stages of evaluation:

1. **Goals:** What is really needed?

2. **HRD design:** What will work?

3. **Program implementation:** How is the training working?

4. **Immediate outcomes:** Did participants learn, what did they learn, and how well did they learn it?

5. **Intermediate or usage outcomes:** Are participants continuing to retain what they learned and continuing to transfer that learning to the workplace?

6. **Impacts and worth:** Ultimately, did the training initiative make a difference to the organization? If so, did it make enough of a difference to be truly worthwhile?

> **NOTE**
>
> If an organization/HR professional/trainer seeks feedback, it is important to ensure that the participants fully understand that they will not experience any sort of negative repercussions for providing candid feedback. Concerns around this might be exacerbated by cultural considerations—organizational or national—or even by past experiences with the employer or with prior employers.

HRD Responsibility 05

RESPONSIBILITY

Develop, implement, and evaluate talent management programs that include assessing talent, developing career paths, and managing the placement of high-potential employees.

Knowledge 28

KNOWLEDGE

Career development and leadership development theories and applications (for example: succession planning, dual career ladders).

Knowledge 29

KNOWLEDGE

Organization development (OD) theories and applications.

Elements of OD

Acknowledging that OD is a values-driven approach, R. T. Golembiewski identified and articulated important characteristics related to OD, some of which follow:

▶ Trust, openness, and collaboration are valued and emphasized.

▶ The needs of individuals as well as the needs of the organization and smaller units of the organization are important and relevant.

▶ Feelings, emotions, ideas, and concepts are important.

▶ Group interaction is emphasized and important with respect to change as well as choice and problem identification and resolution.

Purposes of OD

OD serves a variety of purposes within an organization—purposes that have been defined differently by different individuals and organizations. Some of these purposes are the following:

▶ Enhancing the overall effectiveness of organizations.

- ▶ Promoting openness toward differences and toward resolving the problems that can arise from those differences. (Diversity initiatives, in particular, would deal with matters related to this.)

- ▶ Aligning employee goals with unit and organizational goals.

- ▶ Clarifying individual and organizational goals and objectives.

- ▶ Encouraging, supporting, and facilitating collaborative working relationships between and among managers/leaders, individuals, and teams.

- ▶ Improving decision-making, individually as well as organizationally.

- ▶ Improving employees' work performance and promotability.

- ▶ Supporting the development of new or replacement knowledge and skills.

- ▶ Dealing more effectively with problems of a human as well as of a technical nature.

- ▶ Managing change more effectively.

Role of HR Professionals in OD

Sometimes HR professionals are asked to consult with OD professionals. OD professionals may be employed within the organization or may be brought in from outside the organization to work on a particular assignment. Alternatively, HR professionals may be assigned to work on a specific OD project without the assistance of specialized OD professionals (or, for that matter, specialized OD training). In any of these scenarios, HR's role in the OD process is critical.

OD and Organizational Culture

An important factor to consider when contemplating any OD intervention is the culture of the organization. Organizational culture can be, and has been, defined in myriad ways. Sometimes it is referred to as "the way things are done around here." This seemingly flippant statement actually incorporates a number of important factors, such as the following:

- ▶ The shared values of the organization

- ▶ The external environment in which the organization functions

- ▶ The way the organization responds to specific individual, group, and organization-level behaviors (punishment, rewards, tolerance, and so on)

EXAM ALERT

Organizational culture helps establish organizational identity—one to which employees can relate, to which they can belong, and against which they can measure themselves as one way of ascertaining the degree to which they fit within the organization. The culture of an organization can entice candidates to join an organization and can have a seemingly disproportionate impact on an employee's decision to leave an organization. The culture of the organization is also a unifying force for those who work within it. It provides guidance with respect to the norms and behavioral expectations of the organization—in short, it helps employees figure out how they are supposed to act. Organizational culture also contributes to shaping the goals of an organization and is passed on from one generation of employees to the next through stories, publications, and the like.

Organization culture is powerful. It can be productive as well as counterproductive. It needs to be recognized, acknowledged, and understood by HR professionals—in general and as part of efforts to increase the likelihood that OD interventions will be appropriate and effective.

Career Development

Another way of looking at OD is that it takes a macro, overarching approach to the growth and development of the organization. Career development, on the other hand, takes a more micro approach in that it looks at the development of individuals within the organization. Those two ends of the spectrum are inextricably linked in that they both share the objective of developing the organization. Essentially, the growth and development of individuals within the organization contribute to the overall development and advancement of the organization as a whole.

Career development can be defined as the deliberate preparation for, and unfolding of, the professional pathway along which each individual journeys during his adult working life. Career development can also be described, more simply, as the development of individuals within the organization. In either context, career development is either owned wholly by the employee or co-owned by the employee and the employer. (The latter is more common in learning organizations that are committed to developing high-potential employees.) Rarely, if ever, is career development even the sole responsibility of the employer. (However, that scenario was more common 35 or more years ago.)

Managers can support employees in their career development through coaching, counseling, and offering honest and candid performance feedback and appraisals. The organization can also support and encourage employees who actively seek to grow and enhance their skills through activities such as establishing a skills database or encouraging cross-training, transfers, and other opportunities for employees to expand their skills and knowledge.

Organizations can ensure that resources are allocated to employee career development. In addition to financial resources, employees will need time to develop new skills or attain new knowledge through cross-training or workshops. Organizations also need to ensure that psychological and emotional resources are not withheld—employees may be less likely to avail themselves of development opportunities if they feel that their current supervisors will want to hold them back out of fear of "losing" them (in which case, of course, employees would already likely be seeking opportunities to work for employers who will treat them less like property and more like people).

Ultimately, however, each employee must take responsibility for her own growth and development. An organization cannot force an employee to grow. Learning can't be mandated either. Each employee must determine whether—and how—she wants to grow and follow through on the opportunities that exist to do so.

Leadership Development

Leadership development can be defined as the strategic investment in the managers and leaders who work within the organization.

To understand leadership development, it's first necessary to grasp the concepts of leadership and management. These are explored in depth in Chapter 1, "Business Management and Strategy (BM & S)."

High-Potential Employees

Leadership development can also manifest as organizations invest in high-potential employees. High-potential employees are current employees who demonstrate behaviors—and who perform their responsibilities—in a way that indicates that they are capable of significant growth within the organization. Although they might not possess all the knowledge or skills that they will ultimately need to fulfill higher-level roles, they have been identified as individuals who have the requisite behavioral characteristics as well as the capability to learn what needs to be learned to contribute in more strategic roles and ways.

Dual Career Ladders

When thinking about the topics of high-potential employees and career development, it is crucial to consider the possibility of establishing dual career ladders.

Dual career ladders allow opportunities for employees to grow in terms of pay, skill, responsibility, and authority into supervisory roles or into technical (nonsupervisory roles). Said differently, assuming responsibility for managing others is not the only way to grow vertically within an organization that has established dual career ladders.

Dual career ladders are more commonly found in medical, scientific, or engineering professions. HR professionals, however, should explore the possibility of establishing dual career ladders with their clients (in a consultative, results-driven manner—as always).

Succession Planning

Leadership development can be further supported by a sound succession planning program. Succession planning is the detailed, ongoing process through which an organization identifies individuals who might be able to fill higher-level positions that could become available in the future. Succession plans are "living, breathing" tools that affect individual and group professional development planning and that—through predictive efforts and proactive planning—strive to ensure that the overarching mission and goals of the organization will not be derailed by the inevitable departure of individuals from the organization.

Skill Inventories

Organizations can, and often do, maintain a central database that captures the many KSAs possessed by its employees, even when those KSAs are not being used by an employee in her current position. When a position opens up, the organization can then generate a list of current employees who meet the minimum qualifications for the position.

> **NOTE**
>
> It's important to keep in mind that skill inventory systems may identify employees who meet the minimum qualifications for other positions but who are not interested in applying for them. As long as an employee has not been specifically hired into a particular position as a "feeder pool" for a higher-level position, it's important to ensure that there are no subtle or overt negative consequences for employees who decide not to pursue higher-level positions for which they have been identified as qualified through the skill inventory process. Every organization needs "Steady Eddies" and "Steady Bettys"—employees who are solid contributors in their current roles, who are happy and fulfilled in those roles, and who are not interested in climbing the corporate ladder. Creating a culture in which promotion is the only acceptable career track devalues the contributions of these solid contributors and can subsequently increase the likelihood that these underappreciated employees may eventually leave the organization. It can also increase the likelihood of turnover because of unrealistic expectations that are not fulfilled. The bottom line is that not everyone in an organization can or even wants to be promoted—so it doesn't serve an organization well to imply that "moving up" is the only option available to its employees.

Replacement Charts

Replacement charts identify names of individuals who could potentially fill a particular position if an opening becomes available.

Talent Management

Talent management speaks to the sum total of the organization's efforts, initiatives, and programs to create a targeted employment life cycle experience that attracts, motivates, retains, compensates, and develops valued, high-performing employees.

In a sense, every component of the employment life cycle speaks to, and constitutes a component of, talent management. In the same way, every aspect of HRD is a manifestation of talent management. In this sense, this entire chapter—and much of this book—can be viewed as highly relevant to the topic of talent management.

Teambuilding

Another way in which OD can be incorporated in an organization is through teambuilding exercises. Teambuilding exercises constitute initiatives and activities that seek to help the team learn to function more effectively so that it can attain its overall objective (which must link, of course, to overall organizational objectives). These activities can be set in myriad environments and can be constructed in almost countless ways, all of which should share a common objective: to help the team learn how to function more effectively so that it can attain its overall objectives (which must link, of course, to the overall organizational objectives). Team-building exercises provide teams with an opportunity to explore topics such as trust, communication, problem solving, the role of the individual within the team, and the impact that the team has on its clients. Team-building exercises often provide scenarios through which participants can hone the same skills and learn about the same principles that are required for the team to function effectively at the workplace.

> **NOTE**
>
> Be certain to plan, build, and evaluate potential team-building exercises within the ADDIE framework. Teambuilding activities—especially those described by consultants—can appear to be extremely creative and engaging, but if they do not deliver the desired results and address individual and organizational performance concerns in a measurable way, they will not yield a positive return on investment. This must be assessed through analysis rather than through "gut feeling."

Specific OD Interventions

Although there are a variety of possible OD interventions, two specific ones that HR professionals need to be familiar with are team building and total quality management (TQM).

Total Quality Management

TQM is an OD intervention that is ultimately aimed at meeting or exceeding customer expectations through the commitment of everyone in an organization (often through a team-based approach) to continuous improvement of the production of products or the delivery of services.

Total Quality Pioneers

Several individuals figure prominently in the history of quality management. These are people who have made landmark contributions with respect to quality. This, in turn, relates to the identification of less-than-missionworthy performance and achievement, which in turn leads to the consideration, costing, and development of HRD initiatives.

W. Edwards Deming, a true quality pioneer, began his focus on and study of quality in the 1940s, but, like many prophets, he was not initially appreciated in his homeland. (In Deming's case, that homeland was the United States.) Deming subsequently brought his expertise to Japan in the 1950s, where he has been revered ever since. Deming reemerged as a strong business presence in America in 1980 after an NBC documentary featured him prominently. From that time until his death in 1993, Deming consulted extensively with American organizations, finally disseminating his 14-point quality management program in the nation of his birth—and finally earning the recognition and respect that had previously eluded him.

Joseph M. Juran was another giant in the area of quality. Like Deming, Juran centered his attention on the perspectives and needs of customers. His quality management ideas focused on three key areas: quality planning, quality improvement, and quality control. Juran's commitment to quality is still present today through the Juran Institute, whose stated mission is to "enable our clients to attain quality leadership by achieving sustainable breakthrough results. We focus on improving the 'customer experience' of our clients' clients!"

Philip B. Crosby, a third quality guru, is well known for his "zero defects" standard in contrast to "acceptable quality levels" (AQLs). This management philosophy asserted that employees would perform at whatever level management sets for them. Settling for "goodness"—rather than the full attainment of objectives—would, therefore, effectively preclude the possibility of attaining those objectives.

Crosby, therefore, raised the bar even higher. He established four absolutes of quality management:

▶ Quality means conformance to requirements, not goodness.

▶ Quality is achieved by prevention, not appraisal.

▶ Quality has a performance standard of zero defects, not acceptable quality levels.

▶ Quality is measured by the price of nonconformance, not indexes.

The fourth quality guru we'll look at is Kaoru Ishikawa, who believed in the idea of continued customer service—even after the customer purchases the product. He saw quality as a never-ending process in that it can always be taken one step further. Ishikawa also believed strongly in the criticality of securing top-level management support. He dramatically increased worldwide awareness and acceptance of the idea of quality circles, originally a Japanese philosophy.

Quality Tools

As part of developing a basic understanding and knowledge of TQM, HR professionals need to be familiar with several important quality tools:

▶ **Cause-and-effect, Ishikawa, or Fishbone diagram:** Ishikawa developed an important quality tool called the cause-and-effect diagram, which is also known as an Ishikawa diagram or the fishbone diagram. This tool presents a visual representation of factors that affect whether a desired outcome will be obtained. Ishikawa believed that, by presenting all the possible factors that contribute to a particular result, any potential process imperfections can be identified in advance and eliminated. Figure 3.11 shows an example of an Ishikawa diagram.

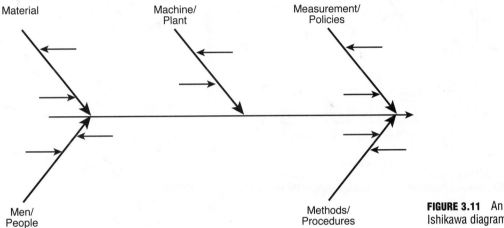

FIGURE 3.11 An Ishikawa diagram.

▶ **Histogram:** Histograms are graphs that depict information about a single factor. In addition to being used to graphically communicate information, they sometimes can help identify patterns or explanations. See Figure 3.12 for an example.

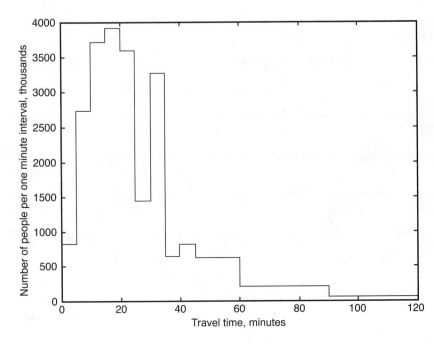

FIGURE 3.12 A histogram.

► **Pareto chart:** The Pareto principle, also referred to as the "80-20 rule," asserts that 80% of effects result from 20% of causes. The Pareto principle and the chart that visually depicts it are intended to help individuals focus efforts where there is the greatest likelihood of maximizing the payoff—that is, where there is greatest likelihood of bringing about positive change. Figure 3.13 shows a Pareto chart.

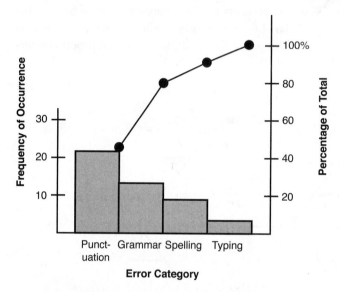

Courtesy of Professor Sid Sytsma, Ferris State University   **FIGURE 3.13** Pareto principle.

RESPONSIBILITY

HRD Responsibility 06

Develop, select, and evaluate performance appraisal processes (for example: instruments, ranking, and rating scales) to increase individual and organizational effectiveness.

RESPONSIBILITY

HRD Responsibility 07

Develop, implement, and evaluate performance management programs and procedures (includes training for evaluators).

KNOWLEDGE

Knowledge 33

Performance appraisal methods (for example: instruments, ranking, and rating scales).

KNOWLEDGE

Knowledge 34

Performance management methods (for example: goal setting, relationship to compensation, job placements/promotions).

Performance Management

Although not always thought of as an HRD intervention, well-executed performance management is wholly consistent with the mission of HRD. Why? Individual performance directly impacts team, unit, and organizational performance. Therefore, performance management is a critical element of an organization's ultimate overall success.

Performance management is the process by which managers and their direct reports communicate about, plan for, and—as the name implies—manage the individual performance of each direct report.

> **NOTE**
>
> Performance management is sometimes confused with performance appraisal. In fact, at some organizations, the terms are used interchangeably. They are not, however, synonymous. Although the two are related, there are important definitional differences. Most important, performance appraisal is, essentially, an event. It is one component of performance management. It speaks to the meeting that takes place at the end of the performance measurement period. During this meeting, the manager and the employee review the employee's performance during the prior year and (often) look ahead to the next year.
>
> Performance management, conversely, consists of a continuous flow of collaborative feedback, coaching, and opportunities for communication during which the manager and the employee engage throughout the entire performance measurement period.

Performance Management: Its Organizational Roots

Effective performance management and appraisal can't take place in a vacuum. Instead, every step of the ongoing performance management process must be rooted in the organization's mission, vision, and values.

Performance Management and Organizational Mission

An organization's mission represents the reason why it exists: its ultimate purpose—the focus that drives (or should drive) every initiative, every employee, and within the context of performance management, every goal. In short, goals cascade throughout the organization, beginning with the mission statement and moving down, and throughout, the hierarchy of the organization. Eventually, that mission statement should affect every goal for every employee in every position within the organization.

In turn, each employee's performance will ultimately contribute to the successful attainment of objectives at every level of the organization, up through and including senior leadership. This combination of top-down/bottom-up goal setting and achievement helps ensure that time, effort, energy, and all other organizational resources are focused upon the ultimate objective: furthering the mission of the organization.

This is the practical, performance-focused definition of mission-driven performance management, within a mission-driven organization, illustrated in Figure 3.14.

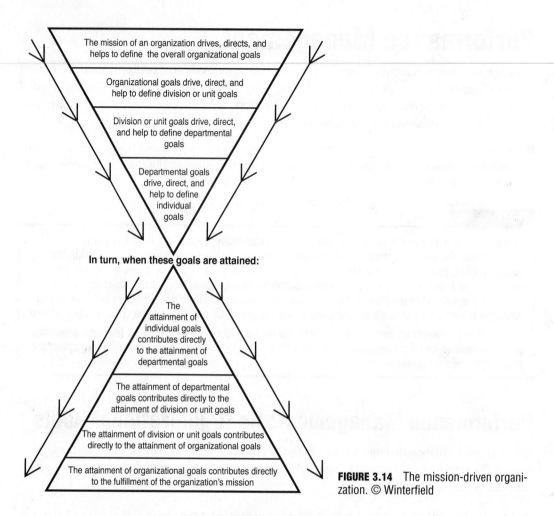

The mission of an organization drives, directs, and helps to define the overall organizational goals

Organizational goals drive, direct, and help to define division or unit goals

Division or unit goals drive, direct, and help to define departmental goals

Departmental goals drive, direct, and help to define individual goals

In turn, when these goals are attained:

The attainment of individual goals contributes directly to the attainment of departmental goals

The attainment of departmental goals contributes directly to the attainment of division or unit goals

The attainment of division or unit goals contributes directly to the attainment of organizational goals

The attainment of organizational goals contributes directly to the fulfillment of the organization's mission

FIGURE 3.14 The mission-driven organization. © Winterfield

Performance Management and Organizational Values

An organization's statement of values reflects its underlying philosophies and its guiding tenets—what it, quite literally, values most closely.

This concept can be difficult to define and even more difficult to link to business objectives. The organization's values, however, must be explicitly clear for several reasons. First, the organization's values contribute significantly to defining the organization's culture. Culture, in turn, has a huge impact on how the organization—and the individuals and teams within the organization—functions on a day-to-day basis.

In thinking about this day-to-day functioning, a link can be made back to performance management. Values, if simply listed as catchy-sounding phrases, can be ambiguous. For instance, what does "integrity" look like? "Professionalism" is no easier to define, nor is "customer commitment" or "loyalty." From a performance management perspective, organizational values only take on their true value when they are defined in behavioral terms. This can be done by providing specific behavioral examples of how each value might manifest itself behaviorally in a particular organization.

In addition to ensuring that an organization's values are truly lived out on a day-to-day basis, the process of defining values behaviorally provides a more objective, productive, and defensible basis from which to incorporate values-related considerations throughout the performance management and appraisal process. This is a critical consideration because values-based performance management is one important way of addressing and appraising how work should be accomplished instead of just what needs to be accomplished.

The Performance Management Process/System

With this foundation of mission and values, let's take a look at a typical performance management process. A performance management process, or system, constitutes a series of steps that, together, comprise an ongoing performance management system or process. These can include the following:

Step 1. Setting and communicating of performance standards

Step 2. Feedback and documentation

Step 3. Written performance appraisal, prepared by manager

Step 4. Performance appraisal meeting

Let's look at each of these.

Step 1: Setting and Communicating of Performance Standards

Performance standards speak to expectations that an organization has for an employee with respect to what she is responsible for accomplishing and the ways in which the employee executes her position.

Performance standards can be expressed in different ways and through different measures, two of which could include these:

▶ Goals/objectives

▶ Competencies

Using the top-down/bottom-up model described previously, performance goals or performance objectives express and communicate expectations in terms of what should be produced. Just like any other OD initiative, performance management goals and objectives must be SMART. (See "ADDIE: 'D' Is for Design.") The "M" in SMART—measurable—is particularly important with respect to setting and communicating performance goals and objectives.

> **NOTE**
>
> At some organizations, "goals" are considered to be "bigger" than objectives. At other organizations, the opposite holds true. The specific verbiage is less crucial than the concepts relating to this.

Like values, competencies describe how employees are expected to perform as they deliver the performance goals/objectives. Unlike goals, however, competencies are more frequently rooted in skills. Competencies (also sometimes referred to as success factors, performance factors, or the like) are often the same for all employees who work in a particular organization. Some organizations establish additional competencies that managers are expected to possess and demonstrate. Examples of competencies for all employees (managers as well as nonmanagers) might be communication, customer focus, and dependability. Examples of additional managerial competencies might be staffing and development and (even better) performance management.

As with values, competencies must be expressed in terms of specific behaviors rather than in terms of attitudes or personality traits. This is the best (and perhaps the only) way to ensure clarity and mutual understanding with respect to competency-based performance expectations. Failure to define competencies in behavioral terms can result in employee (and, sometimes, even managerial) frustration, confusion, resentment, or suspicion.

As an example, let's look at the competency "customer focus." An attitudinal or personality-based approach to customer focus might say that an employee needs to be friendly and helpful. A behavioral approach to customer focus would look more like this:

- ▶ Demonstrates understanding of customers, as well as knowledge of their goals, needs, and wants

- ▶ Accurately anticipates—and communicates an understanding of—the spoken and unspoken needs of customers

- ▶ Seeks out, obtains, and processes information that enables the employee to meet the needs of the customer

- ▶ Responds to customer concerns in a timely, accurate, and thorough manner and confirms that his response meets with the customer's satisfaction

Sometimes the ways in which competencies manifest themselves behaviorally are fairly easy to measure. At other times, however, competencies might manifest themselves through behaviors that are observable but that do not lend themselves as easily to measurement. It is, in part, an organizational decision (that may, to a significant degree, be affected by organizational culture) whether documented observation is an acceptable way of measuring some of these harder-to-quantify competencies.

Step 2: Feedback and Documentation

Feedback encompasses information and input that is provided to (and, ideally, discussed and explored with) an employee relative to her performance and the specific ways in which that performance is meeting or not meeting expectations.

Employees need feedback. So do managers. (This reinforces the value and purpose of a 360-degree appraisal.) Feedback about how each employee performed relative to performance expectations that were set with/for him at the beginning of the performance measurement period should be provided throughout the performance measurement period, not just at the end when it's time to complete the performance appraisal form.

NOTE

It is essential to create an environment in which it is safe to discuss performance and performance-related concerns in a candid and objective manner. Keep in mind that this might be an unfamiliar—or uncomfortable—concept for some individuals, perhaps in light of cultural considerations.

Performance feedback serves a number of important purposes, including the following:

- ▶ Recognizing (and thereby reinforcing) good performance

- ▶ Making the employee aware of performance problems

- ▶ Focusing attention on performance standards, not on nebulous, potentially subjective personality or attitude traits

▶ Furthering the employee's development

▶ Supporting the larger performance culture

It's important for employees to understand (ideally, from the time they are initially interviewed as candidates) that they will be given feedback—positive as well as constructive—and that they are expected to actively participate in the process of discussing and implementing that feedback.

To be effective, feedback needs to be BASIC (behavioral, as soon as possible, specific, interactive, consistent):

▶ **B—Behavioral:** Measurable or observable rather than attitudinal.

▶ **A—As soon as possible:** Do not provide feedback when you are angry or upset and, in most cases, wait until you are alone to have a feedback discussion with employees. This always holds true for constructive feedback and can hold true for positive feedback as well.

▶ **S—Specific and single subject:** The performance expectations you established with and communicated to your employees were specific; the feedback you provide about the employee's performance as compared to those expectations should be specific as well. (Remember the "S" in SMART.) Also, don't let things build up. Communicating about the employee's performance on a regular basis—one behavior at a time—helps increase the likelihood that feedback will be accepted and implemented and that the employee will make the desired behavioral change.

▶ **I—Interactive:** Feedback is a two-way, dynamic interaction, not just a one-way monologue. Use feedback discussions (whether positive or constructive in nature) as an opportunity to collaboratively discuss and explore the employee's performance.

▶ **C—Consistent:** Be consistent in the way you provide feedback to different employees. Consistency, however, does not mean sameness. Also, try to behave and manage in a consistent manner in general. Working for Dr. Jekyll and Mr. Hyde (and trying to figure out who will show up on any given day) can waste a lot of your direct reports' energy that could be better invested in working toward achieving performance expectations, demonstrating desired competencies, and living out the values of the organization (Winterfield).

When you put all this feedback into writing (assuming you do it well and in accordance with the feedback principles listed previously), you've got documentation. Documentation includes, but is not necessarily limited to, formal and informal notes, memos, emails, and all other written or electronic descriptions or comments created at any point during or after the employment life cycle, including those that specifically pertain to employee's performance.

Together with feedback, documentation can provide the basis for creating a shared understanding of how actual performance compares to expected performance. It also might be just what it takes to make your feedback real enough to motivate the employee to act on it appropriately. It creates a paper trail if a performance-related decision is ever challenged.

> **NOTE**
>
> Don't let the previous paragraph fool you—documenting performance isn't always easy. Be sure to familiarize yourself with your organization's practices and policies on documentation (and progressive discipline).
>
> Some union contracts contain specific language pertaining to performance documentation—with respect to substance, as well as with respect to frequency/timing. Management's failure to adhere to such contractual provisions can, if challenged successfully, result in the documentation being dismissed. Proceed with caution, diligence, and a keen and continual awareness of what is in the contract.

Step 3: Written Performance Appraisal

Performance appraisals are often completed to evaluate and document the performance of one employee during a specific period of time (the performance-measurement period). They can also be completed, however, to evaluate the performance of a group of employees. Either way, the performance appraisal should be, in one sense, an anticlimactic conclusion to an ongoing and continuous performance management cycle.

Performance appraisals look backward at the employees' performance over the performance-measurement period. They also look forward to short-term and long-term goals and to development opportunities.

In some organizations, completed performance appraisals may contribute in part—or in whole—to decisions about salary or wage increases. Systems such as this are called pay-for-performance programs. Although many benefits exist to implementing pay-for-performance programs, it's critical that the discussion of performance does not get lost in the discussion of pay when a pay-for-performance program is in place.

Types of Performance Appraisals

Here we'll explore different types of performance appraisal tools. There are three primary methods: comparative methods, narrative methods, and rating methods.

Comparative Methods

Comparison performance appraisal methods are those in which the appraiser compares employees to each other.

> ▶ **Forced distribution method (also known as the forced ranking method):** A comparative performance appraisal method in which the appraiser ranks the performance of his direct reports so that, overall, the performance levels of all of the employees, when looked at together, reflect a bell-shaped curve. Most employees, therefore, will be ranked or evaluated toward the middle of the curve, and a few will be ranked at the high and low ends of the performance spectrum.
>
> Although this technique might be useful in helping to avoid (or at least identify) appraiser errors (see "Performance Appraisal and Management—Pitfalls to Avoid"), it is possible that the mandated ranking levels may not, in fact, reflect employees' actual performance levels. As such, evaluations are being forced into categories that may not be accurate, which can lead to all sorts of complications (for instance, with respect to layoff decisions that are based on performance levels). This is more likely to happen when such distributions must occur within a relatively small group of employees rather than in larger groups of employees where it would be more reasonable to expect a normal distribution to occur.
>
> ▶ **Paired comparison method:** A comparative performance appraisal method in which the appraiser compares every employee in the group, one at a time, to every other employee in the group. In essence, the appraiser ranks his direct reports in terms of overall performance, from "best" to "worst."
>
> Although this method provides more information than simple ranking, it still leaves out the all-important comparison of individual performance to performance standards.
>
> Although fairly simple to use, this method has several shortcomings. First, although it compares employees to each other, ranking does not compare employees' performance

to the objective performance standards that were set for the position. So although it might be nice to be able to know who your best-performing employees are, it's much more important to know which of them meets or exceeds the requirements of the position. Conversely, with the ranking method, it's also possible (although perhaps unlikely in larger groups) that even the lowest-ranked employees might still be meeting the performance requirements of the position; they may just not be as stellar as those employees who were ranked higher.

Narrative Methods

Narrative performance appraisal methods are those in which the appraiser uses a narrative format to write and record observations and assessments of each employee's performance:

▶ **Critical incident:** A narrative performance appraisal method in which the appraiser creates and maintains documentation throughout the year relative to specific situations in which the employee met, and did not meet, the performance expectations of the position.

The effectiveness of this method (which may or may not be combined with rating scales) will vary widely depending on how the appraiser defines "critical incidents." For instance, if an appraiser documents only extreme examples of behavior (ones that either far exceed or fall well below expected performance standards), those performers who are solid (but not outstanding) may receive little attention and thus be provided with insufficient documentation. This method also requires that managers consistently and contemporaneously document critical incidents, which may not always be a realistic expectation. Again, this method relies on the writing skill—as well as the objectivity—of the appraiser.

▶ **Essay method:** A narrative performance appraisal method in which the appraiser writes short essays describing and documenting each employee's performance during the performance measurement period.

Some managers may prefer this method because it gives them ample freedom to accurately and fully evaluate an employee's performance. The method, however, is highly time consuming and requires considerable writing ability—perhaps in a different style than what the manager might be required to use in the normal course of performing her job. Better writers, therefore, might prepare more powerful or convincing performance appraisals than those managers who are not as skilled at expressing themselves in an essay format. This, of course, does not necessarily make those appraisals more accurate. Also, because of the largely unstructured nature of an essay appraisal, it might be easier for rater bias to emerge. Short essays can also become long (and thus time-consuming) essays.

▶ **Field review:** A narrative performance appraisal method in which someone other than the employee's supervisor—someone from HR, for instance—prepares the performance appraisal.

One serious concern with field-review appraisals is that they may unintentionally send a message that performance management and appraisal is an extra part of a supervisor's job rather than an integral part of his day-to-day responsibilities. Instead of being valued as a way of getting work done more productively and in a manner that is consistent with performance expectations, the appraisal process may be perceived as separate, distinct, and therefore less relevant and valuable.

Rating Methods

"Rating methods" include performance appraisal methods in which the appraiser compares the performance of the employee against the expected behavior. Appraisers use rating scales and checklists to appraise employee performance.

▶ **Behavioral anchored ranking scales (BARS):** A rating method type of performance appraisal that starts by identifying the most critical responsibilities or requirements of a position. Then, for each responsibility or requirement, "anchor" statements offering a specific description of a particular type of behavior (which corresponds to a particular level of performance) are written.

For instance, for a programmer analyst, a three-level BARS for responsibilities relating to organizing and planning might look like this:

   ▶ Description of Behaviors

   1. This person normally generates effective plans requiring at least a year of development and a budget of around $750,000. She almost always includes time for unseen emergencies in project timeliness and activities. On most projects, she can schedule the team's activities to coincide with the activities of other teams, users, computer operations personnel, and so on. She normally makes long-term plans to use in effectively adjusting schedules as a project progresses.

   2. This person generally establishes her own goals and the steps to achieve them. She can generally organize a project or task into smaller tasks and time frames. She can generally plan her own and others' efforts on a project but may have difficulty organizing efforts on several concurrent projects. She may sometimes omit lesser elements from a plan that results in underutilization of resources or delays in project completion.

   3. Generally, this person can handle one project, but not multiple projects. She has trouble breaking down a large project into smaller tasks and establishing time frames. She delegates tasks to others but not according to who is best qualified and may not properly coordinate activities with other teams or team members.

▶ **Checklist:** A rating method type of performance appraisal in which the appraiser reviews a series of statements that could describe an employee's performance and literally checks off those statements that are reflective of the employee's performance during the performance measurement period. Sometimes checklists are weighted (called weighted checklists), in which case the weightings are used to generate a mathematically calculated score.

As with other performance appraisal methods, the value of a checklist appraisal is, in part, a function of the skill level of the person completing the appraisal, as well as that person's ability to recognize and manage any rater biases that he might have. (See "Performance Appraisal and Management—Pitfalls to Avoid.")

▶ **Management by objectives (MBOs):** A rating method type of performance appraisal, or a goal-centered OD intervention, that focuses primarily on collaboratively generating individual employee objectives that align with organizational objectives. Measurement is an essential element of an MBO program. As follows logically, MBO is often used as a performance appraisal method because of its strong orientation toward goal establishment and attainment.

An MBO-based performance appraisal process will certainly ensure that individual objectives are aligned with organizational objectives. There are, however, some potential disadvantages. Because MBO focuses exclusively on results (what is produced or delivered), the way goals are accomplished is not given any attention. This could result in an employee choosing to engage in problematic behaviors to achieve goals, including behaviors that are inconsistent with the values of the organization. In addition, an MBO system is time consuming to develop and maintain because it must be continually updated to reflect the current expectations associated with each position. Because jobs change so quickly, this can become a daunting task.

Although several types of performance appraisals incorporate, to a greater or lesser degree, results as part of the measure of success, MBO is driven almost exclusively by this measure.

▶ **Rating scales:** A rating method type of performance appraisal in which the appraiser rates the employee on a variety of different categories using a three-, four-, or five-point scale. Those categories can consist of individual goals, individual competencies, multiple goals, groups of competencies, and the like. Each point on the scale corresponds to a different level of performance against standards.

On a five-point scale, for instance, the numbers might correspond to the following words:

5: Far Exceeds Expectations

4: Exceeds Expectations

3: Successfully Meets Expectations

2: Meets Some, Does Not Fully Meet Expectations

1: Unacceptable

Generally considered to be the least complex and most frequently used type of performance appraisal tool, rating scales can vary significantly in terms of reliability, objectivity, accuracy, and defensibility. This can depend on a number of factors, including the skill level of the person who developed the appraisal as well as the skill level of the individual completing and delivering the appraisal. Skill, in this case, does not refer to the goal or competency that is being evaluated; rather, it refers to the individual's ability to effectively appraise performance.

Step 4: Performance Appraisal Meeting

Knowing the mechanics of performance appraisals is important. But even the best-designed performance appraisal will be rendered ineffective (and perhaps even harmful) if a performance appraisal meeting is executed poorly.

Performance Appraisal and Management—Pitfalls to Avoid

Appraisers of performance must be aware of potential performance appraisal and management pitfalls. These pitfalls relate more to the fact that we are all human and, as such, have biases, beliefs, and reactions that could potentially compromise our ability to manage and appraise performance effectively—that is, if we allow that to happen.

We addressed many of these same potential pitfalls (in a different way) in Chapter 2, "Workforce Planning and Employment," during our exploration of interviewing and employment. In this chapter, we'll now look at them in terms of how they could taint the performance management and appraisal process (see Table 3.4).

TABLE 3.4 Types of Performance Appraisal Errors

Type of Performance Appraisal Errors	How It Manifests in the Performance Appraisal Process
Contrast	The appraiser compares the performance of each employee to the performance of other employees instead of comparing it to the performance standards that were established for the position at the beginning of the performance-measurement period. Please note: this bias is, to a degree, inherent to ranking systems if not combined with other appraisal techniques linked specifically to performance expectations.
First impression	The appraiser forms an impression of the employee's performance early in the performance measurement period (or even worse, early in the individual's employment) and places an inordinate level of emphasis on that impression. Please note: an employee's performance during each performance measurement period should be assessed separately from that employee's performance during any prior performance measurement period(s). In addition, although it's important to recognize performance trends that an employee might demonstrate during a single performance-measurement period, it's also critical to ensure that the performance appraisal reflects the employee's performance during the entire performance-measurement period—not just their level of performance at the end of the performance-measurement period.
Halo	The appraiser evaluates the employee positively on the basis of one outstanding qualification or characteristic that is inherently incomplete and inaccurate. One particularly impressive skill, or one hard-fought goal, does not reflect the employee's overall performance.
Horns	The appraiser evaluates the employee negatively on the basis of one poor qualification or characteristic that is inherently incomplete and inaccurate, in that it will not reflect the employee's overall performance.
Leniency	The appraiser applies an inappropriately lenient standard to one or more employees, resulting in a higher overall assessment of the employee's (or employees') performance. Being "nice" to one or more employees by "giving" inflated performance evaluations doesn't help the organization and doesn't help the employee either. An organization needs to ensure that its employees are provided with honest feedback about performance if the organization is to fulfill its mission and attain its overarching objectives. Evaluating employees in an overly lenient (and thus dishonest) manner undermines those efforts. Employees who are, in fact, performing at or above expectations may be confused or demotivated if (we should actually say "when," to be realistic) they learn that other employees who perform at a level below them are given similar ratings. Those employees who are given inaccurate and overinflated ratings may cease any efforts to improve their performance—after all, they got a good rating. Because other appraisers in the organization will not apply this same degree of leniency, rating consistency across the organization is compromised. In addition to employee (de)motivation and morale issues, this can create problems with respect to internal transfers, promotions, salary and wage increases, disciplinary actions, and layoff decisions. Please also note: generally speaking, when speaking of performance ratings, it is more accurate and effective to say that an employee "earned" a rating than to say that an employee was "given" a rating. After all, performance management is intended to empower employees. When ratings are inflated, however, they have (unfortunately) been given, not earned.

Type of Performance Appraisal Errors	How It Manifests in the Performance Appraisal Process
Strictness	The appraiser applies an inappropriately harsh and demanding standard when evaluating the performance of one or more employees, resulting in a lower overall assessment of the employee(s). Being overly (and inaccurately) strict in one's assessment of the performance of one or more employees doesn't help the organization and is unfair to employees for a number of reasons. An organization needs to ensure that its employees are provided with honest feedback about performance if the organization is to fulfill its mission and attain its overarching objectives. Evaluating employees in an overly strict (and thus dishonest) manner undermines those efforts because it disconnects the employee's performance with any meaningful linkage to the organization's performance. In addition, employees who are, in fact, performing at or above expectations may be confused or demotivated by such unrealistically harsh ratings, in that inaccurate (and manipulative) ratings will inevitably create a "cycle of failure"—a history of never being quite good enough. Because other appraisers in the organization will not apply this same degree of harshness, rating consistency across the organization is compromised. In addition to employee (de)motivation and morale issues, this can also create problems with respect to internal transfers, promotions, salary and wage increases, disciplinary actions, and layoff decisions. Please note: when speaking of performance ratings, it is generally more accurate and effective to say that an employee "earned" a rating rather than saying that an employee was "given" a rating. After all, performance management is intended to empower employees. When ratings are diminished, however, they have (unfortunately) been given, not earned.
Recency	The appraisal places undue emphasis on the employee's most recent performance rather than considering performance demonstrated throughout the entire performance measurement period. Appraisers who find themselves "under the gun" with a looming performance appraisal deadline might be more likely to fall prey to this error—especially if they have not maintained consistent documentation throughout the performance measurement period. But make no mistake: just like children who are anticipating a holiday replete with presents brought by a magical judge (let's face it—those naughty and nice lists have to be based on something), many employees recognize that outstanding performance near the end of the performance measurement period might help to make up for less-than-stellar performance during the earlier portions of the performance measurement period. Don't fall prey to the "Santa Claus" effect.
Similar-to-me	The manager evaluates an employee's performance on the basis of how much a direct report is similar to, or different from, her. If appraisers recognize characteristics, attributes, or performance patterns in an employee that they dislike about themselves, this recognition—whether conscious or unconscious—could cause the appraiser to evaluate the employee inappropriately negatively. Conversely, if appraisers recognize characteristics or attributes in an employee that they like about themselves, this recognition—again, whether conscious or unconscious—could cause the appraiser to evaluate the employee inappropriately positively. Either way, the impression is wholly unrelated to the employee's actual performance and must be compartmentalized from the appraisal process.

RESPONSIBILITY

HRD Responsibility 09

Provide coaching to managers and executives regarding effectively managing organizational talent.

KNOWLEDGE

Knowledge 37

Mentoring and executive coaching.

Coaching and Mentoring

Coaching and mentoring are highly specialized skills. They can only be developed with diligent study, extensive practice, and—some would assert—specialized training.

Coaching is also a profession in much the same way that HR is a profession. The International Coach Federation is a preeminent professional coaching organization. It's website, coachfederation.org, offers extensive resources for those interested in honing their coaching skills or becoming certified in coaching.

Having said all of this, coaching and mentoring are standalone skills that constitute an important subset of those required to be an effective HR professional.

- ▶ **Coaching:** Coaching is a professional relationship in which one individual listens, mirrors, "walks with," and "makes space for" another individual to learn, grow, explore, and make empowered choices.

- ▶ **Executive coaching:** Executive coaching is a professional relationship in which a senior level of the organization works with an individual who helps her identify and eradicate blind spots to explore potentially challenging experiences or relationships or to temper confidence and boldness with other required executive-level professional competencies.

- ▶ **Mentoring:** Mentoring is a professional relationship in which one person shares his insights and personal experiences with individuals who are usually less experienced and who may work at a lower hierarchical level within the organization. Mentors often offer advice, guidance, and direction.

NOTE

The following HRD Responsibilities/Areas of Knowledge pertain to responsibilities and areas of knowledge that are addressed in Pearson's SPHR Exam Prep.

RESPONSIBILITY

HRD Responsibility 04

Evaluate the effectiveness of employee training programs through the use of metrics (for example: participant surveys, pre- and post-testing).

RESPONSIBILITY

HRD Responsibility 08

Develop/select, implement, and evaluate programs (for example: telecommuting, diversity initiatives, repatriation) to meet the changing needs of employees and the organization.

KNOWLEDGE

Knowledge 35

Applicable global issues (for example: international law, culture, local management approaches/practices, societal norms).

Chapter Summary

Responsibilities relating to human resource development afford HR professionals with the opportunity to have a significant impact on the growth and development of the organization and on the people within the organization.

To function successfully with respect to the functional area of human resource development, HR professionals must develop a working knowledge of related legislation. They also must develop facility with the key areas within HRD, specifically the following:

- OD
- Training
- Career development
- Leadership development
- Performance management

As with every other functional area, the ability to execute HRD-related responsibilities effectively is predicated on knowing, understanding, and aligning one's effort with the organization's strategic plan and its mission, vision, and values. Taking those big-picture considerations and translating them into practical HRD applications will enhance the degree to which an HR professional can be effective within the organization.

Key Terms

- Human resource development (HRD)
- Organization development (OD)
- Training
- Career development
- Leadership development
- Performance management
- U.S. Patent Act, 1790
- Copyright Act of 1976
- Copyright holders
- Work-for-hire
- Public domain
- Fair use
- Common law
- Negligent training
- ADDIE
    - A: Analysis/assessment (of needs)
    - D: Design
    - D: Development
- I: Implementation
- E: Evaluation
- McGehee and Thayer
    - Organization-level analysis
    - Task or work (operations)-level analysis
    - Person (man)-level analysis
- Cost-per-trainee/cost-per participant
- SMART
    - Specific
    - Measurable
    - Action-oriented
    - Realistic
    - Time-bound
- Lecture/lecturette
- Demonstration
- Reading
- Small group discussions/instructor-facilitated large group discussions

- Individual, small-group, or large-group activities/applications
- Case study
- Rose play
- The adult learner
- Andragogy
- Pedagogy
- Malcolm Knowles
  - Learner's need to know
  - Learner's self-concept
  - Role of learner's experience
  - Readiness to learn
  - Orientation to learning
- Learning styles
  - Visual learners
  - Auditory learners
  - Tactile/kinesthetic learners
- Learning curves
  - Negatively accelerating learning curve
  - Positively accelerating learning curve
  - S-shaped learning curve
  - Plateau learning curve
- Training modalities/techniques
  - Brick-and-mortar learning
  - On-the-job training
  - E-learning
  - Hybrid learning
- Seating configurations
  - Classroom/theater
  - Chevron
  - Modified restaurant
  - U-shaped
  - Boardroom
- Pilot programs
  - Identical program format
  - Abbreviated program format
- Donald L. Kirkpatrick
  - Summative evaluation

- Reaction-level evaluation
- Learning-level evaluation
  - Pretest
  - Post-test
- Behavior-level evaluation
- Results-level evaluation
- Robert O. Brinkerhoff
  - Formative evaluation
- Talent management
- Organizational culture
- Leadership development
- High-potential employees
- Dual career ladders
- Succession planning
  - Skill inventories
  - Replacement charts
- Teambuilding
- Total quality management (TQM)
- W. Edwards Deming
- Joseph M. Juran
- Philip B. Crosby
- Kaoru Ishikawa
- Cause-and-effect, Ishikawa, or fishbone diagram
- Performance management
- Performance management process/system
- Performance standards
  - Goals/objectives
  - Competencies
- Feedback
- Documentation
- BASIC
- Performance appraisal
  - Comparative methods
    - Forced distribution method
    - Paired comparison method
  - Narrative methods

▶ Critical incident

▶ Essay method

▶ Field review

▶ Rating methods

   ▶ Behavioral anchored rating scales (BARS)

   ▶ Checklist

   ▶ Management by objectives (MBO)

   ▶ Rating scales

▶ Performance appraisal and management pitfalls

   ▶ Leniency error

   ▶ Strictness error

   ▶ Recency error

   ▶ Similar-to-me error

▶ Coaching

▶ Executive coaching

▶ Mentoring

Apply Your Knowledge

This chapter focuses on issues relating to human resource development (HRD). Complete the following review questions and exam questions as a way of reviewing and reinforcing the knowledge and skills you'll need to perform your responsibilities as an HR professional and to increase the likelihood that you will pass the PHR examination.

Review Questions

1. Describe some of the key similarities and differences between performance management and performance appraisal.

2. What does it mean when a document or work is in the public domain?

3. Why is it important that HRD/training objectives remain realistic (the "R" in the acronym SMART)?

4. What are some of the benefits of the case-study methodology?

5. Describe Brinkerhoff's formative evaluation approach.

Exam Questions

1. Which of the following rights is not granted to copyright holders by the Copyright Act of 1976?

   ○ **A.** The right to duplicate/reproduce/copy the work

   ○ **B.** The right to exclude others from making, using, offering for sale, or selling the invention in the United States

   ○ **C.** The right to display the work publicly

   ○ **D.** The right to sell, lease, rent, or otherwise distribute copies of the work to the public

2. All of the following are reasons for conducting needs analysis/assessment except

   ○ **A.** To identify performance-related problems within the organization

   ○ **B.** To increase the likelihood of identifying a solution that will truly bridge the performance gap

   ○ **C.** To begin the initial creation of the HRD/training program before meeting with any organizational resistance that could slow progress

   ○ **D.** To ensure that a legitimate cost-benefit analysis is conducted before a commitment is made to any particular HRD/training solution

3. Which of the following statements about using reading as a training methodology is true?

    ○ **A.** It should be included at least once, whenever possible, in training programs because ideally all training methodologies should be included in every training program.

    ○ **B.** It should be avoided in training programs unless truly necessary because participants generally do not find it engaging or stimulating.

    ○ **C.** It represents a particularly effective methodology for auditory learners.

    ○ **D.** It should be included in training programs when participants would benefit from time to absorb and process detailed materials.

4. Which of the following statements does not reflect a statement by which the presentation effectiveness of instructors/potential instructors could be assessed/evaluated?

    ○ **A.** Summarizes major points throughout and at the conclusion of the workshop

    ○ **B.** Refers to and utilizes training materials (including the participant manual) throughout the program

    ○ **C.** Allows ample time for participants to develop concepts

    ○ **D.** Scores consistently well on post-training evaluation forms

5. Taking a summative approach to evaluation means that

    ○ **A.** The designer/instructor/HRD professional collects, summarizes, and incorporates feedback throughout the program development and implementation phases.

    ○ **B.** The designer/instructor/HRD professional collects, summarizes, and incorporates feedback at the conclusion of the program design and development phases.

    ○ **C.** The designer/instructor/HRD professional collects, summarizes, and incorporates feedback after implementing the HRD/training program.

    ○ **D.** The designer/instructor/HRD professional does not collect, summarize, or incorporate feedback until summary data from a representative number of participants has been collected and analyzed.

6. All of the following statements about Kirkpatrick's behavior-level evaluation are true except

    ○ **A.** It measures transfer of training—the degree to which participants apply the skills and knowledge covered in the training sessions in the workplace.

    ○ **B.** It measures whether and to what degree participants have mastered the skills or acquired the knowledge explored through the learning objectives.

    ○ **C.** It measures changes in behavior that might be the result of factors unrelated to the HRD/training initiative.

    ○ **D.** It measures whether participants' on-the-job behaviors have changed in a manner consistent with training objectives.

7. Which of the following would not be considered to be a major purpose of OD?

    ○ **A.** Identifying and implementing more cost-effective ways of increasing employee retention

    ○ **B.** Enhancing the overall effectiveness of organizations

    ○ **C.** Promoting openness toward differences

    ○ **D.** Aligning employee goals with unit and organizational goals

8. Which of the following is not a key element of the ADDIE model?

   ○ **A.** Needs assessment/analysis

   ○ **B.** Evaluation

   ○ **C.** Data collection

   ○ **D.** Design

9. The Pareto principle says that

   ○ **A.** An organization's commitment to customer service must extend even beyond the point of purchase.

   ○ **B.** Quality is achieved by prevention, not appraisal.

   ○ **C.** In organizations, individuals tend to be promoted up to their "level of incompetence."

   ○ **D.** 80% of consequences can be attributed to 20% of causes.

10. Of the following learning methodologies, which is likely to yield the highest level of participant retention?

   ○ **A.** Discussion

   ○ **B.** Demonstration

   ○ **C.** Application

   ○ **D.** Association

Answers to Exam Questions

1. Answer B is the best answer. The right to exclude others from making, using, offering for sale, or selling the invention in the United States is granted to patent holders under the U.S. Patent Act. Answer A is not the best answer; the Copyright Act of 1976 does grant copyright holders the right to duplicate/reproduce/copy the work. Answer C is not the best answer; the Copyright Act of 1976 does grant copyright holders the right to display the work publicly. Answer D is not the best answer; the Copyright Act of 1976 does grant copyright holders the right to sell, lease, rent, or otherwise distribute copies of the work to the public.

2. Answer C is the best answer. The HRD/training initiative should not be created/developed until the needs analysis/assessment and design phases have been completed (and agreed to in writing). Answers A, B, and D are not the best answers; each one articulates a legitimate reason for conducting a needs analysis/assessment.

3. Answer D is the best answer. Although reading is not always valued as a learning methodology, it does serve a number of valuable purposes, one of which is allowing participants the opportunity to absorb and process detailed information. Answer A is not the best answer; although it is important to use a variety of training methodologies, it is not necessary—and would not always be appropriate—to include all training methodologies in all training programs. Answer B is not the best answer; reading can serve a variety of valuable purposes in training programs. Answer C is not the best answer; reading can be a particularly effective methodology for visual learners—more so than for auditory learners.

4. Answer D is the best answer. Scoring consistently well on post-training evaluation forms is not necessarily a valid measure of training effectiveness. That evaluation technique provides more insight into how well participants liked the trainer than the trainer's effectiveness. Answer A is not the best answer; summarizing major points throughout and at the conclusion of the workshop is one valid measure of presentation effectiveness. Answer B is not the best answer; referring to and utilizing training materials (including the participant manual) throughout the program is one valid measure of presentation effectiveness. Answer C is not the best answer; allowing ample time for participants to develop concepts is one valid measure of presentation effectiveness.

5. Answer C is the best answer. Summative evaluation takes place at the end of the implementation phase. Answer A is not the best answer; it more closely describes the formative evaluation technique. Neither answer B nor answer D is the best answer; both describe evaluation techniques that are not espoused by recognized ISD or HRD experts.

6. Answer B is the best answer. The degree to which participants have mastered the skills or acquired the knowledge explored through the learning objectives is a function of Kirkpatrick's learning-level of evaluation (level 2). Answer A is not the best answer; behavior-level evaluation does measure transfer of training—the degree to which participants apply the skills and knowledge covered in the training sessions in the workplace. Answer C is not the best answer; behavior-level evaluation could measure changes in behavior that might be the result of factors unrelated to the HRD/training initiative. (These changes would taint the evaluation and must somehow be accounted for.) Answer D is not the best answer; behavior-level evaluation does measure whether participants' on-the-job behaviors have changed in a manner consistent with training objectives.

7. Answer A is the best answer. Although effective OD interventions might, in fact, result in increased retention of employees, it would not constitute a major purpose of OD. Answer B is not the best answer; enhancing the overall effectiveness of organizations is a major purpose of OD. Answer C is not the best answer; promoting openness toward differences is a major purpose of OD. Answer D is not the best answer; aligning employee goals with unit and organizational goals is a major purpose of OD.

8. Answer C is the best answer. The five key elements of ADDIE are Needs Assessment/Analysis, Design, Development, Implementation, and Evaluation. Although data collection would be a part of needs assessment and analysis, it does not constitute one of the five key elements (and, therefore, doesn't stand for either of the "Ds" in the acronym ADDIE).

9. Answer D is the best answer. The Pareto principle does assert that 80% of consequences can be attributed to 20% of causes. Answer A is not the best answer; the belief that an organization's commitment to customer service must extend even beyond the point of purchase is part of Kaoru Ishikawa's TQM philosophy and is unrelated to the Pareto Principle. Answer B is not the best answer; the statement that quality is achieved by prevention, not appraisal, is one of Philip B. Crosby's four absolutes of quality management. Answer C is not the best answer; the belief that individuals tend to be promoted up to their "level of incompetence" within organizations is the "Peter Principle" (Laurence J. Peter), not the Pareto principle.

10. Answer C is the best answer. Application is likely to result in a 70% retention level. Answer A is not the best answer; discussion is likely to result in only a 50% retention level. Answer B is not the best answer; demonstration is likely to result in only a 30% retention level. Answer D is not the best answer; association is not a recognized instructional methodology.

Suggested Readings and Resources

Branch, R. (2009). *Instructional Design: The ADDIE Approach*. New York: Springer.

Cummings, T. (2008). *Handbook of Organization Development*. Los Angeles: SAGE Publications.

Dirksen, J. (2012). *Design for How People Learn*. Berkeley, CA: New Riders.

Gibson, C. (2004). *Performance Appraisals*. New York: Barnes & Noble Books.

Gilley, J., and Eggland, S. (2002). *Principles of Human Resource Development* (2nd ed.). Reading, Mass.: Perseus.

Grote, R. (2011). *How to Be Good at Performance Appraisals: Simple, Effective, Done Right*. Boston, MA: Harvard Business Review Press.

Meifert, M. (2013). *Strategic Human Resource Development: A Journey in Eight Stages*. Dordrecht: Springer.

Stolovitch, H., and Keeps, E. (2011). *Telling Ain't Training Updated, Expanded, and Enhanced*, 2nd edition (Updated, expanded, and enhanced, 2nd ed.). Alexandria, Va.: ASTD Press.

Swanson, R., and Holton, E. (2009). *Foundations of Human Resource Development* (2nd ed.). San Francisco: Berrett-Koehler.

Werner, J., and DeSimone, R. (2012). *Human Resource Development* (6th ed.). Mason, OH: South-Western.

CHAPTER FOUR

Compensation and Benefits

Compensation and benefits encompass all the rewards that an organization gives, grants, or otherwise bestows on its employees in exchange for the services those employees have rendered through their employment. It includes more obvious items—such as wages and salaries—as well as mandatory and optional benefits such as Social Security contributions, health and welfare programs, and the like. It also includes items that some, but not all, employees enjoy, such as incentives, bonuses, stock options, and so on.

Those readers who have taken the Professional in Human Resources (PHR) or Senior Professional in Human Resources (SPHR) previously, or those who have older test prep materials, might have noticed that Human Resource Certification Institute (HRCI) has changed the title of this functional area from Compensation and Benefits to Total Rewards and back (again) to Compensation and Benefits. Although this author cannot speak to the specific reasons for these choices, one might speculate that this is because so many—in fact, nearly countless—aspects of the employment relationship and experience contribute to the tangible and intangible benefits that are accrued from working at an organization. Many of these would, perhaps, more logically "roll up" to other functional areas—in particular, workplace planning and employment and human resource development. An argument could be made, however, that every functional area meaningfully contributes to the "total rewards" of working at an organization. For purposes of the reader's test prep and this functional area, keep in mind that this particular functional area is limited to just that—compensation and benefits. These terms will be looked at and explored within the context of the following definitions:

▶ **Benefits:** Noncash or indirect rewards provided to employees in recognition of and in exchange for the performance of their jobs.

▶ **Compensation:** Cash-based rewards provided to employees in recognition of and in exchange for the performance of their jobs.

Together, these concepts comprise total rewards. In more strategic, consultative terms, total rewards speaks to HR's responsibility to ensure that the organization's total compensation and benefits programs, policies, and practices reinforce and support the short-term, long-term, and emerging and strategic objectives of the organization.

C & B Responsibility 01

Ensure that compensation and benefits programs are compliant with applicable federal laws and regulations.

Knowledge 38

Applicable federal laws and regulations related to compensation, benefits, and tax (for example: FLSA, ERISA, FMLA, USERRA).

Worker's Compensation

Worker's compensation (also known as "worker's comp") laws were adopted at the state level between 1911 and 1940. These laws were designed to provide medical care to injured employees and death benefits to families of those who lost their lives in the performance of their jobs. Worker's comp is a no-fault system—injured workers receive medical and compensation benefits regardless of who caused the injury or death.

These laws will be presented and explored in chronological order (except where noted).

Davis-Bacon Act, 1931

The Davis-Bacon Act was the first piece of legislation to consider the topic of—and actually establish—a minimum wage. Davis-Bacon, however, was and still is limited to the construction industry, specifically those contractors and subcontractors on

- Any and all federal government construction contracts
- Nonfederal government construction projects in excess of $2,000 that receive federal funding

Contractors and subcontractors who meet either of these criteria are required to provide laborers and mechanics who are employed at the actual worksite with wages and benefits that are equal to (or better than) what workers on similar local projects receive.

Walsh-Healey Public Contracts Act, 1936

The next significant piece of compensation-related legislation was the Walsh-Healey Public Contracts Act (PCA), enacted in 1936.

The Walsh-Healey PCA requires contractors who have contracts with the federal government that exceed $10,000 to pay an established minimum wage to workers employed through that contract. In addition to minimum wage, Walsh-Healey PCA addressed issues including overtime pay and safe and sanitary working conditions.

Fair Labor Standards Act, 1938

Although it was initially enacted in 1938, the Fair Labor Standards Act (FLSA) still has a profound impact on employees today because of its wide scope and the degree to which it directly affects the lives of nearly every American worker.

The FLSA covers full-time and part-time workers in the private sector and in federal, state, and local governments. It addresses minimum wage, overtime, equal pay, record keeping, and child labor standards (referred to by the government now as "youth employment standards"). For private enterprise employees, it is administered by the Wage and Hour Division of the DOL. For federal employees, the FLSA is administered either by the Wage and Hour Division or the U.S. Office of Personnel Management (which, interestingly, refers to itself as "The Federal Government's Human Resources Agency" on its website).

Let's take a look at each of the areas the FLSA covers, in the following order:

▶ Minimum wage

▶ Overtime pay

▶ Child labor standards (youth employment standards)

▶ Record keeping

Minimum Wage

The FLSA established a federal minimum wage for private sector employees and for all other employees covered by the Act. From time to time, minimum wage has become a hotly debated issue in Congress because Congress has the responsibility for introducing legislation that will change the federal minimum wage. In our nation's system of checks and balances, however, that hotly debated congressional issue quickly becomes a hotly debated presidential issue because it is the president who must either sign or veto legislation to increase the minimum wage.

On July 24, 2009, the federal minimum wage was increased to $7.25 per hour. Many states have established a minimum wage that is higher than the federally established minimum wage. In these circumstances, employees would be entitled to the state minimum wage (because in this case, the state law is more generous than the federal law, and thus supersedes the federal law).

Please review the federal minimum wage poster, included as Figure 4.1.

Want a Good Tip?

Here's one—be sure your tipped employees earn at least the minimum wage.

The FLSA specifically addresses the question of employees who receive tips. According to the Act, an employer of "tipped employees" must pay those employees for every hour worked, even if the employees' tips alone would result in them earning more than the minimum wage. The minimum rate of pay that can be paid to tipped employees (available at www.dol.gov/esa), however, is substantially less ($2.13 as of the date this book was published) than the minimum wage that must be paid to employees who do not receive tips. To be eligible to pay tipped employees this lower hourly rate, the employer must meet certain conditions, including (but not limited to) the following:

▶ The employer must claim a tip credit against its minimum wage obligation.

▶ Each employee's tips combined with the hourly rate that the employer is paying must meet or exceed the federal minimum hourly wage. Otherwise, the employer must make up the difference.

Overtime Pay

According to the FLSA, nonexempt employees must be paid at least the minimum wage for the first 40 hours worked during the workweek. If an employee works more than 40 hours during the workweek (commonly referred to as "overtime"), he must be paid those overtime hours at a rate that is at least 150% (commonly referred to as "time and a half") of his regular rate of pay per hour—which may be different from the employee's stated hourly wage rate.

EMPLOYEE RIGHTS
UNDER THE FAIR LABOR STANDARDS ACT

THE UNITED STATES DEPARTMENT OF LABOR WAGE AND HOUR DIVISION

FEDERAL MINIMUM WAGE
$7.25 PER HOUR
BEGINNING JULY 24, 2009

OVERTIME PAY At least 1½ times your regular rate of pay for all hours worked over 40 in a workweek.

CHILD LABOR An employee must be at least **16** years old to work in most non-farm jobs and at least **18** to work in non-farm jobs declared hazardous by the Secretary of Labor.

Youths **14** and **15** years old may work outside school hours in various non-manufacturing, non-mining, non-hazardous jobs under the following conditions:

No more than
- **3** hours on a school day or **18** hours in a school week;
- **8** hours on a non-school day or **40** hours in a non-school week.

Also, work may not begin before **7 a.m.** or end after **7 p.m.**, except from June 1 through Labor Day, when evening hours are extended to **9 p.m.** Different rules apply in agricultural employment.

TIP CREDIT Employers of "tipped employees" must pay a cash wage of at least $2.13 per hour if they claim a tip credit against their minimum wage obligation. If an employee's tips combined with the employer's cash wage of at least $2.13 per hour do not equal the minimum hourly wage, the employer must make up the difference. Certain other conditions must also be met.

ENFORCEMENT The Department of Labor may recover back wages either administratively or through court action, for the employees that have been underpaid in violation of the law. Violations may result in civil or criminal action.

Employers may be assessed civil money penalties of up to $1,100 for each willful or repeated violation of the minimum wage or overtime pay provisions of the law and up to $11,000 for each employee who is the subject of a violation of the Act's child labor provisions. In addition, a civil money penalty of up to $50,000 may be assessed for each child labor violation that causes the death or serious injury of any minor employee, and such assessments may be doubled, up to $100,000, when the violations are determined to be willful or repeated. The law also prohibits discriminating against or discharging workers who file a complaint or participate in any proceeding under the Act.

ADDITIONAL INFORMATION
- Certain occupations and establishments are exempt from the minimum wage and/or overtime pay provisions.
- Special provisions apply to workers in American Samoa and the Commonwealth of the Northern Mariana Islands.
- Some state laws provide greater employee protections; employers must comply with both.
- The law requires employers to display this poster where employees can readily see it.
- Employees under 20 years of age may be paid $4.25 per hour during their first 90 consecutive calendar days of employment with an employer.
- Certain full-time students, student learners, apprentices, and workers with disabilities may be paid less than the minimum wage under special certificates issued by the Department of Labor.

For additional information:

1-866-4-USWAGE
(1-866-487-9243)   TTY: 1-877-889-5627
WWW.WAGEHOUR.DOL.GOV

U.S. Wage and Hour Division

U.S. Department of Labor | Wage and Hour Division

WHD Publication 1088 (Revised July 2009)

FIGURE 4.1 Minimum Wage Updates poster.

In addition to the all-important questions of who is (and isn't) exempt from the overtime provisions of the FLSA, at least two additional pivotal questions related to overtime must be addressed:

1. How is the number of hours worked calculated?

2. What rate of pay must be used to determine the regular rate of pay per hour (which will, in turn, be used to calculate the overtime pay rate)?

Calculating the Number of Hours Worked During the Workweek

To calculate the number of hours worked during the workweek, it's first necessary to understand the government's definition of and rules regarding workweeks (as published at www.dol.gov):

▶ A workweek is any fixed and regularly recurring period of 168 hours (24 hours in a day, seven days a week).

▶ The employer can select any day (and any hour) of the "calendar week" on which to begin the "workweek." Once chosen, however, that day (and hour) must remain constant (hence, the "fixed" and "recurring" requirement).

▶ The employer can establish different workweeks for different employees or groups of employees.

▶ The hours that an employee works during different workweeks cannot be "averaged" (to avoid overtime payments, or for any other reason).

After you have a handle on what a workweek is, the next step is to understand how to determine what "hours worked" really means.

First of all, "hours worked" means "hours worked"—not "hours paid." In other words, according to the FLSA, hours that have been paid but not worked (vacation time, sick time, holiday time, jury duty time, and the like) do not count toward the 40-hour threshold (although some organizations may voluntarily choose to count these hours toward the 40-hour threshold).

CAUTION

"Hours worked" also doesn't mean "hours approved to work." If an employer "suffers or permits" a nonexempt employee to work, that employee must be compensated for time worked. So whether the employer requires the employee to work or simply allows the employee to work, the time counts as "hours worked" and must be compensated accordingly.

Calculating the Regular Rate of Pay

An employee's regular rate of pay includes more than just her hourly rate of pay; it also includes any incentives and commissions. It does not, however, include bonuses (which, unlike incentive programs, are discretionary), pay for time not worked, premium pay for weekend or holiday work, and the like.

CAUTION

It is critical that employers calculate overtime payments on the basis of each employee's regular rate of pay, not on each employee's hourly rate of pay.

NOTE

As with minimum wage, some states have established more generous overtime laws—for instance, laws that require overtime pay after an employee has worked eight hours in any one day, regardless of how many hours the employee works during the entire workweek. As is the case with minimum wage, a more generous state law would supersede the federal law. Also, be aware that some collective-bargaining agreements provide for more generous overtime-pay arrangements.

Exemptions from Overtime Pay

The FLSA also sets forth guidelines relative to whether, and which, employees are exempt from the overtime provisions of the FLSA. According to the vernacular used in the law (and discussions about it), an employee who is "nonexempt" is covered by the overtime provisions of the FLSA. An employee who is "exempt" is not covered by (and, is thus exempt from) the overtime provisions of the FLSA.

The following poster, available at www.dol.gov, outlines and summarizes the different types of exemptions, as well as the requirements for each: www.dol.gov/whd/overtime/fs17a_overview.pdf.

Safe Harbor Provisions

HR professionals must also be well versed in safe harbor provisions. Under these, an employer that has made improper salary deductions can protect itself from losing the exemption. To do so, the employer would be required to

- Have a clearly communicated policy prohibiting improper deductions and including a complaint mechanism

- Reimburse employees for any improper deductions

- Make a good faith commitment to comply in the future

> **NOTE**
>
> As of the time of publication of this book, revisions to the FLSA are pending. Please review these carefully before taking the PHR exam because they might result in substantial changes—particularly to exemptions.

Child Labor Standards

The child labor provisions of the FLSA restrict the number of hours (and the times of the day) that children under the age of 16 can work, as well as the types of work that children under the age of 18 can perform.

Under the Fair Labor Standards Act (FLSA):

- Children under the age of 14 years cannot be employed (different guidelines exist for certain jobs, such as for farm work or work performed for the child's parent).

- Hours worked by 14- and 15-year-olds are limited to

    - Nonschool hours

    - 3 hours in a school day

    - 18 hours in a school week

    - 8 hours in a nonschool day

    - 40 hours in a nonschool week

    - Hours between 7 a.m. and 7 p.m. (except from June 1 through Labor Day, when evening hours are extended to 9 p.m.)

- Youth who are under 18 years of age may perform nonhazardous jobs. Youth who are 14 and 15 years of age are also restricted from performing manufacturing, mining, and hazardous jobs.

▶ Youth who are 16 years of age and older (and adults) may work an unlimited number of hours per day.

▶ The FLSA does not require work permits or working papers, but certain states do.

Record Keeping

Employers must maintain accurate and complete records for each non-exempt employee of hours worked and wages earned. Certain identifying information (such as Social Security number, address, and so on) is also required. No specific method of timekeeping is required.

Employers must maintain the following basic information:

▶ Employee's full name and Social Security number

▶ Address, including ZIP code

▶ Birth date, if younger than 19

▶ Sex and occupation

▶ Time and day of week when employee's workweek begins

▶ Hours worked each day

▶ Total hours worked each workweek

▶ Basis on which employee's wages are paid (for example, "$9 per hour," "$440 a week," "piecework")

▶ Regular hourly pay rate

▶ Total daily or weekly straight-time earnings

▶ Total overtime earnings for the workweek

▶ All additions to or deductions from the employee's wages

▶ Total wages paid each pay period

▶ Date of payment and the pay period covered by the payment

According to the (DOL), "(e)ach employer shall preserve for at least three years payroll records, collective bargaining agreements, sales and purchase records. Records on which wage computations are based should be retained for two years, i.e., time cards and piecework tickets, wage rate tables, work and time schedules, and records of additions to or deductions from wages. These records must be open for inspection by the Division's representatives, who may ask the employer to make extensions, computations, or transcriptions. The records may be kept at the place of employment or in a central records office" (www.dol.gov).

In addition, depending upon whether there is a collective-bargaining agreement in place and, of course, depending upon what provisions are in such agreement, the employer may be required to keep additional overtime-payment records or share them with the union at certain specified times.

Portal-to-Portal Act, 1947

In May 1947, the FLSA was amended by the Portal-to-Portal Act. Section 254(a) of the Portal-to-Portal Act offered clearer definitions of "hours worked" for purposes of minimum wage and overtime payments. According to the Act, employers are required to compensate workers only for working time that they spend on activities that relate to the performance of their job.

Equal Pay Act, 1963

The Equal Pay Act (EPA) prohibits discrimination on the basis of sex in the payment of wages or benefits to men and women who perform substantially equal (but not identical) work, for the same employer, in the same establishment, and under similar working conditions. (An "establishment" generally refers to one specific physical location.) Similar to the way in which FLSA status is determined, "substantial equality" is determined by job content, not job titles.

More specifically, the substantial equality of job content is assessed on the basis of the following four factors:

▶ **Skill:** The amount or degree of experience, ability, education, and training required to perform the job. Comparisons must be made on the basis of the skills that are required to perform the job—not on the skills that the incumbents happen to possess.

▶ **Effort:** The amount of physical or mental exertion required to perform the job.

▶ **Responsibility:** The degree of responsibility and accountability that an employer entrusts to and expects from a particular person in a specific position.

▶ **Working Conditions:** The physical surroundings of the position, as well as any hazards associated with a particular position.

Employers can, however, set forth "affirmative defenses" to explain inequities in pay between men and women. These arguments can be based on—and must be proven to be—a function of

▶ Seniority

▶ Merit

▶ Quantity or quality of production

▶ Any factors other than sex

Social Security Act, 1935

In August 1935, President Franklin D. Roosevelt signed the Social Security Act (SSA) into law. Social security is a social insurance program (although some would define it differently) that is funded through payroll taxes. Approximately 96% of all workers are covered under the Social Security Act.

Since the program's inception, Social Security has been designed so that employers and the workers they employ contribute equal dollar amounts each pay period. (It was originally 2% of the first $3,000 of the employee's earnings. That cap, along with that percentage, has been raised significantly over the decades.) Independent contractors and self-employed individuals are required to pay both the employer and the employee portions.

Social security is also known as the Old Age, Survivors, and Disability Insurance program (OASDI), in reference to its three primary components, which are now referred to as retirement income, survivor's benefits, and disability benefits.

Retirement Income

Workers earn credits toward Social Security benefits. As of 2005, workers earned one credit for each $920 in earnings—up to a maximum of four credits per year. (The amount of money that a worker must make to earn one credit generally increases each year, but the four-credit-per-year maximum remains the same.) Workers born in 1929 or later need 40 credits to earn retirement benefits. Younger people need fewer credits to be eligible for disability benefits or for their family members to be eligible for survivors' benefits.

Social security tracks each worker's earnings throughout his lifetime. It is the employee's record of earnings—combined with the age at which he retires—that will determine the monetary amount of each worker's monthly benefit.

The earliest age at which a worker can retire and still receive benefits is 62. These benefits, however, are reduced from what they would have been if the worker had worked until her full retirement age. Full retirement age ranges between age 65 (for those who were born in 1937 or earlier) and age 67 (for those who were born in 1960 or later). Those who work beyond their full retirement age will increase their monthly retirement. The longer they work past their full retirement age, the higher their monthly retirement income will be. (Everyone, however, must start receiving retirement benefits at the age of 70—including individuals who continue to work.)

Disability Benefits

Disability benefits were added to the Social Security program in 1956. Under Social Security, workers who become "totally disabled" can receive benefits. Total disability, however, can be a fairly strict standard to meet. Total disability cannot begin until after five full calendar months of continuous disability. Even then, to be considered totally disabled, the worker must be unable to continue in his previous job and unable to adjust to other work; in addition, the disability must be expected to last for at least one year or to result in the worker's death.

In addition to being deemed to have a total disability, the disability eligibility formula requires that the worker has earned a certain number of credits (during her entire working life) and that the worker must have earned a certain number of credits within the 10 years preceding the disability. (Younger workers who haven't had a chance to earn as many credits are held to more lenient requirements than older workers.) Similar to the way in which retirement benefits are calculated, the actual disability benefit that the worker would receive depends on the worker's age and how many credits the worker has earned.

Survivors' Benefits

When a person who has worked and paid Social Security taxes dies, his family members may be eligible to receive survivors' benefits. Depending on the person's age at the time of death, up to 10 years of work is needed for survivors to be eligible for benefits.

As described at www.ssa.gov/pubs, Social Security survivors' benefits can be paid under the following conditions:

▶ Your widow or widower may be able to receive full benefits at age 65 if born before January 1, 1940. (The age to receive full benefits is gradually increasing to age 67 for widows and widowers born January 2, 1940, or later.) Reduced widow or widower benefits can be received as early as age 60. If your surviving spouse is disabled, benefits can begin as early as age 50.

▶ Your widow or widower can receive benefits at any age if she takes care of your child who is entitled to a child's benefit and is age 16 or younger or is disabled.

▶ Your unmarried children who are under age 18 (or up to age 19 if they are attending elementary or secondary school full time) also can receive benefits. Your children can get benefits at any age if they were disabled before age 22 and remain disabled. Under certain circumstances, benefits also can be paid to your stepchildren, grandchildren, or adopted children.

▶ Your dependent parents can receive benefits if they are age 62 or older. (For your parents to qualify as dependents, you would have had to provide at least one-half of their support.)

Unemployment Insurance

The Federal-State Unemployment Insurance Program was established as part of the federal Social Security Act of 1935 and is administered at the state level. Federal rules are developed by the DOL.

In general, the maximum period for receiving benefits is 26 weeks, although the federal government may (and sometimes does) choose to extend the benefit period during difficult economic times.

Unemployment insurance is funded through employer taxes (except in three states, where employees contribute as well). Unemployment insurance is intended to help employees financially "bridge" the time between positions, when a position has been lost through no fault of their own.

Unemployment Insurance—Eligibility

There are a number of requirements for establishing eligibility, two of which follow:

▶ You must meet the state requirements for wages earned or time worked during an established (one-year) period of time referred to as a base period. (In most states, this is usually the first four out of the past five completed calendar quarters prior to the time when your claim is filed.)

▶ It must be determined that you were unemployed through no fault of your own (as determined under state law) and meet other eligibility requirements of state law.

Unemployment benefits are subject to federal income taxes.

Medicare, 1965

Passed in 1965 as an amendment to the Social Security Act, Medicare provides hospital and medical insurance for the elderly and people with disabilities.

There are four parts to Medicare: hospital insurance (sometimes called Part A), medical insurance (sometimes called Part B), Medicare offered through private health insurance companies (Part C), and prescription benefits (sometimes called Part D).

> **NOTE**
> Neither Part A nor Part B pays for all of a covered person's medical costs. In addition, the program contains deductibles and copays (payments due from the covered individual).

Part A: Hospital Insurance

Part A helps pay for inpatient hospital care, skilled nursing care, and other services.

People age 65 or older are eligible for benefits under Part A of Medicare if they meet any of the following criteria:

- Receive Social Security or railroad retirement benefits
- Are not getting Social Security or railroad retirement benefits but have worked long enough to be eligible for them
- Would be entitled to Social Security benefits based on a spouse's (or divorced spouse's) work record
- Worked long enough in a federal, state, or local government job to be insured for Medicare

People under age 65 are eligible for Part A Medicare benefits if they experience certain disabilities (for instance, Lou Gehrig's disease, permanent kidney failure, and so on) and meet other specified criteria (for instance, having worked long enough to receive disability benefits under Social Security).

Part B: Medicare Medical Insurance

Part B helps pay items such as doctor's fees, outpatient hospital visits, and other medical services and supplies.

Almost anyone who is 65 or older or who is under 65 but eligible for hospital insurance can enroll for Medicare medical insurance by paying a monthly premium. People over age 65 don't need Social Security or government work credits for this part of Medicare.

Part C: Medicare Offered Through Private Health Insurance Companies

Part C of Medicare is available to persons who are eligible for Part A and enrolled in Part B. It is a program through which private health insurance companies can contract with the federal government to offer Medicare benefits through their own policies.

Part C: Medicare Prescription Benefits

In December 2003, the Medicare Prescription Drug, Improvement, and Modernization Act (also known as the Medicare Modernization Act, or MMA) was signed into law. This law, which became effective on January 1, 2006, added prescription drug benefits for all individuals eligible for Medicare Part A and enrolled in Medicare Part B.

Although additional information about this plan is available at www.medicare.gov, be certain to familiarize yourself with (at least) the following basic information about this important new protection.

What Is Medicare Prescription Drug Coverage?

Medicare prescription drug coverage is insurance that covers both brand-name and generic prescription drugs at participating pharmacies in your area. Medicare prescription drug coverage provides protection for people who have high drug costs now or believe they'll have unexpected prescription drug bills in the future.

Who Can Get Medicare Prescription Drug Coverage?

Everyone with Medicare is eligible for this coverage, regardless of income and resources, health status, or current prescription expenses.

When Can I Get Medicare Prescription Drug Coverage?

You may sign up when you first become eligible for Medicare (three months before the month you turn age 65 until three months after you turn age 65). If you get Medicare due to a disability, you can join from three months before to three months after your 25th month of cash disability payments. If you don't sign up when you are first eligible, you may pay a penalty.

How Does Medicare Prescription Drug Coverage Work?

Your decision about Medicare prescription drug coverage depends on the kind of health care coverage you have now. There are two ways to get Medicare prescription drug coverage. You can join a Medicare prescription drug plan, or you can join a Medicare Advantage Plan or other Medicare Health Plan that offers drug coverage.

Whatever plan you choose, Medicare drug coverage will help you by covering brand-name and generic drugs at pharmacies that are convenient for you.

Like other insurance, if you join, generally you will pay a monthly premium, which varies by plan, and a yearly deductible. You will also pay a part of the cost of your prescriptions, including a payment or coinsurance. Costs will vary depending on which drug plan you choose. Some plans may offer more coverage and additional drugs for a higher monthly premium. If you have limited income and resources and you qualify for extra help, you may not have to pay a premium or deductible. You can apply or get more information about the extra help by calling Social Security at 1-800-772-1213 (TTY 1–800–325–0778) or visiting www.socialsecurity.gov.

Employee Retirement Income Security Act (ERISA), 1974

The Employee Retirement Income Security Act is perhaps better known by its acronym, ERISA. ERISA's overall purpose is to protect the interests of those who participate—and the beneficiaries of those who participate—in employee benefit plans. ERISA applies only to programs established by private industry employers.

ERISA established minimum participation and vesting standards for retirement programs. (ERISA covers defined benefit plans and defined contribution plans; see "Defined Benefit Plan.") Vesting is the process by which an employee earns a nonforfeitable right to the employer's contribution of his defined benefit/defined contribution plan. There are three types of vesting:

- **Immediate vesting:** An employee is immediately and fully vested in the employer match as soon as it is processed to her account.

- **Cliff vesting:** A vesting arrangement in which an employee earns a nonforfeitable right to 100% of his employer's contributions after a specified number of years (no more than three) but forfeits all rights to those contributions if his employment is terminated before he vests.

- **Graded vesting:** A vesting arrangement in which an employee earns a nonforfeitable right to an increasing percentage of her employer's contributions over a period of years (no more than six years for full vesting).

ERISA also established minimum standards for welfare benefit (including health) plans.

NOTE

It is important to note that the private industry plans that ERISA is designed to regulate are voluntary. ERISA does not require private industry employers to establish pension or health plans. It does, however, impose minimum standards on those employers who choose to do so—all in the interest of protecting plan participants and their beneficiaries.

The Protective Nature of ERISA

The safeguards established by ERISA have a strong, but not exclusive, focus on protecting participants with respect to the financial dimensions of plans. Here are two examples of requirements established by ERISA that demonstrate this effort to protect participants:

Under ERISA, participants must be provided with plan information, specifically about the features and funding of the plan. For instance, when an employee (or beneficiary) becomes a participant in a retirement plan that is covered under ERISA, he is entitled to receive a summary plan description (SPD), at no cost, from the plan administrator. The SPD describes what the plan provides and how it operates. It also provides information relative to when an employee can begin to participate in the plan, how service and benefits are calculated, when benefits become vested, when and in what form benefits are paid, and how to file a claim for benefits. In addition to the SPD, the plan administrator must automatically provide participants with a copy of the plan's summary annual financial report, which includes the same information that employers are required to file with the government on Form 5500.

Ensure Your Organization Follows ERISA Rules

HR professionals must ensure that their organizations follow ERISA participation rules for defined benefit and defined contribution plans. In general, an employee must be allowed to participate in a qualified plan after meeting the following requirements:

▶ **The employee is at least 21 years old**—Note that an employee can be excluded for not having reached a minimum age (which cannot exceed age 21) but cannot be excluded for having reached a maximum age. In other words, no matter how old an employee is, she can still participate in the plan.

▶ **The employee has at least one year of service**—For qualified plans, a year of service is generally 1,000 hours of service performed during the plan year. Employees who do not perform 1,000 hours of service are not considered to have performed one year of service, even if services were performed for a 12-month period. (Note: for plans other than 401(k), this requirement is two years as long as the plan has fully vested after not more than two years of service.)

An employer may, however, choose to implement less restrictive eligibility requirements, such as a minimum age requirement that is younger than 21 or a service requirement of less than one year.

Administrative Responsibility for ERISA

Administrative responsibility for enforcement of ERISA is divided among three government agencies:

▶ **IRS:** The IRS focuses on tax-related dimensions of ERISA.

▶ **DOL:** Within the DOL, ESBA focuses on fiduciary responsibility and transactions that are prohibited by ERISA. Within the DOL, Employee Benefits Security Administration is responsible for administering and enforcing the fiduciary, reporting, and disclosure provisions of ERISA.

▶ **Pension Benefit Guaranty Corporation (PBGC):** The PBGC—a government corporation created by ERISA—functions as an insurer that provides a minimum guaranteed benefit for certain pension plans. PBGC protects participants in most defined benefit plans and cash balance plans (within certain limitations). So, for instance, if a covered plan is terminated, PBGC ensures that participants will receive payment of certain benefits.

The PBGC is funded by insurance premiums that are paid by plan sponsors—not by general tax dollars. Funding also comes from investment income, assets from underfunded pension plans it has taken over, and recoveries from companies formerly responsible for those plans.

Summary Plan Description (SPD)

The summary plan description (SPD) describes what the plan provides and how it operates. It also provides information relative to when an employee can begin to participate in the plan, how service and benefits are calculated, when benefits becomes vested, when and in what form benefits are paid, and how to file a claim for benefits.

Revenue Act, 1978

The Revenue Act brought with it many changes, including a reduction in individual income taxes and a reduction in corporate taxes. It also added two sections to the tax code that essentially resulted in the creation of two new—and ultimately very important—employee benefits: Section 125 plans and 401(k) plans.

Section 125

Section 125 created flexible benefits plans (often referred to as "cafeteria" plans). Section 125 plans can help employers as well as employees save money by reducing payroll taxes.

Before looking at the three types of Section 125 plans, let's consider some of the reasons that an organization might have for implementing a section 125 plan.

Reasons for Considering Section 125 Plans

Thinking back to where we started in this chapter, recall that each organization's total compensation program communicates a great deal to employees—and to potential employees—about what the organization values. As such, Section 125 plans might be one way of communicating some of the following messages (to the degree they are appropriate) to employees:

▶ "We recognize that not everyone's life is the same and that everyone has different needs. Because of that, different employees may want to allocate—or spend—the money they earn in different ways." (Section 125 plans are one way to acknowledge and support these different and changing employee needs.)

▶ "When it comes to benefits, we may not always know what's best for you, but you do. In this sense, our goal becomes to give you tools and information with which you can make benefits-related decisions that are right for you."

▶ "We know you have a choice regarding the company for which you will work. Every day that you choose to remain employed with us, you are casting a vote. We know this, and we appreciate it. Giving you some choice regarding the benefits you select is one way we can say 'thanks.'"

Types of Cafeteria Plans

There are three types of cafeteria plans:

- ▶ **Premium only plans (POPs):** With POPs, the simplest and most transparent (from employees' perspectives) of the three Section 125 plans, employees pay for their portion of certain insurance premiums (health, dental, and so on) on a pretax basis. The net effect is that each employee's taxable income is reduced, which is how employers and employees can reduce taxes—and save money.

- ▶ **Flexible spending accounts (FSAs):** FSAs take POPs one step further. With FSAs, employees can set aside pretax dollars to pay for medical expenses that are not covered by insurance. FSAs can also be set up for dependent care. Employees decide how much money to set aside for the following year, and that amount is automatically deducted from the employee's pay on a pretax basis. After incurring and paying for eligible expenses, employees apply for reimbursement from the FSA.

- ▶ **Full cafeteria plans:** Employers who offer full cafeteria plans provide their employees with a specific amount of money they can use to pick and choose from a variety of benefits.

Although they offer distinct advantages, especially for employees, full cafeteria plans are the most administratively burdensome of the three Section 125 options.

Section 401(k)

The second employee benefit that was created by the Revenue Act is the 401(k) plan. A type of defined contribution plan, 401(k) plans allow employees to set aside pretax dollars to save for their retirement. This can be done through salary deduction, which may or may not be matched in part or (less frequently) in whole by employer contributions. 401(k) dollars can also be set aside through deferral of profit-sharing income.

Like most benefits plans, 401(k)s are more complex than they might initially appear. This is particularly true because of the tax implications associated with 401(k)s. Be sure that your plan is in full compliance with government regulations because lack of compliance can result in significant consequences, financial and otherwise.

Retirement Equity Act (REA), 1984

The Retirement Equity Act (REA), an amendment to ERISA, incorporated a number of key revisions, many of which addressed the concerns of former (in the event of divorce) and surviving (in the event of death) spouses. Specifically, REA enacted a number of important provisions, seven of which are that the REA

1. Lowered the minimum age requirement for pension plan participation.

2. Increased the years of service that "count" for vesting purposes.

3. Allowed for longer breaks in service (with respect to vesting rules).

4. Prohibited plans from counting maternity and paternity leaves as breaks in service for participation and vesting purposes.

5. Required qualified pension plans to provide automatic survivor benefits and allow for waiver of survivor benefits only with the consent of the participant and the spouse.

6. Clarified that pension plans may obey certain qualified domestic relations (court) orders (QDROs) requiring them to make benefit payments to a participant's former spouse or

another alternative payee without violating ERISA's prohibitions against assignment or alienation of benefits. Required information includes the following:

- ▶ The name and last known mailing address of the participant and each alternate payee
- ▶ The name of each plan to which the order applies
- ▶ The dollar amount or percentage (or the method of determining the amount or percentage) of the benefit to be paid to the alternate payee
- ▶ The number of payments or time period to which the order applies

7. Expanded the definition of accrued benefits that are protected against reduction.

Consolidated Omnibus Budget Reconciliation Act (COBRA), 1985

The Consolidated Omnibus Budget Reconciliation Act (COBRA) is technically an amendment to Title I of ERISA and is thus administered by EBSA. COBRA requires employers who employed 20 or more people during the prior year to offer continuation of group health care coverage to employees and their family members who experience certain "qualifying events"—events that would have otherwise resulted in the discontinuation of their health insurance benefits.

COBRA places certain requirements on plan participants who want to extend coverage, and it places certain requirements on the plan provider—in particular with respect to notification requirements.

COBRA Qualifying Events

Employees, their spouses, and their dependent children can experience qualifying events that would immediately entitle them to continue group health insurance coverage under COBRA.

Those who choose to extend coverage are responsible for paying the full cost of the health premium, plus a 2% administrative fee (if the plan sponsor chooses to charge one).

COBRA Qualifying "Life Events" for Employees

The following table describes the different type of life events that would trigger COBRA coverage as well as the corresponding length of time that COBRA can be continued for the employee.

COBRA qualifying events for employees are shown in Table 4.1.

TABLE 4.1   COBRA Qualifying Events for Employees

COBRA Qualifying Event	Length of Continuation Coverage Eligibility
Voluntary or involuntary termination of the covered employee's employment for any reason other than gross misconduct	18 months
Reduction in the hours worked by the covered employee	18 months

COBRA Qualifying "Life Events" for Employees' Spouses

The following table describes the different type of life events that would trigger COBRA coverage as well as the corresponding length of time that COBRA can be continued for the employee's spouse.

COBRA qualifying events for employees' spouses are shown in Table 4.2.

TABLE 4.2   COBRA Qualifying Events for Employees' Spouses

COBRA Qualifying Event	Length of Continuation Coverage Eligibility
Voluntary or involuntary termination of the covered employee's employment for any reason other than gross misconduct	18 months
Reduction in the hours worked by the covered employee	18 months
Covered employees becoming entitled to Medicare	29 months
Divorce or legal separation of the covered employee	36 months
Death of the covered employee	36 months

COBRA Qualifying Events for Employees' Dependent Children

The following table describes the different type of life events that would trigger COBRA coverage as well as the corresponding length of time that COBRA can be continued for the employee's dependent children.

COBRA qualifying events for employees' dependent children are shown in Table 4.3.

TABLE 4.3   COBRA Qualifying Events for Employees' Dependent Children

COBRA Qualifying Event	Length of Continuation Coverage Eligibility
Loss of dependent child status under the plan rules	18 months
Voluntary or involuntary termination of the covered employee's employment for any reason other than gross misconduct	18 months
Reduction in the hours worked by the covered employee	18 months
Covered employee's becoming entitled to Medicare	29 months
Divorce or legal separation of the covered employee	36 months
Death of the covered employee	36 months

> **NOTE**
>
> Extensions of the length of continuation coverage may be available under certain circumstances, such as when a second qualifying event occurs.

> **NOTE**
>
> COBRA is not available to employees, their spouses, or their dependent children when an employee is terminated for gross misconduct.

Older Worker's Benefit Protection Act (OWBPA), 1990

The Older Worker's Benefit Protection Act (OWBPA), passed in 1990, is an amendment to the ADEA that makes it illegal to discriminate against older workers with respect to benefits or to target older workers for layoffs.

Title 2 of OWBPA prohibits individuals from waiving rights or claims under ADEA unless such a waiver is "knowing and voluntary." OWBPA established nine specific criteria for ensuring that such waivers are knowing and voluntary. One particularly important criterion states that employers must allow employees at least 21 days to consider any right-to-sue waivers that the employer offers in exchange for early retirement benefits.

Health Insurance Portability and Accountability Act (HIPAA), 1996

The Health Insurance Portability and Accountability Act (HIPAA) was a more recent amendment to ERISA. HIPAA has two main areas of focus: the security and portability of health care coverage, and privacy considerations.

Security and Portability of Health Care Coverage

One of HIPAA's two key purposes was to help workers experience greater security and portability with respect to health care coverage—even when an employee changes jobs. HIPAA also afforded significantly greater protections for employees who have or who have a family member with a preexisting medical condition. Under HIPAA, a preexisting condition is defined as one for which medical advice, diagnosis, care, or treatment was recommended or received during the 6-month period prior to an individual's enrollment date.

Under HIPAA, in the worst-case scenario, employees (or their family members) with preexisting health conditions can have those conditions excluded from coverage for no more than 12 months (18 months for late enrollees). If an employee maintains health coverage continuously, he can reduce or even eliminate this period of exclusion.

HIPAA also prohibits employers from denying certain employees coverage—or from charging them higher premiums—because of preexisting health conditions. HIPAA affords protection to employers, as well, by mandating that health insurance providers must renew coverage for employers (as long as premium payments are made).

HIPAA Privacy Rule

HIPAA also addresses the issue of privacy for patients and health-care consumers. The three groups of covered entities defined by HIPAA are health plans, health care providers, and health care clearinghouses. Thus, although this rule is not specifically directed at employers, employers who offer group health insurance to employees may be considered a "covered entity" and thus be required to comply with HIPAA's privacy rule.

The primary purpose of the HIPAA privacy rule is to protect patients and other consumers of health care services from the unauthorized disclosure of any personally identifiable health information (also referred to as protected health information, or PHI). Health information is considered to be personally identifiable if it relates to a specifically identifiable individual. The following items would generally be considered PHI (whether communicated electronically, on paper, or verbally):

- ▶ Health care claims or health care encounter information, such as documentation of doctor's visits and notes made by physicians and other provider staff
- ▶ Health care payment and remittance advice
- ▶ Coordination of health care benefits
- ▶ Health care claim status
- ▶ Enrollment and disenrollment in a health plan
- ▶ Eligibility for a health plan
- ▶ Health plan premium payments
- ▶ Referral certifications and authorization
- ▶ First report of injury
- ▶ Health claims attachments

If it is determined that an employer is a "covered entity" under the HIPPA privacy rule, the employer would need to take specific actions, some of which would include these:

- ▶ Enact written PHI privacy procedures.
- ▶ Designate a privacy officer.
- ▶ Require business associates to sign agreements stating that they will respect the confidentiality of PHI.
- ▶ Train all employees in HIPAA privacy rule requirements.
- ▶ Establish a complaint handling and resolution process for issues related to the HIPAA privacy rule.
- ▶ Ensure that PHI is not used for making employment-related decisions.

EXAM ALERT

Like ERISA and COBRA, HIPAA is a highly complex and involved law. Don't let the apparent simplicity of the information presented here mislead you; it's necessary to dig much deeper to truly understand the nuances and subtleties of this law.

Family and Medical Leave Act (FMLA), 1993

The Family and Medical Leave Act (FMLA) (see www.dol.gov) entitles eligible employees (who work for covered employers) up to 12 weeks of unpaid, job-protected leave during any 12-month period for one or more of the following reasons:

- ▶ For the birth and care of the newborn child of the employee
- ▶ For placement with the employee of a son or daughter for adoption or foster care
- ▶ To care for an immediate family member (spouse, child, or parent) with a serious health condition
- ▶ To take medical leave when the employee is unable to work because of a serious health condition

Under some circumstances, leave can be taken intermittently.

The FMLA is administered and enforced by the DOL.

Employee Eligibility for FMLA

To be eligible to take FMLA leave, an employee must

- ▶ Work for a covered employer (public agencies; state, local, and federal employers; local education agencies [schools]; and private-sector employers with 50 or more employees)

- ▶ Have worked for the employer for a total of at least 12 months (this time does not have to have been uninterrupted)

- ▶ Have worked at least 1,250 hours over the previous 12 months

- ▶ Work at a location in the United States or in any territory or possession of the United States where at least 50 employees are employed by the employer within 75 miles

FMLA—Employer Requirements

As described at www.dol.gov, the FMLA places specific requirements upon employers before and during FMLA leaves. Specific requirements pertain to

- ▶ Posting requirements

- ▶ Notifying employees of their rights under FMLA

- ▶ Designating use of leave as FMLA leave

- ▶ Maintaining group health benefits

- ▶ Restoring an employee to her original job or to an equivalent job with equivalent pay, benefits, and other terms and conditions of employment

According to the DOL, all covered employers are required to display and keep displayed a poster summarizing the major provisions of the FMLA and telling employees how to file a complaint. The poster must be displayed in a conspicuous place where employees and applicants for employment can see it—even if there are no FMLA-eligible employees at a particular location. The DOL-approved poster is shown at the following link: www.dol.gov/whd/regs/compliance/posters/fmlaen.pdf.

Notifying Employees of Their Rights Under FMLA

Employers are also required to notify eligible employees of their FMLA rights and responsibilities within five days after the FMLA leave request is made. The DOL updated the Notification of Employee Rights & Responsibilities form in May 2015 (see the following page):

Again, while use of this specific form is optional, notification requirements are mandatory.

This template is valid through May 31, 2018. After that date, check the DOL website for updates.

Notice of Eligibility and Rights &
Responsibilities
(Family and Medical Leave Act)

U.S. Department of Labor
Wage and Hour Division

OMB Control Number: 1235-0003
Expires: 5/31/2018

In general, to be eligible an employee must have worked for an employer for at least 12 months, meet the hours of service requirement in the 12 months preceding the leave, and work at a site with at least 50 employees within 75 miles. While use of this form by employers is optional, a fully completed Form WH-381 provides employees with the information required by 29 C.F.R. § 825.300(b), which must be provided within five business days of the employee notifying the employer of the need for FMLA leave. Part B provides employees with information regarding their rights and responsibilities for taking FMLA leave, as required by 29 C.F.R. § 825.300(b), (c).

[**Part A – NOTICE OF ELIGIBILITY**]

TO: _____
     Employee

FROM: _____ _____
     Employer Representative

DATE: _____ _____

On _____, you informed us that you needed leave beginning on _____ for:

_____ The birth of a child, or placement of a child with you for adoption or foster care;

_____ Your own serious health condition;

_____ Because you are needed to care for your _____ spouse; _____ child; _____ parent due to his/her serious health condition.

_____ Because of a qualifying exigency arising out of the fact that your _____ spouse; _____ son or daughter; _____ parent is on covered active duty or call to covered active duty status with the Armed Forces.

_____ Because you are the _____ spouse; _____ son or daughter; _____ parent; _____ next of kin of a covered servicemember with a serious injury or illness.

This Notice is to inform you that you:

_____ Are eligible for FMLA leave (See Part B below for Rights and Responsibilities)

_____ Are **not** eligible for FMLA leave, because (only one reason need be checked, although you may not be eligible for other reasons):

     _____ You have not met the FMLA's 12-month length of service requirement. As of the first date of requested leave, you will have worked approximately ___ months towards this requirement.
     _____ You have not met the FMLA's hours of service requirement.
     _____ You do not work and/or report to a site with 50 or more employees within 75-miles.

If you have any questions, contact _____ or view the

FMLA poster located in _____.

[**PART B-RIGHTS AND RESPONSIBILITIES FOR TAKING FMLA LEAVE**]

As explained in Part A, you meet the eligibility requirements for taking FMLA leave and still have FMLA leave available in the applicable 12-month period. **However, in order for us to determine whether your absence qualifies as FMLA leave, you must return the following information to us by** _____. (If a certification is requested, employers must allow at least 15 calendar days from receipt of this notice; additional time may be required in some circumstances.) If sufficient information is not provided in a timely manner, your leave may be denied.

_____ Sufficient certification to support your request for FMLA leave. A certification form that sets forth the information necessary to support your request _____ **is/** _____ **is not** enclosed.

_____ Sufficient documentation to establish the required relationship between you and your family member.

_____ Other information needed (such as documentation for military family leave): _____

_____

_____

_____ No additional information requested

Page 1   CONTINUED ON NEXT PAGE   Form WH-381 Revised February 2013

Designating Use of Leave As FMLA Leave

Employers must also notify employees upon determining whether FMLA leave request is approved (or, upon ascertaining that more information is required). Employers may choose to notify employees (and, in particular, designate leave as FMLA qualifying) using the DOL's "Designation Notice." The following form was updated in May 2015, and is valid through May 31, 2018:

Designation Notice
(Family and Medical Leave Act)

U.S. Department of Labor
Wage and Hour Division

OMB Control Number: 1235-0003
Expires: 5/31/2018

Leave covered under the Family and Medical Leave Act (FMLA) must be designated as FMLA-protected and the employer must inform the employee of the amount of leave that will be counted against the employee's FMLA leave entitlement. In order to determine whether leave is covered under the FMLA, the employer may request that the leave be supported by a certification. If the certification is incomplete or insufficient, the employer must state in writing what additional information is necessary to make the certification complete and sufficient. While use of this form by employers is optional, a fully completed Form WH-382 provides an easy method of providing employees with the written information required by 29 C.F.R. §§ 825.300(c), 825.301, and 825.305(c).

To: _____

Date: _____

We have reviewed your request for leave under the FMLA and any supporting documentation that you have provided. We received your most recent information on _____ and decided:

_____ **Your FMLA leave request is approved. All leave taken for this reason will be designated as FMLA leave.**

The FMLA requires that you notify us as soon as practicable if dates of scheduled leave change or are extended, or were initially unknown. Based on the information you have provided to date, we are providing the following information about the amount of time that will be counted against your leave entitlement:

_____ Provided there is no deviation from your anticipated leave schedule, the following number of hours, days, or weeks will be counted against your leave entitlement: _____

_____ Because the leave you will need will be unscheduled, it is not possible to provide the hours, days, or weeks that will be counted against your FMLA entitlement at this time. You have the right to request this information once in a 30-day period (if leave was taken in the 30-day period).

Please be advised (check if applicable):
_____ You have requested to use paid leave during your FMLA leave. Any paid leave taken for this reason will count against your FMLA leave entitlement.

_____ We are requiring you to substitute or use paid leave during your FMLA leave.

_____ You will be required to present a fitness-for-duty certificate to be restored to employment. If such certification is not timely received, your return to work may be delayed until certification is provided. A list of the essential functions of your position ___ **is** ___ **is not** attached. If attached, the fitness-for-duty certification must address your ability to perform these functions.

_____ **Additional information is needed to determine if your FMLA leave request can be approved:**

_____ The certification you have provided is not complete and sufficient to determine whether the FMLA applies to your leave request. You must provide the following information no later than _____, unless it is not
(Provide at least seven calendar days)
practicable under the particular circumstances despite your diligent good faith efforts, or your leave may be denied.

_____
(Specify information needed to make the certification complete and sufficient)

_____

_____ We are exercising our right to have you obtain a second or third opinion medical certification at our expense, and we will provide further details at a later time.

_____ Your FMLA Leave request is Not Approved.
_____ The FMLA does not apply to your leave request.
_____ You have exhausted your FMLA leave entitlement in the applicable 12-month period.

PAPERWORK REDUCTION ACT NOTICE AND PUBLIC BURDEN STATEMENT
It is mandatory for employers to inform employees in writing whether leave requested under the FMLA has been determined to be covered under the FMLA. 29 U.S.C. § 2617; 29 C.F.R. §§ 825.300(d), (e). It is mandatory for employers to retain a copy of this disclosure in their records for three years. 29 U.S.C. § 2616; 29 C.F.R. § 825.500. Persons are not required to respond to this collection of information unless it displays a currently valid OMB control number. The Department of Labor estimates that it will take an average of 10 – 30 minutes for respondents to complete this collection of information, including the time for reviewing instructions, searching existing data sources, gathering and maintaining the data needed, and completing and reviewing the collection of information. If you have any comments regarding this burden estimate or any other aspect of this collection information, including suggestions for reducing this burden, send them to the Administrator, Wage and Hour Division, U.S. Department of Labor, Room S-3502, 200 Constitution Ave., NW, Washington, DC 20210. **DO NOT SEND THE COMPLETED FORM TO THE WAGE AND HOUR DIVISION.**

Form WH-382 January 2009

Again, while use of this specific form is optional, designation requirements are mandatory.

This template is valid through May 31, 2018. After that date, check the DOL website for updates.

FMLA—Employee Requirements
Employees are also subject to certain requirements under the FMLA:

- They must give 30-day advance notice (when foreseeable and practicable).
- Employers may also require employees to provide the following:
    - Medical certification
    - Second or third medical opinions (at the employer's expense) and periodic recertification
    - Periodic reports during FMLA leave regarding the employee's status and intent to return to work
- For intermittent leaves, employees must try to "work around" the needs of the workplace.

Serious Health Condition
The FMLA is a complex and multifaceted law. HR professionals must proceed carefully and should (as always) work with qualified counsel as needed.

As an example of the complexity and the criticality of understanding the language of the FMLA, let's look at one particular term, "serious health condition."

"'Serious health condition' means an illness, injury, impairment, or physical or mental condition that involves:

- any period of incapacity or treatment connected with inpatient care (i.e., an overnight stay) in a hospital, hospice, or residential medical care facility; or
- a period of incapacity requiring absence of more than three calendar days from work, school, or other regular daily activities that also involves continuing treatment by (or under the supervision of) a health care provider;

    or

- any period of incapacity due to pregnancy, or for prenatal care; or
- any period of incapacity (or treatment therefore) due to a chronic serious health condition (e.g., asthma, diabetes, epilepsy, etc.); or
- a period of incapacity that is permanent or long-term due to a condition for which treatment may not be effective (e.g., Alzheimer's, stroke, terminal diseases, etc.); or,
- any absences to receive multiple treatments (including any period of recovery therefrom) by, or on referral by, a health care provider for a condition that likely would result in incapacity of more than three consecutive days if left untreated (e.g., chemotherapy, physical therapy, dialysis, etc.)" (www.dol.gov).

Perhaps ironically, the complexity of the term "serious health condition" (and so many other FMLA terms) is that, despite the large amount of effort and large number of words dedicated to defining it, in practice its meaning remains somewhat ambiguous. As with all other aspects of the FMLA, HR-related law, and the HR profession in general, a significant degree of analysis (coupled with sound judgment and careful monitoring of relevant court interpretations) is essential. In addition, HR professionals should—as always—consult with qualified counsel relative before interpreting and applying the law. (Yes, this bears repeating.)

Employers can/will provide employees who notify them of their need for FMLA because of their own serious health condition with a "Certification of Health Care Provider for Employee's Serious Health Condition," or the equivalent thereof:

Certification of Health Care Provider for Employee's Serious Health Condition (Family and Medical Leave Act)

U.S. Department of Labor
Wage and Hour Division

DO NOT SEND COMPLETED FORM TO THE DEPARTMENT OF LABOR; RETURN TO THE PATIENT

OMB Control Number: 1235-0003
Expires: 5/31/2018

SECTION I: For Completion by the EMPLOYER

INSTRUCTIONS to the EMPLOYER: The Family and Medical Leave Act (FMLA) provides that an employer may require an employee seeking FMLA protections because of a need for leave due to a serious health condition to submit a medical certification issued by the employee's health care provider. Please complete Section I before giving this form to your employee. Your response is voluntary. While you are not required to use this form, you may not ask the employee to provide more information than allowed under the FMLA regulations, 29 C.F.R. §§ 825.306-825.308. Employers must generally maintain records and documents relating to medical certifications, recertifications, or medical histories of employees created for FMLA purposes as confidential medical records in separate files/records from the usual personnel files and in accordance with 29 C.F.R. § 1630.14(c)(1), if the Americans with Disabilities Act applies, and in accordance with 29 C.F.R. § 1635.9, if the Genetic Information Nondiscrimination Act applies.

Employer name and contact: _____

Employee's job title: _____ Regular work schedule: _____

Employee's essential job functions: _____

_____

Check if job description is attached: _____

SECTION II: For Completion by the EMPLOYEE

INSTRUCTIONS to the EMPLOYEE: Please complete Section II before giving this form to your medical provider. The FMLA permits an employer to require that you submit a timely, complete, and sufficient medical certification to support a request for FMLA leave due to your own serious health condition. If requested by your employer, your response is required to obtain or retain the benefit of FMLA protections. 29 U.S.C. §§ 2613, 2614(c)(3). Failure to provide a complete and sufficient medical certification may result in a denial of your FMLA request. 20 C.F.R. § 825.313. Your employer must give you at least 15 calendar days to return this form. 29 C.F.R. § 825.305(b).

Your name: _____
First   Middle   Last

SECTION III: For Completion by the HEALTH CARE PROVIDER

INSTRUCTIONS to the HEALTH CARE PROVIDER: Your patient has requested leave under the FMLA. Answer, fully and completely, all applicable parts. Several questions seek a response as to the frequency or duration of a condition, treatment, etc. Your answer should be your best estimate based upon your medical knowledge, experience, and examination of the patient. Be as specific as you can; terms such as "lifetime," "unknown," or "indeterminate" may not be sufficient to determine FMLA coverage. Limit your responses to the condition for which the employee is seeking leave. Do not provide information about genetic tests, as defined in 29 C.F.R. § 1635.3(f), genetic services, as defined in 29 C.F.R. § 1635.3(e), or the manifestation of disease or disorder in the employee's family members, 29 C.F.R. § 1635.3(b). Please be sure to sign the form on the last page.

Provider's name and business address: _____

Type of practice / Medical specialty: _____

Telephone: (_____)_____ Fax:(_____)_____

Page 1

Form WH-380-E Revised May 2015

This form was updated in May 2015, and expires on May 31, 2018. After this date, please search for updated forms on the DOL website.

If the employee has requested FMLA leave because of a family member's serious health condition, employers can/will provide employees with a "Certification of Health Care Provider for Family Members's Serious Health Condition," or the equivalent thereof:

Certification of Health Care Provider for
Family Member's Serious Health Condition
(Family and Medical Leave Act)

U.S. Department of Labor
Wage and Hour Division

DO NOT SEND COMPLETED FORM TO THE DEPARTMENT OF LABOR; RETURN TO THE PATIENT.

OMB Control Number: 1235-0003
Expires: 5/31/2018

SECTION I: For Completion by the EMPLOYER

INSTRUCTIONS to the EMPLOYER: The Family and Medical Leave Act (FMLA) provides that an employer may require an employee seeking FMLA protections because of a need for leave to care for a covered family member with a serious health condition to submit a medical certification issued by the health care provider of the covered family member. Please complete Section I before giving this form to your employee. Your response is voluntary. While you are not required to use this form, you may not ask the employee to provide more information than allowed under the FMLA regulations, 29 C.F.R. §§ 825.306-825.308. Employers must generally maintain records and documents relating to medical certifications, recertifications, or medical histories of employees' family members, created for FMLA purposes as confidential medical records in separate files/records from the usual personnel files and in accordance with 29 C.F.R. § 1630.14(c)(1), if the Americans with Disabilities Act applies, and in accordance with 29 C.F.R. § 1635.9, if the Genetic Information Nondiscrimination Act applies.

Employer name and contact: _____

SECTION II: For Completion by the EMPLOYEE

INSTRUCTIONS to the EMPLOYEE: Please complete Section II before giving this form to your family member or his/her medical provider. The FMLA permits an employer to require that you submit a timely, complete, and sufficient medical certification to support a request for FMLA leave to care for a covered family member with a serious health condition. If requested by your employer, your response is required to obtain or retain the benefit of FMLA protections. 29 U.S.C. §§ 2613, 2614(c)(3). Failure to provide a complete and sufficient medical certification may result in a denial of your FMLA request. 29 C.F.R. § 825.313. Your employer must give you at least 15 calendar days to return this form to your employer. 29 C.F.R. § 825.305.

Your name: _____
        First   Middle   Last

Name of family member for whom you will provide care:_____
                                        First   Middle   Last
Relationship of family member to you: _____

    If family member is your son or daughter, date of birth:_____

Describe care you will provide to your family member and estimate leave needed to provide care:

_____

_____

_____

_____   _____
Employee Signature   Date

Page 1   CONTINUED ON NEXT PAGE   Form WH-380-F Revised May 2015

This form was updated in May 2015, and expires on May 31, 2018. After this date, please search for updated forms on the DOL website.

Under no circumstances can employers seek more information than what this form requests.

Spouse

Effective March 27, 2015, the DOL updated the definition of "spouse" to include all individuals—including those in same-sex marriages—who are legally married. Specifically, this includes individuals who were married in states where same sex marriages are recognized, even if the married couple does not live in a state in which same-sex marriage is legally recognized.

Uniformed Services Employment and Reemployment Rights Act (USERRA), 1994

The Uniformed Services Employment and Reemployment Rights Act (USERRA) provides reinforcement rights for individuals who miss work because of "service in the uniformed services," which is defined as voluntary or involuntary uniformed service.

Employers are required to inform their employees of their rights under USERRA. This requirement can be met by displaying the following poster, as shown in Figure 4.2, that clearly outlines employees' rights and obligations under USERRA.

YOUR RIGHTS UNDER USERRA
THE UNIFORMED SERVICES EMPLOYMENT AND REEMPLOYMENT RIGHTS ACT

USERRA protects the job rights of individuals who voluntarily or involuntarily leave employment positions to undertake military service or certain types of service in the National Disaster Medical System. USERRA also prohibits employers from discriminating against past and present members of the uniformed services, and applicants to the uniformed services.

REEMPLOYMENT RIGHTS

You have the right to be reemployed in your civilian job if you leave that job to perform service in the uniformed service and:

☆ you ensure that your employer receives advance written or verbal notice of your service;
☆ you have five years or less of cumulative service in the uniformed services while with that particular employer;
☆ you return to work or apply for reemployment in a timely manner after conclusion of service; and
☆ you have not been separated from service with a disqualifying discharge or under other than honorable conditions.

If you are eligible to be reemployed, you must be restored to the job and benefits you would have attained if you had not been absent due to military service or, in some cases, a comparable job.

RIGHT TO BE FREE FROM DISCRIMINATION AND RETALIATION

If you:

☆ are a past or present member of the uniformed service;
☆ have applied for membership in the uniformed service; or
☆ are obligated to serve in the uniformed service;

then an employer may not deny you:

☆ initial employment;
☆ reemployment;
☆ retention in employment;
☆ promotion; or
☆ any benefit of employment

because of this status.

In addition, an employer may not retaliate against anyone assisting in the enforcement of USERRA rights, including testifying or making a statement in connection with a proceeding under USERRA, even if that person has no service connection.

HEALTH INSURANCE PROTECTION

☆ If you leave your job to perform military service, you have the right to elect to continue your existing employer-based health plan coverage for you and your dependents for up to 24 months while in the military.

☆ Even if you don't elect to continue coverage during your military service, you have the right to be reinstated in your employer's health plan when you are reemployed, generally without any waiting periods or exclusions (e.g., pre-existing condition exclusions) except for service-connected illnesses or injuries.

ENFORCEMENT

☆ The U.S. Department of Labor, Veterans Employment and Training Service (VETS) is authorized to investigate and resolve complaints of USERRA violations.

☆ For assistance in filing a complaint, or for any other information on USERRA, contact VETS at **1-866-4-USA-DOL** or visit its **website at http://www.dol.gov/vets**. An interactive online USERRA Advisor can be viewed at **http://www.dol.gov/elaws/userra.htm**.

☆ If you file a complaint with VETS and VETS is unable to resolve it, you may request that your case be referred to the Department of Justice or the Office of Special Counsel, as applicable, for representation.

☆ You may also bypass the VETS process and bring a civil action against an employer for violations of USERRA.

The rights listed here may vary depending on the circumstances. The text of this notice was prepared by VETS, and may be viewed on the internet at this address: http://www.dol.gov/vets/programs/userra/poster.htm. Federal law requires employers to notify employees of their rights under USERRA, and employers may meet this requirement by displaying the text of this notice where they customarily place notices for employees.

U.S. Department of Labor
1-866-487-2365
U.S. Department of Justice
Office of Special Counsel
1-800-336-4590
Publication Date—October 2008

FIGURE 4.2 Employees' rights under USERRA.

Additional information about USERRA is available in Chapter 2, "Workforce Planning and Employment."

Mental Health Parity Act, 1996

The Mental Health Parity Act (MHPA) prohibits group health plan providers, insurance companies, and HMOs that offer mental health benefits from setting annual or lifetime dollar limits on mental health benefits that are lower than any such dollar limits for medical and surgical benefits. This means that plans that don't impose annual or lifetime monetary caps on medical and surgical benefits cannot impose annual or lifetime caps on mental health benefits either. (Benefits for substance abuse or chemical dependency are exempted.) MHPA is under the jurisdiction of the Departments of Labor, Treasury, and Health and Human Services.

> **NOTE**
>
> It is important to note that MHPA does not require health plans to offer mental health benefits. It only applies to plans that voluntarily choose to offer mental health benefits.

Under MHPA, plans can still dictate/define the terms and conditions of benefits provided under mental health plans (for instance, cost sharing, limits on the number of visits or days of coverage, and so forth).

There are certain circumstances under which plan providers that offer mental health benefits are exempt from MHPA, including

- ▶ Small employers who have fewer than 51 employees.

- ▶ Any group health plan whose costs increase 1% or more because of the application of MHPA's requirements. (The increased cost exemption must be based on actual claims data, not on an increase in insurance premiums.)

Sarbanes-Oxley Act, 2002

The Sarbanes-Oxley Act (SOX) was created in the wake of huge corporate accounting scandals, including Enron and Tyco, to name just two. Designed to protect investors, SOX enacted reforms designed to enhance corporate responsibility and financial disclosures and to combat corporate and accounting fraud. For more information on the Sarbanes-Oxley Act, see Chapter 6, "Risk Management."

There are a number of SOX provisions that HR professionals needs to be particularly concerned with, four of which include these:

- ▶ Prohibition against insider trading during certain pension plan blackout periods—section 306(a).

▶ Requirement that plan administrators must provide 30-day written notice in advance of blackout periods to individual account plan participants and beneficiaries—section 306(b).

▶ Requirement to disclose whether the company has adopted a code of ethics that applies to the company's key officers (at a minimum, this code must apply to the company's principal executive officer, principal financial officer, principal accounting officer or controller, or persons performing similar functions)—section 406.

▶ Establishment of whistleblower protection in a variety of situations for employees who report fraud against shareholders—section 806(a).

Pension Protection Act, 2006

The Pension Protection Act (PPA) is a law that brought about "significant changes to section 101(f) of ERISA by enhancing the content of the notice and extending the requirement to provide notice to single-employer plans" (www.dol.gov).

Family and Medical Leave Act and National Defense Authorization Act (NDAA), 2008

The FMLA was amended in 2008, thus establishing two new entitlements for military families: "qualifying exigency leave" and "military caregiver leave." Qualifying exigency leave "may be taken for any qualifying exigency arising out of the fact that a covered military member is on active duty or call to active duty status" (www.dol.gov). Military caregiver leave "may be taken by an eligible employee to care for a covered service member with a serious injury or illness" (www.dol.gov).

Employees can require an employee seeking FMLA leave due to a qualifying exigency to submit a certification. Employers can use the "Certification of Qualifying Exigency For Military Family Leave," or the equivalent thereof:

Certification of Qualifying Exigency
For Military Family Leave
(Family and Medical Leave Act)

U.S. Department of Labor

Wage and Hour Division

OMB Control Number: 1235-0003
Expires: 5/31/2018

SECTION I: For Completion by the EMPLOYER

INSTRUCTIONS to the EMPLOYER: The Family and Medical Leave Act (FMLA) provides that an employer may require an employee seeking FMLA leave due to a qualifying exigency to submit a certification. Please complete Section I before giving this form to your employee. Your response is voluntary, and while you are not required to use this form, you may not ask the employee to provide more information than allowed under the FMLA regulations, 29 CFR 825.309.

Employer name: _____

Contact Information: _____

SECTION II: For Completion by the EMPLOYEE

INSTRUCTIONS to the EMPLOYEE: Please complete Section II fully and completely. The FMLA permits an employer to require that you submit a timely, complete, and sufficient certification to support a request for FMLA leave due to a qualifying exigency. Several questions in this section seek a response as to the frequency or duration of the qualifying exigency. Be as specific as you can; terms such as "unknown," or "indeterminate" may not be sufficient to determine FMLA coverage. Your response is required to obtain a benefit. 29 CFR 825.310. While you are not required to provide this information, failure to do so may result in a denial of your request for FMLA leave. Your employer must give you at least 15 calendar days to return this form to your employer.

Your Name: _____
　　　　　　　　　First　　　　　　　　Middle　　　　　　　　Last

Name of military member on covered active duty or call to covered active duty status:

_____
　　　　　　　　　First　　　　　　　　Middle　　　　　　　　Last

Relationship of military member to you: _____

Period of military member's covered active duty: _____

A complete and sufficient certification to support a request for FMLA leave due to a qualifying exigency includes written documentation confirming a military member's covered active duty or call to covered active duty status. Please check one of the following and attach the indicated document to support that the military member is on covered active duty or call to covered active duty status.

　　　　A copy of the military member's covered active duty orders is attached.

　　　　Other documentation from the military certifying that the military member is on covered active duty (or has been notified of an impending call to covered active duty) is attached.

　　　　I have previously provided my employer with sufficient written documentation confirming the military member's covered active duty or call to covered active duty status.

This form was updated in May 2015, and expires on May 31, 2018. After this date, please search for updated forms on the DOL website. Employers may not request more information than is specified by this template.

The Family and Medical Leave Act (FMLA) provides that an employer may require an employee seeking FMLA leave due to a serious injury or illness of a current servicemember to submit a certification providing sufficient facts to support the request for leave. (www.dol.gov). Employers can use the "Certification for Serious Illness or Injury of a Current Servicemember—For Military Family Leave," or the equivalent thereof:

Certification for Serious Injury or
Illness of a Current
Servicemember - -for Military Family Leave
(Family and Medical Leave Act)

U.S. Department of Labor

Wage and Hour Division

U.S. Wage and Hour Division

DO NOT SEND COMPLETED FORM TO THE DEPARTMENT OF LABOR; RETURN TO THE PATIENT

OMB Control Number: 1235-0003
Expires: 5/31/2018

Notice to the EMPLOYER

INSTRUCTIONS to the EMPLOYER: The Family and Medical Leave Act (FMLA) provides that an employer may require an employee seeking FMLA leave due to a serious injury or illness of a current servicemember to submit a certification providing sufficient facts to support the request for leave. Your response is voluntary. While you are not required to use this form, you may not ask the employee to provide more information than allowed under the FMLA regulations, 29 CFR 825.310. Employers must generally maintain records and documents relating to medical certifications, recertifications, or medical histories of employees or employees' family members created for FMLA purposes as confidential medical records in separate files/records from the usual personnel files and in accordance with 29 CFR 1630.14(c)(1), if the Americans with Disabilities Act applies, and in accordance with 29 CFR 1635.9, if the Genetic Information Nondiscrimination Act applies.

SECTION I: For Completion by the EMPLOYEE and/or the CURRENT SERVICEMEMBER for whom the Employee Is Requesting Leave

INSTRUCTIONS to the EMPLOYEE or CURRENT SERVICEMEMBER: Please complete Section I before having Section II completed. The FMLA permits an employer to require that an employee submit a timely, complete, and sufficient certification to support a request for FMLA leave due to a serious injury or illness of a servicemember. If requested by the employer, your response is required to obtain or retain the benefit of FMLA-protected leave. 29 U.S.C. 2613, 2614(c)(3). Failure to do so may result in a denial of an employee's FMLA request. 29 CFR 825.310(f). The employer must give an employee at least 15 calendar days to return this form to the employer.

SECTION II: For Completion by a UNITED STATES DEPARTMENT OF DEFENSE ("DOD") HEALTH CARE PROVIDER or a HEALTH CARE PROVIDER who is either: (1) a United States Department of Veterans Affairs ("VA") health care provider; (2) a DOD TRICARE network authorized private health care provider; (3) a DOD non-network TRICARE authorized private health care provider; or (4) a health care provider as defined in 29 CFR 825.125

INSTRUCTIONS to the HEALTH CARE PROVIDER: The employee listed on Page 2 has requested leave under the FMLA to care for a family member who is a current member of the Regular Armed Forces, the National Guard, or the Reserves who is undergoing medical treatment, recuperation, or therapy, is otherwise in outpatient status, or is otherwise on the temporary disability retired list for a serious injury or illness. For purposes of FMLA leave, a serious injury or illness is one that was incurred in the line of duty on active duty in the Armed Forces or that existed before the beginning of the member's active duty and was aggravated by service in the line of duty on active duty in the Armed Forces that may render the servicemember medically unfit to perform the duties of his or her office, grade, rank, or rating.

A complete and sufficient certification to support a request for FMLA leave due to a current servicemember's serious injury or illness includes written documentation confirming that the servicemember's injury or illness was incurred in the line of duty on active duty or if not, that the current servicemember's injury or illness existed before the beginning of the servicemember's active duty and was aggravated by service in the line of duty on active duty in the Armed Forces, and that the current servicemember is undergoing treatment for such injury or illness by a health care provider listed above. Answer, fully and completely, all applicable parts. Several questions seek a response as to the frequency or duration of a condition, treatment, etc. Your answer should be your best estimate based upon your medical knowledge, experience, and examination of the patient. Be as specific as you can; terms such as "lifetime," "unknown," or "indeterminate" may not be sufficient to determine FMLA coverage. Limit your responses to the servicemember's condition for which the employee is seeking leave. Do not provide information about genetic tests, as defined in 29 CFR 1635.3(f), or genetic services, as defined in 29 CFR 1635.3(e).

Page 1

Form WH-385 Revised May 2015

Employers may not request more information than is specified by this template.

With respect to recordkeeping, "(e)mployers must generally maintain records and documents relating to medical certifications, recertifications, or medical histories of employees or employees' family members created for FMLA purposes as confidential medical records in separate files/records from the usual personnel files and in accordance with" the ADA and/or GINA (www.dol.gov).

The Family and Medical Leave Act (FMLA) provides that an employer may require an employee seeking military caregiver leave under the FMLA leave due to a serious injury or illness of a covered veteran to submit a certification providing sufficient facts to support the request for leave" (www.dol.gov). Employers can use the "Certification for Serious Injury U.S. Department of Labor or Illness of a Veteran for Wage and Hour Division Military Caregiver Leave," or the equivalent thereof:

Certification for Serious Injury
or Illness of a Veteran for
Military Caregiver Leave
(Family and Medical Leave Act)

U.S. Department of Labor

Wage and Hour Division

DO NOT SEND COMPLETED FORM TO THE DEPARTMENT OF LABOR; RETURN TO THE EMPLOYEE

OMB Control Number: 1235-0003
Expires: 5/31/2018

Notice to the EMPLOYER

The Family and Medical Leave Act (FMLA) provides that an employer may require an employee seeking military caregiver leave under the FMLA leave due to a serious injury or illness of a covered veteran to submit a certification providing sufficient facts to support the request for leave. Your response is voluntary. While you are not required to use this form, you may not ask the employee to provide more information than allowed under the FMLA regulations, 29 CFR 825.310. Employers must generally maintain records and documents relating to medical certifications, recertifications, or medical histories of employees or employees' family members, created for FMLA purposes as confidential medical records in separate files/records from the usual personnel files and in accordance with 29 CFR 1630.14(c)(1), if the Americans with Disabilities Act applies, and in accordance with 29 CFR 1635.9, if the Genetic Information Nondiscrimination Act applies.

SECTION I: For completion by the EMPLOYEE and/or the VETERAN for whom the employee is requesting leave

INSTRUCTIONS to the EMPLOYEE and/or VETERAN: Please complete Section I before having Section II completed. The FMLA permits an employer to require that an employee submit a timely, complete, and sufficient certification to support a request for military caregiver leave under the FMLA leave due to a serious injury or illness of a covered veteran. If requested by the employer, your response is required to obtain or retain the benefit of FMLA-protected leave. 29 U.S.C. 2613, 2614(c)(3). Failure to do so may result in a denial of an employee's FMLA request. 29 CFR 825.310(f). The employer must give an employee at least 15 calendar days to return this form to the employer.

(This section must be completed before Section II can be completed by a health care provider.)

Part A: EMPLOYEE INFORMATION

Name and address of employer (this is the employer of the employee requesting leave to care for a veteran):

_____

Name of employee requesting leave to care for a veteran:

_____
First   Middle   Last

Name of veteran (for whom employee is requesting leave):

_____
First   Middle   Last

Relationship of employee to veteran:

Spouse☐   Parent☐   Son☐   Daughter☐   Next of Kin ☐ (please specify relationship):

Employers may not request more information than is specified by this template. This form was updated in May 2015, and expires on May 31, 2018. After this date, please search for updated forms on the DOL website.

Lilly Ledbetter Fair Pay Act, 2009

The Lilly Ledbetter Fair Pay Act was the first law signed by President Obama during his presidency.

"Under the Act, an individual subjected to compensation discrimination under Title VII of the Civil Rights Act of 1964, the Age Discrimination in Employment Act of 1967, or the Americans with Disabilities Act of 1990 may file a charge within 180 (or 300) days of any of the following:

- ▶ When a discriminatory compensation decision or other discriminatory practice affecting compensation is adopted;

- ▶ When the individual becomes subject to a discriminatory compensation decision or other discriminatory practice affecting compensation; or

- ▶ When the individual's compensation is affected by the application of a discriminatory compensation decision or other discriminatory practice, including each time the individual receives compensation that is based in whole or part on such compensation decision or other practice" (www.eeoc.gov).

According to the EEOC, this Act "codifies the EEOC's longstanding position that each paycheck that contains discriminatory compensation is a separate violation regardless of when the discrimination began. The Ledbetter Act recognizes the 'reality of wage discrimination' and restores 'bedrock principles of American law. Particularly important for the victims of discrimination, the Act contains an explicit retroactivity provision."

Patient Protection and Affordable Care Act, 2010

The Patient Protection and Affordable Care Act (PPACA), also sometimes known as the "ACA" or, more commonly, "Obamacare," requires all Americans to secure healthcare coverage and expands coverage limits (financial and nonfinancial).

> **NOTE**
>
> Regardless of one's political, social, or personal beliefs, it is essential for HR professionals to understand—and adhere to—the myriad changes that the ACA has had, and will continue to have, on ACA benefits coverage guidelines and mandates. As with any other law, it is not necessary to agree with it. However, it is necessary to understand, implement [as appropriate], and abide by it.

The PPACA is a complex and multifaceted law that affects different employers in different ways. HR professionals are strongly encouraged to peruse the resources listed at the end of this chapter to ensure they are well versed and compliant with the many provisions of the PPACA.

In addition, the following URL serves as official .gov portal to many FAQs, and much information, about the PPACA: www.dol.gov. At the time of publication of this book, the specific URL was: http://www.dol.gov/ebsa/healthreform/.

One less-often discussed provision of the PPACA involves nursing mothers who have returned to work. Dol.gov provides information about this dimension of the PPACA and its impact on FLSA requirements.

Nursing Mothers

The PPACA, signed into law on March 23, 2010 (P.L. 111-148), amended Section 7 of the FLSA to provide a break time requirement for nursing mothers.

Employers are required to provide reasonable break time for an employee to express breast milk for her nursing child for one year after the child's birth each time such employee has need to express the milk. Employers are also required to provide a place that an employee can use to express breast milk. The room must be other than a bathroom, shielded from view, and free from intrusion from coworkers and the public.

The FLSA requirement of break time for nursing mothers to express breast milk does not preempt state laws that provide greater protections to employees (for example, providing compensated break time, providing break time for exempt employees, or providing break time beyond one year after the child's birth).

Employers are required to provide a reasonable amount of break time to express milk as frequently as needed by the nursing mother. The frequency of breaks needed to express milk and the duration of each break will likely vary.

A bathroom, even if private, is not a permissible location under the Act. The location provided must be functional as a space for expressing breast milk. If the space is not dedicated to the nursing mother's use, it must be available when needed to meet the statutory requirement. A space temporarily created or converted into a space for expressing milk or made available when needed by the nursing mother is sufficient provided that the space is shielded from view and free from any intrusion from coworkers and the public.

Only employees who are not exempt from the FLSA's overtime pay requirements are entitled to breaks to express milk. Although employers are not required under the FLSA to provide breaks to nursing mothers who are exempt from the overtime pay requirements of Section 7, they may be obligated to provide such breaks under state laws.

Employers with fewer than 50 employees are not subject to the FLSA break time requirement if compliance with the provision would impose an undue hardship. Whether compliance would be an undue hardship is determined by looking at the difficulty or expense of compliance for a specific employer in comparison to the size, financial resources, nature, and structure of the employer's business. All employees who work for the covered employer, regardless of work site, are counted when determining whether this exemption may apply.

Employers are not required under the FLSA to compensate nursing mothers for breaks taken for the purpose of expressing milk. However, where employers already provide compensated breaks, an employee who uses that break time to express milk must be compensated in the same way that other employees are compensated for break time. In addition, the FLSA's general requirement that the employee must be completely relieved from duty or else the time must be compensated as work time applies.

IRS Reporting

While IRS reporting is usually the bailiwick of the tax department, HR professionals do need to have some level of familiarity with the IRS filing implications of the PPACA. Initial filings for CY2015 are required in early 2016. The basics of what HR professionals need to know (at a minimum) are listed here by the IRS:

Basics of Employer Reporting

"1. What are the information reporting requirements for employers relating to offers of health insurance coverage under employer-sponsored plans?

The Affordable Care Act added section 6056 to the Internal Revenue Code, which requires applicable large employers to file information returns with the IRS and provide statements to their full-time employees about the health insurance coverage the employer offered. (For a definition of applicable large employer, see question 5, below.)

Under the regulations implementing section 6056, an applicable large employer may be a single entity or may consist of a group of related entities (such as parent and subsidiary or other affiliated entities). In either case, these reporting requirements apply to each separate entity and each separate entity is referred to as an applicable large employer member (ALE member). See question 7 for more information about the treatment of related entities.

The IRS will use the information provided on the information return to administer the employer shared responsibility provisions of section 4980H. The IRS and the employees of an ALE member will use the information provided as part of the determination of whether an employee is eligible for the premium tax credit under section 36B.

ALE members that sponsor self-insured group health plans also are required to report information under section 6055 about the health coverage they provide (See our section 6055 FAQs). Those ALE members that sponsor self-insured group health plans file with the IRS and furnish to employees the information required under sections 6055 and 6056 on a single form. The IRS and individuals will use the information provided under section 6055 to administer or to show compliance with the individual shared responsibility provisions of section 5000A.

For details about the section 6056 information reporting requirements and additional guidance on how to complete Form 1094-C, Transmittal of Employer-Provided Health Insurance Offer and Coverage Information Returns, and Form 1095-C, Employer-Provided Health Insurance Offer and Coverage, see the Employer Information Reporting FAQs for Forms 1094-C and 1095-C on IRS.gov.

2. When do the information reporting requirements go into effect?

The information reporting requirements under section 6056 are first effective for coverage offered (or not offered) in 2015. An ALE member must file information returns with the IRS and furnish statements to employees beginning in 2016, to report information about its offers of health coverage to its full-time employees for calendar year 2015.

Notice 2013-45 provides transition relief for 2014 from the section 6056 reporting requirements and the section 6055 reporting requirements for health coverage providers and, thus, the section 4980H employer shared responsibility provisions as well. Accordingly, neither the reporting requirements nor the employer shared responsibility provisions apply for 2014. The transition relief applies to all ALE members including for-profit, non-profit, and government entity employers. However, in preparation for the application of the employer shared responsibility provisions beginning in 2015, employers and other affected entities may comply voluntarily for 2014 with the information reporting provisions and are encouraged to maintain or expand coverage in 2014. Returns filed voluntarily will have no impact on the tax liability of the employer. For more information about voluntary filing in 2015, including the requirements for filing electronic returns, see IRS.gov.

3. Is relief available from penalties for incomplete or incorrect returns filed or statements furnished to employees in 2016 for coverage offered (or not offered) in calendar year 2015?

Yes. In implementing new information reporting requirements, short-term relief from reporting penalties frequently is provided. This relief generally allows additional time to develop appropriate procedures for collection of data and compliance with the new reporting requirements. Accordingly, the IRS will not impose penalties under sections 6721 and 6722 on ALE members that can show that they have made good faith efforts to comply with the information reporting requirements. Specifically, relief is provided from penalties under sections 6721 and 6722 for returns and statements filed and furnished in 2016 to report offers of coverage in 2015 for incorrect or incomplete information reported on the return or statement. No relief is provided in the case of ALE members that cannot show a good faith effort to comply with the information reporting requirements or that fail to timely file an information return or furnish a statement. However, consistent with existing information reporting rules, ALE members that fail to timely meet the requirements still may be eligible for penalty relief if the IRS determines that the standards for reasonable cause under section 6724 are satisfied. See question 31 for more information about penalties under sections 6721 and 6722.

4. Where is more detailed information available about these reporting requirements?

The regulations under section 6056 provide further guidance on the information reporting requirements for applicable large employers, and the regulations under section 6055 provide guidance on the information reporting requirements for insurers and other health coverage providers. Regulations on the employer shared responsibility provisions under section 4980H provide guidance on determining applicable large employer status and determining full-time employee status, including defining and providing rules for calculating hours of service. The 1094/1095-C Questions and Answers provide guidance on how to complete Form 1094-C and Form 1095-C."

Additional information, guidelines and requirements can be found at http://www.irs.gov/Affordable-Care-Act.

40% Excise Tax on High Cost Employer-Sponsored Health Coverage

Although many dimensions of the PPACA have been—and continue to be—the subject of intense scrutiny and debate, one of the most hotly debated aspects of this law is the so-called "Cadillac tax," which imposes a 40% employer tax on high-cost employer-sponsored health coverage. Section 4980I, which was added to the Code by the Affordable Care Act, applies to taxable years beginning after December 31, 2017. Under this provision, if the aggregate cost of "applicable employer-sponsored coverage" (referred to in this notice as applicable coverage) provided to an employee exceeds a statutory dollar limit, which is revised annually, the excess is subject to a 40% excise tax" (www.irs.gov).

At the time of this book's publication, legislation has already been proposed to repeal this tax. HR professionals whose organizations might be impacted by Section 4980I should closely monitor developments around this provision of the PPACA.

> **NOTE**
>
> The PPACA cannot be easily abbreviated, summarized, or "shortcutted." This section covers some key (and unfamiliar/particularly noteworthy) components; however, reading this section is not a substitute for reviewing the link above to the DOL's information on this law. It won't be enough to pass the test—and it won't be enough to carry out your responsibilities as an HR professional.

So, roll up your sleeves, fire up your laptop, and dig in to the immense amount of government-published and private data that is available on this all-important HR topic.

A (Foundational) Footnote: Employee or Independent Contractor?

As indicated previously, one of the first steps that an organization needs to take is to ensure that individuals who contribute to the attainment of organizational objectives are accurately designated as either "employees" or "independent contractors."

As with most areas of HR, this question is not as simple as it might initially appear. There is no immediate answer—no single question that resolves the question of whether an individual is an employee or an independent contractor.

To assist in this effort, the Department of Labor (DOL) has published a fact sheet citing U.S. Supreme Court rulings that offer the following seven factors that help to appropriately resolve the seemingly perpetual employee/independent contractor conundrum:

1. The extent to which the services rendered are an integral part of the principal's business

2. The permanency of the relationship

3. The amount of the alleged contractor's investment in facilities and equipment

4. The nature and degree of control by the principal

5. The alleged contractor's opportunities for profit and loss

6. The amount of initiative, judgment, or foresight in open market competition with others required for the success of the claimed independent contractor

7. The degree of independent business organization and operation (www.dol.gov)

The IRS also offers guidance at its website (www.irs.gov) with respect to properly classifying employees and independent contractors. According to the IRS, it is critical to examine the nature of the relationship between the worker and the organization. Specifically, all evidence of "control" and "independence" must be carefully considered. The IRS identifies three categories of control into which facts and evidence can be divided: behavioral control, financial control, and the type of relationship:

- **Behavioral control:** Who controls and directs how the work is done? For instance, it could be argued that the business maintains behavioral control if it provides the individual with training, instructions, and so forth.

- **Financial control:** Does the business have a right to control the financial and business aspects of the worker's job? More specifically

  - To what extent does the worker have unreimbursed business expenses?

  - What is the extent of the worker's investment in the facilities used in performing services?

  - To what extent does the worker make her services available to the relevant market?

  - How does the business pay the worker?

  - To what extent can the worker realize a profit or incur a loss?

▶ **Type of relationship:** Is there a written contract in place? If so, to what extent does it describe

  ▶ The relationship the parties intended to create?

  ▶ The extent to which the worker is available to perform services for other, similar businesses?

  ▶ Whether the business provides the worker with employee-type benefits, such as insurance, a pension plan, vacation pay, or sick pay?

  ▶ The permanency of the relationship?

  ▶ The extent to which services performed by the worker are a key aspect of the regular business of the company?

CAUTION

Great care must be taken to determine whether an individual is classified as an employee or as an independent contractor. Don't make this decision alone. There are many ramifications of misclassification, including the possibility of settlements that have cost some employers millions of dollars.

In many ways, an organization's compensation and benefits philosophy is a clear and direct expression of the organization's mission, vision, and values—whether or not the organization intends it to be so. Even the absence of a clearly defined compensation system or philosophy says something—and nothing can stop those messages from being received, loud and clear, by employees. Just as it is impossible for a person not to communicate, so too it is impossible for an organization's total rewards program (or absence thereof) not to send a clear message to employees and potential employees about what is important to the organization.

Because an organization's total rewards program says so much, it's imperative that it be designed deliberately, intentionally, and with overarching as well as specific objectives in mind.

Those specific objectives will vary from organization to organization, during different phases of the organization's life cycle, and to some degree from position to position. Certain overarching objectives, however, should be kept in mind when crafting a total compensation program—objectives that can be addressed, at least initially, by asking the following questions:

How can—and will—we design a total rewards system that exhibits the following:

▶ Supports and reinforces the mission, vision, and values of the organization

▶ Is consistent with the culture of the organization

▶ Attracts, motivates, and retains targeted/appropriate employees

▶ Ensures internal equity between positions within the organization

▶ Supports our philosophy toward the external labor market

▶ Is affordable, sustainable, and cost effective

▶ Is legally defensible in the event of a challenge

▶ Is appropriate for the organization's current position in its life cycle

▶ Is flexible and easily adaptable

> **NOTE**
>
> For some organizations, there may be great value in attracting, motivating, and retaining high-performing employees who are "in it for the long haul." Keep in mind, however, that holding this intention does not—by itself—change the employment at will relationship. However, be cautious not to say or do anything that could, intentionally or unintentionally, erode that relationship.

In these situations, important considerations may need to be factored in, such as long learning curves, maintaining sensitive and critical client relationships, and so on. For these organizations, there may be a strong focus on designing a total compensation system that would be perceived as very competitive in the relevant labor market and that would encourage high-performing employees to stay with the organization for the long term.

Conversely, some organizations are comfortable with relatively high (or just plain high) levels of turnover. Although these organizations might be interested in developing a total rewards program that will attract employees, motivating and retaining their employees might be of far less importance. Those organizations whose employees do not require much training and whose employees form only transient relationships with customers might develop a total rewards philosophy that positions them less competitively in the relevant labor market.

By itself, neither approach is right nor wrong. However, if you were to switch the two total rewards systems for these two types of organizations, the mismatch could create a significant disconnect—rendering both compensation system ineffective.

In addressing problems and questions that might come up, it's important to keep in mind that what may initially appear to be a compensation problem may, in fact, be wholly unrelated to compensation. Another possibility is that a problem might be related to compensation as well as other issues. For instance, issues pertaining to unfairness (real, or perceived), challenging work conditions, or poor management could easily mask themselves as compensation issues. These misconceptions could be further confirmed—albeit erroneously so—by employees who state during their exit interviews that they are earning more money in their new position, even if compensation was not the factor that initially motivated them to seek employment elsewhere.

So although it is possible that the problem under consideration might be a compensation-related issue, it cannot simply be *assumed* that it is.

> **NOTE**
>
> An organization's total rewards philosophy represents far more than just the amount of cash it pays to employees or even the "fringe benefits" that it provides. Instead, an organization's total rewards philosophy speaks volumes about what the leaders of that organization value, the results they want to attain, the behavior they want to encourage, and their commitment to their employees. It will also have a significant impact on the organization's efforts to attract, motivate, and retain talent.

RESPONSIBILITY

KNOWLEDGE

C & B Responsibility 02

Develop, implement, and evaluate compensation policies/programs (for example: pay structures, performance-based pay, internal and external equity).

Knowledge 39

Compensation and benefits strategies.

Knowledge 42

Job pricing and pay structures.

Compensation: Building and Using Pay Structures

After an organization has identified a total rewards philosophy, it can productively turn its attention to building a compensation system to support that philosophy.

The overarching and specific objectives that the organization has established relative to total are brought to life through the organization's pay structures. Pay structures provide direction relative to wage and salary rates, pay increases, and incentive programs. They operationalize the organization's philosophies relative to internal equity and external competitiveness. In a very real sense, the pay structures that an organization puts in place make the organization's total rewards strategy tangible.

> **EXAM ALERT**
>
> Pay structures provide a reminder about the criticality of effectively communicating with employees about the organization's total rewards philosophy and programs. Familiarize yourself with ways to engage in meaningful and effective communication with employees around these all-important topics.

Elements of Pay Structures

Two important elements of pay structures are grades and salaries, both of which are often referred to as elements of a "salary administration" system.

Grades

Grades (also referred to as "job grades") represent a hierarchy of levels into which jobs of similar internal worth can be categorized. It may be helpful to liken job grades to school grades. Just as students within a particular grade demonstrate similar levels of academic accomplishment, jobs within the same grade share a similar level of value or worth to the organization.

Different organizations will have different numbers of pay grades, with differing degrees of distinction between each of those grades.

Ranges

If grades provide the framework for clustering positions in accordance with their relative value to the organization, ranges provide corresponding compensation levels for each of those clusters.

Ranges specify the lowest (minimum) and the highest (maximum) compensation rates for which positions within each grade are generally paid. The halfway point between those two figures is known as the midpoint and is calculated as follows:

$$\frac{\text{Maximum} + \text{Minimum}}{2}$$

> **NOTE**
>
> As is often the case, exceptions can exist for a variety of reasons. Employees who are paid above the maximum of the range are considered to be "red-circled"; employees who are paid below the minimum of the range are considered to be "green-circled."

The range spread is a percentage that is calculated by subtracting the minimum of the range from the maximum of the range and dividing that number by the minimum of the range. For instance:

Range Minimum:	$40,000
Range Maximum:	$60,000
Range Spread:	$60,000
	−$40,000
	————
	$20,000
	$20,000
	———— = 50%
	$40,000

Range spreads allow organizations to recognize and compensate employees within the same job and within jobs that are in the same grade, for different levels of skill, experience, tenure (if appropriate and consistent with organizational culture) or performance. Of course, the way an organization compensates employees within each range will, to a degree, depend on the total rewards philosophy of the organization.

There is no one "right" percentage for range spreads. Range spreads do, however, tend to grow wider at higher grade levels. Traditionally, range spreads are approximately

- ▶ 35% for nonexempt positions
- ▶ 50% for exempt positions
- ▶ 60% + for senior leadership positions

A series of ranges, along with their accompanying minimums, maximums, and midpoints, is known as a range table. For identification purposes, numbers or letters are often assigned to each grade in a range table.

Broadbanding

Sometimes organizations choose to use a relatively small number of grades, an approach known as *broadbanding*. Organizations might choose to use broadbands to bring about a cultural change (for instance, to support the implementation of a "flatter" organization) or to shift employees' focus away from traditional promotions and place it instead on professional growth. Broadbands typically have range spreads of 100% or more.

Using Pay Structures for Decision-Making

Although it's important to build pay structures, building them—by itself—isn't enough. Organizations also need to develop the policies that will guide day-to-day decisions regarding pay. As alluded to earlier, these policies are reflective of the overarching total rewards philosophies of the organization.

Pay guidelines can be based on performance, experience, seniority, effort, and a variety of other factors. One important consideration to keep in mind is that whatever factor(s) is used to determine how day-to-day pay-related decisions are made will be viewed as having great importance—and will likely become a key driver of employee efforts.

Pay guidelines also need to be developed to guide other types of increases (promotions, adjustments, general increases, cost-of-living increases, and so on) as well as the amount and timing of those increases.

Compa-ratio

Another important tool that can provide valuable information for decision-making is the compa-ratio.

The compa-ratio for each employee is calculated by dividing the employee's pay rate by the range midpoint for his position. For example, if an employee earns $40,000 per year, and the midpoint of his range is $50,000, the compa-ratio is calculated as follows:

$$\frac{\$40,000}{\$50,000} = 80\%$$

Compa-ratios can be a particularly valuable measure for organizations that seek to match the market because in such systems midpoints are often considered to be a close approximation of the "market rate" for a position. By calculating the compa-ratio, therefore, it is possible to compare the employee's rate of pay with the market rate for her position. If you take this percentage in combination with length of service, time in job, performance level, and other employees' earnings, you'll end up with a significant amount of information to help you manage employee compensation.

Total Compensation: Theory and Practice

All the "rewards" that an organization gives, grants, or otherwise bestows upon its employees in exchange for the services those employees have rendered through their employment. It includes more obvious items, such as wages and salaries, that would fall under the subheading "compensation," as well as mandatory and optional benefits such as Social Security contributions, health and welfare programs, and the like. In addition, it includes items that some but not all employees enjoy, such as incentives, bonuses, stock options, and so on. (Note: this includes components—many of which are difficult or impossible to quantify—that are not included in "compensation and benefits" and that would be included in other functional areas. These include flextime, flexplace, and so on.)

Compensation Strategies

Often, individuals and organizations believe that the "right" strategy is to pay for top talent. There are, however, multiple—and more strategic—ways to approach the question of developing an organizational mindset/approach to compensating employees.

"Lead the Market"

When an organization strategically chooses to "lead the market," it offers total compensation packages that are "better" than packages being offered by their labor market competitors. Organizations that lead the market may believe that higher compensation packages will attract higher-performing employees who will, in turn, pay for themselves, and then some. In short, these organizations want the best of the best and are willing to pay for it.

"Lag the Market"

When an organization strategically chooses to "lag the market," it offers total compensation packages that are less competitive than the total compensation packages that are being offered by their labor market competitors. Organizations that lag the market might offset this potential disadvantage by reinforcing and maximizing the intrinsic rewards that it offers—long-term potential growth opportunities, the ability to contribute to a particularly significant organizational mission, and so on.

"Match the Market"

An organization that chooses to "match the market" offers total compensation packages that are comparable to the total compensation packages being offered by their labor market competitors. Organizations that match the market make a conscious choice to be "externally competitive" with respect to total compensation.

> **NOTE**
>
> Maintaining a policy of hiring compensating "better than the best" is not necessarily appropriate for all organizations. Different strategies might be more appropriate for the same organization as it finds itself at different points in the organizational life cycle, for organizations in different sector, or for different organizations. There can be myriad reasons for this, some of which are explored in greater depth in Pearson's PHR and SPHR full length test prep books.

Other Key Compensation Concepts

Be certain you know the following compensation concepts:

- **Direct compensation:** Components of total compensation that are presented to employees in the form of cash:

    - **Commissions:** Compensation paid to employees for the execution of specific transactions or sales.

    - **Hourly wages:** The hourly pay that an employee earns for performing her job, regardless of level of performance demonstrated.

    - **Salary:** A predetermined amount of compensation that an employee will be paid per week.

    - **Shift differentials:** Additional hourly compensation that is paid to employees whose shifts start, end, or are scheduled between or during specified hours. Shift differentials do not exist in all organizations. They represent a way to attract and retain individuals to work shifts that are perceived as less attractive to current or potential employees.

    - **Sign-on bonuses:** Money paid to an employee when he joins the organization. Sign-on bonuses constitute enticements to attract and hire employees.

    - **Variable pay (such as short-term and long-term incentives):** Also known as "pay at risk." It is not guaranteed and is generally tied to the achievement of specific objectives. Variable pay can also take the form of "bonuses." Although the terms "bonus" and "incentive" are often used interchangeably, incentives are tied to the specific achievement of individual, group, and organizational goals, whereas bonuses are more discretionary in nature.

▶ **Indirect compensation:** Components of total compensation that are presented to employees in forms other than cash.

▶ **Perquisites:** Also known as "perks," such as a company car, club memberships, financial planning, legal services, and so on.

▶ **Recognition programs:** Examples include peer recognition programs, noncash spot awards, achievement awards, pizza parties, desirable parking, and so on.

▶ **Compression:** Occurs when employees' pay is clustered so closely together that it does not reflect differences in performance, contribution levels, or seniority. Compression can occur for a variety of reasons, including but not limited to increase in the minimum wage or failure to maintain internal equity while monitoring concerns related to external equity.

▶ **Internal equity:** The degree to which employees within an organization are fairly compensated with respect to how other employees within the same organization are compensated.

▶ **Geographic pay differentials:** Monetary adjustments made to pay/pay structures as a way of adjusting for different cost of living levels in different locations.

▶ **Piece-rate systems:** Compensation programs under which individuals are paid according to their production volume.

C & B Responsibility 05

Conduct compensation and benefits programs needs assessments (for example: benchmarking, employee surveys, trend analysis).

RESPONSIBILITY

In addition to accessing industry and relevant labor market information, follow the ADDIE steps outlined in Chapter 3, "Human Resource Development." And remember, ADDIE isn't just for instructional design; it is relevant to any HR-related needs assessment—including compensation and benefits.

C & B Responsibility 06

Develop/select, implement/administer, update, and evaluate benefit programs (for example: health and welfare, wellness, retirement, stock purchase).

RESPONSIBILITY

Knowledge 47

Benefits programs (for example: health and welfare, retirement, employee assistance programs [EAPs]).

KNOWLEDGE

Some benefits are mandatory, and some are optional. All benefits, to one degree or another, are affected by the law—as described earlier. Yet the nature and content of benefits offers must be looked at through more than just a legal lens. Let's now take a look at some of these.

Retirement Plans

By definition, retirement plans "defer" income—and therefore defer the tax that must be paid on that money until it actually becomes income, which occurs at the time of distribution. Following are some examples of specific retirement plans.

Defined Benefit Plan

Defined benefit plans represent a more traditional type of pension plan in which the employer shoulders the balance of the risk. This risk stems from the non-negotiable fact that defined benefit plans promise to pay the employee a specified monthly benefit at retirement. This "specified monthly benefit" could be expressed as an actual dollar amount, or it could be calculated through some sort of formula. (This is the more common method.) Either way, the PBGC protects participants in defined benefit plans by ensuring that, within certain limitations, the promised benefits will be paid. Please also note that defined benefit plans tend to be more advantageous to longer-term employees.

> **NOTE**
>
> A cash balance plan is a defined benefit plan that expresses the promised benefit in terms of a stated account balance (similar to the way a defined contribution plan works). Most of the time, each participant's cash balance plan account is credited annually with a pay credit (the percentage of compensation that her employer contributes) and an interest credit (either a fixed or a variable rate of interest).

Defined Contribution Plan

Unlike defined benefit plans, defined contribution plans do not "promise" a specific monthly benefit (or total benefit) at retirement. Instead, the employer or the employee contributes to the employee's individual retirement savings account. Those contributions are then invested, and the investments that can either make money or lose money. In this way, defined contribution plans shift the risk away from the employer (which is where it rests for defined benefit plans) and back to the employee. This shift may account for part of the reason why defined contribution plans are increasing in popularity, while defined benefit plans are decreasing in popularity. (Keep in mind that neither of these is legally mandated.)

At the time of retirement, what's there is there. No promises have been made, so no promises about total payouts can be broken. This does not, of course, mean that the ERISA guidelines of fiduciary responsibility are waived; they absolutely apply to defined benefit plans and to defined contribution plans.

Defined contribution plans tend to be more advantageous to shorter-term employees.

Examples of defined contribution plans include 401(k) plans, 403(b) plans (which are similar to 401(k) plans, for employees who work for nonprofit organizations), employee stock ownership plans, and profit-sharing plans.

Employee Stock Ownership Plan

An employee stock ownership plan (ESOP) is a type of defined contribution plan in which investments to individual accounts are made primarily in the form of employer stock. ESOPs offer certain tax advantages to employers as well as to employees.

Profit Sharing Plan

A profit sharing plan is a type of defined contribution plan under which the organization makes contributions to its employees' accounts. These contributions usually come from—and are tied to—organizational profits, and thus also serve as an incentive to performance.

Simplified Employee Pension Plan

A simplified employee pension plan (SEP) allows employers to make contributions on a tax-favored basis to individual retirement accounts (IRAs) that employees set up for this purpose.

Health and Welfare Benefits

Organizations can choose from a array of health and welfare benefits, a few of which are explored here.

Medical Insurance

Employers and employees can choose from several types of medical insurance plans.

Indemnity Insurance

The most traditional type of medical insurance plan, indemnity plans give participants (virtually) unrestricted choices relative to their doctors, hospitals, and other health care providers. Health care providers are paid a fee for the services they actually provide and perform. Hence, the more services that are provided, the greater the fees that will be paid. This is one reason why indemnity plans are usually one of the most expensive types of medical insurance programs from which employers and employees can choose.

Health Maintenance Organizations

Health maintenance organizations, or HMOs, offer a different model of health care—one that is referred to as "managed care." One significant difference between HMOs and indemnity plans centers on "choice." Although participant "choices" are nearly unlimited in indemnity plans, participant choices are more closely managed (and many would argue more limited) with HMOs.

For instance, with indemnity plans, participants make choices relative to which doctors they will visit and how often they will go. In an HMO, each participant chooses a primary care physician, or PCP, who serves as a "gatekeeper." Participants must see their PCPs first, and the PCP then decides whether to refer the patient to a specialist or for additional tests.

In this sense, HMOs truly do "manage" participants' health care experiences. There are advantages and disadvantages to this approach. Some would argue that HMOs are beneficial in that they emphasize preventive care and control health care costs. And because participants can change their PCP, there is still a critical element of choice inherent to the plan. In addition, HMOs provide a full range of health care, including doctor's visits, specialist services, hospitalization, and surgical services.

Others would argue that HMOs are overly restrictive. With an HMO, a referral from a primary care physician is required before a participant can see a specialist or get certain tests done. In addition to being administratively burdensome (and, at times, inconvenient), some would argue that this disempowers participants relative to their own personal health care choices.

Another concern relative to HMOs is capitation, the basis on which doctors are paid. What this means, essentially, is that each PCP is paid each month for every person who chooses that doctor to be her PCP—rather than for the actual amount of care that is provided. In short, providing more care won't generate more revenue—in fact, it dilutes the physician's earnings (not in terms of actual dollars, but in the sense that the physician gets paid the same amount of money for doing "more work"). Some individuals do not feel this is problematic, whereas others believe it motivates physicians to provide patients with fewer services or to spend less time with each patient.

Preferred Provider Organizations

A preferred provider organization (PPO) is a managed care health insurance plan that offers a network of health care providers who band together to offer services at a discounted rate to plan participants. PPOs resemble indemnity plans in that network providers are paid when they render services and plan participants can choose which doctors they want to visit and when they want to visit them. Plan participants can also choose to avail themselves of doctors or other health care providers who are outside the network; however, the costs to the member will be higher than they would have been if the member had chosen a doctor within the network.

Point of Service

Point of service (POS) plans are a combination of the HMO and PPO managed care models. Like the PPO model, there is a network of physicians and health care providers who have agreed to provide services at a discounted rate. Like the HMO model, there is a gatekeeper—a primary care physician who must provide plan members with referrals to specialists and for other services. Unlike the HMO model, however, referrals can be made to physicians who are either inside or outside the network. Although out-of-network referrals will cost participants more, they are permissible.

Dental Insurance

Like medical insurance, dental insurance can be offered through an indemnity program, an HMO network, or a PPO network. There are also some specific categories of coverage within dental plans, each of which is likely to offer a different level of reimbursement.

Preventive Care

"An ounce of prevention is worth a pound of cure"—that adage is perhaps no more apparent than in dental care (with, of course, the possible exception of performance management). Preventive care includes such things as regular dental checkups, exams, cleanings, and sometimes X-rays. It is often reimbursed at 100% of cost (or at 100% of reasonable and customary [R&C] expenses) to encourage plan members to take advantage of measures that encourage good oral health and that potentially decrease long-term costs.

Restorative Care

Restorative care, as its name implies, refers to oral "repairs" that are usually of a relatively minor nature, such as cavities or root canals. The reimbursement for restorative care is generally less than the reimbursement rate for preventive care (perhaps 80% instead of 100%).

Major Restorative Care

For those readers who are thinking, "You think a root canal is minor?" please understand that "minor" is a relative term that is used to describe the degree of restoration that is required, not necessarily the degree of discomfort that is experienced. By comparison, major restorative care—which would be reimbursed at an even lower rate (perhaps 50%)—refers to things such as bridgework and crowns.

Orthodonture

Orthodonture—braces, headgear, retainers, and the like—is a benefit that is often reimbursed at 50%. Unlike the other types of dental insurance discussed previously, orthodonture is often subject to a lifetime cap—perhaps in the vicinity of $1,000–$1,500. Plan members who have multiple children with multiple orthodontic challenges might find that they can burn through this benefit relatively quickly. It still, however, represents a significant savings over full-cost orthodonture and may be highly valued by that segment of your employee population with children to raise, palates to spread, and teeth to straighten.

Vision Coverage

Vision coverage is a little different from the other health and welfare benefits we've looked at so far. Unlike those other plans, an employer will typically offer vision coverage as a discount program (generally around 10%). Vision coverage generally includes items such as exams, contact lenses, and glasses.

Prescription Drug Coverage

As the cost of prescription drugs skyrockets, prescription drug coverage is becoming an even more highly valued employee benefit. Some employers provide prescription drug coverage as part of their medical plan, whereas others provide this coverage under a separate plan. Plan members may be required to pay a copay, to purchase their prescriptions at certain pharmacies, to use generic drugs (when available), or to use mail-order services for maintenance drugs (prescriptions that are prescribed for chronic or longer-term conditions and that are taken on a regular, recurring basis). Even with these restrictions, prescription drug coverage can be a huge benefit to employees.

Life Insurance

Term life insurance is also considered to be a valuable benefit by many employees as a way of ensuring that they can provide their beneficiaries and loved ones with income in the event of their deaths. Many employers offer a certain amount of life insurance at no cost to employees and offer optional supplemental life insurance as well.

Long-Term Disability Insurance

Long-term disability (LTD) insurance replaces a designated percentage of an employee's income that is lost through illness or injury.

Pay for Time Not Worked

As its name implies, pay for time not worked refers to situations in which employees receive compensation for sick days, vacation days, jury duty, personal time, designated holidays, floating holidays, bereavement leave, and the like.

Pay for time not worked is a benefit that is highly valued by many employees, overused by some, and underused by others. "Free time" for employees, however, isn't free of charge to the organization. From the organization's perspective, the true cost of pay for time not worked needs to be calculated just like any other benefit.

Work-Life Programs

The same can be said for work-life ("balance") programs. Programs such as flexible schedules, job sharing, telecommuting, and compressed work weeks can be a great advantage for employees and a great way for employers to market themselves in the relevant labor market. Still, don't institute a program without first conducting careful analysis and assessment (see ADDIE, Chapter 3). Initiatives have to make business sense, and—ideally—should be sustainable for the foreseeable future. Even though there are never guarantees, it's not advisable to implement a program that might need to be revoked in the near time. When this happens, legitimate efforts at enhancing the workplace experience for employees can really backfire.

Employee Assistance Programs

Employee assistance programs (EAPs) offer employees help and resources on a variety of personal issues that can—and often do—have a direct impact on employee job performance. As such, EAPs (which are paid for by organizations) benefit employers as well as employees.

HR professionals should research and calculate the cost of EAPs when proposing changes or expansion to senior leadership. Ultimately, EAPs can offer a positive ROI. It is up to us to ascertain whether this is so for our organization.

Compensation: Job Evaluation

KNOWLEDGE

Knowledge 40

Budgeting and accounting practices related to compensation and benefits.

KNOWLEDGE

Knowledge 41

Job evaluation methods.

Job evaluation is the process through which every job in an organization is assessed and compared to other jobs in the organization. At the conclusion of the job evaluation process, you will be able to ascertain the relative worth of each job within the organization. When this is done, you will have generated an overall job-worth hierarchy.

Job evaluation techniques fall into two categories: nonquantitative and quantitative.

For information on this topic, please see Chapter 1, "Business Management and Strategy (BM & S)."

Nonquantitative Job Evaluation Techniques

Nonquantitative job evaluation techniques, as the name implies, determine the relative value of jobs within the organization without using mathematical techniques. Instead, these methods focus on the "whole job" (which is why these techniques are also referred to as whole job methods).

Whole Job Ranking

In whole job ranking techniques, jobs are ranked from lowest to highest, according to the importance that each job holds (or, stated differently, the value that each job brings) to the organization. In essence, a list is generated that reflects which jobs are more important to the organization and which jobs are less important to the organization, in ranked order.

Whole job ranking is easy to perform and is relatively inexpensive to maintain. It fails, however, to establish specific factors about each job that would need to be considered when comparing jobs to each other, and it can be prone to rater subjectivity. It is also limited to a job-to-job comparison rather than to any specific competencies or responsibilities that are universally valued throughout the organization. Also, if more than just a few positions need to be ranked, this system may prove to be unwieldy within the organization. Finally, although the list that is generated through whole job ranking will show which jobs are most and least important, it will not demonstrate the relative worth of one job to another.

Job Classification

Job classification is a nonquantitative whole job evaluation technique that categorizes jobs into broad categories, or levels, based on the level—and, ultimately, value to the organization—of the work that is performed by jobs within each level. Each level incorporates specific responsibilities and "benchmark statements" that describe the nature, complexity, autonomy, and so on of the work that positions in that level perform.

In addition to being inexpensive, job classification is relatively simple to implement and administer. One potential disadvantage, however, is that jobs may not match perfectly with the benchmark statements listed in each category. In such cases, the evaluator would use her judgment (which can, of course, be imperfect or subjective at times) to choose the best possible classification. Another potential weakness of the job classification method is that raters are also more likely to evaluate jobs on the basis of the current incumbent rather than on the basis of the jobs themselves, thus violating a key principle of sound job evaluation.

Job Slotting

Job slotting incorporates (or "slots") newly created or revised positions into an existing job hierarchy. This process of slotting is accomplished by comparing the new or revised job descriptions to jobs (and job descriptions) that have already been evaluated and slotted within the hierarchy.

Like the other nonquantitative job evaluation methods, job slotting is relatively inexpensive and simple to administer and implement. Job slotting can be used, however, only when a job structure is already in place. As with the other nonquantitative job evaluation methods, there is an increased possibility that rater error and subjectivity can taint the job evaluation process. It is also more likely that jobs will be evaluated on the basis of the current incumbent, rather than on the basis of the jobs themselves, thus violating a key principle of sound job evaluation.

Quantitative Job Evaluation Techniques

Quantitative (or factor based) job evaluation methods are job evaluation techniques that determine the relative value of jobs within the organization by using mathematical techniques.

Point Factor

Point factor-based methods generate a mathematical score that reflects each position's relative worth to the organization Point factor systems first identify specific compensable factors and then establish levels of performance within each of those compensable factors. The relative importance of each compensable factor to the organization is then weighted. A different point value is then assigned to each level within each compensable factor.

After a point factor system has been established, each job is evaluated according to this system by determining which level within each compensable factor is most reflective of the position being evaluated, thus generating a point value for each compensable factor. Some sample compensable factors include education, experience, financial responsibility, and responsibility for contacts.

The evaluator then adds up the points associated with each compensable factor to calculate a total point value. When the point values associated with each job are compared to each other, a mathematical depiction of the relative and absolute value of the jobs will emerge, thus indicating where the job falls within the established job worth hierarchy.

The point factor system affords greater reliability between different raters and minimizes the potential impact of evaluator error or subjectivity. Developing a point factor system, however, can be time consuming and difficult—and purchasing one can be expensive. In addition, using it properly requires some measure of training.

Factor Comparison

Factor comparison is a quantitative job evaluation technique that involves the ranking of each compensable factor of each job. A corresponding monetary value for each level with each factor is subsequently identified. Similar to the point factor method, each job is evaluated with respect to each compensable factor. The appropriate level is then selected. Unlike the point factor method, however, a "dollar value" is associated with each level with each compensable factor. When all the levels that have been selected are added together, a pay rate will emerge for each job.

Although this system affords a degree of objectivity and reliability across raters, it is difficult and expensive to develop. It also requires a great deal of monitoring and updating to ensure that the dollar value associated with each level remains appropriate in a relative as well as in an absolute sense.

KNOWLEDGE

Knowledge 43

External labor markets or economic factors.

Market Pricing

Market-based pricing is a system that takes wage and or salary rates paid by labor market competitors heavily into consideration when determining pay rates.

Market pricing involves looking at the relevant labor market to ascertain what the "going rate" or "market rate" is for a particular position. Market pricing can yield valuable pay data about "benchmark" jobs—jobs for which close matches can be identified in the relevant labor market.

Data collected through market pricing can be used in a number of ways. For example, market data can be obtained about a number of benchmark positions as part of a larger initiative. Market data can also help in the building of a job-worth hierarchy, around which other positions can be placed using a whole job slotting technique. In addition, market data can be used to obtain information for one particular job, in combination with other job evaluation techniques that might be used.

Market Data Considerations

In preparing to collect market data, there are a number of considerations that need to be taken into account and a number of decisions that need to be made. Let's take a look at some of the questions that might be relevant.

What Is the Relevant Labor Market?

We first looked at the topic of relevant labor markets when we started considering the importance of the organization's total rewards philosophy. Within the context of collecting market data, determining an appropriate relevant labor market for each position is foundational to ensuring that the market data we collect—and about which we will be making decisions—is truly relevant.

Who Are Our Labor Market Competitors in General, and for Specific Jobs?

Determining who your labor market competitors are within the relevant labor market is critical. One important consideration is whether you are competing only within your industry for talent or whether you are also competing for talent with organizations in different industries or sectors.

What Sources of Market Data Are Currently Available to You, and What Sources Could You Secure?

Pay surveys provide one important source of market data. These surveys can be developed internally or secured externally either by purchasing existing survey data or by contracting with an outside organization to develop a customized survey.

Market data can also be obtained through the following:

▶ Government resources (the Bureau of Labor Statistics—www.bls.gov—is one excellent resource)

▶ Websites designed for this purpose (for example, onetonline.org, payscale.com, salary.com)

▶ Local economic development councils

▶ Professional associations

▶ Career development offices at college, universities, and tech training schools

▶ Employees (including departing/former employees) and managers

▶ Search firms and employment agencies

TIP

Be familiar with the advantages and disadvantages associated with each of the different methods of securing market data—in particular, the advantages and disadvantages of survey-based methods.

Which Matches Are Appropriate?

As mentioned earlier, matching benchmark positions to available market data provides valuable information. Note that the positions within any organization, however, are benchmark positions. It simply won't be possible to find market data for some positions, in which case you may want to consider other options (for instance, internal job evaluation or a combination of job slotting with benchmark market data).

It's critical to match jobs on the basis of the duties and responsibilities that are performed—not on job titles. Job titles can be misleading or even inaccurate, which could in turn corrupt your analysis and recommendations.

Does the Data Need to Be Adjusted in Any Way?

There are a number of ways to adjust market data, including these:

▶ **Aging:** Ideally, market data should be collected from multiple sources. It is likely that the dates on which these salaries were "effective" will be different for each source of data, so it's necessary to adjust all the data to a common date (usually the date on which the market analysis is being conducted).

▶ **Quality of job match:** Sometimes (perhaps even "often") it's impossible to make a perfect job match, especially for positions that are not benchmark jobs. This can occur because of differences in scope, work conditions, financial responsibility, or a variety of other factors. In situations like this, the best choice you can make is to find the best possible match, even if it is not ideal. After you've made the best possible match, you can then "weight" market data differently as a way of reflecting each source's relative value. "Weighting" market data means putting greater importance on certain data you've collected and less importance on other data you've collected when you use that data to perform calculations or formulate recommendations. This can help account for the inevitable imperfections that you'll come across during the process of job matching.

After the market data has been collected and appropriately adjusted, the recommendations that you'll make on the basis of that data can support sound decision-making. Those recommendations may pertain to one particular position, or they may make a broader contribution toward developing a job-worth hierarchy. It's also important to recognize that market data does not stand alone as the only factor that should be considered—ideally, it should be used in conjunction with existing job evaluation methods, pay structures, and so on. It is also quite possible that externally generated data may present a different perspective than internally generated data; you need to consider and reconcile the two.

| KNOWLEDGE |

Knowledge 44

Pay programs (for example: variable, merit).

External Equity

In summary, market analysis helps to ascertain the degree to which your employees are paid in an externally equitable manner. This means: To what degree are employees within your organization fairly compensated with respect to how employees outside your organization, but within the relevant labor market, are compensated comparably? As you consider this, however, remember that "matching the market" is not the only viable compensation strategy. As we've explored elsewhere in this chapter, lagging the market and leading the market are also potentially appropriate approaches.

To that end, it is important to remember that—as we said near the beginning of this chapter—"total compensation" means more than just pay and benefits. There may be reasons that employees/applicants are attracted to your organization beyond base pay and the value of their benefits. Keep in mind what those "intangibles" might be, and seek to explore the possibility of leveraging those.

After the overall compensation strategy is established, the next step is to determine how that strategy will come to life within the organization. As we discussed earlier, total compensation (rewards) can be divided into direct (cash) and indirect (noncash) elements. In this section, we'll consider two critical elements of direct compensation: base pay and variable pay.

Base Pay

Base pay refers to the fixed rate of pay that an employee receives for performing her job. Base pay does not, however, include earnings obtained through shift differentials, benefits, overtime, incentive premiums, or any pay element other than the employee's fixed rate of pay.

A number of factors go into setting base pay rates, including the relative worth of the job to the organization, the market rate for a particular position, and other special circumstances (for instance, unique skills that are in great demand—also sometimes referred to as "hot skills").

Merit Pay

Merit pay constitutes increases to earnings that are earned by employees on the basis of performance during a specified period of time (the performance measurement period).

Variable Pay

Sometimes organizations choose to compensate employees through variable pay programs in addition to base pay programs. Variable pay is also known as "at risk" pay (but is not often referred to in those terms when such pay programs are being discussed directly with employees, in that "risk" is not universally embraced). Variable pay is cash compensation that fluctuates and is tied, in some way, to the employee's performance.

There are a variety of variable pay programs, each of which can be used on a standalone basis, combined with other variable pay programs, or customized to meet the needs and objectives of an organization's own unique compensation and total rewards philosophy.

Incentive Plans

Incentive plans are variable compensation plans that establish specific financial and nonfinancial goals and targets for individuals, groups, and organizations. For incentive programs to be effective, employees need to believe that they can attain the goals that have been set as part of the incentive program and that the reward that they would earn by attaining those goals is "worth it." (See "Victor Vroom—Expectancy Theory, 1964," in Chapter 1.)

Incentive plans also need to be designed with an awareness of how much downside risk—and upside potential—exists for incentive plan participants. It's also critical to look at the design of the incentive program and the accompanying message that it sends to employees. For instance

- Are "thresholds" in place so that a partial incentive will be paid even if the goal is not fully attained? Or will employees/teams be paid only for meeting or exceeding objectives?

- Is the incentive program an add-on to a current base pay program, or does it truly constitute earnings that are "at risk"? For instance, will participants' base pay be reduced, now or at some point in the future, as a result of participating in the incentive program?

- What is the overall degree of upside potential, and what is the overall degree of downside risk?

Regardless of the answers to these and many other questions, one thing is certain: any incentive program will speak volumes to employees about what the organization values.

There are many types of incentive programs, a few of which are described here.

Short-Term Incentives—Individual

Short-term individual incentive programs are used to financially motivate individual employees to attain specific financial or nonfinancial objectives. Short-term incentive programs are usually one year or less in duration.

Short-Term Incentives—Team/Group

Short-term team/group incentive programs are similar to short-term individual incentive programs except that targets are set for groups of people instead of for individual employees. These incentive programs are intended to foster collaborative efforts and synergies among employees who are pursuing a common goal.

Long-Term Incentive Programs

Long-term incentive programs are similar to short-term individual incentive programs except that they are usually more than one year in duration.

Gainsharing

Gainsharing incentive plans are designed to motivate (or, you could say, to "incent" or "incentivize") employees to reach specific goals relating to cost cutting or revenue generation by offering to share a portion of that savings (or that increased revenue) with the employees who helped to generate it. Gainsharing plans are based on team/group performance rather than on individual performance.

Profit Sharing

Profit-sharing plans are organization-wide plans that establish an organization-wide profit goal. If the goal is reached, the profits are shared with employees. Profits can be shared immediately (cash profit sharing plans) or at a later time (deferred profit sharing plans).

Profit sharing plans are a type of defined contribution plan under which the organization contributes to its employees' accounts. These contributions often come from profits and thus serve as an incentive to performance.

KNOWLEDGE

Knowledge 46

Noncash compensation methods (for example: equity programs, noncash rewards).

Noncash Compensation

Anything that comprises "the total paycheck" (other than cash, of course) could be considered a form noncash compensation. This term speaks to anything and everything of a positive nature that accrues to employees, just because they are employees. This could include a positive organizational culture, sound work/life balance, developmental opportunities—even working for an organization in whose mission an employee believes. In this way, many methods of noncash compensation are real but are not taxable as W2 income.

Let's look at this a bit more closely.

Total rewards consists of a variety of elements, all of which can be divided into direct compensation and indirect compensation.

As we've explored, direct compensation refers to components that are presented to employees in the form of cash, and indirect compensation refers to components that are presented to employees in forms other than cash (noncash).

Some examples of direct compensation would include the following:

- Hourly wages/base salary
- Shift differentials
- Overtime pay
- Commissions
- Sign-on bonuses
- Variable pay (such as short-term and long-term incentives)

Some examples of indirect compensation would include:

- Legally mandated benefits (such as Social Security)
- Medical insurance
- Dental insurance
- Long-term disability insurance
- Vision coverage
- Vacation time
- Holiday time
- Recognition programs (such as peer recognition programs, noncash spot awards, achievement awards, pizza parties, desirable parking, and so on)
- Perquisites (also known as perks, such as a company car, club memberships, financial planning, and so on)

There are numerous forms of cash compensation that organizations can use to reward employees. Some are tangible, and others are intangible (such as those listed previously). One form of tangible noncash compensation is equity compensation.

According to Investopedia.com:

"Equity compensation is a non-cash compensation that represents a form of ownership interest in a company. Due to the complexity of implementing an equity compensation program, companies must plan and use proper legal, accounting, and tax advice and planning.

Companies that offer equity compensations give employees stock options with the right to purchase shares of the companies' stocks at a predetermined price, also referred to as exercise price. This right 'vests' with time, so employees gain control of this option after working for the company for a certain period of time. When the option vests, they gain the right to sell or transfer the option. This method encourages employees to stick with the company for a long term."

Property is another form of noncash compensation. For instance, if an employer has a company car that it no longer uses, this could be given as compensation to an employee. HR professionals must keep in mind, however, that property is another form of compensation and therefore must be declared as earnings on the employees W2 form.

Other possible forms of noncash compensation might be gift cards or travel certificates. As with property, however, these items might be subject to income taxes as income. Consult with counsel before making this determination. Otherwise, your efforts to motivate might have the opposite effect—and might invite legal challenges.

Communicating the Total Rewards Program

It's not enough to "walk the walk"—you've also got to "talk the talk."

Often when we look around our organizations, our country, or even our world, we see people who "talk the talk" but don't "walk the walk." Or, to put it differently, people don't always "put their money where their mouths are." Interestingly, when it comes to total rewards programs, the opposite tends to be true. Organizations often don't communicate enough with employees about the total compensation/benefits programs that they have in place, the benefits of these programs, or what those programs really cost.

For a number of reasons, it's important to change this practice and to communicate with employees. Most employees simply do not know the real costs—let alone the actual value—of their compensation—cash, as well as noncash. Also, in a very real sense, employees earn benefits just like they earn cash compensation—and it's important to ensure that employees understand and recognize that. This holds true for benefits that are voluntarily provided by employers as well as for benefits programs that are mandated by the government. Otherwise, even those benefits that are not entitlements may ultimately begin to feel like entitlements to employees.

There are myriad ways to communicate with employees about the benefits they receive, just a few of which are

- Employee meetings
- DVDs
- Annual total rewards statements
- Internet/intranet
- Newsletters
- Employee handbooks
- Personal letters/emails

Communicate early, and communicate often. Perhaps most important, don't rely on any single method of communication to get your message across. Just as people learn differently in training programs (see Chapter 3), people also process and absorb information differently. Finally, always make sure that at least one of your methods of communication is in writing—something that employees can refer to after the fact.

Making the Connection to Compensation Strategy

Noncash compensation, in any form, is an important component to an organization's total compensation plans. As such, HR professionals, in partnership with senior leadership, would be wise to consider all forms of cash and noncash compensation as part of the organization's total compensation strategy (leading, matching, or lagging the market).

KNOWLEDGE

Knowledge 49

Fiduciary responsibilities related to compensation and benefits.

Fiduciary Responsibility Under ERISA

ERISA provides fiduciary responsibilities for those who manage and control plan assets. Said differently, ERISA establishes fiduciary responsibility for—and designates as a fiduciary—"persons or entities who exercise discretionary control or authority over plan management or plan assets, have discretionary authority or responsibility for the administration of a plan, or provide investment advice to a plan for compensation or have any authority or responsibility to do so are subject to fiduciary responsibilities" (www.dol.gov). Plan fiduciaries could include, for example, plan trustees, plan administrators, and members of a plan's investment committee.

Fiduciaries are charged with running the plan(s) for which they are responsible solely in the interest of participants and beneficiaries. They must ensure that the sole purpose of the plan is and remains providing benefits to participants and beneficiaries and paying plan expenses. Fiduciaries must also act with skill, care, prudence, and diligence. For instance, they must protect plan participants by diversifying plan investments. (In other words, just like any of us, they should diversify.) They must also follow the terms of plan documents to the extent that those terms are consistent with ERISA. In addition, they must avoid conflicts of interest, and, many would argue, even the possibility of an appearance of a conflict of interest (the same standard to which HR professionals should hold themselves).

All this may sound simple—perhaps as though it should be common sense. Common sense, however, is often somewhat uncommon. All it takes is a quick scan of recent headlines trumpeting the news of unethical behavior and defunct pension plans to appreciate the fact that fiduciary responsibility is not something to be taken for granted. According to the Employment Benefits Security Administration (EBSA), ERISA enforcement yielded significant results, as indicated by the following fact sheet:

TABLE 4.4   ERISA Enforcement

Latest Enforcement Statistics	FY 2002	FY 2003	FY 2004
Prohibited transactions corrected	$398M	$460M	$2388.3M
Plan assets restored	$189.7M	$169.8M	$199.7M
Participant benefits restored	$125.3M	$105.4M	$47.8M
Plan assets protected	$168.2M	$662.1M	$141.6M
Voluntary fiduciary correction program	$1.9M	$8.7M	$264.6M
Total monetary results	$883M	$1.4B	$3042M
Individuals indicted	134	137	121

Here's a sample of civil violations:

▶ Failing to operate the plan prudently and for the exclusive benefit of participants

▶ Using plan assets to benefit certain related parties to the plan, including the plan administrator, the plan sponsor, and parties related to these individuals

▶ Failing to properly value plan assets at their current fair market value or to hold plan assets in trust

▶ Failing to follow the terms of the plan (unless inconsistent with ERISA)

▶ Failing to properly select and monitor service providers

▶ Taking adverse action against an individual for exercising her rights under the plan (for example, being fired, fined, or otherwise being discriminated against)

CAUTION

What does this mean? It means plan administrators can be held personally liable for losses that result from breaching their fiduciary responsibility.

ERISA also requires plans to establish a grievance and appeals process for participants and gives participants the right to sue for benefits and for breaches of fiduciary duty.

Fiduciary Responsibility Under the Sarbanes-Oxley Act

The Sarbanes-Oxley Act (SOX) was created in the wake of huge corporate accounting scandals, including Enron and Tyco, to name just two. Designed to protect investors, SOX enacted reforms designed to enhance corporate responsibility and financial disclosures and to combat corporate and accounting fraud. For more information on the Sarbanes-Oxley Act, see Chapter 6. There are a number of SOX provisions that HR professionals needs to be particularly concerned with, four of which are

- ▶ Prohibition against insider trading during certain pension plan blackout periods— section 306(a).

- ▶ Requirement that plan administrators must provide 30-day written notice in advance of blackout periods to individual account plan participants and beneficiaries—section 306(b).

- ▶ Requirement to disclose whether the company has adopted a code of ethics that applies to the company's key officers (at a minimum, this code must apply to the company's principal executive officer, principal financial officer, principal accounting officer or controller, or persons performing similar functions)—section 406.

- ▶ Establishment of whistleblower protection in a variety of situations for employees who report fraud against shareholders—section 806(a).

RESPONSIBILITY

C & B Responsibility 03

Manage payroll-related information (for example: new hires, adjustments, terminations).

Payroll is a specialized and highly technical business function. It requires specific training and knowledge that extends beyond the scope of this chapter and this book.

We suggest that you peruse the payroll-related resources listed at the end of this chapter as well as other payroll-specific publications.

RESPONSIBILITY

C & B Responsibility 04

Manage outsourced compensation and benefits components (for example: payroll vendors, COBRA administration, employee recognition vendors).

For information on this topic, please see Chapter 1.

RESPONSIBILITY

C & B Responsibility 07

Communicate and train the workforce in the compensation and benefits programs, policies, and processes (for example: self-service technologies).

For information on this topic, please see Chapter 3.

NOTE

The following Compensation and Benefits Responsibilities/Areas of Knowledge pertain to responsibilities and areas of knowledge addressed in Pearson's SPHR Exam Prep.

C & B Responsibility 08

Develop/select, implement/administer, update, and evaluate an ethically sound executive compensation program (for example: stock options, bonuses, supplemental retirement plans).

RESPONSIBILITY

C & B Responsibility 09

Develop, implement/administer, and evaluate expatriate and foreign national compensation and benefits programs.

RESPONSIBILITY

Knowledge 45

Executive compensation methods.

KNOWLEDGE

Knowledge 48

International compensation laws and practices (for example: expatriate compensation, entitlements, choice of law codes).

KNOWLEDGE

Chapter Summary

Compensation, benefits, and the synergies created by the combination of those two disciplines are both technically challenging and strategically impactful. Knowledge and insight in both of these areas is critical.

No longer, however, can compensation and benefits programs and strategies be intuitively assessed (if that ever was the case). Rather, knowledge of legal framework, as well as keenly developed skills and competencies, are required to ensure an effective approach strategically, tactically, and transactionally.

In this sense, many organizations have moved away from the HR professional serving as a source of information (especially about benefits) and have instead turned to self-service technology. Although some HR professionals feel that this signals the possibility of even greater outsourcing of positions, another, and perhaps more positive, way to view this development is that HR professionals may be freed from some of their transactional tasks of yesterday and thus may have more time for tactical and strategic interventions.

Thus, HR professionals can increase their value to the organization by enhancing their knowledge and skills in these areas—even if such knowledge and skills do not immediately appear to be relevant to current "primary functions." In addition, this constitutes a crucial portion of the PHR exam. For that reason, start by learning what is included in this chapter, and then go beyond. The value that will accrue to you, and to your organization, is unquestionably worthwhile.

Key Terms

- Compensation
- Benefits
- Total rewards
- Worker's compensation
- Davis-Bacon Act, 1931
- Walsh-Healy Public Contracts Act (PCA), 1936
- Fair Labor Standards Act (FLSA), 1938
    - Minimum wage
    - Overtime pay
    - Child labor standards (youth employment standards)
    - Record keeping
- Workweek
- Regular rate of pay
- Exemptions
    - Executive
    - Administrative
    - Professional
    - Computer employee
- Outside sales
- Highly compensated employees
- Safe harbor provisions
- Portal-to-Portal Act. 1947
- Equal Pay Act (EPA), 1963
- Social Security Act (SSA), 1935
- Unemployment insurance
- Medicare, 1965
    - Part A
    - Part B
    - Part C
    - Part D
- Employee Retirement Income Security Act (ERISA), 1974
- Immediate vesting
- Clift vesting
- Graded vesting
- Pension Benefit Guaranty Corporation (PBGC)
- Summary plan description (SPD)

- Revenue Act, 1978
- Section 125
- Cafeteria plans
- Premium only plans
- Flexible spending accounts
- Full cafeteria plans
- Section 401(k)
- Retirement Equity Act (REA), 1984
- Consolidated Omnibus Budget Reconciliation Act (COBRA), 1985
- COBRA qualifying events
- Older Worker's Benefit Protection Act (OWBPA), 1990
- Health Insurance Portability and Accountability Act (HIPAA), 1996
- HIPAA privacy rule
- Family and Medical Leave Act (FMLA), 1993
- Serious health condition
- Uniformed Services Employment and Reemployment Rights Act (USERRA), 1994
- Mental Health Parity Act (MHPA), 1996
- Sarbanes-Oxley Act (SOX), 2002
- Pension Protection Act (PPA), 2006
- Family and Medical Leave Act and National Defense Authorization Act for FY 2008, 2008
- Lilly Ledbetter Fair Pay Act, 2009
- Patient Protection and Affordable Care Act (PPACA), 2010
- Independent contractor
  - Behavioral control
  - Financial control
  - Type of relationship
- Pay structures
- Grades/job grades
- Ranges/pay ranges
  - Minimum
  - Maximum
  - Midpoint

- Range spread
- Broadbanding
- Compa-ratio
- Compensation strategies
  - "Lead the market"
  - "Lag the market"
  - "Match the market"
- Direct compensation
  - Commissions
  - Hourly wages
  - Salary
  - Shift differentials
  - Sign-on bonuses
  - Variable pay
- Indirect compensation
- Perquisites
- Recognition programs
- Compression
- Internal equity
- Geographic pay differentials
- Piece-rate system
- Retirement plan
- Defined benefit plan
- Cash balance plan
- Defined contribution plan
- Employee stock ownership plan (ESOP)
- Profit sharing plan
- Simplified employee pension plan (SEP)
- Health and welfare benefits
- Medical insurance
  - Indemnity insurance
  - Health maintenance organizations (HMOs)
  - Preferred provider organizations (PPOs)
  - Point of service (POS)
- Dental insurance
  - Preventive care
  - Restorative care

- ► Major restorative care
- ► Orthodonture
- ► Vision coverage
- ► Prescription drug coverage
- ► Life insurance
- ► Long-term disability insurance
- ► Pay for time not worked
- ► Work-life programs
- ► Employee assistance programs (EAPs)
- ► Job evaluation
- ► Nonquantitative job evaluation techniques
  - ► Whole job ranking
  - ► Job classification
  - ► Job slotting
- ► Quantitative job evaluation techniques
  - ► Point factor
  - ► Factor comparison

- ► Market pricing
- ► Relevant labor market
- ► Labor market competitors
- ► Aging
- ► External equity
- ► Base pay
- ► Merit pay
- ► Variable pay
- ► Incentive plans
- ► Short-term incentives
  - ► Individual
  - ► Team/group
- ► Long-term incentive programs
- ► Gainsharing
- ► Profit sharing
- ► Noncash compensation
- ► Equity compensation
- ► Fiduciary responsibility

Apply Your Knowledge

This chapter focuses on issues relating to total rewards. Complete the following review questions and exam questions as a way of reviewing and reinforcing the knowledge and skills you'll need to perform your responsibilities as an HR professional and to increase the likelihood that you will pass the PHR examination.

Review Questions

1. Describe the similarities and differences between defined benefit plans and defined contribution plans.

2. Why is it important to communicate with employees about their compensation and benefits ("total rewards") programs?

3. Define what is meant by "total rewards" and "total rewards philosophy."

4. What is meant by the term "internal equity"?

5. What is meant by the term "relevant labor market"?

Exam Questions

1. Which of the following statements about workweeks is false?

   ○ **A.** A workweek is any fixed and regularly recurring period of 168 hours.

   ○ **B.** The employer can select any day (and any hour) of the calendar week on which to begin the workweek.

○ **C.** The employer can establish different workweeks for different employees or groups of employees.

○ **D.** The hours that an employee works during different workweeks within the same pay period can be "averaged."

2. Which of the following would not be considered an affirmative defense under the Equal Pay Act?

○ **A.** Seniority

○ **B.** Diversity

○ **C.** Quality of production

○ **D.** Merit

3. Which of the following statements about the point factor method of job evaluation is true?

○ **A.** Point factor systems do not establish levels of performance within each compensable factor because that would constitute making the error of evaluating the person instead of the position.

○ **B.** There is a greater likelihood of rater subjectivity with point factor methods of job evaluation than with whole job methods because point factor systems require the evaluator to make more judgments.

○ **C.** The product of a completed job evaluation will generate information that will be helpful to establishing a job worth hierarchy.

○ **D.** Although point factor systems address evaluative information about different compensable factors, they do not address the relative importance of each compensable factor.

4. Which of the following could generate a calculation that represents "range spread"?

○ **A.** $55,000

$$\frac{}{\$61,000} = 90.1\%$$

○ **B.** $80,000–$50,000

$$\frac{}{\$50,000} = \frac{\_\$30,000\_}{} = 60\%$$

○ **C.** $100,000–$40,000 = $60,000

○ **D.** None of the above

5. Which of the following was established by ERISA?

○ **A.** Enhanced protection for plan members with preexisting medical condition

○ **B.** A clearer definition of "hours worked" for purposes of minimum wage and overtime payments

○ **C.** Whistleblower protection for employees who report fraud against shareholders

○ **D.** Minimum participation and vesting standards for retirement programs

6. Fiduciaries must do all the following except

◯ **A.** Protect plan participants by diversifying plan investments.

◯ **B.** Act with skill, care, prudence, and diligence.

◯ **C.** Avoid conflicts of interest.

◯ **D.** Follow the terms of plan documents without deviation.

7. Which of the following did the REA *not* accomplish?

◯ **A.** Lowered the minimum age requirement for pension plan participation and increased the years of service that count for vesting purposes

◯ **B.** Prohibited plans from counting maternity and paternity leaves as breaks in service for participation and vesting purposes

◯ **C.** Required qualified pension plans to provide automatic survivor benefits that could be waived only with the written consent of the plan participant

◯ **D.** Clarified that pension plans may obey certain qualified domestic relations (court) orders (QDROs) without violating ERISA

8. PHI refers to what?

◯ **A.** Health information that relates to a specific individual

◯ **B.** A managed care health option offered to federal and state government employees

◯ **C.** Information that was used as part of the "long form" test under the old provisions of the FLSA

◯ **D.** Information that must be maintained in according with the record-keeping requirements of the FLSA

9. Which of the following is *not* one of the three main provisions of the Social Security Act?

◯ **A.** Retirement income

◯ **B.** Pension protection

◯ **C.** Survivor's benefits

◯ **D.** Disability benefits

10. Which of the following is *not* required of covered entities by the HIPAA privacy rule?

◯ **A.** Designation of a privacy officer

◯ **B.** Creation of a code of ethics that applies to all employees who have access to health-related information

◯ **C.** Establishment of a complaint-handling and resolution process for issues related to the HIPAA privacy rule

◯ **D.** Agreements signed by business associates stating that they will respect the confidentiality of patient information

Answers to Review Questions

1. Some of the differences and similarities between defined benefit and defined contribution plans are summarized in Table 4.5.

TABLE 4.5 Defined Benefit Plans and Defined Contribution Plans Comparison

	DB Plans	DC Plans
Nature of the plan	More traditional type of pension plan	Less traditional type of pension plan
More risk is shouldered by...	The employer	The employee
What will the plan pay out to the employee?	Promises to pay a specified monthly benefit at retirement	Makes no guarantees about the value of the plan as of the time of retirement

2. It is important for organizations to communicate with employees about their total rewards programs with respect to each element of each program and to the program as a whole. First, employees may not truly understand all the benefits that they enjoy as employees of an organization. This leads to a second reason why communicating with employees about total rewards is important: most employees do not know the real costs, let alone the actual value, of the benefits they receive. (This holds true for mandatory as well as optional benefits.) In a very real sense, employees earn benefits, just like they earn cash compensation, and they should know what they are earning. Without this measure of communication, it is more likely that even those benefits that are not entitlements may ultimately begin to feel like entitlements to employees rather than something of value that they have earned in return for their services to the organization.

3. The term "total rewards" refers to all the compensation- and benefits-related elements that employees within an organization earn and enjoy in return for the services they have provided to their employer. An organization's total rewards philosophy, however, represents far more than just the amount of cash it pays to employees or even the "fringe benefits" that it provides. Instead, it speaks volumes about what the leaders of that organization value, the results they want to attain, the behavior they want to encourage, and their commitment to their employees. It is a clear and direct expression of the organization's mission, vision, and values—regardless of whether that was the organization's intention. Even the absence of a clearly defined total rewards or compensation system or philosophy sends a clear message, so be certain that it is the message that your organization truly intends to convey.

4. "Internal equity" refers to fairness (or "equity") within a department or organization with respect to the ways in which jobs are ranked and individuals are compensated.

5. The relevant labor market relates to the size and scope of the geographic area within which an organization would seek to attract qualified candidates. Even within the same organization, the relevant labor market for different positions can vary widely depending on the skills, knowledge, abilities, and behavioral characteristics required to perform each position successfully. Other factors that affect how an organization defines the relevant labor market might be the degree of competition that exists among employers for particular skills and knowledge and the degree to which certain skills and knowledge requirements are industry specific.

Answers to Exam Questions

1. Answer D is the best answer. The hours that an employee works during different workweeks cannot be averaged, even when those weeks are during the same pay period. Answer A is not the best answer; a workweek is any fixed and regularly recurring period of 168 hours. Answer B is not the best answer; the employer can select any day (and any hour) of the calendar week on which to begin the workweek. Answer C is not the best answer; the employer can establish different workweeks for different employees or groups of employees.

2. Answer B is the best answer. Diversity has not been designated as an affirmative defense under the Equal Pay Act. Answer A is not the best answer; seniority would be considered an affirmative defense under the Equal Pay Act. Answer C is not the best answer; quality of production would be considered an affirmative defense under the Equal Pay Act. Answer D is not the best answer; merit would be considered an affirmative defense under the Equal Pay Act.

3. Answer C is the best answer. The information that is generated through the job evaluation process will provide information that is helpful to establishing a job worth hierarchy. Answer A is not the best answer; point factor systems do establish levels of performance within each compensable factor. (As long as evaluations are conducted relative to the performance expected of the position rather than on the basis of the incumbent's individual performance, the job evaluation will still be job-based rather than person-based.) Answer B is not the best answer; the potential for rater subjectivity is lower with the point factor job evaluation method than it is with whole job method of job evaluation. Answer D is not the best answer; point factor systems do address the relative importance of each compensable factor.

4. Answer B is the best answer. The formula to calculate range spread is

Maximum–Minimum

$$\frac{\text{Maximum}-\text{Minimum}}{\text{Minimum}} = \_\%$$

Minimum

Answer A is not the best answer; it represents a calculation that could generate a compa-ratio, not range spread. Answer C is not the best answer; it represents a calculation that could generate the numerator of the range spread formula. Answer D is not the best answer because A was correct.

5. Answer D is the best answer. ERISA did establish minimum participant and vesting standards for retirement programs. Answer A is not the best answer; enhanced protection for plan members with preexisting medical conditions was established by COBRA. Answer B is not the best answer; a clearer definition of "hours worked" for purposes and minimum wage and overtime payments was established by the Portal-to-Portal Act. Answer C is not the best answer; whistleblower protection for employees who report fraud against shareholders was established by Sarbanes-Oxley.

6. Answer D is the best answer. Under ERISA, fiduciaries must follow the terms of plan documents to the extent that those terms are consistent with ERISA, not simply without deviation. Answer A is not the best answer; fiduciaries are required to protect plan participants by diversifying plan investments. Answer B is not the best answer; fiduciaries must act with skill, care, prudence, and diligence. Answer C is not the best answer; fiduciaries must avoid conflicts of interest.

7. Answer C is the best answer. The Retirement Equity Act (REA) requires that the participant and his spouse waive the provision that provides for automatic survivor benefits. (This provision cannot be waived independently by the plan participant, as answer C implies.) Answer A is not the best answer; REA did lower the minimum age requirement for pension plan participation and did increase the years of service that count for vesting purposes. Answer B is not the best answer; REA did prohibit plans from counting maternity and paternity leaves as breaks in service for participation and vesting purposes. Answer D is not the best answer; REA did clarify that pension plans may obey certain qualified domestic relations (court) orders (QDRIs) without violating ERISA.

8. Answer A is the best answer. PHI stands for "protected health information" that relates back to one individual. Answers B, C, and D are not the best answers; each offers a fabricated definition that is wholly unrelated to the real meaning of PHI.

9. Answer B is the best answer. Pension protection is addressed through ERISA, not through the Social Security Act. Answers A, C, and D are not the best answers; retirement income (answer A), survivor's benefits (answer C), and disability benefits (answer D) are the three major provisions of the Social Security Act.

10. Answer B is the best answer. The HIPAA privacy rule requires creation of a code of ethics that applies to the company's key officers (within a "covered entity"). At a minimum, this code must apply to the company's principal executive officer, principal financial officer, principal accounting officer or controller, or persons performing similar functions. It does not, however, have to apply more broadly within the organization. Answer A is not the best answer; the HIPAA privacy rule does require designation of a privacy officer. Answer C is not the best answer; the HIPAA privacy rule does require the establishment of a complaint-handling and -resolution process for issues relating to the HIPAA privacy rule. Answer D is not the best answer; the HIPAA privacy rule does require business associates to sign agreements stating that they will respect the confidentiality of patient information.

Suggested Readings and Resources

The Affordable Care Act: Summary of Employer Requirements.

Berger, L. (2008). *The Compensation Handbook: A State-of-the-Art Guide to Compensation Strategy and Design* (5th ed.). New York: McGraw-Hill.

Bragg, S. (2014). *Payroll Management: 2015 Edition.* Accounting Tools.

Bureau of Labor Statistics. www.bls.gov.

Davis, A., & Shannon, J. (2011). *The Definitive Guide to HR Communication: Engaging Employees in Benefits, Pay, and Performance.* Upper Saddle River, NJ: FT Press.

Department of Labor. www.dol.gov.

Love, P. *The Employer's Payroll Question and Answer Book.* CreateSpace Independent Publishing Platform.

Mitchell, B., & Gamlem, C. (2012). *The Big Book of HR.* Pompton Plains, NJ: Career Press.

O*Net, onetonline.org.

Washington Council Ernst & Young. February, 2013. Retrieved from www.nahu.org/meetings/capitol/2013/attendees/jumpdrive/Employer_ACA_Reference_Deck_02_14_2013.pdf.

World at Work. www.worldatwork.org.

The World at Work Handbook of Compensation, Benefits & Total Rewards: A Comprehensive Guide for HR Professionals. (2007). Hoboken, NJ: John Wiley & Sons.

CHAPTER FIVE

Employee and Labor Relations

Employee relations, labor relations...what are these topics all about, and why are they important to HR professionals? The answers to these questions are sometimes presented in ways that are overly simple and other times presented in ways that are exceedingly complex. In this chapter, we'll try to strike an appropriate balance between these two ends of the spectrum.

Let's first take a look at employee relations because all employees, whether members of a union or not, are, in fact employees.

NOTE

Although this may seem like an axiomatic statement, it warrants mention. Why? Because sometimes, in the midst of the complexities, challenges, and opportunities of dealing with organized labor, organizations (and the people within those organizations, including HR professionals) wrongly perceive "labor" as an amorphous entity, perhaps even an opponent, without a specific identity. In fact, quite the opposite is true. Labor—or a labor organization/union—is a group of people (employees) who happen to be organized to speak with a collective voice.

In its most straightforward sense, the definition of employee relations can be found in the words "employee" and "relations." Within this context, employee relations can be described as

▶ The way in which an organization responds to, handles, or addresses any issue that has impact on employees and their relationships

▶ To and with other employees

▶ To and with managers

▶ To and with those outside the employment in the organization with whom they come in contact as part of their employment experience

For many, this is a new and unfamiliar way of looking at employee relations. Why? Many individuals—HR professionals and non-HR professionals alike—are more accustomed to thinking of employee relations in functional terms. By this, we mean that employees may define employee relations in terms of what the "Employee Relations Department" does within their individual organization. All too often, this perspective can lead to a limited or a misguided definition of what employee relations is all about. Why? Because HR can end up being saddled with the reputation of being "party planners," "personnel police," "the terminators," and other unhelpful, incomplete, and inaccurate stereotypical roles.

In thinking about this broad, more encompassing definition of employee relations, you might be left to wonder whether there is anything that isn't part of employee relations. The answer to this question, as you might expect, is "that depends." In many ways, so much of what happens in our world, our nation, the states and localities in which we live, and the organizations in which we work has an impact, in one way or another, on our workplaces and on the people who work there.

Let's now shift for a moment to labor relations, which, in some ways, is a subset of employee relations. How? Because the term labor relations is most frequently used to refer to those individuals who are "organized"—or, in other words, who belong to and are represented by a union who will collectively bargain on their behalf.

As will be demonstrated in the next section, much of labor relations is governed by law. As we explore this, let's not lose sight of the fact that labor relations still deals with employees and that we should never sacrifice relationship with employees in the face of a contract, a law, or both.

RESPONSIBILITY

ER & LR Responsibility 01

Ensure that employee and labor relations activities are compliant with applicable federal laws and regulations.

KNOWLEDGE

Knowledge 50

Applicable federal laws affecting employment in union and nonunion environments, such as laws regarding antidiscrimination policies, sexual harassment, labor relations, and privacy (for example: WARN Act, Title VII, NLRA).

Laws Governing Employee Relations and Labor Relations

The sections that follow cover the relevant laws (in chronological order). The laws cited here are those that relate specifically and directly to employee and labor relations. Please review every HR-related law, in every functional area of this book, because many of these laws have some impact and relevance to employee and labor relations—whether direct or indirect.

Sherman Antitrust Act, 1890

The Sherman Antitrust Act, named for its sponsor, John Sherman of Ohio, was passed in an effort to curb the growth of monopolies. Under the Act, any business that sought to restrain trade or commerce would, from that time forward, be illegal. Specifically, the Act stated

- ▶ **Section 1:** "Every contract, combination in the form of trust or otherwise, or conspiracy, in restraint of trade or commerce among the several States, or with foreign nations, is declared to be illegal."

- ▶ **Section 2:** "Every person who shall monopolize, or attempt to monopolize, or combine or conspire with any other person or persons, to monopolize any part of the trade or commerce among the several States, or with foreign nations, shall be deemed guilty of a felony."

If, after reading the two sections cited here, you're feeling a bit bemused and confused, you share something in common with those who wrestled to interpret this law more than a century ago. The vague language of the Act, however, proved to be quite challenging—particularly terms such as "trust," "combination," "conspiracy," and "monopoly." This confusion opened the door for the Sherman Antitrust Act to be used against labor unions by those who chose to define those unions as monopolies. For instance, the Act allowed the use of injunctions—court orders that could be issued to restrict certain activities, such as strikes. The first example of this was when an injunction was issued against the American Railway Union in 1894 to end its strike against the Pullman Palace Car Company. George Pullman, the president of this company, decided to reduce his workers' wages. The company refused to arbitrate, and the American Railway Union called a strike, which started in Chicago and spread across 27 states. The attorney general sought and was awarded an injunction against the union.

> **NOTE**
>
> The Sherman Antitrust Act also placed responsibility for pursuing and investigating trusts on government attorneys and district courts.

Clayton Act, 1914

Passed in 1914, the Clayton Act was enacted to build on and clarify the Sherman Antitrust Act.

The provision of the Clayton Act that is most relevant to labor—and therefore to HR professionals—is that Section 6 of the Act specifically exempted labor unions and agricultural organizations from the Sherman Antitrust Act:

> "The labor of a human being is not a commodity or article of commerce. Nothing contained in the antitrust laws shall be construed to forbid the existence and operation of labor, agricultural, or horticultural organizations, instituted for the purposes of mutual help, and not having capital stock or conducted for profit, or to forbid or restrain individual members of such organizations from lawfully carrying out the legitimate objects thereof; nor shall such organizations, or the members thereof, be held or construed to be illegal combinations or conspiracies in restraint of trade, under the antitrust laws."

This section rendered labor unions exempt from the Sherman Antitrust Act and effectively legalized boycotts, peaceful strikes, and peaceful picketing—thus rendering illegal injunctions of the sort that was filed against the American Railway Union during the Pullman strike.

Railway Labor Act, 1926

In 1926, the Railway Labor Act (RLA) was passed. As its name implies, the RLA applied only to interstate railroads and their related undertakings—at the time, the most critical element of the nation's transportation infrastructure. In 1936, it was amended to include airlines engaged in interstate commerce.

The Railway Labor Act was critical in that it provided what was perhaps the first win-win scenario for labor and management. Railroad management wanted to keep the trains moving, which meant they needed to end wildcat strikes. Railroad workers wanted to organize, to be recognized as the exclusive bargaining agent in dealing with the railroad, and to negotiate and enforce agreements.

The Railway Labor Act is also significant in that it is where the "work now, grieve later" rule originated. In an effort to keep the rails running, which Congress felt was in the public's interest, Congress mandated that when disputes arise in the workplace, transportation workers covered by the RLA must "work now and grieve later" (with a few exceptions, such as for safety).

The Railway Labor Act applied only to interstate railroads and their related undertakings—at the time, the most critical element of the nation's transportation infrastructure. In 1936, it was amended to include airlines engaged in interstate commerce.

Norris-LaGuardia Act, 1932

The Norris-LaGuardia Act strengthened unions even more. First, it established the rights of labor unions to organize and to strike. Second, it prohibited federal courts from enforcing "yellow dog" contracts or agreements. (A yellow dog contract is a contract or an agreement between an employer and an employee, the terms of which are essentially that the employer will give the employee a job as long as the employee agrees not to join or have any involvement with a labor union.)

National Industrial Recovery Act, 1933

In 1933, Congress passed the National Industrial Recovery Act (NIRA). Title I of the Act guaranteed laborers the right to organize and bargain collectively. The Act also established that employees could not be required, as a condition of employment, to join or refrain from joining a labor organization.

In May 1935, the National Industrial Recovery Act was held unconstitutional by the U.S. Supreme Court (*Schechter Poultry Corp. v. United States, 1935*). Although this decision was wholly unrelated to labor and collective bargaining, the Supreme Court decision rendered the labor-related provisions illegal as well. The right to organize and bargain reverted, once again, to railway workers and to no one else. This would not, however, be the case for long.

National Labor Relations Act (Wagner Act), 1935

Two months later, Congress passed the National Labor Relations Act (NLRA). Also known as the Wagner Act (named for Senator Robert R. Wagner of New York), the NLRA guaranteed "the right to self-organization; to form, join, or assist labor organizations; to bargain collectively through representatives of their own choosing; and to engage in concerted activities for the purpose of collective bargaining or other mutual aid and protection."

> **NOTE**
>
> Certain groups or categories of employees are excluded under the NLRA from membership in a bargaining unit. Examples would include managers, supervisors, confidential employees (such as secretaries and administrative assistants to managers who can make labor relations decisions), and several other types of positions.

The NLRA also established procedures for selecting a labor organization to represent a unit of employees in collective bargaining and prohibited employers from interfering with that selection. In addition, under the NLRA, the employer would then be required to bargain with the appointed representative of its employees. Although bargaining does not require that either side agree to a proposal or to make concessions, it does require each side to bargain in good faith.

The NLRA also established regulations relative to what tactics (such as strikes, lockouts, and picketing) could be employed during bargaining in an effort to bolster bargaining objectives. The NLRA applied to all employers involved in interstate commerce with the exception of agricultural employees, government employees, and employees covered by the Railway RLA. The NLRA directly affects individuals who are not members of unions as well as those who are. This is particularly relevant—and often misunderstood—with respect to protected concerted activity. As just one example of this, the NLRA often renders policies that prohibit employees from discussing their earnings with each other illegal.

The Act also established the National Labor Relations Board (NLRB), a then-new federal agency that would be (and still is) responsible for administering and enforcing the rights established by the NLRA. As stated on its website, the NLRB has two principle functions:

▶ To determine, through secret-ballot elections, the free democratic choice by employees whether they want to be represented by a union in dealing with their employers and if so, by which union

▶ To prevent and remedy unlawful acts, called unfair labor practices, by either employers or unions

NOTE

Initially, unfair labor practices (ULPs) were identified only for employers. ULPs, as they pertained to unions, were subsequently added through the passage of the Labor-Management Relations Act (also known as the Taft-Hartley Act) in 1947.

The NLRA identified five categories of employer ULPs:

▶ To "interfere with, restrain, or coerce employees" in the exercise of their rights to engage in concerted or union activities or refrain from them

▶ To dominate or interfere with the formation or administration of a labor organization

▶ To discriminate against employees for engaging in concerted or union activities or refraining from them

▶ To discriminate against an employee for filing charges with the NLRB or taking part in any NLRB proceedings

▶ To refuse to bargain with the union that is the lawful representative of its employees

The terms of the NLRA originally permitted closed shops and union shops. A closed shop is one in which an employer agrees to hire only union members. A union shop is one in which an employer agrees to require anyone hired to join the union. These practices were subsequently prohibited, however, through the next major piece of labor-related legislation, the Labor Management Relations Act (also known as the Taft-Hartley Act). Read on....

Labor Management Relations Act (Taft-Hartley Act), 1947

The Labor Management Relations Act (LMRA), also known as the Taft-Hartley Act, was an amendment designed to remedy what the Republican Congress saw as two major omissions in the Wagner Act: first, the identification of behaviors and practices that would be considered ULPs on the part of unions and, second, a provision that would allow the government to issue an injunction against a strike that threatened national interests.

Taft-Hartley identified the following unfair labor practices that could be committed by unions:

- Restraining or coercing employees in the exercise of their rights or an employer in the choice of its bargaining representative.

- Causing an employer to discriminate against an employee.

- Refusing to bargain with the employer of the employees it represents.

- Engaging in certain types of secondary boycotts. Secondary boycotts are defined as efforts to convince others to stop doing business with a particular organization that is the subject of a primary boycott.

- Requiring excessive dues.

- Engaging in featherbedding. Featherbedding agreements require the employer to pay union members wages whether or not their work is needed.

- Picketing for recognition for more than 30 days without petitioning for an election.

- Entering into hot cargo agreements. An employer who makes a hot cargo agreement agrees to stop doing business with another entity. Hot cargo agreements can thus help to protect union work by allowing union members to refuse to handle or process work produced by nonunion entities.

- Striking or picketing a health care establishment without giving the required notice.

In addition, the Taft-Hartley Act imposed these additional changes:

- Reaffirmed that employers have a constitutional right to express their opposition to unions as long as employees are not threatened with reprisal for their union activities or promised benefits for refraining from such activities.

- Expressly excluded supervisors from coverage under the Act.

- Permitted employers to fire supervisors who engaged in union activities or did not support the employer's position.

- Outlawed closed shops, agreements that stated that employers could hire only individuals who were members of labor unions.

- Expressly permitted union shops, in which nonunion workers must join the union within a certain amount of time after being hired.

NOTE

In right-to-work states, union shops are illegal. In other words, no employee is required to join—or to pay dues to—the union. The list of right-to-work states can, and does, change. Be sure to do an online search to confirm the status for any particular state(s).

- Established a 60-day no-strike and no-lockout notice period requiring unions as well as employers to give each other 60 days' notice before strikes (on the part of the union) and lockouts (on the part of the employer) if either party wants to change or cancel an existing collective bargaining agreement.

- Prohibited jurisdictional strikes. A jurisdictional strike is a strike through which a union seeks to pressure an employer to assign particular work to its members rather than to members of other unions or to nonunion workers.

▸ Established the U.S. Conciliation Service and established the Federal Mediation and Conciliation Service (FMCS).

▸ Authorized the president to intervene in strikes or potential strikes that create a national emergency (a provision that President George W. Bush invoked in 2002 in connection with the employer lockout of the International Longshore and Warehouse Union during negotiations with West Coast shipping and stevedoring companies).

Labor Management Reporting and Disclosure Act (Landrum-Griffin Act), 1959

By 1959, it became clear—for some, perhaps, painfully clear—that more guidelines were necessary. Senate committee hearings revealed improper activities by labor as well as by management, uncovered evidence of collusion between labor and management, exposed violent practices used by certain labor leaders, and uncovered the diversion and misuse of labor union funds by senior-level union leaders.

Enter the Labor Management Reporting and Disclosure Act (also known as Landrum-Griffin). This law created additional labor-management guidelines, including these:

▸ A requirement that unions submit annual financial reporting to the Department of Labor (DOL) to document how union members' dues were spent

▸ A bill of rights for union members guaranteeing them freedom of speech and periodic secret elections

▸ The designation of every union official as a fiduciary

▸ Even stronger provisions relative to secondary boycotting and organizational and recognition picketing

Federal Labor Relations Statute, 1978

The Federal Labor Relations Act, also known as Title VII of the Civil Service Reform Act, "allows certain non-postal federal employees to organize, bargain collectively, and to participate through labor organizations of their choice in decisions affecting their working lives. [The Postal Reorganization Act (P.L. 91-375, Aug. 12, 1970) governs labor-management relations in the Postal Service.] The Statute defines and lists the rights of employees, labor organizations, and agencies so as to reflect the public interest demand for the highest standards of employee performance and the efficient accomplishment of Government operations. [5 U.S.C. §7101(a)(2)] Specifically, the Statute requires that its provisions "should be interpreted in a manner consistent with the requirement of an effective and efficient Government." [5 U.S.C. §7101(b)] "The Statue defines the universe of organizations that most directly rely on the FLRA: the Federal agencies that employ workers eligible to be represented by labor organizations and the labor organizations that have been recognized as the exclusive representatives of these employees. The agencies, labor organizations, and federal employees accorded rights by the Statute comprise the individual "customers" of the FLRA. Agency employers subject to the Statute include not only the Executive Branch agencies and the Executive Office of the President but also various independent agencies and certain legislative branch agencies, for instance, the Library of Congress and the Government Printing Office" (www.flra.gov).

This law permits covered employees to negotiate working conditions but does not permit negotiation of wages, hours, employee benefits, and classifications of jobs. It also does not allow employees to strike, and it only permits informational picketing (rather than other forms of picketing in which private sector employees can participate).

Relevant Case Law

The following cases are presented in chronological order:

- ▶ *Schechter Poultry Corp. v. United States, 1935*: A Supreme Court case that rendered the NIRA unconstitutional. Although this decision was wholly unrelated to labor and collective bargaining, the Supreme Court decision rendered the labor-related provisions illegal as well. The right to organize and bargain reverted, once again, to railway workers and no one else. This would not, however, be the case for long.

- ▶ *NLRB v. Mackay Radio and Telegraph Co., 1938*: The Supreme Court case that unrelated established that employers have the right to permanently replace workers who strike during an economic strike.

NOTE

Although it is advisable to avoid using the word "permanent" when describing employment relationships, the term "permanent replacement" is used here because it is the recognized vernacular with respect to strikes.

- ▶ *NLRB v. Weingarten, 1975*: Established the right of unionized employees ("Weingarten Rights") to have union representation at an investigatory unrelated interview with management if the employee reasonably believes that discipline might result from that meeting. Although the NLRB reversed this decision in 2000 (Epilepsy Foundation of Northeast Ohio, 331 NLRB 676) and held that nonunion employees also have the right to have a representative present at a meeting of this sort, in 2004 the NLRB returned to its original determination and held that nonunion employees do not have the right to have a coworker or other representative present in a meeting when the employee reasonably believes it might result in discipline.

- ▶ *Communication Workers of America v. Beck, 1988*: The Supreme Court case that established the right for bargaining unit members to pay only that unrelated portion of union dues that is attributable to mainline union responsibilities (collective bargaining, organizing in the same industry, contract administration, and the like). It is up to the employee, however, to exercise her Beck rights.

- ▶ *Specialty Healthcare and Rehabilitation Center of Mobile, 2011*: The NLRB decision in unrelated this case permits the organization of micro-units in organizations even when the majority of employees do not want or seek union representation.

RESPONSIBILITY

ER & LR Responsibility 02

Assess organizational climate by obtaining employee input (for example: focus groups, employee surveys, staff meetings).

Employee Input

In this section, we'll take a look at the following ways of securing employee input:

- ▶ Employee surveys
- ▶ Focus groups
- ▶ Employee participation groups
- ▶ Open-door policies
- ▶ Suggestion programs
- ▶ Management by walking around (MBWA)

As we do so, keep in mind that although these approaches do secure employee input, they have other impacts as well—ones that can, potentially, be even more lasting that the input that was gathered.

Employee Surveys

Employee surveys (also sometimes called attitude surveys or climate surveys) give employees the opportunity to express their opinions and to share their perspectives. Sometimes employee surveys can even provide a vehicle through which employees can truly contribute in a meaningful and significant way to their organizations by having a voice in shaping the policies, practices, and direction of their organizations.

For employees to fully participate in the survey process and to make truly valuable contributions, they must fully and clearly understand the purpose of the survey, be assured anonymity, and receive feedback relative to the survey results.

Four functional reasons for organizations to conduct surveys follow:

- ▶ To gauge and measure employees' perceptions, viewpoints, and attitudes.
- ▶ To take the pulse of specific current and potential issues that are important to employees.
- ▶ To collect information that can be used by the organization to help set priorities.
- ▶ To provide a benchmark—a snapshot, in a way—of employees' viewpoints and perspectives. This will enable organizations to establish a baseline from which to later draw comparisons.

NOTE

Although they offer many advantages, surveys are neither the only, nor necessarily the best, employee involvement tool for any particular situation. Before you choose whether to use a survey, be sure to consider the advantages and disadvantages of various employee involvement tools. If you work in an organization where a survey has been used in the past, be careful to look thoroughly into that process: what was done, how it was done, and what the outcomes were. This is particularly important because there is a great deal of disparity with respect to the way employee surveys can be conducted, as well as the potential quality of the overall employee survey experience and outcomes.

If you decide that you are going to conduct an employee survey, there are 10 general steps to follow:

1. Secure management buy-in, starting with the senior levels of management.

2. Determine the survey content.

3. Determine the survey methodology (for instance, online, hardcopy, in person, mail, open ended, closed ended, and so on).

4. Develop the survey.

5. "Market" the survey.

6. Conduct the survey.

7. Calculate the results.

8. Interpret the results.

9. Share the results.

10. Act upon the results.

How a survey is designed and how it is conducted are two critically important factors that will contribute significantly to determining the overall success, failure, and value of the survey process. Surveys can be designed or conducted either within the organization or by consultants who reside outside the organization.

Either way, the process of simply conducting an employee survey isn't enough to make it a valuable involvement strategy. First, whether the survey is administered internally or through a consultant, it is essential to ensure that the survey is conducted in an anonymous manner. It is just as important that participants believe in the anonymity of the process. Another critical element that will contribute significantly to determining the ultimate success of a survey is the degree of follow-up that occurs after the survey is administered. This does not mean that all requests expressed through surveys must be granted. It does, however, mean that the summary of survey results must be reported back—in a sanitized manner—to participants and that specific requests and recommendations must be acknowledged and addressed.

Focus Groups

Focus groups provide another means of communicating with and involving employees in the organization. A focus group consists of a small but representative sample of individuals within an organization. Focus group discussions are led by a neutral facilitator who seeks to elicit feedback and input on a specific subject. Focus groups can range in size, with an ideal number of participants ranging from 10 to 15 people. In determining the size of the focus group, the objective is to ensure that you have enough people to generate a dynamic and synergistic discussion, but not so many people that there is insufficient time for participants to meaningfully contribute their ideas—to be, as well as to feel—heard. It's also essential to ensure "groupthink" does not emerge.

Focus groups can be used independently or as a follow-up tool to an employee survey. They afford a degree of flexibility that a survey cannot provide. Successfully facilitating a focus group, however, requires a far greater level of interpersonal skill than is required to administer a survey. In addition, whereas surveys require a significant level of trust if they are to be successful, focus groups require an even greater level of trust. This is true, in part, because anonymity is by definition impossible when people are participating face-to-face in a focus group setting.

If you decide to use a focus group, be sure to thoroughly address the five following steps for success:

1. Develop the right questions.

2. Involve/include all stakeholders.

3. Determine how many focus group sessions you need to conduct. (This may be a function of the size of the population involved, the scope of the issues involved, the number of distinct stakeholder groups, the amount of time you have, the amount of money you have, and the number of skilled and consistent facilitators at your disposal.)

4. Arrange the logistics (who, when, where, how, how long, and so on).

5. Conduct the meetings, select the moderator/facilitator, establish and agree upon ground rules, ensure consistent participation, ask probing questions, ensure continuity across focus groups, and so on.

NOTE

Be familiar with the techniques, advantages, and disadvantages of focus groups. In addition, based on the potential strengths and weaknesses of surveys and focus groups, be prepared to identify situations in which a focus group would be the preferred employee involvement approach, situations in which a survey would be the preferred employee involvement approach, and situations in which a combined approach might be most effective.

Employee Participation Groups

Employee participation groups invite employees to participate actively in the process of managing the organization. Through these groups, employees can contribute ideas and provide feedback. Employee participation groups can also provide an excellent way to encourage creative involvement and enhance commitment.

CAUTION

Under the NLRA, employee participation groups could be found to be "company dominated" and therefore be rendered illegal. Although employee participation groups are neither legal nor illegal by definition, the way in which they are managed/administrated can have a huge impact on whether any particular group is deemed to be legal or illegal. As always, consult with counsel before structuring a group of this sort.

Open-Door Policy

An open-door policy is just what its name implies—a standing invitation for employees to raise their concerns with managers or human resources, face to face. The use of an open door cannot result in penalties, formal or otherwise, against those employees who avail themselves of these resources.

"Betrayer? Me? I Was Only Doing My Job"

Open-door policies highlight another reason why we must not inappropriately promise confidentiality, lest we end up being perceived as betrayers of trust. There are times when we are obligated to reveal information that has been shared with us. Such situations can crop up unexpectedly, especially in organizations where an open-door policy is in effect.

Ensuring discretion and reassuring that you will reveal information only on a "need-to-know basis" is one thing. Promising blanket confidentiality is something entirely different.

Complaint handling and resolution is a skill, an art, and a discipline. Proceed with skill, knowledge, and caution to ensure that you do not unintentionally step into a situation that can damage your credibility, perhaps even beyond repair. Worse yet, do not honor promises of confidentiality if such promises would lead you to run afoul of the law.

Suggestion Programs

Suggestion programs invite employees to submit their ideas, usually anonymously, unless they choose to reveal their identity. Ideas are usually welcomed relative to any work-related topic, such as improving work systems, identifying or eliminating safety concerns, or exposing unethical (or criminal) behavior.

Questions submitted through suggestion programs or "suggestion boxes" (physical or electronic) need to be responded to quickly, regardless of whether the suggestion is implemented. For any suggestion program to be successful, employees must be heard and must feel heard.

Management by Walking Around

MBWA is an acronym that has been around for decades and is just as relevant now as it was when introduced. It is a management approach whereby a manager makes a commitment to spend a dedicated amount of time with employees on a regular basis. By increasing her visibility, the manager creates opportunities to provide feedback to and receive input from employees. MBWA also helps ensure that employees have increased access to "the boss," thereby increasing the potential for spontaneity, creativity, and synergy.

Neither HR professionals nor managers should hide in their offices. If we isolate ourselves, we may end up being marginalized. It is up to each of us, individually and collectively, to make the choice to "get out there" and to keep our finger on the pulse of the workplace and the workforce.

Town Hall/Department/Staff Meetings

Hold them routinely. Share information, and be open to receiving and acting upon feedback.

Employee Relations

Let's take a look at a fundamental premise that applies to employee relations as well as labor relations: the fact that "good employee relations is good employee relations."

What does this mean? Whether or not the employees in question happen to belong to a union, good employee relations is good employee relations. In turn, good employee relations foster enhanced morale, which in turn strengthens the organization's culture. A stronger culture affects and shapes the kinds of employee relations initiatives that will be most effective. When well handled, this circle of influence can evolve positively and productively.

It's hard to think of anything that doesn't influence employee relations. This is just as true of external considerations as it is of internal considerations.

To demonstrate this, we chose an online newspaper at random and scanned the headlines. Within minutes, we compiled a list of factors that can have a direct impact on employee relations (as defined earlier). Just a small portion of that list (in alphabetical order) included the following:

- Aging workforce
- Climate changes
- Credit card debt
- Crime (corporate and otherwise)
- Diversity and inclusion issues
- Drug use in professional sports
- Drug use in schools
- Economic conditions—national, regional, and local
- Energy prices
- Energy supplies
- Ethical breaches
- Executive compensation
- Globalization: management/leadership
- Home prices
- Misappropriation of funds
- Mortgage crisis
- Organ donation
- Outsourcing/offshoring
- Same sex marriage
- School violence/shootings
- Security/homeland security
- Social promotion (in schools)
- Sports
- Student loan repayment crisis
- Supreme Court
- Technology and technological developments
- Terrorism
- Unemployment
- Veterans' issues
- War/international unrest
- Weather-related events and disasters
- Workplace violence

Even with a cursory review of these items, it's relatively easy to make legitimate, meaningful connections that demonstrate how each of these topics could, in one way or another, affect employee relations, as defined earlier.

Even if the organization decides not to respond to factors such as those already listed, make no mistake: the organization is still making a decision. As is mentioned throughout this book, *you can't not communicate.* In that sense, employee relations is defined just as much by what an organization doesn't do as it is by what an organization does do.

RESPONSIBILITY

ER & LR Responsibility 03

Develop and implement employee relations programs (for example: recognition, special events, diversity programs) that promote a positive organizational culture.

KNOWLEDGE

Knowledge 51

Techniques and tools for facilitating positive employee relations (for example: employee surveys, dispute/conflict resolution, labor/management cooperative strategies).

KNOWLEDGE

Knowledge 52

Employee involvement strategies (for example: employee management committees, self-directed work teams, staff meetings).

KNOWLEDGE

Knowledge 58

Positive employee relations strategies and nonmonetary rewards.

Internal Considerations

The considerations listed previously represent external elements that influence employee relations. Although these are critical, it's just as important to consider internal elements that can affect employee relations. Perhaps the most important internal consideration impacting employee relations is organizational culture.

Organizational Culture

Organizational culture casts an expansive, inclusive, and incredibly wide net. It encompasses historical events, current events, and future events (whether potential, likely, or simply rumored). More specifically, organizational culture reflects and embodies the norms, mores, values, beliefs, customs, and attitudes of the organization and of those who work within the organization. It is thought of by some as the "personality" or even the "soul" of the organization.

Culture speaks to "the "way things are done around here"—the formal and informal manifestation of what defines the organization. Organizational culture encompasses historical events, current events, and future events (whether potential, likely, or simply rumored). More specifically, organizational culture reflects and embodies the norms, mores, values, beliefs, customs, and attitudes of the organization and of those who work within it.

Organizational Culture: What It Is

Sometimes we don't fully recognize the importance that organizational culture has on the day-to-day functioning of the organization. There is also sometimes a tendency to think of organizational culture as something nebulous. In reality, the opposite is true.

To begin to get a grasp on this idea, let's consider the work of Terrence E. Deal and Allan A. Kennedy, who have studied culture extensively for decades. Deal and Kennedy's work spans several milestone works, including *Corporate Cultures: The Rites and Rituals of Corporate Life*. Deal and Kennedy identified four specific dimensions of culture:

▸ **Values:** The beliefs that lie at the heart of the corporate culture

▸ **Heroes:** The individuals who embody those values

▸ **Rites and rituals:** Routines, relative to the way people interact, that have strong symbolic qualities

▸ **The culture network:** The information system of communication, or the "hidden hierarchy of power" within an organization

In this sense, Deal and Kennedy's definition of culture helps us recognize the tangible impact and manifestation of organizational culture. This hands-on expression of organizational culture is what employees see and experience every day. To employees, these four dimensions of culture provide a much more meaningful description of culture than any formal organizational communication strategy (by itself) ever could. It is for this reason, in part, that we as HR professionals do a disservice to our clients and ourselves if we limit our awareness of organizational culture solely to its "formal" definitions.

In addition to Deal and Kennedy, Edgard Schein of MIT's Sloan School of Management sheds important insights into organization culture, which, when boiled down to its basics, is about shared assumptions, adapting, integrating, and assimilating new members. In short, Schein seems to be saying that organizational culture speaks to "the way we do things around here."

Like Deal and Kennedy, Schein reaches beyond the formal dimensions of culture to recognize the power and influence inherent in the more subtle dimensions of culture, which in turn begins to speak to the importance of organizational culture.

Another definition of culture is offered by Mary D'Amato of Georgetown University. D'Amato poses the following three questions as a way to understand explore and understand organizational culture:

▸ What behavior does the organization reward?

▸ What behavior does the organization punish?

▸ What behavior does the organization tolerate?

Although these questions may seem simple, the answers are usually profoundly revealing—and often quite surprising.

Organizational Culture: Its Importance

Schein was quite direct about the importance of organizational culture. In his 2004 book *Organizational Culture and Leadership*, Schein wrote about the possibility that a group's very survival could be threatened by the emergence of problems relating to its culture, and the resulting need for leaders to rise to the occasion and address those cultural issues.

At this point, some readers may be wondering, "Threatened survival? Isn't that a bit overly dramatic?" The answer, however, is a clear and unequivocal "No." Deal and Kennedy also identify culture as the single most important factor contributing to an organization's success or failure. And Deal and Kennedy are not alone in their assertion:

▶ In *Ideas Are Free*, Robinson and Schroeder explore the ways in which organizational culture can affect the ideas generated by the organization.

▶ In *HR from the Heart*, Sartain and Finney stress the criticality of culture as a business issue.

▶ In *Reinventing Strategy*, Pietersen links organizational culture to employee performance, and ultimately to the overall success or failure of the organization.

▶ In *The Fast Forward MBA in Business*, O'Brien looks at culture in terms of productivity, profitability, and overall performance.

If we can agree to the premise that culture is a significant factor contributing to the overall success of an organization, the next step that we as HR professionals must take is to focus on how we can leverage effective employee relations initiatives as a way of strengthening an organization's culture and, therefore, moving the organization closer to the attainment of its objectives. Two important ways this can be accomplished are through employee communication programs and employee involvement strategies.

Employee Involvement and Employee Communication

Employee communication and employee involvement are two separate, albeit closely interrelated, types of programs. Said differently, the line between communication strategies and employee involvement strategies is cloudy, as—in many ways—it should be. Both are important components to effective employee relations, and neither is as effective without the other. In addition, when well executed, each can strengthen the role of the other.

For an organization to practice effective employee relations, the employment experience can't just happen to employees. Such an approach implies detachment and disempowerment. Instead, HR professionals must seek to actively and meaningfully involve employees in the experience of their own employment.

Let's take a look at each of these topics, and—more important—the tools and initiatives that can bring them to life.

Employee Communication Strategies

One cornerstone, perhaps *the* cornerstone, of effective employee relations is effective communication. We'll look at communication in terms of communicating with—not just communicating to—employees.

You learned about this in Chapter 1, "Business Management and Strategy," but it's important enough to be repeated here: in the course of performing our jobs, HR professionals need to possess and demonstrate a variety of skills and abilities—analytical, problem-solving, decision-making, interpersonal, intrapersonal, conflict resolution—just to name a few. Underscoring all these is the ability to communicate effectively and strategically. Again, this concept spans all six areas of HR. Doing our jobs well just isn't enough—we have to ensure that the work we do is appropriately communicated to and understood by the people with whom we partner. For instance, we might design a compensation program that is designed to lead the market. (See Chapter 6, "Risk Management," for more information on what this means.) We might accomplish that posture by establishing competitive base-pay rates along with an incentive program that is—potentially—lucrative for employees who meet or exceed certain goals. If we don't communicate with managers and employees about how we designed the program, however, and about how the incentive program really puts us ahead of our labor market competitors in terms of compensation, the impact and power of our design might be unappreciated or, even worse, misunderstood or misapplied.

As discussed in Chapter 1, one way to look at this is to consider the five *W*s and one *H* that news reporters traditionally seek to answer:

▶ *Why* **communicate:** First, think about why you are communicating this message. If you don't clearly convey a reason for the message, others within the organization will undoubtedly ascribe a reason. Not surprisingly, that reason will not always be accurate or positive.

▶ *What to* **communicate:** Balancing employees' "need to know" (and some would say "right to know") against the organization's legal or ethical obligations relative to the dissemination of information presents a delicate and precarious situation. If you find yourself in a situation like this (and it is likely that sooner or later you will), be truthful. Lies or half-truths will always surface. And, once lost, credibility can rarely be regained. Even then, it must be earned—a slow and costly process. Sometimes telling the truth means that you can't reveal every detail of every situation—and that you might need to acknowledge this.

CAUTION

Confidential information is just that—confidential. Confidentiality in this context is what can—and can't—be shared with the employee as opposed to what the employer can—and can't—keep confidential from an employer's obligation to act (investigate sexual-harassment claims, and so on) that we explored earlier in this chapter. Reminding employees (regardless of the nature of your personal relationship with them) of your commitment to maintaining confidentiality is part of truth telling.

▶ *When to* **communicate:** Timing may not be everything when it comes to communication, but it is critically important. First, consider the content of the message you will be communicating. How much urgency is there for communicating the message? Is there a benefit to waiting? Think about other considerations as well. In a micro sense, be aware of the day of the week and the time of the day when you choose to communicate a message. In a macro sense, consider what's going on in the organization, in the industry, in society, and even in the world before you share critical information.

▶ *Where to* **communicate:** Think about where you want people to be when they receive the message: Attending a face-to-face meeting, which is largely presentation driven? Or participating from a satellite location in teleconference/videoconference that permits questions and answers? Or alone, behind their computers, reading an email? There is no one right approach or solution for all situations, so it's important to consider the totality of the exact situation in which you find yourself.

▶ *Who* **will communicate, and to whom:** Sometimes HR professionals prepare messages that they will communicate directly. At other times, HR professionals will collaborate with managers to put together a particular message that the managers will deliver personally. Or HR professionals deliver messages that—in some form or fashion—others have created. And, of course, there are times when we ghost-write information that someone else will actually communicate.

TIP

There's no one right answer for any situation, so think through the cast of characters—those who will construct the message, deliver the message, and receive the message—thoroughly and carefully.

▶ *How to* **communicate:** It's not enough to rely on one method of communication. Identify multiple ways to communicate important messages. Different media are available to you, including in person, print, email, teleconference, and live streaming video, to name just a few.

How to communicate addresses another important consideration: the directional flow of communication. Are methods in place within the organization to ensure that information can flow up as well as down? Can individuals across different units or divisions of the organization communicate with each other? And are meaningful feedback mechanisms in place to enable you to accurately gauge the impact and effectiveness of your communication efforts?

Diversity and Inclusion

A key component of any workplace—and of any workplace culture—is diversity and inclusion. Although related, these topics are not the same. Diversity speaks to the process of recognizing, valuing, and embracing the many ways in which a group or organization embodies differences and leveraging those differences to enhance the overall performance of individuals and groups.

Diversity is a workplace issue, a performance issue, and a human issue. Creating a workplace that recognizes and values diversity in all its forms is essential for organizational health, growth, and (often) survival.

Diversity is sometimes bundled—and confused—with affirmative action or equal-employment opportunities. Although it falls on the same spectrum, diversity is not the same thing.

Diversity is in no way limited to the protected classes that are identified in EEO law—categories such as gender, age, religion, national origin, sexual orientation, color, veteran status, or disability status. Diversity also reaches out to recognize differences in communication styles, thought patterns, and a wide range of other factors that make each of us, as humans, unique.

Diversity vs. Inclusion

Diversity speaks to the many ways in which employees may be different. Inclusion, conversely, takes diversity a step farther and creates a beautiful, living mosaic out of these differences. Inclusion creates a unified whole of many diverse parts.

Imagine, if you will, "memory quilts" that were popular a century or more ago. People (usually women) would turn old clothes that were no longer suitable to wear into lovely, complex patterns and colors. The pieces of these quilts could come from dozens of pieces of clothing. The quilts that were produced were works of art.

And so it is within our organizations that embrace inclusion.

So, since when are quilts business issues? Consider this quotation: "Go where you are celebrated, not tolerated. If they can't see the real value of you, it's time for a new start." —Author Unknown

So it is with many individuals as they make life choices. And so it is with employees who may decide whether to stay with an organization or move on to someplace where they will be truly valued and appreciated (rather than tolerated).

NOTE

Be aware of the benefits that can accrue to an organization that embraces diversity and diversity, offers diversity and inclusion training, or launches diversity and inclusion initiatives. Also be well versed in the differences between equal-employment opportunity (EEO), affirmative action, and diversity. See Chapter 2, "Workforce Planning and Employment," for more information on EEO and affirmative action.

Handbooks

Employee handbooks are an important and frequently used method that organizations use to communicate information about policies, procedures, and rules. Handbooks provide, in a sense, the "rules of the road" in that they ensure that employees are fully informed (in writing) about the obligations, responsibilities, and benefits that are associated with being an employee.

Handbooks will be discussed, in detail, later in this chapter.

ER & LR Responsibility 04

RESPONSIBILITY

Evaluate effectiveness of employee relations programs through the use of metrics (for example: exit interviews, employee surveys, turnover rates).

Measuring Employee Relations Initiatives

As stated throughout the chapter, and as is true for our profession, HR decisions are business decisions. As such, they mandate a structured and deliberate businesslike analysis.

An early part of any analysis is identifying the problem that needs to be solved. This is not always as easy as it seems because symptoms often disguise themselves as problems. From there, careful data collection and data analysis is undertaken, and conclusions are drawn.

As with all other areas of HR, we need to be prepared to use measures when ascertaining the success of employee relations initiatives. Just a few of the measures that might be appropriate to determine the success of employee relations initiatives could include these:

- Turnover levels
- Absenteeism (particularly unplanned)
- Work-related accidents/injuries/"preventable" illnesses
- Productivity
- Quality
- Customer satisfaction

▶ Employee survey results

▶ Return on investment (ROI)

> **NOTE**
>
> Different organizations can prepare many of these calculations in different ways. Remain open to these.

Before exploring these, however, let's take an overarching look at analysis.

Different types of analyses can be clustered into two categories:

▶ Quantitative analysis

▶ Qualitative analysis

Quantitative Analysis

Numeric, mathematical models are utilized in conducting quantitative analysis. Historical data is measured and scrutinized to extract objective and meaningful insights. Correlation and measures of central tendency are two types of quantitative analysis with which you will want to be familiar.

Correlation

Quantitative analysis involves measuring correlation. Through measurement and comparison, correlation mathematically determines whether a demonstrated relationship exists between two factors or entities. A positive correlation or negative correlation indicates that a relationship does exist. The correlation coefficient is a number between –1 and +1 that defines the strength of that relationship. The closer that coefficient is to zero, the weaker the relationship between the two factors.

Measures of Central Tendency

When it comes to quantitative analysis, it's important to look beyond—and even within—what we commonly think of as an average. Three measures of central tendency with which HR professionals need to be familiar are mean, median, and mode.

Mean

Mean most closely corresponds to what people usually imply when they use the word "average." The mean of a set of numbers is calculated as follows:

The total of all the values (or numbers) in a set divided by the number of values that are in that set.

For example, for the set 57, 64, 15, 37, 11, 99, 1, 1, and 19, the mean is calculated as follows:

Total of all values in the set: (57+64+15+37+11+99+1+1+19) = 304

Number of values in the set: 9

Mean: 304/9 = 33.78

Median

The median is derived by putting a set of data in numeric order, from lowest to highest, and identifying the value that is in the middle.

For example, for the set 57, 64, 15, 37, 11, 99, 1, 1, and 19, the median is determined as follows:

Values in numeric order, lowest to highest:

1, 1, 11, 15, 19, 37, 57, 64, 99

Median (middle value): 19

Mode

The mode is the value that appears most frequently in a set.

For example, for the set 57, 64, 15, 37, 11, 99, 1, 1, and 19, the mode is "1" because that is the value that appears most frequently.

> **NOTE**
>
> **Weighted average:** Sometimes not all factors or pieces of data that are being quantitatively analyzed are equally important. Weighted averages allow certain pieces of data to be multiplied by a particular factor to give them greater weight or importance.

Qualitative Analysis

Qualitative analysis does not involve mathematical modeling or calculations. It is based more on judgments that are subjective in nature.

Two examples of qualitative analysis are the Delphi technique and the nominal group technique.

The Delphi Technique

The Delphi technique is an example of a structured nonmathematical technique in which expert opinions from a variety of individuals are sought, distilled, and distilled again. An objective, neutral, uninvolved leader recaps what the experts submit, summarizes that information, and condenses it into a more concise format. (The leader is not one of the "experts" and does not inject his opinions or interpretations into the process.) This happens several times until a final position is identified—one that incorporates the input of many individuals but that does not unduly reflect any one position or viewpoint.

A distinguishing—and critical—element of the Delphi technique is that the "experts" from whom opinions are sought and whose ideas are culled down never meet in person and never discuss their submissions—all of which are made in writing. Rather, their submissions are collected and processed by an objective third party. In this way, the Delphi technique ensures that factors such as group dynamics, overpowering personalities, and just plain politics don't taint the assessment process. The anonymity of the process further encourages individuals to "take a risk" and submit their ideas without fear of reprisal, retribution, or judgment—even if none of those outcomes would ever happen. The sanitized nature of this process puts expert contributors on a more even footing, further ensuring the integrity of this process.

Nominal Group Technique

Like the Delphi technique, the nominal group technique takes a nonmathematical approach to forecasting. The nominal group technique is similar to the Delphi technique in that it calls upon the expertise and predictive ability of experts. Most of the similarities between the two techniques, however, end there. With the nominal group technique, experts meet in person and process their ideas as a group. Led by a facilitator, the meeting begins with each expert writing down her ideas, after which each expert presents those ideas to the group. Discussion of ideas, however, is not permitted at this point; only presentation is acceptable. The group then comes together to discuss each others' ideas, after which each group member is called upon to independently rank the ideas. The meeting facilitator then combines all the individual rankings to determine which are the most important to the group. Through this process, the forecast is made.

An Added Value of Analysis

There is a place in HR for both qualitative and quantitative analysis. Rely too heavily on qualitative analysis, and you may be accused of not having facts to back up your assumptions. Rely exclusively on quantitative analysis, and you may be undervaluing the knowledge and expertise of your seasoned colleagues (or, for that matter, your own).

Both of these approaches, when used exclusively, can damage relationships with your clients and damage your professional credibility within the organization.

Each chapter in this book identifies ways in which the ability to conduct accurate and meaningful quantitative and qualitative analyses will strengthen your effectiveness as an HR professional. Again, this is representative of the ways in which HR has evolved into a true profession, and it supports the important reality that it's simply not enough to be a people person.

With this backdrop, let's return to look at some of the measures listed earlier that might be appropriate to determine the success of employee relations.

Turnover Levels

$$\frac{\text{The number of employees who terminate voluntarily or involuntarily from an organization (during a specified timeframe)}}{\text{The average number of employees employed with the organization (during the same specified timeframe)}}$$

Absenteeism (Particularly Unplanned)

As with all calculations, there is more than one way to approach this calculation. One possible way to determine absenteeism is as follows:

$$\frac{\text{Total number of days on which employees did not work but were scheduled to work (during a specified timeframe)}}{\text{Total number of scheduled workdays (during a specified timeframe)}}$$

Note that this formula can (and, perhaps, should) be adjusted to reflect planned time off, FMLA leave, jury duty, bereavement leave, and more.

Work-Related Accidents/Injuries/"Preventable" Illnesses

When calculating and looking at this metric, it is advisable to avail oneself of reliable and scholarly resources. In particular, check out the following publication when considering using, and managing to, this metric:

▶ *Injury and Illness Prevention Programs, White Paper*, January 2012. https://www.osha.gov/dsg/topics/safetyhealth/OSHAwhite-paper-january2012sm.pdf

Productivity

There are as many productivity metrics as there are, well…let's just say there are many productivity metrics. One cannot determine the most appropriate and suitable one in a vacuum. Ultimately, productivity metrics must be carefully researched and designed to ensure validity and reliability.

Quality

The comments listed earlier with respect to productivity apply equally to quality.

Customer Satisfaction

The comments listed earlier with respect to productivity apply equally to quality.

Employee Survey Results

Employee surveys must be designed to ensure validity and reliability. Design, however, is not enough; surveys must also be administered in a manner that is sound and consistent so that nothing can taint the results. All who design and administer employee surveys—as well as the managers of those who take those surveys—must be well versed in best practices and must be willing to commit to adhering to those practices.

Return on Investment (ROI)

As defined elsewhere in this book, ROI can be calculated as follows:

$$\frac{\text{(Financial gain from investment)} - \text{(cost of investment)}}{\text{Cost of investment}}$$

This formula looks deceptively simple. To ensure validity and reliability, it is particularly important to calculate, include all costs (even those that might be hidden), and ensure that financial gains from an investment legitimately correlate to that investment and not to some other unrelated factor.

> **NOTE**
>
> Organizations can prepare many of these calculations in different ways. Remain open to these.

RESPONSIBILITY

ER & LR Responsibility 05

Establish, update, and communicate workplace policies and procedures (for example: employee handbook, reference guides, or standard operating procedures), and monitor their application and enforcement to ensure consistency.

Employee Handbooks

As discussed previously in this chapter, employee handbooks are an important and frequently used method that organizations use to communicate information about policies, procedures, and rules. Handbooks provide, in a sense, the "rules of the road" in that they ensure that employees are fully informed (in writing) about the obligations, responsibilities, and benefits that are associated with being an employee.

Handbooks can vary widely in terms of the information they contain, their length, the topics they cover, and the tone in which they are written.

The following topics represent a sampling of what employee handbooks can address:

- ▶ Introduction (for example, welcome, history, mission, vision, and values)

- ▶ Statement relating to collective bargaining unit (if applicable)

- ▶ EEO-related policies (for example, statements and policies pertaining to EEO and affirmative action [AA], diversity and inclusion, employees with disabilities, sexual harassment, religious accommodation, and employment eligibility and verification [I-9 form])

- ▶ Job performance (for example, probationary period for new employees/transferred employees, performance management and appraisal, progressive disciplinary process)

- ▶ Behavioral expectations (for example, conduct and work rules, work behavior, appropriate attire, workplace equipment and supplies, and absenteeism and tardiness)

- ▶ Positions (for example, job grading system, job regrading, and nonexempt and exempt FLSA status)

- ▶ Benefits programs (for example, health plans, prescription drug plans, dental plans, retirement plans, flexible spending accounts, life insurance, disability insurance, child care, and elder care)

- ▶ Pay (for example, compensation policy, overtime pay, comp pay, time reporting system, pay procedures, and direct deposit)

- ▶ Workplace as community (for example, transportation, parking, public transportation, carpooling, cafeteria, health and fitness center, ATM, company store, travel agency, bowling league, and softball league)

- ▶ Leave programs (for example, FMLA, jury duty, holiday/sick/vacation leave, and so on)

- ▶ Terminations (for example, voluntary [resignation, retirement]; involuntary [layoff, dismissal, job abandonment, and failure to successfully complete probationary period])

- ▶ Employee records
- ▶ Conflicts of interest
- ▶ Substance abuse policy
- ▶ Smoking policy
- ▶ Inclement weather and other emergency conditions
- ▶ New hire/new transfer orientation
- ▶ Company ID cards
- ▶ Hours of work (workweek, meal/break periods)
- ▶ Safety and security
- ▶ Development and training
- ▶ Employee assistance programs
- ▶ Retirement programs
- ▶ Educational and tuition reimbursement benefits

Although they do not necessarily have to be written in a legalistic manner (and may be even more valuable and effective if they are not), handbooks can have a significant legal impact. If an employment-related decision (for instance, relating to discipline, termination, or other terms or conditions of employment) is questioned or challenged, the handbook will serve as one key piece of evidence that will be closely scrutinized by all parties.

One factor that will significantly affect whether the handbook will more closely support the employer's position or the employee's position is the presence or absence of an employee acknowledgement. From the perspective of the employer, every employee should acknowledge, either in writing or electronically, that she received, read, had the opportunity to ask, and in fact did ask any questions that she might have relative to the information contained within it. This, in effect, removes or greatly diminishes the effectiveness of the "I had no idea" defense. In addition, when policies are added or updated, organizations should strongly consider obtaining a written or electronic acknowledgement from each employee (that, again, confirms that the employee received, read, had the opportunity to ask, and in fact did ask any questions that she might have relative to the new or updated policy).

> **NOTE**
>
> Cultural as well as legal considerations need to be looked at carefully when deciding how to handle the distribution and updating of employee handbooks. As is so often the case with HR, how we handle and communicate relative to a situation is just as important as what we handle and communicate. Sometimes the road to court (and other places) is paved with good intentions.

Because handbooks can have such far-reaching legal impact, it is critical that counsel review and approve handbooks, policies, and updates before they are distributed to employees. In this way, counsel can ensure that legal concerns/problems do not unintentionally arise from the language that is used.

For instance, handbooks sometimes are written using language that can unintentionally create an implied contract and thereby potentially jeopardize "employment at will." The term permanent employee, for example, can raise questions of this sort. For this reason, most attorneys advise that employees should be referred to as "regular" or "ongoing" rather than "permanent." Equal care must be taken when the progressive disciplinary and probationary policies are crafted, for similar reasons.

In addition to all the carefully crafted language that must be included throughout the handbook, organizations often choose to have an attorney draft an overall statement that is included at the beginning of the handbook, on the signed acknowledgement sheet, or in both places. This statement reaffirms that the employment relationship is "at will," that the handbook does not create a contract, and that no other oral or written agreements or statements can override the employment-at-will relationship unless they are specifically designated as doing so.

Despite all this apparent legalese, handbooks must be user friendly. If the culture is the organization's "soul," then the handbook is (in one sense) its voice. It is the document to which employees will refer over and over again, and it must be written in a clear and readable manner. It may even be appropriate to publish the handbook in a variety of languages, depending on the demographics of the workforce.

RESPONSIBILITY

ER & LR Responsibility 06

Develop and implement a discipline policy based on organizational code of conduct/ethics, ensuring that no disparate impact or other legal issues arise.

RESPONSIBILITY

ER & LR Responsibility 07

Create and administer a termination process (for example: reductions in force [RIF], policy violations, poor performance) ensuring that no disparate impact or other legal issues arise.

KNOWLEDGE

Knowledge 54

Workplace behavior issues/practices (for example: absenteeism and performance improvement).

KNOWLEDGE

Knowledge 57

Legal disciplinary procedures.

KNOWLEDGE

Knowledge 60

Legal termination procedures.

Progressive Discipline as Employee Relations

Although not often thought of as an employee relations or employee involvement program, progressive discipline programs can be both. This is despite the fact that the word "discipline" evokes unpleasant associations for many of us. For some, it may elicit thoughts of a relationship in which there is an imbalance of power, a sense of disempowerment or helplessness, or even a tendency to judge or to blame. For others, it may simply conjure up images of "being in trouble" and therefore represent one or more steps along the path to termination. A third possibility is that it may simply equate to punishment.

It is in this context that we must again ensure that we fix the true definition of employee relations in the forefront of our awareness: anything that affects relationships with, among, or for employees. For even—perhaps even especially—through the disciplinary process, our focus on employee relations and relationship building must be maintained.

It is also in this context that we can benefit greatly from remembering Dick Grote's idea of "discipline without punishment" (published in his 1995 book of the same name). Discipline must be seen as a way to give employees the opportunity to help themselves. More specifically, discipline can be used as a tangible way of supporting employees in their efforts to address and resolve their own performance issues. It can, in short, serve as a wake-up call through which an employee will choose to turn around her performance so that it meets or even exceeds expectations.

> **EXAM ALERT**
>
> This vision may be consistent with the culture of your organization and the mindset of the managers whom you support. It is also important to recognize, however, that it might contradict the ideas of managers who might view discipline as a way to "pave a paper trail" that will enable them to terminate an employee (without a whole lot of time-consuming pushback from HR). If you encounter that mindset, move cautiously. Remember your role: you are a consultant and a business partner. You are not there to "just say no," nor are you there to enable behaviors that might eventually prove to be problematic or counterproductive. Keep the ultimate objectives of the organization in mind as you work with your managers; you might be surprised to see just how far a collaborative problem-solving approach can take you.

It is in this spirit that the process of progressive discipline emerges as a truly untapped employee relations opportunity. Progressive discipline is a system that incorporates a series of steps, each more progressively involved, advanced, or serious than the last.

The progressive discipline process is predicated on the belief that each employee *chooses* whether to perform his job satisfactorily (assuming that an employee is at least minimally qualified for the position for which he was hired). There are, of course, other factors involved—for instance, the very assumption that the employee is still at least minimally qualified for the position for which he holds, especially if the minimum requirements for that position have evolved (meaning, increased) over time.

> **NOTE**
>
> Like most of the general concepts that we're exploring in this section, the concept of progressive discipline generally holds true for employees who belong to a union as well as for employees who do not. As always, however, specific progressive disciplinary steps that are outlined in a collective bargaining agreement could overrule the concepts explored here.

It is also important to keep in mind that in 1975, the Supreme Court held in *NLRB v. Weingarten, Inc.* that employees have the right to union representation during investigatory interviews. Although those rights have been extended to—and revoked from—nonunion employees on two different occasions, As of the printing of this book, nonunion employees do not enjoy Weingarten Rights.

Principles of Progressive Discipline

There is no single best approach to the specific steps in progressive discipline; however, there are some important concepts to keep in mind.

"Employees Choose to Discipline—and Even Terminate—Themselves"

Technically speaking, it is true that either the employer or the employee can make a decision to terminate the employment relationship for any lawful reason (assuming, of course, the absence of an employment contract or collective bargaining agreement that stipulates otherwise). Within that range of possibilities, it's also true that an employer can choose to fire an employee who doesn't meet the performance standards of her position.

Another way of looking at this, however, is that, within the structure of progressive discipline, each employee makes choices relative to whether she will meet the expectations of her position. These choices can, ultimately, lead to a larger choice: whether to terminate herself.

What does this mean? Well, let's first say what it *doesn't* mean—we're not talking about employees who "see it coming" and quit before their employer terminates them.

Now let's take a look at what it does mean. An employer's decision to terminate an employee is made, to a greater or lesser degree, because an employee will not, or cannot, bring her performance up to expected levels. Employees have some degree, perhaps even a large degree, of control over that decision. How? An employee may not perform at expected performance levels, for instance, because she has chosen

- ▶ Not to participate in training opportunities

- ▶ Not to turn to her manager for support or assistance

- ▶ Not to change specific counterproductive or problematic behaviors

- ▶ Not to cease certain counterproductive or problematic behaviors

- ▶ Not to "turn over a new leaf" and demonstrate certain positive or productive behaviors

Ultimately, progressive discipline provides multiple opportunities at multiple decision points for employees to make choices that will result in them maintaining their employment in a positive and productive manner. When applied appropriately, therefore, progressive discipline truly is an empowering process.

"Fairness Isn't Sameness"

When it comes to progressive discipline (and, for that matter, many other dimensions of the employment relationship), fairness doesn't mean sameness. Or, in other words, just because you're treating everyone the same way doesn't mean that you're treating everyone fairly.

A concept that needs to be considered during the progressive discipline process, as at other times, is referred to as "similarly situated employees." This term does have a legal meaning and thus needs to be defined by lawyers. However, just for purposes of understanding the concept better, let's look at this concept in an admittedly nonlegal manner. With that caveat, similarly situated employees are employees who are, in one way or another, in the same category. In terms of the ADEA, for instance, this could mean employees who are all over 40 years of age or who are all under 40 years of age. In the context of Title VII of the Civil Rights Act of 1964, similarly situated employees might share the same gender, race, or color. The concept of similarly situated employees, however, isn't limited to civil rights legislation. For example, employees who are being considered for a position and who possess similar credentials could, in one sense, be considered to be similarly situated.

It's also possible, and often advisable, to look at progressive discipline in terms of whether different employees are similarly situated. In this context, being similarly situated could be a function, in part, of each employee's level of performance—ideally, in comparison to the SMART goals that were established for and with the employee at the beginning of the performance measurement period (see Chapter 3, "Human Resource Development"). In addition to performance against goals, it might also be important to consider other factors such as the length of time the employee has been employed with the organization, how long it has been (if ever) since the employee demonstrated any performance that is below predetermined standards, whether there are extraordinary reasons for the substandard performance, and the like.

To reiterate, looking at whether employees are similarly situated doesn't mean that we, as employers and HR representatives, should treat all employees the same. It does mean that we should be, in one sense, "consistently inconsistent." This is part of what makes our profession an art as well as a science.

> **NOTE**
>
> Nothing in this section changes the fact that many organizations (whether unionized or not) identify specific behaviors that can, do, and will result in immediate termination. Those behaviors might be listed in an employee handbook, a collective bargaining agreement, or the like. It is also important to remember that it is not possible to enumerate every behavior that could result in disciplinary action or immediate termination, so situations must also be looked at—in concert with management and with counsel—with an open mind.

Progressive Discipline Steps

Often, progressive discipline processes will include the following steps:

1. **Discussion of the substandard performance issue ("coaching" rather than "counseling"):** If progressive discipline is truly an employee relations initiative, it must be grounded in open communication, collaboration, and an effort to achieve a common objective: the attainment of the organization's objectives and the furtherance of its mission. All this can start with discussion. Sometimes (and there are those who would argue "often") this step, when performed well, may be able to preclude the need to engage in the balance of the progressive discipline process, thereby taking less of a toll on the organization itself and on the employees who work within it.

> **NOTE**
>
> Keep in mind that, for unionized employees, the collective bargaining agreement might speak to specific, additional procedural elements of progressive discipline.

2. **Verbal warning:** The next step in the progressive discipline process is verbal warning. This step moves beyond discussion because the tone is closer to "counseling" than "coaching." In other words, when the process moves to a verbal warning, there is a problem, not just a situation. There are those, however, who say that a verbal warning is "not worth the paper it's not written on." These individuals might assert that the most important aspect of a verbal warning is the message that is conveyed by the tone of the communication rather than the specific words that are used (although we must always

be mindful of the words we use because we never know when we may hear them again, and in what venue). Again, the idea or hope is that in response to the "escalation" from coaching to verbal warning, the employee will choose to bring her behavior up to pre-determined performance standards.

3. **Written warning:** At this point, the counseling has escalated to a formal level. Sometimes the reality of seeing a written warning is enough to help an employee recognize the gravity of a situation. In other words, sometimes messages do not truly seem real until they are written. In addition, a written warning can serve as a formal record of precisely what was communicated to the employee and when if such documentation becomes relevant.

4. **Final written warning or suspension:** This is the final opportunity the employee has to change his behavior before that behavior, if continued, will result in termination. Some organizations will suspend employees with or without pay. (FLSA considerations must be observed for exempt employees so they don't forfeit their exempt status.) Others will present the employee with a date by which he must make a commitment to bring his behavior up to the expected standards.

> **NOTE**
>
> Depending on the organization, step 4 could actually be broken into one, two, or even three substeps. Either way, the written documentation accompanying this step will likely include language to the effect that continuing substandard performance will lead to further disciplinary action, up to and including termination.
>
> Here again, it is particularly important to consult with counsel relative to the language that is used in any warning letters, and particularly in final written warning letters. Take care neither to create any sort of implied contract that the employee's employment will continue for any period of time nor to use language that can limit the employer's response to continued substandard performance.

5. **Involuntary termination:** There comes a point at which it is no longer advisable or productive to continue the employment relationship. It is at this point that managers, with the assistance and support of HR, need to end the employment relationship. Even this, however, must be done with respect, empathy, and dignity.

> **NOTE**
>
> Carrying out a progressive discipline process isn't easy or comfortable. However, tolerating substandard performance or inappropriate behaviors is unacceptable and ill advised for a number of even more compelling reasons. First, those employees who are meeting standards will get a message—a troubling message—loud and clear: "Why should I work so hard? Nothing happens to those who aren't pulling their weight." Those who are not meeting standards will get a message as well: "I guess I can continue to act this way or perform at this level because no one seems to have a problem with it."

Business/Organizational Ethics

Woven throughout this discussion—and underscoring this entire book—is the concept of business and organizational ethics, which speaks to a shared values-based system designed to inculcate within the organization's population a sense of how to conduct business properly.

Organizations must have a well-development awareness of their own ethics—beliefs and values that they actively embrace.

ER & LR Responsibility 08

Develop, administer, and evaluate grievance/dispute resolution and performance improvement policies and procedures.

Discipline and Discharge, and Grievance Handling

Discipline and discharge, and grievance procedures are two critical elements of the collective bargaining agreement that, in one sense, bring together all the other provisions in the agreement. Together with mediation and arbitration, they form the basis for contract administration.

Because of the unique impact of these two types of contract provisions, we will introduce them here.

Discipline and Discharge

Management reserves the right to discipline (a more positive approach than "punishing" or "penalizing") employees for subpar performance and nonperformance. Discharge (the termination of the employment relationship by the employer) is the culmination of unsuccessful discipline—meaning discipline that does not result in the employee bringing her performance up to an acceptable level.

Grievance Handling

Grievance handling is the formal process established by the collective bargaining agreement through which disagreements arising from the administration of the labor agreement are resolved. These difficulties could arise from a number of sources, including but not limited to interpretation of contract language or alleged unfair or inconsistent application of employment provisions. Grievances most often arise out of decisions relating to discipline and discharge.

Contract Administration

The collective bargaining process results in a collective bargaining agreement. In many ways, however, the collective bargaining agreement is more of a beginning than an ending. It is a living document that provides the structure and framework within which the daily happenings of the employment relationship are brought to life. It also provides the language that will govern the employment relationship—language that is at times subject to different interpretations, thereby presenting challenges that need to be resolved.

Grievance Procedure

For employees who belong to a collective bargaining unit, grievance handling is the formal process established by the collective bargaining agreement through which disagreements arising from the administration of the labor agreement are resolved. These difficulties could arise from a number of sources, including but not limited to interpretation of contract language or alleged unfair or inconsistent application of employment provisions. Grievances most often arise out of decisions relating to discipline and discharge.

A procedure/process should also be established so that employees who do not belong to a collective bargaining unit also have a way to raise concerns about actions that they believe are unfair or inappropriate.

> **NOTE**
>
> These avenues already exist outside the organization. It is far wiser for an organization to offer employees a way to address their concerns internally rather than to have no option but to address them externally. In the best-case scenario, this could lead to disgruntled employees, increased turnover, and a tainted reputation in the relevant labor market. It could also lead to formal agency charges or litigation.

Each collective bargaining agreement outlines a grievance procedure for resolving these sorts of differences. This procedure establishes the formal process through which problems and challenges associated with the interpretation or application of the collective bargaining agreement will be addressed and resolved. Sometimes challenges arise out of differences in opinion relative to the interpretation of the language that was used to craft the agreement. Challenges can also emerge when there is a perception that the contract has been applied in an unfair or inconsistent manner, particularly with respect to decisions relating to discipline and discharge.

Although management and labor both have the right to use the grievance process, management does not often choose to do so. Instead, the process is usually initiated by an employee who is a member of the collective bargaining unit or by the union itself. Either way, the grievance alleges that the labor contract has been violated in some way and seeks resolution.

Although the actual grievance procedure will vary widely from one collective bargaining agreement to another, the agreements are similar in that they consist of a series of prescribed steps, each of which has an accompanying time limit for action. The process by which appeals can be filed is also clearly delineated in the agreement.

Many, although not all, agreements outline a four-step grievance procedure:

Step 1: Initiate a complaint.

Step 2: Escalate the complaint internally.

Step 3: Reach the highest level of internal escalation.

Step 4: Participate in binding arbitration.

Step 1: Initiate a Complaint

Either the employee or the union must initiate a complaint within a specified time frame after the date on which the alleged contract violation took place (or, alternatively, the date on which the employee or union became aware of the alleged violation). In some contracts, this step must be formally filed (in writing), whereas other contracts permit this initial complaint to be informal (verbal). This initial complaint is usually filed with the supervisor of the person who experienced the alleged violation. This first-line supervisor then has a prescribed number of days within which to meet with the employee and the union steward to discuss the situation. In most cases, the supervisor will then have a prescribed number of days after that initial meeting to reach a decision relative to the situation. The supervisor can then choose to grant the requested relief in part, in whole, or not at all.

If the employee or the union decides to accept the resolution that the supervisor proposes, the grievance is considered to be settled. If the employee or the union decides not to accept the resolution, the union has a prescribed number of days within which to appeal the grievance to the next step.

In many agreements, management's failure to abide by all prescribed time limits will result in the grievance being automatically appealed to the next level. On the other hand, the union's failure to abide by all prescribed time limits will often result in the immediate dismissal of the grievance and the termination of the grievance process.

Step 2: Escalate the Complaint Internally

Step 2 is similar to step 1 with respect to the actual process and the requirements to abide by prescribed time frames. An important difference at this step, however, is that the meetings occur between higher levels of union and management leadership. At step 2, for instance, the president of the local union might meet with the manager of the plant at which the employee works. If resolution is not reached at step 2, an appeal can be made to move to step 3.

Step 3: Reach the Highest Level of Internal Escalation

Step 3 is similar to step 2 except that the level of the meetings that are being held have escalated even more. At this level, it is quite possible to find someone from the union's national office sitting across from someone from the organization's corporate headquarters.

If step three does not produce a resolution that is acceptable to the union, the union must decide (within a prescribed period of time, of course) whether to appeal to binding arbitration—the final step.

Step 4: Participate in Binding Arbitration

In this step, the disagreement is referred to an outside party—an arbitrator—who will render a decision that will be binding upon the union and management. Most of the time, the collective bargaining agreement will fully outline the arbitration process to which the parties will be held if the grievance is appealed to step 4.

Arbitration that is used to resolve grievances during the administration of the contract (as is described here) is called rights arbitration.

Familiarize Yourself with These Terms and Practices

For the PHR exam, it's important to be familiar with arbitration-related terms and practices. In addition to the rights arbitration process described here, be prepared to respond to questions on the following:

▶ **Interest arbitration:** Arbitration that is used to resolve conflicts around contract language during the collective bargaining process.

▶ **Arbitrator:** An individual selected to participate in the resolution of an agreement and the rendering of a binding decision.

▶ **Arbitrator panels:** Panels that are usually composed of three arbitrators, one of whom is selected by management, one of whom is selected by the union, and one of whom is selected jointly. (This person is referred to as the *neutral arbitrator*.)

▶ **Federal Mediation and Conciliation Service (FMCS):** A source that maintains lists of qualified arbitrators.

▶ **American Arbitration Association (AAA):** A source that maintains lists of qualified arbitrators.

▶ **Arbitration hearing:** A relatively formal process (not wholly unlike a court hearing) that can be conducted by an individual arbitrator or by a panel of arbitrators. The hearing includes the presentation of evidence, the testimony of witnesses, and opening and closing statements from both sides. Lawyers are often present as well, which adds even more to the judicial "feel" of the hearing.

> ▶ **Permanent arbitrators:** An individual arbitration arrangement in which one arbitrator who is selected for a fixed period of time (often the duration of the contract) hears all arbitration cases that arise during that period of time. One advantage to this approach is that the arbitrator becomes very knowledgeable about the contract. One potential disadvantage could emerge if the union, management, or both are dissatisfied with the arbitrator for some reason.
>
> ▶ **Ad hoc arbitrators:** More frequently, each arbitration will result in the selection of an arbitrator. The arbitrator who is selected may specialize in the particular topic with which the arbitration deals, which can be a distinct advantage. Also, neither party will be "stuck" with an arbitrator with whom it is not happy.
>
> ▶ **Decisions:** Arbitrators must resolve grievances on the basis of an objective interpretation of the contract as it was written. If the contract language is unclear, the arbitrator must then work to ascertain where the organization "is," where it needs to be, and how the HR initiative can specifically serve to bridge that gap.

RESPONSIBILITY

ER & LR Responsibility 09

Investigate and resolve employee complaints filed with federal agencies involving employment practices or working conditions, utilizing professional resources as necessary (for example: legal counsel, mediation/arbitration specialists, investigators).

KNOWLEDGE

Knowledge 59

Techniques for conducting unbiased investigations.

Investigating and Resolving Employee Complaints

The skills required to investigate and resolve employee complaints with federal agencies and to conduct unbiased investigations are complex, nuanced, and fraught with potential consequences (legal, financial, and nonlegal). As such, the author and editorial team suggest—in the strongest of terms—that you avail yourself of resources specifically dedicated to learning how to investigate complaints and conduct investigations. We also suggest that you work closely with counsel—in house or outside. In addition to those listed in the resource section of this chapter, here are some additional resources to consider:

▶ Cornell University, School of Industrial and Labor Relations, Employee Relations and Investigations Certificate

▶ Cornell University, School of Industrial and Labor Relations, Advanced Employee Relations and Investigations Certificate

▶ Society for Human Resource Management website, www.shrm.org (the most valuable resources are available on a "members-only" basis)

Unions

HR professionals also need a solid understanding of unions, union structure, and union-related activities. To that end, this section will look at the following subjects:

▶ How unions are structured

▶ Union organizing (the organizing process)

▶ Union decertification and deauthorization

▶ Protected concerted activities

▶ Labor strikes

How Unions Are Structured

Unions are structured democratically, in that union officers are elected. They are also hierarchical.

HR professionals need to be familiar with the following four types of union entities: local unions, national unions, federations, and international unions.

Local Unions

Local unions are largely responsible for the day-to-day administration of the labor agreement and relationship with union members. "Locals" generally have an elected president and elected stewards who represent the workers in the workplace. Larger local unions might have a full-time paid business agent. Most locals belong to and are chartered by a larger national union.

National Unions

National unions bring together all the union locals who are scattered across the country. There are usually different hierarchical levels in between the local union and the national union. National unions have far more power with respect to bargaining and political influence than the union locals could have on their own. National unions also advise and guide local unions and may manage nationwide benefits programs (such as retirement programs and health insurance plans).

Federations

A federation is a group of national unions. Its many members speak with one voice, thus wielding even greater influence and lobbying power. Federations do not, however, get involved with bargaining or contract administration.

Until the summer of 2005, the AFL-CIO was, in many ways, a federation that was the voice of labor in America. In 2005, however, several major national unions quit the AFL-CIO, including the following:

▶ The Service Employees International Union (SEIU)

▶ The International Brotherhood of Teamsters

▶ The United Food and Commercial Workers (UFCW)

▶ UNITE HERE

▶ United Farm Workers

▶ Carpenters Union

Together, these departing unions—representing about 4.5 million workers—nearly 35% of the AFL-CIO's previous members out of the previous total membership of 13 million workers—formed Change to Win (CTW).

International

International labor organizations operate on the international level in much the same manner as federations operate on the national level, only "bigger." For instance, the International Confederation of Free Trade Unions (ICFTU) is an international labor organization that has been in existence for more than 55 years and has a membership of 145 million people across five continents and more than 150 countries. All member unions have a democratic structure. ICFTU consists of three major regional organizations:

- APRO for Asia and the Pacific
- AFRO for Africa
- ORIT for the Americas

The ICFTU is highly active. According to its website, IFCTU's five "priorities for action" include the following:

- Employment and international labor standards
- Tackling the multinationals
- Trade union rights
- Equality, women, race, and migrants
- Trade union organization and recruitment

Union Organizing (The Organizing Process)

Through the organizing process, a union seeks to become the recognized representative of a bargaining unit of individuals within an organization. Members of a bargaining unit share common interests with respect to items that are negotiated through a collective bargaining agreement. A bargaining unit can represent part or all of an organization's workforce (except supervisors or others who are otherwise excluded from membership in unions).

There are five steps involved in the union-organizing process:

1. Make a connection—express interest.
2. Confirm interest—obtain authorization cards.
3. Obtain recognition.
4. The campaign.
5. The election.

Let's take a closer look at each of these steps.

Step 1: Make a Connection—Express Interest

In this step, contact is established. Either the union initiates contact with employees in an effort to begin the process of exploring whether there is interest in forming a union, or one or more employees who have an interest in forming a union initiate contact with the union.

Step 2: Confirm Interest—Obtain Authorization Cards

After contact has been established and cultivated, unions confirm and demonstrate employees' interest by obtaining authorization cards signed by employees. When 30% of the employees who would be in the collective bargaining unit have signed authorization cards, the union can petition NLRB to hold an election. (The 30% threshold demonstrates a "showing of interest" to the NLRB.) Often, however, unions may seek to obtain signed authorization cards from 50% or more employees before petitioning the NLRB to ascertain the seriousness of employees' interest in joining a union.

In general, petitions from the union will not be accepted if an election has been held within the prior year, if a union has been certified within the past year but has not successfully negotiated a contract, or if there is a valid contract (not to exceed three years) in effect.

NOTE

NLRA rules regarding petitioning changed dramatically effective April 14, 2015. The "NLRB Representation Case-Procedures Fact Sheet," published by the NLRA, highlights critical differences and can be found at http://www.nlrb.gov/news-outreach/fact-sheets/nlrb-representation-case-procedures-fact-sheet. HR professionals should be particularly cognizant of the shortened timeframe between when a hearing notice is served and when the hearing will begin, which can be as short as eight days.

Step 3: Obtain Recognition

After the union has obtained recognition—regardless of the way in which that recognition has been obtained—the employer must provide the NLRB with a list of the names and addresses of all the employees who are eligible to vote in the union certification election (the "Excelsior List"). The NLRB will, in turn, give list to the union. The nickname "Excelsior List" is derived from the NLRB decision *Excelsior Underwear, Inc. v. NLRB, 1966*, in which the NLRB considered whether "a fair and free election [can] be held when the union involved lacks the names and addresses of employees eligible to vote in that election, and the employer refuses to accede to the union's request." The NLRB ruled that it could not. As a result, the employer must provide the list of employees' names and addresses within seven days of the NLRB scheduling an election.

Step 4: The Campaign

The NLRB will carry out a secret ballot election 30–60 days after the NLRB determines that an election will be held. As always, unfair labor practices, by employers as well as by unions, are prohibited during the union-organizing campaign. See "Collective Bargaining: The Process," to review specific information about ULPs.

The employer and the union are each permitted to engage in certain activities and prohibited from engaging in other activities during the organizing and campaign processes.

Step 5: The Election

The NLRB conducts the secret ballot election, usually at the workplace, between 30 and 60 days after the NLRB issues its decision. Management and the union are both permitted to have observers present at the election. Observers may object to a vote if they feel that a vote is being cast illegally. The NLRB is responsible for resolving all voter eligibility issues prior to the final vote count.

If a majority of the voters (rather than employees) vote in favor of the proposed bargaining unit, the unit will be established. Even if there is more than one union competing to represent the proposed collective bargaining unit, a simple majority vote is still required for a union to be recognized. If there is no majority vote, the top two choices will have an election to generate a majority vote.

The NLRB can order a new election under certain circumstances if it is determined that the "laboratory conditions" of the secret ballot were disturbed in a way that affected the outcome of the election.

In rare circumstances, the NLRB can require the employer to recognize and bargain with the union if the employer conducted itself in such a seriously egregious manner that the NLRB deems "the holding of a fair election unlikely." This rare situation is referred to as a bargaining order.

Please review the flowchart, available at the following website, which offers a visual representation of this process: www.nlrb.gov/resources/nlrb-process.

Permissible Union Activities

Some of the activities in which unions are permitted to engage are

> **Inside organizing:** Pro-union individuals can seek to influence others at the workplace (unless a no-solicitation rule in effect).

CAUTION

Employers must apply a no-solicitation rule 100% of the time for it to be upheld with respect to any form of inside organizing. Something as simple as selling cookie dough or wrapping paper can be enough to invalidate a no-solicitation rule.

> **Mailing campaign literature to employees' homes.**

> **Leafleting:** This can involve distributing leaflets and flyers offsite or onsite.

> **Local media:** This includes newspaper ads or radio spots.

> **Dedicated websites.**

> **Salting:** A salt is a union organizer who seeks employment with the organization for the express purpose of actively organizing and campaigning within the organization.

> **Organizational picketing:** This is designed to generate interest on the part of employees to vote for union representation.

Permissible Employer Activities

Like unions, employers have the right to engage in certain activities during a union-organizing effort or campaign. Some of those activities include the following:

> Voicing an opinion about unions and the unionization of its operation as long as its communications carry no direct or implied threat toward employees and as long as those communications are in no way coercive. This can be done in a number of ways:

> > Email

> > Hardcopy mail to home addresses

> > Payroll stuffers

- Holding captive audience meetings: The employer can hold mandatory presentations (in the workplace, during regular working hours) during which the employer can share its opinions relative to unions and the unionization of its operations. Unions do not have this opportunity. Captive audience meetings may not be held within 24 hours of the actual election.

- Securing the services of a consultant in its efforts to remain union free.

As always, it is critical to work with counsel—either in house or external—to ensure that the proverbial "legal line" isn't crossed.

Impermissible Union Activities

Like employers, unions are prohibited from engaging in unfair labor practices during a union-organizing campaign. Some activities that would constitute an unfair labor practice on the part of a union would include the following:

- Coercing

- Threatening

- Retaliating or threatening to retaliate

Impermissible Employer Activities

So, too, employers cannot engage in a number of activities during a union campaign—activities that would constitute an unfair labor practice. Some of those activities include the following:

- Telling workers that the employer will fire or punish them if they engage in any union activity

- Laying off or discharging any worker for union activity

- Granting workers wage increases or special concessions in an effort to bribe people from joining a union

- Asking workers about confidential union matters, meetings, members, and so on

- Asking workers about the union or about union representatives

- Asking workers how they intend to vote in a union election

- Asking workers whether they belong to a union or have signed up for a union

- Threatening or coercing workers in an attempt to influence their vote

- Telling workers that existing benefits will be discontinued if the employer is unionized

- Saying unionization will force the employer to lay off workers

- Promising employees promotions, raises, or other benefits if they get out of the union or refrain from joining it

- Spying on union gatherings

Union Decertification and Deauthorization

From time to time, employees may engage in an election process, vote in a union, and ultimately find that things didn't turn out quite the way they expected. It is in situations like this when decertification or deauthorization elections may be held.

Union Decertification

If employees decide that they no longer want to be represented by their union, they must prepare for and hold another election. The process of removing the union's rights to represent the employees is called decertification. This process is similar to certification, only in reverse. It starts with a petition requesting decertification that is signed by at least 30% of employees who belong to the bargaining union being sent to the NLRB. (Decertification cannot occur within the 12-month period following certification after a contract has been negotiated.) The NLRB will then conduct a decertification election if it decides that the petition is in order. If at least 50% of employees who vote (as opposed to 50% of the members of the collective bargaining unit, or CBU) cast a vote to remove the union, then the union will be officially decertified. The union will also be decertified if the vote is exactly even.

Union Deauthorization

Far less frequently, a deauthorization election may be held. Deauthorization revokes the security clause in the contract and effectively creates an "open shop." Deauthorization requires a majority vote of the entire bargaining union, not just the members of the unit who vote in the deauthorization election.

Protected Concerted Activities

Protected concerted activity refers to associational rights that are granted to employees through Section 7 of the NLRA:

> Employees shall have the right to self-organization; to form, join, or assist labor organization; to bargain collectively through representatives of their own choosing; to engage in other concerted activities for the purpose of collective bargaining or other mutual aid or protection; and to refrain from any or all such activities.

> **NOTE**
>
> Through this language, the NLRA protects associational rights for employees who do not belong to a union and for employees who are unionized. This interpretation was confirmed by *NLRB v. Phoenix Mutual Life Insurance Co., 1948*. It is for this reason that employers need to be careful not to interfere with protected concerted activities—even in nonunionized workplaces.

So they don't interfere with concerted activity, employers need to understand what concerted activity is.

Concerted Activity

Any activities undertaken by individual employees who are united in pursuit of a common goal are considered to be concerted activity. For an employee's activity to be concerted, the activity must be engaged in with or on the authority of other employees rather than just on behalf of the individual employee (Meyers Industries, 281 NLRB 882, 1986).

Activity must be concerted before the NLRA can protect it.

Protected Concerted Activity

Section 8 of the NLRA specifically states the following:

> It shall be an unfair labor practice for an employer to interfere with, restrain, or coerce employees in the exercise of the rights guaranteed in [Section 7].

Protected concerted activity can include activity aimed at improving employees' terms and conditions of employment. If an employee is engaged in protected concerted activity, an employer might be considered to have violated the NLRA if all the following are true:

▶ The employer knew of the concerted nature of the employee's activity.

▶ The concerted activity was protected by the Act.

▶ The adverse employment action in question (for instance, termination) was motivated by the employee's protected concerted activity.

Remedies for unfair labor practices include reinstatement with full back pay plus interest. Employers also are required to post a notice to all employees detailing the violation and the remedy.

Example of Protected Concerted Activity

The following are specific cases in which employers were found to have committed an unfair labor practice by interfering with protected concerted activities:

▶ An employer fired a salesman for being an "outspoken critic" against two-hour meetings that sales personnel were required to attend (without compensation) before regular work hours. The employee was awarded reinstatement with full back pay plus interest (*NLRB v. Henry Colder Co., 1990*).

▶ An employer fired two employees who composed a letter protesting a change to the compensation system. The employees were reinstated with full back pay plus interest (*NLRB v. Westmont Plaza, 1990*).

▶ An employer fired employees who mailed a letter to the employer's parent company complaining about working conditions and bonuses. (The employer's president was requiring employees to spend large amounts of time on the president's personal projects.) The employees were reinstated with full back pay plus interest (*NLRB v. Oakes Machine Corp., 1990*).

Labor Strikes

No dialogue about unions would be complete without some discussion of strikes.

There are two very different types of strikes (or work stoppages): unfair labor practice strikes and economic strikes.

Unfair Labor Practice Strikes

Unions sometimes allege, correctly or incorrectly, that the employer has committed a ULP during contract negotiations and call a strike in response to those alleged ULPs. Employers cannot hire permanent strike replacements during a ULP strike, and the striking workers must be returned to their original positions after the strike is over.

It is not enough to assume that a ULP strike is a ULP strike. The courts would need to determine that a strike was, in fact, a ULP strike and not an economic strike in disguise.

Economic Strikes

Any strike that is not directly tied to the employer's commission of a ULP is considered, by law, to be an economic strike. Economic strikes are called in an effort to obtain some sort of economic concession from the employer during collective bargaining negotiations—concessions relating to higher wages, better working conditions, low health-insurance premiums, and the like.

> **NOTE**
>
> Economic strikers cannot be terminated except under highly limited situations, such as if they engage in serious misconduct during the strike. Economic strikers can, however, be permanently replaced by the employer.
>
> Under the Mackay Doctrine, employers have the right to permanently replace workers who strike during an economic strike. This right and its nickname derived from the Supreme Court decision in *NLRB v. Mackay Radio and Telegraph Co., 1938*.
>
> Although it is advisable to avoid using the word "permanent" when describing employment relationships, the term "permanent replacement" is used here because it is the recognized vernacular with respect to strikes.

Perhaps the most renowned example of the use of permanent replacement workers occurred in 1981 when President Ronald Reagan replaced 12,000 striking air traffic controllers. This event had a chilling impact on economic strikes because of concerns relative to employees losing their jobs to permanent replacement workers.

> **NOTE**
>
> The historic impact of this type of strike is not diminished by the fact that workers who have been permanently replaced are entitled to priority status as the employer hires new employees.

Strike-Related Protected Concerted Activities

Economic strikes are considered to be a protected concerted activity under the NLRA. Other protected concerted strike-related activities include sympathy strikes and picketing.

Sympathy Strikes

Employees who are not directly involved in an economic dispute but who choose not to cross a picket line out of support for striking workers are engaging in a sympathy strike. Sympathy strikers do not need to be employed by the same employer as the employees who are actually on strike to engage in a sympathy strike.

Picketing

Picketing is an expression of free speech that takes place when people congregate outside a workplace. To be considered protected concerted activity, picketing must remain nonviolent. Pickets can be used to inform the public, to discourage nonstriking workers from entering the workplace (also referred to as crossing the picket line), and to encourage people to boycott the products or services of the employer who is the subject of the picket.

Double Breasting Picketing

Double breasting picketing, which is actually a type of secondary boycott, takes place when a company that owns or operates union as well as nonunion operations shifts work to the nonunion operation in an effort to diminish the impact of the strike. In this situation, the nonunion operation to which the work has been shifted can be picketed.

Common Situs Picketing

Common situs picketing, which is actually a type of secondary boycott, occurs when members of a labor union picket a workplace in which multiple employers work—the employer with whom the labor union has the dispute, as well as one or more employers with whom the labor union does not have a dispute. Common situs picketing is legal as long as the picket signs indicate the name of the employer with whom the picketers have a dispute.

> **NOTE**
>
> Double breasting picketing and common situs picketing are both examples of secondary boycotts. Secondary boycotts are actions that are ultimately intended to affect a primary party by taking action against a secondary party. Depending on the circumstances, secondary boycotts may or may not be legal.

One specific situation that can clear the way for the union to engage in a secondary boycott is the ally doctrine. The ally doctrine states that a union may expand upon its primary picketing activity to include employers who are allies of the primary employer.

Strike-Related Activity That Is Not Protected Concerted Activity

In addition to strike-related activity that is considered to be protected concerted activity and that is protected by law, there are certain strike-related activities that are not considered to be protected concerted activity.

Wildcat Strikes

If a collective bargaining agreement contains a no-strike clause prohibiting striking during the duration of the agreement, any strikes that occur are considered wildcat strikes. Wildcat strikes are no longer considered to be protected concerted activity.

Jurisdictional Strike

A jurisdictional strike is used to force an employer to assign work to bargaining-unit employees instead of nonbargaining-unit employees. Jurisdictional strikes constitute a ULP, and those who engage in a jurisdictional strike can experience discipline up to and including termination.

> **NOTE**
>
> It is important to check local laws because, for example, some states prohibit strikes of any kind by public employees.

ER & LR Responsibility 11

Direct and/or participate in collective bargaining activities, including contract negotiation, costing, and administration.

RESPONSIBILITY

Knowledge 55

Unfair labor practices.

KNOWLEDGE

Knowledge 56

The collective bargaining process, strategies, and concepts (for example: contract negotiation, costing, and administration).

Collective Bargaining: The Process

Collective bargaining is the process by which an employer and a labor union negotiate the terms of the collective bargaining agreement that will govern the employment relationship for those employees who are represented by the union.

This section will look at a number of specific dimensions of collective bargaining:

► Good faith bargaining

► Subjects of bargaining (required, permissive, and illegal)

► Approaches to collective bargaining

Good Faith Bargaining

According to Section 8(d) of the NLRA, the employer and the union are both required to bargain in good faith. The failure of either the union or the employer to do so is considered to be a ULP. Determining what does and does not constitute good faith bargaining, however, isn't always clear or simple.

Bargaining in good faith doesn't mean that either side is required to reach an agreement or to make concessions. Instead, when ascertaining whether an employer has bargained in good faith, the NLRB will take a more comprehensive look at the activities in which each side has engaged, in their totality.

Sometimes, good faith bargaining is more easily defined by what it's not than by what it is. In other words, good faith bargaining can sometimes be defined by the absence of behaviors that are characteristic of "bad faith bargaining." The following behaviors, when demonstrated by either the union or the employer, could constitute bad faith bargaining:

► Failing to agree to meet at reasonable and convenient places or times

► Failing to show up at the agreed-upon places or times

► Repeatedly canceling meetings

► Failing to maintain an open mind during negotiations

► Surface bargaining: Going through the motions of bargaining, with no real intention of ultimately reaching agreement (in other words, keeping bargaining "at the surface," without moving toward true agreement)

► Repeatedly withdrawing previous positions/concessions

► Refusing to bargain on mandatory items, insisting on bargaining on permissive items, or attempting to bargain on illegal items (see "Illegal Subjects," later in this chapter)

► Committing any sort of ULP(s)

In addition to these items, all of which can be committed by either the employer or the union, there are other examples of bad faith bargaining that the employer could commit:

▶ Taking any action that is deliberately designed to weaken the union's status as the bargaining agent

▶ Presenting proposals directly to employees instead of the union bargaining team

▶ Instituting unilateral changes to wages, hours, and terms and conditions of employment while negotiations are in process

▶ Providing the union with insufficient information with which to make informed proposals and counterproposals

Subjects of Bargaining

The NLRB is empowered to categorize bargaining issues into three categories: required, permissive, and illegal (derived from the Supreme Court decision *NLRB v. Wooster Division of Borg-Warner Corporation, 1958*).

Required Subjects

Required subjects are those that must be bargained in good faith if either the employer or the employees' representative requests it. It's important to keep in mind, however, that according to the NLRA, bargaining in good faith does not require "either party to agree to a proposal or require the making of a concession."

Examples of required subjects include pay, wages, hours of employment, pensions for present employees, bonuses, group insurance, grievance procedures, safety practices, seniority, procedures for discharge, layoff, recall, discipline, and union security.

> **NOTE**
>
> Sometimes, although a certain item may not be considered to be a required subject, implementing that item might have an impact on a required subject. The bargaining that would take place as a result of these impacts is referred to as effects bargaining. For instance, an organization's decision to close a particular plant is not a required subject. The decisions that are made relative to the way employees are treated during—and are affected by—a plant closure is a required subject and is therefore an example of effects bargaining.

Voluntary or Permissive Subjects

Voluntary or permissive subjects are topics that can be submitted to collective bargaining if and only if the employer and the employees' representative are willing to do so. Attempting to force bargaining on a voluntary or permissive subject constitutes a ULP.

For example, voluntary or permissive subjects could include closing plants, shutting down parts of the business, instituting preemployment testing, or modifying retiree benefits.

Illegal Subjects

Certain topics simply cannot be collectively bargained. These would include items that would constitute a violation of the NLRA, labor laws, or, for that matter, any law.

Examples of illegal subjects would include closed-shop agreements, hot cargo clauses, and featherbedding.

Approaches to Collective Bargaining

This section will discuss three primary approaches to collective bargaining: distributive, integrative, and interest based.

Distributive Bargaining

Distributive bargaining takes an approach to bargaining in which each side sets forth its position and does its best to "stick to it." By the end of the process, one side will have won some (or all) of what it wanted, and one side will have lost some (or all) of what it wanted.

Distributive bargaining is essentially adversarial in nature. It assumes that there's only so much to go around. When you divide the pie, therefore, one side will end up with more of the pie, and one side will end up with less of the pie.

By its very nature, the distributive approach to bargaining tends to encourage stubbornness and has a greater likelihood of damaging the parties' relationship with each other.

Integrative Bargaining

The integrative approach to bargaining doesn't look at issues one at a time. Instead, it looks at multiple issues as a whole (hence the term integrative). Integrative bargaining looks at the same pie, but in a different way: instead of just splitting up the pie, it creatively considers how it might be able to make the pie bigger. It looks at how the needs of both sides can be better met when looked at in their entirety and at how a win-win solution can be explored rather than settling for the win-lose scenario that will almost invariably result from distributive bargaining.

In essence, advocates of integrative bargaining believe that an agreement that renders one side "better off" does not necessarily have to result in the other side being "worse off." Instead, through creativity and cooperation, trade-offs are sought that will ultimately benefit both sides.

Interest-Based Bargaining

Roger Fisher and William Ury, authors *of Getting to Yes: Negotiating Agreement Without Giving In*, assert that a "good" agreement is one that is wise and efficient and that ultimately results in everyone involved developing a stronger relationship with each other than they would have had if they had not gone through this negotiation process together.

Fisher and Ury set forth four principles of principled negotiation that can be used effectively in a variety of situations to resolve many types of disputes. Those four principles follow:

- ▶ Separate the people from the problem.
- ▶ Focus on interests rather than positions.
- ▶ Generate a variety of options before settling on one.
- ▶ Resolve disagreements by focusing on objective criteria.

Observing these principles throughout the entire negotiation process will enhance the process as well as the outcome that results from the process. Remaining aware of the other party's perspectives and perceptions throughout the entire process will also greatly strengthen the consensus-building process.

Collective Bargaining Agreements

The output of successful collective bargaining is a collective bargaining agreement (CBA). The CBA contains provisions related to a variety of conditions of employment and outlines the procedures to be used in settling disputes that may arise during the duration of the contract.

Typical Provisions of Collective Bargaining Agreements (Excluding Disciplinary and Grievance Procedures)

Most collective bargaining agreements will include specific guidelines around discipline and discharge, addressing topics such as the following:

- A statement that prohibits discipline or discharge without "cause" or "just cause"

- Establishment of a progressive discipline process (for instance, oral warning, written warning, suspension, discharge) as well as consideration of mitigating factors

- A list of acts that can result in immediate discharge

- A requirement to notify the union of disciplinary actions

- A statement that protects whistleblowers

- Limits on methods that employers may use to conduct investigations (for instance, polygraphs)

- A notification to the employee that he has the right to union representation during a potential disciplinary interview and a guarantee that the interview will not be held until union representation is provided (Weingarten Rights)

NOTE

Weingarten Rights, derived from the Supreme Court decision in *NLRB v. Weingarten, 1975*, established the right of unionized employees to have union representation at an investigatory interview with management if the employee reasonably believes that discipline might result from that meeting. Although the NLRB reversed this decision in 2000 (Epilepsy Foundation of Northeast Ohio, 331 NLRB 676, 2000) and held that nonunion employees also have the right to have a representative present at a meeting of this sort, in 2004 the NLRB returned to its original determination and held that nonunion employees do not have the right to have a coworker or other representative present in a meeting that the employee reasonably believes might result in discipline.

The provisions that are contained within collective bargaining agreements will vary from employer to employer, from union to union, and from situation to situation. Some provisions of a collective bargaining agreement are relatively self-explanatory, and others are less self-evident.

NOTE

For those terms that are relatively self-explanatory, we have indicated either a description or a bullet-point list of the types of stipulations that the provision would seek to address. For those provisions that are somewhat less self-evident, we have also included a definition as well as a sample clause.

The following are the specific provisions that we'll present in this section:

- ▶ Preamble
- ▶ Duration of agreement
- ▶ Nondiscrimination clause
- ▶ Union dues deductions
- ▶ Management rights clause
- ▶ Probation
- ▶ Seniority
- ▶ Bumping rights
- ▶ Hours worked/schedules/rest periods/workdays/overtime
- ▶ No strike/no lockout (also referred to as continuous performance)
- ▶ Wage rates/wage increases
- ▶ Zipper clause
- ▶ Union security clauses (open shop, closed shop, union shop, agency shop, maintenance of membership)
- ▶ Holidays
- ▶ Vacation and personal days
- ▶ Sick days
- ▶ Leaves of absence
- ▶ Performance evaluation/management
- ▶ Layoff and recall

Preamble

A preamble is the introductory and first clause of the collective bargaining agreement. The preamble may articulate the purposes of the agreement, formally recognize the employees' representative, define terms that will be used in the agreement, and basically set the stage for the remaining provisions of the agreement.

Sample preamble clause:

This Agreement is between (the employer), hereinafter called the "Employer" and (the union), hereinafter called the "Union."

This Agreement has as its purpose the joint commitment to achieve the Employer's goals of (A, B, and C) between (the Employer) and the Union; the establishment of an equitable and peaceful procedure for the resolution of differences; and the expression of the full and complete understanding of the parties pertaining to all terms and conditions of employment.

The term "employee" when used hereinafter in this Agreement shall refer to employees represented by the Union in the bargaining unit unless otherwise stated. Any member of the Employer's management referenced in this Agreement may specify a designee.

Titles of articles, sections, and subsections of this Agreement are meant for ease of reading and may not be used to interpret or clarify the text of the language.

Duration of Agreement

The duration of agreement identifies the first date on which the contract is effective and the last date on which the contract is effective.

Sample duration of agreement clause:

> This Agreement shall be effective as of 12:00 a.m. July 1, 2014 and shall continue in full force and effect until midnight, June 30, 2017.

Nondiscrimination Clause

In a nondiscrimination clause, the contract expressly prohibits discrimination on various grounds such as sex, race, creed, color, religion, age, national origin, political affiliation or activity, disability, sexual orientation, or union activity. The nondiscrimination clause might also specifically prohibit sexual harassment.

Sample nondiscrimination clause:

> There shall be no discrimination or intimidation by (the Employer) or by (the employees' representative) against any unit member as a result of, or because of such Member's race, color, creed, sex, age, national origin, disability as qualified by law, or membership/nonmembership in the Union.

Union Dues Deductions

With union dues deductions, employers agree to deduct and forward to the union dues amounts agreed to by workers. By law, employees must agree in writing to this deduction. There is some debate, litigious and otherwise, as to whether dues checkoff constitutes a union security clause.

Sample union dues deductions clause:

> (The Employer) agrees to deduct from the wages of any employee who is a member of the Union a deduction as provided for in written authorization. Such authorization must be executed by the employee and may be revoked by the employee at any time by giving written notice to both (the Employer) and the Union. (The Employer) agrees to remit any deductions made pursuant to this provision promptly to the Union together with an itemized statement showing the name of each employee from whose pay such deductions have been made and the amount deducted during the period covered by the remittance. Deductions shall be sent by the Board to the Union by separate check from membership dues and/or fair share fees.

Management Rights Clause

With a management rights clause, management reserves the right, in terms that are either general or highly specific, to manage the organization as it sees fit unless those rights have been specifically modified in the labor contract through a reserved rights doctrine.

Sample management rights clause:

> The parties agree that only the written specific, express terms of this Agreement bind (the Employer). Except as specifically and expressly provided in this written Agreement, (the Employer) has full and complete discretion to make decisions and implement changes in operations, including those affecting wages, hours, terms, and conditions of employment of members of the bargaining unit, without prior negotiation with or the

agreement of the (employees' representative) except as to the effects of such decisions. The (employees' representative) expressly waives any and all right that it may have to bargain about the decision to make any change in operations, practices, or policies that affect wages, hours, and terms and other conditions of employment of employees in the bargaining unit. Any arbitrators used by the parties under Article (XX) shall give full force and effect to this section.

Probation

Probation is defined as the length of the probationary period, the purpose of the probationary period, and employee status and rights during the probationary period.

Sample probation clause:

▶ A new employee shall be appointed on probation for a period of three months and may be extended for a further three months if deemed necessary by (the Employer) to assess the employee's suitability or otherwise for confirmation in his or her appointment provided such extension shall be made at least one week prior to the completion of his or her probationary period.

▶ At any time during the probationary period, such employment may be terminated by either (the Employer) or the employee on one day's notice being given without any reason being assigned for such termination.

▶ On completion of an employee's probation, (the Employer) shall normally inform the employee in writing whether or not the employee is confirmed in his or her employment. But in the event that (the Employer) has omitted to do so, the appointment of the employee concerned shall be deemed to have been confirmed from the date of the completion of his or her probation and the period of probation shall be deemed as part of the employee's period of service.

Seniority

Seniority is the length of time that an employee has been employed by the employer. Seniority can also be defined, however, as seniority within a position, seniority within a department, seniority within a location, and the like. In collective bargaining agreements, seniority can play an important role with respect to decisions such as promotions layoffs, shift bids, and bumping rights.

Sample seniority clause:

It shall be the policy of the department to recognize the seniority principle. Seniority time shall consist of the total calendar time elapsed since the date of original employment with (the Employer); no time prior to a discharge for cause or a quit shall be included. Seniority shall not be diminished by temporary layoffs or leaves of absence or contingencies beyond the control of the parties to this Agreement.

Bumping Rights

Bumping rights is the process by which a more senior employee whose position is being eliminated may, instead of losing employment with the organization, choose to replace a less senior employee (assuming that the more senior employee is qualified for the position into which she "wants to bump"). This can ultimately lead to a situation in which a person who was not originally slated for job elimination, in fact, loses her job.

Sample bumping rights clause:

> A regular employee who is to be laid off may elect to displace an employee with less service seniority where the laid off employee has the necessary skills, abilities, experience, education, qualifications, and certifications to perform the other position. Where an employee elects to displace another employee with less service seniority, he or she shall notify (the Employer) within ten (10) days of his or her receipt of notice of layoff; or where an employee exercises his or her right to displace an employee with less service seniority, the (employees' representative) shall be notified in writing by copy of the acknowledgement letter to the employee.

Hours Worked/Schedules/Rest Periods/Workdays/Overtime

Clauses related to hours worked, rest period, workdays, and overtime help to further establish the tangible terms and conditions of employment. Topics including shifts worked and changes to scheduled shifts may also be addressed.

Sample hours worked/schedules/rest periods/workdays/overtime clause:

> The standard workweek consists of seven consecutive days and shall begin at 12:01 a.m. Saturday. The standard work schedule for full-time employees shall be forty (40) hours per workweek, normally scheduled in shifts of eight (8) hours. Meal periods shall consist of thirty minutes and shall not count as time worked if the employee is completely relieved from duty. Employees who are completely relieved from duty shall not be required to be accessible during the meal period. Normal hours of work are from 7:00 a.m. to 3:30 p.m. Shifts are: Day, 7:00 a.m. to 3:30 p.m.; Swing, 3:00 p.m. to 11:00 p.m.; and Owl, 11:00 p.m. to 7:00 a.m. Rest periods not to exceed 15 minutes, once during each half of an eight-hour shift, will be granted to employees. The time shall not be taken at the beginning or end of a work period, and rest periods shall not be accumulated. Rest periods shall be taken unless operational necessity requires that they be denied.

No Strike/No Lockout (Also Referred to as "Continuous Performance")

In a no-strike clause, the union agrees not to strike for the duration of the contract. Usually, a union will agree to a no-strike clause in exchange for a clause to engage in binding arbitration in the event that an impasse is reached relative to administration of the contract.

Sample no-strike clause:

> No strike of any kind shall be instigated, encouraged, condoned, or caused by (the employees' representative) during the term of this Agreement.

In a no-lockout clause, the employer agrees not to lock out employees for the duration of the contract. In this context, a lockout is defined as a situation in which the employer prevents some or all employees from working. Usually an employer will agree to a no-lockout clause only in exchange for a no-strike clause.

Sample no-lockout clause:

> No lock out of employees shall be instituted by the Employer during the term of this Agreement.

Wages Rates/Wage Increases

Wage rates and wage increases are defined by how much and when employees will be paid for the various services they render. This clause can also address shift differentials, standby or on-call pay, reporting/call-back pay, and roll-call pay.

Sample wage rates clause:

▶ (The Employer) agrees to pay and the (employees' representative) agrees to accept the schedule of job classifications and wage rates attached hereto as Wage Schedule I and Wage Schedule II for the term of this Agreement.

▶ When an employee is temporarily assigned to a position having a lower rate of pay than his/her regular position, his/her rate of pay shall not be reduced during such temporary assignment. It is understood that this clause does not apply to any situation when the downward assignment has been as a result of a layoff within the Bargaining Unit.

▶ When an employee is temporarily assigned to a position having a higher rate of pay than his/her regular position, and such assignment is in excess of two (2) consecutive hours, he/she shall be paid at the higher rate of pay for the entire time served in such higher assignment.

Sample wage increases clause:

Wages for bargaining unit members are set forth in the Wage Schedule attached as Appendix A. "Steps" set forth in the wage schedule generally reflect a member's years of continuous service with (the Employer) as a regular contract (employee in a particular position), unless placement in the wage schedule was modified upon the employee's initial hiring in accordance with provisions of this Article. Step increases shall be effective on the first day of July following the completion of one (1) year.

Effective July 1, 2015, all members shall advance to the next step in the wage scale each year in accordance with the terms of this Agreement.

Unit members who have transferred from other positions in (the Employer) may be placed at any step on the wage scale not to exceed their years of service in the district.

Each member shall receive written notice of the wage schedule step he or she is placed at effective within thirty (30) days of (Employer) approval of this Agreement, and thereafter shall receive written notice of the step he or she advances to each subsequent July.

Zipper Clause

With a zipper clause, both parties agree that the agreement is an exclusive and complete "expression of consent"—in other words, the only items that can be collectively bargained until the expiration of the agreement are those contained within the agreement. In other words, after the agreement is signed, new subjects cannot be added and existing subjects cannot be reopened for negotiation. The contract has been "zipped" closed.

Sample zipper clause:

All matters within the scope of bargaining have been negotiated and agreed upon. The terms and conditions set forth in this Agreement represent the full and complete understanding and commitment between (the Employer) and (the employees' representative). During the term of this Agreement, there shall be no change in (the Employer's) regulations or departmental policies on matters within the scope of negotiations without notice to the (employees' representative) and providing the (employees' representative) the opportunity to bargain the impacts and effects.

Union Security Clause

Union security clauses are included in some agreements in an effort to protect the interests, strength, and security of the union. Union security clauses regulate membership in the union and, consequently, relate to the payment of dues. Some of the more common types of union security clauses include

- **Open shop:** Employees are required neither to join the union nor to pay union dues. This is the only type of union security clause that is legal in right-to-work states (and for federal government employees).

- **Closed shop:** Employers can hire only employees who are already members of the union. Closed shops were ruled illegal by the Taft-Hartley Act; however, hiring halls do in one sense encourage a closed shop arrangement. A hiring hall is a union-operated placement office that refers registered applicants to jobs on the basis of a seniority or placement system.

- **Union shop:** Newly hired employees must join the union within a specified period of time, usually 30 days, and must remain a member of the union as a condition of employment. In a union shop, employers must terminate employees who are not union members.

  Union shops are illegal in right-to-work states.

- **Agency shop:** Employees are not required to join the union. They must, however, pay a monthly fee that is typically equivalent to union dues.

  Agency shops are illegal in right-to-work states.

- **Maintenance of membership:** Employees who voluntarily choose to join a union must maintain their individual memberships for the duration of the labor contract. Each employee then has a 30-day window at the beginning of the next contract period during which he may terminate membership. Maintenance of membership arrangements are illegal in right-to-work states.

NOTE

Beck Rights are the right for bargaining unit members to pay only that portion of union dues attributable to mainline union responsibilities (collective bargaining, organizing in the same industry, contract administration, and the like). It is up to the employee, however, to exercise her Beck Rights. These rights were established by the Supreme Court decision in *Communication Workers of America v. Beck, 1988.*

Holidays

Terms and conditions that could be delineated in the bargaining agreement clause might include the following:

- Number of holidays granted per year

- Designated holidays (with specific dates) versus "floating" holidays

- Terms of pay for working on a holiday

- Right to equivalent time off for time worked on a holiday

- Procedures for assigning holiday work

- Special circumstances—for example, "one-time" holidays

Vacation and Personal Days

Terms and conditions that could be delineated in the bargaining agreement clause might include the following:

- Number of vacation and personal days accrued per year and procedure for using
- Right to take accrued vacation
- Procedure and time of year for scheduling
- Role of seniority in scheduling vacations and personal days
- Right to carry over vacation to next year, and the amount that can be carried over
- Procedure for payment upon death, resignation, or retirement of employee
- Prorated vacation for part-time employees

Sick Days

Terms and conditions that could be delineated in the bargaining agreement clause might include the following:

- Days accrued per year and maximum accumulation
- Right to use for doctor's appointments
- Right to use for ill family members
- Provision for cash out of sick leave
- Provision for sick leave bank
- Prorated sick leave for part-time employees
- Interaction of sick leave policy with Family and Medical Leave Act (FMLA) and Americans with Disabilities Act (ADA)
- Documentation required for sick leave; protections of employee privacy rights

Leaves of Absence

Terms and conditions that could be delineated in the bargaining agreement clause might include the following:

- Right to take leave, administrative rules for requesting leave, duration of leave, pay during leave, continuation of benefits during leave, and reinstatement after leave
- Parental leave, including adoption leave
- Elder care leave
- Bereavement leave: relatives or household members covered, number of days, extra time when travel required
- Educational leave, leave to attend professional meetings, sabbaticals
- Leave for jury duty
- Military leave with responsibility of employer to hold open same job, shift, and other conditions

- ▶ Leave for union business

- ▶ Leave for voting

- ▶ Family and medical leave: benefits, if any, in addition to those in law (for example, longer period of paid leave than required by law), description of employee and employer rights and responsibilities under law

Performance Evaluation/Management

Terms and conditions that could be delineated in the bargaining agreement clause might include the following:

- ▶ Criteria for evaluations

- ▶ Frequency of evaluations

- ▶ Right of employee to receive copies of evaluations

- ▶ Right to rebut or grieve performance evaluations

- ▶ Limitations on use of performance evaluations (for example, not to determine pay, bidding rights, and so on)

Layoff and Recall

Knowledge 53

Individual employment rights issues and practices (for example: employment at will, negligent hiring, defamation).

KNOWLEDGE

Terms and conditions that could be delineated in the bargaining agreement clause might include the following:

- ▶ Procedures for layoff based on seniority provisions

- ▶ Prior notification to union of layoffs, right of union to offer alternative proposals or plans

- ▶ Rights of employees to bump into positions of less senior employees

- ▶ Procedures for recalling employees; duration of recall list

Earlier in this chapter, we focused on the commonalities that unite employee relations and labor relations. Next, however, we'll begin to look at how these two areas begin to diverge, starting with laws and legal principles.

We'll start by looking at common law and the individual employee rights that accrue from it. We'll then take a closer look at the legal doctrines associated with common law—tort doctrines and contract doctrines. Last, we'll look at some of the legal agreements that employees are asked to make in exchange for securing employment with the organization (specifically, mandatory arbitration agreements, noncompete agreements, and confidentiality agreements).

Common Law

Common law refers to a system of law in which traditions, customs, and precedents have the same force of law as existing laws or statutes that have been enacted as a result of the full legislative process. With a common law system, laws and statutes are quite literally interpreted and reinterpreted on a case-by-case basis. The way this works is that each interpretation and each case sets a precedent, but each can also be reinterpreted, thus setting a new precedent. As it evolves, this continual process of interpretation and reinterpretation results in rights being granted to employees on an individual basis.

> **NOTE**
>
> Although—in a technical sense—common law applies to all employees, common law is eclipsed by the presence of an individual employment contract or collective bargaining agreement. In other words, if there is an employment contract in place, or if an employee belongs to a union that has negotiated an agreement, the terms that are outlined in that contract or agreement will supersede the precedents created by common law.
>
> Unionized employees might also be asked to adhere to one or more of these three types of agreements, in which case corresponding articles would almost certainly be included as part of a larger collectively bargained agreement.

The common law system holds true at the federal and state levels (with the exception of Louisiana, which follows Napoleonic Law). It is composed of two subtypes of law: tort law and contract law.

Common Law—Tort Doctrines

Torts are wrongful acts committed against another individual's property or person. By definition, the commission of a tort infringes on another person's rights.

Torts can include anything from damage or injuries sustained in an automobile accident, to malicious prosecution, to false imprisonment—the list could go on and on. This section, however, will specifically address some of the major tort doctrines that affect individual employee rights in the absence of an employment or labor contract. Specifically, we'll take a look at the following:

- Employment-at-will
- Wrongful termination
- Implied contracts
- Defamation
- Invasion of privacy
- Negligent hiring
- Negligent training
- Negligent retention
- Negligent referral

Employment-at-Will

Under the employment-at-will doctrine, the employer and the employee are both granted broad rights, most of which focus on the right of either party to terminate the employment relationship at any time for any lawful reason. A number of important exceptions to the employment-at-will doctrine exist, some of which are discussed in the following sections.

Lawful Reasons

Although seemingly self-explanatory, lawful reasons deserves a second look. Employees cannot be fired, for instance, for engaging in protected concerted activity or because they belong to a particular protected class.

> **CAUTION**
>
> Although everyone involved in the hiring/employment/termination process shares in this responsibility, HR must be particularly diligent about ensuring that a lawful, legitimate, nondiscriminatory reason exists and can be articulated when a decision is made to terminate an employee.

Public Policy Exception

Most states have adopted the public policy exception, which holds that an employer may not terminate an employee if the termination would violate public policy. For instance, an employee cannot be fired for serving on jury duty, for engaging in protected whistleblower activity, or for reporting safety violations to OSHA.

Wrongful Termination

In certain circumstances, employees who believe that they have been terminated wrongfully— in a legal sense, that is—may pursue a tort action. One possible basis for wrongful termination could exist if an employee was terminated in violation of an individual employment contract in which specific requirements were articulated. Others might apply as well but would vary from state to state.

Implied Contracts

Just because a formal written employment contract isn't in existence doesn't mean that a contract—specifically, an implied contract—is not in force.

There are two primary ways that an implied contract can be created: through documents that the employer has "published" and through oral statements.

Written Documents or Publications

Sometimes the language that is used within employer-published publications (electronic or hardcopy) can be sufficient to create a contract between the employer and the employees. As one example, this can happen because of language that is used in an employee handbook. For instance, language in a handbook stating that an employee will only be terminated for "good cause" or "just cause" could be problematic, in that a court could then interpret that an employer may terminate an employee only when that standard is met.

"Just Cause" or "Good Cause"

"Just cause" or "good cause" refers to a particular legal standard or test that is used to ascertain whether a specific disciplinary action was appropriate. Factors that may be considered in determining whether this standard was met could include the following:

▶ Whether the employee was warned in advance

▶ Whether the rule or standard that was violated was reasonable

▶ Whether a legitimate investigation looking into the totality of the circumstances around the alleged violation was conducted

▶ Whether reasonable "proof" of the violation existed or was obtained through investigation

▶ Whether the rule has been applied consistently

▶ Whether the punishment is proportionate to the violation

Oral Contract

An oral contract can be created when an agent of the employer promises some benefit or right. The term agent is legal and involved, but the point is this—be careful what your supervisors, recruiters, and others say to current (and also to potential) employees. If you have your doubts as to the veracity of this statement, look back at the avalanche of oral contract claims that resulted from the boon of dot-coms—many of which became "dot bombs." Even a cursory glance should dispel any doubts you might have.

Good Faith and Fair Dealing

Good faith and fair dealing is a somewhat less frequently recognized exception to the employment-at-will doctrine. The good faith and fair dealing exception to employment-at-will kicks in when a court decides that an employer has treated an employee unfairly or has failed to provide some benefit to that employee. Two examples of this might be an employer who terminates an employee to avoid paying stock options or one who terminates an employee right before her retirement benefits vest.

Defamation

Defamation is a legal term that, in a general and practical sense, refers to making a false statement that damages someone's character or reputation. Defamation that is in written form is referred to as libel, and defamation that is made through the spoken word is referred to as slander. An employee could sue an employer for libel or slander for a variety of reasons. Just one example of this might be providing a false reference to potential employers.

A key requirement for defamation is that the statement (whether oral or written) must be false.

Invasion of Privacy

The right to privacy is a highly complex doctrine relating to several amendments of the U.S. Constitution, in particular the Fourth Amendment:

> The right of the people to be secure in their persons, houses, papers, and effects, against unreasonable searches and seizures, shall not be violated, and no warrants shall issue, but upon probable cause, supported by oath or affirmation, and particularly describing the place to be searched, and the persons or things to be seized.

The Fourth Amendment, however, addresses and protects individuals only against searches and seizures that the government conducts. Invasions of privacy by individuals who are not state actors (a person who is acting on behalf of the government) must be addressed through private tort law, which is why we are discussing it here. Please also note that public employers must adhere to the Fourth Amendment. As such, compelling all employees to random drug tests as a condition of continued employment might violate the Fourth Amendment and would have to be negotiated into the collective-bargaining agreement

Modern tort law includes four categories of invasion of privacy:

▶ Intrusion of solitude

▶ Public disclosure of private and embarrassing facts

▶ False light

▶ Appropriation of identity

Negligent Hiring

Negligent hiring refers to the process of hiring an employee without engaging in appropriate due diligence into that candidate's credentials, prior work experience, and the like. Negligent hiring tort claims might be filed after an employee who was hired through a flawed hiring process inflicts some sort of harm on another person—harm that could have been predicted (and therefore prevented) if the employer had conducted a background check. A hiring process can be flawed for a number of reasons. For instance, a sound hiring process that is applied in an unsound manner would be flawed, as would a hiring process that is designed in a flawed manner. Flaws could relate to inadequate or poorly conducted reference checks, job requirements that do not reflect the skills or credentials that are truly required for a position, and the like.

Example: *Tallahassee Furniture Co. v. Harrison, 1991*

Tallahassee Furniture Company hired a delivery person without interviewing him, having him fill out an employment application, or conducting any sort of background check. After entering a customer's home to deliver furniture, the delivery person stabbed and raped her. It was subsequently found that this employee had a long history of psychiatric problems (which had been serious enough to result in his hospitalization) and a history of drug abuse. The court ruled that the company should have conducted a background check before giving him a job that afforded him access to customers' homes and awarded $2.5 million.

Negligent Training

Negligent training refers to an employer's failure to provide proper training to an employee when that failure results in some sort of unfit performance by the employee. A negligent training tort claim might be filed, for instance, when an employee inflicts some sort of harm on another person—harm that might not have been inflicted by that employee if the employer had provided him with appropriate training.

Negligent training can emerge as an issue either when an employee who was hired for one position assumes another position for which he may not be fully qualified or appropriately trained or when an employee's job duties and responsibilities change over time, thus requiring additional training if the employee is to continue performing the job in a fit manner.

Example: *Gamble v. Dollar General Corp., 2002*

Heather Gamble went to a Dollar General Store in Purvis, Mississippi, to buy a shirt. At some point, Gamble left the store, returned to her car, and realized that a Dollar General employee had followed her out of the store. The employee subsequently followed Gamble to a Family Dollar store and parked behind Gamble. Gamble stepped out of her car and asked the employee why she was following her. Words were exchanged, and the employee—who decided that Gamble had not (as she had suspected) shoplifted anything from Dollar General—left Gamble in the parking lot of Family Dollar. During the trial, it was shown that although Dollar General had a written shoplifting policy that prohibited employees from leaving the store to pursue suspected shoplifters and from touching shoplifters, Dollar General had not provided its employees with training on how to handle actual or suspected shoplifting situations. The jury awarded Gamble $75,000 in compensatory damages and $100,000 in punitive damages in part on the basis of a finding of negligent training.

Negligent Retention

Negligent retention refers to the continued employment of an individual who is performing in an unfit manner and therefore should have been terminated. Negligent retention tort claims might be filed when an employee who should have been terminated but was not inflicts some sort of harm on another person.

Negligent retention claims are often filed in conjunction with other tort claims, such as negligent training, intentional infliction of emotional distress, and the like.

Negligent Referral

Negligent referral refers to the failure of an organization to reveal truthful, negative information about an employee (or former employee) to a potential employer.

NOTE

Negligent referral highlights the complexities of navigating the choppy waters of tort litigation. The irony in this situation lies in the reality that many organizations confine their remarks about current and former employees to the employee's name, title, and dates of employment—often in an effort to avoid defamation claims. Although this approach may limit the employer's liability for defamation claims, it could simultaneously increase the employer's liability with respect to negligent reference if the employer conceals truthful negative information about an employee.

Once again, these situations are complex, multifaceted, and fraught with potential legal pitfalls. Consult with counsel—in house or outside—with any and all questions.

> **Example:** *Randi W. v. Muroc Joint Unified School Dist., 1997*
>
> Officials at several school districts recommended a former employee even although that employee had been the subject of several complaints relating to sexual misconduct with students. Two situations were so serious that the employee was forced to resign. Despite all this, the employee moved from one school district to another, bolstered in large part by recommendations from the school districts for which he had worked. Letters from the former employers recommended the employee "for almost any administrative position he wishes to pursue" and commended his efforts to make "a safe, orderly and clean environment for students and staff." He was hired at another school district and ultimately molested a 13-year-old girl in his office. The court found that these misleading employment recommendations amounted to "an affirmative misrepresentation presenting a foreseeable and substantial risk of physical harm to a third person" and that the student who filed the complaint had successfully established a prima facie case of negligent misrepresentation.

Common Law—Contract Doctrines

Another way in which common law directly affects the employment relationship is through contract doctrines. A contract is an agreement that is enforceable by law. Contracts can be either oral or written.

Employment contracts are made between an employer and an employee. They can include topics such as term or length of employment, compensation and benefits, job responsibilities, and termination.

> **NOTE**
>
> The terms and conditions under which an employee can be terminated constitute a critical element of any employment contract. Specifically, the contract should state whether the employee is employed under the employment-at-will doctrine, or—conversely—whether the employee can be terminated only for just cause.

Employees are often asked to sign specific agreements in exchange for the opportunity to work for the employer. Three agreements that we'll look at in this section include the following:

- Mandatory arbitration agreements
- Noncompete agreements
- Confidentiality agreements

Mandatory Arbitration Agreements

More and more, potential employees are being asked to agree in writing to mandatory arbitration. This means that, in return for the opportunity to be employed by the organization, the employee agrees to resolve employment-related issues through a neutral third party (the arbitrator/s) instead of filing a private lawsuit against the employer.

The landmark U.S. Supreme Court case that confirmed the legality of mandatory arbitration agreements was *Circuit City Stores, Inc. v. Adams, 2001*, in which the court ruled that requiring employees to sign mandatory arbitration agreements as a condition of employment is legal and that such agreements are enforceable under the Federal Arbitration Act (FAA).

Less than 10 months later, in *EEOC v. Waffle House, Inc., 2002*, the court ruled that although the existence of a signed mandatory arbitration agreement precluded the employee from being allowed to file a private lawsuit, it did not preclude the EEOC from seeking its own independent action against an employer because the EEOC cannot be bound by a private arbitration agreement to which it was not a party. More specifically, the EEOC is not required to "relinquish its statutory authority if it has not agreed to do so" and that, as "the master of its own case," the EEOC can independently determine whether it will commit resources to specific cases.

Noncompete Agreements

Noncompete agreements prohibit current and (within stated limitations) former employees from competing against the employer.

Noncompete agreements are addressed more thoroughly in Chapter 2.

Confidentiality Agreements

Confidentiality agreements prohibit employees from revealing any confidential information to which they might be exposed during the course of their employment.

Confidentiality agreements are addressed more thoroughly in Chapter 2.

NOTE

The following Employee and Labor Relations Responsibility pertains to responsibilities and areas of knowledge addressed in Pearson's *SPHR Exam Prep*.

RESPONSIBILITY

ER & LR Responsibility 10

Develop and direct proactive employee relations strategies for remaining union-free in nonorganized locations.

Chapter Summary

Often, HR professionals think that the purpose or "bottom line" of effective employee relations is making employees happy. It isn't. Even setting aside the fact that no one can make anyone else happy, there are problems with this premise. First, using the goal of making employees happy as our benchmark of success merely reaffirms the erroneous perception of HR professionals as "people people" rather than as business people. Second, it ignores the organization's measures of success. It is against these organizational measures of success that we must be prepared to measure our employee relations initiatives. So, to be considered successful, an employee relations initiative must bring the organization closer to achieving its objectives, furthering its mission, and attaining its vision—all while remaining consistent with the organization's values. In short, the bottom line is that employee relations must measurably support and reinforce the bottom line of the organization.

Employee relations and labor relations are terms that encompass practices and responsibilities that are far reaching and of critical importance. They are also terms that can sometimes evoke strong feelings and reactions.

In the beginning of this chapter, we described employee relations as

- The way in which an organization responds to, handles, or addresses any issue that has impact on employees and their relationships

- To and with other employees

- To and with managers

- To and with those outside the organization with whom they come in contact as part of their employment experience

Throughout this chapter, we attempted to explore the myriad ways in which these relationships can manifest themselves, as well as the many factors that need to be considered when it comes to relationships with employees. We also looked at the history, legality, processes, tools, and importance of labor relations.

It is our hope that, after having journeyed through this chapter, you will understand the true impact of your role more fully—and, therefore, be better equipped to perform it even more effectively. (We also hope that you perform exceedingly well in your role as PHR candidate.)

Key Terms

- Employee relations

- Labor relations

- Sherman Antitrust Act, 1890

- Clayton Act, 1914

- Railway Labor Act, 1926

- Norris-LaGuardia Act, 1932

- National Industrial Recovery Act, 1933

- National Labor Relations Act (Wagner Act), 1935

- Unfair labor practice

- National Labor Relations Board

- Closed shop

- Union shop

- Labor Management Relations Act (Taft-Hartley Act), 1947

- Primary boycott

- Secondary boycott

- Dues

- Featherbedding
- Picketing
- Recognition picketing
- Hot cargo agreements
- Right-to-work states
- Strike
- Jurisdictional strike
- U. S. conciliation service
- Federal Mediation and Conciliation Service (FMCS)
- Labor Management Reporting and Disclosure Act (Landrum-Griffin Act), 1959
- Federal Labor Relations Statute (Title VII of the Civil Service Reform Act), 1978
- *Schechter Poultry Corp. v. United States, 1935*
- *NLRB v. Mackay Radio and Telegraph Co., 1938*
- *NLRB. v. Weingarten, 1975*
- *Communication Workers of America v. Beck, 1988*
- Specialty Healthcare and Rehabilitation Center of Mobile, 2011
- Employee surveys
- Focus groups
- Employee participation groups
- Open-door policies
- Suggestion programs
- Management by walking around (MBWA)
- Confidentiality
- Organizational culture
- Employee involvement strategies
- Employee communication strategies
- Diversity
- Inclusion
- Employee handbook
- Turnover
- Absenteeism
- Work-related accidents/injuries/ "preventable" illnesses

- Productivity
- Quality
- Customer satisfaction
- Employee survey results
- Return on investment (ROI)
- Quantitative analysis
- Correlation
- Measures of central tendency
  - Mean
  - Median
  - Mode
- Qualitative analysis
- The Delphi technique
- Nominal group technique
- Progressive discipline
  - Discussion of substandard performance issue
  - Verbal warning
  - Written warning
  - Final written warning or suspension
  - Involuntary termination
- Business/organizational ethics
- Discipline and discharge
- Grievance handling
- Contract administration
- Grievance procedure
  - **Step 1:** Initiate a complaint.
  - **Step 2:** Escalate the complaint internally.
  - **Step 3:** Reach the highest level of internal escalation.
  - **Step 4:** Participate in binding arbitration.
- Contract negotiation
- Contract administration
- Local unions
- National unions
- Federations
- International labor organizations
- Union organizing

▸ Authorization cards

▸ Recognition

▸ Campaign

▸ Election

▸ Salting

▸ Organizational picketing

▸ Captive audience meetings

▸ Union decertification

▸ Union deauthorization

▸ Protected concerted activity

▸ Labor strikes

▸ Unfair labor practice (ULP) strikes

▸ Economic strikes

▸ Sympathy strikes

▸ Double breasting picketing

▸ Common situs picketing

▸ Wildcat strikes

▸ Jurisdictional strikes

▸ Collective bargaining

▸ Good faith bargaining

▸ Surface bargaining

▸ Required subjects

▸ Voluntary of permissive subjects

▸ Illegal subjects

▸ Distributive bargaining

▸ Integrative bargaining

▸ Interest-based bargaining

▸ Collective bargaining agreements

▸ Bumping rights

▸ Zipper clause

▸ Union security clause

▸ Agency shop

▸ Beck Rights

▸ Common law

▸ Tort doctrines

    ▸ Employment-at-will

    ▸ Wrongful termination

    ▸ Implied contracts

    ▸ Defamation

    ▸ Invasion of privacy

    ▸ Negligent hiring

    ▸ Negligent training

    ▸ Negligent retention

    ▸ Negligent referral

▸ Just cause

▸ Good cause

▸ Oral contract

▸ Good faith and fair dealing

▸ Common law—*Contract Doctrines Circuit City Stores, Inc. v. Adams, 2001*

▸ Federal Arbitration Act (FAA)

▸ Noncompete agreements

Apply Your Knowledge

This chapter focuses on issues relating to employee and labor relations. Complete the following review questions and exam questions as a way of reviewing and reinforcing the knowledge and skills you'll need to perform your responsibilities as an HR professional and to increase the likelihood that you will pass the PHR examination.

Review Questions

1. Explore and discuss "progressive discipline" within the context of its role as an employee involvement program.

2. Describe and compare local unions and national unions.

3. Compare and contrast distributive and integrative approaches to collective bargaining.

4. Describe negligent hiring.

5. Describe and discuss grievance handling.

Exam Questions

1. All the following represent measures that could be helpful in measuring the effectiveness of employee relations initiatives except

   ○ **A.** Turnover

   ○ **B.** Absenteeism

   ○ **C.** Unionization

   ○ **D.** Work-related accidents/injuries/"preventable" illnesses

2. Employers should not create policies prohibiting employees from discussing their earnings/compensation with each other for the following reason:

   ○ **A.** Doing so constitutes poor employee relations and could result in higher turnover and lower morale.

   ○ **B.** Doing so could constitute a violation of the NLRA.

   ○ **C.** Doing so could constitute a violation of Title VII of the Civil Rights Act of 1964.

   ○ **D.** This question contains a false assertion; there is no substantive reason why employers cannot establish a policy prohibiting employees from discussing earnings.

3. The NLRA identified all the following as unfair labor practices (for employers) except

   ○ **A.** To dominate or interfere with the formation or administration of a labor organization

   ○ **B.** To discriminate against employees for engaging in concerted or union activities or refraining from them

   ○ **C.** To discriminate against an employee for filing charges with the FMCS or taking part in any FMCS proceedings

   ○ **D.** To refuse to bargain with the union that is the lawful representative of its employees

4. Yellow dog agreements

   ○ **A.** Occur when employers agree to give an employee a job as long as the employee agrees not to join or be involved with a union

   ○ **B.** Occur when employers agree to give an employee a job as long as the employee agrees to join a union and to advocate on the employer's behalf

   ○ **C.** Occur when a union agrees not to seek recognition at a particular employer

   ○ **D.** Occur when a union agrees not to advocate on behalf of an employee in a particular grievance

5. Featherbedding refers to

   ○ **A.** A requirement that anyone who is hired by the organization must join the union

   ○ **B.** An agreement that requires the employer to pay wages to union members whether or not their work is needed

   ○ **C.** A requirement to pay "prevailing wages" on federal government construction contracts and most contracts for federally assisted construction greater than $2,000

   ○ **D.** An agreement that an employer will stop doing business with another entity (most frequently a nonunion entity)

6. Weingarten Rights, derived from the U.S. Supreme Court decision in *NLRB v. Weingarten, 1975*, established the right of unionized employees to

  ○ **A.** Have union representative at meetings with supervisors/management if the employee chooses to do so

  ○ **B.** Have union representation at investigatory meetings with management if the employee reasonably believes that discipline might result

  ○ **C.** Have the EEOC take its own independent action even when a binding arbitration agreement is in place

  ○ **D.** Pay only that portion of union dues that is attributable to mainline union responsibilities

7. Many, although not all, agreements outline a grievance procedure that includes all the following steps except

  ○ **A.** Initiating a formal complaint

  ○ **B.** Notifying the NLRB of the complaint

  ○ **C.** Escalating the complaint internally

  ○ **D.** Participating in binding arbitration

8. All the following statements about defamation are false except

  ○ **A.** An employer cannot be sued for making negative statements about a current or former employee unless those statements have been recorded.

  ○ **B.** Defamation that is in written form is referred to as slander.

  ○ **C.** Defamation that is made verbally is referred to as libel.

  ○ **D.** Employers can be sued for defamation for providing a false reference to potential employers.

9. All the following are important steps to take to ensure the success of a focus group except

  ○ **A.** Develop effective questions.

  ○ **B.** Involve/include all stakeholders.

  ○ **C.** Arrange the logistics.

  ○ **D.** Conduct the survey.

10. Which of the following would be least likely to be considered an employee involvement strategy?

  ○ **A.** Open-door policy

  ○ **B.** Progressive discipline

  ○ **C.** Suggestion programs

  ○ **D.** Captive audience meetings

Answers to Review Questions

1. Progressive discipline programs can, in fact, function as a type of employee involvement (and employee relations) program if we keep the true definition of employee relations in mind: anything that affects a relationship with an employee. Even throughout the progressive discipline process, there should be a focus on building a relationship. Discipline can and should be seen as a way to give employees every opportunity to help themselves in their efforts to address their performance issues and, in short, "turn them around" so that they can meet or exceed performance expectations.

2. Local unions, which truly operate at the "local" level, are largely responsible for the day-to-day administration of the labor agreement and relationship with union members. Locals generally have an elected president and elected stewards who represent the workers in the workplace. Larger local unions might have a full-time paid business agent. Most locals belong to and are chartered by a larger national union.

   National unions, conversely, bring together all the union locals for a particular group that are scattered across the country. There are usually different hierarchical levels in between the local union and the national union. National unions have far more power with respect to bargaining and with respect to political influence than the union locals could have on their own. They also advise and guide local unions and may manage nationwide benefits programs (such as retirement programs and health insurance plans).

3. Distributive bargaining takes an approach to bargaining in which each side sets forth its position, and at the end of the process one side has "won" some (or all) of what it wanted, and the other has "lost" some (or all) of what it wanted. Distributive bargaining is adversarial in nature. It assumes that there's only so much to go around, so when you divide up the pie, one side will get more and one side will get less.

   Integrative bargaining doesn't look at bargaining issues one at a time; instead, it looks at multiple issues as a whole (hence, the term integrative). Integrative bargaining looks at that same pie in a different way. Instead of just splitting up the pieces, it creatively considers how it might be able to make that pie bigger; how the needs of both sides can be better met when looked at in their entirety; and how a win-win solution can be explored, rather than settling for the win-lose scenario that will inevitably result from distributive bargaining.

   In essence, integrative bargaining is predicated on the idea that an agreement that renders one side better off does not necessarily have to result in the other side being worse off. Instead, through creativity and cooperation, trade-offs of some sort are sought that will ultimately benefit both parties to the agreement.

4. Negligent hiring refers to the process of hiring an employee without engaging in appropriate "due diligence" into that candidate's credentials, prior work experience, and the like. Negligent hiring tort claims might be filed when an employee who was hired through a flawed process inflicts some sort of harm on another person—harm that could have been predicted and therefore prevented if the employer had conducted the background check. A hiring process can be flawed for a number of reasons, such as the application of a sound hiring process in an unsound manner or the use of a hiring process that was originally designed in a flawed manner. Flaws could relate to inadequate or poorly conducted reference checks, job requirements that do not reflect the skills or credentials that are truly required for a position, and the like.

5. Grievance handling is the formal process established by the collective bargaining agreement through which disagreements arising from the administration of the labor agreement are resolved. These difficulties could arise from a number of sources, including but not limited to interpretation of contract language or alleged unfair or inconsistent application of employment provisions. Grievances most often arise out of decisions relating to discipline and discharge.

Answers to Exam Questions

1. Answer C is the best answer. The presence or absence of a union should not be used as a way to measure the success or failure of employee relations initiatives. Unions provide a voice, and the right to join a union is afforded to most workers under the NLRA. The choice to exercise that right must not be used to draw unrelated conclusions. Answers A, B, and D are not the best answers; turnover, absenteeism (especially unplanned), and work-related accidents/injuries/"preventable" illnesses can all provide valid measures of the effectiveness of employee relations initiatives.

2. Answer B is the best answer. Employees who discuss earnings with each other could be found to be engaging in protected concerted activity, which is protected by the NLRA—even for employees who do not belong to a union. Answer A is not the best answer; although this may be true, it is not the most compelling response to this question. Answer C is not the best answer; this would not hold true unless different members of protected classes were subjected to different rules. Answer D is not the best answer; employers should not adopt a policy preventing employees from discussing their earnings/compensation with each other.

3. Answer C is the best answer. Discriminating against an employee for filing charges with the FCMS or taking part in any FCMS proceedings does not constitute an unfair labor charge. (FCMS stands for the Federal Mediation and Conciliation Service and is a source that maintains lists of qualified arbitrators. Charges, therefore, cannot be filed with the FCMS.) Answers A, B, and D are not the best answers; each one has been specifically identified as an unfair labor practice (ULP) by the NLRA.

4. Answer A is the best answer. A yellow dog contract is a contract or an agreement between an employer and an employee, the terms of which are essentially that the employer will give the employee a job as long as the employee agrees not to join or have any involvement with a labor union. Answers B, C, and D are not the best answers; they are fabricated and do not reflect realistic scenarios.

5. Answer B is the best answer. Featherbedding refers to an agreement that the employer will pay wages to union members whether or not their work is needed. Answer A is not the best answer; a requirement that anyone who is hired by the organization must join the union refers to a union shop. Answer C is not the best answer; the requirement to pay prevailing wages on federal government construction contracts and most contracts for federally assisted construction over $2,000 refers to the Davis-Bacon Act. Answer D is not the best answer; an agreement that an employer will stop doing business with another entity is a hot cargo agreement.

6. Answer B is the best answer. Weingarten Rights refer to the rights of unionized employees to have union representation at investigatory meetings with management if the union member reasonably believes that discipline might result. Answer A is not the best answer; unionized employees do not have the right to have a representative at a meeting with a supervisor/manager unless the employee reasonably believes that discipline might result from that meeting. Answer C is not the best answer; the EEOC's right to take its own independent action even when a binding arbitration agreement is in place refers to *EEOC v. Waffle House, Inc.*, not *NLRB v. Weingarten, 1975*. Answer D is not the best answer; the right of unionized employees to pay only that portion of union dues that is attributable to mainline union responsibility is known as Beck Rights, not Weingarten Rights.

7. Answer B is the best answer. A grievance procedure would not include a requirement to notify the NLRB. Answers A, C, and D are not the best answers; each represents a common step in many grievance processes.

8. Answer D is the best answer. Employers can be sued for defamation for providing a false reference to potential employers. Answer A is not the best answer; statements do not need to be recorded for a defamation suit to be filed. Answer B is not the best answer; defamation that is in written form is referred to as libel. Answer C is not the best answer; defamation that is made verbally is referred to as slander.

9. Answer D is the best answer. Although focus groups can be used as follow-up to an employee survey, they can also be used independently from a survey. Answers A, B, and C are not the best answers; each represents an important step that must be taken to ensure the success of a focus group.

10. Answer D is the best answer. Although captive audience meetings involve employees (in that the "captive audience" consists of employees), such meetings are held in response to efforts to organize and are not considered to be a true employee involvement strategy. In addition, they are mandatory meetings, which undermines the element of choice that is inherent to authentic employee involvement strategies. Answers A, B, and D are not the best answers; each represents a legitimate employee involvement strategy.

Suggested Readings and Resources

Aylott, E. (2014). *Employee Relations*. Kogan Page.

Budd, J. (2013). *Labor Relations: Striking a Balance* (4th ed.). New York: McGraw-Hill/Irwin.

Cihon, P., and Castagnera, J. (n.d.). *Employment & Labor Law* (8th ed.).

Department of Labor. www.dol.gov.

Fisher, R., and Ury, W. (1991). *Getting to Yes: Negotiating Agreement Without Giving In* (2nd ed.). New York: Penguin Books.

Grote, R. (2006). *Discipline Without Punishment: The Proven Strategy That Turns Problem Employees into Superior Performers* (2nd ed.). New York: Amacom-American Management Association.

Guerin, L. (n.d.). *The Essential Guide to Workplace Investigations: How to Handle Employee Complaints & Problems* (3rd ed.).

Kearney, R. (2014). *Labor Relations in the Public Sector* (5th ed.). CRC.

National Labor Relations Board, www.nlrb.gov.

Rodriguez, E. (2012). *Managing Employee Relations: Leading HR Executives on Developing Talent, Monitoring Morale, and Maximizing Employee Engagement*. Boston: Aspatore.

CHAPTER SIX

Risk Management

We've said it before, and we'll say it again here—HR is an ever-evolving, ever-expanding profession. Perhaps nowhere is this more evident than in this functional area—formerly known as "occupational health, safety and security" and now renamed/reclassified as "risk management." This shift represents far more than just a change in title; rather, it reflects a shift in focus that recognizes HR's role in the proactive identification, anticipation, mitigation, and management of risks. It's also important to keep in mind that this shift in focus represents an expansion of HR's former role rather than a replacement of it; our prior, more transactional responsibilities still remain.

Like every other functional area in HR, risk management has a wide-ranging influence on the day-to-day—as well as the long-term—operations of the organization. This impact is real, direct, and significant—even for those HR professionals who don't have formal responsibility for risk management. Why? Because, ultimately, as HR professionals, we all share a degree of accountability for these critical, highly impactful dimensions of the workplace experience.

Risk management, and the results thereof, can affect the workplace (along with the organization's bottom line) in myriad ways—some of which are obvious, and others that are subtler. On a somewhat mundane level, productivity and performance can be derailed by health-related concerns, security breaches, or noncompliance with mandatory government requirements. But risk management means much more than this.

As we've seen time and time again in recent years, risk can manifest itself in many forms—some of which seem unthinkable (and are therefore difficult, if not impossible, to predict) until they are either experienced or witnessed firsthand, as was the case with the tragedy of September 11, 2001, or Hurricane Katrina in August 2005. In cases such as these, although it is imperative to deal swiftly and competently with the immediate aftermath of the situation, we cannot stop there. We must also work with our business partners and clients to learn as many lessons and glean as much knowledge as possible—lessons and knowledge that will enable us to prepare to deal more effectively with other similar situations that we might encounter in the future. For, although it might be impossible to predict the specifics of such situations, it is somewhat possible to anticipate that something (even if we do not know what) unspeakably horrific and intensely disruptive can happen.

In light of all of this, it becomes even clearer that risk management issues are business issues, which means they are HR issues. As HR professionals, we must consider these issues from a proactive perspective as well as from a reactive perspective. We must also recognize the specific ways in which having a better understanding of risk management issues can bolster our efforts to advance the mission of the organization and to contribute meaningfully to achieving its overarching organizational objectives.

So, starting from the beginning, what, specifically, is meant by risk management? According to the 2015 online edition of the Random House Dictionary, risk management refers to "the technique or profession of assessing, minimizing and preventing accidental loss to a business, as through the use of insurance, safety measures, etc."

There is, however, another dimension to risk management—and it incorporates the potential for a slightly more positive perspective: risk can also refer to choices and decisions that are made taking into account upside as well as downside potential. These are choices that—whether made with the utmost degree of caution, by throwing caution to the wind, or something in between—can have, by their very nature, significant impact on the organization, its operations, and its employees.

> **NOTE**
>
> Let us be clear on this point. In no way are we implying that risk is something that should be avoided at all costs or in all circumstances. If that were the case, this functional area would be called "risk avoidance" rather than "risk management." In the words of Lorayne Fiorillo, author of *Financial Fitness in 45 Days*, "Risk is uncertainty, and in uncertainty lies opportunity. Without uncertainty, there's little chance to profit." This is true for individuals, and it's true for organizations. As HR professionals, we must not seek solely to avoid risk; rather, we must strive to wisely navigate the waters of risk—acting in a manner that is consistent with our organization's mission and overarching objectives.

> **NOTE**
>
> Of the six functional areas, this one is, perhaps, the least "fact driven" and the most driven by skills, processes, protocols, culture, and strategy. It is also, oddly and a bit ironically, significantly affected by a strange and variable combination of both fear and apathy—both of which HR professionals must address.

First, however, it's necessary for HR professionals to understand the important legislation relating to risk management. The following topics will be covered in the next section.

RESPONSIBILITY

RM Responsibility 01

Ensure that workplace health, safety, security, and privacy activities are compliant with applicable federal laws and regulations.

KNOWLEDGE

Knowledge 61

Applicable federal laws and regulations related to workplace health, safety, security, and privacy (for example: OSHA, Drug-Free Workplace Act, ADA, HIPAA, Sarbanes-Oxley Act).

Key Legislation

Each HR professional must have a solid understanding of—and familiarity with—key legislation relating to risk management and with the relevant overarching legal dimensions to be able to effectively handle routine and nonroutine health, safety, and security-related situations.

Some of the laws that influence risk management were crafted specifically around health and safety concerns, whereas others address these topics more tangentially (for instance, through worker's compensation laws). Congress passed three laws to encompass other dimensions of risk management, including privacy, security, and credit-related issues.

In this section of the chapter, we'll take a look (in chronological order) at some of the key legislation most traditionally associated with occupational health, safety, and security, as well as legislation that extends into the broader definition of risk management described previously:

► Occupational Safety and Health Act (OSH Act), 1970

► Mine Safety and Health Act (MSHA), 1977

► Drug-Free Workplace Act, 1988

► USA PATRIOT Act, 2001

► Homeland Security Act, 2002

► Sarbanes-Oxley Act, 2002

NOTE

In addition to these six laws, there are other areas of legislation that (although they do have an impact on risk management) fall more directly within other functional areas:

► Labor-Management Relations Act, 1947 (Chapter 5, "Employee and Labor Relations")

► Fair Credit Reporting Act, 1970 (Chapter 2, "Workforce Planning and Employment")

► Privacy Act, 1974 (Chapter 2)

► Employee Polygraph Protection Act, 1988 (Chapter 2)

► Health Insurance Portability and Accountability Act, 1996 (Chapter 4, "Compensation and Benefits")

► Fair and Accurate Credit Transactions Act, 2003 (Chapter 2)

Occupational Safety and Health Act, 1970

The Occupational Safety and Health (OSH) Act was the first law to establish consistent workplace health and safety standards. The Act's opening words communicate the reason for its creation—which is, essentially, to protect workers by ensuring safe and healthful workplaces.

This purpose is also reflected in the mission statement of OSHA, which is "to assure the safety and health of America's workers by setting and enforcing standards; providing training, outreach, and education; establishing partnerships; and encouraging continual improvement in workplace safety and health."

According to various governmental reports, the OSH Act has been successful. A 2003 Department of Labor (DOL) report, for example, states that workplace deaths have decreased by 62% and occupational injury and illness rates have dropped 40% since the passage of OSH Act—all while the size of the workforce has doubled. Nonetheless, according to www.dol.gov, there is still much work to do because each day nearly 16 workers die on the job and more than 14,000 experience an injury or illness. Using these results as a place from which to look forward, rather than solely as a place from which to review the past.

OSHA has established the following strategic objectives for 2010—2016:

"OSHA is focusing on actively promoting safe and healthy working conditions for working men and women by: setting and enforcing workplace safety and health standards; delivering effective enforcement; providing outreach, education and compliance assistance; and encouraging continual improvement in workplace safety and health."

▶ Our strategies to achieve these goals include:

   ▶ ~~Strengthen enforcement capabilities—target the most egregious and persistent violators.~~

   ▶ Strengthen regulatory capabilities.

   ▶ Increase OSHA's presence in the workplace.

   ▶ Protect workers in high-hazard occupations.

   ▶ Protect vulnerable and hard-to-reach worker populations.

   ▶ Review and restructure penalties to ensure that penalties imposed are consistent with the seriousness of the violation and act as effective deterrence to violators.

   ▶ Maintain a strong outreach and education program.

   ▶ Enhance and strengthen compliance assistance program for small businesses."

(Source: http://www.dol.gov/_sec/stratplan/2010/osha/osha.ppt)

OSHA plays a critical role in supporting the DOL Quality Workplaces goal by carrying out programs designed to save lives, prevent injuries and illnesses, and protect the health of America's workers. These programs include the following:

▶ Developing guidance and standards for occupational safety and health

▶ Inspecting places of employment and working with employers and employees

▶ Offering consultation services to small businesses

▶ Providing compliance assistance, outreach, education, and other cooperative programs for employers and employees

▶ Providing matching grants to assist states in administering consultation projects and approved occupational safety and health enforcement programs

▶ Fostering relationships with other agencies and organizations to address critical safety and health issues

Consistent with the DOL's emphasis on managing for results, the OSHA Strategic Management Plan focuses on serious hazards and dangerous workplaces. The plan includes strategies that emphasize the following

▶ Exercising strong, fair, and effective enforcement

▶ Expanding partnerships and voluntary programs

▶ Expanding outreach, education, and compliance assistance

OSHA covers more than 114 million workers at 7 million worksites, twice the number under the agency's jurisdiction when it began operations in 1971. These workplaces and the working population are becoming increasingly diverse. New safety and health issues continually emerge. Workplace violence and work-related motor vehicle accidents now account for more than 40% of workplace fatalities. OSHA also must be ready to assist with emergency preparedness and national security concerns.

Purpose of OSHA

Why was OSHA established? In short, because there was a need. Specifically, "The Congress finds that personal injuries and illnesses arising out of work situations impose a substantial burden upon, and are a hindrance to, interstate commerce in terms of lost production, wage loss, medical expenses, and disability compensation payments" (www.osha.gov). Within this context, work-related illnesses are defined as those resulting from an event or condition in the work environment that falls into any one of the following four categories: skin diseases or disorders, respiratory conditions, poisoning, hearing loss, or "all other illnesses." Work-related illnesses result from an event or condition in the work environment that falls into any one of the following four categories: skin diseases or disorders, respiratory conditions, poisoning, hearing loss, or "all other illnesses." Work-related injuries refer to any wound or damage to the body resulting from an event in the work environment.

OSHA has identified 13 specific objectives, shown in Section 2 of the Act ("Congressional Findings and Purpose"), as follows.

SEC. 2. Congressional Findings and Purpose

(a) The Congress finds that personal injuries and illnesses arising out of work situations impose a substantial burden upon, and are a hindrance to, interstate commerce in terms of lost production, wage loss, medical expenses, and disability compensation payments.

(b) The Congress declares it to be its purpose and policy, through the exercise of its powers to regulate commerce among the several States and with foreign nations and to provide for the general welfare, to assure so far as possible every working man and woman in the Nation safe and healthful working conditions and to preserve our human resources—

(1) by encouraging employers and employees in their efforts to reduce the number of occupational safety and health hazards at their places of employment, and to stimulate employers and employees to institute new and to perfect existing programs for providing safe and healthful working conditions;

(2) by providing that employers and employees have separate but dependent responsibilities and rights with respect to achieving safe and healthful working conditions;

(3) by authorizing the Secretary of Labor to set mandatory occupational safety and health standards applicable to businesses affecting interstate commerce, and by creating an Occupational Safety and Health Review Commission for carrying out adjudicatory functions under the Act;

(4) by building upon advances already made through employer and employee initiative for providing safe and healthful working conditions;

(5) by providing for research in the field of occupational safety and health, including the psychological factors involved, and by developing innovative methods, techniques, and approaches for dealing with occupational safety and health problems;

(6) by exploring ways to discover latent diseases, establishing causal connections between diseases and work in environmental conditions, and conducting other research relating to health problems, in recognition of the fact that occupational health standards present problems often different from those involved in occupational safety;

(7) by providing medical criteria which will assure insofar as practicable that no employee will suffer diminished health, functional capacity, or life expectancy as a result of his work experience;

(8) by providing for training programs to increase the number and competence of personnel engaged in the field of occupational safety and health; affecting the OSH Act since its passage in 1970 through January 1, 2004.

(9) by providing for the development and promulgation of occupational safety and health standards;

(10) by providing an effective enforcement program which shall include a prohibition against giving advance notice of any inspection and sanctions for any individual violating this prohibition;

(11) by encouraging the States to assume the fullest responsibility for the administration and enforcement of their occupational safety and health laws by providing grants to the States to assist in identifying their needs and responsibilities in the area of occupational safety and health, to develop plans in accordance with the provisions of this Act, to improve the administration and enforcement of State occupational safety and health laws, and to conduct experimental and demonstration projects in connection therewith;

(12) by providing for appropriate reporting procedures with respect to occupational safety and health which procedures will help achieve the objectives of this Act and accurately describe the nature of the occupational safety and health problem;

(13) by encouraging joint labor-management efforts to reduce injuries and disease arising out of employment.

The OSH Act also (also known as OSHA). Residing within the Department of Labor, OSHA administers and enforces OSH Act.

OSHA Coverage

The OSH Act offers broad coverage. In a 1999 letter, OSHA defined its coverage as including "employees of an organization." Unlike most other employment laws, smaller employers are not exempt from OSHA. Exceptions do exist, however. For instance, family farms that do not employ anyone outside the family are not covered under OSHA. Also excluded from the Act are self-employed individuals, state government employees, and local government employees. State and local government employees, however, are often covered by state-sponsored OSHA legislation. Employees who work in specific industries (such as mining) that are covered by their own industry-specific laws are also exempt from OSHA.

General Duty Clause—Section 5(a)

The General Duty Clause of the Act identifies two primary duties for employers and one for employees on which all subsequent requirements (called standards) are ultimately built:

1. Employers must ensure a safe workplace. The Act defines "safe workplace" as one that is "free from recognized hazards that are causing or are likely to cause death or serious physical harm to his employees."

2. Employers must comply with all current and future OSHA-related standards.

The General Duty Clause comes into play when there are no existing standards covering a particular job or industry. Standards will be discussed later in this chapter.

The General Duty Clause also identifies a duty for employees—that they must follow all safety and health-related rules stemming from the Act. This duty is defined broadly, as well, in that it would include

▶ Reporting hazardous conditions to their supervisor

▶ Immediately reporting any and all job-related injuries or illnesses to their employer

▶ Cooperating in the event of an OSHA inspection or investigation

Employee Rights Under OSHA

The OSHA 3165 poster (see Figure 6.1)—which must be displayed in a conspicuous place that is easily visible to employees and applicants for employment—lists each employee's rights.

**Job Safety and Health
IT'S THE LAW!**

All workers have the right to:

- A safe workplace.
- Raise a safety or health concern with your employer or OSHA, or report a work-related injury or illness, without being retaliated against.
- Receive information and training on job hazards, including all hazardous substances in your workplace.
- Request an OSHA inspection of your workplace if you believe there are unsafe or unhealthy conditions. OSHA will keep your name confidential. You have the right to have a representative contact OSHA on your behalf.
- Participate (or have your representative participate) in an OSHA inspection and speak in private to the inspector.
- File a complaint with OSHA within 30 days (by phone, online or by mail) if you have been retaliated against for using your rights.
- See any OSHA citations issued to your employer.
- Request copies of your medical records, tests that measure hazards in the workplace, and the workplace injury and illness log.

This poster is available free from OSHA.

Contact OSHA. We can help.

Employers must:

- Provide employees a workplace free from recognized hazards. It is illegal to retaliate against an employee for using any of their rights under the law, including raising a health and safety concern with you or with OSHA, or reporting a work-related injury or illness.
- Comply with all applicable OSHA standards.
- Report to OSHA all work-related fatalities within 8 hours, and all inpatient hospitalizations, amputations and losses of an eye within 24 hours.
- Provide required training to all workers in a language and vocabulary they can understand.
- Prominently display this poster in the workplace.
- Post OSHA citations at or near the place of the alleged violations.

FREE ASSISTANCE to identify and correct hazards is available to small and medium-sized employers, without citation or penalty, through OSHA-supported consultation programs in every state.

1-800-321-OSHA (6742) • TTY 1-877-889-5627 • **www.osha.gov**

FIGURE 6.1 The OSHA 3165 poster.

Employer Requirements Under OSHA—Recordkeeping, Reporting, and Posting Requirements

HR professionals must have a solid understanding of recordkeeping, reporting, and posting requirements under the OSH Act. The first step for any organization is to determine whether it needs to maintain such records.

Determining Whether an Employer Is Required to Maintain Records

Most organizations employing fewer than 11 employees are exempt from OSHA recordkeeping requirements. In addition, OSHA publishes a list of specific low-risk industries that are exempt from this requirement, even if they employ more than 10 people. Please note that this list of exempt industries was updated effective January 1, 2015:

> "The previous list of partially exempt industries was based on the old Standard Industrial Classification (SIC) system and injury and illness data from the Bureau of Labor Statistics (BLS) from 1996, 1997, and 1998. The new list of partially exempt industries in the updated rule (link) is based on the North American Industry Classification System (NAICS) and injury and illness data from the Bureau of Labor Statistics (BLS) from 2007, 2008, and 2009" (www.osha.gov).

Recordkeeping—Updated Requirements Effective January 1, 2015

OSHA instituted the following changes to recordkeeping requirements effective January 1, 2015:

> "The Occupational Safety and Health Administration's revised recordkeeping rule includes two key changes:"

> "First, the rule updates the list of industries that are exempt from the requirement to routinely keep OSHA injury and illness records, due to relatively low occupational injury and illness rates. The previous list of industries was based on the old Standard Industrial Classification (SIC) system and injury and illness data from the Bureau of Labor Statistics (BLS) from 1996, 1997, and 1998. The new list of industries that are exempt from routinely keeping OSHA injury and illness records is based on the North American Industry Classification System (NAICS) and injury and illness data from the Bureau of Labor Statistics (BLS) from 2007, 2008, and 2009. Note: The new rule retains the exemption for any employer with ten or fewer employees, regardless of their industry classification, from the requirement to routinely keep records."

> "Second, the rule expands the list of severe work-related injuries that all covered employers must report to OSHA. The revised rule retains the current requirement to report all work-related fatalities within 8 hours and adds the requirement to report all work-related in-patient hospitalizations, amputations, and loss of an eye within 24 hours to OSHA."

> "Establishments located in States under Federal OSHA jurisdiction must begin to comply with the new requirements on January 1, 2015. Establishments located in states that operate their own safety and health programs (State Plan States) should check with their state plan for the implementation date of the new requirements. OSHA encourages the states to implement the new coverage provisions on 1/1/2015, but some may not be able to meet this tight deadline."

> "The final rule will allow OSHA to focus its efforts more effectively to prevent fatalities and serious work-related injuries and illnesses. The final rule will also improve access by employers, employees, researchers and the public to information about workplace safety and health and increase their ability to identify and abate serious hazards" (www.osha.gov).

Reporting—Updated Requirements as of January 1, 2015

Certain OSHA reporting requirements were updated as of January 1, 2015. These changes are reflected in the OSHA Fact Sheet shown in Figure 6.2.

Updates to OSHA's Recordkeeping Rule: Reporting Fatalities and Severe Injuries

OSHA's updated recordkeeping rule expands the list of severe injuries that all employers must report to OSHA. Establishments located in states under Federal OSHA jurisdiction must begin to comply with the new requirements on January 1, 2015. Establishments located in states that operate their own safety and health programs should check with their state plan for the implementation date of the new requirements.

What am I required to report under the new rule?

Previously, employers had to report the following to OSHA:

- All work-related fatalities
- Work-related hospitalizations of three or more employees

Starting in 2015, employers will have to report the following to OSHA:

- All work-related fatalities
- All work-related inpatient hospitalizations of one or more employees
- All work-related amputations
- All work-related losses of an eye

Who is covered under the new rule?

All employers under OSHA jurisdiction must report all work-related fatalities, hospitalizations, amputations and losses of an eye to OSHA, even employers who are exempt from routinely keeping OSHA injury and illness records due to company size or industry.

An amputation is defined as the traumatic loss of a limb or other external body part. Amputations include a part, such as a limb or appendage, that has been severed, cut off, amputated (either completely or partially); fingertip amputations with or without bone loss; medical amputations resulting from irreparable damage; and amputations of body parts that have since been reattached.

How soon must I report a fatality or severe injury or illness?

Employers must report work-related fatalities within **8 hours of finding out about them.**

Employers only have to report fatalities that occurred within 30 days of a work-related incident.

For any inpatient hospitalization, amputation, or eye loss **employers must report the incident within 24 hours of learning about it.** Employers only have to report an inpatient hospitalization, amputation or loss of an eye that occurs within 24 hours of a work-related incident.

How do I report an event to OSHA?

Employers have three options for reporting the event:

- By telephone to the nearest OSHA Area Office during normal business hours.
- By telephone to the 24-hour OSHA hotline at 1-800-321-OSHA (6742).
- OSHA is developing a new means of reporting events electronically, which will be available soon at www.osha.gov.

What information do I need to report?

For any fatality that occurs within 30 days of a work-related incident, employers must report the event **within 8 hours** of finding out about it.

FIGURE 6.2 The OSHA fact sheet.

Required Forms

Covered employers must maintain records using OSHA Form 300, OSHA Form 300A, and OSHA Form 301 for each worksite.

OSHA's Form 300: Log of Work-Related Injuries and Illnesses

OSHA's Form 300 is used to record the "what," "how," "when," "where," and "who" of work-related injuries and illnesses. The employer has seven working days from the time it learns of a work-related injury or illness to record it on this form. Please also note that work-related deaths or inpatient hospitalizations of three or more employees resulting from a work-related incident must be reported to OSHA within eight hours.

CAUTION

> Care must be taken to preserve employee privacy when completing these forms. Under certain circumstances—including upon employee request—the words "privacy case" should be substituted for the employee's name. In these cases, a separate document must be maintained matching case numbers with employee names (for identification purposes).

OSHA's Form 300A: Summary of Work-Related Injuries and Illnesses

Employers use Form 300A to record a numeric summary of all work-related injuries and illnesses logged in OSHA's Form 300 over the course of each calendar year. This form indicates the number of cases, the number of workdays impacted, and the numbers and types of work-related injuries and illnesses. A worksheet is also available to assist employers in filling out this summary. Each year, a completed Form 300 must be posted conspicuously for three months (between February 1 and April 30).

OSHA's Form 301: Injury and Illness Incident Report

A separate Form 301 (see Appendix A, "OSHA Forms for Recording Work-Related Injuries and Illnesses") must be completed for each work-related injury or illness within seven calendar days of the date on which the employer learns of the work-related injury or illness. Completed forms must be maintained by the employer for five years following the year in which the incident or illness occurred.

TIP

> Detailed instructions on how to complete these forms, as well as actual downloadable forms, can be found at www.osha.gov.

Optional Calculations

OSHA provides formulas for calculating incidence rates. (Search www.osha.gov for this information.) An employer would then compare its incidence rate to incidence rates for other employers of similar size or other employers in their industry.

TABLE 6.1 Incidence Rate Worksheet for _____ Company (Optional)

Incidence Rate	Columns from OSHA 300 Log 300 Log Column Entry	Calculation	(Year) Company Rate _____	(Year) BLS Rate for SIC _____
Total Injury and Incidence Rate	G _____	_____ cases		
	H + _____	x 200,000		
	I + _____	÷ _____ (hours)		
	J + _____	= _____ (rate)		
	Total = _____			
DART Rate [Was Lost Workday Injury and Illness Rate (LWDII)]	H _____	_____ cases		
	I + _____	x 200,000		
	Total = _____	÷ _____ (hours)		
		= _____ (rate)		
Day Count Rate	K _____	_____ days		No comparable rate available from BLS
	L + _____	x 200,000		
	Total = _____	÷ _____ (hours)		
		= _____ (rate)		

Posting and Access Requirements

All employers covered by OSHA must display the OSHA 3165 poster. In addition, all employers covered by OSHA must provide employees, their designated representatives, and OSHA with access to employee exposure and medical records (29 CFR 1910.1020). Exposure records must be maintained for 30 years, and medical records must be maintained for 30 years after the employee's period of employment ends.

The Needlestick Safety and Prevention Act of 2000

The Needlestick Safety and Prevention Act of 2000 was, essentially, a compliance directive for enforcing the Bloodborne Pathogens Standard. The Act added three key requirements to the existing standard:

▶ Evaluation and implementation of safer needle devices (as they become available). Reviews of—and searches for—such enhancements must be done annually.

▶ Actively involving employees who actually use needles and needle devices in this evaluation and selection process.

▶ Maintenance of a log of all injuries resulting from contaminated sharps.

TIP

The PHR exam may cover any or all of these in greater detail. Increase your knowledge of all of them, especially if they do not apply to your particular industry.

OSHA Priorities

OSHA recognizes that its compliance officers can't be everywhere all the time. For this reason, OSHA has established a tiered priority system for workplace inspections. Listed in order of importance (from highest to lowest), OSHA's priorities are

1. "A written, signed complaint by a current employee or employee representative with enough detail to enable OSHA to determine that a violation or danger likely exists that threatens physical harm or that an imminent danger exists;

2. An allegation that physical harm has occurred as a result of the hazard and that it still exists;

3. A report of an imminent danger;

4. A complaint about a company in an industry covered by one of OSHA's local or national emphasis programs or a hazard targeted by one of these programs;

5. Inadequate response from an employer who has received information on the hazard through a phone/fax investigation;

6. A complaint against an employer with a past history of egregious, willful or failure-to-abate OSHA citations within the past three years;

7. Referral from a whistle blower investigator; or

8. Complaint at a facility scheduled for or already undergoing an OSHA inspection" (www.osha.gov).

OSHA Inspections

OSHA inspections consist of the display of the inspector's credentials, an opening conference, the physical inspection (walk-through), and a closing conference.

Inspector's Credentials

When the OSHA compliance officer arrives at the establishment, he displays official credentials and asks to meet an appropriate employer representative. Employers should always ask to see the compliance officer's credentials. Employers may verify the OSHA federal or state compliance officer credentials by calling the nearest federal or state OSHA office. Compliance officers may not collect a penalty at the time of the inspection or promote the sale of a product or service at any time; anyone who attempts to do so is impersonating a government inspector, and the employer should contact the FBI or local law enforcement officials immediately.

Opening Conference

In the opening conference, the compliance officer explains how the establishment was selected and what the likely scope of the inspection will be. The compliance officer also will ascertain whether an OSHA-funded consultation visit is in progress or whether the facility is pursuing or has received an inspection exemption through the consultation program; if so, the inspection may be limited or terminated.

The compliance officer explains the purpose of the visit, the scope of the inspection, and the standards that apply. The compliance officer gives the employer information on how to get a copy of applicable safety and health standards as well as a copy of any employee complaint that may be involved (with the employee's name deleted, if the employee requests anonymity).

The compliance officer asks the employer to select an employer representative to accompany the compliance officer during the inspection.

The compliance officer also gives an authorized employee representative the opportunity to attend the opening conference and accompany the compliance officer during the inspection. If a recognized bargaining agent represents the employees, the agent ordinarily will designate the employee representative to accompany the compliance officer. Similarly, if there is a plant safety committee, the employee members of that committee will designate the employee representative (in the absence of a recognized bargaining agent). Where neither employee group exists, the employees themselves may select an employee representative, or the compliance officer may determine if any employee suitably represents the interest of other employees.

The Act does not require an employee representative for each inspection. Where there is no authorized employee representative, however, the compliance officer must consult with a reasonable number of employees concerning safety and health matters in the workplace.

Walk-Through

After the opening conference, the compliance officer and accompanying representatives proceed through the establishment to inspect work areas for safety and health hazards.

The compliance officer determines the route and duration of the inspection. While talking with employees, the compliance officer makes every effort to minimize work interruptions. The compliance officer observes safety and health conditions and practices; consults with employees privately, if necessary; takes photos, videotapes, and instrument readings; examines records; collects air samples; measures noise levels; surveys existing engineering controls; and monitors employee exposure to toxic fumes, gases, and dusts.

An inspection tour may cover part or all of an establishment, even if the inspection resulted from a specific complaint, fatality, or catastrophe. If the compliance officer finds a violation in open view, he may ask permission to expand the inspection.

The compliance officer keeps all trade secrets observed confidential.

The compliance officer consults employees during the inspection tour. He may stop and question workers, in private, about safety and health conditions and practices in their workplaces. Each employee is protected under the Act from discrimination by the employer for exercising his safety and health rights.

OSHA places special importance on posting and recordkeeping requirements. The compliance officer will inspect records of deaths, injuries, and illnesses that the employer is required to keep. He will check to see that a copy of the totals from the last page of OSHA Form Number 300 are posted as required and that the OSHA workplace poster (OSHA 3165), which explains employees' safety and health rights, is prominently displayed. Where records of employee exposure to toxic substances and harmful physical agents are required, the compliance officer will examine them for compliance with the recordkeeping requirements.

The compliance officer also requests a copy of the employer's Hazard Communication Program. Under OSHA's Hazard Communication Standard, employers must establish a written, comprehensive communication program that includes provisions for container labeling, material safety data sheets, and an employee training program. The program must contain a list of the hazardous chemicals in each work area and the means the employer will use to inform employees of the hazards associated with these chemicals.

During the course of the inspection, the compliance officer will point out to the employer any unsafe or unhealthful working conditions observed. At the same time, the compliance officer will discuss possible corrective action if the employer so desires.

Some apparent violations detected by the compliance officer can be corrected immediately. When the employer corrects them on the spot, the compliance officer records such corrections to help in judging the employer's good faith in compliance. Although corrected, the apparent violations will serve as the basis for a citation and, if appropriate, a notice of proposed penalty. OSHA may reduce the penalties for some types of violations if they are corrected immediately.

Closing Conference

At the conclusion of the inspection, the compliance officer conducts a closing conference with the employer, employees, or the employees' representative.

The compliance officer gives the employer and all other parties involved a copy of "Employer Rights and Responsibilities Following an OSHA Inspection" (OSHA 3000) for their review and discussion.

The compliance officer discusses with the employer all unsafe or unhealthful conditions observed during the inspection and indicates all apparent violations for which he may issue or recommend a citation and a proposed penalty. The compliance officer will not indicate specific proposed penalties but will inform the employer of appeal rights.

During the closing conference, the employer may want to produce records to show compliance efforts and provide information that can help OSHA determine how much time may be needed to abate an alleged violation.

When appropriate, the compliance officer may hold more than one closing conference. This is usually necessary when the inspection includes an evaluation of health hazards, after a review of additional laboratory reports, or after the compliance officer obtains additional factual evidence while concluding an accident investigation.

The compliance officer explains that OSHA area offices are full-service resource centers that inform the public of OSHA activities and programs. This includes information on new or revised standards, the status of proposed standards, comment periods, or public hearings. Additionally, area offices provide technical experts and materials and refer callers to other agencies and professional organizations as appropriate. The area offices promote effective safety and health programs through Voluntary Protection Programs (VPP) and provide information about study courses offered at the OSHA Training Institute or its satellite locations nationwide.

If an employee representative does not participate in either the opening or the closing conference held with the employer, the compliance officer holds a separate discussion with the employee representative, if requested, to discuss matters of direct interest to employees.

Federal OSHA Complaint-Handling Process

When OSHA receives a complaint, it makes a determination as to whether its investigation will be conducted onsite or offsite. This determination is made on the basis of eight predetermined criteria, at least one of which must be met for OSHA to conduct an onsite inspection:

- A written, signed complaint by a current employee or employee representative with enough detail to enable OSHA to determine that a violation or danger likely exists that threatens physical harm or that an imminent danger exists
- An allegation that physical harm has occurred as a result of the hazard and that it still exists
- A report of an imminent danger
- A complaint about a company in an industry covered by one of OSHA's local or national emphasis programs or a hazard targeted by one of these programs
- Inadequate response from an employer who has received information on the hazard through a phone/fax investigation
- A complaint against an employer with a past history of egregious, willful, or failure-to-abate OSHA citations within the past three years
- Referral from a whistle-blower investigator
- Complaint at a facility scheduled for or already undergoing an OSHA inspection (www.osha.gov)

Workers who complain have the right to have their names withheld from their employers. OSHA will not reveal this information.

If none of these criteria is met or if the employee or employee representative requests, OSHA may investigate via phone/fax method. In such cases, OSHA will call the employer, describe the alleged hazards, and follow up with either a fax or a letter. According to www.osha.gov:

> "The employer must respond within five days, identifying in writing any problems found and noting corrective actions taken or planned. If the response is adequate, OSHA generally will not conduct an inspection. The employee who filed the original complaint will receive a copy of the employer's response. If still not satisfied, the complainant may then request an on-site inspection" (wsw.osha.gov).

TIP

At times, OSHA will investigate an employee complaint with a phone/fax investigation instead of an onsite inspection. Know the circumstances under which this can happen, and know what an employer needs to do.

OSHA Violations and Penalties

OSHA has established five categories of violations—and five levels of accompanying penalties. Table 6.2 highlights these penalties.

TABLE 6.2   OSHA Violations and Penalties

Violation	Description of Violation of Standard	Penalty
Willful	Deliberate and intentional.	Up to $70,000 per violation. Will escalate in the event of employee death. Incarceration is possible.
Serious	Death or serious injury probable. The employer either knew or should have known about the violation.	Up to $7,000 for each violation.
Other-than-serious	Unlikely to result in serious injury or death.	Up to $7,000 for each violation.
De minimis	No direct or immediate relationship to safety or health.	NA. They are documented but are not included on the citation.
Failure to abate prior violation	Violation continues beyond the prescribed abatement date.	Up to $7,000 per day.
Repeat	Same or substantially similar violation as was found during a previous inspection.	Up to $70,000 for each violation.

TIP

With the exception of those that are de minimis, violations result in citations. Know the process that must be followed upon receipt of a citation, and know the appeal process.

Mine Safety and Health Act, 1977

The Mine Safety and Health (MSH) Act is the second piece of legislation created specifically to protect employee health and safety—this time, for underground and surface miners working in coal, as well as noncoal, mines. Unlike OSHA, inspections of mines are mandatory—at least four times a year for underground mines and at least twice a year for surface mines. MSHA.gov has published the following MSHA fact sheet: www.msha.gov/MSHAINFO/ MSHA_Informational_Flyer.pdf.

Drug-Free Workplace Act, 1988

The Drug-Free Workplace Act requires federal contractors (with contracts of $100,000 or more) and individuals and organizations who are awarded federal grants (of any size) to agree to maintain a workplace free from drugs. Like the OSH and MSH Acts, the Drug-Free Workplace Act is administered and enforced by the Department of Labor.

Three key requirements that the Act imposes on employers are as follows:

▶ Publish a statement notifying employees that the manufacture, distribution, dispensation, possession, or use of a controlled substance in the workplace is prohibited. This statement must also include a description of the consequences of violating this policy.

▶ Establish a drug-free awareness program addressing the dangers of drug use in the workplace, the employer's drug-free policy (including the consequences of violating that policy), and information about programs that are available to employees who use drugs.

▶ Distribute a copy of the workplace substance abuse policy to all employees.

NOTE

You can find more information about the Drug-Free Workplace Act in Chapter 3.

USA PATRIOT Act, 2001

Just one month after the terrorist attacks of September 11, 2001, President Bush signed the USA PATRIOT Act (Uniting and Strengthening America by Providing Appropriate Tools Required to Intercept and Obstruct Terrorism). Each of the titles in the PATRIOT Act (along with a final title called "miscellaneous") gives insight into the focus of this Act:

▶ Title I: Enhancing Domestic Security Against Terrorism

▶ Title II: Enhanced Surveillance Procedures

▶ Title III: International Money Laundering Abatement and Anti-Terrorist Financing Act of 2001 (the title's sections primarily amend portions of the Money Laundering Control Act of 1986 and the Bank Secrecy Act of 1970)

▶ Title IV: Protecting the Border

▶ Title V: Removing Obstacles to Investigating Terrorism

▶ Title VI: Providing for Victims of Terrorism, Public Safety Officers and Their Families

▶ Title VII: Increased Information Sharing for Critical Infrastructure Protection

▶ Title VIII: Strengthening the Criminal Laws Against Terrorism

▶ Title IX: Improved Intelligence

▶ Title X: Miscellaneous

In 2011, President Obama signed PATRIOT Sunsets Extension Act of 2011. This Act extended three key provisions of the original PATRIOT Act: roving wiretaps, searches of business records (the "library records provision"), and conducting surveillance of "lone wolves" (individuals acting independently from organized terrorist organizations).

NOTE

Review resources listed at the end of this chapter for information on how the PATRIOT Act could affect employers.

Homeland Security Act, 2002

The Homeland Security Act, passed 13 months after the September 11, 2001, terrorist attacks, established the Department of Homeland Security, a cabinet-level agency composed of 22 previously independent federal agencies.

The vision, mission, and strategic goals of DHS—an entity inextricably linked to risk management of the highest order—are as follows (www.dhs.gov):

Vision

Preserving our freedoms, protecting America…we secure our homeland.

Mission

We will lead the unified national effort to secure America. We will prevent and deter terrorist attacks and protect against and respond to threats and hazards to the nation. We will ensure safe and secure borders, welcome lawful immigrants and visitors, and promote the free-flow of commerce.

Strategic Goals

▶ **Awareness:** Identify and understand threats, assess vulnerabilities, determine potential impacts and disseminate timely information to our homeland security partners and the American public.

▶ **Prevention:** Detect, deter and mitigate threats to our homeland.

▶ **Protection:** Safeguard our people and their freedoms, critical infrastructure, property and the economy of our Nation from acts of terrorism, natural disasters, or other emergencies.

▶ **Response:** Lead, manage and coordinate the national response to acts of terrorism, natural disasters, or other emergencies.

▶ **Recovery:** Lead national, state, local and private sector efforts to restore services and rebuild communities after acts of terrorism, natural disasters, or other emergencies.

▶ **Service:** Serve the public effectively by facilitating lawful trade, travel and immigration.

▶ **Organizational Excellence:** Value our most important resource, our people. Create a culture that promotes a common identity, innovation, mutual respect, accountability and teamwork to achieve efficiencies, effectiveness, and operational synergies.

Sarbanes-Oxley Act, 2002

On July 30, 2002, President Bush signed into law the Sarbanes-Oxley Act, which he characterized as "the most far reaching reforms of American business practices since the time of Franklin Delano Roosevelt." The Act mandated a number of reforms to increase corporate responsibility, expand financial disclosures, and combat corporate and accounting fraud. The Act also created the Public Company Accounting Oversight Board, or PCAOB, to oversee the activities of the auditing profession. The full text of the Act is available at www.sec.gov/about/laws/soa2002.pdf. You can find links to all commission rulemaking and reports issued under the Sarbanes-Oxley Act at www.sec.gov/spotlight/sarbanes-oxley.htm (www.sec.gov).

RESPONSIBILITY

RM Responsibility 02

Conduct a needs analysis to identify the organization's safety requirements.

RESPONSIBILITY

RM Responsibility 06

Communicate and train the workforce on security plans and policies.

RESPONSIBILITY

RM Responsibility 08

Communicate and train the workforce on the business continuity and disaster recovery plans.

Although the topic of these particular responsibilities pertains specifically to safety, security, and business continuity, the skills and competencies required to carry out these responsibilities are outlined in detail in Chapter 3.

Thus, develop a strong and solid understanding of the topic of the training program, and proceed with solid adherence to the principles of and steps outlined in ADDIE. The following topics will be discussed in the next section.

RESPONSIBILITY

RM Responsibility 03

Develop/select and implement/administer occupational injury and illness prevention programs (that is, OSHA, workers' compensation).

KNOWLEDGE

Knowledge 68

General health and safety practices (for example: evacuation, hazard communication, ergonomic evaluations).

Occupational Health

At their core, occupational health programs and initiatives help to ensure that workplaces remain healthy. Within that framework, organizations need to consider the physical, psychological, and emotional dimensions of health. Organizations also need to realize that although maintaining a healthy work environment is critical to maintaining a healthy workplace, it isn't enough. Employers also need to address—and be prepared to respond to—health-related issues that can develop in the workplace because of conditions, issues, or problems that don't originate in the workplace.

One area of responsibility related to occupational health involves identifying, preventing, or minimizing health hazards in the workplace. Another dimension involves developing appropriate responses if a health hazard or health risk does emerge.

Health Hazards

A health hazard refers to anything in the workplace that creates or increases the possibility of work-related injuries. There are several types of health hazards with which HR professionals must be familiar.

Environmental Health Hazards

Environmental health hazards originate in—and exist because of—"something" in the workplace. Environmental health hazards refer to a wide spectrum of conditions, circumstances, objects, or organisms in the workplace that can create or increase the likelihood of employee illness or injury. In this chapter, we'll cluster environmental health hazards into three categories: physical, chemical, and biological.

Physical Hazards: Objects/Conditions

One type of physical health hazard results from actual, tangible "things" or conditions in the workplace that increase the risk of work-related illnesses or injuries. This type of hazard may be caused by or related to a variety of factors. Table 6.3 highlights some of these factors.

TABLE 6.3 Causes of Physical Hazards

Cause/Contributing Factor	Example
Failure to properly maintain or repair equipment or other physical objects	A tear in carpeting is not repaired, increasing the likelihood of trips and falls.
Failure to address and resolve potentially dangerous conditions	A puddle of water collects on the floor because of a leaking freestanding freezer unit, increasing the likelihood of slips and falls.
Poor process design	Bus drivers (such as for rental car companies) enter information into portable computer terminals while in transit, increasing the likelihood of accidents.
Physical conditions relating to the actual performance of the job	A road paving crew installs or resurfaces asphalt in high heat conditions, increasing the likelihood of dehydration or heatstroke.
Physical conditions resulting from the actual operators who are exposed to high noise	A carpenter is exposed to dangerously high levels of sound for extended periods of time, increasing the likelihood of temporary or permanent hearing loss.

Physical Hazards: Design

Physical hazards can also result from the way in which the workplace or workspace is designed (also referred to as ergonomics). Ergonomic problems can result from poor workplace design; for instance, doors in hallways that have no windows increase the likelihood of collisions between employees who don't know that a door is about to swing in their direction. Ergonomic problems can also result from poor workspace design—for instance, LCD monitors that are placed above eye level increase the likelihood of back or neck injury because employees frequently need to look up.

Another significant area of concern involves work-related musculoskeletal disorders (MSDs). MSDs are perhaps better known as repetitive stress injuries (RSIs), cumulative trauma syndrome (CTS), or cumulative trauma disorders (CTDs). Specific examples of MSDs are the following:

▶ Carpal tunnel syndrome

▶ Trigger finger

▶ Chronic lumbar strain

▶ Tendonitis

▶ Bursitis

MSDs are caused, or exacerbated, by forceful exertions, awkward postures, repetitive movements, or exposure to extreme environmental conditions (for example, heat, cold, humidity, or vibration). MSDs represent a serious and expensive workplace problem. In 1998, the National Academy of Sciences published a report estimating that financial costs from MSDs were in the vicinity of $20 billion annually.

OSHA has adopted a four-pronged approach to address MSDs and other ergonomics-related issues:

▶ Industry-specific or task-specific guidelines

▶ Enforcement

▶ Outreach and assistance (to businesses)

▶ National Advisory Committee

Chemical Health Hazards

Chemicals represent another potential workplace hazard. Many—perhaps even most—businesses use some type of chemicals in the course of their operations (for instance, gasoline at a service station, acetone at a nail salon, or certain cleaning supplies in an office). The Hazard Communication Standard–in place since 1983–used to require that employers have material safety data sheets for all chemicals located in the workplace. Although that requirement is still in place, new and significantly expanded requirements went into effect on June 15, 2015. These requirements are outlined in the OSHA Fact Sheet–Hazard Communication Standard Final Rule, which can be found at https://www.osha.gov/dsg/hazcom/HCSFactsheet.html.

Material Safety Data Sheets

In general, the material safety data sheets (MSDSs) must provide information about chemical hazards in the workplace as well as protective measures that are available. Although OSHA does not mandate use of any specific MSDS format (unlike the I-9 form), the agency does provide the following sample MSDS on its website. (This form, OSHA 174, includes and reflects all information that is required to comply with MSDS guidelines.)

> **NOTE**
>
> Although Form 174 is still available (https://www.osha.gov/Publications/OSHA3514.html), OSHA is moving toward a separate American National Standards Institute (ANSI) standard, Z129.1, for labeling of hazardous chemicals. This, too, gives employers guidance on how to provide information on a label, including standardized phrases and other information that can improve the quality of labels. Because they are voluntary standards, however, the ANSI approach has not been adopted by all chemical manufacturers and importers. As a result of the diverse formats and language used, consistent and understandable presentation of information has not been fully achieved (source: https://www.osha.gov/dsg/hazcom/finalmsdsreport.html#considerations).

> **TIP**
>
> Be familiar with required—and suggested—elements of MSDSs.

Chemical Health Hazards: Teratogens

One specific group of chemicals, called teratogens, will not harm pregnant women but do have the potential to harm fetuses. To deal with this category of chemicals, some organizations have developed fetal protection policies. In some cases these organizations—and policies—are well intentioned; in others, establishing such policies could constitute an attempt to minimize potential legal exposure. Fetal protection policies are intended to protect fetuses from the possibility of being harmed by teratogens. The impact of most (if not all) of these policies, as ruled by the Supreme Court, is unlawful gender discrimination.

The landmark case that resulted in this Supreme Court ruling was *Automobile Workers v. Johnson Controls (1990)*. Johnson Controls manufactured batteries, a process that exposed employees to high levels of lead. The Supreme Court ruled that Johnson Controls' policy constituted a violation of Title VII of the Civil Rights Act of 1964, as amended by the Pregnancy Discrimination Act. The Act states that women cannot be discriminated against

> "Because of or on the basis of pregnancy, childbirth, or related medical conditions; and women affected by pregnancy, childbirth, or related medical conditions shall be treated the same for all employment-related purposes."

In the Johnson case, Supreme Court Associate Justice Byron White wrote in his opinion that "decisions about the welfare of the next generation must be left to the parents who conceive, bear, support, and raise them, rather than to the employers who hire those parents."

Biological Health Hazards

Biological health hazards can be introduced into the workplace by people—employees, customers, vendors, and so forth. Biological health hazards can also be caused by some factor other than person-to-person transmission.

Under the ADA, infectious diseases are considered to be disabilities. As such, employers must determine what reasonable accommodations—specifically, ones that do not cause undue hardship—must be afforded to individuals with infectious diseases. Infectious diseases also pose unique challenges in that employers must take great care to ensure that the health of all individuals in the workplace is not threatened by possible person-to-person transmission. Essentially, the rights of people with infectious diseases must be balanced against the obligation to protect those who work with them.

Determinations relative to what constitutes "reasonable accommodation," "undue hardship," and "threat" must be made carefully. Such decisions cannot be made on the basis of misinformation or coworkers' irrational—albeit genuine—fears. Employers should educate employees, as appropriate, while protecting the confidentiality of people with disabilities. Please review Chapter 2 for a closer look at these considerations.

HR professionals need to be familiar with certain infectious diseases. In the following sections, we will discuss HIV/AIDS, Hepatitis B and C, tuberculosis, and pandemics.

HIV/AIDS

Human Immunodeficiency Virus (HIV) and Acquired Immune Deficiency Syndrome (AIDS) are transmitted person to person through blood or other bodily fluids. Transmission of HIV/AIDS is of particular importance in the health care industry because of the nature of the work performed in that industry.

Employees with HIV/AIDS are afforded protection under the Americans with Disabilities Act. Like any other person with a disability, a person with HIV/AIDS may continue to hold her position as long as she can perform the essential functions of the position with or without reasonable accommodation (that does not cause undue hardship to the organization).

Bias against individuals with HIV/AIDS may exist in the workplace—and that bias is often based on misinformation. HR professionals must be alert to signs of such bias and must be prepared to take appropriate action.

HBV

The Hepatitis B virus (HBV) causes Hepatitis B, a potentially serious (and potentially fatal) form of liver inflammation. People with HBV may experience a wide range of symptoms—anything from no symptoms to serious damage to the liver. Like HIV/AIDS, HBV is transmitted through blood and other bodily fluids and is therefore of particular concern to those in the health care industry. Unlike HIV/AIDS, a vaccine for HBV exists—and must be made available to "all occupationally exposed employees." The term "made available" reflects the fact that an employee cannot be required to get an HBV vaccination.

HCV

The Hepatitis C virus (HCV) causes Hepatitis C, a viral infection of the liver. Transmitted by blood or bodily fluids, HCV has been identified by the Center for Disease Control and Prevention as the most chronic bloodborne infection in the United States.

Although most people with HCV will experience no symptoms for many years, over time that can change. After 10, 20, or as many as 40 years, people with Hepatitis C can develop cirrhosis or cancer of the liver. There is no vaccine for HCV, so the best protection is afforded through prevention, such as protective personal equipment (PPE).

Tuberculosis

Tuberculosis, or TB, is a highly infectious bacterial disease. Although TB usually affects the lungs, it can also impact other organs.

TB can be spread by sneezing or coughing and is thus an important workplace issue. An increase in drug-resistant strains of TB in the 1980s—along with an increased population of individuals with suppressed immune systems—led to a renewed focus on TB. The number of cases of TB has decreased dramatically in the past decade; in fact, according to OSHA, the number of cases of TB is now at its lowest level since reporting began in 1953.

Pandemics

The government defines a pandemic as "a global disease outbreak. A flu pandemic occurs when a new influenza virus emerges for which people have little or no immunity and for which there is no vaccine. The disease spreads easily person to person, causes serious illness, and can sweep across the country and around the world in very short time" (www.pandemciflu.gov). Concerns relative to pandemics currently focus on avian H5N1 virus (commonly referred to as "avian flu" or "bird flu"). The H5N1 virus has raised concerns about a potential human pandemic because

▶ It is especially virulent.

▶ It is being spread by migratory birds.

▶ It can be transmitted from birds to mammals and in some limited circumstances to humans.

▶ Like other influenza viruses, it continues to evolve.

According to the government, since 2003 a growing number of human H5N1 cases have been reported in Azerbaijan, Cambodia, China, Djibouti, Egypt, Indonesia, Iraq, Lao Democratic People's Republic, Nigeria, Thailand, Turkey, and Vietnam. More than half of the people infected with the H5N1 virus have died, and most of these cases are believed to have been caused by exposure to infected poultry. Although there has been no sustained human-to-human transmission of the disease, there is concern that H5N1 will evolve into a virus capable of human-to-human transmission.

Avian flu represents, in some ways, a confluence of different dimensions of risk management pertaining to infectious disease and emergency preparedness. Although it is critical for organizations to prepare, just as they would do with any sound emergency preparedness plan, it is equally critical that organizations not overreact or allow fear to fuel their actions or reactions.

Health and Wellness Programs

Health and wellness programs offer employees the opportunity to enhance the quality of their lives through healthier lifestyle choices. Health and wellness programs take a proactive approach to health of body, mind, and spirit.

Although prevention is a key element, health and wellness programs can also provide assistance to employees who are dealing with existing health issues (for instance, weight problems or smoking).

Wellness programs, however, are not (and should not be) positioned to HR's business partners as something that is "nice to do" for employees. Instead, health and wellness programs constitute a solid business investment that benefits the organization as well as its employees. According to Ron Goetzel, Ph.D., Director of the Cornell University Institute for Health and Productivity Studies, wellness programs have been shown to yield a 3-to-1 return on investment (ROI). In that same article, published in the November/December 2006 edition of the *North Carolina Medical Journal*, Goetzel references one specific success story, in which Citibank reported a savings of $8.9 million in medical expenditures from their health promotion program after investing 1.9 million in the program—thereby generating an ROI of 4.56 to 1.

Like employee assistance programs (EAPs), health and wellness programs benefit employers as well as employees. As with EAPs, HR professionals must be prepared to demonstrate the specific financial and nonfinancial benefits that would accrue to their employers as a result of implementing health and wellness programs.

Health and Wellness Programs and the ADA

On April 20, 2015, the U.S. Equal Employment Opportunity Commission (EEOC) published a Notice of Proposed Rulemaking (NPRM) in the Federal Register that describes how Title I of the Americans with Disabilities Act (ADA) applies to employee wellness programs that are part of group health plans and that include questions about employees' health (such as questions on health risk assessments) or medical examinations (such as screening for high cholesterol, high blood pressure, or blood glucose levels). The NPRM is available at https://www.federalregister.gov/articles/2015/04/20/2015-08827/regulations-under-the-americans-with-disabilities-act-amendments. A fact sheet explaining the contents of the NPRM can be found at http://www1.eeoc.gov//laws/regulations/facts_nprm_wellness.cfm?renderforprint=1.

Chemical Use and Dependency

The statistics regarding costs associated with chemical/substance use, abuse, and dependency—particularly as related to the workplace, are economically staggering. As published on the DOL website (www.dol.gov):

▶ More than 6 percent of the population over 12 years of age (13.9 million people) has used drugs within the past 30 days. Rates of use remain highest among persons aged 16 to 25—the age group entering the workforce most.

▶ Seventy-three percent of all current drug users aged 18 and older (8.3 million adults) were employed in 1997. This includes 6.7 million full-time workers and 1.6 million part-time workers.

▶ More than 14 percent of Americans employed full time and part time report heavy drinking, which is defined as five or more drinks on five or more days in the past 30 days. The heaviest drinking occurred among persons between the ages of 18 and 25 years.

▶ According to a national survey conducted by the Hazelden Foundation, more than 60 percent of adults know people who have gone to work under the influence of drugs or alcohol.

The Impact of Drug and Alcohol Use in the Workplace

The economic and human costs of drug and alcohol use are staggering. The following fact sheet offers more insight into the expansiveness of this crisis, and its impact.

Substance Abuse Programs

According to the U.S. Department of Labor's Working Partners for an Alcohol- and Drug-Free Workplace initiative, a comprehensive substance program consists of the following five components:

▶ Drug-free workplace policy

▶ Supervisor training

▶ Employee education

▶ Employee assistance

▶ Drug testing

One more critical element (in many ways perhaps the most critical element) must be added to this list: management buy-in and support. Without this, the likelihood that the program will be successful is greatly diminished—and HR is more likely to be seen as an enforcer rather than as a strategic partner.

As with all workplace initiatives to which HR contributes, it is important to quantify the benefits of establishing a substance abuse program.

Symptoms of Chemical and Substance Abuse

HR professionals need to be able to recognize the warning signs of chemical and substance abuse:

▶ Sudden decline in quality or quantity or work performed for no apparent reason

▶ Increased errors

▶ Increased accidents

▶ Inconsistent behavior

▶ Emotional unpredictability

It is important to note, however, that any of these symptoms could result from a variety of other factors, so guard against jumping to any conclusions. In addition, always check state laws that may be in place in their jurisdiction as well as collective-bargaining contracts if and when the employer is contemplating dismissal of the employee.

Drug Testing

Drug testing in the workplace is a hotly debated topic. Some states restrict certain types of drug testing, and some federal laws require drug testing of certain employees. Drug testing programs must be administered fairly and consistently to similarly situated employees.

CAUTION

HR professionals should consult with senior leadership and with legal counsel before implementing or changing a drug-testing program. Such changes can have unforeseen legal and employee relations ramifications.

Various types of drug-testing programs exist, each of which has different goals and objectives. Table 6.4 highlights these programs further.

TABLE 6.4 Types of Drug Tests

Type of Drug Test	Purpose/Description
Pre-employment	Decrease the likelihood of hiring someone who is currently using/abusing drugs. To ensure that similarly situated candidates are being treated consistently, it is important to ensure that all candidates applying for a particular position(s) participate in pre-employment drug tests. To ensure even greater consistency, conduct the test at the same point in the pre-employment process.
Prepromotion	Decrease the likelihood of promoting an employee who is currently using/abusing drugs.
Annual physical tests	Drug testing is performed as part of each employee's annual physical exam to identify current drug users/abusers for assistance or disciplinary action.

Type of Drug Test	Purpose/Description
Reasonable suspicion and for cause	For cause tests are conducted when an employee shows obvious signs of not being fit for duty. Reasonable suspicion tests are conducted when employee has a documented pattern of unsafe work behavior. These tests are conducted to protect the safety and well-being of employees and coworkers and to identify opportunities for rehabilitation.
Random	Unannounced tests are conducted at random for reasons related to safety or security.
Postaccident	Employees who are involved in an accident or unsafe practice incident are tested to determine whether alcohol or some other drug was a factor. These tests are intended to protect the safety of employees (users and nonusers) and to identify opportunities for rehabilitation.
Treatment follow-up	Employees who return to work after participating in an alcohol or drug treatment program are periodically tested to ensure that they remain free of illegal substances.

TIP

Be familiar with drug-testing techniques as well as appropriate intervention strategies.

Work-Related Stress

Stress is a significant workplace issue. In its 1999 report titled "Stress at Work," the National Institute for Public Safety and Health (NIOSH) defined stress as the "harmful physical and emotional responses that occur when the requirements of the job do not match the capabilities, resources, or needs of the worker." Stress can be more than disquieting; it can actually cause illness and injury. And stress is expensive. The American Institute of Stress estimates a $300 billion annual price tag for stress, which includes costs relating to accidents; absenteeism; employee turnover; diminished productivity; direct medical, legal, and insurance costs; workers' compensation awards; and tort and FELA (Federal Employers' Liability Act) judgments. In the book *Stress Costs*, author Ravi Tangri presents a formula for tabulating the actual costs of stress, which he asserts account for the physical, psychological, and mental manifestations of stress:

- ▶ 19% of absenteeism
- ▶ 40% of turnover
- ▶ 30% of short- and long-term disability
- ▶ 10% of drug plan costs
- ▶ 60% of total workplace accidents

HR professionals must also be able to identify, implement, and evaluate interventions designed to prevent or eradicate job stress. NIOSH outlines a valuable three-step approach to this in "Stress at Work," www.cdc.gov/niosh/.

TIP

Stress, left unchecked or unresolved, can lead to burnout. Know the symptoms of employee burnout.

Worker's Compensation

Worker's compensation laws are state laws intended to provide medical care to injured employees and death benefits to families of those who died. HR professionals also need to be highly familiar with the worker's compensation laws within the states in which their employees work. Worker's comp is a no-fault system—injured workers receive medical or compensation benefits regardless of who caused the job-related accident.

RM Responsibility 04

Establish and administer a return-to-work process after illness or injury to ensure a safe workplace (for example: modified duty assignment, reasonable accommodations, independent medical exam).

RESPONSIBILITY

Knowledge 64

Return to work procedures (for example: interactive dialog, job modification, accommodations).

KNOWLEDGE

The U.S. DOL offers a highly useful resource titled "Return-to-Work Toolkit for Employees & Employers." This is available online through www.dol.gov.

RM Responsibility 05

Develop/select, implement, and evaluate plans and policies to protect employees and other individuals and to minimize the organization's loss and liability (for example: emergency response, workplace violence, substance abuse).

RESPONSIBILITY

Knowledge 71

Employer/employee rights related to substance abuse.

KNOWLEDGE

Risk Management: A Process Model

One way to begin to gain a better understanding of almost any topic, including risk management, is to look at models. Although many risk management models have been developed, one particularly thought-provoking model was developed by the Nonprofit Risk Management Center (www.nonprofitrisk.org).

Although designed specifically for nonprofit organizations, this model provides a valuable starting point for organizations within the for-profit (and perhaps even the municipal) sector. Their model of the risk management process contains the following five steps:

1. **Establish the context:** It's important to begin a risk management program by setting goals and identifying any potential barriers or impediments to the implementation of the program. In the goal-setting exercise, ask, "what are we trying to accomplish by integrating risk management into our operations?"

2. **Acknowledge and identify risks:** There are many ways to undertake risk identification; the key is using a framework or strategy that allows you to identify all major risks facing your nonprofit.

3. **Evaluate and prioritize risks:** The third step in the process helps you keep things in perspective and establish a list of action items in priority order. The risk of an asteroid crashing into your organization's annual Black Tie Event is remote, so it probably makes more sense to work on a more likely risk—that someone could slip and hurt herself on a waxed dance floor.

4. **Select appropriate risk management strategies and implement your plan:** We'll discuss four risk management techniques that can be used individually or in combination to address many different types of risk.

5. **Monitor and update the risk management program:** Organizations constantly face new challenges and opportunities. Risk management techniques and plans should be reviewed periodically to ensure they remain the most appropriate strategy given the organization's needs and circumstances.

Risk Management: Techniques

As this model and these techniques begin to demonstrate, risk is part of the everyday fabric of organizational life. It spans every workplace responsibility from hiring a new employee, to serving a customer, to expanding into a new market, to launching an advertising campaign, to making a charitable contribution. In a broader sense, however, risk management also speaks to being prepared to weather the storms of unavoidable (or unavoided) risk, in part through emergency and business continuity planning.

This model also identifies a variety of risk management techniques—each of which (or a combination of which) might be more appropriate under different circumstances.

Avoidance

Whenever an organization cannot offer a service while ensuring a high degree of safety, it should choose avoidance as a risk management technique. Do not offer programs that pose too great a risk. In some cases avoidance is the most appropriate technique if an organization doesn't have the financial resources required to fund adequate training, supervision, equipment, or other safety measures. Always ask, "Is there something we could do to deliver this program/conduct this activity safely?" If you answer "yes," risk modification may be the more practical techniques.

Modification

Modification is changing an activity to make it safer for all involved. Policies and procedures are examples of risk modification. For instance, an organization concerned about the risk of using unsafe drivers may add DMV record checks to its screening process or an annual road test for all drivers.

Retention

There are two ways to retain risk. The first is by design. An organization may decide that other available techniques aren't suitable and it will therefore retain the risk of harm or loss. Organizations make conscious decisions to retain risk every day. For example, when an organization purchases liability insurance and elects a $1,000 deductible or self-insured retention, it's retaining risk. This can be a rational and appropriate approach to managing risk. Organizations get into trouble when risk is retained unintentionally. The unintentional retention of risk can be the result of failure to understand the exclusions of an insurance policy, insufficient understanding of the scope of risk an organization faces, or not taking the time to consider the risk and how it can be addressed.

Sharing

Risk sharing involves apportioningrisk with another organization through a contract. Two common examples are insurance contracts that require an insurer to pay for claims expenses and losses under certain circumstances, and service contracts whereby a provider (such as a transportation service or caterer) agrees to perform a service and assume liability for potential harm occurring in the delivery of the service.

Employment Practices Liability Insurance

Employment practices liability insurance (EPLI) can help employers prepare for facing such situations and for withstanding the costs associated with them.

As HR professionals and as human beings, there are some things that are within our control and other things that are outside it. One of the things that falls outside our control, to a significant degree, is the fact that U.S. organizations must operate within a culture that—whether right or wrong, whether good or bad, and whether justified or unjustified—is highly litigious.

Regardless of who prevails in litigation, there are many costs—financial and otherwise—associated with employment litigation. EPLI can help employers be prepared for facing such situations and the costs associated with them.

As described by the Insurance Information Institute (www.iii.org), EPLI covers businesses against claims by workers who allege that their legal rights as employees of the company have been violated. Some insurers provide this coverage as an endorsement to their business owners policy (BOP), whereas others offer EPLI as a standalone coverage.

EPLI provides protection against many kinds of employee lawsuits, including claims of

- ► Sexual harassment
- ► Discrimination
- ► Wrongful termination
- ► Breach of employment contract
- ► Negligent evaluation
- ► Failure to employ or promote
- ► Wrongful discipline
- ► Deprivation of career opportunity
- ► Wrongful infliction of emotional distress
- ► Mismanagement of employee benefit plans

The cost of EPLI coverage depends on the type of business, the number of employees, and various risk factors such as whether the company has been sued over employment practices in the past. The policies will reimburse your company against the legal costs of defending a lawsuit in court and for judgments and settlements, regardless of whether your company wins or loses the suit. Policies typically do not pay for punitive damages or civil or criminal fines. Liabilities covered by other insurance policies such as workers compensation are excluded from EPLI policies.

Employee Rights Related to Substance Abuse

An excellent source of information on this complex and multifaceted topic can be found at www.usccr.gov/pubs/ada/ch4.htm: "Sharing the Dream: Is the ADA Accommodating All?," Chapter 4, Substance Abuse under the ADA.

RESPONSIBILITY

RM Responsibility 07

Develop, monitor, and test business continuity and disaster recovery plans.

KNOWLEDGE

Knowledge 69

Organizational incident and emergency response plans.

KNOWLEDGE

Knowledge 72

Business continuity and disaster recovery plans (for example: data storage and backup, alternative work locations, procedures).

The business impact of most emergencies can be minimized if organizations have developed, distributed, and rehearsed business continuity and disaster recovery plans in advance.

Emergency/Business Continuity Planning

So what's an emergency? In its "Emergency Management Guide for Business and Industry," Federal Emergency Management Agency (FEMA) offers a relatively all-encompassing definition of emergency:

> "An emergency is an unplanned event that can cause deaths or significant injuries to employees, customers or the public; or that can shut down your business, disrupt operations, cause physical or environmental damage, or threaten the facility's financial standing or public image."

Nearly limitless types of emergencies could fall within the broad scope of this definition—natural, chemical, biological, terrorist, technological. The list could go on and on.

Knowing what an emergency is, however, is only part of this equation. It's also critical to have a working knowledge of emergency management, which this same FEMA document describes as follows:

> "Emergency management is the process of preparing for, mitigating, responding to and recovering from an emergency.... Emergency planning is a dynamic process. Planning, though critical, is not the only component. Training, conducting drills, testing equipment, and coordinating activities with the community are other important functions."

Interestingly, this same document—although not written directly for HR professionals—goes on to address emergency planning in a way that speaks to the essence of our role as HR business partners—partners who must function tactically and strategically as well as transactionally:

"To be successful, emergency management requires upper management support. The chief executive sets the tone by authorizing planning to take place and directing senior management to get involved."

When presenting the case for emergency management, avoid dwelling on the negative effects of an emergency (deaths, fines, criminal prosecution) and emphasize the positive aspects of preparedness. For example:

▶ It helps companies fulfill their moral responsibility to protect employees, the community, and the environment.

▶ It facilitates compliance with requirements of federal, state, and local agencies.

▶ It enhances a company's ability to recover from financial losses, regulatory fines, loss of market share, damage to equipment/products, or business interruption.

▶ It reduces exposure to civil or criminal liability in the event of an incident.

▶ It enhances a company's image and credibility with employees, customers, suppliers, and the community.

▶ It may reduce your insurance premiums.

Continuity of HR-Related Operations

When looking at the areas of emergency management and business continuity, be careful not to unintentionally overlook the continuity of HR-related operations. On the transactional, tactical, and transformational levels, HR professionals must have a method in place to continue functioning and to continue meeting the fast-changing needs of the organization.

Many HR departments were unexpectedly faced with extreme situations of this nature in the wake of the terrorist attacks of September 11, 2001. In an instant, HR professionals had to think—and live—the unthinkable and had to function effectively in unimaginable circumstances. Some gave their lives in service to their organizations and to their colleagues. Now, in the wake of September 11, it is incumbent upon us to ensure that those sacrifices were not in vain. We must do all that we can to prepare for the unthinkable, in whatever form it could ultimately take.

Knowledge 62
Occupational injury and illness prevention (safety) and compensation programs.

KNOWLEDGE

Knowledge 63
Investigation procedures of workplace safety, health, and security enforcement agencies.

KNOWLEDGE

Knowledge 65
Workplace safety risks (for example: trip hazards, bloodborne pathogens).

KNOWLEDGE

Knowledge 66

Workplace security risks (for example: theft, corporate espionage, sabotage).

Safety

Workplace safety can be defined in many ways. In essence, a "safe workplace" can be defined as one in which employees are free from risks of injury or illness. Call it prevention or call it avoidance, either way, workplace safety requires that companies take a proactive approach to accidents, injury, and illness:

1. Organizations must minimize the likelihood that work-related injuries or illnesses will occur.

2. Organizations must proactively establish response plans in the event that injuries or illnesses do occur.

OSHA and Workplace Safety

OSHA, as its name implies, is the government agency charged with ensuring a safe and healthy workplace. OSHA recommends a four-module approach to safety and health management.

Module 1—Safety and Health Payoffs

Work-related injuries are expensive, financially and otherwise. According to the National Safety Council, workplace injuries cost $198.2 billion in 2012. The cost is also human—according to OSHA, an average of 3.3 out of every 100 workers is injured each day.

Module 2—Management System

Organizations must create and cultivate a culture of safety. Safety can't be separate from the culture; rather, it must be an integral component of the culture. Within this culture of safety, four specific elements can then be created and integrated:

▶ Management leadership and employee involvement

▶ Worksite analysis

▶ Hazard prevention and control

▶ Safety and health training

Module 3—Conducting a Safety and Health Checkup

Organizations must then assess their own safety and health—take a good hard look at themselves with respect to each of those four areas identified in Module 2.

Module 4—Creating Change

The roadmap is in place, and the self-analysis has been conducted. The next step is to implement necessary change. To do this, obstacles will need to be identified and overcome, and a process implementation strategy—beginning with the buy-in of top management—must be developed and implemented.

Safety Committees

Safety committees provide a means by which employees and managers can collaboratively work toward increasing workplace safety. Safety committees can also support HR professionals as they research, develop, select, and implement safety training and incentive programs.

Some of the purposes of safety committees include

▶ Building and maintaining interest in health and safety issues

▶ Ensuring that managers and employees recognize that they are primarily responsible for preventing workplace accidents

▶ Reinforcing safety as part of the fabric of the organization's culture

▶ Providing a forum for discussing health- and safety-related issues

▶ Informing, educating, and training employees about emerging safety-related information or guidelines

Functions that safety committees might carry out in support of these objectives could include the following:

▶ Analyzing accidents/incidents to identify trends and to plan corrective action

▶ Conducting periodic (such as monthly) safety inspections

▶ Planning and carrying out training

▶ Reporting and analyzing accomplishments as well as current safety concerns

▶ Setting annual safety objectives

▶ Ensuring that an effective safety program is in place

OSHA—Inspections and Investigations

OSHA compliance officers can conduct inspections or investigations without prior notice or warning. Upon showing proper identification, a compliance officer is free to conduct reasonable inspections and investigations during regular working hours.

There are certain limited circumstances under which OSHA may give employers 24-hours advance notice:

▶ In cases of apparent imminent danger to enable the employer to abate the danger as quickly as possible

▶ In circumstances where the inspection can most effectively be conducted after regular business hours or where special preparations are necessary for an inspection

▶ Where necessary to assure the presence of representatives of the employer and employees or the appropriate personnel needed to aid in the inspection

▶ In other circumstances where the Area Director determines that the giving of advance notice would enhance the probability of an effective and thorough inspection (www.osha.gov)

Giving advanced notice is an involved process that triggers a series of requirements and guidelines:

"In the situations described in paragraph (a) of this section, advance notice of inspections may be given only if authorized by the Area Director, except that in cases of apparent imminent danger, advance notice may be given by the Compliance Safety and Health Officer without such authorization if the Area Director is not immediately available. When advance notice is given, it shall be the employer's responsibility promptly to notify the authorized representative of employees of the inspection, if the identity of such representative is known to the employer. (See §1903.8(b) as to situations where there is no authorized representative of employees.) Upon the request of the employer, the Compliance Safety and Health Officer will inform the authorized representative of employees of the inspection, provided that the employer furnishes the Compliance Safety and Health Officer with the identity of such representative and with such other information as is necessary to enable him promptly to inform such representative of the inspection. An employer who fails to comply with his obligation under this paragraph promptly to inform the authorized representative of employees of the inspection or to furnish such information as is necessary to enable the Compliance Safety and Health Officer promptly to inform such representative of the inspection, may be subject to citation and penalty under section 17(c) of the Act. Advance notice in any of the situations described in paragraph (a) of this section shall not be given more than 24 hours before the inspection is scheduled to be conducted, except in apparent imminent danger situations and in other unusual circumstances" (www.osha.gov).

It is also important to note that "(t)he Act provides in section 17(f) that any person who gives advance notice of any inspection to be conducted under the Act, without authority from the Secretary or his designees, shall, upon conviction, be punished by fine of not more than $1,000 or by imprisonment for not more than 6 months, or by both" (www.osha.gov).

Employer Rights

Employers have certain rights with respect to inspections, including the right to

- ▶ Request proper identification from compliance officers
- ▶ Ask the compliance officer for the reason for the inspection or investigation—and get an answer
- ▶ Have an opening conference with the compliance officer
- ▶ Accompany the compliance officer as she conducts the inspection
- ▶ Have a closing conference with the compliance officer
- ▶ File a "notice of contest" to dispute the results of the inspection
- ▶ Request an informal settlement agreement process after an inspection
- ▶ Protect the confidentiality of trade secrets
- ▶ Require the compliance officer to obtain a search warrant

Employer Responsibilities—Standards

OSHA's standards, or requirements, apply to one or more of the four industries designated by OSHA:

- General industry

- Maritime

- Construction

- Agriculture

OSHA identifies six standards that apply to most general industry employers:

- **Hazard Communication Standard ("Employee Right-to-Know"):** This standard ensures that employers and employees have knowledge and awareness about hazardous chemicals located in the workplace and that they know how to protect themselves. Specifically, this standard requires all employers having hazardous materials at the workplace to implement a written Hazard Communication Program. Four important key elements of this program are MSDSs, orientation, training, and container labeling requirements.

- **Emergency Action Plan Standard:** Although recommended for all employers, an emergency action plan is mandatory only if required by a separate OSHA standard.

- **Fire Safety Standard:** Although recommended for all employers, a fire safety plan is mandatory only if required by a separate OSHA standard.

- **Exit Routes Standard:** Mandatory for all employers, the exit route standard defines exit requirements and addresses maintenance, safeguarding, and operational dimensions of exit routes. OSHA defines an exit route as "a continuous and unobstructed path of exit travel from any point within a workplace to a point of safety" (source: OSHA Fact Sheet, Exit Routes).

- **Walking/Working Surfaces Standard:** Mandatory in all permanent places of employment (with few exceptions), this standard seeks to minimize or eliminate slips, trips, and falls in the workplace. Its coverage impacts surfaces such as floors, platforms, ladders, and steps.

- **Medical and First Aid Standard:** OSHA requires employers to provide medical and first aid personnel and supplies in accordance with the hazards of the workplace. The specifics of each program, however, will differ from workplace to workplace and from employer to employer.

In a list that OSHA specifically describes as "not comprehensive," OSHA identifies nine additional standards that may apply to workplaces. These are described in Table 6.5.

TABLE 6.5   Nine OSHA Standards

Standard	Employers May Be Covered If...
Machine Guarding	Employees operate machinery such as saws, slicers, power presses, and so on.
Lockout/Tagout	Employees work with equipment that can start up without warning or that release hazardous energy.
Electrical Hazards	Any electrical systems are present.

Standard	Employers May Be Covered If...
Personal Protective Equipment (PPE)	Mandatory employer assessment determines that PPE is necessary. If so, the employer must provide, maintain, and require the use of PPE.
Respirators	Respirators are necessary to protect the health of employees. If so, the employer must provide respirators.
Hearing Conservation	Employees are exposed to excessive noise.
Confined Spaces	Employees work in confined spaces, thereby increasing the likelihood of entrapment or placing the employee in close physical proximity to hazards (such as machinery with moving parts).
Bloodborne Pathogens	Employees are exposed to blood or other bodily fluids through the performance of their regular duties.
Powered Industrial Tools	Powered industrial tools, such as forklifts, are used.

Security

Security refers to protection of the workplace and of the employees who work there. Security threats can come from a range of possible sources, just a few of which are

- Natural disasters, such as earthquakes
- Theft
- Workplace violence
- Terrorism (including biological terrorism)
- Identity theft
- Fire
- Flood
- Hazardous materials
- Computer viruses/hackers

HR professionals need a working knowledge of these and other threats that can jeopardize workplace security.

EXAM ALERT

A cursory review of the preceding list reinforces the fact that security issues are business issues—ones that can jeopardize an organization's existence. As such, it is critical for organizations to conduct a SWOT analysis—strengths, weaknesses, opportunities, and threats—of security-related issues.

Threats are often perceived as coming from outside the organization. Overlooking internal threats, however, can be disastrous. For instance, even a company's own employees can present a security threat. Disgruntled employees, departing employees, or former employees can present threats in the form of sabotage, theft, espionage, or violence.

HR must partner with internal or external security experts to protect the tangible—and intangible—assets of the organization. Of primary importance are the organization's human assets—its employees. Other assets, such as technology, facilities, and financial assets, must also be protected.

When Prevention Isn't Enough

The criticality of emergency preparedness planning was perhaps among the most painful—and the most valuable—of the many lessons learned from the 9/11 terrorist attacks. On that day, the unthinkable became real. Now it is a part of our shared history. As HR professionals, however, we must not allow any degree of complacency to creep back into our business operations. HR must work ceaselessly and collaboratively to develop emergency response plans should a situation arise in which security is breached. Although the plans we collaboratively develop may never be utilized, failing to do so will surely place employers, employees, and all other assets at significant risk.

It is here, during a discussion of workplace security, that we are naturally led to where this chapter began—an in-depth review of risk management. Security is, at its core, all about assessing, preparing for, addressing, and in a holistic sense, managing various types of risk. This applies to any imaginable type of asset—technical, human, financial, or physical. The reality is that it is not possible to remove all risk. Nor would that necessarily be advisable because security so often finds itself perched on the opposite of the pendulum from freedom. In other words, total security might be possible, but there is a cost—a cost that may not represent an acceptable choice to senior leadership. Risk is real—whether it emanates from within or outside the organization, or even from within or outside the nation. It is unavoidable, and whether it takes the form of issues pertaining to health, safety, or security, it must be addressed and managed to the best of the organization's—and our profession's—collective ability.

RM Responsibility 09

Develop policies and procedures to direct the appropriate use of electronic media and hardware (for example: email, social media, and appropriate website access).

RESPONSIBILITY

Knowledge 74

Technology and applications (for example: social media, monitoring software, biometrics).

KNOWLEDGE

HR professionals need to be familiar with the following terms and concepts:

- ▶ **Social media:** Online websites that individuals/employees use for personal as well as professional networking purposes.

- ▶ **Monitoring software:** Software that employers often install to block or report when employees/contractors have accessed websites that could cause the organization risk. This risk can take many forms, ranging from lost productivity, to the introduction of viruses, to corporate espionage.

- ▶ **Biometrics:** Unique biological characteristics or attributes (such as a fingerprints, retina scanning, or DNA) that are matched to one specific individual for purposes of identification.

In addition, familiarize yourself with the terms and concepts explored in Chapter 1, "Business Management and Strategy," and carefully review the resources cited at the end of this chapter.

RESPONSIBILITY

RM Responsibility 10

Develop and administer internal and external privacy policies (for example: identity theft, data protection, workplace monitoring).

KNOWLEDGE

Knowledge 70

Internal investigation, monitoring, and surveillance techniques.

KNOWLEDGE

Knowledge 73

Data integrity techniques and technology (for example: data sharing, password usage, social engineering).

KNOWLEDGE

Knowledge 75

Financial management practices (for example: procurement policies, credit card policies and guidelines, expense policies).

Human resource professionals must remain cognizant of, and ideally participate in, the shaping of financial management and other policies that influence policies affecting employees and that could expose the organization to risk (financial or nonfinancial).

Familiarize yourself with the terms and concepts explored in Chapter 1 and carefully review the resources cited at the end of this chapter.

KNOWLEDGE

Knowledge 67

Potential violent behavior and workplace violence conditions.

Workplace violence has become a progressively more serious concern for employers, and for HR professionals in particular. Although many incidents are reported in the media, many other incidents are only locally reported or may not be reported in mainstream media (especially if the incident does not result in a death). According to OSHA:

> "Nearly 2 million American workers report having been victims of workplace violence each year. Unfortunately, many more cases go unreported. The truth is, workplace violence can strike anywhere, anytime, and no one is immune. Research has identified factors that may increase the risk of violence for some workers at certain worksites. Such factors include exchanging money with the public and working with volatile, unstable people. Working alone or in isolated areas may also contribute to the potential for violence. Providing services and care, and working where alcohol is served may also impact the likelihood of violence. Additionally, time of day and location of work, such as working late at night or in areas with high crime rates, are also risk factors that should be considered when addressing issues of workplace violence. Among those with higher risk are workers who exchange money with the public, delivery drivers, healthcare professionals, public service workers, customer service agents, law enforcement personnel, and those who work alone or in small groups" (www.osha.gov).

OSHA defines workplace violence as:

> "any act or threat of physical violence, harassment, intimidation, or other threatening disruptive behavior that occurs at the work site. It ranges from threats and verbal abuse to physical assaults and even homicide. It can affect and involve employees, clients, customers and visitors. Homicide is currently the fourth-leading cause of fatal occupational injuries in the United States. According to the Bureau of Labor Statistics Census of Fatal Occupational Injuries (CFOI), of the 4,547 fatal workplace injuries that occurred in the United States in 2010, 506 were workplace homicides. Homicide is the leading cause of death for women in the workplace. However it manifests itself, workplace violence is a major concern for employers and employees nationwide" (www.osha.gov).

Ultimately, therefore, no employer is immune from addressing potential workplace violence concerns. As such, HR professionals must be committed to proactively—and, as necessary—reactively addressing this pressing concern.

OSHA has published a fact sheet on workplace violence (available at www.osha.gov) that can be seen in Appendix B, "OSHA Fact Sheet."

Chapter Summary

Knowledge and skill in the area of risk management present another significant opportunity for HR professionals to add value to the organization. As such, HR professionals must understand and be able to respond effectively to all issues—proactive, reactive, and regulatory—relating to risk management.

This holds true even if risk management does not seem to fall directly within an HR professional's formal job description. HR professionals cannot be prepared to handle only those situations that are predictable or routine. We need look no further than the wake of the terror attacks of 9/11 to see examples of how HR professionals can—and will—be called upon to bring their knowledge and expertise to situations that are predictable, as well as to situations that are unpredictable. Knowledge and skill in the areas of risk management will ensure that we are poised to rise to the challenges with which we will inevitably be presented.

Key Terms

- Risk management
- Occupational health, safety, and security
- Occupational Safety and Health Act (OSHA), 1970
- Fair Credit Reporting Act (FCRA), 1970
- Mine Safety and Health Act (MSHA)
- Drug-Free Workplace Act, 1988
- USA PATRIOT Act, 2001
- Homeland Security Act, 2002
- Sarbanes-Oxley Act, 2002
- Work-related illness
- Work-related injury
- General Duty Clause
- OSHA 3165 poster
- OSHA Form 300—Log of Work-Related Injuries and Illnesses
- OSHA Form 300A—Summary of Work-Related Injuries and Illnesses
- OSHA Form 301—Injury and Illness Incident Report
- Incidence rates
- Needlestick Safety and Prevention Act of 2000
- Opening conference
- Walk-through
- Closing conference
- Willful violation

- Serious violation
- Other-than-serious violation
- De minimis violation
- Failure to abate violation
- Repeat violation
- Environmental health standards
- Physical health hazards
- Physical design hazards
- Musculoskeletal disorders (MSDs)
- Cumulative trauma syndrome (CTS)
- Chemical health hazards
- Teratogens
- *Automobile Workers v. Johnson Controls, 1990*
- Material safety data sheets (MSDSs)
- Biological health hazards
- HIV/AIDS
- HBV
- HCV
- Tuberculosis
- Pandemics
- Health and wellness programs
- Chemical use and dependency
- Substance abuse programs
- Drug testing
- Work-related stress

- ▸ Worker's compensation
- ▸ Return-to-work process
- ▸ Employment practices liability insurance (EPLI)
- ▸ Continuity and disaster recovery plans
- ▸ Emergency response plans
- ▸ Safety committees
- ▸ Hazard Communication Standard ("Employee Right-to-Know")

- ▸ Emergency Action Plan Standard
- ▸ Fire Safety Standard
- ▸ Exit Routes Standard
- ▸ Walking/Working Surfaces Standard
- ▸ Medical and First Aid Standard
- ▸ Security
- ▸ Monitoring software
- ▸ Biometrics
- ▸ Workplace violence

Apply Your Knowledge

This chapter focuses on risk management issues. Complete the following exercises, review questions, and exam questions as a way of reviewing and reinforcing the knowledge and skills you'll need to perform your responsibilities as an HR professional.

Review Questions

1. What three employer requirements were added to the Bloodborne Pathogens Standard by the Needlestick Safety and Prevention Act of 2000?

2. In what way was the *Automobile Workers v. Johnson Controls (1990)* Supreme Court ruling significant?

3. The General Duty Clause identified three responsibilities: two for employers, and one for employees. What are they?

4. What is the best way to prevent Hepatitis C/HCV from being transmitted in the workplace?

5. What are the six critical components of a comprehensive substance program? Of these, which is the most important?

Exam Questions

1. Which of the following laws was not created specifically to address occupational safety and health issues?

   ❍ **A.** Drug-Free Workplace Act

   ❍ **B.** MSHA

   ❍ **C.** OSHA

   ❍ **D.** WARNA

2. Which of the following is exempt from coverage under OSHA?

   ❍ **A.** Family farms that employ fewer than 11 employees

   ❍ **B.** Federal government employees

   ❍ **C.** Self-employed individuals

   ❍ **D.** Certain low-risk industries specified by OSHA

3. Which of the following statements about health and wellness programs is most true?

- ○ **A.** They are of primary benefit to employers.
- ○ **B.** They are of primary benefit to employees.
- ○ **C.** They take a proactive approach to health and wellness issues.
- ○ **D.** They take a reactive approach to health and wellness issues.

4. All the following are likely functions of a safety committee except

- ○ **A.** Investigating accidents and incidents
- ○ **B.** Conducting inspections
- ○ **C.** Instituting PPE enhancements
- ○ **D.** Identifying safety concerns

5. Which of the following is not a category of workplace drug testing?

- ○ **A.** Pre-employment
- ○ **B.** Reasonable cause
- ○ **C.** Post-accident
- ○ **D.** Random

6. Which of the following statements does not reflect a security-related HR responsibility?

- ○ **A.** Develop/select, implement, and evaluate security plans to protect the company from liability.
- ○ **B.** Develop/select, implement, and evaluate recordkeeping tools for reporting internal and external breaches of security to OSHA.
- ○ **C.** Develop/select, implement, and evaluate security plans to protect employees (for example, injuries resulting from workplace violence).
- ○ **D.** Develop/select, implement, and evaluate incident and emergency response plans.

7. Which of the following is most likely to cause or contribute to the onset of an MSD?

- ○ **A.** Improper use of PPE
- ○ **B.** Poor ergonomic design
- ○ **C.** Poor ventilation
- ○ **D.** Improper use of MSDS

8. An employee who has just learned that he is HIV positive

- ○ **A.** Is entitled to continue performing his job as long as he can perform the essential functions of that job
- ○ **B.** May continue to perform his job until he begins to develop visible or other outward symptoms
- ○ **C.** Should strongly consider informing coworkers about his HIV status to address any fears or concerns in a proactive manner
- ○ **D.** Constitutes a direct threat to coworkers' health and should therefore be strongly encouraged to take a leave of absence

9. According to the OSH Act, which of the following statements is true?

○ **A.** Employers must correct workplace hazards by the date indicated on the citation and must certify that these hazards have been reduced or eliminated.

○ **B.** Employees have the right to copies of medical records of coworkers who have been exposed to toxic and harmful substances or conditions.

○ **C.** Employers must submit a plan to reduce or eliminate workplace hazards by the date indicated on the citation.

○ **D.** Employees have the right to review, but not to photocopy, their medical records or records of their exposure to toxic and harmful substances or conditions.

10. Under OSHA, employees enjoy all the following rights except

○ **A.** The right to notify their employer or OSHA about workplace hazards

○ **B.** The right to ask OSHA to maintain your confidentiality

○ **C.** The right to request an OSHA inspection if you believe that there are unsafe and unhealthful conditions in your workplace

○ **D.** The right to file a complaint with OSHA within 45 days of discrimination by your employer for making safety and health complaints or for exercising your rights under the OSH Act

Answers to Review Questions

1. The Needlestick Safety and Prevention Act of 2000 added the following three employer requirements to the Bloodborne Pathogens Standard:

   ▶ Maintaining a log of all injuries resulting from contaminated sharps

   ▶ Evaluating—and implementing—safer needle devices (as they become available)

   ▶ Involving employees who use needles and needle devices in the evaluation and selection of needles and needle devices

2. The *Automobile Workers v. Johnson Controls (1990)* Supreme Court ruling established that most, if not all, fetal protection policies result in gender discrimination. It also affirmed that parents—not employers—bear the obligation of protecting fetuses from chemical risk.

3. The General Duty clause established that employers are responsible for ensuring a safe workplace and for complying with all current and future OSHA-related standards. It also established that employees are responsible for following all safety and health-related rules stemming from the Act.

4. Because no vaccine is available for HCV, the best way to prevent the transmission of Hepatitis C/HCV in the workplace is to ensure the proper use of personal protective equipment (PPE).

5. The six critical components of a comprehensive substance abuse program are

   ▶ Management buy-in and support

   ▶ Drug-free workplace policy

   ▶ Supervisor training

   ▶ Employee education

   ▶ Employee assistance

   ▶ Drug testing

   Of these, management buy-in and support is the most important.

Answers to Exam Questions

1. Answer D is the best answer. WARNA, the Worker Adjustment and Retraining Notification Act, addresses plant closings and mass layoffs. The Drug-Free Workplace Act, MSHA (Mine Safety and Health Act), and OSHA (Occupational Safety and Health Act) were all created specifically to address issues of health and safety in the workplace.

2. Answer C is the best answer. Answer A is not the best answer because family farms are exempt from OSHA coverage only if they do not employ anyone who is not a family member. Answer B is not the best answer because federal government employees are covered under the OSH Act (however, state and local government employees are not). Answer D is not the best answer because although OSHA designates certain low-risk industries as exempt from OSHA reporting requirements, those industries are still covered by the OSH Act.

3. Answer C is the best answer. Health and wellness programs take a more proactive—rather than reactive—approach. Answer D is not the best answer; although health and wellness programs do address some issues "reactively" (for instance, smoking cessation or weight loss), health and wellness programs are more frequently proactive in nature. Answers A and B are not the best answers because health and wellness programs can significantly benefit employees and employers.

4. Answer C is the best answer. Although safety committees could very likely formulate recommendations relative to personal protective equipment (PPE) enhancements, they are far less likely to have final decision-making authority. Safety committees, therefore, would not likely find themselves in a capacity to institute their own recommendations. Safety committees, however, do play an essential role relative to investigating accidents and incidents (Answer A), conducting inspections (Answer B), and proactively identifying safety concerns (Answer D).

5. Answer B is the best answer. "Reasonable suspicion" is one category of drug test, and "for cause" is another. Preemployment (Answer A), post-accident (Answer C), and random (Answer D) are all categories of drug tests.

6. Answer B is the best answer. OSHA requires most employers to maintain records and submit reports relative to work-related injuries and accidents but not specifically in response to security breaches (unless, of course, those breaches result in work-related injuries or accidents). Answers A, C, and D do represent security-related HR responsibilities.

7. Answer B is the best answer. Poor ergonomic design can result in employees assuming awkward postures or having to move in problematic ways. In turn, and over time, this can lead to the development of an MSD (musculoskeletal disorder). Answers A and C are not the best answers because neither use of PPE (personal protective equipment) nor poor ventilation is identified as a significant contributing factor to MSDs. Answer D is not the best answer; although MSDS is a similar acronym, it refers to materials data safety sheets, which are generally unrelated to MSDs.

8. Answer A is the best answer. A person who is HIV positive or who has AIDS is considered a person with a disability under the ADA (Americans with Disabilities Act) and is therefore entitled to perform the essential functions of his job as long as he can do so with or without reasonable accommodation (that does not cause undue hardship to the organization). Developing visible or outward symptoms (Answer B)—as long as those symptoms are unrelated to the person's ability to perform the essential functions of his position—does not preclude an individual from continuing to work. Answer C is not the best answer because an employee who is HIV positive or who has AIDS is entitled to maintain confidentiality relative to either of those conditions. Answer D is not the best answer because the belief that a person who is HIV positive or who has AIDS poses a direct threat to coworkers is unfounded.

9. Answer A is the best answer. Answer B is not the best answer; although each employee has a right to copies of her own medical records or records of her exposure to toxic and harmful substances or conditions, employees do not have the right to copies of coworkers' medical records. Answer

C is not the best answer; employers must correct workplace hazards by the date indicated on the citation—not just create or submit a plan to do so. Answer D is not the best answer because an employee does have the right to photocopies of her medical records or records of her exposure to toxic and harmful substances or conditions.

10. Answer D is the best answer. You have 30 days to file a complaint with OSHA if your employer has discriminated against you for making safety and health complaints or for exercising your rights under the OSH Act. Answers A, B, and C are not the best answers because each identifies rights that employees enjoy under OSHA.

Suggested Readings and Resources

Agnew, J., and Snyder, G. (2002). *Removing Obstacles to Safety: A Behavior-Based Approach*. Tucker, GA: Performance Management Publications.

Centers for Disease Control and Prevention. www.cdc.gov.

Department of Labor. www.dol.gov.

Insurance Information Institute (III). www.iii.org.

Kavianian, H., and Wentz, C. (1990). *Occupational and Environmental Safety Engineering and Management*. New York: John Wiley and Sons.

Mendelsohn, M. (1998). *Biomarkers Medical and Workplace Applications*. Washington, D.C.: Joseph Henry Press.

National Council for Occupational Safety and Health. www.coshnetwork.org/.

National Institute for the Prevention of Workplace Violence. www.workplaceviolence911.com/.

Nixon, W., and Kerr, K. (2008). *Background Screening and Investigations: Managing Hiring Risk from the HR and Security Perspectives*. Amsterdam: Butterworth-Heinemann.

Occupational Health and Safety Administration. www.osha.gov.

"The OSHA Inspection: A Step-by-Step Guide." (n.d.). National Council for Occupational Safety and Health. Retrieved from https://www.osha.gov/dte/grant_materials/fy10/sh-20853-10/osha_inspections.pdf.

Safety and Health Topics—Workplace Violence. (n.d.). Retrieved from https://www.osha.gov/SLTC/workplaceviolence/.

Sall, R. (2004). *Strategies in Workers' Compensation*. Dallas: Hamilton Books.

Schneid, T. (2014). *Workplace Safety and Health Assessing Current Practices and Promoting Change in the Profession*. Boca Raton, FL: CRC Press, Taylor and Francis.

Stanton, J., and Stam, K. (2006). *The Visible Employee Using Workplace Monitoring and Surveillance to Protect Information Assets—Without Compromising Employee Privacy or Trust*. Medford, NJ: Information Today.

Stricoff, R., and Groover, D. (2012). *The Manager's Guide to Workplace Safety*. Ojai, CA: Safety in Action Press.

Practice Exam

1. Which of the following is not one of the four categories of modern tort law as it pertains to invasion of privacy?

   ○ **A.** Intrusion of solitude

   ○ **B.** Public disclosure of private and embarrassing facts

   ○ **C.** Unbecoming light

   ○ **D.** Appropriation of identity

2. Which of the following is not mandated by the General Duty Clause?

   ○ **A.** Employers must ensure a safe workplace.

   ○ **B.** Employers must comply with all current and future OSHA-related standards.

   ○ **C.** Employees must report all work-related injuries resulting in hospitalization (emergency room or in-patient) to their employer.

   ○ **D.** Employees must follow all safety and health-related rules stemming from the OSH Act.

3. The Retirement Equity Act enacted a number of important provisions, including

   ○ **A.** Increasing the minimum age requirement for pension plan participation

   ○ **B.** Requiring qualified pension plans to provide automatic survivor benefits and allow for waiver of survivor benefits without the consent of the participant or the spouse

   ○ **C.** Clarifying that pension plans are prohibited from obeying qualified domestic relations (court) orders (QDROs) requiring them to make benefit payments to a participant's former spouse (or another alternative payee) if that order violates ERISA's prohibitions against assignment or alienation of benefits

   ○ **D.** Prohibiting plans from counting maternity and paternity leaves as breaks in service for participation and vesting purposes

4. Which of the following is the least important factor in ensuring that an employee survey is a valuable employee involvement strategy?

   ○ **A.** Ensure confidentiality by administering the survey through an external consultant

   ○ **B.** Ensure that the survey input is maintained in a fully confidential manner

   ○ **C.** Ensure that employees believe in the confidentiality of the survey

   ○ **D.** Ensure management buy-in and support

5. Which of the following characteristics is most likely to first manifest itself during the development (or growth) stage in the organizational life cycle?

   ○ **A.** A core group of highly talented employees who focus fixedly on the founder for direction and inspiration

   ○ **B.** Resistance to OD and change initiatives

   ○ **C.** Resistance to the process of formalizing policies and procedures

   ○ **D.** An entitlement mentality toward pay and benefits

6. Of the following four types of pay that an employee could earn, which one would not need to be included in an employee's regular rate of pay?

 - ○ **A.** Overtime pay

 - ○ **B.** Premium pay (for weekend work)

 - ○ **C.** Bonus pay

 - ○ **D.** Incentive pay

7. All of the following statements about OD are true except

 - ○ **A.** OD refers to the process through which the overall performance, growth, and effectiveness of an organization is enhanced through strategic, deliberate, and integrated initiatives.

 - ○ **B.** OD incorporates the following four academic disciplines: psychology, sociology, anthropology, and management.

 - ○ **C.** OD helps maintain the organization's focus on the belief that the systems that have been enacted within organizations are ultimately responsible for whether the work of the organization is accomplished.

 - ○ **D.** OD interventions are intended to identify an organization's competitive advantages and to ensure the organization's success.

8. Which of the following statements about ULP strikes is untrue?

 - ○ **A.** ULP strikes are called during contract negotiations.

 - ○ **B.** Striking workers must be returned to their original positions after the strike is over.

 - ○ **C.** ULP strikes are called when the employer has committed an unfair labor practice.

 - ○ **D.** Employers cannot hire permanent strike replacements during a ULP strike.

9. All of the following are required by the Hazard Communication Standard except

 - ○ **A.** Material safety data sheets

 - ○ **B.** Signed employee acknowledgement forms

 - ○ **C.** Container labeling requirements

 - ○ **D.** Training and orientation

10. Which of the following occurs during a jurisdictional strike?

 - ○ **A.** Employees who are not directly involved in an economic dispute choose not to cross a picket line out of support for striking workers.

 - ○ **B.** A union seeks to pressure an employer to assign particular work to its members rather than to members of other unions or to nonunion workers.

 - ○ **C.** The strike occurs even though the collective bargaining agreement contains a no-strike clause prohibiting striking during the duration of the agreement.

 - ○ **D.** A union seeks to pressure an employer to grant some sort of concession from the employer during collective bargaining negotiations.

11. Copyrights are granted for which period of time?

○ **A.** The lifetime of the author

○ **B.** The lifetime of the author, unless there are heirs to whom the copyright has been deeded

○ **C.** The lifetime of the author plus 70 years

○ **D.** The lifetime of the author plus 95 years

12. When conducting panel interviews, it is generally advisable to do all of the following except

○ **A.** Let the candidate know ahead of time that she will be participating in a panel interview.

○ **B.** Plan in advance who will ask which questions and in which order and arrange for "handoffs" from one interviewer to another.

○ **C.** Interview in a room that has a round table, if possible.

○ **D.** Place all the interviewers on one side of the table and the candidate on the other.

13. According to OSHA, which of the following does not need to be recorded?

○ **A.** Days away from work

○ **B.** Injuries that result in bleeding

○ **C.** Restricted work or job transfer

○ **D.** Loss of consciousness

14. If an employee is engaged in protected concerted activity, an employer might be considered to have violated the NLRA if all but which of the following conditions are met?

○ **A.** The employee or collective bargaining unit advised the employer of the concerted nature of the employee's activity.

○ **B.** The employer knew of the concerted nature of the employee's activity.

○ **C.** The concerted activity was protected by the NLRA.

○ **D.** The adverse employment action in question (for instance, termination) was motivated by the employee's protected concerted activity.

15. Henry Fayol was a guru in the area of

○ **A.** Quality

○ **B.** Management

○ **C.** Strategic human resources

○ **D.** Human behavior

16. *General Dynamics Land Systems v. Cline, 2004*, a case that addressed age discrimination, established/clarified that

○ **A.** The ADEA prohibits favoring the old over the young.

○ **B.** The ADEA prohibits favoring the old over the young, and it prohibits favoring the young over the old.

○ **C.** Younger employees (even if they are over the age of 40) cannot allege age discrimination because of programs that favor older employees.

○ **D.** Younger employees (even if they are over the age of 40) can allege age discrimination because of programs that favor older employees.

17. What method of job evaluation is this: "A nonquantitative job evaluation technique that categorizes jobs into broad categories, or levels, based on the level—and, ultimately, value to the organization—of the work that is performed by jobs within each level. Each level incorporates specific responsibilities and benchmark statements that describe the nature, complexity, autonomy, and so forth of the work that is performed by positions in that level."

○ **A.** Job classification

○ **B.** Job slotting

○ **C.** Whole job ranking

○ **D.** Factor comparison

18. An organization's total compensation/total rewards program should do all of the following except

○ **A.** Support and reinforce the mission, vision, and values of the organization

○ **B.** Be consistent with the culture of the organization

○ **C.** Be competitive with the total compensation programs offered by labor market competitors

○ **D.** Attract, motivate, and retain targeted/appropriate employees

19. Which of these individuals is least likely to create an oral contract?

○ **A.** A full-time recruiter

○ **B.** A hiring manager who interviews candidates for open positions in his area

○ **C.** An employee's current supervisor

○ **D.** An employee's current coworker

20. Which case established the following relative to what constitutes a sexually hostile work environment: "This standard, which we reaffirm today, takes a middle path between making actionable any conduct that is merely offensive and requiring the conduct to cause a tangible psychological injury. Conduct that is not severe or pervasive enough to create an objectively hostile or abusive work environment—an environment that a reasonable person would find hostile or abusive—is beyond Title VII's purview. Likewise, if the victim does not subjectively perceive the environment to be abusive, the conduct has not actually altered the conditions of the victim's employment, and there is no Title VII violation."

○ **A.** *Taxman v. Board of Education of Piscataway, 1993*

○ **B.** *Meritor Savings Bank v. Vinson, 1986*

○ **C.** *St. Mary's Honor Center v. Hicks, 1993*

○ **D.** *Harris v. Forklift Systems, 1993*

21. Which of the following is true of Ishikawa's fishbone diagram?

   ○ **A.** Demonstrates how 20% of causes account for 80% of effects

   ○ **B.** Identifies factors that ultimately affect whether a desired outcome will be attained

   ○ **C.** Assesses the potential impact of utilizing quality circles in a particular situation

   ○ **D.** Depicts information about a single factor

22. All of the following statements about the ADEA are true except

   ○ **A.** ADEA prohibits discrimination based on age, for individuals age 18 and older (to ensure that individuals are not discriminated against based on being too young, as well as based on being too old).

   ○ **B.** ADEA covers private employers with 20 or more employees, state and local governments (including school districts), employment agencies, and labor organizations.

   ○ **C.** ADEA does not establish an upper cap, or an age at which it once again becomes legal to discriminate against individuals based on age.

   ○ **D.** ADEA is subject to certain exceptions and places certain requirements on employers, particularly with respect to benefits plans, coverages, and early retirement incentives.

23. In the acronym KSAs, A refers to

   ○ **A.** An attitudinal predilection toward the type of work performed in the position

   ○ **B.** Specific information that the incumbent either needs to know or with which she needs to be familiar

   ○ **C.** The ability to perform a particular task

   ○ **D.** Specific traits required to successfully perform a position

24. A manager with whom you have not previously worked comes to you for help with implementing solutions she has come up with to address a turnover problem in her department. Your first response should be to

   ○ **A.** Communicate your commitment to implementing the manager's solution.

   ○ **B.** Offer alternative solutions based on experience you have had with similar situations.

   ○ **C.** Ask questions to obtain more information about the problems the manager is experiencing.

   ○ **D.** Ask questions to obtain information that will help you implement the manager's solution more effectively.

25. Of the following four options, the best way to avoid or minimize the likelihood of a negligent referral claim against the organization is to

   ○ **A.** Refuse to provide employee references

   ○ **B.** Provide only titles, dates of employment, and final salary when providing references

   ○ **C.** Outsource the process of providing employee references to a third party

   ○ **D.** Require a signed release form from the employee or former employee before providing a reference

26. Which of the following statements about defined contribution plans is untrue?

   ○ **A.** Unlike defined benefit plans, defined contribution plans do not promise a specific monthly benefit (or total benefit) at retirement.

   ○ **B.** Defined contribution plans shift the risk away from the employer (which is where it rests for defined benefit plans) and back onto the employee.

   ○ **C.** Defined contribution plans are decreasing in popularity, whereas defined benefit plans are increasing in popularity.

   ○ **D.** Examples of defined contribution plans include 401(k) plans, employee stock ownership plans, and profit-sharing plans.

27. In which case did the U.S. Supreme Court rule that, in the absence of underrepresentation as demonstrated and documented through an affirmative action plan, organizations cannot take race into account when making decisions relative to who will be laid off and who will be retained (and that doing so would constitute a violation of Title VII of the Civil Rights Act of 1964)?

   ○ **A.** *Taxman v. Board of Education of Piscataway, 1993*

   ○ **B.** *Meritor Savings Bank v. Vinson, 1986*

   ○ **C.** *St. Mary's Honor Center v. Hicks, 1993*

   ○ **D.** *Harris v. Forklift Systems, 1993*

28. Which law implemented changes in two sections of the United States tax code that resulted in the creation of two new—and ultimately important—employee benefits?

   ○ **A.** Consolidated Omnibus Budget Reconciliation Act (COBRA), 1985

   ○ **B.** The Revenue Act

   ○ **C.** Health Insurance Portability and Accountability Act (HIPAA)

   ○ **D.** Retirement Equity Act (REA)

29. A cash balance plan is

   ○ **A.** A defined benefit plan that expresses the promised benefit in terms of a stated account balance

   ○ **B.** A defined benefit plan that expresses the promised benefit in terms of a specific monthly benefit

   ○ **C.** A defined contribution plan that expresses the promised benefit in terms of a stated account balance

   ○ **D.** A defined contribution plan that expresses the promised benefit in terms of a specific monthly benefit

30. Which of the following statements about the Civil Rights Act of 1991 is untrue?

   ○ **A.** It expanded employees' rights.

   ○ **B.** It expanded employees' remedies.

   ○ **C.** It capped damages at $500,000 per employee.

   ○ **D.** It allowed for jury trials for discrimination cases.

31. Joseph M. Juran's focus on quality addresses three key areas, which include all of the following except

   ○ **A.** Quality planning

   ○ **B.** Quality circles

   ○ **C.** Quality improvement

   ○ **D.** Quality control

32. Strategic planning is a step-by-step process through which an organization does all of the following except

   ○ **A.** Ensures its individual and organizational readiness for the future

   ○ **B.** Generates a statement that articulates what the organization wants to become in the future

   ○ **C.** Identifies where it wants to be and what it wants to accomplish in the long term (often 3–5 years)

   ○ **D.** Begins to map out how its vision and mission for the long term will be attained

33. Which of the following factors is least relevant to creating and sustaining credibility during the implementation of a strategic plan?

   ○ **A.** Securing the support and commitment of senior leadership

   ○ **B.** Clear, complete, and appropriate documentation of the process

   ○ **C.** A commitment to follow through on every step of the process

   ○ **D.** Representative participation from all levels of the organization

34. For the set of numbers 5, 29, 194, 87, 645, 42, 29, 334, and 97, the mean is

   ○ **A.** 162.4

   ○ **B.** 645

   ○ **C.** 29

   ○ **D.** 87

35. A manager within your organization sends you an email asking you to help her with terminating an employee. This is the first time you've heard about the situation. The manager has specifically asked for your help with pulling together the COBRA paperwork, calculating the final paycheck, and making sure that the employee turns over his company ID and corporate credit card. The manager tells you how much she needs and appreciates your help and is glad she can count on you.

   This manager probably views HR primarily in terms of the following dimension:

   ○ **A.** Operational/tactical

   ○ **B.** Strategic

   ○ **C.** Administrative

   ○ **D.** Transformational

36. The difference between job posting systems and job bidding systems is

    ○ **A.** Job bidding systems deal with jobs that are currently open, whereas job posting systems deal with jobs that might open at some point in the future.

    ○ **B.** Job bidding systems are directed at internal candidates, whereas job posting systems are directed at external candidates.

    ○ **C.** Job bidding systems deal with jobs that might open at some point in the future, whereas job posting systems deal with jobs that are currently open.

    ○ **D.** Job bidding systems are directed at internal candidates, whereas job posting systems are directed at internal as well as external candidates.

37. According to the Older Worker's Benefit Protection Act (OWBPA), individuals are prohibited from waiving their rights or claims under ADEA unless such a waiver is "knowing and voluntary." OWBPA established nine specific criteria for ensuring that such waivers are knowing and voluntary, one of which requires that employers allow employees time to consider any right-to-sue waivers that the employer offers in exchange for early retirement benefits. How many days must an employer allow?

    ○ **A.** At least one week

    ○ **B.** At least two weeks

    ○ **C.** At least three weeks

    ○ **D.** At least one week for each year of service

38. The progressive discipline process is predicated on a belief that includes which of the following ideas/assumptions?

    ○ **A.** An employee decides whether to perform his job satisfactorily.

    ○ **B.** The employee, when hired, was at least minimally qualified for the position.

    ○ **C.** Both A and B.

    ○ **D.** Neither A nor B.

39. An organization conducts an employee survey and finds that many employees are bored with their jobs, are unhappy with their pay, and feel as though they don't get enough vacation time. If the organization's primary goal is to motivate employees, what is the first step that should be taken?

    ○ **A.** Conduct an external survey to determine pay rates and vacation allotments among labor market competitors.

    ○ **B.** Identify ways in which employees' jobs can be enriched, and implement them.

    ○ **C.** Give everyone an across-the-board raise and an extra week of vacation, and let employees know that you will be conducting a salary/benefits survey to see if further adjustments are needed.

    ○ **D.** Before you take any action, conduct another employee survey to ensure that results of the second survey are consistent with the results of the first survey.

40. According to Hersey and Blanchard's model, effective leaders

    ○ **A.** Identify the leadership style that is best suited to them and use that style consistently.

    ○ **B.** Determine the quadrant into which each employee falls and manage employees in each quadrant according to the corresponding leadership style.

◯ **C.** Place emphasis on ensuring that an employee has the ability to execute the technical or functional skills required to complete a task.

◯ **D.** Utilize different leadership approaches, with different employees, at different times.

41. Which of the following was not one of Knowles's five key assumptions about how adults learn?

◯ **A.** The learner's need to know

◯ **B.** The learner's readiness to learn

◯ **C.** The learner's self-concept

◯ **D.** The learner's willingness to change

42. When would a plan provider that offers mental health benefits be exempt from MHPA?

◯ **A.** If the plan provider is a small employer with fewer than 15 people

◯ **B.** If a plan provider's costs (measured in terms of actual claims) increase 1% or more because of the application of MHPA's requirements

◯ **C.** If a plan provider's costs (in terms of insurance premiums) increase 1% or more due to the application of MHPA's requirements

◯ **D.** Never

43. Under COBRA, plan providers must offer plan participants the opportunity to continue participating in

◯ **A.** Group health care plans, wellness programs, and long-term disability insurance

◯ **B.** Group health care plans

◯ **C.** All health and welfare plans for which the plan participant cannot secure coverage through another individual's group plan

◯ **D.** All health and welfare plans

44. According to the Equal Pay Act, the substantial equality of job content is assessed based on four factors:

◯ **A.** Working conditions, effort, skill, and scope

◯ **B.** Effort, skill, responsibility, and working conditions

◯ **C.** Scope, accountability, responsibility, and working conditions

◯ **D.** Responsibility, skills, working conditions, and scope

45. An approach in which an organization chooses to utilize a relatively small number of grades is known as

◯ **A.** Flattening

◯ **B.** Growthbanding

◯ **C.** Broadbanding

◯ **D.** Gradesharing

46. Which of the following statements is least reflective of an organization's statement of vision?

- ○ **A.** It is a descriptive and inspirational statement that articulates where the organization wants to be and what it wants to become in the future.

- ○ **B.** It gives employees an awareness that they have a meaningful opportunity to be part of something bigger than themselves.

- ○ **C.** It motivates and inspires employees to aspire to the legacy that the vision can create and that it ultimately can leave behind.

- ○ **D.** It speaks to the nature of the organization's business or purpose, its customers, and sometimes even its employees and its role in the community.

47. After the House of Representatives and the Senate have approved a bill in identical form, the legislation will die unless

- ○ **A.** The president takes no action for 10 days while Congress is not in session.

- ○ **B.** The president takes no action for 10 days while Congress is in session.

- ○ **C.** The president sends the legislation back for Conference Committee Action.

- ○ **D.** The president overrides Congress.

48. Preemployment medical exams can only be conducted

- ○ **A.** If all candidates who apply for a position are required to partake in a preemployment medical exam

- ○ **B.** If the medical exam is job related and consistent with business necessity

- ○ **C.** If the medical exam is conducted by a physician who is not employed or retained by the employer

- ○ **D.** If the candidate reveals a disability that might require a reasonable accommodation

49. EO 11246 requires covered employers to develop and implement an auditing system that periodically measures the effectiveness of its total affirmative action program. This requirement could include all the following actions except

- ○ **A.** Monitor records of all personnel activity, including referrals, placements, transfers, promotions, terminations, and compensation, at all levels to ensure the nondiscriminatory policy is carried out

- ○ **B.** Require internal reporting on a scheduled basis as to the number of charges of discrimination that have been filed based on race, gender, and veterans status during the length of each AAP degree to which equal employment opportunity and organizational objectives are attained

- ○ **C.** Review report results with all levels of management

- ○ **D.** Advise top management of program effectiveness and submit recommendations to improve unsatisfactory performance

50. Which of the following statements about trend analysis is true?

- ○ **A.** It can provide information that can be helpful in developing a better understanding of business cycles.

- ○ **B.** It can become the basis for a number of applications, including forecasting staffing needs.

◯   **C.** It looks at how two variables have changed over time.

◯   **D.** It looks at the relationship between one dependent variable and more than one independent variable.

51. WARNA covers which employers?

◯   **A.** Employers with 15 or more employees

◯   **B.** 100 or more full-time employees

◯   **C.** All private employers

◯   **D.** Private employers with 20 or more employees

52. Learning organizations are best described as those within which

◯   **A.** The HRD/training budget is equivalent to (or exceeds) the merit budget.

◯   **B.** Employees at all levels of the organization commit to attaining knowledge and skills that will enable them to perform better and attain more.

◯   **C.** Employees at all levels of the organization participate in training initiatives—either individually or through organizational initiatives—at least annually.

◯   **D.** Each employee's performance appraisal incorporates a goal relative to completing specific training or development activities.

53. Which of the following managers is most likely to experience the recency effect?

◯   **A.** A manager who recently observed a direct report performing her position

◯   **B.** A manager who recently placed an employee on a performance improvement plan

◯   **C.** A manager who maintained consistent documentation during earlier portions of the performance measurement period

◯   **D.** A manager who has not consistently documented the direct report's performance during the performance measurement period

54. For overtime purposes, hours worked includes

◯   **A.** All hours for which an employee received compensation

◯   **B.** All hours for which an employee was granted prior to, or subsequent to, approval to work

◯   **C.** All hours during which an employee performed work

◯   **D.** All hours during which an employee was required or allowed to perform work

55. The Equal Pay Act prohibits discrimination based on sex in the payment of wages or benefits to men and women who

◯   **A.** Perform the same work for the same employer

◯   **B.** Perform substantially equal (but not identical) work for the same employer

◯   **C.** Perform substantially equal (but not identical) work for different employers within the same relevant labor market

◯   **D.** Perform the same work for different employers within the same relevant labor market

56. Which of the following statements about job grades is not true?

   ○ **A.** Grades represent a hierarchy of levels into which jobs of similar internal worth are categorized.

   ○ **B.** Jobs within the same grade share a similar level of value or worth to the organization.

   ○ **C.** Jobs within the same grade are paid according to a corresponding compensation range.

   ○ **D.** Grades represent a hierarchy of levels into which jobs of similar external worth are categorized.

57. Which of the following terms best describes transactional leaders?

   ○ **A.** Enforcers

   ○ **B.** Coaches

   ○ **C.** Captains

   ○ **D.** Directors

58. Which of the following statements about the nominal group technique is true?

   ○ **A.** It constitutes a nonmathematical forecasting technique that draws on the insights of subject matter experts.

   ○ **B.** It is similar to the Delphi technique in that it affords experts the opportunity to interact with each other.

   ○ **C.** It is self-directing, self-governing, and relies on the facilitative abilities of the experts who are participating in the forecasting process.

   ○ **D.** It permits and encourages discussion and collaboration throughout the forecasting process.

59. The Drug-Free Workplace Act requires all of the following except

   ○ **A.** Establishing an EAP (or equivalent program) to which employees who use drugs can turn for assistance and rehabilitation

   ○ **B.** Publishing a statement notifying employees that the manufacture, distribution, dispensation, possession, or use of a controlled substance is prohibited in the workplace

   ○ **C.** Establishing a drug-free awareness program addressing the dangers of drug use in the workplace and the employer's drug-free policy, and information about programs that are available to employees who use drugs

   ○ **D.** Distributing a copy of the workplace substance abuse policy to all employees

60. Which of the following statements about unemployment insurance is not true?

   ○ **A.** Unemployment insurance is a mandatory benefit program.

   ○ **B.** In general, the maximum period for receiving unemployment insurance benefits is 26 weeks.

○ **C.** Except in three states (in which only employers contribute), unemployment insurance is funded through employer and employee taxes.

○ **D.** Unemployment insurance was established as part of the federal Social Security Act and is administered at the state level.

61. Which of the following is not a disadvantage of the nonquantitative job evaluation method known as job slotting?

○ **A.** Job slotting is somewhat expensive and difficult to administer.

○ **B.** It is more likely that jobs will be evaluated based on the person, not the position.

○ **C.** Job slotting can be used only when a job structure is already in place.

○ **D.** There is a greater chance that rater error and subjectivity can taint the job evaluation process.

62. Which of the following statements about protected concerted activities is not true?

○ **A.** Protected concerted activity refers to associational rights that are granted to employees through the NLRA.

○ **B.** The NLRA protects associational rights for employees who belong to a union.

○ **C.** The NLRA does not protect associational rights unless an employee belongs to a union.

○ **D.** Employees have the right to refrain from engaging in protected concerted activities.

63. When there is a FEPA, all of the following statements are true except

○ **A.** Charges must be filed with the EEOC within 180 days of the alleged discriminatory act.

○ **B.** The EEOC usually maintains responsibility for handling charges that are filed with it if the basis for the charge is also protected under state or local law.

○ **C.** The FEPA usually maintains responsibility for handling charges that are filed with it if the basis for the charge is also protected under federal law.

○ **D.** A charge may not be filed with the EEOC when state or local EEO law is more protective than the corresponding federal law.

64. COBRA covers employers who employ

○ **A.** 2 or more employees during the prior year

○ **B.** 15 or more employees as of the close of the most recent payroll period

○ **C.** 20 or more employees during the prior year

○ **D.** 50 or more employees as of the close of the most recent payroll period

65. The defining case for employment tests and disparate impact was

○ **A.** *McDonnell Douglas Corp v. Green, 1973*

○ **B.** *Griggs v. Duke Power, 1971*

○ **C.** *Meritor Savings Bank v. Vinson, 1986*

○ **D.** *Washington v. Davis, 1976*

66. Which of the following activities would be least likely to happen during onboarding?

- ○ **A.** Tour of the facility

- ○ **B.** Background investigation

- ○ **C.** Opportunity to meet with current employees

- ○ **D.** Review of the mission of the organization and of how that mission relates to the position

67. Three of the following terms refer to the same sort of instrument or tool, and one does not. Which one of these terms means something different from the other three?

- ○ **A.** Employee surveys

- ○ **B.** Multirater surveys

- ○ **C.** Attitude surveys

- ○ **D.** Climate surveys

68. The LMRA, also known as the Taft-Hartley Act, was an amendment designed to remedy what the Republican Congress saw as two major omissions in the Wagner Act, including

- ○ **A.** The identification of behaviors and practices that would be considered ULPs on the part of employers

- ○ **B.** The identification of behaviors and practices that would be considered ULPs on the part of unions

- ○ **C.** The identification of behaviors and practices that would be considered ULPs on the part of employees

- ○ **D.** The identification of behaviors and practices that would be considered ULPs on the part of managers

69. The landmark Supreme Court case that confirmed the legality of mandatory arbitration agreements was

- ○ **A.** *NLRB v. Phoenix Mutual Life Insurance Co., 1948*

- ○ **B.** *EEOC v. Waffle House, Inc., 2002*

- ○ **C.** *Circuit City Stores, Inc. v. Adams, 2001*

- ○ **D.** *NLRB v. Henry Colder Co., 1990*

70. OSHA did all of the following except

- ○ **A.** Establish relief for employees who suffer work-related injuries and illnesses

- ○ **B.** Establish a means of enforcement

- ○ **C.** Encourage and assist states to take steps to ensure safe and healthful workplaces

- ○ **D.** Provide for relevant research, information, education, and training

71. Change interventions that focus on improving what work is done, as well as the ways and processes through which the work is done, are considered

- ○ **A.** Human processual interventions

- ○ **B.** Technostructural interventions

○ **C.** Sociotechnical interventions

○ **D.** Organization transformation change interventions

72. Which of the following statements about the PBGC is not true?

○ **A.** PBGC is a government corporation created by ERISA.

○ **B.** PBGC is funded by a combination of employer and employee payroll taxes.

○ **C.** PBGC protects participants in most defined benefit plans and cash balance plans (within certain limitations).

○ **D.** PBGC ensures that participants will receive payments of certain benefits if a covered plan is terminated.

73. In conducting a SWOT analysis, the strengths and weaknesses portion of the analysis is directed

○ **A.** Internally

○ **B.** Externally

○ **C.** Both internally and externally

○ **D.** Neither internally nor externally

74. The landmark case *McKennon v. Nashville Banner Publishing Co., 1995*, established that

○ **A.** An employer will be held accountable for discriminatory employment actions unless it discovers evidence after taking the discriminatory employment action that would have led the employer to that same employment action for legitimate, nondiscriminatory reasons.

○ **B.** An employer will be held accountable for discriminatory employment actions even if it discovers evidence after taking the discriminatory employment action that would have led the employer to that same employment action for legitimate, nondiscriminatory reasons.

○ **C.** An employer will not be held accountable for discriminatory employment actions if it discovers evidence after taking the discriminatory employment action that would have led the employer to that same employment action for legitimate, nondiscriminatory reasons.

○ **D.** An employer will not be held accountable for discriminatory employment actions even if it discovers evidence after taking the discriminatory employment action that would have led the employer to a different employment action for legitimate, nondiscriminatory reasons.

75. FMLA entitles eligible employees (who work for covered employers) up to 12 weeks of unpaid, job-protected leave during any 12-month period for all of the following reasons except

○ **A.** For the birth and care of the newborn child of the employee

○ **B.** For placement of a son or daughter for adoption or foster care with the employee

○ **C.** To care for an immediate family member (spouse, child, sibling, or parent) with a serious health condition

○ **D.** To take medical leave when the employee is unable to work because of a serious health condition

76. Which of the following statements about factor comparison is untrue?

    ⭕ **A.** Factor comparison provides a degree of objectivity and reliability across raters.

    ⭕ **B.** Factor comparison evaluates each job with respect to each compensable factor.

    ⭕ **C.** Factor comparison assigns a point value to each level within each factor.

    ⭕ **D.** Factor comparison involves ranking each compensable factor of each job.

77. Which of the following activities would not constitute an unfair labor practice on the part of an employer during a union organizing campaign?

    ⭕ **A.** Tell workers that the organization will fire or punish them if they engage in any union activity.

    ⭕ **B.** Grant workers wage increases or special concessions in an effort to bribe people from joining a union.

    ⭕ **C.** Require employees to attend presentations to listen to the employer's opinions about the unionization of its operations

    ⭕ **D.** Tell workers that existing benefits will be discontinued if the workplace is unionized.

78. An employer who makes a hot cargo agreement has done all of the following except

    ⭕ **A.** Agreed to stop doing business with another entity

    ⭕ **B.** Refused to stop doing business with another entity

    ⭕ **C.** Committed a ULP

    ⭕ **D.** Helped the union

79. All of the following statements about negligent hiring are true except

    ⭕ **A.** Negligent hiring refers to the process of hiring an employee without engaging in appropriate due diligence.

    ⭕ **B.** Appropriate due diligence includes looking into items such as the candidate's credentials and prior work experience.

    ⭕ **C.** An organization can prevent negligent hiring tort claims—or can ensure that it will prevail in any such claim—by performing due diligence on all employees before they are hired.

    ⭕ **D.** Negligent hiring tort claims might be filed after an employee who was hired through a flawed hiring process inflicts some sort of harm on another person.

80. Which of the following statements about focus groups is least true?

    ⭕ **A.** Skillfully facilitated focus groups can generate a great deal of valuable data.

    ⭕ **B.** The synergy of the group dynamics can contribute to a more valuable data collection experience.

    ⭕ **C.** When facilitated by the same individual, participants across multiple focus groups will have a similar data collection experience.

    ⭕ **D.** Focus groups can provide a qualitative approach to data collection.

81. Which of the following factors should have the least impact on how base pay for newly hired employees is set?

   ○ **A.** The relative worth of the job to the organization

   ○ **B.** Each incumbent's rate of pay in her current/most recent position

   ○ **C.** The market rate for the position in the marketplace

   ○ **D.** Whether the job requires hot skills

82. An agreement between an employer and an employee that states that the employer will give the employee a job as long as the employee agrees not to join or have any involvement with a labor union is known as a

   ○ **A.** Yellow dog contract

   ○ **B.** Hot cargo agreement

   ○ **C.** Featherbedding agreement

   ○ **D.** Union shop agreement

83. Which of the following would not describe a purpose of a safety committee?

   ○ **A.** Building and maintaining interest in health and safety issues

   ○ **B.** Satisfying the OSHA requirement that covered organizations establish cross-functional safety committees

   ○ **C.** Reinforcing safety as part of the fabric of the organization's culture

   ○ **D.** Providing a forum for discussing health- and safety-related issues

84. Which of the following cases established that gender can be used as a factor in the selection process if there is underrepresentation in a particular job classification as long as the AAP does not set forth a quota?

   ○ **A.** *Johnson v. Santa Clara County Transportation Agency, 1987*

   ○ **B.** *Martin v. Wilks, 1988*

   ○ **C.** *Harris v. Forklift Systems, 1993*

   ○ **D.** *Taxman v. Board of Education of Piscataway, 1993*

85. Which of the following statements about diversity is true?

   ○ **A.** Diversity is a legally mandated program, similar to affirmative action.

   ○ **B.** Diversity initiatives require the preparation and filing of specific reports to the federal government on an annual basis.

   ○ **C.** Diversity can encompass attributes or characteristics such as communication styles, regional backgrounds, or affiliation with unions.

   ○ **D.** Diversity programs represent an extension of EEO programs and thus should be limited to the same protected classes that are defined by EEO laws.

86. Which of the following statements about Social Security retirement benefits is untrue?

   ○ **A.** The earliest age at which a worker can retire and still receive benefits is 62.

   ○ **B.** Full retirement age ranges between ages 65 and 67.

   ○ **C.** Workers who work beyond their full retirement age will increase their monthly retirement income.

   ○ **D.** There is no requirement to start receiving retirement benefits by any particular age.

87. An employee who was constructively discharged

   ○ **A.** Was forced to quit due to intolerable working conditions

   ○ **B.** Was terminated at the conclusion of a progressive disciplinary process

   ○ **C.** Was afforded the opportunity to resign (instead of being fired)

   ○ **D.** Was laid off through no fault of his own and is eligible for rehire

88. Placement goals

   ○ **A.** Must be established for areas in which underutilization exists

   ○ **B.** Must be pursued through good faith efforts

   ○ **C.** Must be set at an annual percentage rate equal to the availability figure for women or minorities

   ○ **D.** Must be established for each specific minority group when underutilization is found to exist

89. According to Hersey and Blanchard's situational leadership model, low task and low relationship dimensions correspond to which quadrant?

   ○ **A.** Telling

   ○ **B.** Selling

   ○ **C.** Participating

   ○ **D.** Delegating

90. Which of the following statements about correlation is true?

   ○ **A.** A negative correlation indicates that a relationship does not exist between two factors.

   ○ **B.** Correlation mathematically determines whether there is a demonstrated relationship between two factors or entities.

   ○ **C.** The correlation coefficient is a number between 0 and 1 that defines the strength of a relationship between two factors.

   ○ **D.** The closer the correlation coefficient is to 1, the greater the likelihood that there is a causative relationship between the two factors.

91. FLSA established standards affecting full-time and part-time workers in the private sector and in federal, state, and local governments pertaining to the following four areas:

   ○ **A.** Minimum wage, overtime, recordkeeping, and child labor

   ○ **B.** Minimum wage, overtime, worker's compensation, and unemployment insurance

○ **C.** Minimum wage, overtime, child labor, and wage garnishments

○ **D.** Minimum wage, overtime, unemployment insurance, and wage garnishments

92. Which of the following is not a requirement under Sarbanes-Oxley (SOX)?

○ **A.** Prohibition against insider trading during certain pension plan blackout periods.

○ **B.** Establishment of whistleblower protection in a variety of situations for employees who report fraud against shareholders.

○ **C.** Plan administrators must provide 30-day written notice in advance of blackout periods to individual account plan participants and beneficiaries.

○ **D.** Requirement to disclose whether the company has adopted a companywide code of ethics.

93. One key potential problem with employee participation groups is that, under the NLRA, it is possible that employee participation groups could be found

○ **A.** To interfere with employees' ability to affiliate with a collective bargaining unit

○ **B.** To interfere with employees' associational rights

○ **C.** To be company dominated

○ **D.** To have an adverse impact upon members of a protected class

94. Which of the following four statements offers the best definition of slander?

○ **A.** A statement that damages someone's character or reputation

○ **B.** A false statement that damages someone's character or reputation

○ **C.** A false spoken statement that damages someone's character or reputation

○ **D.** A false written statement that damages someone's character or reputation

95. In the landmark case *Meritor Savings Bank v. Vinson, 1986*, the Supreme Court ruling stated all of the following except

○ **A.** Unwelcome sexual advances at work create a hostile work environment, which constitutes gender discrimination under Title VII of the Civil Rights Act of 1964.

○ **B.** The employer isn't responsible for the sexually harassing behavior of supervisors in its employ even if it didn't know about the behavior.

○ **C.** One way for employers to avoid liability is to prove that a sexually harassed employee had reasonable opportunities to take advantage of a good, clear complaint procedure (without fear of retaliation) but had failed to do so.

○ **D.** Employers are automatically liable for sexual harassment by their supervisors.

96. All of the following represent advantages of whole job ranking except

○ **A.** Whole job ranking is easy to perform.

○ **B.** Whole job ranking establishes factors about each job that need to be taken into consideration when comparing jobs to each other.

○ **C.** Whole job ranking is relatively inexpensive to maintain.

○ **D.** Whole job ranking produces a list that shows which jobs are most and least important.

97. There are five management functions, one of which speaks particularly to the ways in which the manager obtains and arranges resources. Those resources could include people, facilities, materials, and the like. While executing this function, the manager must also make decisions about reporting relationships within the organization. In short, the manager must work to establish linkages between people, places, and things. According to Henri Fayol, this management function is known as

  ○ **A.** Organizing

  ○ **B.** Controlling

  ○ **C.** Planning

  ○ **D.** Coordinating

98. An interviewer truly enjoys interviewing because he feels as though it gives him the opportunity to make a difference in the world by helping individuals who are unemployed find gainful employment. Which of the following four interviewer biases/errors might this interviewer be most likely to experience?

  ○ **A.** Compassion

  ○ **B.** Urgency

  ○ **C.** Leniency

  ○ **D.** Recency

99. Title VII of the Civil Rights Act of 1964 was a landmark piece of legislation prohibiting employment discrimination based on

  ○ **A.** Race, color, religion, sex, and national origin

  ○ **B.** Race, color, age, sex, and national origin

  ○ **C.** Race, age, sex, religion, and handicapping status (renamed to disability upon the passage of the ADA)

  ○ **D.** Race, religion, sex, and national origin

100. An undue hardship is one that does all of the following except

  ○ **A.** Creates significant difficulty (enough to disrupt business operations)

  ○ **B.** Requires a financial outlay that exceeds 25% of the employee's annual salary

  ○ **C.** Changes something about the (essential) nature of the business

  ○ **D.** Results in a significant financial outlay

101. Which of the following statements about teambuilding is least true?

  ○ **A.** Building on the idea that there is no I in team, teambuilding exercises focus primarily on the role of the team rather than on the role of each team member.

  ○ **B.** Teambuilding is an effective means through which team members can explore issues such as communication, problem solving, and trust.

  ○ **C.** Teambuilding exercises are most effective when they are linked directly and specifically to organizational objectives.

  ○ **D.** Teambuilding exercises can be of value even if the activity itself doesn't seem to bear any immediate resemblance to the actual workplace.

102. Taft-Hartley identified all but which of the following as unfair labor practices that could be committed by unions:

- ○ **A.** Striking or picketing an employer without giving the required notice
- ○ **B.** Picketing for recognition for more than 30 days without petitioning for an election
- ○ **C.** Causing an employer to discriminate against an employee
- ○ **D.** Refusing to bargain with the employer of the employees it represents

103. All but which of the following constitute protections that were instituted through the Labor Management Reporting and Disclosure Act (also known as Landrum-Griffin)?

- ○ **A.** A requirement that unions submit annual financial reporting to the DOL to document how union members' dues were spent
- ○ **B.** A bill of rights for union members guaranteeing them freedom of speech and periodic secret elections
- ○ **C.** The designation of every union official as an agent of the union
- ○ **D.** Even stronger provisions relative to secondary boycotting and organizational and recognition picketing

104. When a company that owns or operates union as well as nonunion operations shifts work to the nonunion operation in an effort to diminish the impact of the strike, this is referred to as

- ○ **A.** Featherbedding
- ○ **B.** Double breasting
- ○ **C.** Yellow dogging
- ○ **D.** Single roofing

105. The following formula calculates

$$\frac{\text{Total of all costs associated with the HRD/training initiative}}{\text{Number of individuals who participate in the HRD/training initiative}}$$

- ○ **A.** ROI
- ○ **B.** Cost per trainee
- ○ **C.** Cost per hire
- ○ **D.** Cost/benefit analysis

106. The significance of *Martin v. Wilks, 1988*, was

- ○ **A.** Current employees who are negatively impacted by consent decrees that were established in an earlier time and which sought to resolve discrimination that was present in an earlier time may not challenge the validity of such decrees.
- ○ **B.** Current employees who are negatively impacted by consent decrees that were established in an earlier time and which sought to resolve discrimination that was present in an earlier time may challenge the validity of such decrees.
- ○ **C.** Gender can be used as a factor in the selection process if there is underrepresentation in a particular job classification as long as the AAP does not set forth a quota.
- ○ **D.** Gender can be used as a factor in the selection process if there is underrepresentation in a particular job classification as long as the AAP does not set forth specific good faith efforts in which the organization will engage to attain that quota.

107. Organizations who lead the market

◯ **A.** Choose to offer total rewards/total compensation packages that incorporate a variety of indirect compensation components in addition to a competitive direct compensation component.

◯ **B.** Choose to offer variable pay components with greater upside potential than those that are being offered by their labor market competitors and offer base compensation components that are less competitive than what their labor market competitors are offering.

◯ **C.** Choose to offer total rewards/total compensation packages that are more generous than the total rewards/total compensation packages being offered by their labor market competitors.

◯ **D.** Choose to offer total compensation packages that are more innovative, creative, atypical, and usually nontraditional than packages being offered by their labor market competitors.

108. The five distinct, yet overlapping, project management processes are (in order):

◯ **A.** Establishing, developing, implementing, evaluating, and controlling.

◯ **B.** Initiation, planning, controlling, executing, and closing

◯ **C.** Planning, organizing, coordinating, directing, and controlling

◯ **D.** Initiation, planning, executing, controlling, and closing

109. An HR audit is likely to yield information about all of the following except

◯ **A.** The usefulness, appropriateness, and effectiveness of the employee handbook

◯ **B.** Strategies for decreasing noncompliance with legal requirements

◯ **C.** Grievances, their causes, and their impact

◯ **D.** The degree to which the organization complies with HR-related legal requirements

110. Which of the following is a mandatory OSHA standard for all covered employers?

◯ **A.** Emergency Action Plan Standard

◯ **B.** Fire Safety Standard

◯ **C.** Exit Route Standard

◯ **D.** Hazard Communication Standard

111. The Mine Safety and Health Act (MSH Act)

◯ **A.** Applies only to underground mines

◯ **B.** Requires that all mines be inspected at least twice a year (and sometimes four times)

◯ **C.** Applies only to coal mines

◯ **D.** Provides protections in addition to those afforded by OSHA

112. An organization creates affinity groups. Which of the following of Maslow's needs does this initiative primarily address?

- ○ **A.** Safety and security
- ○ **B.** Belonging and love
- ○ **C.** Esteem
- ○ **D.** Self-actualization

113. Which of the following is not an example of direct compensation?

- ○ **A.** Hourly wages/base salary
- ○ **B.** Shift differentials
- ○ **C.** Flexible spending accounts
- ○ **D.** Variable pay

114. Which of the following does not represent a potential disadvantage of an employee referral program?

- ○ **A.** If the current organization is not particularly diverse (with respect to gender, age, race, education background, or a host of other factors), employee referral programs might perpetuate that lack of diversity.
- ○ **B.** If the organization needs to fill multiple openings for the same position during a short period of time, using employee referrals has the potential to significantly increase the cost-per-hire.
- ○ **C.** If an affirmative action plan is in place, and if there are areas of underutilization, an employee referral program is not likely to demonstrate good faith efforts to recruit candidates who are women or minorities.
- ○ **D.** If the organization has prior patterns of hiring discrimination, employee referral programs are likely to reinforce those patterns.

115. Job specs can be expressed as all but which of the following?

- ○ **A.** KSAs
- ○ **B.** Credentials (years of experience, educational requirements, and so on)
- ○ **C.** Physical or mental requirements
- ○ **D.** Qualifications possessed by the best qualified candidate

116. To what dimension of the organization is Edgard Schein referring when he writes

"…a pattern of shared basic assumptions that the group learns as it solved its problems of external adaptation and internal integration, that has worked well enough to be considered valid and, therefore, to be taught to new members as the correct way you perceive, think, and feel in relation to those problems."

- ○ **A.** Vision
- ○ **B.** Mission
- ○ **C.** Culture
- ○ **D.** Values

117. Managers who use performance appraisal systems based on rating scales

   ○ **A.** Rate employees against each other

   ○ **B.** Rate employees against performance expectations

   ○ **C.** Identify statements that are reflective of employees' performance

   ○ **D.** Write a narrative assessment of employees' performance

118. The key issues in *Albemarle Paper v. Moody, 1975*, were

   ○ **A.** Job relatedness and validity

   ○ **B.** Disparate impact and disparate treatment

   ○ **C.** Reasonable accommodations and undue hardship

   ○ **D.** Negligent hiring and negligent retention

119. All of the following represent reasons to establish an ethics program except

   ○ **A.** To prevent or minimize aggression/violence

   ○ **B.** To prevent or minimize organizational politics

   ○ **C.** To prevent or minimize the erosion of trust

   ○ **D.** To prevent or minimize cynicism

120. Which of the following statements about the Uniform Guidelines on Employee Selection Procedures is not true?

   ○ **A.** One of its key purposes is to address the concept of adverse impact.

   ○ **B.** One of its key purposes is to address the concept of adverse treatment.

   ○ **C.** One important objective of the Uniform Guidelines is to ensure that interview and selection processes are reliable.

   ○ **D.** One important objective of the Uniform Guidelines is to ensure that interview and selection processes are valid.

121. The Davis-Bacon Act of 1931

   ○ **A.** Was the first piece of legislation to consider the topic of—and to actually establish—a minimum wage

   ○ **B.** Was rendered obsolete by the minimum wage provisions of the FLSA of 1938

   ○ **C.** Applies only to federal contractors and subcontractors with contracts in excess of $20,000

   ○ **D.** Applies to construction projects that receive federal funding

122. Youth workers (also known as "children") who are 14 or 15 years old may work

   ○ **A.** Up to 4 hours on a school day

   ○ **B.** Up to 20 hours during a school week

   ○ **C.** Up to 7 hours on a nonschool day

   ○ **D.** Up to 40 hours during a nonschool week

123. Which of these questions is the most appropriate to ask?

   ○ **A.** "Tell me about any restriction you have that would prevent you from lifting 30-pound metal sheets onto a conveyor belt for about four hours each day."

   ○ **B.** "This job requires lifting 30-pound metal sheets onto a conveyor belt for about four hours each workday. Do you have any problems doing this?"

   ○ **C.** "This job requires lifting 30-pound metal sheets onto a conveyor belt for about four hours each workday. Can you meet this requirement of the position?"

   ○ **D.** "Although it's technically not part of the job, the person who used to hold this job would help out everyone once in a while with lifting 30-pound metal sheets onto a conveyor belt. Can we count on you to follow in her footsteps and help out if we need you to do so?"

124. Which of the following statements about the Portal-to-Portal Act is not true?

   ○ **A.** The Portal-to-Portal Act offered a clearer definition of hours worked for purposes of minimum wage and overtime calculations.

   ○ **B.** It established that employers must compensate workers for the time that they spend performing their jobs but not for time spent on activities that only relate to the performance of their job.

   ○ **C.** It addresses topics such as travel time, preshift work, postshift work, idle waiting time, overnight travel, training time, and the like.

   ○ **D.** The Portal-to-Portal Act was an amendment of the FLSA.

125. Common law refers to a system of law in which all of the following statements are true except

   ○ **A.** Traditions, customs, and precedents have the same force of law as existing laws or statutes.

   ○ **B.** Laws and statutes are, quite literally, interpreted and reinterpreted on a case-by-case basis.

   ○ **C.** Contracts, including employment, are eclipsed by the prevailing common law.

   ○ **D.** Each interpretation and each case sets a precedent but can also be reinterpreted, thus setting a new precedent.

126. The key issue in *Griggs v. Duke Power, 1971*, was

   ○ **A.** Replacing striking workers

   ○ **B.** Employment testing

   ○ **C.** Adverse treatment

   ○ **D.** Adverse impact

127. Taken together, the two 1998 landmark Supreme Court cases *Faragher v. City of Boca Raton* and *Ellerth v. Burlington Northern Industries* established all of the following except

   ○ **A.** If an employee is subjected to a tangible adverse employment action because of a supervisor's sexually harassing behavior, the employer is liable.

   ○ **B.** The employer is vicariously liable when its supervisors create a sexually hostile work environment, even if the employee is not subjected to an adverse employment action.

○ **C.** If the employee is not subjected to tangible adverse employment action, the employer may be able to raise as a defense that he acted reasonably to prevent or promptly correct any sexually harassing behavior and that the plaintiff unreasonably failed to take advantage of the employer's preventive or corrective opportunities.

○ **D.** If the employee is subjected to tangible adverse employment action, the employer may be able to raise as a defense that he acted reasonably to prevent or promptly correct any sexually harassing behavior and that the plaintiff unreasonably failed to take advantage of the employer's preventive or corrective opportunities.

128. To be eligible to take FMLA leave, an employee must meet four requirements. Which of the following does not constitute one of those requirements?

○ **A.** The employee must work for a covered employer (public agencies; federal, state, and local employers; local education agencies [schools]; and private-sector employers with 50 or more employees).

○ **B.** The employee must have worked for the employer for a total of at least 12 months. (This time does not have to have been uninterrupted.)

○ **C.** The employee must have worked at least 1,250 hours over the previous 12 months.

○ **D.** The employee must work at a location in the United States or in any territory or possession of the United States where at least 75 employees are employed by the employer within 50 miles.

129. The ruling in the landmark case *Automobile Workers v. Johnson Controls, 1990*, determined that

○ **A.** Employers have an obligation to establish policies to protect unborn fetuses from possible harm resulting from chemical exposure.

○ **B.** Most, if not all, fetal protection policies result in gender discrimination.

○ **C.** The government has the obligation to protect unborn fetuses from chemical risk, even if the parents who conceived them do not choose to do so.

○ **D.** Most, if not all, fetal protection policies constitute a legitimate BFOQ.

130. The process of maintaining awareness of opportunities and threats is known as

○ **A.** SWOT analysis

○ **B.** Environmental scanning

○ **C.** Strategic planning

○ **D.** Contingency planning

131. The significance of *Regents of California v. Bakke, 1978*, was

○ **A.** The permissibility of quotas in college admissions affirmative action programs is irrelevant and nontransferable to the workplace.

○ **B.** The permissibility of quotas in college admissions affirmative action programs is relevant and transferable to the workplace.

○ **C.** The impermissibility of quotas in college admissions affirmative action programs is irrelevant and nontransferable to the workplace.

○ **D.** The impermissibility of quotas in college admissions affirmative action programs is relevant and transferable to the workplace.

132. In the acronym SMART, M stands for

○ **A.** Marketable

○ **B.** Meaningful

○ **C.** Measurable

○ **D.** Motivational

133. During an organizing campaign, unions are permitted to engage in all of the following activities except

○ **A.** Inside organizing

○ **B.** Salting

○ **C.** Surface organizing

○ **D.** Organizational picketing

134. Which of the following statements about strikes is not true?

○ **A.** Employers cannot hire permanent strike replacements during an economic strike.

○ **B.** Employers cannot hire permanent strike replacements during a ULP strike.

○ **C.** Workers must be returned to their original positions after a ULP strike is over.

○ **D.** Workers cannot be terminated for participating in an economic strike.

135. Which of the following statements about focus groups is untrue?

○ **A.** A focus group is more of a communication tool than an involvement tool.

○ **B.** Focus groups consist of a representative sample of employees.

○ **C.** Focus groups need to include enough people to generate a dynamic and synergistic discussion.

○ **D.** Focus groups are led by a neutral facilitator.

136. Which of the following considerations would be least valuable to ask while you are preparing to collect market data?

○ **A.** What is the relevant labor market for this position?

○ **B.** What sources of market data do you already have, and what additional sources could you get?

○ **C.** How does the position compare to others within the existing job worth hierarchy?

○ **D.** Who are our labor market competitors in general and for specific jobs?

137. You've been hired as the HR manager of a start-up company that produces a new type of alternative fuel. Which of the following conditions are you least likely to experience in your new role?

○ **A.** A request to publish an employee handbook

○ **B.** The need to develop total rewards packages that lead the market

○ **C.** The need to develop total rewards packages that lag the market

○ **D.** A high level of excitement and energy

138. An employee who prefers to learn about HR practices by attending a guest lecture series is probably a(n)

    ◯ **A.** Visual learner

    ◯ **B.** Auditory learner

    ◯ **C.** Kinesthetic learner

    ◯ **D.** Vicarious learner

139. Which of the following statements does not constitute a consideration for determining what constitutes fair use?

    ◯ **A.** Whether the work will be used for commercial purposes or for not-for-profit or educational purposes

    ◯ **B.** The nature or way in which the work will be used

    ◯ **C.** How much of the work is used, both in terms of the aggregate amount of work that is being used as well as the percentage of the total work that is being used

    ◯ **D.** Specific permissions that the copyright holder has previously granted, if those permissions are deemed to be precedent-setting in nature

140. The most renowned example of the Mackay Doctrine in use was

    ◯ **A.** In 2005, when President George W. Bush waived the requirement to pay a prevailing wage rate to government contractors and subcontractors involved in the rebuilding of New Orleans

    ◯ **B.** In 1996, when President William Jefferson "Bill" Clinton signed legislation permitting employers to require all employees to agree to binding arbitration in exchange for the opportunity to be employed with the organization

    ◯ **C.** In 1992, when President George H. W. Bush passed an executive order that required more than 11,000 troops returning from the (first) Gulf War be reinstated to the positions that they would have held if they had not experienced a break in service due to their military service

    ◯ **D.** In 1981, when President Ronald Wilson Reagan replaced 12,000 striking air traffic controllers

141. Which of the following is least likely to be considered an action-oriented program?

    ◯ **A.** Recruiting at colleges or universities traditionally attended by minorities

    ◯ **B.** Increasing the cash awards granted through the organization's employee referral program

    ◯ **C.** Reaching out to professional organizations whose membership criteria is designed to attract women or minorities

    ◯ **D.** Posting job openings at resource centers for displaced homemakers

142. An employee is hired as a telesales representative for a sports apparel company. She performs exceptionally well in that position and is promoted to the position of field sales manager. Two months later, this employee is injured in a serious automobile accident in which she loses both of her legs. To everyone's amazement, she is ready to return to work two months later. She is told, however, that she will not be able to return to her position as sales manager but is welcome

to return to her former position as telesales representative. Although she is not initially given a reason, she is finally told "off the record" that although the customers feel very bad for what happened to her, they just aren't comfortable having a wheelchair-bound field sales manager and that, ultimately, "the customer is always right." Would this decision likely be upheld as legal under EEO law?

- ○ **A.** Yes, because of the BFOQ exception to EEO laws.
- ○ **B.** No, because this would not qualify under the BFOQ exception to EEO laws.
- ○ **C.** Yes, because of the customer preference exception to EEO laws.
- ○ **D.** No, because there are no exceptions to EEO laws.

143. The following formula

$$\frac{\text{Number of terminations during a specified period of time}}{\text{The average number of employees in the workforce during that same period of time}}$$

calculates which of the following?

- ○ **A.** Time to hire
- ○ **B.** Turnover
- ○ **C.** ROI
- ○ **D.** Cost per hire

144. All of the following statements offer sound advice to follow relative to offer letters except

- ○ **A.** State that the only agreements or promises that are valid are those that are included in the offer letter.
- ○ **B.** Use the offer letter as an opportunity to reaffirm that the employment relationship is at-will.
- ○ **C.** For exempt positions, avoid expressing earnings in weekly, bimonthly, or monthly terms (depending upon your payroll cycle) so you don't jeopardize the nonexempt FLSA status.
- ○ **D.** Avoid language that hints of any sort of long-term employment relationship as well as any statements that indicate that the employer is "like a family."

145. Which of the following types of tests is most frequently considered to be illegal on a preemployment basis?

- ○ **A.** Agility tests
- ○ **B.** Aptitude tests
- ○ **C.** Honesty tests
- ○ **D.** Polygraph tests

146. To be concerted, activity must be

- ○ **A.** Undertaken by individual employees who are acting in pursuit of an individual goal
- ○ **B.** Undertaken by individual employees who are acting in an independent manner
- ○ **C.** Protected before it can be concerted
- ○ **D.** Engaged in with or on the authority of other employees

147. If an employer does not choose to seek a settlement agreement when a charge of discrimination is first filed, the EEOC can handle the charge in all of the following ways except

   ○ **A.** Investigate it

   ○ **B.** Settle it

   ○ **C.** Arbitrate it

   ○ **D.** Dismiss it

148. A protected class is best described as

   ○ **A.** A group of individuals who have, historically, experienced discrimination (for instance, women, people of color, people with disabilities, and so on)

   ○ **B.** A group of individuals who share a common characteristic and who are protected from discrimination and harassment based on that shared characteristic

   ○ **C.** A group of individuals who have filed charges with the NLRB or are taking part in any NLRB proceedings

   ○ **D.** Employees who have engaged in an economic strike and who, therefore, under the Mackay Doctrine, cannot be permanently replaced by the employer

149. If you notice a change in a candidate's nonverbal behavior during the interview

   ○ **A.** Probe for more information around whatever question the candidate was answering when that change occurred.

   ○ **B.** Be familiar with what specific nonverbal communication cues mean (for instance, folded arms indicate aloofness) so you know how to interpret the behavior.

   ○ **C.** Without assessing judgment, point out and describe the changed nonverbal behavior and ask her to help you understand what it means.

   ○ **D.** Mirror the candidate's nonverbal behavior to see if she continues to display that behavior.

150. Recruiting is

   ○ **A.** The process of creating a pool of candidates and selecting the final candidate

   ○ **B.** The process of attracting and creating a pool of qualified candidates

   ○ **C.** The process of identifying the candidate(s) to whom the position will be offered

   ○ **D.** The process of selecting the candidate to whom the position will be offered

151. After you decide that you are going to conduct an employee survey, what is the first step that you should take?

   ○ **A.** Select an internal or external consultant.

   ○ **B.** Determine the survey methodology.

   ○ **C.** Secure management buy-in.

   ○ **D.** Decide upon the survey content.

152. Union deauthorization

    ○ **A.** Is the process of removing the union's rights to represent the employees

    ○ **B.** Revokes the union security clause in the contract

    ○ **C.** Requires that 50% or more of those who vote during the union deauthorization election support the deauthorization

    ○ **D.** Is far more common than union decertification

153. Preemployment realistic job previews can be conveyed and communicated in a number of ways. Which of the following is the least effective way of providing candidates with a realistic job preview?

    ○ **A.** Verbal descriptions of the work, the work environment, or the work conditions

    ○ **B.** The opportunity to read the employee handbook

    ○ **C.** The opportunity to speak with current employees, particularly those who would be the incumbent's peers or colleagues

    ○ **D.** The opportunity to interact with other candidates and to compare perceptions of the organization with each other

154. Which of the following statements about IRCA is inaccurate?

    ○ **A.** IRCA prohibits discrimination against job applicants based on national origin.

    ○ **B.** IRCA imposes penalties for knowingly committing recordkeeping errors.

    ○ **C.** IRCA prohibits giving employment preference to U.S. citizens.

    ○ **D.** IRCA imposes penalties for hiring illegal aliens.

155. All of the following are valuable guidelines for managing a vendor and a relationship with a vendor except

    ○ **A.** Giving the vendor constructive and positive feedback

    ○ **B.** Setting clear and reasonable expectations

    ○ **C.** Converting full-time vendors from independent contractors to employees to foster greater esprit de corps

    ○ **D.** Incorporating upside potential and downside risk into your negotiated agreements with vendors

156. The four Ps refer to

    ○ **A.** Priorities, posting, places, and people (the four Ps of recruiting)

    ○ **B.** Perception, perspective, proportion, and perseverance (the four Ps of employee relations)

    ○ **C.** Prospect, persistence, proposal, and project (the four Ps of project management)

    ○ **D.** Product, place, price, and promotion (the four Ps of marketing)

157. Which of the statements about common situs picketing is not true?

   ○ **A.** Common situs picketing is a type of secondary boycott.

   ○ **B.** Common situs picketing is generally legal.

   ○ **C.** Common situs picketing occurs when members of a labor union picket a workplace in which multiple employers work.

   ○ **D.** Common situs picketing is permissible when double breasting has occurred.

158. All of the following statements about essential functions are true except

   ○ **A.** To be considered essential, a function must be inherently fundamental and necessary to a position.

   ○ **B.** To be considered essential, a function must constitute part or all of the reason the job exists.

   ○ **C.** The elimination of an essential function would substantially alter the nature of the job.

   ○ **D.** They must be identified in the job description.

159. *McDonnell Douglas Corp v. Green, 1979*, determined that the initial burden of proof for establishing a prima facie case of discrimination against an employer (or potential employer) under Title VII of the Civil Rights Act of 1964 rests with the employee (or applicant), who must be able to establish four key elements. Which one of these elements is not one of those four elements that the employee must have to establish a prima facie case?

   ○ **A.** The person is a member of a protected class.

   ○ **B.** The person applied for a job for which the employer was seeking applicants.

   ○ **C.** The person was rejected despite being the most qualified for the position.

   ○ **D.** After this rejection, the employer continued to seek other applicants with similar qualifications.

160. All of the following are possible reasons to conduct prescreen phone interviews except

   ○ **A.** To identify legitimate job-related factors that could cause the employer to decide to eliminate the candidate from consideration

   ○ **B.** To share (with every candidate) job-related information that could lead one or more candidates to self-select out of the selection process

   ○ **C.** To interact with a candidate in a more informal manner to ascertain whether he is likely to be a good fit with the organization

   ○ **D.** To ascertain whether the candidate's desired salary/wage rate is close to the salary/wage range that the organization has established for the position

161. Which of the following situations would be least likely to result in disparate impact?

   ○ **A.** An employer requires all employees to live within a 30-mile radius of an employer to ensure quick response if employees need to report to work immediately.

   ○ **B.** An employer will not hire candidates who have experienced a gap in employment.

    ○ **C.** An employer establishes a high potential program, in which participants are required to relocate every 9–12 months until they have completed five rotational assignments in five different locations.

    ○ **D.** An employer creates a cross-training program in which all nonmanagement employees who meet or exceed performance expectations of their current positions would be able to participate.

162. Although it is difficult to establish good measures of validity, it is possible to make a case for validity if the interview process has certain characteristics. Which of these processes/attributes contributes the least to enhancing the validity of an interview process?

    ○ **A.** The same interviewer conducts every interview for a particular job opening.

    ○ **B.** The interview is based on job analysis.

    ○ **C.** The interviewer asks questions that provide evidence about important job-related skills.

    ○ **D.** The information shared, discussed, and collected during an interview relates to a specific job.

163. In behavioral leadership theories, the dimension of leadership behavior known as initiating structure refers to

    ○ **A.** The interpersonal relationships that managers must first establish with employees before attempting to ensure completion of the actual work

    ○ **B.** What employees need to do, and how they need to do it, to attain objectives

    ○ **C.** The training in which managers need to participate to develop the skills needed to be an effective leader

    ○ **D.** The degree to which an individual demonstrates an innate ability to being an effective leader

164. According to the Copyright Act of 1976, which of the following statements is true?

    ○ **A.** Most of the time, the employer owns/retains the copyright to the work product that an employee generates during the normal course of her employment.

    ○ **B.** Most of the time, an independent contractor owns/retains the copyright to the work product that she generates for the organization with which she has contracted.

    ○ **C.** Most of the time, an employee owns/retains the copyright to the work product that she generates in the normal course of her employment.

    ○ **D.** Most of the time, a consulting firm owns/retains the copyright to the work product that the consultant generates for the organization with which she is consulting.

165. The formative evaluation model

    ○ **A.** Seeks feedback during and after the development and implementation phases

    ○ **B.** Uses feedback, analysis, and assessment conducted at one phase of the process to make enhancements in other phases

    ○ **C.** Was initially developed by Donald L. Kirkpatrick

    ○ **D.** Measures participants' responses and reactions to the program immediately after the program has been delivered

166. Which of the following would not be considered a form of indirect compensation?

    ○ **A.** Legally mandated benefits (such as social security)

    ○ **B.** Vacation time

    ○ **C.** Perquisites

    ○ **D.** Vacation buyout programs

167. Which of the following statements about the MHPA is untrue?

    ○ **A.** MHPA requires employers that offer health care plans with medical benefits to offer mental health benefits.

    ○ **B.** Under MHPA, plans can still dictate/define the terms and conditions of benefits provided under mental health plans (for instance, cost-sharing, limits on the number of visits or days of coverage, and so on).

    ○ **C.** Under MHPA, plans that don't impose annual or lifetime monetary caps on medical and surgical benefits cannot impose annual or lifetime caps on mental health benefits.

    ○ **D.** Benefits for substance abuse or chemical dependency are excluded from MHPA's requirements relative to annual or lifetime caps.

168. Generally speaking, when an employee handbook is submitted as legal evidence, which of the following factors is usually most important?

    ○ **A.** EEO/AA statement

    ○ **B.** Sexual harassment policy

    ○ **C.** Records retention policy

    ○ **D.** Employee acknowledgement

169. Which of the following is least likely to be a reason that an organization would conduct an employee survey?

    ○ **A.** To gauge and measure employees' perceptions, viewpoints, and attitudes

    ○ **B.** To take the pulse on specific current or potential employee issues

    ○ **C.** To collect information that can be used to address an individual's employee relations issues

    ○ **D.** To collect information that can be used by the organization to help set priorities

170. For a bargaining unit to be established, which of the following has to happen during the election?

    ○ **A.** A simple majority of the voters must cast a vote in favor of the proposed bargaining unit.

    ○ **B.** A simple majority of the individuals who would be members of the proposed bargaining unit must cast a vote in favor of the proposed bargaining unit.

    ○ **C.** When there is more than one bargaining unit competing in the election, a proposed bargaining unit must obtain more votes than other bargaining units obtain.

    ○ **D.** At least 30% of the voters must cast a vote in favor of the bargaining unit.

171. Of the following situations, which one represents the highest priority for OSHA?

  ○ **A.** Referrals from the media

  ○ **B.** Planned inspections in high-hazard industries

  ○ **C.** Employee complaints

  ○ **D.** Catastrophes and fatal accidents

172. With respect to selection procedures, reliability can be defined as

  ○ **A.** The degree to which a selection procedure assesses a candidate's ability to perform representative and significant parts of the job

  ○ **B.** The degree to which incumbents' scores or ratings on a particular selection procedure correlate with their actual job performance

  ○ **C.** The degree to which a selection process or instrument is consistent and generates consistent information that can be used for decision making

  ○ **D.** The degree to which a clear relationship exists between performance on the selection procedure and performance on the job

173. "The degree of responsibility and accountability which an employer entrusts to—and expects from—a particular position" refers to the definition of which of the four factors used by the Equal Pay Act to assess substantial equality?

  ○ **A.** Skill

  ○ **B.** Trust

  ○ **C.** Accountability

  ○ **D.** Responsibility

174. Taft-Hartley accomplished all of the following except

  ○ **A.** Reaffirmed that employers have a constitutional right to express their opposition to unions so long as employees are not threatened with reprisal for their union activities or promised benefits for refraining from such activities

  ○ **B.** Prohibited employers from taking adverse employment actions against supervisors who did not support the employer's position

  ○ **C.** Outlawed closed shops, agreements that stated that employers could only hire individuals who were members of labor unions

  ○ **D.** Expressly permitted union shops, in which nonunion workers must join the union within a certain amount of time after being hired

175. The list of the names and addresses of all the employees who are eligible to vote in the union certification election is known as

  ○ **A.** The Excelsior List

  ○ **B.** The Davis-Bacon List

  ○ **C.** The Hot Cargo List

  ○ **D.** The Waffle House List

Answers to Practice Exam

Answers at a Glance to Practice Exam

1.	C	36.	C	71.	B	106.	B	141.	B
2.	C	37.	C	72.	B	107.	C	142.	B
3.	D	38.	C	73.	A	108.	D	143.	B
4.	A	39.	A	74.	B	109.	B	144.	C
5.	C	40.	D	75.	C	110.	C	145.	D
6.	C	41.	D	76.	C	111.	B	146.	D
7.	C	42.	B	77.	C	112.	B	147.	C
8.	C	43.	B	78.	B	113.	C	148.	B
9.	B	44.	B	79.	C	114.	B	149.	A
10.	B	45.	C	80.	C	115.	D	150.	B
11.	C	46.	D	81.	B	116.	C	151.	C
12.	D	47.	B	82.	A	117.	B	152.	B
13.	B	48.	B	83.	B	118.	A	153.	D
14.	A	49.	B	84.	A	119.	B	154.	B
15.	B	50.	A	85.	C	120.	B	155.	C
16.	C	51.	B	86.	D	121.	A	156.	D
17.	A	52.	B	87.	A	122.	D	157.	D
18.	C	53.	D	88.	D	123.	C	158.	D
19.	D	54.	D	89.	D	124.	B	159.	C
20.	D	55.	B	90.	B	125.	C	160.	C
21.	B	56.	D	91.	A	126.	D	161.	D
22.	A	57.	A	92.	D	127.	D	162.	A
23.	D	58.	A	93.	C	128.	D	163.	B
24.	C	59.	A	94.	C	129.	B	164.	A
25.	D	60.	C	95.	D	130.	B	165.	B
26.	C	61.	A	96.	B	131.	D	166.	D
27.	A	62.	C	97.	A	132.	C	167.	A
28.	B	63.	A	98.	C	133.	C	168.	D
29.	A	64.	C	99.	A	134.	A	169.	C
30.	C	65.	D	100.	B	135.	A	170.	A
31.	B	66.	B	101.	A	136.	C	171.	D
32.	B	67.	B	102.	A	137.	A	172.	C
33.	A	68.	B	103.	C	138.	B	173.	D
34.	C	69.	C	104.	B	139.	D	174.	B
35.	C	70.	A	105.	B	140.	D	175.	A

Answers with Explanations

1. Answer C is the best answer. Unflattering light does not constitute one of the four categories of invasion of privacy; however, false light does. Answer A is not the best answer; intrusion of solitude does constitute one of the four categories of invasion of privacy. Answer B is not the best answer; public disclosure of private and embarrassing facts does constitute one of the four categories of invasion of privacy. Answer D is not the best answer; appropriation of identity does constitute one of the four categories of invasion of privacy.

2. Answer C is the best answer. Employees must report all work-related injuries to their employer—whether or not the injury results in in-patient hospitalization. Answers A, B, and D are not the best answers; each identifies responsibilities that are mandated by the General Duty Clause.

3. Answer D is the best answer. The Retirement Equity Act did prohibit plans from counting maternity and paternity leaves as breaks in service for participation and vesting purposes. Answer A is not the best answer; REA lowered, rather than increased, the minimum age requirement for pension plan participation. Answer B is not the best answer; REA required qualified pension plans to provide automatic survivor benefits and allow for waiver of survivor benefits only with the consent of the participant and the spouse. Answer C is not the best answer; REA clarified that pension plans may obey certain qualified domestic relations (court) orders (QDROs) requiring them to make benefit payments to a participant's former spouse (or another alternative payee) without violating ERISA's prohibitions against assignment or alienation of benefits.

4. Answer A is the best answer. Whether a survey is designed and conducted by someone from inside or outside the organization is not nearly as important as the other considerations that are listed in the other answers. A survey can be successful or unsuccessful whether it is conducted by someone inside, or outside, the organization. The way the survey is designed and conducted is generally much more important. Answer B is not the best answer; ensuring that survey input is maintained in a fully confidential manner is an important determinant of the overall success of an employee survey. Answer C is not the best answer; ensuring that employees believe in the confidentiality of the survey is an important determinant of the overall success of an employee survey. Answer D is not the best answer; ensuring buy-in and support from management is an important determinant of the overall success of an employee survey.

5. Answer C is the best answer. Resistance to the process of formalizing policies and procedures is most likely to first manifest itself during the development (or growth) stage in the organizational life cycle. Answer A is not the best answer; having a core group of highly talented employees who focus on the founder is more likely to first manifest itself during stage 1 of the organizational life cycle (introduction or birth). Answer B is not the best answer; resistance to OD and change initiatives is more likely to first manifest itself during stage 3 of the organizational life cycle (maturity). Answer D is not the best answer; an entitlement mentality toward pay and benefits is most likely to first manifest itself during stage 3 of the organizational life cycle (maturity).

6. Answer C is the best answer. Bonus pay (which, unlike incentive pay, is discretionary) would not be included in an employee's regular rate of pay.

7. Answer C is the best answer. OD helps maintain the organization's focus on the belief that it is the people within organizations (not the systems within organizations) who perform and accomplish the work of the organization. Answer A is not the best answer; OD does refer to the process through which the overall performance, growth, and effectiveness of the organization is enhanced through strategic, deliberate, and integrated initiatives. Answer B is not the best answer; OD does incorporate psychology, sociology, anthropology, and management. Answer D is not the best answer; OD interventions are designed to identify an organization's competitive advantages.

8. Answer C is the best answer. A ULP is called when a union alleges that an employer has committed a ULP. This does not necessarily mean that the employer actually did, in fact, commit a ULP. (The courts would need to subsequently determine that a strike was, in fact, a ULP strike and not an economic strike

in disguise.) Answer A is not the best answer; ULP strikes stem from an allegation that the employer has committed a ULP during contract negotiations. Answer B is not the best answer; an employer must return striking workers to their original positions after the strike is over. Answer D is not the best answer; employers cannot hire permanent strike replacements during a ULP strike.

9. Answer B is the correct answer. The Hazard Communication Standard has no requirement pertaining to obtaining signed employee acknowledgement forms, although it is always a good idea to obtain signed documentation that participants have attended a training session (especially when such training is required by law). This standard does, however, require MSDSs (answer A), container labeling requirements (answer C), and training and orientation requirements (answer D).

10. Answer B is the best answer. A jurisdictional strike is one through which a union seeks to pressure an employer to assign particular work to its members rather than to members of other unions or to nonunion workers. Answer A is not the best answer; employees who are not directly involved in an economic dispute who choose not to cross a picket line out of support for striking workers are engaging in a sympathy strike, not a jurisdictional strike. Answer C is not the best answer; a strike that occurs even though the collective bargaining agreement contains a no-strike clause is a wildcat strike, not a jurisdictional strike. Answer D is not the best answer; a strike used by a union to pressure an employer to grant some sort of concession (namely, an economic concession) from the employer during collective bargaining negotiations is an economic strike, not a jurisdictional strike.

11. Answer C is the best answer. Copyrights are granted for the lifetime of the author, plus 70 years (assuming that the work was not created anonymously). Answer A is not the best answer; the copyright does not end when the author dies. Answer B is not the best answer; copyrights cannot be deeded to heirs. Answer D is not the best answer; this answer alludes to copyrights for anonymous works and works that were created under work-for-hire agreements that enter the public domain 95 years after the first year of publication or 120 years after the year in which it was created, whichever comes first.

12. Answer D is the best answer. In general, placing all the interviewers on one side of the table and the candidate on the other can unintentionally create an adversarial atmosphere even if this arrangement makes it easier for the candidate to make eye contact with the interviewers. Answer A is not the best answer; it is a good idea to let the candidate know ahead of time if shewill be participating in a panel interview to help minimize—or avoid—the anxiety that a surprise of this sort could cause. Answer B is not the best answer; it is a good idea to plan who will ask what questions in advance, and in what order. Answer C is not the best answer; a round table will help create an atmosphere that is conducive to the exchange of information.

13. Answer B is the best answer. As long as they fall under the category of "first aid," injuries resulting in bleeding do not need to be recorded unless they also result in death, days away from work (answer A), restricted work or job transfer (answer C), or loss of consciousness (answer D).

14. Answer A is the best answer. The question of whether the employee or the collective bargaining unit advised the employer of the concerted nature of the employee's activity is irrelevant to whether the employer might be considered to have violated the NLRA. The only three requirements that would need to be met for an employer to be considered to have possibly violated the NLRA are whether the employer knew of the concerted nature of the employee's activity (answer B), whether the concerted activity was actually protected by NLRA (answer C), and whether the adverse employment action in question (for instance, termination) was motivated by the employee's protected concerted activity (answer D).

15. Answer B is the best answer. Henry Fayol is known as the father of modern management. Answers A, C, and D are not the best answers; Fayol was not known as a guru in any of these areas.

16. Answer C is the best answer. In *General Dynamics Land Systems v. Cline, 2004*, the Supreme Court ruled that younger employees (even if they are over the age of 40) cannot allege age discrimination because of programs that favor older employees. Answer A is not the best answer; *General Dynamics Land Systems v. Cline, 2004*, established that the ADEA does not prohibit favoring the old over the young. Answer B is not the best answer; although the ADEA prohibits favoring the young over the old,

it has not been interpreted to prohibit favoring the old over the young. Answer D is not the best answer; younger employees (even if they are over the age of 40) cannot allege age discrimination because of programs that favor older employees.

17. Answer A is the best answer. Job classification is a nonquantitative job evaluation technique that categorizes jobs into broad categories, or levels, based on the level—and, ultimately, value to the organization—of the work that is performed by jobs within each level. Each level incorporates specific responsibilities and benchmark statements that describe the nature, complexity, autonomy, and so forth of the work that is performed by positions in that level. Answer B is not the best answer; job slotting is a nonquantitative job evaluation technique that incorporates, or slots, newly created or revised positions into an existing job hierarchy. Answer C is not the best answer; in whole job ranking techniques (nonquantitative), jobs are ranked, from lowest to highest, according to the importance that each job holds (or, stated differently, the value that each job brings) to the organization. Answer D is not the best answer; factor comparison is a quantitative job evaluation technique that involves the ranking of each compensable factor of each job.

18. Answer C is the best answer. The decision whether to lag, match, or lead the market with respect to total compensation/total rewards is just that—a decision. It is not universally true that an organization's total compensation program should be competitive with (in other words, match) the total compensation programs offered by labor market competitors. Answer A is not the best answer; an organization's total compensation/total rewards program should support and reinforce the mission, vision, and values of the organization. Answer B is not the best answer; an organization's total compensation/total rewards program should be consistent with the culture of the organization. Answer D is not the best answer; an organization's total compensation program should attract, motivate, and retain targeted/appropriate employees.

19. Answer D is the best answer. An oral contract can be created when an agent of the employer promises some benefit or right. The term agent is legal, and involved, but of the four individuals listed in the question, the one who is least likely to be considered an agent would be a coworker. Answer A is not the best answer; a full-time recruiter would be more likely than a coworker to create an oral contract. Answer B is not the best answer; a hiring manager—even if he interviews only for his open positions—is more likely than a coworker to create an oral contract. (It only takes one interview, and maybe even one comment, to create an oral contract.) Answer C is not the best answer; an employee's current supervisor is more likely to create an oral contract than an employee's current coworker is.

20. Answer D is the best answer. *Harris v. Forklift Systems, 1993*, established the reasonable person standard. Answer A is not the best answer; in *Taxman v. Board of Education of Piscataway, 1993*, the Supreme Court ruled that, in the absence of underrepresentation as demonstrated and documented through an affirmative action plan, organizations cannot take race into account when making decisions relative to who will be laid off and who will be retained (and that doing so would constitute a violation of Title VII of the Civil Rights Act of 1964). Answer B is not the best answer; in *Meritor Savings Bank v. Vinson, 1986*, the Supreme Court ruled that a claim of "hostile environment" sexual harassment does constitute a form of sex discrimination actionable under Title VII of the 1964 Civil Rights Act. Answer C is not the best answer; in *St. Mary's Honor Center v. Hicks, 1993*, the Supreme Court ruled that to ultimately prevail in an allegation of discrimination under Title VII of the Civil Rights Act of 1964, the charging party must go beyond a prima facie case and actually prove that the employer's reasons for an employment action are, in fact, discriminatory.

21. Answer B is the best answer. Ishikawa's fishbone diagram (also known as the cause-and-effect diagram or the Ishikawa diagram) presents a visual representation of factors that impact whether a desired outcome will be obtained. Ishikawa believed that, by presenting all the possible factors that can contribute to a particular result, any potential process imperfections can be identified in advance and eliminated. Answer A is not the best answer; the Pareto Chart (based on the Pareto Principle) visually depicts the 80–20 rule. Answer C is not the best answer; although Ishikawa dramatically increased worldwide awareness and acceptance of the idea of quality circles, quality circles are not directly related to his fishbone diagram. Answer D is not the best answer; histograms depict information about a single factor, whereas the Ishikawa diagram depicts information about multiple factors.

22. Answer A is the best answer. ADEA prohibits discrimination based on age for individuals age 40 (not age 18) and above. Some states, however, have established age thresholds that are lower. Answer B is not the best answer; the ADEA does cover private employers with 20 or more employees, state and local governments (including school districts), employment agencies, and labor organizations. Answer C is not the best answer; the ADEA does not establish an upper cap, or an age at which it again becomes legal to discriminate against individuals based on age (although it did at one time). Answer D is not the best answer; ADEA is subject to certain exceptions and does place certain requirements on employers, particularly with respect to benefits plans, coverage, and early retirement incentives.

23. Answer D is the best answer. The A in KSAs refers to abilities, which can be defined as specific traits required to successfully perform a position. Answer A is not the best answer; the A in KSAs does not refer to attitude. Answer B is not the best answer; this answer defines knowledge, the K in KSAs. Answer C is not the best answer; this answer defines skill, the S in KSAs.

24. Answer C is the best answer. HR adds value to this process by asking our clients questions

    ▶ That enable us to collect information

    ▶ That help us to collaboratively ascertain the underlying problems

    ▶ That can help us work with managers to distinguish problems from symptoms

    Answer A is not the best answer; although a manager might be convinced of what the problem is or what the solution should be, the manager's assessment is not necessarily 100% complete or correct, so it is not advisable to automatically commit to implementing it. (Instead, find another way to demonstrate your commitment to that manager, to her problem, and—ultimately—to building a relationship with her.) Answer B is not the best answer for a related reason; at this point, you don't truly know what the problem is, so it is not possible to suggest a solution. Additionally, if you use this approach, you are dismissing the manager's opinions and experience, and you risk damaging your relationship with the manager. (Narcissism won't get you very far in your role as an HR professional.) Answer D is not the best answer; it assumes that the manager's assessment of the problem is 100% complete and correct and that the proposed solution is the best possible intervention.

25. Answer D is the best answer. In concert with counsel, develop a policy requiring that current and former employees sign a carefully worded release before information can be released to a third party. This might include designating what information can be released, as well as acknowledging what information must be released (for instance, to avoid a claim that the organization withheld truthful negative information about the employee). Answer A is not the best answer; refusing to provide any employee references could result in the employer concealing truthful negative information about the employee. Answer B is not the best answer; providing only titles, dates of employment, and final salary information when providing references could still result in a tort claim alleging that the employer concealed truthful negative information about an employee. Answer C is not the best answer; although outsourcing might anesthetize an organization to the fear of litigation, it will not immunize the organization from its consequences.

26. Answer C is the best answer. Defined contribution plans are increasing, not decreasing, in popularity. Answer A is not the best answer; it is true that, unlike defined benefit plans, defined contribution plans do not promise a specific monthly benefit (or total benefit) at retirement. Answer B is not the best answer; defined contribution plans do shift the risk away from the employer (which is where it rests for defined benefit plans) and back onto the employee. Answer D is not the best answer; 401(k) plans, employee stock ownership plans, and profit-sharing plans are examples of defined contribution plans.

27. Answer A is the best answer. In *Taxman v. Board of Education of Piscataway, 1993*, the Supreme Court ruled that, in the absence of underrepresentation as demonstrated and documented through an affirmative action plan, organizations cannot take race into account when making decisions relative to who will be laid off and who will be retained (and that doing so would constitute a violation of Title VII of the Civil Rights Act of 1964).

28. Answer B is the best answer. The Revenue Act of 1978 resulted in the creation of two important employee benefits: section 125 plans and 401(k) plans. Answer A is not the best answer; passed in 1985, COBRA requires employers who employed 20 or more people during the prior year to offer continuation of group health care coverage to employees and their family members who experience certain qualifying events—events that would have otherwise resulted in the discontinuation of their health insurance benefits. Answer C is not the best answer; HIPAA has two main focuses: the security and portability of health care coverage and privacy considerations. Answer D is not the best answer; an amendment to ERISA, REA incorporated a number of key revisions, many of which addressed the concerns of former spouses (in the event of divorce) and surviving spouses (in the event of death).

29. Answer A is the best answer. A cash balance plan is a defined benefit plan that expresses the promised benefit in terms of a stated account balance. Answer B is not the best answer; a cash balance plan is a defined benefit plan, but it doesn't express the promised benefit in terms of a specific monthly benefit (like other defined benefits plans do). Answer C is not the best answer; a cash balance plan is not a defined contribution plan. Answer D is not the best answer; a cash balance plan is not a defined contribution plan, and it doesn't express the promised benefit in terms of a specific monthly benefit.

30. Answer C is the best answer. The Civil Rights Act of 1991 capped damages at $300,000 per employee, not at $500,000 per employee. Answer A is not the best answer; the Civil Rights of 1991 expanded employees' rights. Answer B is not the best answer; the Civil Rights Act of 1991 expanded employees' remedies. Answer D is not the best answer; the Civil Rights Act of 1991 did allow for jury trials for discrimination cases.

31. Answer B is the best answer. Quality circles were brought to the attention of the world by Ishikawa. Answers A, C, and D encompass Juran's three-point quality focus: quality planning, quality improvement, and quality control.

32. Answer B is the best answer. The statement that articulates what the organization wants to become in the future is the vision statement. The vision statement should be one important tool used to guide strategic planning rather than a product of strategic planning. Answers A, C, and D are not the best answers; each one makes a true statement about strategic planning.

33. Answer A is the best answer. Securing the support and commitment of senior leadership is critical with respect to demonstrating commitment to the strategic planning process rather than with respect to creating and sustaining credibility during the implementation of a strategic plan. Answer B is not the best answer; clear, complete, and appropriate documentation of the process is particularly relevant to creating and sustaining credibility during the implementation of a strategic plan. Answer C is not the best answer; a commitment to following through on every step of the process is particularly relevant to creating and sustaining credibility during the implementation of a strategic plan. Answer D is not the best answer; representative participation from all levels of the organization is particularly relevant to creating and sustaining credibility during the implementation of a strategic plan.

34. Answer C is the best answer. Answer A, 162.4, is the mean of the numbers in this set. Answer B, 645, is the highest number in this set. Answer D, 87, is the median of the numbers in this set.

35. Answer C is the best answer. The paperwork-type functions described here are administrative and task oriented in nature and are reflective of the way HR was viewed in the past. Answer A is not the best answer; the functions (as described) do not even rise to an operational or tactical level; they are purely administrative in nature. Answers B and D are the best answers; strategic and transformational dimensions of HR focus on a long-term, future-focused approach to the ways in which HR will work with the organization to attain its organizational mission. It looks at business and organizational issues rather than at more traditional HR issues.

36. Answer C is the best answer. Job bidding systems deal with jobs that might open at some point in the future, whereas job posting systems deal with jobs that are currently open. Answer A is not the best answer; job bidding systems deal with jobs that might open at some point in the future, whereas job posting systems deal with jobs that are currently open. Answers B and D are not the best answers; job bidding and job posting systems are both directed solely at internal candidates.

37. Answer C is the best answer. Employers must allow at least 21 days to consider any right-to-sue waivers that the employer offers in exchange for early retirement benefits. Thus, answers A, B, and D are incorrect.

38. Answer C is the best answer. The progress discipline process is predicated on the belief that (assuming that an employee is at least minimally qualified for the position for which he was hired) an employee can choose whether to perform his job satisfactorily. It is in this way that we establish the foundation for thinking of progressive discipline as an employee relations initiative. Thus, answers A, B, and D are incorrect.

39. Answer A is the best answer. According to Herzberg's motivation-hygiene theory, motivation factors have a positive impact on an employee's motivation level if, and only if, hygiene factors are acceptable. In this situation, it appears as though neither motivation nor hygiene factors are acceptable. According to Herzberg's theory, it's important to address hygiene factors first to ensure that motivation factors will have a positive impact. Answer B is not the best answer; it jumps straight to motivation factors. Answer C is not the best answer; it takes a "ready, fire, aim" approach. Although employees have communicated that they are unhappy with their pay, that does not necessarily mean that pay levels are inappropriate, that they need to be increased, or that 5% would be the right number to use. Answer D is not the best answer; although it will probably be necessary to collect more information (perhaps through follow-up meetings), it would not be effective (or even well received) to ask employees to give you the same information, in the same way, through the same type of instrument.

40. Answer D is the best answer. Hersey and Blanchard's situational leadership model is predicated on the idea that effective leaders are able to demonstrate different leadership styles, with different employees, at different times, under different circumstances. Answer A is not the best answer; picking one leadership style and sticking to it in a resolute fashion violates that principle. Answer B is not the best answer; the same employee can fall into two, three, or even four quadrants at the same time because quadrants are determined based on each employee's ability to perform a specific function or task, not based on an employee's overall performance. Answer C is not the best answer; an effective leader focuses on an employee's maturity—the degree to which she possesses and demonstrates the nontechnical skills required to bring the task to successful completion—as much as that leader focuses on the technical skills required to perform the function or task.

41. Answer D is the best answer. Willingness to change is not one of Knowles's five key assumptions about how adults learn. Answer A is not the best answer; the learner's need to know is one of Knowles's five key assumptions about how adults learn. Answer B is not the best answer; the learner's readiness to learn is one of Knowles's five key assumptions about how adults learn. Answer C is not the best answer; the learner's self-concept is one of Knowles's five key assumptions about how adults learn.

42. Answer B is the best answer. A plan provider that offers mental health benefits would be exempt from MHPA requirements if actual claims costs increase 1% or more because of the application of MHPA's requirements. Answer A is not the best answer; a plan provider with fewer than 51 people (not 15 people) would be exempt from MHPA requirements. Answer C is not the best answer; a plan provider's costs would need to increase more than 1% in terms of actual claims—not in terms of insurance premiums—for that plan provider to be exempt from MPHA. Answer D—"never"—is not the best answer because answer B provides a legitimate example of when a plan provider that offers mental health benefits would be exempt from MHPA.

43. Answer B is the best answer. COBRA requires plan providers to offer plan participants the opportunity to continue participating in the plan provider's group health care plans. Answer A is not the best answer; COBRA does not require plan providers to offer plan participants the opportunity to continue participating in wellness programs or long-term disability insurance. Answer C is not the best answer; a plan participant's ability to join a different group health care plan is irrelevant to the plan provider's obligation to offer the plan participant the opportunity to continue participating in its group healthcare plan. Answer D is not the best answer; COBRA does not require plan providers to offer plan participants the opportunity to continue participating in any benefit programs other than group health care plans.

44. Answer B is the best answer. According to the Equal Pay Act, the substantial equality of job content is assessed based on effort, skill, responsibility, and working conditions (more often listed in the order of skill, effort, responsibility, and working conditions). Neither answer A nor answer D is the best answer; scope is not one of the four factors used by the Equal Pay Act to assess substantial equality. Answer C is not the best answer; neither scope nor accountability is among the four factors used by the Equal Pay Act to assess substantial equality.

45. Answer C is the best answer. Broadbanding is an approach in which organizations choose to establish and use a relatively small number of grades. Answer A is not the best answer; although one reason that organizations might choose to use broadbands could be to support the implementation of a flatter organization, this process or approach is not known as flattening. Answer B is not the best answer; although one reason that organizations might choose to use broadbands could be to shift employees' focus away from traditional promotions and place it instead on career growth, this process or approach is not known as growthbanding. Answer D is not the best answer; although the institution of broadbanding might result in the collapsing and combining of a large number of grades into a smaller number of grades, this process or approach is not known as gradesharing.

46. Answer D is the best answer. It is the mission statement, not the vision statement, that should speak to the nature of the organization's business or purpose, its customers, and sometimes even its employees and its role in the community. Answer A is not the best answer; an organization's statement of vision is a descriptive and inspirational statement that articulates where the organization wants to be and what it wants to become in the future. Answer B is not the best answer; an organization's vision statement should give employees an awareness that they have a meaningful opportunity to be part of something bigger than themselves. Answer C is not the best answer; a vision statement should motivate and inspire employees to aspire to the legacy that the vision can create and that it ultimately can leave behind.

47. Answer B is the best answer. If the president takes no action for 10 days while Congress is in session, the legislation automatically becomes law. Answer A is not the best answer; if the president takes no action for 10 days while Congress is not in session, the legislation dies. (This is called a pocket veto.) Answer C is not the best answer; the president does not have the option of sending legislation back for more committee work. Answer D is not the best answer; if Congress sends a bill to the president, there is nothing to override. In addition, the president cannot override Congress; rather, it is Congress that could override a bill that the president vetoes.

48. Answer B is the best answer. Preemployment medical exams can be conducted only if the medical exam is job related and consistent with business necessity. Answer A is not the best answer; an organization cannot require all candidates who apply for a position to take a preemployment medical exam because an employer can only require a candidate to take a medical exam if an offer or conditional offer of employment has already been extended. Answer C is not the best answer; the ADA does not specify who can or cannot conduct a preemployment medical exam. Answer D is not the best answer; a candidate's self-disclosures about a disability that might require a reasonable accommodation is unrelated to whether and when a preemployment medical exam can be conducted.

49. Answer B is the best answer. Employers covered under EO 11246 are not required to file internal reports relative to the number of charges of discrimination that have been filed based on race, gender, and veterans status during the length of each AAP (this might be a good moment to point out, once again, that affirmative action is different from, and should not be confused with, protections against discrimination afforded by EEO laws). Answer A is not the best answer; the internal audit system does require covered employers to monitor records of all personnel activity, including referrals, placements, transfers, promotions, terminations, and compensation at all levels to ensure the nondiscriminatory policy is carried out. Answer C is not the best answer; the internal audit system does require covered employers to review report results with all levels of management. Answer D is not the best answer; the internal audit system does require covered employers to advise top management of program effectiveness and submit recommendations to improve unsatisfactory performance.

50. Answer A is the best answer. Trend analysis can provide information that can be helpful in developing a better understanding of business cycles. Answer B is not the best answer; ratio analysis, rather than trend analysis, can become the basis for a number of applications, including forecasting staffing needs. Answer C is not the best answer; ratio analysis, not trend analysis, looks at how variables can change over time. Answer D is not the best answer; multiple regression analysis, not trend analysis, looks at the relationship between one dependent variable and more than one independent variable.

51. Answer B is the best answer. WARNA covers employers with 100 or more full-time employees. (This is a somewhat oversimplified explanation; see www.dol.gov for more details.) Answer A is not the best answer; the ADA covers employers with 15 or more employees. (This is a somewhat oversimplified explanation; see www.eeoc.gov for more details.) Answer C is not the best answer; Title VII of the Civil Rights Act of 1964 covers all private employers, among others. (This is a somewhat oversimplified explanation; see www.eeoc.gov for more details.) Answer D is not the best answer; the ADEA covers private employers with 20 or more employees. (This is a somewhat oversimplified explanation; see www.eeoc.gov for more details.)

52. Answer B is the best answer. In learning organizations, employees at all levels do strive to acquire knowledge and develop skills that will enable them, individually and collectively, to attain higher levels of performance. Answer A is not the best answer; the size of an HRD/training budget does not necessarily correlate to the degree to which an organization is truly a learning organization. Answer C is not the best answer; although learning organizations often manifest their commitment through training, training is not the only type of HRD initiative through which an organization can demonstrate that commitment. Answer D is not the best answer; linking performance appraisal to training and development is not the only way in which an organization can demonstrate its commitment to being a learning organization (although it is often a good idea).

53. Answer D is the best answer. Managers who have not consistently maintained documentation throughout the entire performance measurement period are more likely to rely upon recent events when preparing an employee's performance appraisal. Answer A is not the best answer; although it is possible for a manager who has recently observed a direct report to experience the recency effect, managers who did not maintain consistent documentation throughout the performance measurement period are even more likely to experience the recency effect. Answer B is not the best answer, for a similar reason. Answer C is not the best answer; a manager who maintained documentation during earlier portions of the performance measurement period is less likely to experience the recency effect than a manager who did not maintain such documentation.

54. Answer D is the best answer. For overtime purposes under the FLSA, hours worked would include all hours during which an employee was required or allowed (suffered or permitted) to perform work. Answer A is not the best answer; the hours for which an employee receives compensation might include hours during which an employee was not suffered or permitted to work (such as vacation pay, jury duty pay, and so on). Answer B is not the best answer; whether an employee was granted approval to work (prior or subsequent) is irrelevant to calculating hours worked. Answer C is not the best answer; hours worked would include hours that an employee is suffered or permitted to work, not just those hours during which the employee actually performs work.

55. Answer B is the best answer. The Equal Pay Act prohibits discrimination based on sex in the payment of wages or benefits to men and women who perform substantially equal (but not identical) work for the same employer and within the same establishment. Answer A is not the best answer; the work in question has to be substantially equal, not the same or identical. Answer C is not the best answer; the work in question must be performed for the same employer and within the same establishment. Answer D is not the best answer; the work in question must be substantially equal (not the same or identical) and must be performed for the same employer and within the same establishment.

56. Answer D is the best answer. Grades represent a hierarchy of levels into which jobs of similar internal, not external, worth are categorized. Because of this distinction, answer A is not the best answer; grades do represent a hierarchy of levels into which jobs of similar internal worth are categorized. Answer

B is not the best answer; jobs within the same grade do share a similar level of value or worth to the organization. Answer C is not the best answer; jobs within the same grade are paid according to a corresponding compensation range.

57. Answer A is the best answer. Transactional leaders use a system built on the carrot and the stick method—and mainly the stick part of it. Answer B is not the best answer; coaching is more characteristic of the transformational leadership style. Answer C is not the best answer; the image of a captain might more closely reflect the role a leader plays in the selling quadrant of Hersey and Blanchard's situational leadership model. Answer D is not the best answer; the image of a director could imply a wider variety of leadership approaches under transactional as well as transformational styles.

58. Answer A is the best answer. The nominal group technique does take a nonmathematical approach to forecasting that draws on the insights of subject matter experts. Answer B is not the best answer; although it is true that the nominal group technique affords experts the opportunity to meet in person and process their ideas from the group, this is not a characteristic that is shared with the Delphi technique (in which the experts do not meet in person). Answer C is not the best answer; the nominal group technique is not self-directing—it is led by a facilitator. Answer D is not the best answer; although the nominal group technique permits collaboration at certain points of the process, collaboration is not permitted at all points in the process. Specifically, at the beginning of the meeting, each expert writes down her ideas, after which each expert presents those ideas to the group. Discussion of ideas is not permitted at this point; only presentation is acceptable.

59. Answer A is the best answer. The Drug-Free Workplace Act does not require employers to establish an EAP (employee assistance program). If an organization does have an EAP (or equivalent program), however, information about that program must be included as part of the employer's drug-free awareness program (answer C). Answer B is not the best answer; the Drug-Free Workplace Act does require employers to establish a drug-free awareness program addressing the dangers of drug use in the workplace and the employer's drug-free policy, and information about programs that are available to employees who use drugs. Answer D is not the best answer; the Drug-Free Workplace Act does require employers to distribute a copy of the workplace substance abuse policy to all employees.

60. Answer C is the best answer. Unemployment insurance is funded solely through employer taxes (except in only three states, where employees contribute as well). Answer A is not the best answer; unemployment insurance is a mandatory benefit program. Answer B is not the best answer; in general, the maximum period for receiving unemployment insurance benefits is 26 weeks (although the federal government may choose to extend the benefit period during difficult economic times). Answer D is not the best answer; unemployment insurance was established as part of the federal Social Security Act of 1935 and is administered at the state level.

61. Answer A is the best answer. Job slotting is not expensive or difficult to administer. (In fact, its inexpensive cost and ease of administration are two of its advantages.) Answer B is not the best answer; job slotting increases the likelihood that a job will be evaluated based on the person, not the position. Answer C is not the best answer; job slotting can be used only when a job structure is already in place. Answer D is not the best answer; as with any nonquantitative job evaluation method, there is a greater chance with job slotting that rater error and subjectivity can taint the job evaluation process.

62. Answer C is the best answer. Section 7 of the NLRA does protect associational rights for employees who belong to a union, as well as for those who do not. Employers need to be careful not to interfere with protected concerted activities even in workplaces that are nonunionized. Answer A is not the best answer; protected concerted activity refers to associational rights that are granted to employees through the NLRA. Answer B is not the best answer; the NLRA does protect associational rights for employees who belong to a union. Answer D is not the best answer; employees have the right to refrain from engaging in protected concerted activities.

63. Answer A is the best answer. Charges must be filed with the EEOC within 180 days of the alleged discriminatory act when there is no FEPA. Answer B is not the best answer; the EEOC usually maintains responsibility for handling charges that are filed with it if the basis for the charge is also protected

under state or local law. Answer C is not the best answer; the FEPA usually maintains responsibility for handling charges that are filed with it if the basis for the charge is also protected under federal law. Answer D is not the best answer; a charge may not be dual filed with the EEOC when state or local EEO law is more protective than the corresponding federal law.

64. Answer C is the best answer. Passed in 1985, COBRA covers employers who employed 20 or more employees during the prior year. Thus, answers A, B, and D are incorrect.

65. Answer D is the best answer. *Washington v. Davis, 1976*, determined that a test that has an adverse impact on a protected class is still lawful, as long as the test can be shown to be valid and job related. Answer A is not the best answer; the key issue in *McDonnell Douglas Corp v. Green, 1973*, was disparate treatment and establishing a prima facie case. Answer B is not the best answer; the key issue in *Griggs v. Duke Power, 1971*, was adverse impact. Answer C is not the best answer; the key issue in *Meritor Savings Bank v. Vinson, 1986*, was sexual harassment.

66. Answer B is the best answer. Onboarding refers to the new hire orientation process, and a background investigation is far more likely to occur during the preemployment reference checking phase than during the new hire orientation process. Answer A is not the best answer; the onboarding process often includes a tour of the facility. Answer C is not the best answer; the onboarding process often gives newly hired employees the opportunity to meet with current employees. Answer D is not the best answer; the onboarding process should include a review of the mission of the organization and of how that mission relates to the position.

67. Answer B is the best answer. A multirater survey refers to a performance feedback and management tool in which one individual receives feedback on his performance from a variety of people, holding a variety of perspectives. A multirater, or 360-degree, survey is different from employee surveys (answer A), attitude surveys (answer C), and climate surveys (answer D), all of which refer to surveys that are distributed throughout the organization to collect information on a variety of topics that are relevant to the entire organization—not just to one single person.

68. Answer B is the best answer. One of the two omissions that the Wagner Act sought to address was the identification of behaviors and practices that would be considered ULPs on the part of unions. Neither answer A nor answer D is the best answer; the Wagner Act did identify behaviors and practices that would be considered ULPs on the part of employers/managers. Answer C is not the best answer; an employee cannot commit a ULP unless she is acting on behalf of a union or an employer, in which case her role in that capacity would eclipse the significance of her role as an individual and is therefore already addressed through the Wagner Act.

69. Answer C is the best answer. In *Circuit City Stores, Inc. v. Adams, 2001*, the court ruled that requiring employees to sign mandatory arbitration agreements as a condition of employment is legal and that such agreements are enforceable under the Federal Arbitration Act (FAA). Answer A is not the best answer; in *NLRB v. Phoenix Mutual Life Insurance Co., 1948*, it was confirmed that union and nonunion employees enjoy associational rights afforded under the NLRA. Answer B is not the best answer; less than 10 months after the Circuit City case, the court ruled in *EEOC v. Waffle House, Inc., 2002*, that although the existence of a signed mandatory arbitration agreement precluded the employee from being allowed to file a private lawsuit, it did not preclude the EEOC from seeking its own independent action against an employer. Answer D is not the best answer; *NLRB v. Henry Colder, 1990*, was a case in which an employer was found to have committed an unfair labor practice by interfering with protected concerted activities.

70. Answer A is the best answer. Workers' compensation programs (not the OSH Act) are designed to enable workers to obtain relief (in particular, monetary relief) for work-related injuries. Answer B is not the best answer; the OSH Act did establish a means of enforcement. Answer C is not the best answer; the OSH Act did encourage and assist states to take steps to ensure safe and healthful workplaces. Answer D is not the best answer; the OSH Act did provide for relevant research, information, education, and training.

71. Answer B is the best answer. Technostructural interventions focus on improving what work is done as well as the ways and processes through which the work is done. This category of OD intervention looks at job design, job redesign, job restructuring, work content, workflow, work processes, and the like. Answer A is not the best answer; human processual interventions seek to effect change and impact relationships within (and between) groups and individuals on more of an interpersonal level. Answer C is not the best answer; sociotechnical interventions focus on groups in the workplace and the ways in which those groups can become more (or semi) autonomous with respect to the performance and execution of the work. Answer D is not the best answer; organization transformation change interventions focus on the organization as a complex human system that must be continually examined and reexamined.

72. Answer B is the best answer. The PBGC (Pension Benefit Guaranty Corporation) is funded by insurance premiums that are paid by plan sponsors, not by tax dollars (payroll or otherwise). Funding for the PBGC also comes from investment income, assets from underfunded pension plans it has taken over, and recoveries from companies formerly responsible for those plans. Answer A is not the best answer; the PBGC is a government corporation created by ERISA. Answer C is not the best answer; the PBGC protects participants in most defined benefit plans and cash balance plans (within certain limitations). Answer D is not the best answer; the PBGC ensures that participants will receive payments of certain benefits if a covered plan is terminated.

73. Answer A is the best answer. Assessing strengths and weaknesses is an inward-looking process. Answer B is not the best answer; the external portion of the SWOT analysis refers to assessing opportunities and threats. By default, then, neither answer C nor answer D can be the best answer.

74. Answer B is the best answer. *McKennon v. Nashville Banner Publishing Co., 1995*, established that an employer will be held accountable for discriminatory employment actions even if it discovers evidence after taking the discriminatory employment action that would have led the employer to that same employment action for legitimate, nondiscriminatory reasons. Thus, answers A, C, and D are incorrect.

75. Answer C is the best answer. Although FMLA entitles employees to take job-protected leave to care for an immediate family member, siblings are not included in the definition of an immediate family member. Answer A is not the best answer; FMLA does entitle employees to take job-protected leave for the birth and care of the newborn child of the employee. Answer B is not the best answer; FMLA does entitle employees to take job-protected leave for placement of a son or daughter for adoption or foster care with the employee. Answer D is not the best answer; FMLA does entitle employees to take job-protected leave when the employee is unable to work because of a serious health condition.

76. Answer C is the best answer. Factor comparison assigns a monetary value, not a point value, to each level within each factor. Answer A is not the best answer; the factor comparison method of job evaluation does provide a degree of objectivity and reliability across raters. Answer B is not the best answer; factor comparison does evaluate each job with respect to each compensable factor. Answer D is not the best answer; factor comparison involves ranking each compensable factor of each job.

77. Answer C is the best answer. Employers can require employees to attend mandatory presentations during which management will present its opinions about unions in general and about the unionization of its operations. There are certain limitations to this, however, to which the employer must adhere. (For instance, these "captive audience meetings" cannot be held within 24 hours of the actual election.) It is also worth noting that although an employer can require an employee to attend captive audience meetings, the employer cannot truly require the employee to listen. Answer A is not the best answer; telling workers that the organization will fire or punish them if they engage in any union activity would constitute a ULP. Answer B is not the best answer; granting workers wage increases or special concessions in an effort to bribe people from joining a union would constitute a ULP. Answer D is not the best answer; telling workers that existing benefits will be discontinued if the workplace is unionized would constitute a ULP.

78. Answer B is the best answer. An employer who makes a hot cargo agreement has not refused to stop doing business with another entity; instead, it has agreed to stop doing business with another entity (answer A), thus helping to protect union work (answer D) by allowing union members to refuse to

handle or process work produced by nonunion entities. Answer C is not the best answer; an employer who makes a hot cargo agreement has committed a ULP.

79. Answer C is the best answer. Although it is important to perform due diligence, performing due diligence does not insulate an organization from exposure relating from negligent hiring claims. One way in which this can happen is if stated job requirements for a particular position that are used as a guide through the hiring process do not reflect the skills or credentials that are actually required to perform a particular position. Answer A is not the best answer; negligent hiring does refer to the process of hiring an employee without engaging in appropriate due diligence. Answer B is not the best answer; appropriate due diligence could include looking into items such as the candidate's credentials and prior work experience. Answer D is not the best answer; it is quite possible that negligent hiring tort claims might be filed after an employee who was hired through a flawed hiring process inflicts some sort of harm on another person.

80. Answer C is the best answer. It can be challenging to replicate identical conditions across various focus groups, even when focus group meetings are conducted by the same individual. These differences in conditions could taint/affect the consistency of the data that is collected. Answer A is not the best answer; skillfully facilitated focus groups can generate a great deal of valuable data. Answer B is not the best answer; the dynamics that exist in focus groups often can lead to a more synergistic and productive data collection experience. Answer D is not the best answer; focus groups do, in fact, provide a qualitative approach to data collection.

81. Answer B is the best answer. Although some organizations do choose to consider each incumbent's most recent salary or wage rate when setting base pay rates for new hires, this should be the least important of the four factors listed (if it is even factored in at all). Many variables could render the newly hired employee's most recent rate of pay irrelevant—for instance, the employee might have held a different position, in a different sector, in a different city, in a different industry, at a different time, and so on. Answer A is not the best answer; the relative worth of the job to the organization is likely to affect the way base pay for new hires is set. Answer C is not the best answer; the market rate for the position in the marketplace is likely to affect how base pay for new hires is set. Answer D is not the best answer; whether the job requires hot skills is likely to affect how base pay for new hires is set.

82. Answer A is the best answer. A yellow dog contract is a contract or agreement between an employer and an employee that states that the employer will give the employee a job as long as the employee agrees not to join or have any involvement with a labor union. Answer B is not the best answer; an employer who makes a hot cargo agreement agrees to stop doing business with another entity (thus helping to protect union work by allowing union members to refuse to handle or process work produced by nonunion entities). Answer C is not the best answer; a featherbedding agreement states that the employer will pay wages to union members whether or not their work is needed. Answer D is not the best answer; a union shop agreement exists when an employer agrees that anyone who is hired by the organization must join the union.

83. Answer B is the best answer. There is no specific OSHA requirement mandating the creation of a safety committee. Many organizations, however, do find that safety committees can make significant contributions toward achieving other health and safety objectives or mandates. Answer A is not the best answer; one purpose of a safety committee is to build and maintain interest in health and safety issues. Answer C is not the best answer; one purpose of a safety committee is to reinforce safety as part of the fabric of the organization's culture. Answer D is not the best answer; one purpose of a safety committee is to provide a forum for discussing health- and safety-related issues.

84. Answer A is the best answer. *Johnson v. Santa Clara County Transportation Agency, 1987*, established that gender can be used as a factor in the selection process if there is underrepresentation in a particular job classification, as long as the AAP does not set forth a quota. Thus, answers B, C, and D are incorrect.

85. Answer C is the best answer. Diversity can—and, some would argue, should—encompass attributes or characteristics such as communication styles, regional backgrounds, or affiliation with unions, to name just a few examples. Answer A is not the best answer; diversity is not legally mandated (although it makes sound sense from an organizational and business perspective). Answer B is not the best answer; diversity initiatives do not have governmentally mandated reporting requirements. Answer D is not the best answer; diversity can, and should, extend well beyond the boundaries of legally protected classes.

86. Answer D is the best answer. Although there is no mandatory retirement age (with few exceptions, such as pilots who must retire from that particular position at age 60), there is a requirement that everyone must start receiving retirement benefits by age 70. Answer A is not the best answer; the earliest age at which a worker can retire and still receive benefits is 62. Answer B is not the best answer; full retirement age ranges between age 65 and age 67, depending on the year of birth. Answer C is not the best answer; workers who work beyond their full retirement age will increase their monthly retirement. The longer they work past their full retirement age, the more their monthly retirement income will be.

87. Answer A is the best answer. An employee who was constructively discharged was subjected to such intolerable working conditions that remaining employed with the organization was impossible. Answers B, C, and D are not the best answers because none of those definitions accurately defines constructive discharge.

88. Answer D is the best answer. Unless significant underutilization exists, placement goals are set for minorities (in total). If, however, significant underutilization exists, it might be necessary to set goals for particular minority groups. Answer A is not the best answer; placement goals must be established for areas in which underutilization exists. Answer B is not the best answer; placement goals must be pursued through good-faith efforts. Answer C is not the best answer; placement goals must be set at an annual percentage rate that is equivalent to the availability figure for women or minorities.

89. Answer D is the best answer. According to Hersey and Blanchard's situational leadership model, low task and low relationship dimensions correspond to the "delegating" quadrant. Answer A is not the best answer; "telling" corresponds to high task and low relationship. Answer B is not the best answer; "selling" corresponds to high task and high relationship. Answer C is not the best answer; "participating" corresponds to high relationship and low task.

90. Answer B is the best answer. Correlation mathematically determines whether there is a demonstrated relationship between two factors or entities. Answer A is not the best answer; a negative correlation does indicate that a relationship exists between two factors. Answer C is not the best answer; the correlation coefficient is a number between −1 and 1 that defines the strength of a relationship between two factors. Answer D is not the best answer; the correlation coefficient speaks to the strength of a relationship, not to causative dimensions of that relationship.

91. Answer A is the best answer. The FLSA established minimum standards affecting full-time and part-time workers in the private sector and in federal, state, and local governments pertaining to minimum wage, overtime, recordkeeping, and child labor. Answer B is not the best answer; the FLSA does not address or establish standards relating to worker's compensation or unemployment insurance. Answer C is not the best answer; FLSA does not address or establish standards relating to wage garnishments. Answer D is not the best answer; the FLSA does not address or establish standards relating to unemployment insurance and wage garnishments.

92. Answer D is the best answer. Sarbanes-Oxley (SOX) establishes a requirement to disclose whether the company has adopted a code of ethics that applies to the company's key officers, not to the company as a whole. Key officers include, at a minimum, the company's principal executive officer, principal financial officer, principal accounting officer or controller, or persons performing similar functions. Answer A is not the best answer; SOX does prohibit insider trading during certain pension plan blackout periods. Answer B is not the best answer; SOX does require the establishment of whistleblower protection in a variety of situations for employees who report fraud against shareholders. Answer C is not the best answer; SOX does require plan administrators to provide 30-day written notice in advance of blackout periods to individual account plan participants and beneficiaries.

93. Answer C is the best answer. One key potential problem that HR professionals need to be aware of is the possibility that employee groups could be found to be company dominated and, therefore, be rendered illegal. Although employee participation groups are neither legal nor illegal by definition, the way in which they are administrated can have a huge impact on whether any particular group is deemed to be legal or illegal. Answers A, B, and D are not the best answers; none of these answers identifies a frequently identified key potential problem with employee participation groups.

94. Answer C is the best answer. Of the four choices in this question, slander is best defined as "a false spoken statement that damages someone's character or reputation." Answer A is not the best answer; even if it damages someone's character or reputation, a statement must be false to be considered slanderous. Answer B is not the best answer; "a false statement that damages someone's character or reputation" is more general in that it encompasses spoken and written statements and is therefore a better definition of the term defamation than it is of the term slander. Answer D is not the best answer; "a false written statement that damages someone's character or reputation" constitutes libel, not slander.

95. Answer D is the best answer. Answer B is not the best answer; the Supreme Court found that an employer is responsible if its supervisors engage in sexually harassing others even if it didn't know about that behavior. The court did point out, however, that it isn't enough for an organization to have a policy prohibiting discrimination; one way for employers to reduce this liability is to prove that a sexually harassed employee had reasonable opportunities to take advantage of a good, clear complaint procedure (without fear of retaliation) but had failed to do so (answer C). Answer A is not the best answer; in *Meritor Savings Bank v. Vinson, 1986*, the Supreme Court ruled for the first time that sexual harassment (whether quid pro quo or hostile environment) constitutes a violation of Title VII of the Civil Rights Act of 1964. The Supreme Court specifically rejected the lower court's view that employers are not automatically liable for sexual harassment by their supervisors.

96. Answer B is the best answer. Whole job ranking does not establish factors about each job that need to be taken into consideration when comparing jobs to each other. (This is one of the disadvantages of whole job ranking.) Answer A is not the best answer; whole job ranking is easy to perform. Answer C is not the best answer; whole job ranking is relatively inexpensive to maintain. Answer D is not the best answer; whole job ranking does produce a list that will show which jobs are most and least important.

97. Answer A is the best answer. These functions describe the organizing management function, which speaks particularly to the ways in which the manager obtains and arranges resources. Those resources could include people, facilities, materials, and the like. While executing this function, the manager must also make decisions about reporting relationships within the organization. In short, the manager must work to establish linkages between people, places, and things. Answer B is not the best answer; the controlling function is the one through which the manager assumes more of an oversight role and ascertains the degree to which the planning in which she engaged actually produced the desired results. Answer C is not the best answer; planning consists of laying the groundwork for how managers will work toward accomplishing the organization's goals. Answer D is not the best answer; the coordinating function consists of activities through which the manager brings together all the resources that she has organized to accomplish the stated plan.

98. Answer C is the best answer. In the context of interviewing, the leniency bias/error occurs when an interviewer applies an inappropriately lenient standard to one or more candidates, resulting in a higher overall assessment of the candidate. Neither answer A nor answer B is the best answer; neither is a legitimate and recognized interviewing bias/error. Answer D is not the best answer; the recency error occurs when the interviewer recalls the most recently interviewed candidates more vividly than candidates who were interviewed earlier in the process.

99. Answer A is the best answer. Title VII of the Civil Rights Act of 1964 established five areas of protection: race, color, religion, sex, and national origin. Answer B is not the best answer; age did not become a protected class until the passage of the Age Discrimination in Employment Act (ADEA) in 1967. Answer C is not the best answer; Title VII of the Civil Rights Act of 1964 did not address the question of disability (under any appellation). Answer D is not the best answer; Title VII of the Civil Rights Act of 1964 included color as a protected class.

100. Answer B is the best answer. The ADA does not directly define "undue hardship" in terms of a person's salary. Answer A is not the best answer; the ADA does describe an undue hardship as one that creates significant difficulty (enough to disrupt business operation). Answer C is not the best answer; the ADA does describe an undue hardship as one that changes something about the (essential) nature of the business. Answer D is not the best answer; the ADA describes undue hardship as one that requires a significant financial outlay, but it does not specifically define what significant financial outlay means, as answer B asserts.

101. Answer A is the best answer. Although teambuilding is team focused, it also recognizes the criticality of addressing and enhancing the role of the individual within the team. Answer B is not the best answer; teambuilding is an effective means through which team members can explore issues such as communication, problem solving, and trust. Answer C is not the best answer; teambuilding exercises are most effective when they are linked directly and specifically to organizational objectives or to the mission, vision, or values of the organization. Answer D is not the best answer; parallels between teambuilding scenarios and their relevance to the workplace might not always be immediately apparent. Sometimes teambuilding exercises are intentionally designed so that they are not immediately recognized as being analogous to the workplace; in this way, participants may gain greater insights after they do identify those similarities.

102. Answer A is the best answer. Taft-Hartley was more specific, in that it identified striking or picketing a health care establishment (not just any employer) without giving the required notice as a ULP that could be committed by a union. Answer B is not the best answer; Taft-Hartley did identity picketing for recognition for more than 30 days without petitioning for an election as a ULP that could be committed by a union. Answer C is not the best answer; Taft-Hartley did identify causing an employer to discriminate against an employee as a ULP that could be committed by a union. Answer D is not the best answer; Taft-Hartley did identify refusing to bargain with the employer of the employees it represents as a ULP that could be committed by a union.

103. Answer C is the best answer. The Labor Management Reporting and Disclosure Act (also known as the Landrum-Griffin Act) specifically designated every union official as a fiduciary, not as an agent of the union. Answer A is not the best answer; the Landrum-Griffin Act did institute a requirement that unions submit annual financial reporting to the DOL, to document how union members' dues were spent. Answer B is not the best answer; the Landrum-Griffin Act did institute a bill of rights for union members guaranteeing them freedom of speech and periodic secret elections. Answer D is not the best answer; the Landrum-Griffin Act did institute even stronger provisions relative to secondary boycotting and organizational and recognition picketing.

104. Answer B is the best answer. Double breasting occurs when a company that owns or operates union as well as nonunion operations shifts work to the nonunion operation in an effort to diminish the impact of the strike. Answer A is not the best answer; featherbedding occurs when an employer agrees to pay wages to union members whether or not their work is needed. Answer C is not the best answer; there is no such expression as yellow dogging in labor relations. (A yellow dog contract, however, is one in which an employer agrees to give the employee a job, as long as the employee agrees not to join or have any involvement with a labor union.) Answer D is not the best answer; there is no such expression as single roofing in labor relations.

105. Answer B is the best answer. This formula calculates the cost per trainee, also known as the cost per participant. Answer A is not the best answer; this formula does not yield a calculation of return on investment. Answer C is not the best answer; this formula is unrelated to hiring costs. Answer D is not the best answer; this formula does not represent a cost/benefit analysis.

106. Answer B is the best answer. Current employees who are negatively impacted by consent decrees that were established in an earlier time and which sought to resolve discrimination that was present in an earlier time may challenge the validity of such decrees. Answer A is not the best answer; it asserts the opposite. Answer C is not the best answer; *Johnson v. Santa Clara County Transportation Agency, 1987*, established that gender can be used as a factor in the selection process if there is underrepresentation in a particular job classification, as long as the AAP does not set forth a quota. Answer D is not the best answer; there is no case that resulted in this finding.

107. Answer C is the best answer. The bottom line is this: organizations that lead the market with respect to total rewards/compensation offer better total rewards/total compensation packages than their competitors do. It's that simple. For purposes of determining whether an organization leads the market in this way, the balance of direct and indirect compensation pay components is not relevant (answer A), nor is the mix of variable and base pay (answer B), nor is the level of innovation or creativity of the total rewards/total compensation package. All that matters is the total (and multifaceted) value of the package. Answer D is not the best answer; organizations that lead the market do not necessarily choose to offer total compensation packages that are more innovative, creative, typical, and nontraditional than packages being offered by their labor market competitors.

108. Answer D is the best answer. The five distinct, yet overlapping, project management processes are initiation, planning, executing, controlling, and closing. Answer A is not the best answer; establishing, developing, implementing, and evaluating are the four steps of strategic planning. Answer B is not the best answer; although it cites the five project management processes, they are not presented in the right order. Answer C is not the best answer; planning, organizing, coordinating, directing, and controlling are the five management functions.

109. Answer B is the best answer. HR audits cannot yield strategies; conversely, they yield information that the organization can subsequently use to draw conclusions and develop strategies. Answer A is not the best answer; an HR audit is likely to yield information relative to the usefulness, appropriateness, and effectiveness of the employee handbook. Answer C is not the best answer; an HR audit is likely to yield information about grievances, their causes, and their impact. Answer D is not the best answer; an HR audit is likely to yield information about the degree to which the organization complies with HR-related legal requirements.

110. Answer C is the best answer. The exit route standard is a mandatory OSHA standard covering all employers. Answers A and B are not the best answers; although the Emergency Action Plan Standard and Fire Safety Standard are both recommended for all employers, they are not mandatory unless required under a separate OSHA standard. Answer D is not the best answer; the Hazard Communication Standard applies only to those workplaces where there are hazardous materials or chemicals.

111. Answer B is the best answer. MSH Act requires at least four inspections per year of underground mines and at least two inspections per year of surface mines. Answer A is not the best answer; MSH Act applies to underground and surface mines. Answer C is not the best answer; MSH Act applies to coal and noncoal mines. Answer D is not the best answer; employees who are covered by MSH Act are exempt from OSH Act.

112. Answer B is the best answer. Affinity groups bring together people who share common interests, goals, or backgrounds. Answer A is not the best answer; affinity groups do not primarily address safety and security needs. Although members might derive benefits that affect their esteem (answer C) or that enable them to self-actualize (answer D), affinity groups primarily address the need for belonging and love.

113. Answer C is the best answer. Direct compensation refers to components that are presented to employees in the form of cash, and indirect compensation refers to components that are presented to employees in forms other than cash (noncash). A flexible spending account is an example of a benefit, not an example of direct compensation. Answer A is not the best answer; hourly wages/base salary is a form of direct compensation. Answer B is not the best answer; shift differentials are a form of direct compensation. Answer D is not the best answer; variable pay is a form of direct compensation.

114. Answer B is the best answer. Employee referral programs can result in significant savings in cost-per-hire, not significant increases in cost-per-hire. Answers A is not the best answer; one potential disadvantage of an employee referral program is that if the organization is not particularly diverse (with respect to gender, age, race, education background, or a host of other factors), employee referral programs might perpetuate that lack of diversity. Answer C is not the best answer; one potential disadvantage of an employee referral program is that if an affirmative action plan is in place, and if there are areas of underutilization, an employee referral program is not likely to demonstrate good faith efforts to recruit candidates who are women or minorities. Answer D is not the best answer; one potential disadvantage of an employee referral program is that if the organization has prior patterns of hiring discrimination, employee referral programs are likely to reinforce those patterns.

115. Answer D is the best answer. Just as it is critical to distinguish between the position and the incumbent, so too it is important not to confuse actual job requirements—such as KSAs (answer A), credentials (answer B), and physical or mental requirements (answer C)—with any particular candidate's or incumbent's qualifications.

116. Answer C is the best answer. Schein recognized and appreciated the formal, as well as the informal, dimensions and expressions of culture. As HR professionals, so must we. Thus, answers A, B, and D are incorrect.

117. Answer B is the best answer. Performance appraisal tools that use rating scales require managers (or any other appraisers) to evaluate employee performance on a variety of categories using a multiple-point scale (often three, four, or five points). Those categories can consist of individual goals, individual competencies, multiple goals, groups of competencies, and the like. Each point on the scale corresponds to a different level of performance against standards. Answer A is not the best answer; performance appraisal systems that require managers to compare employees against each other are called ranking methods, not rating methods. Answer C is not the best answer; the performance appraisal method that requires managers to indicate statements that are reflective of the employee's performance is called a checklist method. Answer D is not the best answer; the performance appraisal method that requires managers to write a narrative assessment of employee's performance is called the essay method.

118. Answer A is the best answer. The key issues in *Albemarle Paper v. Moody, 1975*, were job relatedness and job validity. This case established that any tests that are used as part of the hiring or promotional decision-making process must be job related. This applies to any instrument that is used as a test, even if that was not its original purpose. This case also established that employment tests must demonstrate predictive validity, consistent with the Uniform Guidelines for Employee Selection Procedures. Thus, answers B, C, and D are incorrect.

119. Answer B is the best answer. An ethics program cannot prevent or minimize organizational politics. Let's be realistic; there aren't many things that can prevent or minimize organizational politics. However, an ethics program can prevent or minimize dysfunctional manifestations of organizational politics—manifestations that can become destructive or even dangerous. Answer A is not the best answer; preventing or minimizing aggression/violence represents one reason to establish an ethics program. Answer C is not the best answer; preventing or minimizing the erosion of trust represents one reason to establish an ethics program. Answer D is not the best answer; preventing or minimizing cynicism represents one reason to establish an ethics program.

120. Answer B is the best answer. Adverse treatment was not one of the key topics that the Uniform Guidelines on Employee Selection Procedures was designed to address. Answer A is not the best answer; one of the key purposes of the Uniform Guidelines was to address the concept of adverse impact. Answer C is not the best answer; one important objective of the Uniform Guidelines is to ensure that interview and selection processes are reliable. Answer D is not the best answer; one important objective of the Uniform Guidelines is to ensure that interview and selection processes are valid.

121. Answer A is the best answer. The Davis-Bacon Act of 1931 was the first piece of legislation to consider the topic of—and to actually establish—a minimum wage. Davis-Bacon, however, was (and still is) limited to federal government construction projects and nonfederal government construction projects in excess of $2,000 that receive federal funding (hence, neither answer C nor answer D is the best answer). Answer B is not the best answer; the Davis Bacon Act was not rendered obsolete by the minimum wage provisions of the FLSA; Davis-Bacon requires that covered contractors and subcontractors provide laborers and mechanics who are employed at the actual worksite with wages and benefits that are equal to (or better than) what workers on similar local projects receive.

122. Answer D is the best answer. Children who are 14 or 15 years old may work up to 40 hours during a nonschool week. Answer A is not the best answer; children who are 14 or 15 years old may work up to 3 (not 4) hours on a school day. Answer B is not the best answer; children who are 14 or 15 years old

may work up to 18 (not 20) hours during a school week. Answer C is not the best answer; children who are 14 or 15 years old may work up to 8 (not 7) hours on a nonschool day.

123. Answer C is the best answer. As articulated, the question states the requirement in specific, measurable, job-related terms and asks the candidate (in a closed-ended manner) whether he can meet that requirement of the position. Answer A is not the best answer; as phrased, this question seeks information that may reveal the existence or nature of a medical condition or disability. Answer B is not the best answer; using the phrase "Do you have any problems doing this" is more likely to elicit information relating to a disability than the closed-ended question "Can you meet this requirement of the position?" Answer D is not the best answer; as described, it does not appear as though this function would be considered "essential." (In fact, it does not even appear as though this responsibility falls within this function of this position.) In addition, interview questions should be based on the requirements of the job itself, not on the basis of the performance of prior incumbents.

124. Answer B is the best answer. In actuality, the Portal-to-Portal Act clarified that employers are required to compensate workers for working time that they spend performing their jobs and for working time that they spend on activities that relate to the performance of their jobs. Answer A is not the best answer; the Portal-to-Portal Act did offer a clearer definition of hours worked for purposes of minimum wage and overtime calculations. Answer C is not the best answer; the Portal-to-Portal Act did address topics such as travel time, preshift work, postshift work, idle waiting time, overnight travel, training time, and the like. Answer D is not the best answer; the Portal-to-Portal Act was an amendment of the Fair Labor Standards Act.

125. Answer C is the best answer. In a common law system, contracts that govern the terms and conditions of employment (including employment contracts and collective bargaining agreements) take precedence over traditions, customs, and precedents. For example, a collective bargaining agreement could modify employment-at-will status even though that concept exists in common law. Answer A is not the best answer; in common law systems, traditions, customs, and precedents have the same force of law as existing laws or statutes. Answer B is not the best answer; in a common law system, laws and statutes are interpreted and reinterpreted on a case-by-case basis. Answer D is not the best answer; in a common law system, each interpretation and each case sets a precedent that can subsequently be reinterpreted, thus setting a new precedent.

126. Answer D is the best answer. *Griggs v. Duke Power, 1971*, established that discrimination did not need to be deliberate or intentional to be real. Instead, it can exist even when a particular policy or practice has a statistically significant adverse impact upon members of a protected class. Thus, answers A, B, and C are incorrect.

127. Answer D is the best answer. If the employee is subjected to tangible adverse employment action, the employer may not raise a defense that it acted reasonably to prevent or promptly correct any sexually harassing behavior. Answer A is not the best answer; Faragher and Ellerth did establish that an employer is liable if the employee is subjected to an adverse employment action. Answer B is not the best answer; the employer is vicariously liable when its supervisors create a sexually hostile work environment, even if the employee is not subjected to an adverse employment action. Answer C is not the best answer; if the employee is not subjected to tangible adverse employment action, the employer may be able to raise as a defense that he acted reasonably to prevent or promptly correct any sexually harassing behavior and that the plaintiff unreasonably failed to take advantage of the employer's preventive or corrective opportunities.

128. Answer D is the best answer. To be eligible to take FMLA leave, an employee must meet four requirements, one of which is that the employee must work at a location in the United States or in any territory or possession of the United States where at least 50 (not 75) employees are employed by the employer within 75 (not 50) miles. Answer A is not the best answer; the employee must work for a covered employer—public agencies; state, local, and federal employers; local education agencies (schools); and private-sector employers with 50 or more employees. Answer B is not the best answer; the employee must have worked for the employer for a total of at least 12 months. (This time does not have to have

been uninterrupted.) Answer C is not the best answer; the employee must have worked at least 1,250 hours over the previous 12 months.

129. Answer B is the best answer. The ruling in the landmark case *Automobile Workers v. Johnson Controls, 1990*, determined that most, if not all, fetal protection policies result in gender discrimination. Answer A is not the best answer; the Supreme Court ruled that these sorts of decisions must be left to parents, not to employers. Answer C is not the best answer; the Supreme Court ruled that government does not have the obligation to protect unborn fetuses from chemical risk, even if the parents who conceived them do not choose to do so. Answer D is not the best answer; few, if any, fetal protection policies would qualify for a bona fide occupational qualification exception.

130. Answer B is the best answer. Environmental scanning refers to the process of maintaining awareness of opportunities and threats. Answer A is not the best answer; although maintaining awareness of opportunities and threats is part of SWOT analysis, SWOT analysis also incorporates maintaining awareness of strengths and weaknesses. Answer C is not the best answer; although conducting a SWOT analysis is an essential part of strategic planning, it does not encompass everything that is involved with strategic planning. Answer D is not the best answer; although an organization's awareness of threats is likely to highlight the need for contingency planning, those two concepts are not synonymous.

131. Answer D is the best answer. The Supreme Court ruled in *Regents of California v. Bakke, 1978*, that race could be a factor in college admission decisions but that quotas are impermissible. Although this case was based on a college admission program, its significance has extended to the workplace. Neither answer A nor answer B is the best answer; both those choices assume that the Supreme Court ruled in *Regents of California v. Bakke, 1978*, that quotas are permissible in college affirmative action programs. Answer C is not the best answer; although it acknowledges that quotas are impermissible in college admission decisions, it asserts that this ruling is not transferable to the workplace.

132. Answer C is the best answer. In the acronym SMART, M stands for measurable. Objectives—whether related to performance management or any other HRD (or, for that matter, HR) initiative—must be measurable. Answer A is not the best answer; although goals should be marketable to the degree that they relate to the overarching objectives of the organization and are, therefore, hopefully widely embraced, marketability is not one of the key driving forces behind goal setting. Answers B and D are not the best answers for similar reasons.

133. Answer C is the best answer. This is the best answer in part because there is no commonly recognized activity known as surface organizing. Rather, surface bargaining is an impermissible activity during the bargaining (rather than the organizing) process. Surface bargaining refers to going through the motions of bargaining, with no real intent of ultimately reaching agreement (in other words, keeping bargaining at the surface, without moving toward true agreement). Answer A is not the best answer; unions may engage in inside organizing, an activity through which prounion individuals can seek to influence others at the workplace, unless a valid no-solicitation rule is in effect 100% of the time. Answer B is not the best answer; unions may engage in salting, the process through which a salt (a union organizer) seeks employment with the organization for the express purpose of actively organizing and campaigning within the organization. Answer D is not the best answer; unions may engage in organizational picketing, which is designed to generate interest on the part of employees to vote for union representation.

134. Answer A is the best answer. Employers can hire permanent strike replacements during an economic strike. This is different from ULP strikes, in which employers cannot hire permanent strike replacements (answer B). Answer C is not the best answer; workers must be returned to their original positions after a ULP strike is over. Answer D is not the best answer; workers cannot be terminated for participating in an economic strike.

135. Answer A is the best answer. A focus group is an employee involvement tool as much as it is a communication tool. Answer B is not the best answer; focus groups consist of a representative sample of employees. Answer C is not the best answer; focus groups need to include enough people to generate

a dynamic and synergistic discussion (but not so many people that not everyone has a chance to participate). Answer D is not the best answer; focus groups are led by a neutral facilitator whose role is to elicit feedback and input on a specific topic.

136. Answer C is the best answer. Asking how the position compares to others within the existing job worth hierarchy is a valuable question, but it pertains to internal, rather than external, considerations. That question is addressed through the job evaluation process and is not as appropriate to ask when you are preparing to collect market data. Answer A is not the best answer; it is valuable and appropriate to ask about the relevant labor market for a position when you are preparing to collect market data. Answer B is not the best answer; it is valuable and appropriate to ask about what sources of market data you already have, and about what other sources you could get, when you are preparing to collect market data. Answer D is not the best answer; it is valuable and appropriate to ask about labor market competitors in general, as well as for a specific job, when you are preparing to collect market data.

137. Answer A is the best answer. HR might or might not have a presence during the introduction or birth stage of the organizational life cycle. If you are fortunate enough to have a presence, you might find that the formalization of policies and procedures (as would be found in a handbook) is not the most valued or appreciated dimension of your role. (Give it time.) Answer B is not the best answer; during the introductory phase of the organizational life cycle, employees might find themselves paid above market rates as a reflection of the founder's desire to lure them on board. Answer C is not the best answer; struggling start-ups often find themselves searching for solid financial footing. In such situations, employees might earn less cash compensation and have those diminished earnings offset by other non-cash rewards (equity, intrinsic rewards, and so on). Answer D is not the best answer; you are likely to find—and experience—a high level of excitement and energy in your new role.

138. Answer B is the best answer. Auditory learners learn most effectively through their sense of hearing. Answer A is not the best answer; visual learners learn most effectively through their sense of sight/vision. Answer C is not the best answer; kinesthetic (or tactile) learners learn most effectively through their sense of touch (or, in a more general sense, through hands-on experiences). Answer D is not the best answer; vicarious learners are not among the three recognized learning styles. The term vicarious learner, however, does exist and is defined as one who learns best by observing others participating in learning, which is not reflected in the scenario described in the question.

139. Answer D is the best answer. When determining what constitutes fair use, any permissions that the copyright holder has previously granted are not relevant to a determination of fair use. Answer A is not the best answer; whether the work will be used for commercial purposes or for not-for-profit or educational purposes does constitute a consideration for determining what constitutes fair use. Answer B is not the best answer; the nature or way in which the work will be used does constitute a consideration for determining what constitutes fair use. Answer C is not the best answer; how much of the work is used, both in terms of the aggregate amount of work that is being used as well as the percentage of the total work that is being used, does constitute a consideration for determining what constitutes fair use.

140. Answer D is the best answer. The most famous real-life example of the Mackay Doctrine occurred in 1981 when President Ronald Reagan replaced 12,000 striking air traffic controllers. Answer A is not the best answer; President George W. Bush's decision to waive the requirement to pay a prevailing wage rate to government contractors and subcontractors involved in the rebuilding of New Orleans suspended the Davis-Bacon Act for the first time in its 74-year history. (This action was wholly unrelated to the Mackay Doctrine.) Answers B and C are not the best answers because actions such as these would not fall under the Mackay Doctrine and because they never happened.

141. Answer B is the best answer. Employee referral programs are not likely to bring in candidates who would address issues of underutilization because employees are less likely to refer candidates who are of a different race or gender than they are to refer candidates who are of the same race or gender. Answer A is not the best answer; recruiting at colleges or universities traditionally attended by minorities is likely to be considered an action-oriented program (if the job group or organization is underutilized with respect to race). Answer C is not the best answer; reaching out to professional organizations whose membership criteria

are designed to attract women or minorities is likely to be considered an action-oriented program. Answer D is not the best answer; posting job openings at resource centers for displaced homemakers is likely to be considered an action-oriented program (if the job group or organization is underutilized with respect to gender).

142. Answer B is the best answer. The BFOQ (bona fide occupational qualification) exception to EEO laws would refer to certain job requirements that are mandated by business necessity that might have an unintended discriminatory (disparate) impact upon applicants or employees on the basis of gender, religion, or national origin. The scenario described in the question would not be likely to fall under that exception. Neither answer A nor answer C is the best answer; this decision would not likely be upheld as legal under EEO law. Answer D is not the best answer; there are certain permissible exceptions to EEO laws (for instance, BFOQ, professionally developed test of skill or ability, seniority systems, and piece rate systems).

143. Answer B is the best answer. The formula used to calculate turnover is this:

$$\frac{\text{Number of terminations during a specified period of time}}{\text{The average number of employees in the workforce during that same period of time}}$$

144. Answer C is the best answer. It is advisable to express earnings in short-term increments in offer letters; however, this has nothing to do with forfeiting the exempt FLSA status. Instead, this should be done without unintentionally creating an implied contract. Answer A is not the best answer; it is advisable to specifically state in an offer letter that the only agreements or promises that are valid are those that are included in the offer letter. Answer B is not the best answer; it is advisable to use the offer letter as an opportunity to reaffirm that the employment relationship is at-will. Answer D is not the best answer; it is advisable to avoid language that hints of any sort of long-term employment relationship as well as any statements that indicate that the employer is "like a family."

145. Answer D is the best answer. With very few exceptions (such as for armored car services or pharmaceutical distributors), it is almost always illegal to administer polygraph tests on a preemployment basis. Answers A (agility tests), B (aptitude tests), and C (polygraph tests) are not the best answers; each can be used, under specific circumstances, within specific prescribed parameters, on a preemployment basis.

146. Answer D is the best answer. To be concerted, activity must be engaged in with or on the authority of other employees. Neither answer A nor answer B is the best answer; to be concerted, activity must be undertaken by individual employees who are united in pursuit of a common goal. Answer C is not the best answer; activity must be concerted before it can be protected by the NLRA (rather than the other way around).

147. Answer C is the best answer. Arbitration is not one of the ways in which the EEOC can handle charges of discrimination. Mediation, however, is one possible option. Answer A is not the best answer; the EEOC can handle a charge of discrimination by investigating it. Answer B is not the best answer; settlement remains one possible, ongoing option, even if this option is not utilized (or successfully utilized) when the charge of discrimination is first filed. Answer D is not the best answer; the EEOC can choose to dismiss the charge of discrimination.

148. Answer B is the best answer. A protected class is a group of individuals who share a common characteristic and who are protected from discrimination and harassment on the basis of that shared characteristic. Answer A is not the best answer; antidiscrimination laws protect everyone from discrimination on the basis of a shared characteristic, even if a particular group of individuals has not, historically, experienced discrimination on the basis of that shared characteristic. (For instance, both women and men are protected from discrimination and harassment based on sex even though men have experienced gender discrimination far less frequently on a historical basis.) Answer C is not the best answer; although employers may not discriminate against an employee who has filed charges with the NLRB or who has taken part in any NLRB proceeding because this would be considered an unfair labor practice, these individuals would not be considered members of a protected class as that term is traditionally

defined. Answer D is not the best answer; employees who have engaged in an economic strike can be permanently replaced by the employer (according to the Mackay Doctrine); however, this is unrelated to "protected class."

149. Answer A is the best answer. A nonverbal communication cue could be an indicator of many things, only some of which might be job related. If you notice a change, use job-related questions to probe for more information about the question that you were asking when you noticed the new or changed nonverbal communication cue. Answer B is not the best answer; there is no one, single "dictionary" of nonverbal behaviors (and, even if someone claims to have written one, it is not advisable to apply it to employment or preemployment interactions). Answer C is not the best answer; it is not advisable to point out and describe the changed nonverbal behavior to the candidate or to ask her to help you understand what it means. (It won't do much to build rapport, and it won't help the interviewer obtain the information she needs.) Answer D is not the best answer; mirroring the candidate's nonverbal behavior to see if she continues to display that behavior will not yield helpful job-related information and might even create an uncomfortable interpersonal dynamic.

150. Answer B is the best answer. Recruiting—a separate and distinct process from selection—is the process of attracting and creating a pool of qualified candidates. Answer A is not the best answer; recruiting does not include the process of selecting the final candidate. Answer C is not the best answer; selection, not recruiting, involves the process of identifying the candidate(s) to whom the position will be offered. Answer D is not the best answer; selection, not recruiting, involves the process of selecting the candidate to whom the position will be offered.

151. Answer C is the best answer. The first thing that needs to be done after you decide to conduct an employee survey is to ensure that you have management support—up through and including top levels of management. Answers A (selecting an internal or external consultant), B (determining the survey methodology), and D (deciding upon the survey content) are not the best answers; although each represents an important step in the survey process, none of these should be the first step in that process.

152. Answer B is the best answer. Union deauthorization revokes the union security clause in the contract, thereby effectively creating an open shop. Answer A is not the best answer; the process of removing the union's rights to represent the employee is union decertification, not union deauthorization. Answer C is not the best answer; union deauthorization requires that 50% or more of the members of the collective bargaining unit (not 50% or more of those who vote in the deauthorization election) support the deauthorization. Answer D is not the best answer; union deauthorization is far less common than union decertification.

153. Answer D is the best answer. Providing candidates with opportunities to interact with each other is not an effective way of giving them a realistic job preview. (Generally speaking, it's just not a good idea.) Answer A is not the best answer; providing verbal descriptions of the work, the work environment, or the work conditions can be a good way of giving candidates a realistic job preview. Answer B is not the best answer; providing candidates with the opportunity to read the employee handbook can be a good way of giving candidates a realistic job—and organizational—preview. Answer C is not the best answer; providing candidates with the opportunity to interact with current employees, particularly those who would be the incumbent's peers or colleagues, can be a good way of giving candidates a realistic job preview.

154. Answer B is the best answer. IRCA imposes penalties for recordkeeping errors, whether those errors were committed knowingly or unknowingly. Answer A is not the best answer; IRCA does prohibit discrimination against job applicants based on national origin. Answer C is not the best answer; IRCA does prohibit giving employment preference to U.S. citizens. Answer D is the best answer; IRCA does impose penalties for hiring illegal aliens.

155. Answer C is the best answer. Vendors, by definition, are not employees. The decision to classify individuals as employees or contractors is a legal determination, not an emotional or psychological one. And although fostering an esprit de corps is essential, that sense of team is separate and distinct from whether an individual is an employee or an independent contractor. Answer A is not the best answer;

providing positive and constructive feedback is an important part of effectively managing relationships with vendors. Answer B is not the best answer; setting clear and reasonable expectations is an important part of effectively managing relationships with vendors. Answer D is not the best answer; incorporating upside potential and downside risk into negotiated agreements with contractors is an important part of effectively managing relationships with vendors.

156. Answer D is the best answer. The four Ps of marketing (or the marketing mix) are product, place, price, and promotion. These refer to the variables that need to be addressed and controlled to best satisfy customers in an organization's target market. Answer A is not the best answer; there are no generally recognized four Ps of recruiting. Answer B is not the best answer; there are no generally recognized four Ps of employee relations. Answer C is not the best answer; there are no generally recognized four Ps of project management.

157. Answer D is the best answer. Common situs picketing is unrelated to double breasting because the employers in question with double breasting picketing share common ownership, whereas the employers in question with common situs picketing share a common work location. Answer A is not the best answer; common situs picketing is a type of secondary boycott. Answer B is not the best answer; common situs picketing is legal as long as the picket signs indicate the name of the employer with whom the picketers have a dispute. Answer C is not the best answer; common situs picketing occurs when members of a labor union picket a workplace in which multiple employers work.

158. Answer D is the best answer. The ADA states that "consideration shall be given to the employer's judgment as to what functions of a job are essential, and if an employer has prepared a written description before advertising or interviewing applicants for the job, this description shall be considered evidence of the essential functions of the job." So, although the failure to have a job description in place that identifies essential job functions could significantly diminish the strength of the employer's position in defending an allegation that an employee or applicant has been discriminated against based on disability, this does not necessarily equate to a mandatory legal requirement to do so. Answer A is not the best answer; to be considered essential, a function must be inherently fundamental and necessary to the position. Answer B is not the best answer; to be considered essential, a function must constitute part, or all, of the reason the job exists. Answer C is not the best answer; the elimination of an essential function would substantially alter the nature of the job.

159. Answer C is the best answer. *McDonnell Douglas Corp v. Green, 1979*, determined that the initial burden of proof for establishing a prima facie case of discrimination against an employer (or potential employer) under Title VII of the Civil Rights Act of 1964 rests with the employee (or applicant), who must be able to establish four key elements. "The person was rejected despite being the most qualified for the position" is NOT one of those key elements. Rather, the relevant key element reads: "The person was rejected, despite being qualified for the position." Establishing that a candidate was the most qualified candidate, therefore, is not required to establish a prima facie case… However, establishing that a qualified is qualified IS required. Answers A, B and D are not the best answers; each establishes an element that an individual must be able to establish in order to establishing a prima facie case.

160. Answer C is the best answer. Just like in-person interviews, prescreen phone interviews should be professional, consistent, and stick to job-related factors. Any assessment of informal "fit" that is made through informal interactions is more likely to be based on factors that are not specifically related to the job-related knowledge, skills, abilities, and behavioral characteristics that are required for a position. Answer A is not the best answer; a prescreen phone interview can be an effective way to identify legitimate job-related factors that could cause the employer to decide to eliminate the candidate from consideration. Answer B is not the best answer; a prescreen phone interview can be an effective way to share job-related information (with every candidate) that could lead one or more candidates to self-select out of the selection process. Answer D is not the best answer; a prescreen phone interview can be an effective way to ascertain whether the candidate's desired salary/wage rate is close to the salary/wage range that the organization has established for the position.

161. Answer D is the best answer. (For this discussion, keep the definition of disparate or adverse impact in mind: disparate or adverse impact occurs when a seemingly neutral policy or practice has a disproportionately negative impact on a member of a protected class.) Although it is conceivable that this scenario could result in adverse impact, of the four situations described, creating a cross-training program in which all nonmanagement employees who meet or exceed performance expectations of their current positions would be able to participate is the least likely to have an adverse impact on a protected class. Answer A is not the best answer; requiring employees to live within a certain radius of an employer could have an adverse impact if it screens out individuals based on membership in a protected class, for instance, race. (This policy could also eliminate people from consideration based on socioeconomic status; although socioeconomic status does not constitute a protected class, it could be discriminatory depending on the characteristics shared by individuals who have been eliminated because of this requirement. Employers would be better advised to consult with counsel relative to the appropriateness of requiring specific response times for specific positions.) Answer B is not the best answer; excluding candidates who have gaps in employment could have an adverse impact on women (who are more likely to experience a gap in employment than men) and individuals over the age of 40 (who are more likely to have experienced a layoff or other involuntary termination). Answer C is not the best answer; any program that requires people to relocate frequently could have an adverse impact based on gender or age.

162. Answer A is the best answer. Of all these factors, having the same interviewer perform every interview contributes the least to ensuring that the interview process will have validity. Why? Because if the interview is not based on job analysis (answer B), if the interviewer (even if it is the same person) does not ask questions that elicit information about important job-related skills (answer C), or if the information that is shared, discussed, and collected during an interview does not relate to a specific job (answer D), having the same person conduct the interview isn't going to do anything to enhance validity. What will contribute to validity is if the interview(s) incorporates these processes/attributes into the interview process.

163. Answer B is the best answer. This dimension of leadership relates to the dimensions of leadership that speak specifically to ensuring that employees successfully perform the work associated with the position. Answer A is not the best answer; "the interpersonal relationships that managers must first establish with employees before attempting to ensure completion of the actual work" refers to the dimension identified through behavioral leadership theories, known as consideration or employee centered. Answer C is not the best answer; "the training in which managers need to participate to develop the skills needed to be an effective leader" does not reflect one of the two leadership dimensions. Answer D is not the best answer; "the degree to which an individual demonstrates an innate ability to being an effective leader" articulates a belief that is ascribed to the trait leadership theories, not the behavioral leadership theories.

164. Answer A is the best answer. Employers do normally own/retain the copyright to work product that is generated by an employee during the normal course of her employment. Neither answer B nor answer D is the best answer; independent contractors/consulting firms do not normally own/retain the copyright to the work product generated for the organization for which they are consulting. (From the perspective of the organization, however, it is important to have a signed written agreement that states that a work-for-hire arrangement has been established and that the organization owns/retains all work product that is produced.) Answer C is not the best answer; an employee does not normally own/retain the copyright to the work product that she generates in the normal course of her employment.

165. Answer B is the best answer. The formative evaluation model uses feedback, analysis, and assessment conducted at one phase of the process to make enhancements in other phases. Answer A is not the best answer; the formative evaluation model seeks feedback throughout—rather than at the end of—the development and implementation phases. Answer C is not the best answer; the formative evaluation model was developed by Robert Brinkerhoff. Answer D is not the best answer; it refers to Kirkpatrick's reaction-level analysis (which measures participants' answers and reactions to a program immediately after the program has been delivered).

166. Answer D is the best answer. A vacation buyout program (a program through which an employer will buy back a certain amount of unused vacation time) constitutes cash compensation and therefore is not a form of indirect compensation. Answer A is not the best answer; whether legally mandated or not, benefits are a form of indirect compensation. Answer B is not the best answer; vacation time (or any program that grants employees paid time off) is a form of indirect compensation. Answer C is not the best answer; perquisites (also known as "perks"), such as a company car, club memberships, financial planning, and the like are a form of indirect compensation.

167. Answer A is the best answer. MHPA (the Mental Health Parity Act) does not require health plans to offer mental health benefits; rather, it applies only to plans that do offer mental health benefits. Answer B is not the best answer; under MHPA, plans can still dictate/define the terms and conditions of benefits provided under mental health plans (for instance, cost sharing, limits on the number of visits or days of coverage, and so forth). Answer C is not the best answer; under MHPA, plans that don't impose annual or lifetime monetary caps on medical and surgical benefits cannot impose annual or lifetime caps on mental health benefits either. Answer D is not the best answer; benefits for substance abuse or chemical dependency are excluded from MHPA's requirements relative to annual or lifetime caps.

168. Answer D is the best answer. The single-most important factor that is most likely to impact whether the handbook will support the employer's position or the employee's position is the presence or absence of a signed employee acknowledgement. Without it, even the most carefully crafted handbook, including one with a carefully (and effectively) written EEO/AA statement (answer A) or sexual harassment policy (answer B), will be less relevant because it cannot be proven that the employee received, read, understood, and had the opportunity to ask questions about it. Answer C is not the best answer; employee handbooks usually don't include a records retention policy.

169. Answer C is the best answer. To collect information that could be used to address an individual's employee relations issues, the employee survey could not remain anonymous, rendering it useless and ineffective. Answer A is not the best answer; an organization would conduct an employee survey to gauge and measure employees' perceptions, viewpoints, and attitudes. Answer B is not the best answer; an organization would conduct an employee survey to take the pulse on specific employee current or potential issues. Answer D is not the best answer; an organization would conduct an employee survey to collect information that the organization can use to help set priorities.

170. Answer A is the best answer. For a bargaining unit to be established, a simple majority of those who choose to vote in the election must vote in favor of the proposed bargaining unit. Answer B is not the best answer; a simple majority of voters (not of potential members) is required for a bargaining unit to be established. Answer C is not the best answer; even when there is more than one bargaining unit competing in an election, a proposed bargaining unit must still obtain a simple majority of the votes. (This is significant for two reasons. First, a runoff election might be required. Second, in that runoff election, the bargaining unit could find itself competing either with another bargaining unit or with the option of remaining union free). Answer D is not the best answer; the relevant distinction here is that at least 30% of the employees who would be in the collective bargaining unit must sign authorization cards before the union can petition the NLRB to hold an election—all of which takes place, of course, long before the actual election.

171. Answer D is the best answer. Of the four choices listed in the question, catastrophes and fatal accidents would represent the highest priority, followed by employee complaints (answer C); referrals from the media or other individuals, agencies, or organizations (answer A); and planned inspections in high-hazard industries (answer B). Imminent danger, however, poses an even higher priority for OSHA than any of the situations listed in this explanation.

172. Answer C is the best answer. The degree to which a selection process or instrument is consistent and generates consistent information that can be used for decision making determines the degree to which that instrument is reliable. Answer A is not the best answer; the degree to which a selection procedure assesses a candidate's ability to perform representative and significant parts of the job measures its content validity, not its reliability. Answer B is not the best answer; the degree to which incumbents'

scores or ratings on a particular selection procedure correlate with their actual job performance measures its criterion-related validity, not its reliability. Answer D is not the best answer; the degree to which a clear relationship exists between performance on the selection procedure and performance on the job measures (in a more general sense) its validity.

173. Answer D is the best answer. With respect to the Equal Pay Act, the definition of responsibility is "the degree of responsibility and accountability which an employer entrusts to and expects from a particular position." Answer A is not the best answer; with respect to the Equal Pay Act, the definition of skill is "the amount or degree of experience, ability, education, and training required to perform the job." Neither answer B nor answer C is the best answer; the Equal Pay Act does not designate trust or accountability as one of the four factors used to assess substantial equality.

174. Answer B is the best answer. Taft-Hartley enacted provisions that permitted (not prohibited) employers to fire supervisors who engaged in union activities or who did not support the employer's position. Answer A is not the best answer; Taft-Hartley did reaffirm that employers have a constitutional right to express their opposition to unions so long as employees are not threatened with reprisal for their union activities or promised benefits for refraining from such activities. Answer C is not the best answer; Taft-Hartley did outlaw closed shops, agreements that stated that employers could only hire individuals who were members of labor unions. Answer D is not the best answer; Taft-Hartley did expressly permit union shops, in which nonunion workers must join the union within a certain amount of time after being hired.

175. Answer A is the best answer. The list of the names and addresses of all the employees who are eligible to vote in the union certification election is also known as the Excelsior List. This nickname comes from the NLRB decision *Excelsior Underwear, Inc. v. NLRB, 1966*, in which the NLRB considered whether "a fair and free election [can] be held when the union involved lacks the names and addresses of employees eligible to vote in that election, and the employer refuses to accede to the union's request…." The NLRB ruled that it could not. As a result, the employer must provide the list of employees' names and addresses within seven days after the NLRB has scheduled an election. Thus, answers B, C, and D are incorrect.

Glossary

Numbers

4 Ps   The categories into which components of marketing plans can be divided:

▶ **Product:** The item (tangible) or service (intangible) that is being marketed

▶ **Place:** Any location, real or virtual, at which a product or service can be purchased/procured

▶ **Price:** The amount that a customer pays/will pay for a product or service

▶ **Promotion:** All the ways in which an organization seeks to communicate with customers and potential customers about its products and services and the benefits thereof

80–20 rule (also known as the Pareto Principle)   A principle that asserts that 80% of effects result from 20% of causes. The 80–20 rule, and the chart that visually depicts it, is intended to help individuals focus their efforts where there is the greatest likelihood of bringing about the desired change.

A

acceptable quality levels (AQLs)   According to Phil Crosby's zero defect philosophy, acceptable quality levels refer to the acceptable level of errors that are sometimes permitted—and that thus preclude the possibility of fully attaining quality objectives through the "zero defects" standard that Crosby alternatively espoused.

accounts payable   Money that the organization owes to others. This could include—but is not necessarily limited to—outstanding bills from vendors, suppliers, lenders, and the like. Accounts payable constitutes a liability to the organization and is reflected as such on an organization's balance sheet.

accounts receivable   Money that is owed to the organization. Accounts payable refers to invoices that have been sent/given to customers but which have not yet paid. Accounts receivable constitutes an asset and is generally recorded as such on an organization's balance sheet.

acid test   A mathematical calculation/metric that divides current liabilities into the sum of the following: cash, accounts receivable, and short-term investments. This calculation is intended to measure an organization's ability to cover liabilities without selling off inventory or liquidating other long-term investments.

action-oriented programs   Programs that are specifically designed to correct any areas of underutilization and, thereby, attain established placement goals (with respect to affirmative action).

activity-based budgeting An approach to budgeting in which the costs of individual activities are individually assessed compared to other activities performed within the organization and looked at within the context of the overarching organizational objectives and the degree to which those activities contribute to the attainment of those objectives.

ADDIE A five-phase model (often used within a context of instructional design) that includes analysis/assessment (of needs), design, development, implementation, and evaluation.

administrative professional exemption An exemption under the FLSA. To qualify for an administrative exemption

- The employee's primary duty must be the performance of office or nonmanual work directly related to the management or general business operations of the employer or the employer's customers.

- The employee's primary duty includes the exercise of discretion and independent judgment with respect to matters of significance.

adult learner An individual who has exceeded the primary/secondary levels of education (United States) and who is engaged in learning activities in an academic or organizational setting.

adverse impact (also known as disparate impact) Occurs when a seemingly neutral policy or practice has a disproportionately negative impact on a member(s) of a protected class. Adverse impact that results from policies or practices that are not job related and that have a statistically significant impact on members of a protected class can constitute unlawful discrimination.

Affirmative Action Plans (AAPs) Programs created under Executive Order 11246 to overcome the effects of past societal discrimination by identifying areas of underutilization. AAPs set forth (and require documentation of) good faith efforts to address and resolve that underutilization. Federal contractors and subcontractors with 50

employees and $50,000 or more in contracts during any 12-month period are also required to design and implement formal AAPs.

affirmative defenses Legitimate explanations that employers can set forth to explain inequities in pay between men and women under the Equal Pay Act of 1963. These arguments can be based on—and must be proven to be—a function of

- Seniority

- Merit

- Quantity or quality of production

- Any factors other than sex

Age Discrimination in Employment Act, 1967 A law that prohibits discrimination on the basis of age for individuals age 40 and above. There is no upper cap on age limit (although there originally was). The ADEA covers private employers with 20 or more employees, state and local governments (including school districts), employment agencies, and labor organizations.

agency shop Employees are not required to join the union. They must, however, pay a monthly fee that is typically equivalent to union dues if they choose not to join the union. Agency shops are illegal in right-to-work states.

agility tests Preemployment tests that are used to ascertain whether the candidate can perform the physical requirements of the position for which he is applying.

aging The process of mathematically adjusting market data collected during the market pricing process to a common date (usually the date on which the market analysis is being conducted).

agriculture One of the major industries designated by Occupational Safety and Health Administration (OSHA).

AIDS (acquired immune deficiency syndrome) An infectious disease that is transmitted from person to person through blood or other bodily fluids.

Albemarle Paper v. Moody, 1975 Key issue: job relatedness and validity of employment tests. Significance: Any tests that are used as part of the hiring or promotional decision-making process must be job related. This applies to any instrument that is used as a "test," even if that was not its original purpose. This case also established that employment tests must demonstrate predictive validity, consistent with the Uniform Guidelines for Employee Selection Procedures.

ally doctrine   A doctrine that states that a union can expand on its primary picketing activity to include employers who are "allies" of the primary employer. One specific situation that can permit the union to conduct a secondary boycott is the ally doctrine.

Americans with Disabilities Act (ADA), 1992   A law that guarantees equal opportunity for qualified individuals with disabilities in public accommodations, employment, transportation, state and local government services, and telecommunications.

Americans with Disabilities Act Amendments Act (ADAAA), 2008   A law that amended the ADA of 1990. ADAAA codifies a broader interpretation of the ADA, particularly with respect to the definition of a disability. Specifically, "(t)he Act emphasizes that the definition of disability should be construed in favor of broad coverage of individuals to the maximum extent permitted by the terms of the ADA and generally shall not require extensive analysis."

"The Act makes important changes to the definition of the term 'disability' by rejecting the holdings in several Supreme Court decisions and portions of EEOC's ADA regulations. The effect of these changes is to make it easier for an individual seeking protection under the ADA to establish that he or she has a disability within the meaning of the ADA" (www.eeoc.gov).

andragogy   The study and science of how adults learn.

aptitude tests   Preemployment tests that are used to ascertain whether the candidate possesses the skills or knowledge required to perform the position for which she is applying.

assessment centers   Facilities that assess candidates' absolute and relative qualifications for open positions within an organization or with respect to overall potential/talent.

asset   Anything owned by an organization that has, or has the ability to generate, economic value to that organization.

attitude surveys (also sometimes called employee or climate surveys)   A vehicle through which employees can express their opinions or share their perspectives. Sometimes attitude surveys can even provide a vehicle through which employees can truly contribute in a meaningful and significant way to their organizations by having a voice in shaping the policies, practices, and directions of their organizations.

auditory learners   Those who learn most effectively by processing information that they hear.

authorization cards   Cards that, once signed by employees, demonstrate and confirm employees' interest in joining a union. After 30% of the employees who would be in the collective bargaining unit have signed authorization cards, the union can petition the National Labor Relations Board (NLRB) to hold an election. (The 30% threshold demonstrates a "showing of interest" to the NLRB.) Often, however, unions seek to obtain signed authorization cards from 50% or more employees before petitioning the NLRB. In addition, under the National Labor Relations Act (NLRA), after 50% or more employees who would be in a collective bargaining unit have signed authorization cards, the employer could choose to recognize the union as the representative of all workers in that bargaining unit (although this process, referred to as a "card check," rarely happens).

Automobile Workers v. Johnson Controls, 1990   The case in which the Supreme Court ruled that Johnson Controls' fetal protection policy constituted a violation of Title VII of the Civil Rights Act of 1964, as amended by the Pregnancy Discrimination Act.

availability analysis   The section of an Affirmative Action Plan that determines the availability of minorities and women for jobs in their establishments, compares incumbency to availability, declares underutilization, and establishes goals to eliminate the underutilization.

B

background check   A process through which the specifics of an individual's past history are explored and revealed.

balance sheet   A financial statement that itemizes assets, liabilities, and shareholder/owners' equity as of a particular point (date) in time. On a balance sheet, the total of the assets must equal the sum of the liabilities + shareholder/owners' equity. A balance sheet is sometimes referred to as a statement of financial position.

balanced scorecard   An approach to strategic management that seeks increased clarity and specificity by offering a clear and unequivocal prescription of what companies should measure to appropriately balance financial measures of success with/against nonfinancial measures of success.

base pay   The fixed rate of pay that an employee receives for performing his job. Base pay does not include earnings obtained through shift differentials, benefits, overtime, incentive premiums, or any pay element other than the employee's fixed rate of pay.

BASIC (behavioral, as soon as possible, specific, interactive, consistent)   An acronym that outlines the principles that should be followed when providing feedback to, and discussing feedback with, employees.

Beck Rights   The right for bargaining unit members to pay only that portion of union dues attributable to mainline union responsibilities (collective bargaining, organizing in the same industry, contract administration, and the like). It is up to the employee, however, to exercise her Beck Rights. Beck Rights were established by the 1988 Supreme Court decision in *Communication Workers of America v. Beck, 1988.*

behavior-based interviews   Interviews that require the candidate to describe past experiences that demonstrate the degree to which he possesses the knowledge, skills, and abilities required to successfully perform the position for which he is applying.

behavior-level evaluation   Measures whether participants' on-the-job behaviors have changed in a manner consistent with training objectives. In short, it measures transfer of training—the degree to which participants apply the skills and knowledge covered in the training sessions in the workplace. This level of evaluation takes place some period of time (weeks, or perhaps even months) after the training is completed.

behavioral anchored ranking scales (BARS)   A rating method type of performance appraisal that starts by identifying the most critical responsibilities or requirements of a position. Then, for each responsibility or requirement, "anchor" statements offering a specific description of a particular type of behavior (which corresponds to a particular level of performance) are written.

benchmark positions   Jobs that are frequently found in the relevant labor market and that can be compared, with confidence, to highly similar positions in other organizations.

benefits   Noncash, or indirect, rewards provided to employees in recognition of and in exchange for the performance of their jobs.

bills   Statutes, in their draft format, while they are on their way to becoming law.

biological health hazards   Dangers of a biological origin or nature that are introduced into the workplace.

biometrics   Unique biological characteristics or attributes (such as fingerprints, retina scanning, or DNA) that are matched to one specific individual for purposes of identification.

bona fide occupational qualification (BFOQ)   Legitimate job requirements mandated by business necessity that can have an unintended discriminatory (disparate) impact on applicants or employees.

boundaryless organization   An organizational model that relies little on a traditional, hierarchical approach and instead functions with little attention to reporting lines or relationships, functional distinctions or siloes, or barriers (real, or imagined) between or even outside the organization.

brick-and-mortar learning   A training/learning program that is delivered face to face and in person.

Brinkerhoff, Robert   Brinkerhoff's evaluation model incorporates "formative evaluation."

broadbanding   An approach to pay systems that includes a relatively small number of grades. Organizations might choose to use broadbands to bring about a cultural change (for instance, to support the implementation of a flatter organization) or to shift employees' focus away from traditional promotions and place it instead on professional growth and development. Broadbands typically have range spreads of 100% or more.

budgeting   The process by which a financial plan is developed for an organization, or one or more portions of an organization, for a specified period of time. A budget includes expected costs and expenses and revenues within the specific context of resource requirements (human and nonhuman). Budgets are created as a way of further supporting organizational objectives and stated milestones.

bureaucracy   An organizational model in which clearly defined lines of authority and areas of responsibility are created within a hierarchical structure. Bureaucracies are often characterized by many rules, approval guidelines, and—often—a degree of rigidity.

business activity ratios   Mathematical calculations/metrics that provide information on the pace at which different balance sheet items have been converted into either cash or sales (depending upon which balance sheet item is being measured).

business case development   The process of developing a proposal in support of the modification of an existing business approach or the introduction of a new program/initiative. The business case must be made on the basis of careful and supported analysis, sound projections, financial metrics, realistic assessments, and always—always—with an eye toward how the initiative will advance the overarching business objectives and attainment of the organization's mission in a manner that is consistent with the values of the organization.

business (or organizational) ethics   A shared values-based system designed to inculcate within the organization's population a sense of how to conduct business properly, appropriately, and consistently with the underlying values of the organization.

business process perspective   One of the four perspectives of the balanced scorecard. This perspective scrutinizes key internal business processes so as to measure and ascertain how well those processes generate business results (that is, products and services) that meet customer expectations. The business process perspective ascertains performance levels through specific measures that are unique to each particular organization.

C

capacity   A manufacturing term that speaks to the maximum volume of goods or services that can be produced/delivered within a specified timeframe based on current human and nonhuman organizational resources.

captive audience meeting   A mandatory meeting held by management, in the workplace, during regular working hours, during which the employer can share its opinions relative to unions and the unionization of its operations. Captive audience meetings cannot be held within 24 hours of the actual election.

career development   The deliberate preparation for, and unfolding of, the professional pathway along which each individual travels during her adult working life. Career development can also be described, more simply, as the development of individuals within the organization. In either context, career development is either "owned" wholly by the employee or is co-owned by the employee and the employer. The latter is more common in learning organizations that are committed to developing high-potential employees. Rarely, if ever, is career development even the sole responsibility of the employer. (However, that scenario was more common 40 or more years ago.)

case study A training method through which participants are presented with a real-life situation that allows them to apply the knowledge they have learned and practice the skills they have developed during the training session.

cash balance plan A type of defined benefit plan that expresses the promised benefit in terms of a stated account balance (similar to the way a defined contribution plan does).

cash flow statement (statement of cash flows) A financial tool that captures the inflows and outflows of cash during a stated period of time. A cash flow statement is one tool that can be used to ascertain and predict the financial soundness and strength of an organization.

cause-and-effect diagram (also known as the Ishikawa or fishbone diagram) An important quality tool developed by Ishikawa that presents a visual representation of factors that impact whether a desired outcome will be obtained. Ishikawa believed that, by presenting all the possible factors that contribute to a particular result, any potential process imperfections can be identified in advance and eliminated.

centralization The concentration/organization of power and authority within one primary (and usually small) group of individuals within the organization. Centralization is often geographically focused (the individuals—and the power—often residing in one central location).

certification The process by which HR professionals earn formal recognition by a professional certifying body, the Human Resource Certification Institute (HRCI).

chain of command The reporting relationships existing at specific levels within an organization, starting at the highest levels and defined to encompass and incorporate every position throughout the organization, in every department, unit, division, or geographical location.

change management Activities involved in "(1) defining and instilling new values, attitudes, norms, and behaviors within an organization that support new ways of doing work and overcome resistance to change; (2) building consensus among customers and stakeholders on specific changes designed to better meet their needs; and (3) planning, testing, and implementing all aspects of the transition from one organizational structure or business process to another" (as defined by the Government Accounting Office).

change process theory The theory that looks at the dynamics behind how change happens within organizations.

charge A formal complaint, submitted to an agency, that alleges unlawful discrimination.

charging party (also called the complainant) A person who alleges that she has experienced unlawful discrimination.

checklist A rating method type of performance appraisal in which the appraiser reviews a series of statements that could describe an employee's performance and literally checks off those statements that are reflective of the employee's performance during the performance measurement period. Sometimes checklists are weighted (called weighted checklists), in which case the weightings are used to generate a mathematically calculated score.

chemical health hazards Any chemical in the workplace for which evidence exists that acute or chronic health effects may occur in exposed employees.

child labor The child labor provisions of the Fair Labor Standards Act (FLSA) restrict the number of hours (and the times of the day) that children under the age of 16 can work, as well as the types of work that children under the age of 18 can perform.

Circuit City Stores, Inc. v. Adams, 2001 The landmark Supreme Court case that confirmed the legality of requiring employees to sign mandatory arbitration agreements as a condition of employment and that such agreements are enforceable under the Federal Arbitration Act (FAA).

Civil Rights Act of 1991 A law that significantly expanded employees' rights and remedies under Title VII of the Civil Rights Act of 1964. In addition to establishing the right for plaintiffs in Title VII cases to enjoy jury trials, it allowed plaintiffs to be awarded compensatory and punitive damages.

Clayton Act, 1914 A law enacted to build on and clarify the Sherman Act. The provision of the Clayton Act that is most relevant to labor—and therefore to HR professionals—is Section 6, which specifically exempts labor unions and agricultural organizations from the Sherman Antitrust Act.

cliff vesting A vesting arrangement in which an employee earns a nonforfeitable right to 100% of his employer's contributions after a specified number of years but forfeits all rights to those contributions if his employment is terminated before he vests.

climate survey (also sometimes called attitude survey or employee survey) A vehicle through which employees can express their opinions or share their perspectives. Sometimes climate surveys can even provide a mechanism through which employees can truly contribute in a meaningful and significant way to their organizations by having a voice in shaping the policies, practices, and direction of their organizations.

closed shop Employers can hire only employees who are already members of the union. Closed shops were ruled illegal by the Taft-Hartley Act; however, hiring halls do, in one sense, encourage a closed-shop arrangement. A hiring hall is a union-operated placement office that refers registered applicants to jobs on the basis of a seniority or placement system.

closing processes Those processes (within project management) that mark the end of the project, including the sign-off process. As part of closing processes, stakeholders must determine whether, and to what degree, the project met its obligations. In general, closing processes are considered the fifth of five project management processes, although there can be considerable overlap between those five distinct processes.

coaching A professional relationship in which one individual listens, mirrors, "walks with," and "makes space" for another individual to learn, to grow, to explore, and to make empowered choices.

COBRA qualifying event Events that would have otherwise resulted in the discontinuation of health insurance benefits for employees, their spouses, and dependent children.

cognitive ability tests Preemployment tests that are used to assess the candidate's intelligence or current skill level with respect to a job-related function. Cognitive tests could be administered to assess skills such as problem-solving, mathematical skill, or numerical ability.

collective bargaining agreement (CBA) The output of a successful collective bargaining process. The CBA contains provisions related to a variety of conditions of employment and outlines the procedures to be used in settling disputes that might arise throughout the duration of the contract.

commissions Compensation paid to employees for the execution of specific transactions or sales.

common law A system of law in which traditions, customs, and precedents have the same force of law as existing laws or statutes that have been enacted as a result of the full legislative process. With a common law system, laws and statutes are, quite literally, interpreted and reinterpreted on a case-by-case basis. In practice, each interpretation (and each case) sets a precedent but can also be reinterpreted, thus setting a new precedent. As it evolves, this process results in rights being granted to employees on an individual basis.

common situs picketing A type of picketing that is actually a type of secondary boycott. Common situs picketing occurs when members of a labor union picket a workplace in which multiple employers work: the employer with whom the labor union has the dispute, as well as one or more employers with whom the labor union does not have a dispute. Common situs picketing is legal as long as the picket signs indicate the name of the employer with whom the picketers have a dispute.

communication The exchange or conveyance of information, ideas, feelings, thoughts, or questions between two or more individuals or groups. Communication can take many forms and can be accomplished with or without technical or mechanical devices. Communication can also vary in its level of effectiveness and creates a shared responsibility between the person who conveys the communication and the person who receives the communication.

***Communication Workers of America v. Beck,
1988*** The Supreme Court case that established
the right for bargaining unit members to pay only
that portion of union dues that is attributable
to mainline union responsibilities (collective
bargaining, organizing in the same industry,
contract administration, and the like). It is up
to the employee, however, to exercise her Beck
Rights.

community partnership Relationships that are
forged between employers and community
organizations (usually not-for-profit or municipal)
in support of the mission of the community-based
organization. These relationships often benefit the
community organization, the organization, and its
employees.

compa-ratio The compa-ratio for each employee is
calculated by dividing the employee's pay rate by the
range midpoint for his position. Compa-ratios can
be a particularly valuable measure for organizations
that seek to match the market because, in such
systems, midpoints are often considered to be
a close approximation of the market rate for a
position. By calculating the compa-ratio, therefore,
you can compare the employee's rate of pay with
the market rate for his position.

comparative methods Performance appraisal
methods in which the appraiser compares
employees to each other.

compensable factors Skills, abilities,
characteristics, or areas of responsibility that an
organization values and for which it is willing to
pay. Some sample compensable factors include
education, experience, financial responsibility,
responsibility for contacts, and so on.

compensation Cash-based rewards provided to
employees in recognition of and in exchange for
the performance of their jobs.

competencies Skills or behaviors that reflect
the way employees are expected to deliver
performance goals/objectives.

competitive advantage A way in which an
organization can operate, sell, manage, produce,
or somehow function in a way that is measurably
and meaningfully superior to that of its
competitors.

complainant (also called the charging party) A
person who alleges that she has experienced
unlawful discrimination.

compression When employees' pay is clustered
so closely together that it does not reflect
differences in performance, contribution levels,
or seniority. Compression can occur for a variety
of reasons, including but not limited to increase
in the minimum wage and failure to maintain
internal equity while monitoring concerns related
to external equity.

computer employee exemption An exemption
under the FLSA. To qualify for a computer
employee exemption

▶ The employee must be compensated either
on a salary or fee basis (as defined in the
regulations) at a rate not less than $455 per
week or, if compensated on an hourly basis, at
a rate not less than $27.63 an hour.

▶ The employee must be employed as a
computer systems analyst, computer
programmer, software engineer, or other
similarly skilled worker in the computer field
performing the duties described next.

▶ The employee's primary duty must
consist of

  ▶ The application of systems analysis
  techniques and procedures, including consulting with users to determine
  hardware, software, or system functional
  specifications

  ▶ The design, development,
  documentation, analysis, creation,
  testing, or modification of computer
  systems or programs, including
  prototypes, based on and related to user
  or system design specifications

  ▶ The design, documentation, testing,
  creation, or modification of computer
  programs related to machine operating
  systems

  ▶ A combination of the aforementioned
  duties, the performance of which
  requires the same level of skills

concentrated industry An industry that consists of only a few dominant—and usually behemoth—organizations. These organizations often mold, as well as dominate, the industry.

concerted activities Any activities undertaken by individual employees who are united in pursuit of a common goal are considered to be concerted activity. For an employee's activity to be concerted, the activity must be engaged in with, or on the authority of, other employees, rather than just on behalf of only herself (Meyers Industries, 281 NLRB 882 [1986]).

concurrent resolutions A legislative measure that addresses a concern that pertains to the Senate as well as to the House of Representatives. Concurrent resolutions, however, are not submitted to the president and thus do not have the force of law.

confidentiality agreement A type of employment agreement that prohibits employees from revealing any confidential information to which they might be exposed during the course of their employment. This could include trade secrets, patent information, and the like. It also usually prohibits employees from using confidential information in any way other than the purposes for which it was intended, and which is necessary, within the context of their jobs.

Congressional Accountability Act (CAA), 1995 Expanded coverage of the following 12 laws to congressional employees:

- ▶ Fair Labor Standards Act (FLSA), 1938
- ▶ Title VII of the Civil Rights Act of 1964, as amended
- ▶ Age Discrimination in Employment Act of 1967
- ▶ Occupational Safety and Health Act of 1970
- ▶ Rehabilitation Act of 1973
- ▶ Civil Service Reform Act of 1978
- ▶ Employee Polygraph Protection Act of 1988
- ▶ Worker Adjustment and Retraining Notification Act of 1988
- ▶ Americans with Disabilities Act of 1990

- ▶ Family and Medical Leave Act of 1993
- ▶ Veterans Reemployment Act of 1994
- ▶ Uniformed Services Employment and Reemployment Rights Act of 1994

Consolidated Omnibus Budget Reconciliation Act (COBRA), 1985 An amendment to Title I of ERISA that requires employers who employed 20 or more people during the prior year to offer continuation of group health care coverage to employees and their family members who experience certain qualifying events—events that would have otherwise resulted in the discontinuation of their health insurance benefits. COBRA places certain requirements on plan participants who want to extend coverage and places certain requirements on the plan provider, in particular with respect to notification requirements.

construct validity The degree to which a selection procedure measures the degree to which the test taker possesses a particular psychological trait (if, of course, it can be shown that the trait is required for successful performance of the position).

construction One of the major industries designated by Occupational Safety and Health Administration (OSHA).

constructive discharge An employee who alleges constructive discharge asserts that he was subjected to such intolerable working conditions that remaining employed with the organization would be impossible. Essentially, an employee who alleges that he was constructively discharged is alleging that he was forced to quit.

content validity The degree to which a selection procedure assesses a candidate's ability to perform significant parts of the job.

contingency employment agencies Search firms to whom an organization pays a fee only if that firm's efforts result in the organization actually hiring a candidate. The services of this type of agency are more often secured in an effort to fill entry-level professional or supervisory-level positions.

contract doctrines Another way in which common law directly impacts the employment relationship. A contract is an agreement that is enforceable by law. Employment contracts are made between an employer and an employee and can be either oral or written. They can include topics such as term or length of employment, compensation and benefits, job responsibilities, and termination.

contrast error/bias (interviewing)   An interviewing error/bias that occurs when the interviewer compares candidates to each other instead of comparing them to the requirements of the position.

contrast error/bias (performance management)   A performance management error/bias in which the appraiser compares the performance of each employee to the performance of other employees instead of comparing it to the established performance standards for the position.

controlling function   Identified by Fayol as one of the five management functions, the controlling function is the one during which the manager ascertains the degree to which the planning in which she was engaged actually produced the desired results. If the manager determines that there is a gap between the targeted goals and the actual results, the manager must then focus on ways to bridge that gap.

controlling processes   Those processes (within project management) that include managing the scope of the project and ensuring that the project stays in line with the original objectives. A significant degree of follow-up is required to carry out controlling processes. In general, controlling processes are considered the fourth of five project management processes, although there can be considerable overlap between those five distinct processes.

coordinating function   Identified by Fayol as one of the five management functions. Through the coordinating function, the manager brings together all the resources that she has organized to accomplish the stated plan.

Copyright Act of 1976   A law protecting the work of authors, artists, and others who create original materials. This law also addresses fair use and public domain questions.

cost per trainee/cost per participant   A formula that calculates the following:

- ▶ Total of all costs associated with the HRD/training initiative
- ▶ Number of individuals who participate in the HRD/training initiative

corporate responsibility   An organization's choice to share responsibility for the environment—physical as well as social—in which it operates. Corporate responsibility constitutes a form of corporate citizenship, commitment to, and engagement that is optional and that, presumably, will result in a better quality of life in the community.

counsel   An attorney or a lawyer who has been admitted to the bar and is thus legally permitted to practice law.

creative professional exemption   An exemption under the Fair Labor Standards Act (FLSA). To qualify for a creative professional exemption, the employee's primary duty must be the performance of work requiring invention, imagination, originality, or talent in a recognized field of artistic or creative endeavor.

criterion-related validity   The degree to which a selection procedure correlates with employees' subsequent job performance.

critical incident   A narrative performance appraisal method in which the appraiser creates and maintains documentation throughout the year relative to specific situations in which the employee met and did not meet the performance expectations of the position.

Crosby, Philip B.   A quality guru known for his zero defects standard (in contrast to acceptable quality levels [AQLs]). This management philosophy asserts that employees will perform at whatever level management sets for them.

culture/organizational culture   The "way things are done around here"; the formal and informal manifestation of what the organization "is all about." Organizational culture encompasses historical events, current events, and future events (whether potential, likely, or simply rumored).

More specifically, organizational culture reflects and embodies the norms, mores, values, beliefs, customs, and attitudes of the organization and of those who work within it.

cumulative trauma disorders (CTDs) (also known as repetitive stress injuries [RSIs] or cumulative trauma syndrome [CTS])   Injuries that result from placing too much stress (often through overuse) on a part of the body.

cumulative trauma syndrome (CTS) (also known as repetitive stress injuries [RSIs] or cumulative trauma disorders [CTDs])   Injuries that result from placing too much stress (often through overuse) on a part of the body.

current ratio   A mathematical calculation/metric that divides current assets by current liabilities. This calculation is considered to reflect the organization's ability to pay its creditors and meet its current and short-term financial obligations.

customer perspective   One of the four perspectives of the balanced scorecard. This perspective focuses on the criticality of customer focus and customer satisfaction. Dissatisfied customers will eventually look to others who will meet their needs and expectations (often without ever sharing their reasons for doing so), which, if the numbers are large enough, can ultimately lead to organizational decline.

D

Davis-Bacon Act, 1931   The first piece of legislation to consider the topic of, and actually establish, a minimum wage. Davis-Bacon, however, was (and still is) limited to the construction industry—specifically, those contractors and subcontractors on

- ▶ Any and all federal government construction contracts
- ▶ Nonfederal government construction projects in excess of $2,000 that receive federal funding

Contractors and subcontractors who meet either of these criteria are required to provide laborers and mechanics who are employed at the actual worksite with wages and benefits that are equal to (or better than) what workers on similar local projects receive.

debt ratios   A mathematical calculation/metric that divides total debt by total assets. Debt ratios are often one tool (of several) used to assess the level of risk associated with moving forward with a financial transaction/venture with an organization.

decentralization   The dispersion of power and authority to different areas within the organization.

decline   The fourth stage of the organizational life cycle, after which—if inertia has set in and if atrophy has begun—demise might not be far behind.

defamation   A tort doctrine that, in a general and practical sense, refers to making a false statement that damages someone's character or reputation. Defamation that is in written form is referred to as libel, and defamation that is made through the spoken word is referred to as slander. An employee could sue an employer for libel or slander for a variety of reasons, such as the provision of a false reference to potential employers.

defined benefit plan   A more traditional type of pension plan in which the employer promises to pay the employee a specified monthly benefit at retirement. Under defined benefit retirement plans, employers shoulder more of the risk than employees.

defined contribution plan   A type of retirement plan that does not promise a specific monthly benefit (or total benefit) at retirement. Instead, the employer or the employee contribute to the employee's individual retirement savings account. Those contributions are then invested, and these investments can either make money or lose money. In this way, defined contribution plans shift the risk away from the employer (which is where it rests for defined benefit plans) and back onto the employee.

The Delphi Technique   A structured, nonmathematical (qualitative) forecasting technique in which opinions from a variety of experts are sought, distilled, and distilled again. An objective, neutral, uninvolved leader recaps what the experts submit, summarizes that information, and condenses it into a more concise format. (The leader is not one of the experts and does not inject his opinions or interpretations into the process.) This happens several times until a final position is identified—one that incorporates the input of many individuals but that does not unduly reflect any one position or viewpoint.

Deming, W. Edwards   A true quality pioneer who, although unappreciated in America until the 1980s, brought his expertise to Japan, where he was revered until—and long after—his death. One of Deming's most noteworthy contributions is his 14-point quality management program.

demonstration   A training method during which the instructor/facilitator shows the participants how to perform a particular function, duty, or role.

Departmentalization ("departmentation")   The process of dividing related tasks and responsibilities between different units within the organization. Such units are often referred to as "departments." Although each department might address a variety of tasks, all those tasks are related in some meaningful way.

design patents   Granted for the invention of a new, original, and ornamental design for an article of manufacture.

designation of responsibility   The section of an affirmative action plan that identifies the person who has overall responsibility for ensuring the successful implementation of the affirmative action plan.

development/growth   The second stage of the organizational life cycle, during which the organization grows in so many ways. Market share, facilities, equipment, revenues, and the number of employees are all likely to expand, to varying degrees. Along with that growth, the organization is likely to experience some growing pains.

direct compensation   Components of total compensation that are presented to employees in the form of cash.

directing function   Identified by Fayol as one of the five management functions, the directing function is the one during which the actual work is performed—goods are produced or services are provided. In addition to ensuring that things go smoothly from a technical perspective, in the directing phase, the manager must focus attention on leading and motivating the human resources who are actually performing the work.

directive interviews   Highly structured interviews in which interviewers maintain control, in significant part by asking consistent questions of all candidates.

disability   A medical condition or disorder that substantially limits a person's ability to perform major life activities.

disability benefits   One of the three primary components of the Social Security Act.

discrimination   Discrimination, in the truest sense of the word, is not necessarily illegal. To discriminate is to make a distinction or to discern. When distinctions or discernments are made on the basis of factors, traits, or characteristics that are protected by law, however, discrimination becomes unlawful.

disparate impact (also known as adverse impact)   Occurs when a seemingly neutral policy or practice has a disproportionately negative impact on a member (or members) of a protected class. Disparate impact that results from policies or practices that are not job related and that have a statistically significant impact on members of a protected class can constitute unlawful discrimination.

disparate treatment   A type of unlawful discrimination that occurs when an employer intentionally treats one or more applicants or employees differently on the basis of their race, color, sex, religion, national origin, age, disability, or any other characteristic that is protected by law.

distributive bargaining   An approach to collective bargaining in which each side sets forth its position and does its best to stick to it. By the end of the process, one side will have won some (or all) of what it wanted and one side will have lost some (or all) of what it wanted. Distributive bargaining is essentially adversarial in nature. It assumes that "there's only so much to go around." When you divide the pie, one side will end up with more and one side will end up with less.

diversity   Diversity refers to the process of recognizing, valuing, and embracing the many ways in which a group or organization embodies differences and leveraging those differences to enhance the overall performance of individuals and groups.

documentation   Formal and informal notes, memos, emails, and all other written or electronic descriptions or comments created at any point during or after the employment lifecycle, including those that specifically pertain to employee's performance.

double-breasting picketing   A type of picketing that is actually a type of secondary boycott. Double-breasting picketing occurs when a company that owns or operates union as well as nonunion operations shifts work to the nonunion operation in an effort to diminish the impact of the strike. In this situation, the nonunion operation to which the business has been shifted can be picketed.

Drug-Free Workplace Act, 1988   A law that requires federal contractors (with contracts of $100,000 or more) and individuals and organizations who are awarded federal grants (of any size) to agree to maintain a workplace free of illegal drugs.

drug testing   Analysis that ascertains whether drugs are present within a person's body.

E

E-Verify   "An Internet-based system that compares information from an employee's Form I-9, Employment Eligibility Verification, to data from U.S. Department of Homeland Security and Social Security Administration records to confirm employment eligibility" (www.uscis.gov). E-Verify is a voluntary program for some employers and is mandatory for others, such as federal contracts.

economic strike   Any strike that is not directly tied to the union's allegation that the employer has committed a ULP. Economic strikes are

called in an effort to obtain some sort of economic concession from the employer during collective bargaining negotiations—concessions relating to higher wages, better working conditions, lower health insurance premiums, and the like. Economic strikers cannot be terminated except under highly limited situations, such as if they engage in serious misconduct during the strike. (However, note that under the Mackay doctrine, the employer can permanently replace economic strikers.)

effects bargaining   Bargaining that takes place when nonmandatory subjects would have an impact that does fall under the category of required subjects.

effort   One of the four factors used as a basis to assess the substantial equality of job content under the Equal Pay Act of 1963. Effort refers to the amount of physical or mental exertion required to perform the job.

***Ellerth v. Burlington Northern Industries, 1998* (along with *Faragher v. City of Boca Raton, 1998*)**   Key issue: Sexual harassment. Significance: If an employee is subjected to a tangible adverse employment action because of a supervisor's sexually harassing behavior, the employer is liable. The employer is also vicariously liable when its supervisors create a sexually hostile work environment, even if the employee is not subjected to an adverse employment action. This is true regardless of whether the employer itself was negligent or otherwise at fault. However, if the employee is not subjected to tangible adverse employment action, the employer might be able to raise as a defense that it acted reasonably to prevent or promptly correct any sexually harassing behavior and that the plaintiff unreasonably failed to take advantage of the employer's preventive or corrective opportunities.

emergency   An unplanned event that can cause deaths or significant injuries to employees, customers, or the public or that can shut down a business, disrupt operations, cause physical or environmental damage, or threaten the facility's financial standing or public image.

Nearly limitless types of emergencies could fall within the broad scope of this definition—natural, chemical, biological, terrorist, technological. The business impact of most of these can be minimized if organizations have developed, distributed, and rehearsed business continuity and disaster recovery plans in advance.

emergency action plan standard   Although recommended for all employers, an emergency action plan is mandatory only if required by a separate OSHA standard.

employee   An individual who has been hired by an organization to perform work for that organization and who is compensated directly on that employer's payroll system.

employee and labor relations   Employee and labor relations encompass every dimension of relationships at the workplace, with the overall objective of balancing employee's needs and rights with the employer's need to attain short-term, long-term, emerging, and strategic objectives.

employee assistance programs (EAPs)   Employee assistance programs provide employees with help and resources on a variety of personal issues that can—and often do—direct affect employee job performance. As such, EAPs (which are paid for by organizations) benefit employers as well as employees.

employee communication strategies   One cornerstone—perhaps *the* cornerstone— of effective employee relations. Effective communication can't happen by accident; it must be strategized and executed. Organizations must be deliberate about communicating with, and not just communicating to, employees.

employee handbooks   An important and frequently used method that organizations use to communicate information about policies, procedures, and rules. Handbooks provide, in a sense, the "rules of the road" in that they ensure that employees are fully informed (in writing) about the obligations and benefits that are associated with being an employee.

Handbooks can vary widely in terms of the information they contain, their length, the topics they cover, and the tone in which they are written. Organizational culture must be taken into consideration when decisions of this sort are made.

employee hazard communication standard (also known as right-to-know)   Ensures that employers and employees have knowledge and awareness about hazardous chemicals located in the workplace and that they know how to protect themselves. Specifically, this standard requires all employers having hazardous materials at the workplace to implement a written Hazard Communication Program. Four important key elements of this program are material safety data sheets (MSDSs), orientation, training, and container labeling requirements.

employee involvement strategies   Deliberate efforts to actively and meaningfully involve employees in the experience of their own employment. HR professionals must seek to actively and meaningfully involve employees in the experience of their own employment.

employee participation groups   Groups through which employees are invited to participate actively in the process of managing the organization by contributing ideas and providing feedback. Employee participation groups can also provide an excellent way of encouraging creative involvement and enhancing commitment. Although employee participation groups are neither legal nor illegal by definition, the way in which they are administrated can have a huge impact on whether any particular employee participation group is deemed to be legal or illegal under the NLRA.

employee referral   A recruiting technique through which current employees are used as a source for recruiting external candidates into the applicant pool.

employee relations   The way in which an organization responds to, handles, or addresses any issue that has impact on employees and their relationships

- To and with other employees
- To and with managers
- To and with those outside the employment in the organization with whom they come into contact as part of their employment experience

Employee Retirement Income Security Act (ERISA), 1974 A law that was established to protect the interests of those who participate, and the beneficiaries of those who participate, in employee benefit plans. ERISA applies only to programs established by private industry employers. ERISA establishes minimum participation and vesting standards for retirement programs and minimum standards for welfare benefit (including health) plans.

employee stock ownership plans (ESOPs) A type of defined contribution plan in which investments to individual accounts are made primarily in the form of employer stock.

employee surveys (also sometimes called attitude surveys or climate surveys) A vehicle through which employees can express their opinions or share their perspectives. Sometimes employee surveys can even provide a vehicle through which employees can truly contribute in a meaningful and significant way to their organizations by having a voice in shaping the policies, practices, and directions of their organizations.

employer branding The process by and through which organizations deliberately and intentionally decide on the marketing strategy that will be used to promote the employer's brand within the labor market.

employment application Documents/forms (paper or electronic) that seek consistent job-related information from candidates relative to their work history, education, and qualifications.

employment-at-will A common-law tort doctrine under which the employer and the employee are both granted broad rights, most of which focus on the right of either party to terminate the employment relationship at any time for any lawful reason. A number of important exceptions to the employment-at-will doctrine exist, including lawful reasons, public policy exceptions, wrongful terminations, and implied contracts.

Although everyone involved in the hiring/ employment/termination process shares in this responsibility, HR must be particularly diligent about ensuring that a lawful, legitimate, nondiscriminatory reason exists and can be articulated when a decision to terminate an employee is being contemplated.

employment contracts An agreement that addresses and outlines various aspects of the employment relationship and that is binding on the organization as well as on the employee.

employment practices liability insurance (EPLI) Protects businesses in the event of claims by workers or applicants who allege that their legal rights as employees of (or applicants to) the company have been violated. Some insurers provide this coverage as an endorsement to their Businessowners Policy (BOP), whereas others offer EPLI as a standalone coverage.

employment testing Preemployment tests, tools, or instruments used to ascertain the degree to which a candidate possesses and can demonstrate the knowledge, skills, and abilities required to successfully perform the position for which she is applying.

environmental health hazards A type of health hazard that originates in and exists because of something in the workplace. Environmental health hazards refer to a wide spectrum of conditions, circumstances, objects, and organisms in the workplace that can create or increase the likelihood of employee illness or injury.

environmental scanning The process through which organizations maintain awareness of the opportunities and threats presented by the surroundings—both macro and micro—within which they operate.

Equal Employment Opportunity (EEO) Laws, regulations, structures, and processes that are designed to ensure that all employment-related decisions are based solely on job-related factors and without regard to factors including race, color, religion, sex, age, national origin, disability, or other factors protected by law.

Equal Employment Opportunity Act, 1972 Expanded the reach of Title VII of the Civil Rights Act of 1964 to include educational institutions; state, local and federal governments; and private employers who employ 15 or more employees. This Act also allows charging parties a longer period of time within which to file claims and "amends its sex discrimination guidelines to prohibit employers from imposing mandatory leaves of absence on pregnant women or terminating women because they become pregnant. EEOC also states it is sex discrimination for an employer to give women disabled by pregnancy less favorable health insurance or disability benefits than that provided to employees disabled by other temporary medical conditions" (www.eeoc.gov).

Equal Employment Opportunity Commission (EEOC)   The government agency responsible for enforcing Title VII of the Civil Rights Act of 1964 (Title VII), the Equal Pay Act (EPA), the Age Discrimination in Employment Act (ADEA), and the Americans with Disabilities Act (ADA).

Equal Pay Act, 1963   A law that prohibits discrimination on the basis of sex in the payment of wages or benefits to men and women who perform substantially equal (but not identical) work, for the same employer, in the same establishment, and under similar working conditions. (An establishment generally refers to one specific physical location.) Four different factors are used as bases to assess the substantial equality of jobs under the EPA:

- ► Responsibility: The degree of responsibility and accountability that an employer entrusts to and expects from a particular position

- ► Skill: The amount or degree of experience, ability, education, and training required to perform the job.

- ► Working conditions: The physical surroundings of the position, as well as any hazards that are associated with a particular position

- ► Effort: The amount of physical or mental exertion required to perform the job

Similar to the way in which Fair Labor Standards Act (FLSA) status is determined, substantial equality is determined by job content, not job titles.

equity   The value (in financial terms) of the owners' interest in an organization.

ergonomics   The way in which the workplace or workspace is designed.

essay method   A narrative performance appraisal method in which the appraiser writes short essays describing and documenting each employee's performance during the performance measurement period.

ethics   A shared values-based system that serves to guide, channel, shape, and direct the behavior of individuals in organizations in an appropriate and productive direction that is consistent with the values of the organization.

Excelsior List   The list of names and addresses of all employees who are eligible to vote in the union certification election. After the union has obtained recognition, regardless of the way in which that recognition is obtained, the employer must provide the NLRB with this list, which the National Labor Relations Board will in turn provide to the union. The nickname "Excelsior List" is derived from the 1966 NLRB decision *Excelsior Underwear, Inc. v. NLRB.*

Excelsior Underwear, Inc. v. NLRB, 1966   The NLRB case in which the NLRB considered whether "a fair and free election [can] be held when the union involved lacks the names and addresses of employees eligible to vote in that election, and the employer refuses to accede to the union's request." The NLRB ruled that it could not. As a result, the employer must provide the list of employees' names and addresses within seven days after the NLRB has scheduled an election.

executing processes   Those processes (within project management) that "bring everything together," including the project's scope, objectives, and deliverables. In general, executing processes are considered the third of five types of project management processes, although there can be considerable overlap between those five distinct processes.

executive coaching   A professional relationship in which a senior level of the organization works with an individual who helps him to identify and eradicate blind spots, to explore potentially challenging experiences or relationships, or to temper confidence and boldness with other required executive-level professional competencies.

executive exemption   An exemption under the Fair Labor Standards Act (FLSA). To qualify for an executive exemption

- The employee's primary duty must be managing the enterprise or managing a customarily recognized department or subdivision of the enterprise.

- The employee must customarily and regularly direct the work of at least two or more other full-time employees or their equivalent.

- The employee must have the authority to hire or fire other employees, or the employee's suggestions and recommendations as to the hiring, firing, advancement, promotion, or any other change of status of other employees must be given particular weight.

Executive Order 11246   EO 11246, the first employment-related EO, established two key requirements for federal contractors and subcontractors that have contracts in excess of $10,000 during any one-year period:

- These employers are prohibited from discriminating in employment decisions on the basis of race, creed, color, or national origin. This requirement reconfirmed the nondiscrimination requirements established by Title VII of the Civil Rights Act of 1964.

- These employers must take affirmative steps or actions in advertising open positions, recruiting, employment, training, promotion, compensation, and termination of employees to ensure the elimination of employment barriers for women and minorities (people whom we might refer to today as "people of color").

exempt   An employee who is exempt from the overtime (and minimum wage) provisions of the Fair Labor Standards Act (FLSA).

exit interviews   Conversations with employees who are leaving the organization in an effort to obtain helpful, fact-based, job-related information about the departing employee's experience with the organization.

exit routes standard   Mandatory for all employers, the exit route standard defines exit requirements and addresses maintenance, safeguarding, and operational dimensions of exit routes. OSHA defines an exit route as "a continuous and unobstructed path of exit travel from any point within a workplace to a point of safety" (source: OSHA Fact Sheet, Exit Routes).

external equity   The degree to which employees within an organization are fairly compensated with respect to how employees outside of the organization, but within the relevant labor market, are compensated.

external recruiting   The process of creating a pool of qualified candidates who are not currently employed with the organization.

F

factor comparison   A quantitative job evaluation system that involves the ranking of each compensable factor of each job. A monetary value for each level with each factor is subsequently identified. Similar to the point factor method, each job is evaluated with respect to each compensable factor, and the appropriate level (with an accompanying dollar value) is selected. When all the levels that have been selected are added together, a pay rate for each job will emerge.

Failure to Abate Prior Violation   A violation that continues beyond the prescribed abatement date. Occupational Safety and Health Administration (OSHA) may propose a fine of up to $7,000 per day for each failure to abate prior violation.

fair employment practices agencies (FEPAs)   State or local agencies that are responsible for enforcing Equal Employment Opportunity (EEO) laws that are specific to their respective jurisdiction.

Fair Labor Standards Act (FLSA)   A law that establishes standards with respect to minimum wage, recordkeeping, child labor standards, and overtime pay.

Fair Labor Standards Act (FLSA): child labor   The child labor provisions of the FLSA restrict the number of hours (and the times of the day) that children under the age of 16 can work, as well as the types of work that children under the age of 18 can perform.

Fair Labor Standards Act (FLSA): Recordkeeping requirements
Employers must maintain the following basic information:

- Employee's full name and Social Security number

- Address, including ZIP Code

- Birth date, if younger than 19

- Sex and occupation

- Time and day of week when employee's workweek begins

- Hours worked each day

- Total hours worked each workweek

- Basis on which employee's wages are paid (for example, "$9 per hour," "$440 a week," "piecework")

- Regular hourly pay rate

- Total daily or weekly straight-time earnings

- Total overtime earnings for the workweek

- All additions to or deductions from the employee's wages

- Total wages paid each pay period

- Date of payment and the pay period covered by the payment

According to the Department of Labor (DOL), "(e)ach employer shall preserve for at least three years payroll records, collective bargaining agreements, sales and purchase records. Records on which wage computations are based should be retained for two years, i.e., time cards and piecework tickets, wage rate tables, work and time schedules, and records of additions to or deductions from wages. These records must be open for inspection by the Division's representatives, who may ask the employer to make extensions, computations, or transcriptions. The records may be kept at the place of employment or in a central records office" (www.dol.gov).

FairPay   The nickname for the 2004 revisions of the Fair Labor Standards Act (FLSA).

fair use   The right to use copyrighted works without the permission of the author under certain circumstances, such as "criticism, comment, news reporting, teaching (including multiple copies for classroom use), scholarship, or research."

Family and Medical Leave Act (FMLA), 1993   FMLA entitles eligible employees (who work for covered employers) up to 12 weeks of unpaid, job-protected leave during any 12-month period for one or more of the following reasons:

- The birth and care of the newborn child of the employee

- Placement with the employee of a son or daughter for adoption or foster care

- Care for an immediate family member (spouse, child, or parent) with a serious health condition

- Medical leave when the employee is unable to work because of a serious health condition

The FMLA was amended in 2008, thus establishing two new entitlements for military families: "qualifying exigency leave" and "military caregiver leave." Qualifying exigency leave "may be taken for any qualifying exigency arising out of the fact that a covered military member is on active duty or call to active duty status" (www.dol.gov). Military caregiver leave "may be taken by an eligible employee to care for a covered servicemember with a serious injury or illness" (www.dol.gov).

***Faragher v. City of Boca Raton, 1998* (along with *Ellerth v. Burlington Northern Industries, 1998*)**   Key issue: Sexual harassment. Significance: If an employee is subjected to a tangible adverse employment action because of a supervisor's sexually harassing behavior, the employer is liable. The employer is also vicariously liable when its supervisors create a sexually hostile work environment even if the employee is not subjected to an adverse employment action. This is true whether the employer itself was negligent or otherwise at fault. However, if the employee is not subjected to tangible adverse employment action, the employer may be able to raise a defense that it acted reasonably to prevent or promptly correct any sexually harassing behavior and that the plaintiff unreasonably failed to take advantage of the employer's preventive or corrective opportunities.

Fayol, Henri   Known as the father of modern management, Fayol identified five functions of a manager, now referred to as planning, organizing, coordinating, directing, and controlling.

featherbedding   An agreement that requires the employer to pay wages to union members whether or not their work is needed.

Federal Mediation and Conciliation Service (FMCS)   A resource that maintains lists of qualified arbitrators. FMCS was created by the Labor Management Relations Act (LMRA), also known as the Taft-Hartley Act.

federation   A formal group of national unions that choose to affiliate with each other. Its many members speak with one voice, thus wielding even greater influence and lobbying power. Federations do not, however, get involved with bargaining or contract administration.

feedback   Information that is provided to and discussed with an employee relative to her performance and the specific ways in which that performance is meeting or not meeting expectations.

fetal protection policies   Policies that are intended to protect unborn fetuses from the possibility of being harmed by teratogens. The impact of most (if not all) of these policies, as ruled by the Supreme Court, is unlawful gender discrimination.

fiduciary   According to Employee Retirement Income Security Act (ERISA), fiduciaries are those persons or entities "who exercise discretionary control or authority over plan management or plan assets, have discretionary authority or responsibility for the administration of a plan, or provide investment advice to a plan for compensation or have any authority or responsibility to do so are subject to fiduciary responsibilities" (www.dol.gov).

Plan fiduciaries could include, for example, plan trustees, plan administrators, and members of a plan's investment committee.

fiduciary responsibility   Fiduciaries are charged with running the plan(s) for which they are responsible solely in the interest of participants and beneficiaries. They must ensure that the sole purpose of the plan is and remains providing benefits to participants and beneficiaries and paying plan expenses. Fiduciaries must also act with skill, care, prudence, and diligence. For instance, they must protect plan participants by diversifying plan investments and must follow the terms of plan documents to the extent that those terms are consistent with Employee Retirement Income Security Act (ERISA). They also must avoid conflicts of interest, and, many would argue, even the possibility of an appearance of a conflict of interest (the same standard to which HR professionals should hold themselves).

field review   A narrative performance appraisal method in which someone other than the employee's supervisor—someone from HR, for instance—prepares the performance appraisal.

financial perspective   One of the four perspectives of the balanced scorecard. The financial perspective is the most traditional of Kaplan's and Norton's four perspectives.

financial ratios   Mathematical calculations/ metrics in which different items from the financial statement are divided, one into another, to provide information on organizational performance. This information can subsequently be analyzed to reach conclusions and inform organizational decision-making.

fire safety standard   Although recommended for all employers, a fire safety plan is mandatory only if required by a separate Occupational Safety and Health Administration (OSHA) standard.

first-impression error/bias (interviewing)   An interviewing error/bias that occurs when the interviewer places an inordinate level of emphasis on the impression that the candidate makes on him during the first few minutes, seconds, or even moments of the interview.

first-impression error/bias (performance management)   A performance management error/ bias in which the appraiser forms an impression of the employee's performance early in the performance measurement period (or, even worse, early in the individual's employment) and places an inordinate level of emphasis on that impression.

fishbone diagram (also known as the cause-and-effect diagram or Ishikawa diagram)   An important quality tool developed by Ishikawa that presents a visual representation of factors that impact whether a desired outcome will be obtained. Ishikawa believed that by presenting all the possible factors that contribute to a particular result, any potential process imperfections can be identified in advance and eliminated.

flexible spending accounts (FSAs)   A type of Section 125 plan. Flexible spending accounts (FSAs) enable employees to set aside pretax dollars to pay for medical expenses that are not covered by insurance. FSAs can also be set up for dependent care. Employees decide how much money to set aside for the following year, and that amount is automatically deducted from the employee's pay on a pretax basis. After incurring and paying for eligible expenses, employees apply for reimbursement from the FSA.

focus groups   An important vehicle for communicating with and involving employees in the organization. A focus group consists of a small but representative sample of individuals within an organization. Within each focus group, discussions are led by a neutral facilitator who seeks to elicit feedback and input on a specific subject.

for-cause drug testing   Drug testing that is conducted when an employee shows obvious signs of not being fit for duty, in an effort to protect the safety and well-being of employees and coworkers and to identify opportunities for rehabilitation.

forced distribution method (also known as the forced ranking method)   A comparative performance appraisal method in which the appraiser ranks the performance of her direct reports so that, overall, the performance levels of all the employees, when looked at together, reflect a bell-shaped curve.

forced ranking method (also known as the forced distribution method)   A comparative performance appraisal method in which the appraiser ranks the performance of his direct reports so that, overall,

the performance levels of all of the employees, when looked at together, reflect a bell-shaped curve.

formalization, or formal authority   The rights, privileges, and power that is inherent to a particular position, and which thus is granted to an individual upon selection for or appointment to a particular position. This type of authority is often codified in some way. It is often historically present in the same position, but such authority can be imbued to—or even taken away from—positions as intentional organizational changes are implemented.

formative evaluation   A process by which evaluative feedback and input is sought throughout the development and implementation phases in an effort to strengthen the ultimate training initiative through real-time incorporation of evaluative feedback.

formula budgeting   An approach to budgeting in which the proposed budget is developed by applying a consistent formula to the current budget figures (for instance, 3% increase).

four absolutes of quality management   Phil Crosby's four absolutes of quality management include

▶ Quality means conformance to requirements, not goodness.

▶ Quality is achieved by prevention, not appraisal.

▶ Quality has a performance standard of zero defects, not acceptable quality levels.

▶ Quality is measured by the price of non-conformance, not indexes.

full cafeteria plan   The most comprehensive and administratively burdensome of the three types of Section 125 plans. Employers who offer full cafeteria plans provide their employees with a specific amount of money they can use to pick and choose from a variety of benefits programs.

functional structure   An organizational structure in which positions (and, consequently, employees who hold those positions) are grouped according to the relatedness of the functions they perform.

G

gainsharing   Incentive plans that are designed to motivate employees to reach specific goals relating to cost cutting or revenue generation and that share a portion of that savings (or that increased revenue) with the employees who helped to achieve it. Gainsharing plans are based on team/group performance, not individual performance.

General Duty Clause   Part of the Occupational Health and Safety Act (OSHA) that identifies two primary duties for employers (ensuring a safe workplace and complying with all current and future OSHA-related standards) and one for employees (following all safety and health-related rules stemming from the Act).

General Dynamics Land Systems v. Cline (2004)   Key issue: Age dscrimination (relative). Significance: Younger employees (even if they are over the age of 40) cannot allege age discrimination because of the establishment of programs or decisions that favor older employees. As Justice David Souter wrote in the opening of his opinion, "The Age Discrimination in Employment Act of 1967 (ADEA or Act), 81 Stat. 602, 29 U.S.C. [section] 621 et seq., forbids discriminatory preference for the young over the old. The question in this case is whether it also prohibits favoring the old over the young. We hold it does not."

general industry   One of the major industries designated by OSHA.

Genetic Information Nondiscrimination Act (GINA), 2008   Under Title II of GINA, it is "illegal to discriminate against employees or applicants because of genetic information. Title II of GINA prohibits the use of genetic information in making employment decisions, restricts employers and other entities covered by Title II (employment agencies, labor organizations and joint labor-management training and apprenticeship programs—referred to as 'covered entities') from requesting, requiring or purchasing genetic information, and strictly limits the disclosure of genetic information" (www.eeoc.gov).

"The law forbids discrimination on the basis of genetic information when it comes to any aspect of employment, including hiring, firing, pay, job assignments, promotions, layoffs, training, fringe benefits, or any other term or condition of employment. An employer may never use genetic information to make an employment decision because genetic information is not relevant to an individual's current ability to work" (www.eeoc.gov).

geographic pay differentials   Monetary adjustments made to pay/pay structures as a way of adjusting for different cost of living levels in different locations.

Global Professional in Human Resources (GPHR)   The Global Professional in Human Resources certification, granted by and issued through Human Resource Certification Institute (HRCI). The GHPR focuses on cross-border HR functions.

goals/objectives   Statements that express and communicate performance expectations in terms of "what" is expected to be produced.

good faith bargaining   Refraining from behaviors during the collective bargaining process that could constitute bad faith bargaining. The following behaviors, when demonstrated by either the union or the employer, could constitute bad faith bargaining:

- Failing to agree to meet at reasonable and convenient places or times
- Failing to show up at the agreed-upon places or times
- Repeatedly canceling meetings
- Failing to maintain an "open mind" during negotiations
- Surface bargaining: going through the motions of bargaining, with no real intent of ultimately reaching agreement (in other words, keeping bargaining "at the surface," without moving toward true agreement)
- Repeatedly withdrawing previous positions/concessions
- Refusing to bargain on mandatory items, insisting on bargaining on permissive items, or attempting to bargain on illegal items
- Committing any sort of unfair labor practices (ULPs)

graded vesting   A vesting arrangement in which an employee earns a nonforfeitable right to an increasing percentage of her employer's contributions over a period of years.

grades (also referred to as pay grades or job grades)   "Levels" into which jobs of similar internal worth can be categorized. Jobs within the same grade share a similar level of value or worth to the organization. Different organizations will have different numbers of pay grades, with differing degrees of distinction between each of those grades.

green circle rates   A pay rate for an hourly or salaried employee that is set below the maximum rate of the range for the position that the employee holds.

Griggs v. Duke Power, 1971   Key issue: Adverse impact. Significance: Discrimination need not be deliberate or observable to be real. Rather, it can exist if a particular policy or practice has a statistically significant adverse impact upon members of a protected class. This is true even when the same requirement applies to all employees or applicants, as was the situation in this case. When a particular requirement does have an impact on members of a protected class, the burden of proof rests with the employer to demonstrate that the requirement is, in fact, job related and consistent with business necessity.

gross profit margin   A mathematical calculation/ metric that divides gross profit by revenues. The resulting quotient is a measure of the organization's profitability.

group interviews   An interview in which more than one candidate is participating.

Some organizations use the term "group interview" to describe a "panel interview." These are, however, two different types of interviews— the group interview being the less common of the two types.

Grutter v. Bollinger and Gratz v. Bollinger (2003)   Barbara Grutter was applying for admission to the University of Michigan Law School, and Jennifer Gratz was applying for the University of Michigan as an undergraduate student. Lee Bollinger was the president of the University of Michigan.

Key issue: Affirmative action. Significance: Race can be taken into account as an admissions factor because it furthers the establishment of diversity—a "compelling state interest"—as long as the admissions process is "narrowly tailored" to achieve the objective of achieving a diverse student body.

Interestingly, Supreme Court Justice Sandra Day O'Connor indicated that cases of this sort will likely be ruled differently in the future: "Race-conscious admissions policies must be limited in time. The Court takes the Law School at its word that it would like nothing better than to find a race-neutral admissions formula and will terminate its use of racial preferences as soon as practicable. The Court expects that 25 years from now, the use of racial preferences will no longer be necessary to further the interest approved today."

These cases fall under the category of "reverse discrimination" because they alleged race discrimination and were brought by people who were not minorities/people of color.

H

halo error/bias (interviewing)   An interviewing error/bias that occurs when the interviewer evaluates the candidate positively on the basis of one outstanding qualification or characteristic.

halo error/bias (performance management)   A performance management error/bias in which the appraiser evaluates the employee positively on the basis of one outstanding qualification or characteristic.

Harris v. Forklift Systems, 1993   Key issue: Sexual harassment. Significance: The court clarified the standard relative to what constitutes a sexually hostile work environment: "This standard, which we reaffirm today, takes a middle path between making actionable any conduct that is merely offensive and requiring the conduct to cause a tangible psychological injury. Conduct that is not severe or pervasive enough to create an objectively hostile or abusive work environment—an environment that a reasonable person would find hostile or abusive—is beyond Title VII's purview. Likewise, if the victim does not subjectively perceive the environment to be abusive, the conduct has not actually altered the conditions of the victim's employment, and there is no Title VII violation."

hazard communication standard (also known as employee right-to-know)   Ensures that employers and employees have knowledge and awareness about hazardous chemicals located in the workplace and that they know how to protect themselves. Specifically, this standard requires all employers having hazardous materials at the workplace to implement a written hazard communication program. Four important key elements of this program are material safety data sheets (MSDS), orientation, training, and container labeling requirements.

HBV (hepatitis B virus)   The virus that causes Hepatitis B, a potentially serious (and potentially fatal) form of liver inflammation.

HCV (hepatitis C virus)   The virus that causes Hepatitis C, a viral infection of the liver.

health and welfare benefits   A variety of nonretirement, nonmandatory benefits that can be effective ways of attracting, motivating, and retaining employees.

health and wellness programs   Programs that offer employees the opportunity to enhance the quality of their lives (usually proactively, but also reactively) through healthier lifestyle choices.

health hazards   Anything in the workplace that creates or increases the possibility of work-related injuries.

Health Insurance Portability and Accountability Act (HIPAA), 1996   An amendment to Employee Retirement Income Security Act (ERISA) that has two primary focuses: the security and portability of health care coverage, and privacy considerations.

With respect to the security and portability of health care coverage, HIPAA was intended to help

workers experience greater security and portability with respect to health care coverage, even when an employee changes jobs. HIPAA also afforded significantly greater protections for employees who have or who have a family member with a preexisting medical condition.

health maintenance organization (HMO)   A managed care model of health care and health insurance. In an HMO, each participant chooses a primary care physician, or PCP, who serves as a gatekeeper. Participants must see their PCPs first, and the PCP then decides whether to refer the patient to a specialist or for additional tests.

high-potential employees   Current employees who demonstrate behaviors and who perform responsibilities in a way that indicates that they are capable of significant growth within the organization. Although they might not possess all the knowledge or skills they will ultimately need to fulfill higher level roles, they have been identified as individuals who have the requisite behavioral characteristics, as well as the capability to learn what needs to be learned to contribute in more strategic roles and ways.

highly compensated employee exemption   An exemption under the FLSA. To qualify for a highly compensated employee exemption, an employee must

▶ Earn $100,000 or more annually (of which at least $455 per week must be paid on a salary or fee basis)

▶ Perform office or nonmanual work

▶ Customarily and regularly perform at least one of the duties of an exempt executive, administrative, or professional employee identified in the standard tests for exemption

HIPAA covered entity   One of three groups of individuals or corporate entities (health plans, health care providers, and health care clearinghouses) that are covered by Health Insurance Portability and Accountability Act's (HIPAA's) privacy rule, which thus requires specific actions regarding protected health information (PHI):

▶ Enact written PHI privacy procedures

▶ Designate a privacy officer

▶ Require business associates to sign agreements stating they will respect the confidentiality of PHI

▶ Train all employees in HIPAA privacy rule requirements

▶ Establish a complaint handling and resolution process for issues related to the HIPAA privacy rule

▶ Ensure that PHI is not used for making any employment-related decisions

HIPAA privacy rule   Designed to protect patients and other consumers of health care services from the unauthorized disclosure of any personally identifiable health information (protected health information, or PHI). Health information is considered to be personally identifiable if it relates to a specifically identifiable individual.

histogram   A graph that depicts information about a single factor. In addition to being used to graphically communicate information, histograms can sometimes help identify patterns or explanations.

HIV (human immunodeficiency virus)   The virus that causes AIDS (acquired immune deficiency syndrome).

horns error/bias (interviewing)   An interviewing error/bias that occurs when the interviewer evaluates the candidate negatively on the basis of one poor characteristic or dimension of performance.

horns error/bias (performance management)   A performance management error/bias in which the appraiser evaluates the employee negatively on the basis of one poor qualification or characteristic.

hostile work environment   A form of sexual harassment that occurs when unwelcome sexual conduct unreasonably interferes with an individual's job performance or creates a hostile, intimidating, or offensive work environment. Hostile work environment harassment can be found to exist whether the employee experiences

(or runs the risk of experiencing) tangible or economic work-related consequences. By definition, hostile work environments can be created by virtually anyone with whom an employee might come in contact in the workplace.

hot cargo agreements   An agreement entered into by an employer in which the employer agrees to stop doing business with another entity. Hot cargo agreements can thus help to protect union work by allowing union members to refuse to handle or process work produced by nonunion entities. Hot cargo agreements were made illegal by the Landrum-Griffin Act.

hourly wages   The hourly pay that an employee earns for performing her job, regardless of level of performance demonstrated.

hours worked   "Hours worked" means "hours worked," not "hours paid." In other words, according to the Fair Labor Standards Act (FLSA), hours that have been paid but not worked (vacation time, sick time, holiday time, jury duty time, and the like) do not count toward the 40-hour overtime threshold (although some organizations may voluntarily choose to count these hours toward the 40-hour threshold). "Hours worked" also doesn't mean "hours approved to work." If an employer "suffers or permits" a nonexempt employee to work, that employee must be compensated for that time. So, whether the employer requires the employee to work or simply allows the employee to work, the time counts as "hours worked" and must be compensated appropriately.

HR audit   The primary tool that many HR departments use to assess their own effectiveness and efficiency with respect to ascertaining how well they have aligned themselves with the organization's strategic objectives.

HRIS   An integrated computer-based system that collects, processes, analyzes, stores, maintains, and retrieves information relating to all dimensions of the HR function.

human processual interventions   Organization development (OD) interventions that seek to effect change and impact relationships within (and between) groups and individuals.

Human Resource Certification Institute (HRCI) HRCI is the credentialing organization of the HR profession.

human resource development Human resource development employs effective training, development, change management, and performance management functions and initiatives to ensure that the skills, knowledge, abilities, and performance of the workforce will meet the short-term, long-term, emerging, and strategic objectives of the organization.

I

I-9 The form (mandated by IRCA) that documents an employee's identity and eligibility to legally work in the United States.

Identification of Problem Areas The section of an affirmative action plan that provides an in-depth analysis of its total employment process to determine whether and where impediments to equal employment opportunity exist.

illegal subjects Topics that simply cannot be the subject of collective bargaining. These would include items that would constitute a violation of the NLRA, subsequent labor laws, or (for that matter) any law.

Immigration Reform and Control Act (IRCA), 1986 A law that prohibits employers from discriminating against job applicants on the basis of national origin and from giving preference to U.S. citizens. IRCA also established penalties for those who knowingly hire illegal aliens (people who are referred to, by some individuals and organizations, as "undocumented workers," rather than "illegal aliens").

imminent danger Occupational Safety and Health Administration's (OSHA's) highest priority for investigation, and defined in the Act as "any conditions or practices in any place of employment which are such that a danger exists which could reasonably be expected to cause death or serious physical harm immediately or before the imminence of such danger can be eliminated through the enforcement procedures otherwise provided by this Act."

implementation theory A theory that focuses on carrying out specific strategies—in this case, organization development (OD) interventions—that are designed to bring about the unfreezing, moving, and refreezing through Lewin's change process theory.

implied contracts A tort doctrine under which an employee can allege that a promise of employment has been created, even when that promise is not explicitly written or articulated. Sometimes the language that is used within employer-published documents (electronic or hardcopy) can actually be sufficient to create a contract between the employer and the employees. An oral contract can be created when an "agent" of the employer "promises" some benefit or right. The term "agent" is legal and involved, but the point is this: be careful what your supervisors, recruiters, and others say to current, and especially to potential, employees.

incentive plans Variable compensation plans that establish specific financial and nonfinancial goals and targets for individuals, groups, and organizations. For incentive programs to be effective, employees need to believe that they can attain the goals that have been set as part of the incentive program and that the reward that they would earn by attaining those goals is sufficiently worthwhile.

income statement A financial instrument that enumerates and documents revenues and expenses over a particular period of time.

incremental budgeting A process by which a new budget is developed using the budget for the current period as a starting point. This form of budgeting constitutes a "tweaking" of the current budget, rather than an approach that starts from the beginning.

indemnity insurance The most traditional type of medical insurance plan. Indemnity plans provide participants with (virtually) unrestricted choices relative to their doctors, hospitals, and other health care providers. Health care providers are paid a fee for the services they actually provide and perform.

independent contractor   An individual who has been retained by an organization to perform work for that organization and who is not compensated directly on that employer's payroll system.

indirect compensation   Components of total compensation that are presented to employees in forms other than cash. This could include but is not necessarily limited to

- ▶ Legally mandated benefits (such as social security)

- ▶ Medical insurance

- ▶ Dental insurance

- ▶ Long-term disability insurance

- ▶ Vision coverage

- ▶ Vacation time

- ▶ Holiday time

- ▶ Recognition programs (such as peer recognition programs, noncash spot awards, achievement awards, "pizza parties," desirable parking, and so on)

- ▶ Perquisites (also known as "perks," such as a company car, club memberships, financial planning, legal services, and so on)

individual, small group, or large group activities/ applications   A training method during which the instructor provides participants with an opportunity to immediately apply the knowledge they have learned or the skills they have developed through hands-on application.

industrial relations   One of the earlier monikers by which the HR profession was known.

infectious diseases   Viral or bacterial diseases that can be transmitted from person to person.

initiating processes   Those processes (within project management) that secure approval or authorization to undertake the project. In general, initiating processes are considered the first of five project management processes, although there can be considerable overlap between those five distinct processes.

initiative   A series of programs that, together, support a multipronged approach to attain specific organizational objectives. An initiative constitutes an investment that should have a positive ROI and that should further the overarching mission and objectives of the organization, while remaining consistent with its values and vision.

Injury and Illness Incident Report (also known as the OSHA Form 301)   A form that must be completed for each work-related injury or illness within seven calendar days of the date on which the employer learns of the work-related injury or illness and that must be maintained by the employee for five years following the year in which the incident or illness occurred.

integrative bargaining   An approach to collective bargaining that looks at multiple issues as a whole. Instead of just splitting up the pie, it creatively considers how it might be able to "make the pie bigger." It looks at how the needs of both sides can be better met when looked at in their entirety and at how a win-win solution can be explored, rather than settling for the win-lose scenario that will almost invariably result from distributive bargaining. In essence, advocates of integrative bargaining believe that an agreement that renders one side "better off" does not necessarily have to result in the other side being "worse off." Instead, through creativity and cooperation, trade-offs are sought that will ultimately benefit both sides.

integrity, or honesty, tests   Preemployment tests that are used to ascertain the degree to which a candidate would be likely to engage in behavior that is dishonest or that reflects a potential lack of integrity.

internal audit and reporting system   An auditing system that periodically measures the effectiveness of an organization's total affirmative action program.

internal equity   The degree to which employees within an organization are fairly compensated with respect to how other employees within the same organization are compensated.

internal recruiting   The process of creating a pool of qualified candidates from individuals who are already employed with the organization.

Two primary mechanisms for seeking internal candidates for positions within the organization are job posting and job bidding.

international labor organizations   A formal group of labor organizations that operates on the international level in much the same manner as federations operate on the national level, only bigger.

interviewing error/bias   Factors that are not related to a job that (when not identified and managed) can taint or affect an interviewer's assessment of a candidate.

introduction/birth   The first stage of the organizational life cycle, during which excitement and energy are high and cash flow may be low. Struggling start-ups often find themselves searching for solid footing, financially as well as operationally. The core group of highly talented employees who join the organization during the introduction/birth stage of the organizational life cycle may focus fixedly on the founder as a source of direction, wisdom, and inspiration.

intrusion of solitude   A tort doctrine that refers to one person's invasion of another person's privacy either with or without electronic devices, when such intrusion would be highly offensive to a reasonable person.

invasion of privacy   The right to privacy is a key issue in the workplace and "workspace" (meaning the electronic dimensions of the workplace as well as the physical ones). Modern tort law includes four categories of invasion of privacy, all of which employers need to be aware:

▸ Intrusion of solitude

▸ Public disclosure of private and embarrassing facts

▸ False light

▸ Appropriation of identity

inventory   The supply of goods and materials that is poised for production, sales, or to support customer service.

involuntary terminations   A decision, initiated by the employer, to end the employment relationship.

Ishikawa diagram (also known as the "cause-and-effect" diagram or "fishbone" diagram)   An important quality tool developed by Ishikawa that presents a visual representation of factors that affect whether a desired outcome will be obtained. Ishikawa believed that, by presenting all the possible factors that contribute to a particular result, any potential process imperfections can be identified in advance and eliminated.

Ishikawa, Kaoru   A quality guru committed to the idea of continued customer service, even after the customer purchases the product. Ishikawa also believed strongly in the criticality of securing top-level management support and dramatically increased worldwide awareness and acceptance of the idea of quality circles, originally a Japanese philosophy.

J

job analysis   The process by which information about a specific position is collected and through which (up to) three important outputs are generated: a job description, job specifications, and job competencies.

job bidding   A system that invites employees to express interest in any internal position at any time, even if a position is not currently available.

job classification   A nonquantitative, whole job evaluation technique that categorizes jobs into broad categories, or "levels," based on the level—and, ultimately, value to the organization—of the work that is performed by jobs within each job level. Each level incorporates specific responsibilities and benchmark statements that describe the nature, complexity, autonomy, and so on of the work that is performed by positions in that level.

job competencies   Broad categories of behavioral characteristics that are required to perform successfully in a particular position, department, or organization. They are often referred to by organizations as "key success factors," "competencies for success," or "performance factors." They could include things such as "communication skills," "teamwork," or "judgment."

job description   A document that contains information about a job, such as the essential functions, expected outputs, key accountabilities, requirements, and so forth of the position. This information is collected through the job analysis process.

job evaluation   The process through which every job in an organization is assessed and compared to other jobs in the organization. At the conclusion of the job evaluation process, it will be possible to knowledgeably ascertain the relative worth of each job within the organization. When this is done for positions, an overall job worth hierarchy has been created.

job group analysis   The section of an affirmative action plan that nonconstruction contractors use to begin the process of comparing the employer's representation of women and minorities to the estimated availability of qualified women and minorities who are available to be employed.

job match   An external position to which an internal job is compared during the market pricing process.

job posting   A system that announces position openings to current employees within the organization.

job slotting   A nonquantitative, whole job evaluation technique that incorporates or "slots" newly created or revised positions into an existing job hierarchy. This process of slotting is accomplished by comparing the new or revised job descriptions to job descriptions of positions that have already been evaluated and assigned within the hierarchy.

job-specific employment applications   Employment applications that are tailored to seek highly specific and relevant information pertaining to one specific position.

job specifications   The skills, knowledge, abilities, behavioral characteristics, and other credentials and experience necessary to perform a position successfully.

Johnson v. Santa Clara County Transportation Agency, 1987   Key issue: Affirmative action. Significance: Gender can be used as a factor in the selection process if there is underrepresentation in a particular job classification, as long as the AAP does not set forth a quota.

This case falls under the category of "reverse discrimination" because it alleged sex discrimination and was brought by a man.

joint resolutions   A resolution passed by the Senate as well as the House of Representatives that has the force of law after it has been either signed by the president or passed over the veto of the president.

Juran, Joseph M.   A giant in the area of quality who focused on the perspectives and the needs of customers and whose quality management ideas focused on three key areas: quality planning, quality improvement, and quality control.

jurisdictional strikes   A strike through which a union seeks to pressure an employer to assign particular work to its members rather than to members of other unions or to nonunion workers.

K–L

Kirkpatrick, Donald L.   Kirkpatrick's theory takes a "summative" approach to evaluation in that it is predicated on the interpretation of data that is collected after the initiative has been implemented. Kirkpatrick's approach, therefore, allows for a complete analysis of the entire initiative on four levels: reaction, learning, behavior, and results.

Knowles, Malcolm   Identified five key assumptions about how adults learn:

- ▶ Learner's need to know
- ▶ Learner's self-concept
- ▶ Role of learner's experience
- ▶ Readiness to learn
- ▶ Orientation to learning

Kolstad v. American Dental Association, 1999   Key issue: Punitive damages under the Civil Rights Act of 1991. Significance: Punitive damages can be awarded only when the employer has acted with malice and reckless indifference to the employee's federally protected rights. This subjective standard was considered to be easier to establish than the more objective standard that would be required if employees had to prove that the nature of the actual behavior to which they had been subjected reached a level where it would be considered "egregious."

KSAs The minimally acceptable levels of knowledge, skills, and abilities required to successfully perform a position.

Labor Management Relations Act (also known as the Taft-Hartley Act), 1947 An amendment designed to remedy what the Republican Congress saw as two major omissions in the National Labor Relations Act (NLRA) (Wagner Act): first, the identification of behaviors and practices that would be considered unfair labor practices (ULPs) on the part of unions, and second, a provision that would allow the government to issue an injunction against a strike that threatened national interests. The Labor-Management Relations Act identified the following unfair labor practices that could be committed by unions:

- Restraining or coercing employees in the exercise of their rights or an employer in the choice of its bargaining representative

- Causing an employer to discriminate against an employee

- Refusing to bargain with the employer of the employees it represents

- Engaging in certain types of secondary boycotts

- Requiring excessive dues

- Engaging in featherbedding

- Picketing for recognition for more than 30 days without petitioning for an election

- Entering into hot cargo agreements

- Striking or picketing a health care establishment without giving the required notice

Labor Management Reporting and Disclosure Act (also known as the Landrum-Griffin Act), 1959 A law that created additional labor-management guidelines, including

- A requirement that unions submit annual financial reporting to the Department of Labor (DOL) to document how union members' dues were spent

- A bill of rights for union members guaranteeing them freedom of speech and periodic secret elections

- The designation of every union official as a fiduciary

- Even stronger provisions relative to secondary boycotting and organizational and recognition picketing

labor market competitors Other employers with whom you are competing for talent.

labor relations Labor relations speaks to the many dimensions and facets of the relationship between management and groups of workers who happen to be represented by a labor union. In some ways, labor relations can be thought of as a subset of employee relations. (See the definition for employee relations.)

lag the market A compensation approach in which an organization chooses, by design, or simply because of budgetary constraints, to offer total compensation packages that are less competitive than the total compensation packages that are being offered by their labor market competitors. Organizations that lag the market might offset this potential disadvantage by reinforcing and maximizing the intrinsic rewards that it offers— long-term potential growth opportunities, the ability to contribute to a particularly significant organizational mission, and so on.

Landrum-Griffin Act (also known as the Labor Management Reporting and Disclosure Act), 1959 A law that created additional labor-management guidelines, including

- A requirement that unions submit annual financial reporting to the Department of Labor (DOL) to document how union members' dues were spent

- A bill of rights for union members guaranteeing them freedom of speech and periodic secret elections

▶ The designation of every union official as a fiduciary

▶ Even stronger provisions relative to secondary boycotting and organizational and recognition picketing

lead the market   A compensation approach in which an organization offers total compensation packages that are "better" than packages being offered by their labor market competitors. Organizations that lead the market may believe that higher compensation packages will attract higher-performing employees who will, in turn, pay for themselves and then some. In short, these organizations want the best of the best and are willing to pay for it.

leadership development   The strategic investment in the managers and leaders who work within the organization.

leafleting   The onsite or offsite distribution of leaflets and flyers.

learned professional exemption   An exemption under the FLSA. To qualify for a learned professional exemption

▶ The employee's primary duty must be the performance of work requiring advanced knowledge, defined as work that is predominantly intellectual in character and which includes work requiring the consistent exercise of discretion and judgment.

▶ The advanced knowledge must be in a field of science or learning.

▶ The advanced knowledge must be customarily acquired by a prolonged course of specialized intellectual instruction.

learning and growth perspective   One of the four perspectives of the balanced scorecard. This perspective looks at employee training as well as attitudes toward individual and corporate growth. It emphasizes the criticality of the knowledge worker, of people as the organization's primary resource, and of the need for employees to continually grow and learn so they can perform in a manner that will truly support the attainment of organizational goals.

learning level evaluation   Measures whether and to what degree participants have mastered the skills or acquired the knowledge explored through the learning objectives. "Pre-tests" and "post-tests," which are frequently seen in e-learning applications, are one means of assessing skills development and knowledge acquisition.

learning organization   An organization in which individuals at all levels strive to acquire knowledge and develop skills that will enable them, individually and collectively, to attain higher levels of performance. The concept of a learning organization is fundamental to human resource development (HRD) and is often supported through training initiatives.

learning styles   Different ways that people learn and process ideas and information. There are three different learning styles: visual, auditory, and tactile/kinesthetic.

lecture/lecturette   A training method that includes presenting information to participants. Lecturettes are simply shorter versions of lectures.

leniency error/bias (interviewing)   An interviewing error/bias that occurs when the interviewer applies an inappropriately lenient standard to one or more candidates, resulting in a higher overall assessment of the candidate(s).

leniency error/bias (performance management)   A performance management error/bias in which the appraiser applies an inappropriately lenient standard to one or more employees, resulting in a higher overall assessment of the employee's (or employees') performance.

Lewin, Kurt   Lewin first described the change process as one that involves three stages: unfreezing, moving, and refreezing.

liability   Any financial obligation that an organization must pay, either presently or in the future.

life insurance   A health and welfare benefit that helps employees provide their beneficiaries and loved ones with income in the event of their deaths. Many employers offer a certain amount of life insurance at no cost to employees and offer optional supplemental life insurance, as well.

Lilly Ledbetter Fair Pay Act, 2009 "Under the Act, an individual subjected to compensation discrimination under Title VII of the Civil Rights Act of 1964, the Age Discrimination in Employment Act of 1967, or the Americans with Disabilities Act of 1990 may file a charge within 180 (or 300) days of any of the following:

▶ When a discriminatory compensation decision or other discriminatory practice affecting compensation is adopted;

▶ When the individual becomes subject to a discriminatory compensation decision or other discriminatory practice affecting compensation; or

▶ When the individual's compensation is affected by the application of a discriminatory compensation decision or other discriminatory practice, including each time the individual receives compensation that is based in whole or part on such compensation decision or other practice" (www.eeoc.gov).

liquidity A calculation of available cash or assets that could be quickly converted to cash with no loss in value.

lobbying The process of reaching out to elected officials to express beliefs and opinions with the hope of influencing a governmental body.

local union A specific level of a union organization that is largely responsible for the day-to-day administration of the labor agreement and relationship with union members. "Locals" generally have an elected president and elected stewards who represent the workers in the workplace. Larger local unions might have a full-time paid business agent. Most locals belong to and are chartered by a larger national union.

lockout A scenario in which an employer refuses to allow unionized employees to work.

Log of Work-Related Injuries and Illnesses (also known as the OSHA Form 300) A form used to record the "what," "how," "when," "where," and "who" of all work-related injuries and illnesses. It must be completed within seven calendar days from the time the organization learns of a work-related injury or illness.

long-form employment applications Employment applications that require candidates to provide more detailed and comprehensive information about their work history, education, and qualifications.

long-term disability insurance (LTD) A health and welfare benefit that provides employees with the opportunity to replace a designated percentage of an employee's income that is lost through illness or injury.

long-term incentive programs Incentive programs that are usually more than one year in duration.

M

Mackay Doctrine The doctrine that grants employers the right to permanently replace workers who strike during an economic strike. This right and this nickname are derived from the 1938 Supreme Court decision in *NLRB v. Mackay Radio and Telegraph Co.*

maintenance of membership Employees who voluntarily choose to join a union must maintain their individual memberships for the duration of the labor contract. Each employee then has a 30-day window at the beginning of the next contract period during which she may terminate membership. Maintenance of membership arrangements are illegal in right-to-work states.

major life activities Include but are not necessarily limited to walking, seeing, hearing, breathing, caring for oneself, performing manual tasks, sitting, standing, lifting, learning, and thinking. Major bodily functions are also considered to be a major life activity. Furthermore, according to the Equal Employment Opportunity Commission (EEOC), "the determination of whether an individual's (condition) substantially limits a major life activity is based on the limitations imposed by the condition when its symptoms are present (disregarding any mitigating measures that might limit or eliminate the symptoms)" (www.eeoc.gov).

major restorative care A category of dental care or coverage that includes more involved procedures such as bridgework and crowns and that usually has a lower reimbursement percentage (perhaps 50%).

management by objectives (MBO) A rating method type of performance appraisal, or a goal-centered organization development (OD) intervention, that focuses primarily on collaboratively generating individual employee objectives that align with organizational objectives. Measurement is an essential element of an MBO program. As follows logically, MBO is often used as a performance appraisal method because of its strong orientation toward goal establishment and attainment.

management by walking around (MBWA) A management approach where a manager makes a commitment to spend a dedicated amount of time with employees on a regular basis. By increasing her visibility, the manager creates opportunities to provide feedback to and receive input from employees. MBWA also helps ensure that employees have increased access to "the boss," thereby increasing the potential for spontaneity, creativity, and synergy.

mandatory arbitration agreements A type of employment agreement that stipulates that, in return for the opportunity to be employed by the organization, the employee agrees to resolve employment-related issues through a neutral third party (the arbitrator/s) instead of filing a private lawsuit against the employer.

mandatory subjects (also known as required subjects) Subjects that must be bargained in good faith if either the employer or the employees' representative requests it. Examples of required subjects include pay; wages; hours of employment; pensions for present employees; bonuses; group insurance; grievance procedures; safety practices; seniority; procedures for discharge, layoff, and recall; discipline; and union security.

maritime One of the major industries designated by Occupational Safety and Health Administration (OSHA).

market data Data that is collected through the process of market pricing. Market data can be obtained about a number of benchmark positions as part of a larger initiative and can be used in a number of ways. For instance, market data can help in the building of a job-worth hierarchy, around which other positions can be placed using a whole job slotting technique. Market data can also be used to obtain information for one particular job in combination with other job evaluation techniques that might be used.

market pricing A process of looking at the relevant labor market to ascertain what the going rate or market rate is for a particular position. Market pricing can yield valuable pay data about "benchmark" jobs—jobs for which close matches can be identified in the relevant labor market.

Martin v. Wilks, 1988 Key issue: Affirmative action. Significance: Current employees who are negatively impacted by consent decrees that were established in an earlier time and which sought to resolve discrimination that was present in an earlier time may challenge the validity of such decrees.

This case falls under the category of "reverse discrimination" because it alleged race discrimination and was brought by individuals who were not minorities/people of color.

mass layoff Occurs (under Worker Adjustment and Retraining Notification Act [WARNA]) when one of the following two events happens within a 30-day period at a single worksite: 500 full-time employees are laid off or at least 33 percent of the workforce is laid off (if and only if that 33% includes between 50 and 499 full-time employees).

match the market A compensation approach in which an organization chooses to offer total compensation packages that are comparable to the total compensation packages being offered by their labor market competitors. Organizations that match the market make a conscious choice to be "externally competitive" with respect to total compensation.

material safety data sheet (MSDS) Required (by the Hazard Communication Standard) for all chemicals located in the workplace.

matrix structure An organizational structure in which individuals have two reporting relationships. The first usually relates to function, whereas the second often relates to the project assignment or geographical location.

maturity The third stage of the organizational life cycle, during which the growing pains have passed and the culture is well established. It's important to ensure that certain elements of the culture do not become a bit too well established. If this were to happen, an "entitlement mentality" could begin to emerge relative to pay or benefits. The organizational structure could evolve in a somewhat rigid manner, and resistance to organization development (OD) and change initiatives could be high.

McDonnell Douglas Corp v. Green, 1973 Key issue: Disparate treatment/prima facie. Significance: The initial burden of proof for establishing a prima facie (Latin for "at first view") case of discrimination against an employer (or potential employer) under Title VII of the Civil Rights Act of 1964 rests with the employee (or applicant), who must be able to establish four key elements:

► The person is a member of a protected class.

► The person applied for a job for which the employer was seeking applicants.

► The person was rejected despite being qualified for the position.

► After this rejection, the employer continued to seek other applicants with similar qualifications.

After the employee establishes a prima facie case for disparate treatment, the burden of proof then shifts to the employer, which must provide a nondiscriminatory reason for its decision.

McGehee and Thayer Identified three levels of human resource development (HRD)/training needs analysis and assessment: organizational analysis, task or work (operations) analysis, and individual or person (man) analysis.

McKennon v. Nashville Banner Publishing Co., 1995 Key issue: After-acquired evidence. Significance: An employer will be held accountable for discriminatory employment actions even if it discovers evidence after taking the discriminatory employment action that would have led the employer to that same employment action for legitimate, nondiscriminatory reasons.

mechanistic organizations An organizational model that is characterized by a clear hierarchical structure, centralization, and clear and unambiguous lines of authority and responsibility. Mechanistic organizations are similar to bureaucracies but are often less complex, simpler, and smaller.

medical tests Preemployment medical tests, or exams, that can be conducted only if the exam is job related and consistent with business necessity, and even then only after an offer (or a conditional offer) of employment has been extended to the candidate.

medical and first aid standard Occupational Safety and Health Administration (OSHA) requires employers to provide medical and first aid personnel and supplies in accordance with the hazards of the workplace. The specifics of each program, however, will differ from workplace to workplace and from employer to employer.

Medicare (1966) An amendment to the Social Security Act that provides hospital and medical insurance for the elderly and people with disabilities. There are four parts to Medicare: hospital insurance (sometimes called Part A), medical insurance (sometimes called Part B), Medicare advantage plans (sometimes called Part C), and prescription benefits (sometimes called Part D).

► **Medicare—Part A** The portion of Medicare that helps pay for inpatient hospital care, skilled nursing care, and other services

► **Medicare—Part B** The portion of Medicare that helps pay for items such as doctor's fees, outpatient hospital visits, and other medical services and supplies

► **Medicare—Part C** The portion of Medicare available to persons who are eligible for Part A and enrolled in Part B through which private health insurance companies can contract with the federal government to offer Medicare benefits through their own policies

► **Medicare—Part D** The portion of Medicare that added prescription drug benefits for all individuals eligible for Medicare Part A and enrolled in Medicare Part B

Mental Health Parity Act (MHPA), 1996 A law that prohibits group health plans providers, insurance companies, and health maintenance organizations (HMOs) that offer mental health benefits from setting annual or lifetime dollar limits on mental health benefits that are lower than any such dollar limits for medical and surgical benefits.

mentoring A professional relationship in which one person shares his insights and personal experiences with individuals who are usually less experienced and who may work at a lower hierarchical level within the organization. Mentors often offer advice and guidance and may even provide direction.

merit pay Increases to earnings that are given to employees on the basis of performance during a specified period of time (such as a performance measurement period) that is ideally aligned with the performance appraisal system.

Meritor Savings Bank v. Vinson, 1986 Key issue: Sexual harassment. Significance: This was the first ruling to establish that sexual harassment (whether quid pro quo or hostile environment) constitutes a violation of Title VII of the Civil Rights Act of 1964. In addition, the court ruled that it isn't enough for an organization to have a policy prohibiting discrimination. Instead, the ruling stated that "reasonable care requires effective communication of policies and training. The employer has the burden of proof."

Mine Safety and Health Act (MSH Act), 1977 The second piece of legislation created specifically to protect employee health and safety—this time for underground and surface miners working in coal as well as non-coal mines.

minimum wage The lowest hourly rate of pay that an employer can legally pay an employee.

mission A statement that articulates, in essence, why the organization is in existence. It may speak to the nature of the organization's business or purpose, its customers, and sometimes even its employees and its role in the community. A mission statement should be broad (but not overly generalized), brief, clear, unambiguous, and designed to last for "the long haul."

modeling In this context, modeling refers to individuals at all levels of the organization—especially the upper levels, in organizations that are not flat—demonstrating behaviors that are reflective of the organization's values and the behaviors that are considered to be appropriate and consistent with and supportive of the organization's overarching vision and mission.

monitoring software Software that employers often install to block or report when employees/contractors have accessed websites could cause the organization risk. This risk can take many forms, ranging from lost productivity, to the introduction of viruses, to corporate espionage.

moving The second stage in Lewin's change process theory. Through the moving stage, people are brought to accept the change and experience the "new state" that the change was designed to bring about.

multiple linear regression A mathematical technique that examines the past relationship between several variables, determines the statistical strength of that relationship, and, on the basis of that analysis, projects future conditions.

musculoskeletal disorders (MSDs) Work-related illnesses or injuries that affect one or more parts of the musculoskeletal system.

N

narrative method Performance appraisal method in which the appraiser uses a narrative format to write and record observations and assessments of each employee's performance.

National Industrial Recovery Act, 1933 A law that guaranteed laborers the right to organize and bargain collectively (Title I). The Act also established that employees could not be required, as a condition of employment, to join or refrain from joining a labor organization. In May 1935, the National Industrial Recovery Act was held unconstitutional by the U.S. Supreme Court (*Schechter Poultry Corp. v. United States*). Although this decision was wholly unrelated to labor and collective bargaining, the Supreme Court decision rendered the labor-related provisions illegal as well. The right to organize and bargain reverted, once again, to railway workers and no one else. This would not, however, be the case for long.

National Labor Relations Act (also known as the Wagner Act), 1935   A law that guaranteed "the right to self-organization, to form, join, or assist labor organizations, to bargain collectively through representatives of their own choosing, and to engage in concerted activities for the purpose of collective bargaining or other mutual aid and protection." Certain groups or categories of employees are excluded under the NLRA from membership in a bargaining unit. Examples would include managers, supervisors, confidential employees (essentially secretaries and administrative assistants to managers who can make labor relations decisions), and several others.

National Labor Relations Board (NLRB)   A federal agency created by the National Labor Relations Act (NLRA) that is responsible for administering and enforcing the rights established by the NLRA. As stated on its website, the NLRB has two principle functions:

▶ To determine, through secret-ballot elections, the free democratic choice by employees whether they want to be represented by a union in dealing with their employers and if so, by which union

▶ To prevent and remedy unlawful acts, called unfair labor practices, by either employers or unions

national union   A specific level of a union organization that brings together all the union locals for a particular group that is scattered across the country. There are usually different hierarchical levels in between the local union and the national union. National unions have far more power with respect to bargaining and political influence than the union locals could have on their own. National unions also advise and guide local unions and may manage nationwide benefits programs (such as retirement programs and health insurance plans).

The Needlestick Safety and Prevention Act of 2000   A compliance directive for enforcing the Bloodborne Pathogens Standard that added three key requirements to the existing standard:

▶ Evaluation and implementation of safer needle devices (as they become available). Reviews of and searches for such enhancements must be done annually.

▶ Actively involving employees who actually use needles and needle devices in this evaluation and selection process of safer needle devices.

▶ Maintenance of a log of all injuries resulting from contaminated sharps.

negligent hiring   A tort doctrine that speaks to an employer's decision to hire an individual without engaging in appropriate "due diligence" into that candidate's credentials, prior work experience, and the like. In essence, negligent hiring claims arise after an individual is hired through a flawed hiring process. A hiring process can be flawed for a number of reasons. For instance, a sound hiring process that is applied in an unsound manner would be flawed, as would a hiring process that is designed in a flawed manner. Flaws could relate to inadequate or poorly conducted reference checks, job requirements that do not reflect the skills or credentials that are truly required for a position, and the like.

negligent referral   A tort doctrine that speaks to the failure of an organization to reveal truthful, negative information about an employee (or former employee) to a potential employer.

negligent retention   A tort doctrine that speaks to the continued employment of an individual who is performing in an unfit manner and, therefore, should have been terminated. Negligent retention tort claims might be filed when an employee who should have been terminated but was not inflicts some sort of harm on another person. Negligent retention claims are often filed in conjunction with other tort claims, such as negligent training, intentional infliction of emotional distress, and the like.

negligent training   A tort doctrine that refers to an employer's failure to provide proper training to an employee when that failure results in some sort of unfit performance by the employee.

Negligent training can emerge as an issue either when an employee who was hired for one position assumes another position for which she may not be fully and appropriately trained or when an employee's job duties and responsibilities change over time, thus requiring additional training if the employee is to continue performing the job in a fit manner.

NLRB v. Mackay Radio and Telegraph Co., 1938   The Supreme Court case that established that employers have the right to permanently replace workers who strike during an economic strike.

NLRB v. Weingarten, 1975   Weingarten Rights, derived from the Supreme Court decision in *NLRB v. Weingarten, 1975*, established the right of unionized employees to have union representation at an investigatory interview with management if the employee reasonably believes that discipline might result from that meeting. Although the NLRB reversed this decision in 2000 (Epilepsy Foundation of Northeast Ohio, 331 NLRB 676) and held that nonunion employees also have the right to have a representative present at a meeting of this sort, in 2004 the NLRB returned to its original determination and held that nonunion employees do not have the right to have a coworker or other representative present in a meeting when the employee reasonably believes it might result in discipline.

nominal group technique   A nonmathematical, qualitative forecasting technique that calls upon the expertise and predictive ability of experts who meet in person and process their ideas as a group. Led by a facilitator, the meeting begins with each expert writing down his ideas, after which each expert presents those ideas to the group. The group then comes together to discuss everyone's ideas, after which each group member is called upon to independently rank the ideas. The meeting facilitator will then combine all the individual rankings to determine which are the most important to the group.

noncompete agreements   A type of employment agreement that prohibits current and (within stated limitations) former employees from competing against the employer. "Competing" can manifest itself in a number of ways and must be defined within the agreement.

nondirective interviews   Relatively unstructured interviews through which the candidate, not the interviewer, guides and controls the flow and content of information discussed.

nonexempt   An employee who is covered by the overtime (and minimum wage) provisions of the Fair Labor Standards Act (FLSA).

nonquantitative job evaluation techniques   Job evaluation techniques that determine the relative value of jobs within the organization without using mathematical techniques. Instead, these methods focus on the "whole job" (which is why these techniques are also referred to as "whole job" methods).

nontraditional staffing alternatives   Work arrangements that do not fall clearly within "internal" or "external" recruiting methods because they could be used as a retention tool for existing employees, as a way to attract candidates, or as a way to outsource current assignments. Examples of nontraditional staffing alternatives could include the use of temporary help, temp-to-hire arrangements, or consultants. Current or newly hired employees can also participate in flexible staffing programs through part-time employment, telecommuting, job sharing arrangements, or seasonal employment.

nonverbals   Also known as "body language" or "nonverbal communication cues," nonverbals refer to communication that is not based on spoken language.

Norris-LaGuardia Act, 1932   A law that strengthened unions even more by establishing the rights of labor unions to organize and to strike. It also prohibited federal courts from enforcing "yellow dog" contracts or agreements.

O

occupational health, safety, and security Occupational health, safety, and security promotes employees' physical and mental well-being while maintaining a reasonably safe and nonviolent work environment, all in support of the employer's short-term, long-term, emerging, and strategic objectives.

Occupational Safety and Health Act (OSH Act), 1970 The first law to establish consistent health and safety standards for the workplace.

Occupational Safety and Health Administration (OSHA) The federal agency created to administer and enforce the Occupational Safety and Health Administration Act (OSH Act).

offshoring A specific type of outsourcing that uses vendors that are located overseas.

Old Age, Survivors, and Disability Insurance (OASDI) (also known as the Social Security Act) OASDI is a social insurance program (although some would define it differently) that is funded through payroll taxes. Its three primary components are retirement income, disability benefits, and survivor's benefits.

Older Worker's Benefit Protection Act (OWBPA), 1990 An amendment to the Age Discrimination in Employment Act (ADEA) that makes it illegal to discriminate against older workers with respect to benefits or to target older workers for layoffs.

onboarding (also known as orientation) The process by which a new employee transitions into the organization.

open-door policy A "standing invitation," and a genuine one, for employees to raise their concerns with managers or human resources, face to face. The use of an "open door" cannot result in penalties, formal or otherwise, against those employees who avail themselves of this resource.

open shop Employees are required neither to join the union nor to pay union dues. This is the only type of union security clause that is legal in right-to-work states (and for federal government employees).

operational/tactical HR Somewhere in between the administrative functions that must be performed to keep our organizations going and the inventive and creative life force that is part of strategic management lies the operational or tactical dimension of the HR function. The operational, tactical, or day-to-day performance and execution of the HR role can be accomplished in many ways, some of which do more to define us toward the administrative end of the spectrum, and others that demonstrate more vividly how and whether the overarching strategic objectives of HR (and, therefore, of the organization) are being brought to life. Operational/tactical level HR is one leg of the HR stool; the other two legs are strategic HR and transformational HR.

organic organizations An organizational model characterized by fluidity, responsiveness, agility, and decentralization. This is accomplished through a relatively flat organizational structure, coupled with full engagement in and commitment to nurturing a culture that is free from siloes (or a "siloed mind-set").

organization development (OD) The planned and structured process through which the overall performance, growth, and effectiveness of an organization is enhanced through strategic, deliberate, and integrated initiatives. The interesting and complex area of OD incorporates four academic disciplines: psychology, sociology, anthropology, and management.

organization transformation change Organizational development (OD) interventions that focus on the organization as a complex human system that must be continually examined and reexamined.

organizational branding The process by which an organization creates, establishes, and maintains a distinct and differentiating image of itself in the minds and memories of consumers in an effort to create positive associations and, in turn, increase brand loyalty.

organizational culture The "way things are done around here"; the formal and informal manifestation of what the organization "is all about." Organizational culture encompasses historical events, current events, and future events (whether potential, likely, or simply rumored). More specifically, organizational culture reflects and embodies the norms, mores, values, beliefs, customs, and attitudes of the organization and of those who work within the organization.

organizational display   The section of an affirmative action plan that essentially provides an organization chart that depicts the contractor's workforce in terms of incumbents' race, gender, and wages. The organization display is the newer, shorter, and simpler version of the "workforce analysis."

organizational (or business) ethics   A shared values-based system designed to inculcate within the organization's population a sense of how to conduct business properly.

organizational-level analysis   Level 1 of McGehee and Thayer's three levels of human resource development (HRD)/training needs analysis and assessment. Organizational-level analysis determines where HRD/training can and should be used within the overall organization.

organizational life cycle   Four evolutionary stages of birth, growth, maturity, and decline experienced by organizations over the course of time. These phases or stages are roughly approximate to the phases of life experienced by humans, thereby further bolstering the perspective of the organization as a living, breathing entity. Each phase of the organizational life cycle will warrant different HR systems or interventions.

organizational picketing   Picketing that is designed to generate interest on the part of employees to vote for union representation.

organizational structure   The various ways in which organizations can be designed to attain maximum levels of effectiveness and efficiency.

organizing function   Identified by Fayol as one of the five management functions, organizing speaks to the ways in which the manager obtains and arranges the resources that she needs to implement the plans (the output of the "planning" function). Those resources could include people, facilities, materials, and so on.

orientation (also known as onboarding)   The process by which a new employee is supported as he transitions into the organization.

orthodonture   A specialty type of dental coverage that is often covered at a relatively low percentage (perhaps 50%) and that often has a lifetime cap per covered employee.

OSHA 3165   A poster that lists each employee's rights related to health and safety. This poster must be displayed in a conspicuous place that is easily visible to employees and applicants for employment.

OSHA Form 300 (also known as the Log of Work-Related Injuries and Illnesses)   A form used to record the "what," "how," "when," "where," and "who" of certain work-related injuries and illnesses and that must be completed within seven calendar days from the time the organization learns of a work-related injury or illness.

OSHA Form 300A (also known as the Summary of Work-Related Injuries and Illnesses)   A form used to record a numeric summary of all work-related injuries and illnesses logged in OSHA's Form 300 over the course of each calendar year. This form indicates the number of cases, the number of workdays impacted, and the numbers and types of work-related injuries and illnesses. A worksheet is also available to assist employers in filling out this summary. Each year, a completed Form 300 must be posted conspicuously for three months (between February 1 and April 30).

OSHA Form 301 (also known as the Injury and Illness Incident Report)   A form that must be completed for each work-related injury or illness within seven calendar days of the date on which the employer learns of the work-related injury or illness and that must be maintained by the employee for five years following the year in which the incident or illness occurred.

other-than-serious violation   A violation that is unlikely to result in serious injury or death. OSHA may propose a fine of up to $7,000 for each other-than-serious violation.

outside sales exemption   An exemption under the FLSA. Unlike the other types of exemptions, a minimum salary is not required to establish an exemption on the basis of outside sales. The following criteria, however, must be met:

▶ The employee's primary duty must be making sales (as defined in the FLSA) or obtaining orders or contracts for services or for the use of facilities for which a consideration will be paid by the client or customer.

▶ The employee must be customarily and regularly engaged away from the employer's place or places of business.

outplacement support   Assistance provided to employees who are being involuntarily terminated for reasons unrelated to cause. The purpose of this assistance is to empower departing employees to find new employment. This could include resume preparation, mock interviewing, networking assistance, coaching, and more.

outsourcing   The reassignment of responsibilities, functions, or jobs that had been performed within the organization to now be carried out by resources that are outside the organization ("third-party contractors").

overtime   Hours worked in excess of 40 per week.

overtime pay   Compensation paid to employees who are not exempt from the overtime provisions of the FLSA, and who work in excess of 40 hours/week, at a rate of 1-1/2 times the employee's regular rate of pay.

P

paired comparison method   A comparative performance appraisal method in which the appraiser compares every employee in the group, one at a time, to every other employee in the group.

panel interviews   Interviews in which more than one person interviews a candidate at the same time.

Patient Protection and Affordable Care Act (PPACA, ACA), 2010   The ACA, also sometimes known as "Obamacare," requires all Americans to secure healthcare coverage and expands coverage limits (financial and nonfinancial).

Pareto Principle (also known as the 80–20 rule)   A principle asserting that 80% of effects result from 20% of causes. The Pareto principle and the chart that visually depicts it are intended to help individuals focus their efforts where there is the greatest likelihood of bringing about the desired change.

pay for time not worked   Programs that pay employees for time that they did not actually work (for instance, sick days, vacation days, jury duty, personal time, designated holidays, floating holidays, bereavement leave, and the like).

pay grades (also referred to as grades or job grades)   Levels into which jobs of similar internal worth can be categorized. Jobs within the same pay grade share a similar level of value or worth to the organization. Different organizations will have different numbers of pay grades, with differing degrees of distinction between each of those grades.

pay structures   The "building blocks" that are used to create compensation systems that will support the total compensation philosophy of the organization, and that will, in turn, support the attainment of the organization's objectives.

pedagogy   The study and science of how children learn.

Pension Benefit Guaranty Corporation (PBGC)   A government corporation created by ERISA that functions as an insurer that provides a minimum guaranteed benefit for certain pension plans. PBGC protects participants in most defined benefit plans and cash balance plans (within certain limitations). PBGC is funded by insurance premiums that are paid by plan sponsors, not by general tax dollars. Funding also comes from investment income, assets from underfunded pension plans it has taken over, and recoveries from companies formerly responsible for those plans.

Pension Protection Act (PPA), 2006   A law that brought about "significant changes to section 101(f) of ERISA by enhancing the content of the notice and extending the requirement to provide notice to single-employer plans (www.dol.gov).

performance appraisal   The form that is reviewed during the meeting that takes place at the end of the performance measurement period, during which the manager and the employee review the employee's performance during the prior year and look ahead to the next year.

performance management   Day-to-day activities in which managers engage with their employees as they work to collaboratively accomplish organizational objectives.

performance management process/system   A series of steps that, together, comprise an ongoing performance management system or process.

performance standards/expectations   The expectations that an organization has for an employee with respect to what she is responsible for accomplishing and the ways in which the employee executes her position.

permissive subjects (also known as voluntary subjects)   "Permissive" subjects of bargaining are topics that can be submitted to collective bargaining if and only if the employer and the employees' representative are willing to do so. Attempting to force bargaining on a voluntary or permissive subject constitutes an unfair labor practice (ULP).

perpetuating past discrimination   Unlawful discrimination that occurs when an employer's past discriminatory practices are perpetuated through current policies or practices—even those that appear to be nondiscriminatory. When linked in some way with past discrimination, seemingly nondiscriminatory practices can have a discriminatory effect.

person (man) level analysis   Level 3 of McGehee and Thayer's three levels of human resource development (HRD)/training needs analysis and assessment. Person (man) level analysis assesses the performance of a particular individual.

personality tests   Preemployment tests that are used to gather information about a candidate's personality traits, motivation, discipline, and other characteristics.

phone interviews   A telephone-based prescreen interview that is used as one important tool to determine which candidates will be invited in for a face-to-face interview.

physical hazards—design   A physical hazard that results from the way in which the workplace or workspace is designed (also referred to as ergonomics).

physical health hazards   A type of health hazard that results from actual, tangible things or conditions in the workplace that increase the risk of work-related illnesses or injuries.

picketing   An expression of free speech that takes place when people congregate outside a workplace. To be considered protected concerted activity, picketing must remain nonviolent.

piece-rate systems   Compensation programs under which individuals are paid according to their production volume.

pilot programs   A training program that is generally delivered to a subsection of the population of individuals who would ultimately be expected to participate in the training initiative. Others who might participate in a pilot program could be decision makers, senior management (from whom you want to secure buy-in), and key stakeholders.

placement goals   The section of an affirmative action plan that establishes goals for areas in which underutilization exists.

plaintiff   A party who files a lawsuit alleging unlawful discrimination.

planning function   Identified by Fayol as one of the five management functions, planning lays the groundwork for the way managers will work toward accomplishing the organization's goals. Through planning, managers decide what needs to get done, when it needs to get done, who will do it, how it will get done, and where it will be done.

planning processes   Those processes (within project management) through which objectives are established, along with the best alternatives that will support the attainment of those objectives. In general, planning processes are considered the second of five project management processes, although there can be considerable overlap between those five distinct processes.

plant closing   Occurs (under Worker Adjustment and Retraining Notification Act [WARNA]) when a facility or operating unit is shut down for more than six months or when 50 or more employees at a worksite lose their jobs during any 30-day period.

plant patents   Granted for the invention, discovery, or asexual reproduction of any distinct and new variety of plant.

point factor   A quantitative job evaluation system that first identifies specific compensable factors and then establishes levels of performance within each of those compensable factors. The relative importance of each compensable factor to the organization is "weighted," and a different point value is then assigned to each level within each compensable factor.

point of service (POS)   A type of managed healthcare plan that is a combination of the health maintenance organization (HMO) and the preferred provider organization (PPO) managed care models. Like the PPO model, there is a network of physicians and health care providers who have agreed to provide services at a discounted rate. Like the HMO model, there is a gatekeeper, a primary care physician who must provide plan members with referrals to specialists and for other services. Unlike the HMO model, however, referrals can be made to physicians who are either inside or outside the network. Although out-of-network referrals will cost participants more, they are permissible.

Portal to Portal Act, 1947   An amendment to the Fair Labor Standards Act (FLSA) that offered clearer definitions of "hours worked" for purposes of minimum wage and overtime payments. According to the Act, employers are only required to compensate workers for working time that they spend on activities that relate to the performance of their job.

postaccident drug testing   Drug testing that is conducted for employees who are involved in an accident or unsafe practice incident to determine whether alcohol or some other drug was a factor, protect the safety of employees (users and nonusers), and identify opportunities for rehabilitation.

predictive validity   The degree to which the predictions made by a selection procedure actually manifest themselves through future performance.

preemployment drug testing   Drug testing that is conducted to decrease the likelihood of hiring someone who is currently using/abusing illegal drugs.

preexisting condition   Under Health Insurance Portability and Accountability Act (HIPAA), a condition for which medical advice, diagnosis, care, or treatment was recommended or received during the six-month period prior to an individual's enrollment date.

preferred provider organization (PPO)   A managed care health care plan that offers a network of health care providers who band together to offer services at a discounted rate to plan participants. PPOs resemble indemnity plans, in that network providers are paid when they render services and plan participants can choose which doctors they want to visit and when they want to visit them. Plan participants can also choose to avail themselves of doctors or other health care providers who are outside the network; however, the costs to the member will be higher than they would have been if the member had chosen a doctor within the network.

Pregnancy Discrimination Act, 1978   A law that amended Title VII of the Civil Rights Act of 1964 to specifically prohibit discrimination on the basis of pregnancy, childbirth, or related medical conditions.

premium only plans (POPs)   The simplest and most transparent (from employees' perspectives) of the three Section 125 plans. With POPs, employees pay for their portion of certain insurance premiums on a pretax basis. The net effect is that each employee's taxable income is reduced, which is how employers and employees can reduce taxes and save money.

prepromotion drug testing   Drug testing that is conducted to decrease the likelihood of promoting someone who is currently using/abusing illegal drugs. This may not apply to public-sector employers unless permitted by the collective-bargaining agreement or for safety-sensitive positions.

prescreen interviews   An interview used early in the selection process to determine which candidates meet specific predetermined job requirements.

prescription drug coverage   A health and welfare benefit that affords employees with discounted or (less frequently) free prescription drugs. Some employers provide prescription drug coverage as part of their medical plan, whereas others provide this coverage under a separate plan. Plan members may be required to pay a copay, to purchase their prescriptions at certain pharmacies, to use generic drugs (when available), or to use mail order services for maintenance drugs (prescriptions that are prescribed for chronic, long-term conditions and that are taken on a regular, recurring basis).

preventive care   A category of dental care or coverage that includes things such as regular dental checkups, exams, cleanings, and sometimes X-rays. It is often reimbursed at 100% of cost or at 100% of reasonable and customary (R&C) expenses to encourage plan members to take advantage of measures that encourage good oral health and that potentially decrease long-term costs.

primary care physician (PCP)   A member's primary physician, who in health maintenance organization (HMO) and point of service (POS) models is the "gatekeeper" who must provide plan members with referrals to specialists and for other services.

primary duty   The principal, main, major, or most important duty that the employee performs. Determination of an employee's primary duty must be based on all the facts in a particular case, with the major emphasis being on the character of the employee's job as a whole.

primary questions   Questions that are asked of all candidates for a particular position during a particular interview process. They are designed to elicit relevant information about how well the candidate possesses and would demonstrate the skills, knowledge, abilities, behavioral characteristics, and other requirements of the position.

primary research   A process that involves collecting data firsthand from the original source from which it emanates.

principled negotiation   Roger Fisher and William Ury, authors of *Getting to Yes: Negotiating Agreement Without Giving In*, assert that a good agreement is one that is wise and efficient and that ultimately results in everyone involved developing a stronger relationship with each other than they would have had if they had not gone through this negotiation process together.

Fisher and Ury set forth four principles of principled negotiation that can be used effectively in a variety of situations to resolve many types of disputes. Those four principles are

- ▶ Separate the people from the problem.
- ▶ Focus on interests rather than positions.
- ▶ Generate a variety of options before settling on one.
- ▶ Resolve disagreements by focusing on objective criteria.

privacy case   In an effort to preserve privacy, under certain circumstances (including upon employee request), the words "privacy case" should be substituted for the employee's name in the OSHA Form 300 (also known as the Log of Work-Related Injuries and Illnesses). In these cases, a separate document must be maintained that matches case numbers with employee names (for identification purposes).

probing questions   The questions that an interviewer asks as a way of following up to the candidate's response to primary questions. Because they are asked in response to each candidate's initial response to the primary question, probing questions will vary from interview to interview. Interviews can still ensure consistency, however, by asking probing questions that relate only to each original primary question.

Professional in Human Resources (PHR)   The PHR certification, granted by and issued through Human Resource Certification Institute (HRCI).

profit sharing   Organizationwide incentive plans that establish an organizationwide profit goal. If the goal is reached, the profits are shared with employees. Profits can be shared either immediately (cash profit-sharing plans) or later (deferred profit-sharing plans).

profit sharing plans   A type of defined contribution plan under which the organization contributes to its employees' accounts. These contributions often come from profits and thus serve as an incentive to performance.

profitability ratio   A mathematical calculation/metric that measures how well an organization has been able to generate profit (revenues less expenses) during a particular period of time.

progressive discipline   A system that incorporates a series of steps—each more progressively involved, advanced, or serious, than the last—for addressing performance or behavior that does not meet expectations. Progressive discipline provides multiple opportunities, at multiple decision points, for employees to make decisions that will result in them maintaining their employment. When applied appropriately, therefore, progressive discipline can be an empowering process as well as an employee relations initiative.

project management   "The application of knowledge, skills, tools, and techniques to a broad range of activities in order to meet the requirements of a particular project" (Project Management Institute).

protected class   A group defined by a common characteristic that is protected from discrimination and harassment on the basis of law. People who share a common characteristic and who are protected from discrimination and harassment on the basis of that shared characteristic are said to belong to a protected class.

protected concerted activity   Protected concerted activity refers to associational rights that are granted to employees through Section 7 of the NLRA. Protected concerted activity can include activity aimed at improving employees' terms and conditions of employment. Through this language, the NLRA protects associational rights for employees who do not belong to a union as well as for employees who are unionized. This interpretation was confirmed by 1948. As such, employers need to be careful not to interfere with protected concerted activities even in workplaces that are nonunionized.

public domain   Copyrights eventually expire, upon which the work enters the public domain. This means that the work is available and free for all to use. In addition, many federal government works are considered to be in the public domain.

Q

qualified domestic relations order (QDRO)   Court orders that require employers to make benefit payments to a participant's former spouse (or another alternative payee) without violating Employee Retirement Income Security Act's (ERISA's) prohibitions against assignment or alienation of benefits. Required information for a QDRO includes

- The name and last known mailing address of the participant and each alternate payee
- The name of each plan to which the order applies
- The dollar amount or percentage (or the method of determining the amount or percentage) of the benefit to be paid to the alternate payee
- The number of payments or time period to which the order applies (www.dol.gov)

qualified person   A candidate who meets minimum job requirements (education, experience, licenses, and so on) and can perform the essential functions of the position with or without reasonable accommodation.

qualified retirement plans   Offer benefits to employees and employers by allowing employees to contribute funds to a retirement savings account on a pre-tax basis. Employers also receive a tax benefit for making contributions to these plans (sometimes "matching" what an employee has contributed, up to a certain percentage of her salary). Qualified retirement plans can be structured as either defined contribution or defined benefit plan.

quantitative job evaluation techniques   Job evaluation techniques that determine the relative value of jobs within the organization without using mathematical techniques. Quantitative (or "factor-based") job evaluation methods identify the degree to which each position is responsible for or requires specific "compensable factors."

quid pro quo   A form of sexual harassment that occurs when an individual's submission to or rejection of sexual advances or conduct of a sexual nature is used as the basis for employment-related decisions. Quid pro quo harassment, by nature, originates from a supervisor or from others who have the authority to influence or make decisions about the terms and conditions of the employee's employment.

R

Railway Labor Act, 1926   A law that provided what was perhaps the first "win-win scenario" for labor and management. Railroad management wanted to keep the trains moving, which meant they needed to end "wildcat" strikes. Railroad workers wanted to organize, to be recognized as the exclusive bargaining agent in dealing with the railroad, and to negotiate and enforce agreements. The Railway Labor Act addressed both issues. The Railway Labor Act is also significant in that it is where the "work now, grieve later" rule originated. In an effort to keep the rails running, which Congress felt was in the public's interest, Congress mandated that when disputes arise in the workplace, transportation workers covered by the RLA must "work now and grieve later" (with a few exceptions, such as for safety).

The Railway Labor Act applied only to interstate railroads and their related undertakings—at the time, the most critical element of the nation's transportation infrastructure. In 1936, it was amended to include airlines engaged in interstate commerce.

random drug testing   Unannounced drug tests that are conducted at random, for reasons related to safety or security.

range spread   The percentage that is calculated by subtracting the minimum of the range from the maximum of the range and dividing that number by the minimum of the range. Range spreads allow organizations to recognize and compensate

employees within the same job and within jobs that are in the same grade, for different levels of skill, experience, or performance.

ranges   A range of compensation rates that correspond to grades and that guide the pay rates for jobs within that grade. Ranges specify the lowest (minimum) and the highest (maximum) compensation rates for which positions within each grade are generally paid. The halfway point between those two figures is known as the midpoint.

range spread   The percentage that is calculated by subtracting the minimum of the range from the maximum of the range and dividing that number by the minimum of the range. Range spreads allow organizations to recognize and compensate employees within the same job and within jobs that are in the same grade, for different levels of skill, experience, or performance.

ranking method   A comparative performance appraisal method in which the appraiser "ranks" his direct reports in terms of overall performance, from "best" to "worst."

rapport   The process of helping a candidate to relax and feel comfortable and welcome at the beginning of the interview.

rapport building questions   The process of asking simple questions or making "small talk" with the intention of helping a candidate to relax and feel comfortable and welcome at the beginning of the interview.

rating methods   Performance appraisal methods in which the appraiser compares the performance of the employee against the expected behavior.

rating scales   A rating method type of performance appraisal in which the appraiser rates the employee on a variety of different categories using a three-, four-, or five-point scale. Those categories can consist of individual goals, individual competencies, multiple goals, groups of competencies, and the like. Each point on the scale corresponds to a different level of performance against standards.

ratio analysis   A mathematical technique that examines changes, movements, and trends over a period of time. Instead of looking at just one variable, however, it looks at two variables and how the relationship between those two variables has evolved over time.

reaction level evaluation   Measures participants' responses and reactions to a program immediately after it has been delivered. This level of evaluation often takes the form of a short survey that participants are asked to complete at the end of a training session.

reading   A training method during which the instructor/facilitator directs the participants to read specific printed materials.

realistic job preview   A realistic picture of the position and the organization (that is provided to candidates). This, in turn, will help the candidate make a realistic and accurate assessment of whether she will be willing or able to function effectively within the day-to-day realities of the position, the department or unit, and the organization.

reasonable accommodation   A change in the way that one (or more) responsibilities relating to the execution of a position is performed, so as to enable a person with a disability to perform the essential functions of the position. Accommodations do not necessarily have to be adopted if they are unreasonable—in other words, if they cause undue hardship to the organization.

reasonable cause   A determination made by the Equal Employment Opportunity Commission (EEOC) relative to whether discrimination has occurred. If the EEOC determines that there is no reasonable cause, the case is closed, the parties are notified, and the charging party is given a "right to sue" letter. The charging party then has 90 days to file a private lawsuit.

If the EEOC determines that there is reasonable cause, the EEOC will attempt conciliation with the employer in an effort to develop a remedy for the discrimination. If the EEOC cannot conciliate the case, the EEOC will decide whether to take the case to court. (This happens in a small percentage of cases.) If the EEOC does not take the case to court, it will close the case and issue the charging party a "right to sue" letter.

reasonable suspicion drug testing   Drug testing that is conducted when an employee has a documented pattern of unsafe work behavior in an effort to protect the safety and well-being of employees and coworkers and to identify opportunities for rehabilitation.

recency error/bias (interviewing)   An interviewing error/bias that occurs when the interviewer recalls recently interviewed candidates more vividly than candidates who were interviewed earlier in the process.

recency error/bias (performance management)   A performance management error/bias in which the appraiser places undue emphasis on the employee's most recent performance rather than considering performance demonstrated throughout the entire performance measurement period.

recertification   The process by which HR professionals who have earned Professional in Human Resources (PHR), Senior Professional in Human Resources (SPHR), or Global Professional in Human Resources (GPHR) certification maintain the currency of that status.

recruiting   The process of attracting and creating a pool of qualified candidates.

red circle rates   A pay rate for an hourly or salaried employee that is set above the maximum rate of the range for the position that the employee holds.

refreezing   The third and final stage in Lewin's change process theory. Through the refreezing stage, people come to experience that what once represented a change has now become, in simplest terms, the norm.

Regents of California v. Bakke, 1978   Key issue: Affirmative action. Significance: The Supreme Court ruled that although race could be a factor in college admission decisions, quotas could not be established.

Although this case was based on a college admissions program, its significance extended to workplace affirmative action programs.

This case falls under the category of "reverse discrimination" because it alleged race discrimination and was brought by someone who was not a minority/person of color.

regular rate of pay An employee's regular rate of pay includes more than just her hourly rate of pay; it would also include any incentives and commissions. It would not, however, include bonuses (which, unlike incentive programs, are discretionary), pay for time not worked, premium pay for weekend or holiday work, and the like.

Rehabilitation Act, 1973 A law that prohibits discrimination on the basis of physical and mental disabilities.

Section 503 of the Act requires affirmative action and prohibits employment discrimination by federal government contractors and subcontractors with contracts of more than $10,000.

Section 504 of the Act states that "no otherwise qualified individual with a disability in the United States shall be excluded from, denied the benefits of, or be subjected to discrimination under" any program or activity that either receives federal financial assistance or is conducted by any executive agency or the United States Postal Service.

Section 508 requires that federal agencies' electronic and information technology is accessible to people with disabilities, including employees and members of the public.

relevant labor market The size and scope of the geographic area within which an organization would seek to attract qualified candidates for a particular position(s). Even within the same organization, the relevant labor market for different positions can vary widely depending upon the skills, knowledge, abilities, and behavioral characteristics required to perform each position successfully. Other factors that impact how an organization defines the relevant labor market might be the degree of competition that exists among employers for particular skills or knowledge and the degree to which certain skills or knowledge requirements are industry specific.

reliability The degree to which a selection process or instrument is consistent.

relief When a plaintiff prevails in an Equal Employment Opportunity (EEO) lawsuit, she may be awarded various forms of "relief" or remedies.

relocation The process of moving a current or existing (or, less frequently, newly hired) employee's primary residence from one location to another.

remedies When a plaintiff prevails in an EEO lawsuit, he may be awarded various forms of remedies or "relief."

repeat violation A violation that is the same or substantially similar to a violation that was found during a previous inspection. Occupational Safety and Health Administration (OSHA) may propose a fine of up to $70,000 for each repeat violation.

repetitive stress injuries (RSIs) (also known as cumulative trauma syndromes [CTSs] or cumulative trauma disorders [CTDs]) Injuries that result from placing too much stress (often through overuse) on a part of the body.

replacement charts Tools that identify names of individuals who could potentially fill a particular position if an opening were to occur.

request for proposal (RFP) A request to potential vendors to propose solutions to address specific requirements (which are identified in the RFP document, and to which potential vendors respond in writing).

required subjects Subjects that must be bargained in good faith if either the employer or the employees' representative requests it. Examples of required subjects include pay; wages; hours of employment; pensions for present employees; bonuses; group insurance; grievance procedures; safety practices; seniority; procedures for discharge, layoff, recall, or discipline; and union security.

research Finding answers to questions.

respondent The person or party against whom a charge of unlawful discrimination has been filed.

responsibility One of the four factors used as a basis to assess the substantial equality of job content under the Equal Pay Act of 1963. "Responsibility" refers to the degree of responsibility and accountability that an employer entrusts to and expects from a particular position.

restorative care   A category of dental care or coverage that refers to oral "repairs" that are usually of a relatively minor nature, such as cavities or root canals. The reimbursement for restorative care is generally less than the reimbursement rate for preventive care (perhaps 80% instead of 100%).

results level evaluation   Looks specifically at whether the business or organizational results that were expected to occur as a result of training did in fact occur. This level of results-based evaluation is measurable, concrete, and usually of keen interest to the leaders of the organization because results speak volumes.

retained employment agencies   Search firms to whom an organization pays a fee whether or not the organization actually hires a candidate referred by the firm. The services of this type of agency are more often secured in an effort to fill executive-level positions.

retirement benefits   One of the three primary components of the Social Security Act.

return on investment (ROI)   A metric that calculates the absolute or relative worth, value, and effectiveness.

Retirement Equity Act, 1984   An amendment to Employee Retirement Income Security Act (ERISA) that incorporated a number of key revisions, many of which addressed the concerns of former (in the event of divorce) and surviving (in the event of death) spouses.

Revenue Act, 1978   Among many other changes, the Revenue Act added two sections to the tax code that essentially resulted in the creation of two new and ultimately very important employee benefits: Section 125 plans and 401(k) plans.

Ricci v. DeStafano, 2009   Key issue: disparate impact. Significance: The Supreme Court confirmed that "fear of litigation alone cannot justify an employer's reliance on race to the detriment of individuals who passed the examinations and qualified for promotions."

right-to-know (also known as the employee hazard communication standard)   Ensures that employers and employees have knowledge and awareness about hazardous chemicals located in the workplace and that they know how to protect themselves. Specifically, this standard requires all employers having hazardous materials at the workplace to implement a written Hazard Communication Program. Four important key elements of this program are material safety data sheets (MSDS), orientation, training, and container labeling requirements.

right to sue letter   A letter issued by the Equal Employment Opportunity Commission (EEOC) that entitles the recipient (the charging party) to bring a private lawsuit within the specified time frame.

right-to-work states   States in which union shops and closed shops are illegal. In a right-to-work state, no employee has to join the union.

role play   A training method that is similar to case studies and can even be designed to be the natural "culmination" of a case study. Role plays, in one sense, take case studies one step further, in that participants actually "act out" the ways in which they would apply the knowledge and practice the skills in particular situations.

S

safe harbor provisions   Provisions under which an employer that has made improper salary deductions can protect itself from losing the exemption. To do so, the employer would be required to

▶ Have a clearly communicated policy prohibiting improper deductions and including a complaint mechanism

▶ Reimburse employees for any improper deductions

▶ Make a good faith commitment to comply in the future

safety committees   A vehicle through which employees and managers can collaboratively work to increase workplace safety.

salary   A predetermined amount of compensation that an employee will be paid per week.

salting   Activity engaged in by a "salt," a union organizer who seeks employment with the organization for the express purpose of actively organizing and campaigning within the organization.

Sarbanes-Oxley Act (SOX), 2002   A law designed to protect investors, SOX enacted reforms designed to enhance corporate responsibility and financial disclosures and to combat corporate and accounting fraud.

Schechter Poultry Corp. v. United States, 1935   A Supreme Court case that rendered the National Industrial Recovery Act unconstitutional. Although this decision was wholly unrelated to labor and collective bargaining, the Supreme Court decision rendered the labor-related provisions illegal as well. The right to organize and bargain reverted, once again, to railway workers and no one else. This would not, however, be the case for long.

scientific method   A form of primary research that consists of a systematic approach of testing hypotheses and using the knowledge generated to strengthen the degree to which HR can support the overall objectives of the organization.

secondary boycott   Efforts to convince others to stop doing business with a particular organization that is the subject of a primary boycott.

secondary research   A process that involves collecting information "secondhand," meaning not directly from the original source of the data. Secondary research assimilates data that has already been collected by others and thus allows the secondary researcher to "stand on the shoulders" of those who conducted the primary research.

Section 125   The tax code created by the Revenue Act of 1978 that created flexible benefits plans (often referred to as "cafeteria" plans). Section 125 plans can help employers as well as employees save money by reducing payroll taxes.

Section 401(k)   The second employee benefit that was created by the Revenue Act. A type of defined contribution plan, 401(k) plans allow employees to set aside pretax dollars to save for their retirement. This can be done through salary deduction, which may or may not be matched in part or (less frequently) in whole by employer contributions. 401(k) dollars can also be set aside through deferral of profit sharing income.

security   Protection of the workplace and of the employees who work there.

selection   The process of choosing the candidate(s) to whom the position will be offered.

selection criteria   The "shopping list" of what you're looking for in the individuals who will populate your candidate pool (and, ultimately, the employees who will join the organization). This could and often will include knowledge, skills, and abilities (KSAs), job specifications, behavioral characteristics, required credentials, and specific requirements stemming from job competencies.

Senior Professional in Human Resources (SPHR)   The Senior Professional in Human Resources certification, granted by and issued through Human Resource Certification Institute (HRCI).

seniority systems   Bona fide seniority or merit-based systems that are not intended or designed to discriminate unlawfully.

serious violation   A violation that the employer either knew about or should have known about and from which death or serious injury is probable. Occupational Safety and Health Administration (OSHA) may propose a fine of up to $7,000 per serious violation.

severance package   Monies granted to an involuntarily terminated employee for reasons unrelated to individual performance in recognition of the end of the employment relationship and of the years that the employee worked for her employer.

sexual harassment   A form of sex discrimination rendered illegal by Title VII of the Civil Rights Act of 1964. There are two categories of sexual harassment: quid pro quo and hostile work environment.

Sherman Antitrust Act, 1890   A law passed in an effort to curb the growth of monopolies. Under the Act, any business combination that sought to restrain trade or commerce would from that time forward be illegal. Specifically, the Act states that

▶ Section 1: "Every contract, combination in the form of trust or otherwise, or conspiracy, in restraint of trade or commerce among the several States, or with foreign nations, is declared to be illegal."

▶ Section 2: "Every person who shall monopolize, or attempt to monopolize, or combine or conspire with any other person or persons, to monopolize any part of the trade or commerce among the several States, or with foreign nations, shall be deemed guilty of a felony."

The Sherman Antitrust Act also placed responsibility for pursuing and investigating trusts on government attorneys and district courts.

The Sherman Antitrust Act is relevant to compensation's impact on recruitment and retention because an improperly conducted salary survey (or even information attempts to gather data on competitor's wage rates) can constitute a violation of this Act.

shift differentials   Additional hourly compensation that is paid to employees whose shifts start, end, or are scheduled during specified hours. Shift differentials do not exist in all organizations. They represent a way to attract and retain individuals to work shifts that are perceived as less attractive to current or potential employees.

short-form employment applications   Shorter versions of an organization's standard employment application.

short-term incentive programs   Incentive programs that are usually one year or less in duration.

short-term incentives—individual   Variable incentive programs (usually one year or less in duration) that are used to motivate employees to attain specific individual financial or nonfinancial objectives.

short-term incentives—team/group   Variable incentive programs (usually one year or less in duration) that are used to motivate teams/ groups to attain specific team/group financial or nonfinancial objectives. Short-term team/ group incentive programs are intended to foster collaborative efforts and synergy among employees who are pursuing a common goal.

sign-on bonuses   Money paid to an employee when she joins the organization. Sign-on bonuses constitute enticements to attract and hire employees.

similar-to-me error/bias (interviewing)   An interviewing error/bias that occurs when the interviewer evaluates a candidate on the basis of how much a candidate is similar to, or different from, him.

similar-to-me error/bias (performance management)   A performance management error/bias in which the appraiser evaluates an employee's performance on the basis of how much a candidate is similar to, or different from, her.

simple linear regression   A mathematical forecasting technique that examines the past relationship between two factors; determines the statistical strength of that relationship; and, on the basis of that analysis, projects future conditions.

simple resolutions   A legislative measure that pertains to either the Senate or the House of Representatives. Simple resolutions offer a nonbinding opinion, are not submitted to the president, and do not have the force of law.

simplified employee pension plan (SEP)   A defined contribution plan that allows employers to contribute on a tax-favored basis to individual retirement accounts (IRAs) that employees set up for this purpose.

simulations   A mathematical forecasting technique that creates scenarios through which different "realities" can be tested to see what could happen under a variety of changing conditions.

skill   One of the four factors used as a basis to assess the substantial equality of job content under the Equal Pay Act of 1963. Skill refers to the amount or degree of experience, ability, education, and training required to perform the job.

skill inventories   A central database that captures the knowledge, skills, and abilities (KSAs) possessed by its employees, even when those KSAs are not being used by an employee in her current position.

small group discussions/instructor-facilitated large group discussions   A training method during which the facilitator encourages learning by drawing upon the experiences and insights of the participants. This is used as a way of reinforcing the adult learning principle that says that adult learners believe that they have a significant amount of valuable experience from which they can draw to enhance their own learning and from which others can learn as well.

SMART   An acronym that can be applied to performance management (as well as other objectives that are developed and used within HR). The acronym speaks to the following attributes: specific, measurable, action-oriented, realistic, and time bound.

social media   Online websites that individuals/ employees use for personal as well as professional networking purposes.

Social Security Act (SSA), 1935 (also known as Old Age, Survivors and Disability Insurance [OASDI])   Social security is a social insurance program (although some would define it differently) that is funded through payroll taxes. Social security has three primary components, which are now referred to as retirement income, disability benefits, and survivor's benefits.

sociotechnical interventions   Organization development (OD) interventions that focus on the ways in which groups can become more (or semi) autonomous with respect to the performance and execution of the work.

span of control   The number of individuals ("direct reports") who report to a specific supervisor/manager/leader within an organization.

Specialty Healthcare and Rehabilitation Center of Mobile, 2011   The National Labor Relations Board (NLRB) decision in this case permits the organization of micro-units in organizations, even when the majority of employees do not want or seek union representation.

St. Mary's Honor Center v. Hicks, 1993   Key issue: Burden of proof. Significance: To prevail in an allegation of discrimination under Title VII of the Civil Rights Act of 1964, an employee goes beyond a prima facie case and actually proves that the employer's true reasons for an employment action are, in fact, discriminatory.

standards   Requirements created by the Occupational Health and Safety Administration (OSHA) as a way of ensuring the health and safety of employees.

strategic HR   The transactions, the tasks, the procedural functions that need to be done. Strategic-level HR is one leg of the HR stool; the other two legs are operational/tactical HR and transformational HR.

strategic management   Strategic HR management speaks to HR's overall commitment, in both word and deed, to meeting the ever-evolving short-term, long-term, and strategic objectives of the organization.

strategic planning   The process by which an organization defines and describes its long-term mission and vision and engages in expansive, far-reaching, and systematic planning to achieve that mission and vision.

stress   According to Public Safety and Health (NIOSH), the "harmful physical and emotional responses that occur when the requirements of the job do not match the capabilities, resources, or needs of the worker."

stress interviews   Interviews in which the interviewer(s) deliberately creates a high-stress environment in an effort to ascertain how the candidate would respond in a similarly stressful situation in the workplace post hire.

strictness error/bias (interviewing)   An interviewing error/bias that occurs when the interviewer applies an inappropriately harsh and demanding standard to one or more candidates, resulting in a lower overall assessment of the candidate(s).

strictness error/bias (performance management)   A performance management error/bias in which the appraiser applies an inappropriately harsh and demanding standard when evaluating the performance of one or more employees, resulting in a lower overall assessment of the employee(s).

strike   A "concerted stoppage" of work by employees.

substance use/abuse programs   A comprehensive program that consists of a drug-free workplace policy, supervisor training, employee education, employee assistance, and drug testing.

succession planning   The detailed, ongoing process through which an organization identifies individuals who might be able to fill higher-level positions that could become available in the future. Succession plans are "living, breathing" tools that impact individual and group professional development planning and that—through predictive efforts and proactive planning—strive to ensure that the overarching mission and goals of the organization will not be derailed by the inevitable departure of individuals from the organization.

suggestion programs   Programs that invite employees to submit their ideas (often anonymously) relative to any work-related topic, such as improving work systems, identifying or eliminating safety concerns, or even exposing unethical (or criminal) behavior. Questions submitted through suggestion programs or "boxes" need to be responded to quickly, regardless of whether the suggestion is implemented. Employees must be heard and feel heard for any suggestion program to be successful.

Summary of Work-Related Injuries and Illnesses (also known as the OSHA Form 300A)   A form used to record a numeric summary of all work-related injuries and illnesses logged in OSHA's Form 300 over the course of each calendar year. This form indicates the number of cases, the number of workdays impacted, and the number and types of work-related injuries and illnesses. A worksheet is also available to assist employers in filling out this summary. Each year, a completed Form 300 must be posted conspicuously for three months (between February 1 and April 30).

summary plan description (SPD)   A document that employees (or beneficiaries) who become

participants in a retirement plan that is covered under ERISA are entitled to receive, at no cost, from the plan administrator. The SPD describes what the plan provides and how it operates. It also provides information relative to when an employee can begin to participate in the plan, how service and benefits are calculated, when benefits become vested, when and in what form benefits are paid, and how to file a claim for benefits.

summative evaluation   An approach that is predicated on the interpretation of data that is collected after the initiative has been implemented. Summative evaluation allows for a complete analysis of the entire initiative on four different levels: reaction, learning, behavior, and results.

sunset provision   A clause that places a time limit/end date on the agreement.

survivor's benefits   One of the three primary components of the Social Security Act.

SWOT analysis (strengths, weaknesses, opportunities, threats)   An analysis that is conducted to ascertain the strengths and weaknesses that are inherent to an organization, as well as the opportunities and threats that it faces from external forces.

sympathy strikes   A type of strike that occurs when employees who are not directly involved in an economic dispute choose not to cross a picket line out of support for striking workers. Sympathy strikers do not need to be employed by the same employer as the employees who are actually on strike to engage in a sympathy strike. A sympathy strike is considered protected concerted activity.

T

tactile/kinesthetic learners   Those who learn most effectively by processing information with which they can interact in a hands-on manner, in the most literal sense of the word. They like to touch, feel, explore, and experience the world around them.

Taft-Hartley Act (also known as the Labor Management Relations Act), 1947   An amendment designed to remedy what the Republican Congress saw as two major omissions in the National Labor

Relations Act (NLRA) (Wagner Act): first, the identification of behaviors and practices that would be considered unsafe labor practices (ULPs) on the part of unions, and second, a provision that would allow the government to issue an injunction against a strike that threatened national interests. Taft-Hartley identified the following unfair labor practices that unions could commit:

▶ Restraining or coercing employees in the exercise of their rights or an employer in the choice of its bargaining representative

▶ Causing an employer to discriminate against an employee

▶ Refusing to bargain with the employer of the employees it represents

▶ Engaging in certain types of secondary boycotts

▶ Requiring excessive dues

▶ Engaging in featherbedding

▶ Picketing for recognition for more than 30 days without petitioning for an election

▶ Entering into hot cargo agreements

▶ Striking or picketing a health care establishment without giving the required notice

talent management   The sum-total of the organization's efforts, initiatives, and programs to create a targeted employment life-cycle experience that attracts, motivates, retains, compensates, and develops valued, high-performing employees.

task or work (operations) level analysis   Level 2 of McGehee and Thayer's three levels of human resource development (HRD)/training needs analysis and assessment. Task or work (operations) level analysis collects and addresses data about a particular job or group of jobs.

Taxman v. Board of Education of Piscataway, 1993   Key issue: Affirmative action. Significance: The U.S. Court of Appeals for the Third Circuit ruled that, in the absence of underrepresentation as demonstrated and documented through an affirmative action plan, organizations cannot consider race when making decisions relative to who will be laid off and who will be retained.

Doing so would constitute a violation of Title VII of the Civil Rights Act of 1964.

This case falls under the category of "reverse discrimination" because it alleged race discrimination and was brought by a person who was not a minority/person of color.

teambuilding   Exercises and initiatives that seek to help the team learn to function more effectively so that it can attain its overall objective (which must link, of course, to overall organizational objective).

technostructural interventions   Organization development (OD) interventions that focus on improving what work gets done as well as the ways and processes through which the work gets done. It looks at job design, job redesign, job restructuring, work content, workflow, work processes, and the like.

teratogens   A specific group of chemicals that will not harm pregnant women but that do have the potential to harm unborn fetuses.

third-party vendor   An entity or person outside the organization to whom work can be outsourced.

Title VII of the Civil Rights Act, 1964   A landmark piece of legislation prohibiting employment discrimination on the basis of race, color, religion, sex, and national origin.

tort doctrines   Torts are wrongful acts committed against another individual's property or person. By definition, the commission of a tort infringes on another person's rights.

Some of the major tort doctrines that affect individual employee rights in the absence of an employment or labor contract are

▶ Employment-at-will

▶ Wrongful termination

▶ Implied contracts

▶ Defamation

▶ Invasion of privacy

▶ Negligent hiring

▶ Negligent training

▶ Negligent retention

▶ Negligent referral

total compensation   All the "rewards" that an organization gives, grants, or otherwise bestows upon its employees in exchange for the services those employees have rendered through their employment. It includes more obvious items, such as wages and salaries, that would fall under the subheading "compensation," as well as mandatory and optional benefits such as Social Security contributions, health and welfare programs, and the like. It also includes items that some but not all employees enjoy, such as incentives, bonuses, and stock options.

total quality management (TQM)   An organization development (OD) intervention that is ultimately aimed at meeting or exceeding customer expectations through the commitment of everyone in an organization (often through a team-based approach) to continuous improvement of products or services.

total rewards   Total rewards speaks to HR's responsibility to ensure that the organization's total compensation and benefits programs, policies, and practices reinforce and support the short-term, long-term, and emerging and strategic objectives of the organization.

transformational HR   Takes a long-term, future-focused approach to the ways in which HR will work with the organization to attain its organizational mission. It looks at business and organizational issues rather than "HR issues." It fosters and cultivates change and is dynamic, impactful, and ever evolving.

treatment follow-up drug testing   Drug testing that is conducted periodically for employees who return to work after participating in an alcohol or drug treatment program to ensure that they remain substance free.

trend analysis   A mathematical technique that looks at and measures how one particular factor changes over a period of time.

tuberculosis (TB)   A highly infectious bacterial disease that usually affects the lungs and that can also affect other organs.

turnover analysis   Measures the percentage of the workforce that has left the organization during a specified period of time.

U

ULP strike   A strike called by a union that alleges, correctly or incorrectly, that the employer has committed an unfair labor practice during contract negotiations. Employers cannot hire permanent strike replacements during an unfair labor practice (ULP) strike, and the striking workers must be returned to their original positions when the strike is over.

undue hardship   A hardship created by a requested accommodation that creates significant difficulty (enough to disrupt business operations), results in a significant financial outlay, or changes something about the (essential) nature of the business.

unemployment insurance   A program intended to help employees financially "bridge" the gap between positions when an employee has lost his job through no fault of his own. Unemployment insurance was established as part of the federal Social Security Act of 1935 but is administered at the state level. Unemployment insurance is funded through employer taxes (except in three states, where employees contribute as well).

unfair labor practice (ULP)   Unlawful acts that can be committed by either employers or unions. The National Labor Relations Act (NLRA) (Wagner Act) identified five categories of employer unfair labor practices:

▶ To "interfere with, restrain, or coerce employees" in the exercise of their rights to engage in concerted or union activities or refrain from them

▶ To dominate or interfere with the formation or administration of a labor organization

▶ To discriminate against employees for engaging in concerted or union activities or refraining from them

▶ To discriminate against an employee for filing charges with the NLRB or taking part in any NLRB proceedings

▶ To refuse to bargain with the union that is the lawful representative of its employees

Unfair labor practices that could be committed by unions were identified in 1947, in the Labor Management Relations Act (also known as the Taft-Hartley Act):

▸ Restraining or coercing employees in the exercise of their rights or an employer in the choice of its bargaining representative

▸ Causing an employer to discriminate against an employee

▸ Refusing to bargain with the employer of the employees it represents

▸ Engaging in certain types of secondary boycotts

▸ Requiring excessive dues

▸ Engaging in featherbedding

▸ Picketing for recognition for more than 30 days without petitioning for an election

▸ Entering into hot cargo agreements

▸ Striking or picketing a health care establishment without giving the required notice

unfreezing The first stage in Lewin's change process theory. Through the unfreezing stage, everyone who is involved with and impacted by the change must be brought to the point where she can understand and accept that a particular change will happen.

Uniform Guidelines on Employee Selection Procedures, 1978 A law that establishes a uniform set of principles relative to all elements of the selection process, including but not limited to interviewing, preemployment testing, and performance appraisal. A key purpose of the Uniform Guidelines is to deal with the concept of "adverse impact" (also known as "disparate impact") as it pertains to the employment process and to ensure that interview and selection processes are reliable (consistent) and valid.

Uniformed Services Employment and Reemployment Rights Act (USERRA), 1994 A law that provides reinforcement rights for individuals who miss work because of "service in the uniformed services," which is defined as voluntary or involuntary uniformed service.

union deauthorization The revocation of the union security clause in the contract, which thereby creates an "open shop." Deauthorization requires a majority vote of the entire bargaining unit, not just the members of the unit who vote in the deauthorization election.

union decertification The process by which employees vote to remove the union's rights to represent the employees. This process is similar to certification, only in reverse. Decertification requires 50% (or more) of individuals who vote in the decertification election.

union security clauses Articles that are included in some agreements in an effort to protect the interests, strength, and security of the union. Union security clauses regulate membership in the union and, consequently, relate to the payment of dues. Some of the more common types of union security clauses include

▸ Open shop

▸ Closed shop

▸ Union shop

▸ Agency shop

▸ Maintenance of membership

union shop Newly hired employees must join the union within a specified period of time, usually 30 days, and must remain a member of the union as a condition of employment. In a union shop, employers must terminate employees who are not union members. Union shops are illegal in "right to work" states.

United Steelworkers v. Weber, 1979 Key issue: Affirmative action. Significance: Affirmative action plans that establish voluntary quotas that have been jointly agreed to by an organization as well as its collective bargaining unit do not constitute race discrimination under Title VII of the Civil Rights Act of 1964 if they are designed to remedy past discrimination that has resulted in current underutilization.

This case falls under the category of "reverse discrimination" because it alleged race discrimination and was brought by someone who was not a minority/person of color.

U.S. Patent Act Patents confer certain rights upon the individual to whom the patent is granted. Specifically, a patent holder has "the right to exclude others from making, using, offering for sale, or selling" the invention in the United States or "importing" the invention into the United States.

utility patents Granted for the invention or discovery of any new and useful process, machine, article of manufacture, composition of matter, or any new and useful improvement thereof.

utilization analysis The section of an affirmative action plan that compares the percentage of qualified women and minorities available to be employed in a particular job group to the percentage of women and minorities who are actually employed in that job group.

V

validity The degree to which selection processes measure skills that relate meaningfully and clearly to the skills that are required to perform a particular job.

values Beliefs on which the organization has been built. They are the tenets that shape and guide strategic and day-to-day decision making, as well as the behaviors that are exhibited in the organization. Organizations identify values, in part, as a way to clearly guide those decisions and behaviors. Values are often represented in terms and principles such as integrity, honesty, and respect.

variable pay Also known as "at risk" pay, variable pay is cash compensation that fluctuates and is tied, in some way, to the employee's performance. It is not guaranteed and is generally tied to the achievement of specific objectives. Variable pay can also take the form of "bonuses." While the terms "bonus" and "incentive" are often used interchangeably, incentives are tied to the specific achievement of individual, group, or organizational goals, whereas bonuses are more discretionary in nature.

vesting The process by which an employee earns a nonforfeitable right to the employer's contribution of her defined benefit/defined contribution plan.

VETS-100 The Federal Contractor Veterans' Employment Report that must be filed annually by those having federal contracts or subcontracts of $100,000 or more.

Vietnam Era Veterans' Readjustment Assistance Act (VEVRAA), 1974 A law that requires employers with federal contracts or subcontracts of $25,000 or more to provide equal opportunity and affirmative action for Vietnam era veterans, special disabled veterans, and veterans who served on active duty during a war or in a campaign or expedition for which a campaign badge has been authorized.

virtual organization An organizational model in which the organization does not reside in any one particular "brick and mortar" location but rather exists and conducts business on the Internet.

vision A brief yet comprehensive descriptive and inspirational statement that articulates where the organization wants to be and what it wants to become in the future.

vision coverage A type of health and welfare benefit. An employer will typically offer vision coverage as a discount program (generally around 10%). Vision coverage generally includes items such as exams, contact lenses, and glasses.

visual learners Those who learn most effectively by processing information that they see.

voluntary subjects (also known as permissive subjects) Voluntary subjects of bargaining are topics that can be submitted to collective bargaining if and only if the employer and the employees' representative are willing to do so. Attempting to force bargaining on a voluntary or permissive subject constitutes an unsafe labor practice (ULP).

voluntary terminations A decision initiated by the employee to end the employment relationship.

W–X

Wagner Act (also known as the National Labor Relations Act), 1935 A law that guaranteed "the right to self-organization, to form, join, or assist labor organizations, to bargain collectively through representatives of their own choosing, and to engage in concerted activities for the purpose of collective bargaining or other mutual aid and protection." Certain groups or categories of employees are excluded under the Wagner Act from membership in a bargaining unit. Examples would include managers, supervisors, confidential employees (essentially secretaries and administrative assistants to managers who can make labor relations decisions), and several others.

walking/working surfaces standard Mandatory in all permanent places of employment (with few exceptions), this standard seeks to minimize or eliminate slips, trips, and falls in the workplace. Its coverage affects surfaces such as floors, platforms, ladders, and steps.

Walsh-Healey Public Contracts Act, 1936 The Walsh-Healey Public Contracts Act requires contractors who have contracts with the federal government that exceed $10,000 to pay an established minimum wage to workers employed through that contract. In addition to minimum wage, Walsh-Healey PCA addressed issues including overtime pay and safe and sanitary working conditions.

Washington v. Davis, 1976 Key issue: Employment tests and disparate impact. Significance: A test that has an adverse impact on a protected class is still lawful as long as the test can be shown to be valid and job related.

weighted employment applications Employment applications that assign relative weights to different portions of the application in an effort to facilitate the process of evaluating candidates' qualifications in a consistent and objective manner.

Weingarten Rights The right of a unionized employee to have union representation during a potential disciplinary interview.

whole job methods Nonquantitative job evaluation techniques that determine the relative value of jobs within the organization without using mathematical techniques.

whole job ranking A whole job evaluation technique that ranks, from lowest to highest, according to the importance that each job holds (or, stated differently, the value that each job brings) to the organization. In essence, a whole job ranking is a list that reflects which jobs are more important to the organization and which jobs are least important to the organization, in rank order.

wildcat strikes A type of strike that occurs when a strike is called even when a collective bargaining agreement contains a no-strike clause that prohibits striking during the duration of the agreement. Wildcat strikes are not protected concerted activity.

willful violation A violation that is deliberate and intentional. Occupational Safety and Health Administration (OSHA) may impose a fine of up to $70,000 per willful violation (more in the event of the employee's death), and possibly incarceration.

Worker Adjustment and Retraining Notification Act (WARNA), 1988 A law that mandates employer notification requirements under specific circumstances involving mass layoffs and plant closings, thus giving displaced workers time to make arrangements for other employment. WARNA covers employers with 100 or more full-time employees.

worker's compensation State laws intended to provide medical care to injured employees and death benefits to families of those who died. Worker's comp is a "no fault" system—injured workers receive medical or compensation benefits regardless of who caused the job-related accident.

workforce analysis The section of an affirmative action plan that essentially depicts the contractor's workforce in terms of incumbents' race, gender, and wages. The workforce analysis is the older, longer, and more complex version of the "organizational display."

workforce planning and employment Workforce planning and employment speaks to HR's responsibility to ensure integrated, seamless, and effective recruitment, hiring, orientation, and exit processes that support the short-term, long-term, emerging, and strategic objectives of the organization.

working conditions One of the four factors used as a basis to assess the substantial equality of job content under the Equal Pay Act of 1963. Working conditions refer to the physical surroundings of the position, as well as any hazards that are associated with a particular position.

work-life programs Programs that provide employees with the opportunity to combine or "balance" professional and nonprofessional dimensions of their lives, including flexible schedules, job sharing, telecommuting, and compressed work weeks. Work-life programs offer advantages for employees as well as employers who want to market themselves in the relevant labor market.

work-related illness Illnesses resulting from an event or condition in the work environment that fall into any one of the following five categories: skin diseases or disorders, respiratory conditions, poisoning, hearing loss, or "all other illnesses."

work-related injury Any wound or damage to the body resulting from an event in the work environment.

workweek Any fixed and regularly recurring period of 168 hours (24 hours in a day, seven days a week).

wrongful termination A tort doctrine that speaks to the employer having ended the employment relationship for wrongful reasons. One possible basis for wrongful termination could exist if an employee was terminated in violation of an individual employment contract. Others could apply as well and would vary from state to state.

Y–Z

"yellow dog" contract A contract or an agreement between an employer and an employee in which the employer agrees to give the employee a job as long as the employee agrees not to join or have any involvement with a labor union.

zero-based budgeting A process by which the proposed budget is not based on current or prior expenses, revenues, or performance. Rather, the budgeting process begins, each time, "from scratch."

zero defects Phil Crosby's philosophy, which asserts that employees will perform at whatever level management sets for them. For that reason, settling for "goodness," rather than the full attainment of objectives, would effectively preclude the possibility of attaining those objectives.

zipper clause A collective bargaining article through which both parties agree that the agreement is an exclusive and complete "expression of consent"—in other words, that the only items that can be collectively bargained until the expiration of the agreement are the ones that are actually included in the agreement. After the agreement is signed, new subjects cannot be added, and existing subjects cannot be reopened for negotiation. The contract has been zipped closed.

APPENDIX A

OSHA Forms for Recording Work-Related Injuries and Illnesses

U.S. Department of Labor
Occupational Safety and Health Administration

OSHA Forms for Recording Work-Related Injuries and Illnesses

Dear Employer:

This booklet includes the forms needed for maintaining occupational injury and illness records for 2004. These new forms have changed in several important ways from the 2003 recordkeeping forms.

In the December 17, 2002 Federal Register (67 FR 77165-77170), OSHA announced its decision to add an occupational hearing loss column to OSHA's Form 300, Log of Work-Related Injuries and Illnesses. This forms package contains modified Forms 300 and 300A which incorporate the additional column M(5) Hearing Loss. Employers required to complete the injury and illness forms must begin to use these forms on January 1, 2004.

In response to public suggestions, OSHA also has made several changes to the forms package to make the recordkeeping materials clearer and easier to use:

- On Form 300, we've switched the positions of the day count columns. The days "away from work" column now comes before the days "on job transfer or restriction."
- We've clarified the formulas for calculating incidence rates.
- We've added new recording criteria for occupational hearing loss to the "Overview" section.
- On Form 300, we've made the column heading "Classify the Case" more prominent to make it clear that employers should mark only one selection among the four columns offered.

The Occupational Safety and Health Administration shares with you the goal of preventing injuries and illnesses in our nation's workplaces. Accurate injury and illness records will help us achieve that goal.

Occupational Safety and Health Administration
U.S. Department of Labor

What's Inside...

In this package, you'll find everything you need to complete OSHA's *Log* and the *Summary of Work-Related Injuries and Illnesses* for the next several years. On the following pages, you'll find:

▼ **An Overview: Recording Work-Related Injuries and Illnesses** — General instructions for filling out the forms in this package and definitions of terms you should use when you classify your cases as injuries or illnesses.

▼ **How to Fill Out the Log** — An example to guide you in filling out the *Log* properly.

▼ **Log of Work-Related Injuries and Illnesses** — Several pages of the *Log* (but you may make as many copies of the *Log* as you need). Notice that the *Log* is separate from the *Summary*.

▼ **Summary of Work-Related Injuries and Illnesses** — Removable *Summary* pages for easy posting at the end of the year. Note that you post the *Summary* only, not the *Log*.

▼ **Worksheet to Help You Fill Out the Summary** — A worksheet for figuring the average number of employees who worked for your establishment and the total number of hours worked.

▼ **OSHA's 301: Injury and Illness Incident Report** — A copy of the OSHA 301 to provide details about the incident. You may make as many copies as you need or use an equivalent form.

Take a few minutes to review this package. If you have any questions, *visit us online at www.osha.gov OR call your local OSHA office.* We'll be happy to help you.

OSHA's Form 301

Injury and Illness Incident Report

U.S. Department of Labor
Occupational Safety and Health Administration

Form approved OMB no. 1218-0176

This *Injury and Illness Incident Report* is one of the first forms you must fill out when a recordable work-related injury or illness has occurred. Together with the *Log of Work-Related Injuries and Illnesses* and the accompanying *Summary*, these forms help the employer and OSHA develop a picture of the extent and severity of work-related incidents.

Within 7 calendar days after you receive information that a recordable work-related injury or illness has occurred, you must fill out this form or an equivalent. Some state workers' compensation, insurance, or other reports may be acceptable substitutes. To be considered an equivalent form, any substitute must contain all the information asked for on this form.

According to Public Law 91-596 and 29 CFR 1904, OSHA's recordkeeping rule, you must keep this form on file for 5 years following the year to which it pertains.

If you need additional copies of this form, you may photocopy and use as many as you need.

Completed by _____

Title _____

Phone (___) ___ - ___   Date ___ / ___ / ___

Information about the employee

1) Full name _____

2) Street _____
   City _____ State _____ ZIP _____

3) Date of birth ___ / ___ / ___

4) Date hired ___ / ___ / ___

5) ☐ Male
   ☐ Female

Information about the physician or other health care professional

6) Name of physician or other health care professional _____

7) If treatment was given away from the worksite, where was it given?
   Facility _____
   Street _____
   City _____ State _____ ZIP _____

8) Was employee treated in an emergency room?
   ☐ Yes
   ☐ No

9) Was employee hospitalized overnight as an in-patient?
   ☐ Yes
   ☐ No

Information about the case

10) Case number from the *Log* _____ *(Transfer the case number from the Log after you record the case.)*

11) Date of injury or illness ___ / ___ / ___

12) Time employee began work _____ AM / PM

13) Time of event _____ AM / PM   ☐ Check if time cannot be determined

14) **What was the employee doing just before the incident occurred?** Describe the activity, as well as the tools, equipment, or material the employee was using. Be specific. *Examples:* "climbing a ladder while carrying roofing materials"; "spraying chlorine from hand sprayer"; "daily computer key-entry."

15) **What happened?** Tell us how the injury occurred. *Examples:* "When ladder slipped on wet floor, worker fell 20 feet"; "Worker was sprayed with chlorine when gasket broke during replacement"; "Worker developed soreness in wrist over time."

16) **What was the injury or illness?** Tell us the part of the body that was affected and how it was affected; be more specific than "hurt," "pain," or sore." *Examples:* "strained back"; "chemical burn, hand"; "carpal tunnel syndrome."

17) **What object or substance directly harmed the employee?** *Examples:* "concrete floor"; "chlorine"; "radial arm saw." *If this question does not apply to the incident, leave it blank.*

18) **If the employee died, when did death occur?** Date of death ___ / ___ / ___

U.S. Department of Labor
Occupational Safety and Health Administration

If You Need Help...

If you need help deciding whether a case is recordable, or if you have questions about the information in this package, feel free to contact us. We'll gladly answer any questions you have.

▼ Visit us online at www.osha.gov

▼ Call your OSHA Regional office and ask for the recordkeeping coordinator

or

▼ Call your State Plan office

Federal Jurisdiction

Region 1 - 617 / 565-9860
Connecticut; Massachusetts; Maine; New Hampshire; Rhode Island

Region 2 - 212 / 337-2378
New York; New Jersey

Region 3 - 215 / 861-4900
DC; Delaware; Pennsylvania; West Virginia

Region 4 - 404 / 562-2300
Alabama; Florida; Georgia; Mississippi

Region 5 - 312 / 353-2220
Illinois; Ohio; Wisconsin

Region 6 - 214 / 767-4731
Arkansas; Louisiana; Oklahoma; Texas

Region 7 - 816 / 426-5861
Kansas; Missouri; Nebraska

Region 8 - 303 / 844-1600
Colorado; Montana; North Dakota; South Dakota

Region 9 - 415 / 975-4310

Region 10 - 206 / 553-5930
Idaho

State Plan States

Alaska - 907 / 269-4957

Arizona - 602 / 542-5795

California - 415 / 703-5100

*Connecticut - 860 / 566-4380

Hawaii - 808 / 586-9100

Indiana - 317 / 232-2688

Iowa - 515 / 281-3661

Kentucky - 502 / 564-3070

Maryland - 410 / 527-4465

Michigan - 517 / 322-1848

Minnesota - 651 / 284-5050

Nevada - 702 / 486-9020

*New Jersey - 609 / 984-1389

New Mexico - 505 / 827-4230

*New York - 518 / 457-2574

North Carolina - 919 / 807-2875

Oregon - 503 / 378-3272

Puerto Rico - 787 / 754-2172

South Carolina - 803 / 734-9669

Tennessee - 615 / 741-2793

Utah - 801 / 530-6901

Vermont - 802 / 828-2765

Virginia - 804 / 786-6613

Virgin Islands - 340 / 772-1315

Washington - 360 / 902-5554

Wyoming - 307 / 777-7786

*Public Sector only

U.S. Department of Labor
Occupational Safety and Health Administration

Have questions?

If you need help in filling out the *Log* or *Summary*, or if you have questions about whether a case is recordable, contact us. We'll be happy to help you. You can:

▲ Visit us online at: **www.osha.gov**

▲ Call your regional or state plan office. You'll find the phone number listed inside this cover.

U.S. Department of Labor
Occupational Safety and Health Administration

An Overview:
Recording Work-Related Injuries and Illnesses

The Occupational Safety and Health (OSH) Act of 1970 requires certain employers to prepare and maintain records of work-related injuries and illnesses. Use these definitions when you classify cases on the Log. OSHA's recordkeeping regulation (see 29 CFR Part 1904) provides more information about the definitions below.

The *Log of Work-Related Injuries and Illnesses* (Form 300) is used to classify work-related injuries and illnesses and to note the extent and severity of each case. When an incident occurs, use the *Log* to record specific details about what happened and how it happened.

The *Summary* — a separate form (Form 300A) — shows the totals for the year in each category. At the end of the year, post the *Summary* in a visible location so that your employees are aware of the injuries and illnesses occurring in their workplace.

Employers must keep a *Log* for each establishment or site. If you have more than one establishment, you must keep a separate *Log and Summary* for each physical location that is expected to be in operation for one year or longer.

Note that your employees have the right to review your injury and illness records. For more information, see 29 Code of Federal Regulations Part 1904.35, *Employee Involvement.*

Cases listed on the *Log of Work-Related Injuries and Illnesses* are not necessarily eligible for workers' compensation or other insurance benefits. Listing a case on the *Log* does not mean that the employer or worker was at fault or that an OSHA standard was violated.

When is an injury or illness considered work-related?

An injury or illness is considered work-related if an event or exposure in the work environment caused or contributed to the condition or significantly aggravated a preexisting condition. Work-relatedness is presumed for injuries and illnesses resulting from events or exposures occurring in the workplace, unless an exception specifically applies. See 29 CFR Part 1904.5(b)(2) for the exceptions. The work environment includes the establishment and other locations where one or more employees are working or are present as a condition of their employment. See 29 CFR Part 1904.5(b)(1).

Which work-related injuries and illnesses should you record?

Record those work-related injuries and illnesses that result in:

▶ death,
▶ loss of consciousness,
▶ days away from work,
▶ restricted work activity or job transfer, or
▶ medical treatment beyond first aid.

You must also record work-related injuries and illnesses that are significant (as defined below) or meet any of the additional criteria listed below.

You must record any significant work-related injury or illness that is diagnosed by a physician or other licensed health care professional. You must record any work-related case involving cancer, chronic irreversible disease, a fractured or cracked bone, or a punctured eardrum. See 29 CFR 1904.7.

What are the additional criteria?

You must record the following conditions when they are work-related:

▶ any needlestick injury or cut from a sharp object that is contaminated with another person's blood or other potentially infectious material;

▶ any case requiring an employee to be medically removed under the requirements of an OSHA health standard;

▶ tuberculosis infection as evidenced by a positive skin test or diagnosis by a physician or other licensed health care professional after exposure to a known case of active tuberculosis.

▶ an employee's hearing test (audiogram) reveals 1) that the employee has experienced a Standard Threshold Shift (STS) in hearing in one or both ears (averaged at 2000, 3000, and 4000 Hz) and 2) the employee's total hearing level is 25 decibels (dB) or more above audiometric zero (also averaged at 2000, 3000, and 4000 Hz) in the same ear(s) as the STS.

What is medical treatment?

Medical treatment includes managing and caring for a patient for the purpose of combating disease or disorder. The following are not considered medical treatments and are NOT recordable:

▶ visits to a doctor or health care professional solely for observation or counseling;

What do you need to do?

1. Within 7 calendar days after you receive information about a case, decide if the case is recordable under the OSHA recordkeeping requirements.

2. Determine whether the incident is a new case or a recurrence of an existing one.

3. Establish whether the case was work-related.

4. If the case is recordable, decide which form you will fill out as the injury and illness incident report.

   You may use *OSHA's 301: Injury and Illness Incident Report* or an equivalent form. Some state workers compensation, insurance, or other reports may be acceptable substitutes, as long as they provide the same information as the OSHA 301.

How to work with the Log

1. Identify the employee involved unless it is a privacy concern case as described below.

2. Identify when and where the case occurred.

3. Describe the case, as specifically as you can.

4. Classify the seriousness of the case by recording the **most serious outcome** associated with the case, with column G (Death) being the most serious and column J (Other recordable cases) being the least serious.

5. Identify whether the case is an injury or illness. If the case is an injury, check the injury category. If the case is an illness, check the appropriate illness category.

U.S. Department of Labor
Occupational Safety and Health Administration

- diagnostic procedures, including administering prescription medications that are used solely for diagnostic purposes; and
- any procedure that can be labeled first aid. (See below for more information about first aid.)
- using finger guards;
- using massages;
- drinking fluids to relieve heat stress

What is first aid?

If the incident required only the following types of treatment, consider it first aid. Do NOT record the case if it involves only:

- using non-prescription medications at non-prescription strength;
- administering tetanus immunizations;
- cleaning, flushing, or soaking wounds on the skin surface;
- using wound coverings, such as bandages, Band-Aids™, gauze pads, etc., or using SteriStrips™ or butterfly bandages.
- using hot or cold therapy;
- using any totally non-rigid means of support, such as elastic bandages, wraps, non-rigid back belts, etc.;
- using temporary immobilization devices while transporting an accident victim (splints, slings, neck collars, or back boards);
- drilling a fingernail or toenail to relieve pressure, or draining fluids from blisters;
- using eye patches;
- using simple irrigation or a cotton swab to remove foreign bodies not embedded in or adhered to the eye;
- using irrigation, tweezers, cotton swab or other simple means to remove splinters or foreign material from areas other than the eye;

How do you decide if the case involved restricted work?

Restricted work activity occurs when, as the result of a work-related injury or illness, an employer or health care professional keeps, or recommends keeping, an employee from doing the routine functions of his or her job or from working the full workday that the employee would have been scheduled to work before the injury or illness occurred.

How do you count the number of days of restricted work activity or the number of days away from work?

Count the number of calendar days the employee was on restricted work activity or was away from work as a result of the recordable injury or illness. Do not count the day on which the injury or illness occurred in this number. Begin counting days from the day after the incident occurs. If a single injury or illness involved both days away from work and days of restricted work activity, enter the total number of days for each. You may stop counting days of restricted work activity or days away from work once the total of either or the combination of both reaches 180 days.

Under what circumstances should you NOT enter the employee's name on the OSHA Form 300?

You must consider the following types of injuries or illnesses to be privacy concern cases:

- an injury or illness to an intimate body part or to the reproductive system,
- an injury or illness resulting from a sexual assault,
- a mental illness,
- a case of HIV infection, hepatitis, or tuberculosis,
- a needlestick injury or cut from a sharp object that is contaminated with blood or other potentially infectious material (see 29 CFR Part 1904.8 for definition), and
- other illnesses, if the employee independently and voluntarily requests that his or her name not be entered on the log.

You must not enter the employee's name on the OSHA 300 Log for these cases. Instead, enter "privacy case" in the space normally used for the employee's name. You must keep a separate, confidential list of the case numbers and employee names for the establishment's privacy concern cases so that you can update the cases and provide information to the government if asked to do so.

If you have a reasonable basis to believe that information describing the privacy concern case may be personally identifiable even though the employee's name has been omitted, you may use discretion in describing the injury or illness on both the OSHA 300 and 301 forms. You must enter enough information to identify the cause of the incident and the general severity of the injury or illness, but you do not need to include details of an intimate or private nature.

What if the outcome changes after you record the case?

If the outcome or extent of an injury or illness changes after you have recorded the case, simply draw a line through the original entry or, if you wish, delete or white-out the original entry. Then write the new entry where it belongs. Remember, you need to record the most serious outcome for each case.

Classifying injuries

An injury is any wound or damage to the body resulting from an event in the work environment.

Examples: Cut, puncture, laceration, abrasion, fracture, bruise, contusion, chipped tooth, amputation, insect bite, electrocution, or a thermal, chemical, electrical, or radiation burn. Sprain and strain injuries to muscles, joints, and connective tissues are classified as injuries when they result from a slip, trip, fall or other similar accidents.

U.S. Department of Labor
Occupational Safety and Health Administration

Classifying illnesses

Skin diseases or disorders

Skin diseases or disorders are illnesses involving the worker's skin that are caused by work exposure to chemicals, plants, or other substances.

Examples: Contact dermatitis, eczema, or rash caused by primary irritants and sensitizers or poisonous plants; oil acne; friction blisters, chrome ulcers; inflammation of the skin.

Respiratory conditions

Respiratory conditions are illnesses associated with breathing hazardous biological agents, chemicals, dust, gases, vapors, or fumes at work.

Examples: Silicosis, asbestosis, pneumonitis, pharyngitis, rhinitis or acute congestion; farmer's lung, beryllium disease, tuberculosis, occupational asthma, reactive airways dysfunction syndrome (RADS), chronic obstructive pulmonary disease (COPD), hypersensitivity pneumonitis, toxic inhalation injury, such as metal fume fever, chronic obstructive bronchitis, and other pneumoconioses.

Poisoning

Poisoning includes disorders evidenced by abnormal concentrations of toxic substances in blood, other tissues, other bodily fluids, or the breath that are caused by the ingestion or absorption of toxic substances into the body.

Examples: Poisoning by lead, mercury,

cadmium, arsenic, or other metals; poisoning by carbon monoxide, hydrogen sulfide, or other gases; poisoning by benzene, benzol, carbon tetrachloride, or other organic solvents; poisoning by insecticide sprays, such as parathion or lead arsenate; poisoning by other chemicals, such as formaldehyde.

Hearing Loss

Noise-induced hearing loss is defined for recordkeeping purposes as a change in hearing threshold relative to the baseline audiogram of an average of 10 dB or more in either ear at 2000, 3000 and 4000 hertz, and the employee's total hearing level is 25 decibels (dB) or more above audiometric zero (also averaged at 2000, 3000, and 4000 hertz) in the same ear(s).

All other illnesses

All other occupational illnesses.

Examples: Heatstroke, sunstroke, heat exhaustion, heat stress and other effects of environmental heat; freezing, frostbite, and other effects of exposure to low temperatures; decompression sickness; effects of ionizing radiation (isotopes, x-rays, radium); effects of nonionizing radiation (welding flash, ultra-violet rays, lasers); anthrax; bloodborne pathogenic diseases, such as AIDS, HIV, hepatitis B or hepatitis C; brucellosis; malignant or benign tumors; histoplasmosis; coccidioidomycosis.

When must you post the Summary?

You must post the *Summary* only — not the *Log* — by February 1 of the year following the year covered by the form and keep it posted until April 30 of that year.

How long must you keep the Log and Summary on file?

You must keep the *Log* and *Summary* for 5 years following the year to which they pertain.

Do you have to send these forms to OSHA at the end of the year?

No. You do not have to send the completed forms to OSHA unless specifically asked to do so.

How can we help you?

If you have a question about how to fill out the *Log,*

☐ **visit us online at www.osha.gov** or

☐ **call your local OSHA office.**

U.S. Department of Labor
Occupational Safety and Health Administration

Optional

Calculating Injury and Illness Incidence Rates

What is an incidence rate?

An incidence rate is the number of recordable injuries and illnesses occurring among a given number of full-time workers (usually 100 full-time workers) over a given period of time (usually one year). To evaluate your firm's injury and illness experience over time or to compare your firm's experience with that of your industry as a whole, you need to compute your incidence rate. Because a specific number of workers and a specific period of time are involved, these rates can help you identify problems in your workplace and/or progress you may have made in preventing work-related injuries and illnesses.

How do you calculate an incidence rate?

You can compute an occupational injury and illness incidence rate for all recordable cases or for cases that involved days away from work for your firm quickly and easily. The formula requires that you follow instructions in paragraph (a) below for the total recordable cases or those in paragraph (b) for cases that involved days away from work, and for both rates the instructions in paragraph (c).

(a) To find out the total number of recordable injuries and illnesses that occurred during the year, count the number of line entries on your OSHA Form 300, or refer to the OSHA Form 300A and sum the entries for columns (G), (H), (I), and (J).

(b) To find out the number of injuries and illnesses that involved days away from work, count the number of line entries on your OSHA Form 300 that received a check mark in column (H), or refer to the entry for column

(H) on the OSHA Form 300A.

(c) The number of hours all employees actually worked during the year. Refer to OSHA Form 300A and optional worksheet to calculate this number.

You can compute the incidence rate for all recordable cases of injuries and illnesses using the following formula:

Total number of injuries and illnesses × 200,000 ÷ Number of hours worked by all employees = Total recordable case rate

(The 200,000 figure in the formula represents the number of hours 100 employees working 40 hours per week, 50 weeks per year would work, and provides the standard base for calculating incidence rates.)

You can compute the incidence rate for recordable cases involving days away from work, days of restricted work activity or job transfer (DART) using the following formula:

(Number of entries in column H + Number of entries in column I) × 200,000 ÷ Number of hours worked by all employees = DART incidence rate

You can use the same formula to calculate incidence rates for other variables such as cases involving restricted work activity (column (I) on Form 300A), cases involving skin disorders (column (M-2) on Form 300A), etc. Just substitute the appropriate total for these cases, from Form 300A, into the formula in place of the total number of injuries and illnesses.

What can I compare my incidence rate to?

The Bureau of Labor Statistics (BLS) conducts a survey of occupational injuries and illnesses each year and publishes incidence rate data by

various classifications (e.g., by industry, by employer size, etc.). You can obtain these published data at www.bls.gov/iif or by calling a BLS Regional Office.

Worksheet

| Total number of injuries and illnesses | × 200,000 | ÷ | Number of hours worked by all employees | = | Total recordable case rate |

| Number of entries in Column H + Column I | × 200,000 | ÷ | Number of hours worked by all employees | = | DART incidence rate |

How to Fill Out the Log

U.S. Department of Labor
Occupational Safety and Health Administration

The *Log of Work-Related Injuries and Illnesses* is used to classify work-related injuries and illnesses and to note the extent and severity of each case. When an incident occurs, use the *Log* to record specific details about what happened and how it happened.

If your company has more than one establishment or site, you must keep separate records for each physical location that is expected to remain in operation for one year or longer.

We have given you several copies of the *Log* in this package. If you need more than we provided, you may photocopy and use as many as you need.

The *Summary* — a separate form — shows the work-related injury and illness totals for the year in each category. At the end of the year, count the number of incidents in each category and transfer the totals from the *Log* to the *Summary*. Then post the *Summary* in a visible location so that your employees are aware of injuries and illnesses occurring in their workplace.

You don't post the Log. You post only the Summary at the end of the year.

OSHA's Form 300 (Rev. 01/2004)

Log of Work-Related Injuries and Illnesses

You must record information about every work-related death and about every work-related injury or illness that involves loss of consciousness, restricted work activity or job transfer, days away from work, or medical treatment beyond first aid. You must also record work-related injuries and illnesses that are diagnosed by a physician or licensed health care professional. You must also record work-related injuries and illnesses that meet any of the specific recording criteria listed in 29 CFR Part 1904.8 through 1904.12. Feel free to use two lines for a single case if you need to. You must complete an injury and illness incident report (OSHA Form 301) or equivalent form for each injury or illness recorded on this form. If you're not sure whether a case is recordable, call your local OSHA office for help.

Attention: This form contains information relating to employee health and must be used in a manner that protects the confidentiality of employees to the extent possible while the information is being used for occupational safety and health purposes.

Year 20___
U.S. Department of Labor
Occupational Safety and Health Administration
Form approved OMB no. 1218-0176

Establishment name _XYZ Company_
City _Anywhere_   State _MA_

(A) Case no.	(B) Employee's name	(C) Job title (e.g. Welder)	(D) Date of injury or onset of illness	(E) Where the event occurred (e.g. Loading dock north end)	(F) Describe injury or illness, parts of body affected, and object/substance that directly injured or made person ill (e.g. Second degree burns on right forearm from acetylene torch)
1	Mark Bagin	Welder	5 / 25	basement	fracture, left arm and left leg; fell from ladder
2	Shana Alexander	Foundry man	7 /2	pouring deck	poisoning from lead fumes
3	Sam Sander	Electrician	8 /15	2nd floor storeroom	broken left foot, fell over box
4	Ralph Bacola	Laborer	9 /17	packaging dept.	Back strain lifting boxes
5	Jarrod Daniels	Machine opr.	10 /23	production floor	dust in eye

Be as specific as possible. You can use two lines if you need more room.

Revise the log if the injury or illness progresses and the outcome is more serious than you originally recorded or serious than you originally recorded for the case. Cross out, erase, or white-out the original entry.

Classify the case
CHECK ONLY ONE box for each case based on the most serious outcome for that case.

| (G) Death | (H) Days away from work | (I) Job transfer or restriction | (J) Other record-able cases |

Remained at Work

(K) Away from work
12 days / 15 days
7 days / 30 days
3 days / 30 days
___ days / ___ days
___ days / ___ days

(L) On job transfer or restriction

Choose ONLY ONE of these categories. Classify the case by recording the most serious outcome of the case, with column G (Death) being the most serious and column J (Other recordable cases) being the least serious.

Check the "Injury" column or choose one type of illness:
(M)
(1) Injury
(2) Skin disorder
(3) Respiratory conditions
(4) Poisoning
(5) Hearing loss
(6) All other illnesses

Note whether the case involves an injury or an illness.

OSHA's Form 300 (Rev. 01/2004)

Log of Work-Related Injuries and Illnesses

Attention: This form contains information relating to employee health and must be used in a manner that protects the confidentiality of employees to the extent possible while the information is being used for occupational safety and health purposes.

Year 20____

U.S. Department of Labor
Occupational Safety and Health Administration

Form approved OMB no. 1218-0176

You must record information about every work-related death and about every work-related injury or illness that involves loss of consciousness, restricted work activity or job transfer, days away from work, or medical treatment beyond first aid. You must also record significant work-related injuries and illnesses that are diagnosed by a physician or licensed health care professional. You must also record work-related injuries and illnesses that meet any of the specific recording criteria listed in 29 CFR Part 1904.8 through 1904.12. Feel free to use two lines for a single case if you need to. You must complete an Injury and Illness Incident Report (OSHA Form 301) or equivalent form for each injury or illness recorded on this form. If you're not sure whether a case is recordable, call your local OSHA office for help.

Establishment name _____

City _____   State _____

Identify the person

(A) Case no.	(B) Employee's name	(C) Job title (e.g., Welder)

Describe the case

(D) Date of injury or onset of illness	(E) Where the event occurred (e.g., Loading dock north end)	(F) Describe injury or illness, parts of body affected, and object/substance that directly injured or made person ill (e.g., Second degree burns on right forearm from acetylene torch)
month/day		
month/day		
month/day		
month/day		
month/day		
month/day		
month/day		
month/day		
month/day		
month/day		
month/day		
month/day		
month/day		

Classify the case

CHECK ONLY ONE box for each case based on the most serious outcome for that case:

(G) Death	Remained at Work		
	(H) Days away from work	(I) Job transfer or restriction	(J) Other record- able cases

Enter the number of days the injured or ill worker was:

(K) Away from work	(L) On job transfer or restriction
____ days	____ days
____ days	____ days
____ days	____ days
____ days	____ days
____ days	____ days
____ days	____ days
____ days	____ days

Check the "injury" column or choose one type of illness:

(M)
(1) Injury	(2) Skin disorder	(3) Respiratory condition	(4) Poisoning	(5) Hearing loss	(6) All other illnesses

Page totals ▶

(1) Injury
(2) Skin disorder
(3) Respiratory condition
(4) Poisoning
(5) Hearing loss
(6) All other illnesses

Be sure to transfer these totals to the Summary page (Form 300A) before you post it.

Page ____ of ____

Public reporting burden for this collection of information is estimated to average 14 minutes per response, including time to review the instructions, search and gather the data needed, and complete and review the collection of information. Persons are not required to respond to the collection of information unless it displays a currently valid OMB control number. If you have any comments about these estimates or any other aspects of this data collection, contact: US Department of Labor, OSHA Office of Statistical Analysis, Room N-3644, 200 Constitution Avenue, NW, Washington, DC 20210. Do not send the completed forms to this office.

OSHA's Form 300A (Rev. 01/2004)

Summary of Work-Related Injuries and Illnesses

Year 20___

U.S. Department of Labor
Occupational Safety and Health Administration

Form approved OMB no. 1218-0176

All establishments covered by Part 1904 must complete this Summary page, even if no work-related injuries or illnesses occurred during the year. Remember to review the Log to verify that the entries are complete and accurate before completing this summary.

Using the Log, count the individual entries you made for each category. Then write the totals below, making sure you've added the entries from every page of the Log. If you had no cases, write "0."

Employees, former employees, and their representatives have the right to review the OSHA Form 300 in its entirety. They also have limited access to the OSHA Form 301 or its equivalent. See 29 CFR Part 1904.35, in OSHA's recordkeeping rule, for further details on the access provisions for these forms.

Number of Cases

Total number of deaths	Total number of cases with days away from work	Total number of cases with job transfer or restriction	Total number of other recordable cases
_____ (G)	_____ (H)	_____ (I)	_____ (J)

Number of Days

Total number of days away from work	Total number of days of job transfer or restriction
_____ (K)	_____ (L)

Injury and Illness Types

Total number of . . .
(M)

(1) Injuries _____

(2) Skin disorders _____

(3) Respiratory conditions _____

(4) Poisonings _____

(5) Hearing loss _____

(6) All other illnesses _____

Post this Summary page from February 1 to April 30 of the year following the year covered by the form.

Public reporting burden for this collection of information is estimated to average 58 minutes per response, including time to review the instructions, search and gather the data needed, and complete and review the collection of information. Persons are not required to respond to the collection of information unless it displays a currently valid OMB control number. If you have any comments about these estimates or any other aspects of this data collection, contact: US Department of Labor, OSHA Office of Statistical Analysis, Room N-3644, 200 Constitution Avenue, NW, Washington, DC 20210. Do not send the completed forms to this office.

Establishment information

Your establishment name _____

Street _____

City _____ State _____ ZIP _____

Industry description (e.g., Manufacture of motor truck trailers)
_____

Standard Industrial Classification (SIC), if known (e.g., 3715)
_ _ _ _

OR

North American Industrial Classification (NAICS), if known (e.g., 336212)
_ _ _ _ _ _

Employment information *(If you don't have these figures, see the Worksheet on the back of this page to estimate.)*

Annual average number of employees _____

Total hours worked by all employees last year _____

Sign here

Knowingly falsifying this document may result in a fine.

I certify that I have examined this document and that to the best of my knowledge the entries are true, accurate, and complete.

_____
Company executive   Title

(_____) _____ - _____   ___/___/___
Phone   Date

Optional

Worksheet to Help You Fill Out the Summary

At the end of the year, OSHA requires you to enter the average number of employees and the total hours worked by your employees on the summary. If you don't have these figures, you can use the information on this page to estimate the numbers you will need to enter on the Summary page at the end of the year.

How to figure the average number of employees who worked for your establishment during the year:

1. **Add** the total number of employees your establishment paid in all pay periods during the year. Include all employees: full-time, part-time, temporary, seasonal, salaried, and hourly.

   The number of employees paid in all pay periods = ❶ _____

2. **Count** the number of pay periods your establishment had during the year. Be sure to include any pay periods when you had no employees.

   The number of pay periods during the year = ❷ _____

3. **Divide** the number of employees by the number of pay periods.

   ❶ ÷ ❷ = ❸ _____

4. **Round the answer** to the next highest whole number. Write the rounded number in the blank marked *Annual average number of employees.*

   The number rounded = ❹ _____

For example, Acme Construction figured its average employment this way:

For pay period...	Acme paid this number of employees...
1	10
2	0
3	15
4	30
5	40
▼	▼
24	20
25	15
26	+10
	830

Number of employees paid = 830   ❶

Number of pay periods = 26   ❷

830 ÷ 26 = 31.92   ❸

31.92 rounds to 32

32 is the annual average number of employees   ❹

How to figure the total hours worked by all employees:

Include hours worked by salaried, hourly, part-time and seasonal workers, as well as hours worked by other workers subject to day to day supervision by your establishment (e.g., temporary help services workers).

Do not include vacation, sick leave, holidays, or any other non-work time, even if employees were paid for it. If your establishment keeps records of only the hours paid or if you have employees who are not paid by the hour, please estimate the hours that the employees actually worked.

If this number isn't available, you can use this optional worksheet to estimate it.

Optional Worksheet

Find the number of full-time employees in your establishment for the year.   _____

Multiply by the number of work hours for a full-time employee in a year.   × _____

This is the number of full-time hours worked.   _____

Add the number of any overtime hours as well as the hours worked by other employees (part-time, temporary, seasonal)   + _____

Round the answer to the next highest whole number. Write the rounded number in the blank marked *Total hours worked by all employees last year.*   _____

U.S. Department of Labor
Occupational Safety and Health Administration

OSHA**FACT** *Sheet*

Workplace Violence

What is workplace violence?

Workplace violence is violence or the threat of violence against workers. It can occur at or outside the workplace and can range from threats and verbal abuse to physical assaults and homicide, one of the leading causes of job-related deaths. However it manifests itself, workplace violence is a growing concern for employers and employees nationwide.

Who is vulnerable?

Some 2 million American workers are victims of workplace violence each year. Workplace violence can strike anywhere, and no one is immune. Some workers, however, are at increased risk. Among them are workers who exchange money with the public; deliver passengers, goods, or services; or work alone or in small groups, during late night or early morning hours, in high-crime areas, or in community settings and homes where they have extensive contact with the public. This group includes health-care and social service workers such as visiting nurses, psychiatric evaluators, and probation officers; community workers such as gas and water utility employees, phone and cable TV installers, and letter carriers; retail workers; and taxi drivers.

What can these employers do to help protect these employees?

The best protection employers can offer is to establish a zero-tolerance policy toward workplace violence against or by their employees. The employer should establish a workplace violence prevention program or incorporate the information into an existing accident prevention program, employee handbook, or manual of standard operating procedures. It is critical to ensure that all employees know the policy and understand that all claims of workplace violence will be investigated and remedied promptly. In addition, employers can offer additional protections such as the following:

- Provide safety education for employees so they know what conduct is not acceptable, what to do if they witness or are subjected to workplace violence, and how to protect themselves.

- Secure the workplace. Where appropriate to the business, install video surveillance, extra lighting, and alarm systems and minimize access by outsiders through identification badges, electronic keys, and guards.

- Provide drop safes to limit the amount of cash on hand. Keep a minimal amount of cash in registers during evenings and late-night hours.

- Equip field staff with cellular phones and hand-held alarms or noise devices, and require them to prepare a daily work plan and keep a contact person informed of their location throughout the day. Keep employer-provided vehicles properly maintained.

- Instruct employees not to enter any location where they feel unsafe. Introduce a "buddy system" or provide an escort service or police assistance in potentially dangerous situations or at night.

- Develop policies and procedures covering visits by home health-care providers. Address the conduct of home visits, the presence of others in the home during visits, and the worker's right to refuse to provide services in a clearly hazardous situation.

How can the employees protect themselves?

Nothing can guarantee that an employee will not become a victim of workplace violence. These steps, however, can help reduce the odds:

- Learn how to recognize, avoid, or diffuse potentially violent situations by attending personal safety training programs.

- Alert supervisors to any concerns about safety or security and report all incidents immediately in writing.

- Avoid traveling alone into unfamiliar locations or situations whenever possible.

- Carry only minimal money and required identification into community settings.

What should employers do following an incident of workplace violence?

- Encourage employees to report and log all incidents and threats of workplace violence.

- Provide prompt medical evaluation and treatment after the incident.

- Report violent incidents to the local police promptly.

- Inform victims of their legal right to prosecute perpetrators.

- Discuss the circumstances of the incident with staff members. Encourage employees to share information about ways to avoid similar situations in the future.

- Offer stress debriefing sessions and post-traumatic counseling services to help workers recover from a violent incident.

- Investigate all violent incidents and threats, monitor trends in violent incidents by type or circumstance, and institute corrective actions.

- Discuss changes in the program during regular employee meetings.

What protections does OSHA offer?

The *Occupational Safety and Health Act's* (*OSH Act*) General Duty Clause requires employers to provide a safe and healthful workplace for all workers covered by the *OSH Act*. Employers who do not take reasonable steps

to prevent or abate a recognized violence hazard in the workplace can be cited. Failure to implement suggestions in this fact sheet, however, is not in itself a violation of the General Duty Clause.

How can you get more information?

OSHA has various publications, standards, technical assistance, and compliance tools to help you, and offers extensive assistance through its many safety and health programs: workplace consultation, voluntary protection programs, grants, strategic partnerships, state plans, training, and education. Guidance such as *OSHA's Safety and Health Management Program Guidelines* identify elements that are critical to the development of a successful safety and health management system. This and other information are available on OSHA's website at **www.osha.gov**.

- For a free copy of OSHA publications, send a self-addressed mailing label to this address: OSHA Publications Office, P.O. Box 37535, Washington, DC 20013-7535; or send a request to our fax at (202) 693-2498, or call us at (202) 693-1888.

- To file a complaint by phone, report an emergency, or get OSHA advice, assistance, or products, contact your nearest OSHA office under the "U.S. Department of Labor" listing in your phone book, or call us toll-free at **(800) 321-OSHA (6742)**. The tele-typewriter (TTY) number is (877) 889-5627.

- To file a complaint online or obtain more information on OSHA federal and state programs, visit OSHA's website.

Workplace Violence

Index

Q